Contested Spaces
of Early America

EARLY AMERICAN STUDIES

Series editors
Daniel K. Richter, Kathleen M. Brown,
Max Cavitch, and David Waldstreicher

Exploring neglected aspects of our colonial, revolutionary, and early national history and culture, Early American Studies reinterprets familiar themes and events in fresh ways. Interdisciplinary in character, and with a special emphasis on the period from about 1600 to 1850, the series is published in partnership with the McNeil Center for Early American Studies.

A complete list of books in the series
is available from the publisher.

CONTESTED SPACES
of EARLY AMERICA

~

EDITED BY
Juliana Barr and Edward Countryman

PENN

UNIVERSITY OF PENNSYLVANIA PRESS

PHILADELPHIA

Published in Cooperation with the William P. Clements Center
for Southwest Studies, Southern Methodist University

Copyright © 2014 University of Pennsylvania Press

All rights reserved. Except for brief quotations used
for purposes of review or scholarly citation, none of this
book may be reproduced in any form by any means without
written permission from the publisher.

Published by
University of Pennsylvania Press
Philadelphia, Pennsylvania 19104-4112
www.upenn.edu/pennpress

Printed in the United States of America
on acid-free paper

10 9 8 7 6 5 4 3 2 1

Library of Congress Cataloging-in-Publication Data
Contested spaces of early America / edited by Juliana Barr and Edward Countryman.—1st ed.
   p. cm.— (Early American studies)
"Published in Cooperation with the William P. Clements Center for Southwest Studies, Southern Methodist University"—T.p. verso.
  Includes bibliographical references and index.
  ISBN 978-0-8122-4584-4 (hardcover : alk. paper)
  1. Borderlands—America—History. 2. America—History—To 1810. 3. Indians—Land tenure. 4. America—Colonization. 5. America—Historical geography. I. Barr, Juliana. II. Countryman, Edward. III. William P. Clements Center for Southwest Studies. IV. Series: Early American studies.
E18.75.C68 2014
970.01—dc23

2013035998

In David's memory

CONTENTS

Introduction. Maps and Spaces, Paths to Connect, and Lines to Divide 1
JULIANA BARR AND EDWARD COUNTRYMAN

PART I. SPACES AND POWER

Chapter 1. The Shapes of Power: Indians, Europeans, and North American Worlds from the Seventeenth to the Nineteenth Century 31
PEKKA HÄMÄLÄINEN

Chapter 2. Dispossession in a Commercial Idiom: From Indian Deeds to Land Cession Treaties 69
ALLAN GREER

PART II. SPACES AND LANDSCAPES

Chapter 3. The Mandans: Ecology, Population, and Adaptation on the Northern Plains 95
ELIZABETH FENN

Chapter 4. Colonial Spaces in the Fragmented Communities of Northern New Spain 115
CYNTHIA RADDING

Chapter 5. Transformations: The Rio de la Plata During the Bourbon Era 142
RAÚL JOSÉ MANDRINI

PART III. SPACES AND RESETTLEMENTS

Chapter 6. Blurred Borders: North America's Forgotten Apache Reservations 163
MATTHEW BABCOCK

Chapter 7. The Forced Transfer of Indians in Nueva Vizcaya and Sinaloa: A Hispanic Method of Colonization 184
CHANTAL CRAMAUSSEL

Chapter 8. Remaking Americans: Louisiana, Upper Canada, and Texas 208
ALAN TAYLOR

PART IV. SPACES AND MEMORY

Chapter 9. Blood Talk: Violence and Belonging in the Navajo–New Mexican Borderland 229
BRIAN DELAY

Chapter 10. Toward a New Literary History of the West: Etahdleuh Doanmoe's Captivity Narrative 257
BIRGIT BRANDER RASMUSSEN

Chapter 11. Toward an Indigenous Art History of the West: The Segesser Hide Paintings 276
NED BLACKHAWK

Chapter 12. The Borderlands and Lost Worlds of Early America 300
SAMUEL TRUETT

Notes 325

List of Contributors 409

Index 413

Acknowledgments 427

Contested Spaces
of Early America

INTRODUCTION

Maps and Spaces, Paths to Connect, and Lines to Divide

JULIANA BARR AND EDWARD COUNTRYMAN

"In the last decades of the twentieth century," argued David J. Weber, "American historians discovered America." Scholars of New Spain, New France, and New England began to look toward other colonial regions for connections and comparisons. Ethnohistorians explored the commonalities and contrasts in histories of indigenous people from Peru to Greenland. We cannot speak of "early America" anymore with only the East Coast British colonies, the St. Lawrence River Valley, or Mexico and Peru in mind. The topic has grown vastly larger.

This volume suggests that we should think of "early" or "colonial" America on the largest possible scale.[1] In its own historical time, our subject stretched from north of Quebec to south of Buenos Aires and from the Atlantic littoral to the Pacific coast. It needs to stretch just as far in modern understanding. This book brings together scholars and scholarly perspectives from the entirety of that zone around the organizing theme of contested spaces, places throughout the hemisphere where people who had been total strangers met, mingled, and clashed, creating colonial societies unlike any that the world had seen to that time. Our original intention was to honor David Weber's career and achievements upon his retirement, but his death in August 2010 turned this project into a memorial. The book thus has emerged both from Weber's lifework and from a larger turn in the study of early America to which he contributed mightily. David offered a bridge—in scholarship and among scholars—to link together the historic Americas and to see beyond borderlands, borders, and territorial crossings to imagine that history as a hemispheric project. The authors here are based at institutions not just across the United States but also in Canada, Mexico, Argentina, and Great Britain, and we hope that the essays will in some way embody the scope and breadth of David's vision to bring together the histories of early America.

In geographical terms, our writers deal largely but not exclusively with the areas that now compose the U.S. Southwest and the northern parts of Mexico. But their discussions also extend to what now forms Canada; the western, northern, and eastern United States; and Argentina. Our interest is with contestation over places that did not yet bear their modern names, not with any kind of precursor to the modern nation-states whose seemingly timeless boundaries are the main subject of conventional classroom and textbook political maps. For our purposes those nations and their internal divisions into states and provinces do not exist. Instead, a really good map of the colonial situation of the early western hemisphere would show a set of sometimes fluid, sometimes unbending fields of force, all of them dealing with the issue of space. We need not look for such an ideal map. Instead, we can turn to the maps that people who were caught up in colonial interactions generated as they tried to make sense of one another. The potential set of such maps is enormous, and no single map within that set is perfect. But taken together they bring out the theme of contested spaces that is our subject here.

Let's first look at the map that appears on the cover of this book and also in Figure I.1, drawn by the Portuguese adventurer-soldier Antonio Pereira half a century after the first voyage of Christopher Columbus in 1492. Pereira certainly saw America all of a piece, as did most cartographers of his age. His depiction of the western hemisphere as a single extensive landmass is part of an illuminated vellum map of the world in his time. What Pereira showed represented the sum of knowledge gained from Spanish and Portuguese explorers, primarily by sea, and from travel reports, notably regarding the Amazon River, and that information dates the map almost precisely to the year 1545. Scattered throughout North, South, and Meso-America appear three Portuguese flags, two flags sporting the French fleur-de-lis, and thirteen Spanish standards—all along the coastlines. To Pereira the vast interior remained unknown and apparently undeveloped, uncontrolled, or simply unpopulated. A caravel carries the Portuguese cross of Christ across to South America, another approaches the Strait of Magellan, and five Spanish ships navigate the Pacific Ocean. This is a space preeminently about Europeans

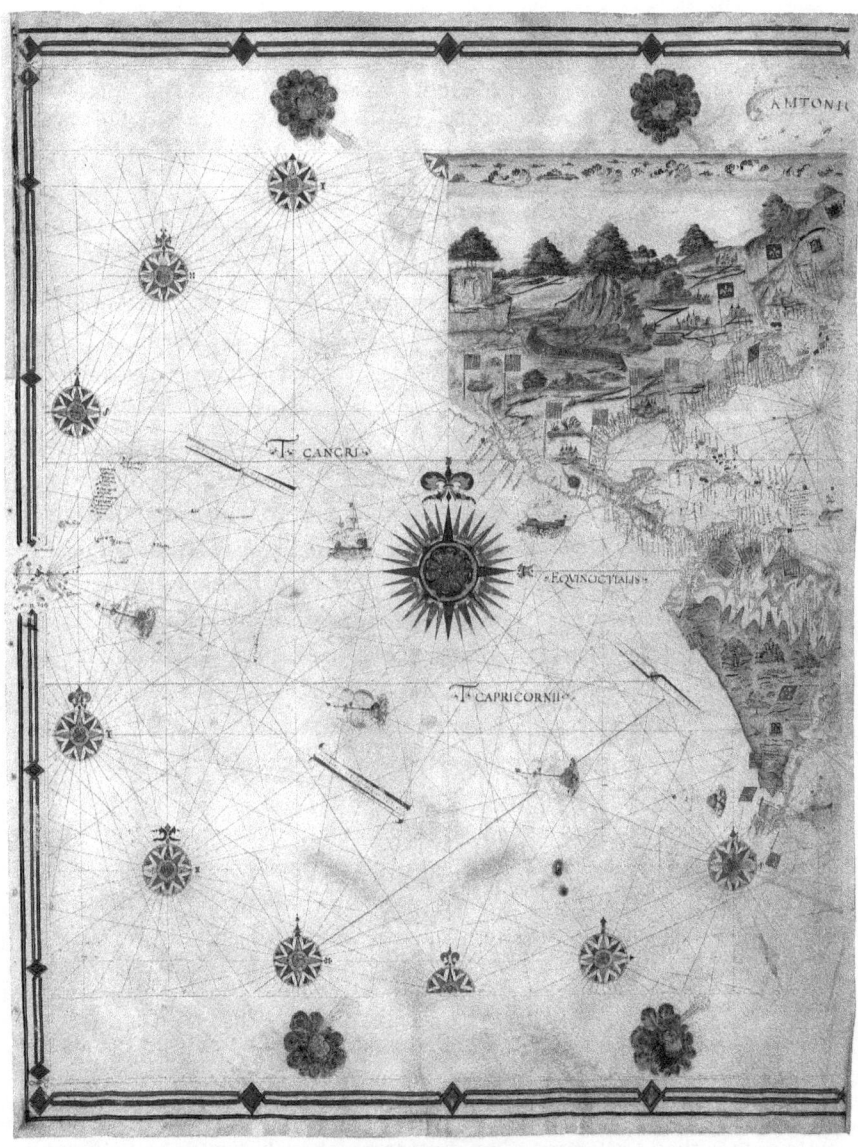

FIGURE I.1. Hand-colored map of North and South America by Antonio Pereira (1545).

Courtesy of the John Carter Brown Library at Brown University.

in motion, transforming oceans from barriers into highways, while creating Portuguese and Spanish commercial empires built "literally on water."[2]

Early modern European cartography reflected not just the advancement of knowledge but also the machinations of geopolitics. Geographic information (or sometimes the lack of it) determined the power and fate of nations. The flags and ships of Pereira's map proclaim America to be a world of competing European nations already divvying up rights within the hemisphere, and a blue banner unfurled across North America asserts possession by declaring the land there to be "Nova España." Early modern maps such as Pereira's thus created a landscape for colonialism, both anticipating the territory that vying European nations claimed in America and licensing plans to appropriate, conquer, and colonize. Visualizing a "breathless progression from 'I see' to 'I possess,'" colonial maps were expressions of desire, not reality. The names "New Spain," "New France," and "New England" appeared on maps long before the lands claimed became active zones of European invasion and settlement. European rulers legitimated colonial authority in America through cartography just as they had previously done with state systems in Europe; they used it primarily as a "political discourse concerned with the acquisition and maintenance of power" within national borders and across them. Maps were part and parcel of military intelligence, commercial activity, and territorial and proprietary rights and, in America, maps were "tools of imperialism as much as guns and warships."[3]

In the hands of rulers, as scholars beginning with the late Brian Harley taught us to understand, such maps gave the illusion of control over distant lands and of powers claimed vis-à-vis other European nations; in the hands of colonizers, they promoted the lands to would-be settlers, proprietors, and investors. Such maps were not accurate, mirrorlike representations of objective reality. They were intensely political documents, boasts of power that were open to contestation and that could not be definitively enforced, despite all the might of the distant monarchs whose American dominions they purported to depict. Looked at carefully, they reveal tension and dispute, rather than settlement. One dimension of such dispute pitted European claimants against one another in a paper war of differently colored spaces and supposed borderlines. But other dimensions also are present, if we look. One such dimension involves all the Europeans, taken as a group despite their differences in language, religion, culture, and politics, vis-à-vis all Natives, also taken as a group, despite differences that dwarf the ones that separated Europeans. Another dimension takes those differences into account, showing how different sorts of Native people and different sorts of invaders cooperated in some situations and clashed in others.

A key quality in colonial-era European and later Euro-American maps of America was the attempted erasure of indigenous populations from the land and its history, viewing American space in purely European terms. Maps charted voyages of "discovery" in an "age of exploration" in which Europeans moved across spaces, and the land and sea became surfaces for European action. Such spatial narratives reduced Indian places, people, and cultures to "phenomena *on* this surface." They appeared as if always in one place, unbounded from one another yet simultaneously unconnected to one another. Their lands seemingly had no borders, and their towns and communities no names. They were not in movement—Europeans were— and, in that immobilization, Indians were denied their own trajectories, histories, and "potential for their own, perhaps different, futures."

The story of these cartographic landscapes is one of beginnings, the first acts in "the one and only narrative it is possible to tell." Just as in maps of Europe itself, political priorities imposed a silence on subject populations (or soon-to-be subject populations). Promotional visions flattened out the American landscapes that European readers and observers sought to possess into ones that were comfortably safe, familiar, and homogeneous. In its inventions of "New Spain," "New France," "New Netherlands," and "New England," and its "engulfing [of Indians] with blank spaces," cartography anachronistically rewrote historical spaces as "new" European creations while simultaneously denying the presence and the past of America's indigenous populations.[4]

But none of the European maps could fully repress the large reality that Native people possessed the land, knowing it, using it, understanding it, and either ruling it or remembering how it had been entirely theirs. The British scholar G. Malcolm Lewis taught students of early American maps to recognize that much of what those maps depicted actually was Native knowledge that Europeans were appropriating, rather than the result of direct European exploration. Barbara Mundy demonstrates that both Nahua knowledge and Nahua spatial and cultural understanding underpinned the map of Tenochtitlan (published in Germany in 1524) that Hernán Cortés sent back to the King of Spain. John Smith showed on the first map that he drew of Virginia (1612) precisely where what Smith had seen gave way to what the people of the land they knew as Tsenacommacah had

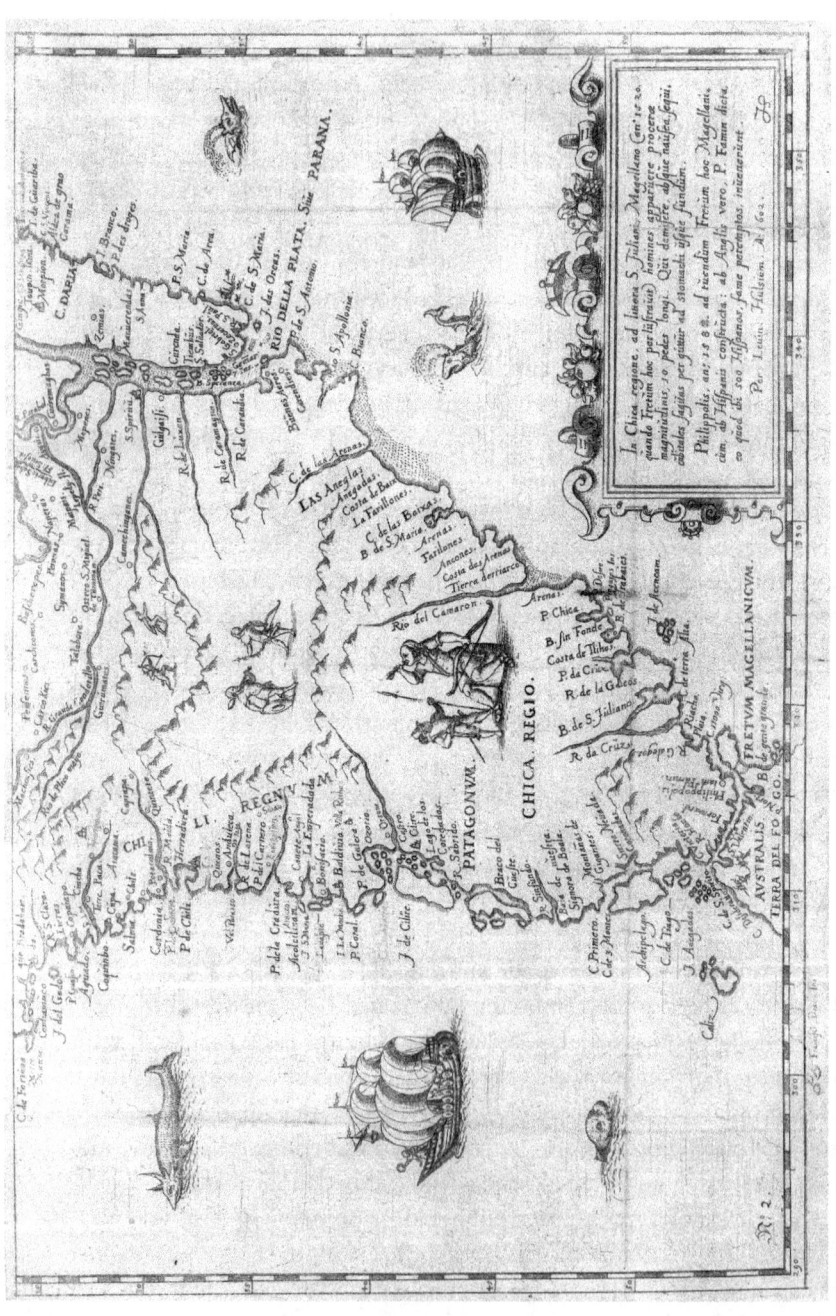

FIGURE I.2. Many early European maps symbolized Native power with outsized Indians, such as this Patagonian "giant" squaring off against a European man. Map of southern South America and Tierra del Fuego (1602).

Courtesy of the John Carter Brown Library at Brown University.

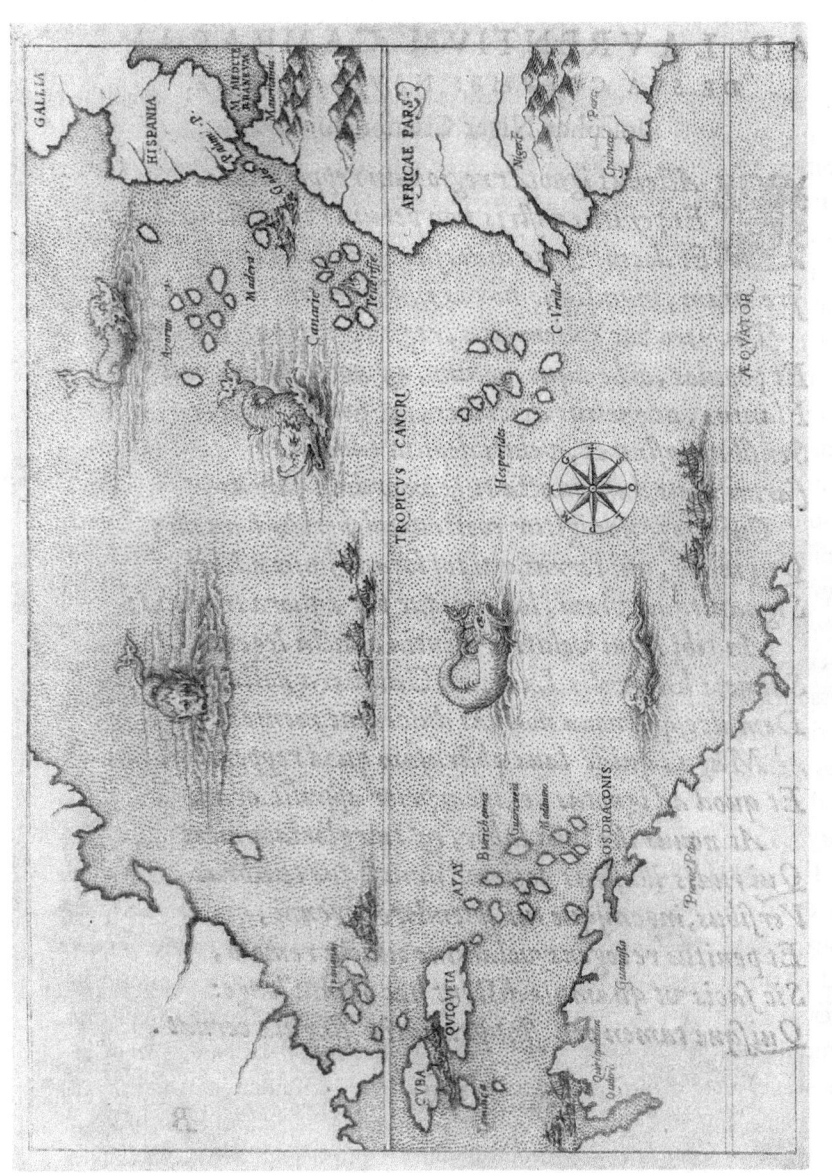

FIGURE I.3. Monsters fill the Atlantic Ocean and huge blank spaces await travelers who make it to the other side. Courtesy of the John Carter Brown Library at Brown University.

taught him. In 1673 Illinois Indians told the French Jesuit missionary Jacques Marquette, in effect, that if he ascended the Missouri and Platte rivers he could portage to the upper Colorado and descend it to the Pacific Ocean.[5]

Giving the lie completely to European claims, Indians, too, charted their visions of America via the borders, experiences, and histories that gave meaning to the spaces they inhabited. Using written, carved, and narrative forms to represent the world as they saw it, Indians located themselves in celestial, cosmographic, and terrestrial terms. The landscape itself carried inscriptions of Indian history and identity. Indigenous maps and place-names give linguistic, cognitive, and visual testimony to the communities and cultures that created those sites through their material practices, claimed and developed them economically and politically, and defended them in diplomacy and war. Rock-art cartography found throughout North America provides carved and painted narratives of the pre-Columbian landscape. The oldest North American cartographic representation is found in southeastern Missouri. There, a Mississippian map at Commerce Quarry combines a meandering line representing the Mississippi River with interconnected dotted lines (thoroughfares) and dotted clusters and glyphs (towns and surrounding settlements). Other rock-art panels marked the extensive borders of the Cahokia polity, centered near the point where the Missouri River joins the Mississippi. For the people they served, such maps carried multiple functions. They provided guides to routes, signposts, trespass warnings, markers of conquest, and signs of territorial possession. For modern scholars, surviving Native maps present historical and political storyboards.[6]

In contrast to European cartography that made Indians stationary in place and across time, Indian maps tell of old spaces, as deeply layered with history, movement, and meaning as any in Europe, spaces where empires and communities sat on the sites of previous ones. Native communities offer just as rich a story as the contemporaneous rise and fall of cultures, communities, and empires in Europe, Africa, and Asia. Some American landscapes were highly urbanized. The city-state of Tenochtitlan, so coveted and then conquered by Hernán Cortés, dwarfed Madrid and equaled Rome or Constantinople with its monumental sculpture and architecture, temples, palaces, marketplaces, suburbs, and roads radiating out in all directions. But prior to Tenochtitlan there had been Teotihuacan, and before Teotihuacan there had been other rich cultures and empires. With a total

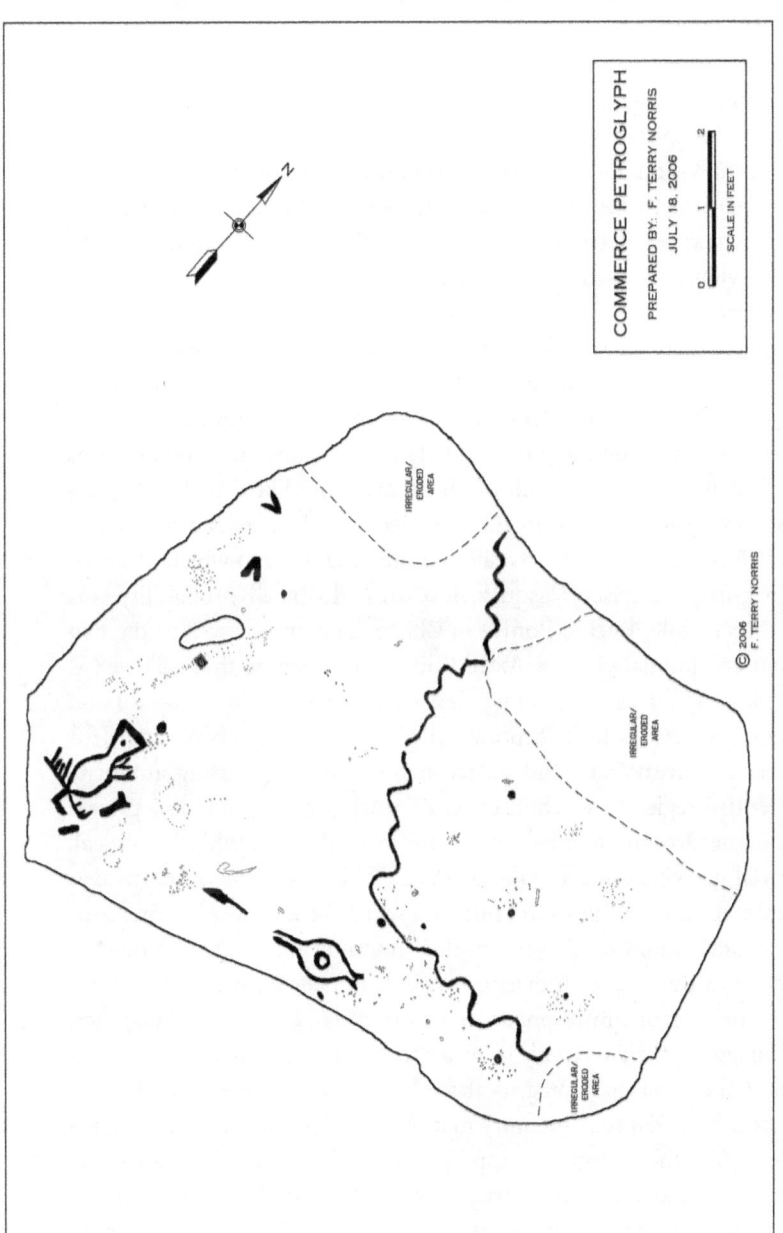

FIGURE I.4. This ancient Native map, inscribed on stone and dating from 1200–1400 CE, shows the Mississippi River and nearby highways, towns, and settlements.

Commerce Petroglyph, prepared by F. Terry Norris, July 18, 2006; reproduced in F. Terry Norris and Timothy R. Pauketat, "A Pre-Columbian Map of the Mississippi?" *Southeastern Archaeology* 27 (Summer 2008), 78–92.

mileage of more than fourteen thousand miles, the Peruvian highway system offered eloquent testimony to "the scale and precision of Inca geographic conceptions" and the imperial control needed to "keep track of their wide-flung possessions." Distance markers, roadside shelters, and storehouses—all spaced at regular intervals along the roads—gave further evidence of the vision and authority behind the roads' operation.[7]

In comparison to the more readily recognized Indian cities of South and Meso-America, metropolis building north of the Rio Grande until recently fell victim to a scholarly tendency to set "a glass ceiling on ancient Native American history." Consider the monumental earthen structures of the Mississippi and Ohio valleys. A "myth of the mound builders" long denied that Native American peoples had built them. Now, we understand that people north of the Rio Grande created many paramount chiefdoms that sometimes amounted to city-states. The largest and most notable was Cahokia, but it did not stand alone. It seems quite likely that Cahokia's power and influence lingered in the knowledge and memories of Indians some three hundred years after its fall; the site of Quivira to which El Turco sought to guide Francisco Vásquez de Coronado in all probability was Cahokia. Meanwhile, Pueblo Bonito in Chaco Canyon—as well as the two subsequent ceremonial cities at Aztec Ruins and Paquimé that followed—operated as a capital where a ruling class of Chacoans built canonical and monumental structures to incorporate elite residence and governance (for and by rulers, bureaucrats, and palace functionaries exercising authority over the entire region), warehouses, craft workshops, public and private ritual sites, guardrooms, and barracks. Commercial, geographical, political, and imperial markers filled and defined pre-Columbian American space.[8]

Indian mapping traditions did not stop when those spaces became contested by a new round of challenges, this time not among Native peoples but rather from Europeans. Indigenous people in post-Columbian America most often made maps in response to European land claims and disputes, creating images of their territory in order to substantiate their borders and the political and economic integrity those borders represented. Local Peruvian communities adapted "memory mapping" to Spanish boundary marking by walking the course of topographical features and man-made signposts that marked the boundaries of a *pueblo de indios*, creating cartographic art that visualized the routes and recorded Native place-names. From early in their encounters with French, Dutch, and English invaders, representatives of the powerful Iroquois Confederacy repeatedly met with colonial officials to direct the drawing of maps with demarcations for their sovereign borders, first showing the land as they understood it and eventually using the cartographic methods of Europeans to protect their territories from incursive English settlers. Indian communities dealing with New England methods of land acquisition not only incorporated their own graphic and written representations into land deeds but also used them to define by their own traditions the rights granted their European neighbors within and across territorial boundaries. In these ways, Indians often adapted their own mapping images to European idioms in order to attain their political ambitions and secure their lands.[9]

In some instances we can see European and Native views in direct conflict. By the early eighteenth century European cartographers such as the Frenchman Guillaume de L'Isle and the Englishman Henry Popple had enough information to create reasonably accurate maps of much of North America, bar the northwest quadrant, which (to Europeans at least) remained "unknown." Both cartographers used bold lines, large typefaces, and, in some iterations, splashes of color to indicate European claims of authority and possession across very large areas. But neither de L'Isle nor Popple could deny who really possessed most of the land: the names of many Native communities lie beneath the color washes on their maps.

Still, the fundamental project of both cartographers was to show imperial possession and boundaries in European terms.[10] Native people had other ideas. In 1723 Chickasaw Indians presented to the newly arrived governor of South Carolina, Francis Nicholson, a map drawn on their terms and conceived on an equally large scale. Spatially, their map stretched from East Texas to westernmost New York. They, too, showed geographical features and many peoples, both European and Native. But rather than a mass of tiny names, so small they appear only like a gray wash, the Chickasaw cartographer used two characteristic Native mapping devices. One was representing separate Native communities as circles. The other was to use lines not to indicate boundaries in the European fashion but rather to show paths that connected Native and European peoples to one another in a huge web.[11]

Many staked their claims *within* the spaces they now shared with Europeans, asserting co-ownership of the land and its communities. Representing the time both before and after European arrival, these images often aimed not so much at convincing European officials as retaining Native memory, inscribing ideology from the past and for the present and future.

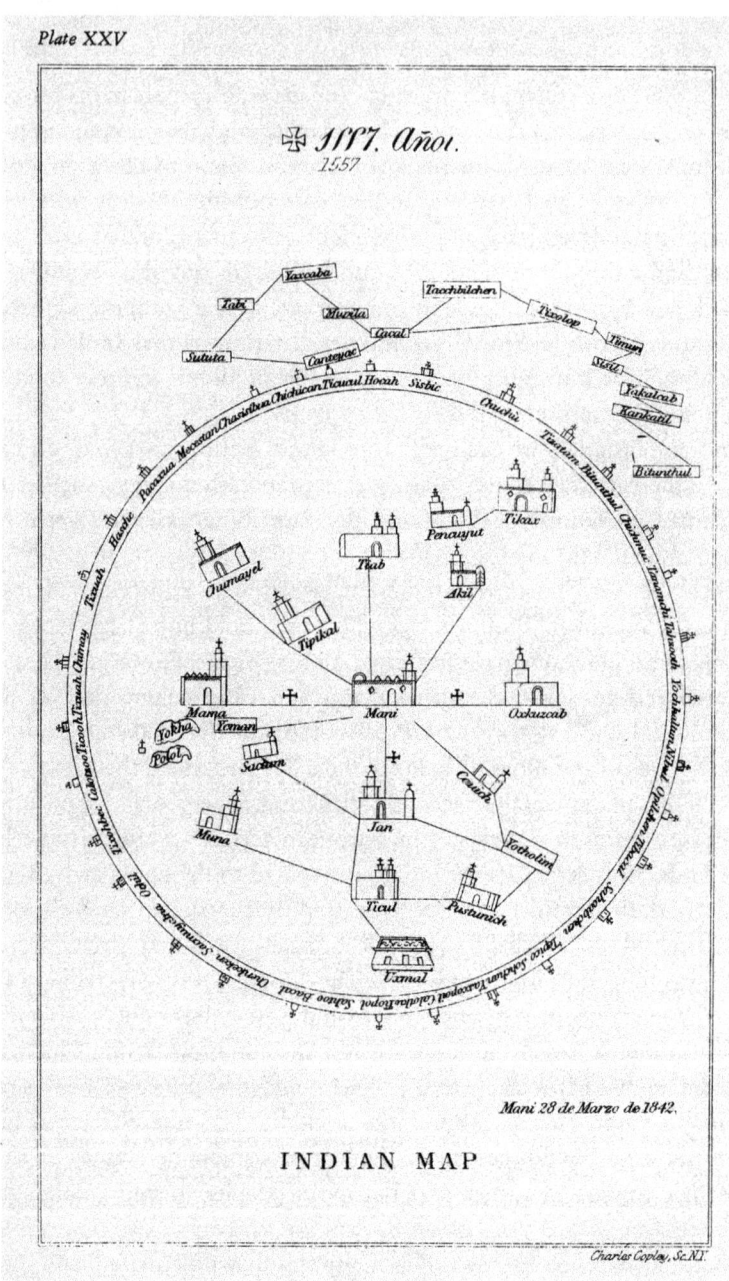

FIGURE I.5. Copied from the 1557 Mani Land Treaty, this nineteenth-century map shows where Yucatec leaders stationed guards in order to secure their sovereign territories.

Engraving 35 from *Incidents of Travel in Yucatan*, vol. 2, by John Lloyd Stephens, 1848.

Perhaps the most famous colonial image from the New World—the 1524 map of the Aztec capital Tenochtitlan that was published in Nuremberg to accompany the publication of Hernán Cortés's letters—reveals a Native hand at the center of its design. Ethnographic analysis shows the map to be far closer to an Aztec idea of the city as a "cosmic linchpin, a place where the human world brushed up against the divine" rather than to the European idealization of the conquered metropolis enriching Spanish coffers. Others, like the Peruvian Felipe Guamán Poma de Ayala, encoded their maps with protest. Guamán Poma de Ayala's 1613 *mapa mundi* of the Indies, drawn for King Philip III, conveyed a polemic for Native viewers against the imposition of Spanish rule, using the geometrical grid of the Andean universe to show the superior nobility of the Inca over the Spanish Crown.[12]

Meanwhile, across Mexico, cartographic reports commissioned by the Spanish government circa 1580 produced maps from sixty-nine Native cities, villages, or provinces within the *gobierno de Nueva España*. The project had originated with the goal of combining the reports into a representational whole in visualizing the implementation of Spanish rule via new programs of land and resource use and constructing a national identity for New Spain, as one of the many separate kingdoms possessed by the Spanish Crown. Instead, the maps preserve cartographic histories of Nahua migrations, communal foundations, alliances, and conquests that had given them their corporate identity as the possessors and managers of specific territory. Indians in the North American Southeast similarly continued to draw maps to plot the social and political relationships among kin, allies, and trading partners on the ground, choosing between continuous or broken lines to register open relations or ones disrupted by war. One archaeologist even used the eighteenth-century maps of Guillaume de L'Isle to explore the origins of the Choctaw polity. In de L'Isle's efforts to map as closely as possible the Native political geography in order to serve French economic and diplomatic aspirations in the Louisiana Valley, he unknowingly imitated Native cartographic "sociograms" in conveying geographic data from Native informants and incorporated into his maps locations reflecting their historical migration legends.[13]

Across a plurality of spaces, post-Columbian maps thereby tell of diverse trajectories of Native resistance, accommodation, and even the expansive power of Indian nations whose territorial power grew rather than diminished in response to a European presence. Independent groups like

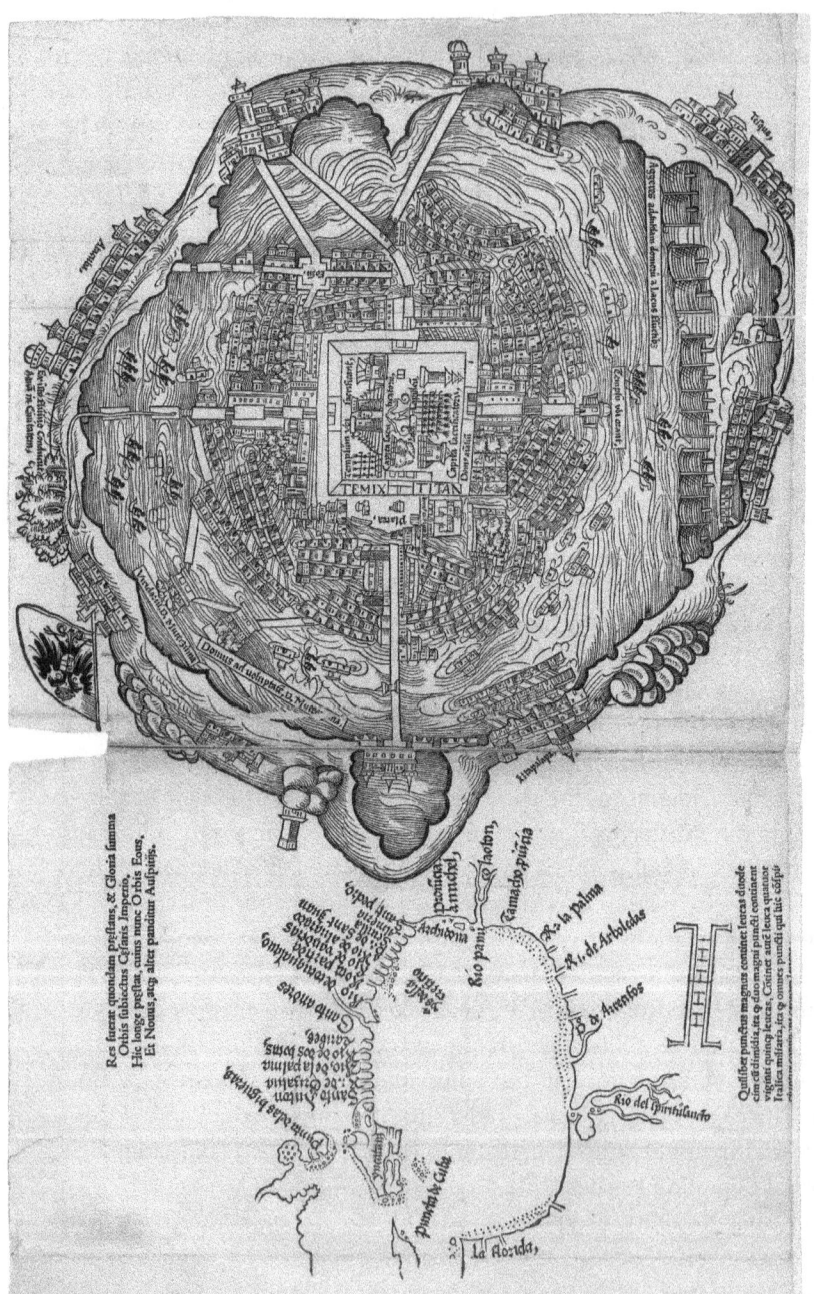

FIGURE I.6. This 1524 Spanish map of Tenochtitlan contains within it idealized Aztec geometries that patterned the city to reflect the order of the cosmos.

Courtesy of the John Carter Brown Library at Brown University.

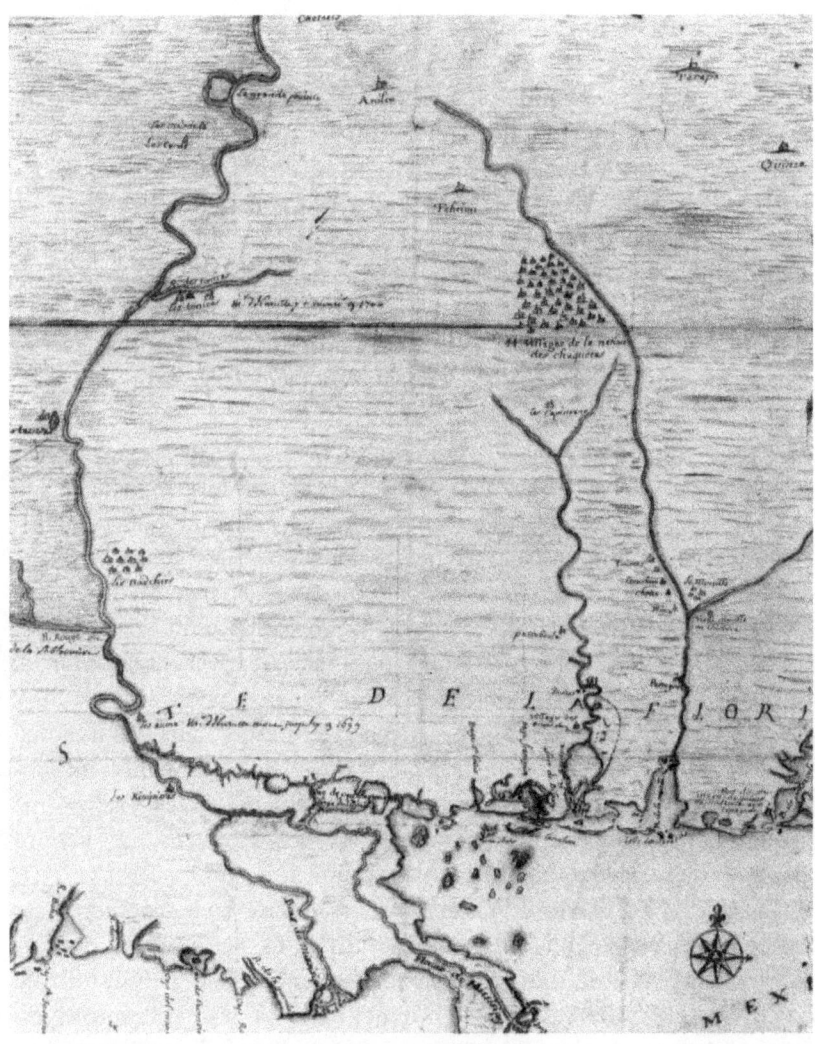

FIGURE I.7. Guillaume de L'Isle's map of the lower Mississippi Valley asserts a French claim based on "discovery," but it shows Native symbols for communities whose peoples already possessed, defined, and understood their land.

Circa 1700, Edward E. Ayer Collection.

Iroquois, Apaches, and Comanches in North America and Araucanians and Pampas in South America commanded the attention of officials as they expanded their own boundaries and threatened European ones.[14] Europeans who crossed the Atlantic to conquer, trade, and settle had little choice but to recognize the undeniably sovereign Indian presence. Give Pereira's map another look. At the same time that he proclaimed America was there for the taking, he highlighted the existence of Indian cities and populaces, prominently marking their placement across North America to convey Spanish expectations about Indians throughout America.

Pereira was far from the first or last European to incorporate Indian geographies into his maps. The cartographic knowledge represented by such maps came equally if not more often from Indian informants and guides as it did from European exploration. European narratives and *relaciones* reported that Indians regularly drew maps at the behest of their foreign visitors. The very oldest extant North American example of such indigenous cartography comes from an Indian known only as Miguel, who was taken captive by Juan de Oñate's expedition out of New Mexico onto the Southern Plains in 1601. He drew the map the following year during interrogations in Mexico City to show indigenous highways, rivers, water sources, and settlements (with power and population denoted by each town's size), and with travel time and distances noted across more than one hundred thousand square miles from Mexico City to the Plains. His Spanish interrogators sought not only geographic data but also information about the region's geopolitics and the economic relations among Indian nations there—knowledge that might serve their colonial designs.[15]

Spanish and French visions of America always included Indians as their policies made Native populations intrinsic to their imperial projects and as knowledge of Indian locations, economies, and politics proved crucial to their colonial success. Samuel de Champlain's map of New France (1632) emphasized the locations of the Indian nations whose political and economic alliances aided the French fur trade and protected the French against the dominant Iroquois Confederacy. Colonial French officials throughout the seventeenth and eighteenth centuries had little choice but to recognize "that the territory of New France was not a physical space so much as a set of relationships that bound the French to their various Indian allies." Indian power to defend their borders—be they geopolitical or socioeconomic—made such information essential to European survival across landscapes they could not claim. Moving through another's land

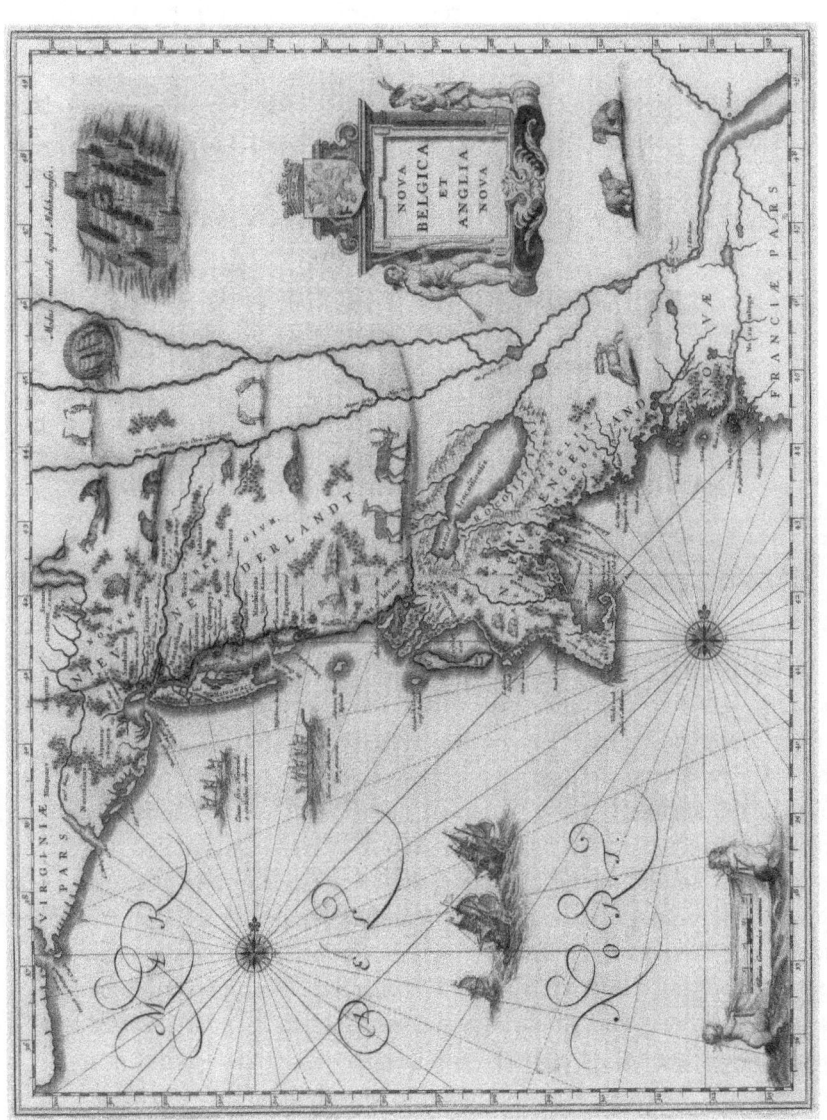

FIGURE I.8. The palisaded Indian town dominating the upper right recognizes Native power in relation to early Dutch and English settlers. Map of New Netherland by Willem Janszoon Blaeu, 1635.

Courtesy of the John Carter Brown Library at Brown University.

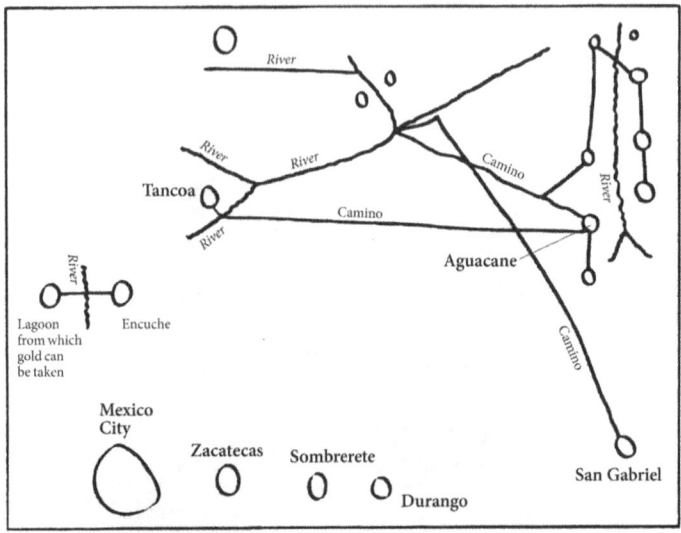

FIGURE I.9. "Indian Miguel's" map, originally drawn for Spanish officials, shows indigenous communities and roadways plotted across an area of more than one hundred thousand square miles.

Redrawn from G. Malcolm Lewis, "Indian Maps: Their Place in the History of Plains Cartography," *Great Plains Quarterly* 4 (Spring 1984), 101.

necessitated knowing whose borders you were trespassing and when and where one became safe or endangered because it was an ally's or enemy's territory.[16] For their part, Native people learned not only to keep Europeans out of their homelands, but also to deny the Europeans any real knowledge about such places.[17]

In contrast to the French and Spanish, English maps increasingly became "declaration[s] of exclusion for the Indian occupation of the land," giving visual representation to English legal presumptions of *vacuum domicilium* that proclaimed forfeit any lands they deemed not properly occupied or "settled" to those who would attach themselves to it in a "civilized" manner. As early as 1616, John Smith expunged all Indian place-names from his map of New England, replacing them with English substitutes before any Englishman had set foot in the region. Following the 1637 Pequot massacre, English officials renamed their destroyed village "New London," redubbed the Pequot River the "Thames," and forbid the use of the older name by any surviving individuals. If and when English maps indicated an

FIGURE I.10. Samuel Champlain's map of New France depicts a landscape blanketed with Native settlements, towns, and agricultural fields.

Courtesy of the John Carter Brown Library at Brown University.

Indian presence on the land, they invariably put them beyond a so-called *frontier* or *wilderness* demarcation. It can be no coincidence that the English philosopher John Locke once famously wrote that "in the beginning all the world was *America*," meaning it was almost empty, undeveloped, waiting to be taken.[18]

Accompanying this erasure, the reduction of bounded Indian polities and nations into a single "Indian Country" began to appear on English maps by 1700, along with the first reservations in North America. The same spirit of "dispossession by degrees" continued with the creation of the United States. Anglo-Americans "delineated both material and imagined borders for the nation, and they placed Indian people on the outside." Henry Popple's great map of the British Empire in America did show Native communities, but John Mitchell's 1755 map virtually ignored them and extended East Coast provincial boundary lines beyond the Mississippi River to boot.[19] It would be only in the late nineteenth century that Indians made a significant reappearance on United States maps. At that point, cartography documented the spatial segregation achieved by U.S. colonialism—in the form of reservations that served as a "concentration camp for the containment of dangerous people" and a "reeducation camp" for the remaking of Indians into a subaltern class. Dispossession meant not simply the loss of lands for Indians but also "deplacialization: the systematic destruction of regional landscapes that served as the concrete settings for local culture."[20]

The de L'Isle, Popple, Chickasaw, and Mitchell maps all were public statements, intended to be seen and to have an impact on the understanding of the people who saw them. The contrast between what the anonymous Chickasaw cartographer drew and the work of the other three points to one of the largest issues of spatial contestation in the colonial era. The Europeans were agents of and participants in the Westphalian system of nation-states that had effectively swept feudalism, the notion of a universal church, and the notion of universal empire off the European political map. The actual European colonies were outposts of that system, and the emergence of the United States began that system's full extension into the western hemisphere. But people like Chickasaws and Choctaws were outsiders to that system. They were caught up in the hemisphere-spanning colonial formation, not simply as victims but in many ways as active participants. But their terms of participation were not the same as those of their settler-colonist neighbors. The different Europeans contested with one another

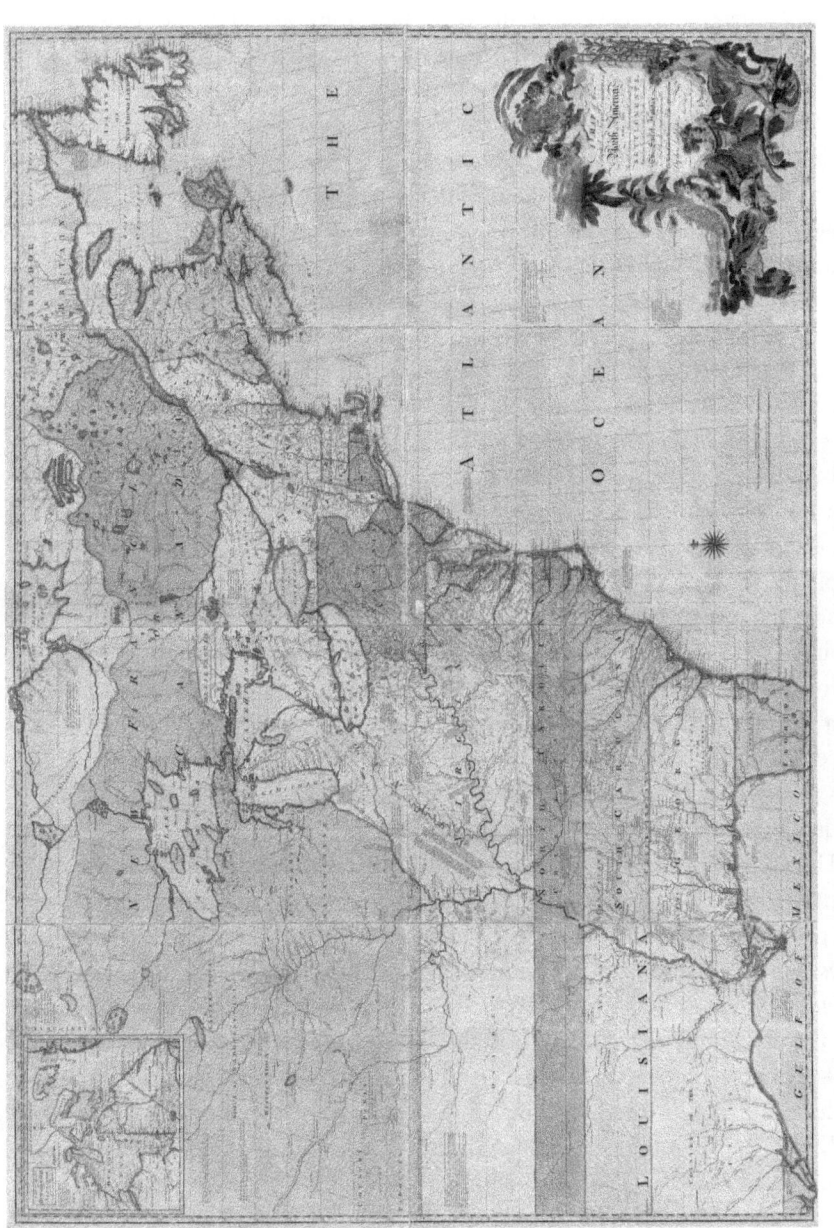

FIGURE I.11. John Mitchell's map of British America in 1755 extended eastern boundaries across the continent, ignoring both resident Native communities and other European claimants. Reproduced by the Library of Congress.

over American space within a general framework of understanding, ultimately expressed in law, a framework that they all understood and accepted. Europeans contested with indigenous people not just about land but about the entire framework of possession. The conventional distinction between "state" and "non-state" societies was yet another Euro-American attempt to draw differences. Beginning in the nineteenth century, then, nation-states like Mexico, Brazil, and the United States used mapping surveys and legislation to stamp out traditional Indian land uses and communal landholding whether they be deemed "domestic dependent nations" or peasant villagers within the modern body politic.[21]

It is from Euro-American rather than American Indian cartographic images that there developed the *terra cognita* so familiar to us and to our students when we visualize the geography of colonial America in textbook and classroom maps: the waters and lands of the western hemisphere covered with the shaded hatch marks and sharply drawn lines of vying European border claims. These renamed, defined, and possessed regions are connected to the world across the Atlantic, from which were coming the people who, supposedly, were the sole makers of early American history.[22] As such maps evolved over time, the lines increased and spread across the continent, and the maps describe how Europeans came to define, use, and control American spaces. We thus have clear origins for the progression from imperial visions of early modern states to the modern national borders of Peru, Brazil, Mexico, Canada, the United States and the many countries in between. We are also left with a specifically plural "Americas," divided into imperial zones that led inexorably to national ones.[23]

The casting of early America as proto-nationalist spaces whose stories are the seedbed for modern nation-states has in turn led us down the garden path to a "hierarchy of geographical spaces"—with different colonial zones ranked as centers or peripheries when judged from European frames of reference across the Atlantic World. The frames make Indians superfluous because within them the historical narrative has only one skewed storyline—that of the processes by which supposedly pristine wilderness became productive space through colonial development and "civilization." We imply the "inevitability of the modern map" and modern states when we "succumb to the temptation to superimpose these lines on earlier historical periods, when they did not yet exist." To attempt to fit the history of America and its indigenous population into the smaller and shorter histories of modern nations is to be teleological, understanding colonial or early

America not on its own terms but only in terms of what now has succeeded it. It is as if we were to try to understand the ancient Roman Empire in terms of the modern European Union. It is to let the modern tail wag the historical dog.[24]

IN an effort to reclaim early America from such modern conceptions, the original essays collected here seek to bring together the parallel histories and historiographies of European and Indian spaces created throughout the hemisphere during the "colonial era." The hemispheric perspective of Pereira's that we have discussed is critical to ensuring that Indians "are at the starting point of any analysis of colonization." David J. Weber, to whom this volume is dedicated, was one in a long line of Latin American and Iberian historians calling for hemispheric history, and he made the most persuasive case yet that the Americas do have a common history. Joining Herbert E. Bolton, Silvio Zavala, J. H. Elliott, and others, Weber added a crucial modifier to the call, arguing most persuasively in his last book, *Bárbaros*, that the Indian population was the defining commonality to European experience, throughout all of colonial America, North, Central, and South, whatever Europeans those Indians encountered. European officialdom might place all Indians—even *indios no sometidos* ("Indians who had not submitted")—within their rule and polity, but that claim remained a mere boast in most places and cases. Policy flowed from Indian lands to the metropolis as Indian power and authority thwarted or bent imperial goals to their own ends. Rather than imposing firm lines, creoles and Indians created porous boundaries that they crossed regularly in order to trade, live, and marry. In comparisons of New Spain, New England, and New France, scholars "tend to attribute the differences they find primarily to the national characters of European kingdoms," yet "wherever we analyze colonial enterprise in the Americas, we must begin with the realization that Native American societies gave those efforts their essential shape." Put simply, in building new empires and nations on the sites of those that had come before, European societies took their form and shape from the Indian spaces they inhabited (and often shared with them).[25]

Following that lead, we have consciously chosen to define early America as a single unified space defined by indigenous experiences with colonialism. At the heart of this book is a search for a human geography of colonial relations. Our first step is to redefine its space and borders, ridding the historical landscape of imperial cores, Native peripheries, and modern national borders that "obfuscat[e] the colonization and dispossession of Native peoples" as part of the "ideological work performed by national history in a settler state." We shift our gaze from the water and from coastal European perspectives in order to focus on Indian cores within America. This will not merely help us to understand early America equally from an Indian perspective; it also allows us to come to grips with the everyday realities of those long-ago worlds.[26]

The history of American space is an old one, with narrative roots dating back long before European arrivals in the early modern period. Moving away from European cartographic visions frees us to reimagine space not as a surface to be crossed and conquered but rather as the product of interrelations, be they local or global, "a place where people came together to coexist as best they could." Interrelations are by definition plural, and space then is clearly co-constitutive—a "sphere in which distinct trajectories coexist" with "dynamic simultaneity." The space called early America is where we will find the meeting up of multiple stories and histories, brought together by contemporaneous European and Indian journeying, each with their own spaces and geographies.[27]

Bringing our story of America literally down to earth helps us to see how European ventures in America far more often reflected locally driven systems negotiated with Indians rather than metropolitan designs. The reality of colonial spaces thus had little to do with imperial cores in Europe. It is not surprising that recent historiography has produced many geographical metaphors for colonial processes in early America—borderlands, middle grounds, Native grounds—but we can only trace the shifts and evolutions of those spaces once we have restored Indian landscapes, not as static places outside history but as developing within their own history, before and after contact. When we pay more attention to the perspectives of America's Indian inhabitants, it quickly becomes clear that many more borders and borderlands existed than current historiographical discussion allows for, and the borders and borderlands that scholars do recognize often arose as much from indigenous forms of territorial control as from European assertions of authority. Our histories must recognize the sovereignty of Indian nations and that "their claims to sovereignty rest on a simple fact: in one form or another, they were here before Columbus." Most fundamentally, that power was made manifest on the land and within unequivocal borders so that the effects of and responses to colonialism would be "rooted deeply in place."[28]

Nor did colonialism (and the history of contested spaces) end with the creation of new Euro-American nation-states in the nineteenth century. If we are engaged in reversing an image of early America as proto-nationalist, we might also ask whether America has entered a postcolonial age. Nationalism finally succeeded in breaking apart "colonial America" in historical understanding, but, on the ground, independent Indians maintained sovereign polities (as do many today) and had controlled far more than half the landmass from Canada to Peru until well into the nineteenth century— much of it within the borders claimed by Euro-American nations. In some ways, the American hemisphere may be just as much a colonial space today as it was in 1700, considering as we might the Indian reservations still dotting the maps of Canada and the United States and the continued battles fought by independent Indians in Chiapas and Brazil. The legacy of early America remains with us, as several of the essays will attest, because a sense of place also represents a culling of experience, of "what has accrued—and never stops accruing."[29]

PART I of the book, "Spaces and Power," is large and conceptual. Its first two essays seek to contribute to a portrait of the colonial era hemisphere's "vernacular landscape."[30] Pekka Hämäläinen poses the problem of how to integrate the overarching and the local, seeking to explore how different power dynamics emanated out from the indigenous interior and spread to the continent's edges where they gave shape and limits to European ambitions. Allan Greer, like Weber, ranges widely in both space and time while zooming in to a tight focus on one specific issue. This is how "Indian" land became "European" land in different colonial situations of French, Spanish, and English usurpation and, in particular, among English colonizers. He asks how their United States and Canadian successors transformed Native land into a marketplace commodity, as opposed to what Native people understood when they "sold" it. Reaching into both the Spanish and French zones, Greer (again like Weber) makes a strong argument against the "black legend" that has led to regarding Spanish practice as inherently more violent than that of the English.

In Part II, "Spaces and Landscapes," Elizabeth Fenn deals with a place that lay at the heart of the North American Native world. Writing about the Mandan villages at the Great Bend of the Missouri River, she poses questions about their long, vital survival amid the transformations that contact with Europeans set loose and about their sudden collapse in the middle of the nineteenth century. She shows that, to understand the tiny point that the Mandans occupied within the vast space of the continental interior, one must understand both their space and their time on a large scale. Cynthia Radding takes on the theme of "creating space" directly. Like Fenn, she examines the rhythm of advance and retreat of different groups' domains. But whereas Fenn tracks the expansion and retraction of Native populations and the spaces they inhabited as they responded to changing contours of the land's resources and the ravages of European disease, Radding explains how Indian communities maintained territorial and ethnic integrity even as the arrival of mines, missions, labor migrations, and Native enslavement led to overlapping Spanish and Indian societies. Writing from the perspective of residents of Buenos Aires and of the Pampas that sprawled to its south, Raúl José Mandrini continues the theme of overlapping societies, in this case based on people who enjoyed great mobility. In his essay the Pampas indigenes south of and surrounding Buenos Aires seem much like people of the Great Plains, except that wild cattle, rather than bison, figured in their lives. Like the people studied by Fenn, Radding, and Greer, they contested the understanding, control, possession, and use of space with invaders who would not go away.

Part III turns from long-lasting and relatively fluid contestation to "Space and Resettlements." Matthew Babcock's essay on Apache reservations under Spanish and Mexican dominion achieves two separate purposes. One is to break with received general notions of Apache people as simply warlike wanderers and hunters. On the contrary, like Mandans, they practiced agriculture, which required that they occupy settled spaces. The other is to complicate the very notion of an "Indian reservation." The Apache settlements that Babcock studies emerged from negotiation, not from imprisonment, and they were bases from which their people often ranged widely in pursuit of their own purposes.

Much farther south, but also reaching into the country that Radding and Babcock consider, Chantal Cramaussel faces directly a theme that runs through many of the other essays: forced labor and outright enslavement. Understanding of American Indian enslavement has increased enormously in recent scholarship. Colonizers practiced it one way or another throughout the hemisphere, parallel in geographical scale if not in outright numbers to the enslavement of Africans for American labor. Spaniards did so despite the supposed prohibition on enslaving Indians legislated as early as the New Laws of 1542. Like African enslavement, Indian bondage took many specific forms, but again like African enslavement, it came to form a pan-American pattern. In particular, Cramaussel brings out Greer's point that Spanish colonizers wanted labor rather than land. Alan Taylor concludes Part III with an examination of contestation among the colonizers, not on the level of imperial conflict but among the "pioneers" and "settlers" who rapidly extended the dominion of the United States westward after the era of independence. Their object was land. Unlike Greer's early colonial New Englanders, who used the discourse of law to dispossess Native people, Taylor's subjects contested with one another, both for land and for the power to define, delimit, and control that land for their own benefit.

The four essays that make up Part IV, "Spaces and Memory," address how contestation moved from "real" or "historical" affairs and events into the realm of memory, and how the memories linger on. Brian DeLay opens this part of the discussion by showing how both long-standing and recent memories persisted in folklore and custom during the nineteenth century in the newly conquered American Southwest. Those memories guided people who were facing the problem of how and when a conflict might "legitimately" become violent. The literary scholar Birgit Brander Rasmussen reaches in a different direction, exploring the artistic achievement and the consciousness of a late nineteenth-century Kiowa man. Many scholars have explored how "white" captivity stories can take their readers at least partly into the world of the Native captors. A fair number of those people "went Native" themselves, to the point that the image of a captive white person, usually a woman, has become familiar in American popular culture. Few have reversed the perspective, as Rasmussen does, exploring captivity from the viewpoint of a male Native.

Ned Blackhawk likewise deals with Native people expressing their own thoughts. Closely examining two enormous and relatively well-known hide paintings from the early eighteenth-century Southwest, he shows how they depicted violence that swept over the land, pitting Native people against Spaniards (in a battle that the Indians won) and also against one another. He also shows how the paintings address the problem of identity in a world of turmoil, both as experienced and as represented for others to see. Finally, Samuel Truett deals with the question of memory both during the age of conflicting empires and after the shooting finally stopped. Starting with efforts early in the colonial era to find an "ancient" American past written into the very landscape, he traces the theme of conflicting or complex memories about American space into the age of capitalist exploitation by an emergent tourism industry.

Taken together, these essays demonstrate that the geography of the western hemisphere's landscapes is covered by layer after layer of historical detritus, just as surely as any place in the so-called Old World. The notion of such "layered history" is beginning to find currency in writings on the American past, or pasts, developing Nobel Prize–winning novelist William Faulkner's famous dictum that "the past is never dead. It's not even past."[31] The essays do not at all exhaust the topic. The hard, clearly drawn boundaries that appear on modern geopolitical maps of the western hemisphere suggest a permanent fixity that contrasts strikingly with the fluidity and uncertainty of the American landscapes that the writers here consider. Those older landscapes were as much a human creation as modern boundaries. The many sorts of people who inscribed those landscapes with their presence, their actions, their plans, their successes, and their failures were not precursors or pioneers of a future they could not foresee, a future of which they had not even dreamed. They were contestants in their own world. What they wrought and how they wrought it still lingers, and the contestation is not at all over.

PART I
Spaces and Power

CHAPTER 1

The Shapes of Power: Indians, Europeans, and North American Worlds from the Seventeenth to the Nineteenth Century

Pekka Hämäläinen

In 1948, Carl Bridenbaugh, the director of the Institute of Early American History, reported that his field was in crisis. The history of colonial America, he lamented, had been eclipsed by the attention-grabbing Revolutionary era, and nonspecialists thought that almost all of colonial history had already been written. Today, more than sixty years later, the field faces a different kind of challenge. If in Bridenbaugh's time there did not seem to be enough history for the field to endure, today there seems to be too much of it. The history of colonial America has been nudged out of its Anglocentric trenches and extended deep into the nineteenth century under the rubric of early American history.[1] Anchored in multiple historiographies and spatial coordinates, today's scholarship produces so much new history that we do not quite know where to put it all. And so we have broken it into pieces and sprinkled the pieces around: first on the Atlantic, then on indigenous America, and now on borderlands and the Pacific.

In doing so, we might be pushing the field into yet another impasse. By tracing early America to its varied global origins and slicing it up for analytical purposes, historians are atomizing their subject. If the long-dominant Atlantic paradigm integrated early America into multidirectional transoceanic networks, the current stretching of early America across the continent has coincided with what might be called a localist turn in the field. Historians have moved early American history beyond British America not so much with broad strokes than with countless, tightly focused monographs that have illuminated nearly every obscured corner of the continent. Wonderfully space- and time-specific, these works have abandoned the pointed teleology of the Anglocentric master story for a patchwork of localized narratives and microworlds—some of them colonial, some of them Native, some something in between. This is an intellectual overhaul of vast proportions—a continent that was but half-illuminated is now filled with detail and texture—but it has come with a price. With the increased specialization, something has been lost: a sense of the whole, a sense of connections among peoples, places, and periods. In the early twenty-first century, it seems impossible to talk about "early American history," at least in the singular. Viewed through the local lens, North America seems little more than a fictional unit of analysis, an artificial container for countless small stories and center points that have little in common beyond basic geographical proximity.[2]

The early America that now dominates academic histories is nuanced and inclusive, but it is also blurred and curiously one-dimensional. Like a pointillist painting observed close-up, it overwhelms: dots stretch out to all directions, but they do not seem to blend together into shapes. We know that the dots *were* linked—every homeland was also a borderland, a zone of contestation and intermixing—but that awareness only heightens our sense of disorientation. A "mosaic [of] a hundred different colours," "a kaleidoscopic array of people migrating and merging in dizzying profusion," a "mixed and mixed-up world where frontier cultures coincided as well as collided": early America as it is viewed today is a protean medley of animated pieces, each arresting in its own light, all unique in a vaguely similar way. The persistent recycling of stock elements—microcontingencies, face-to-face encounters, small group agency—has built a paradox in the heart of early American history. Individual works may celebrate the particularity of different places, but as a collective they impart a conspicuous sense of déjà vu. And the irony runs deeper still. Local and continental approaches to early American history are two sides of the same historiographical coin, but increasingly they seem to be at cross-purposes. Together, they have allowed historians to reclaim a larger continental setting from the shadows of Anglo- and Atlantic-centered histories, but the localist turn might lead them to lose it once again, this time to overwhelming specificity. If older paradigms glossed over larger continental developments, localism is splintering and hiding them from plain sight.[3]

This fragmentation of early American history reflects the relativist mood of our times. Suspicious of grand narratives and generalization, historians feel comfortable with this pulverized edition, believing that it captures the essence of the early American experience: the immediacy and inherent provincialism of everyday life, the primacy of familial and communal ties in shaping social identities.[4] And yet early America was neither flat nor amorphous: there were cohering loyalties, large patterns, and transcending trajectories. Each small niche was part of larger circuits—political, economic, cultural, biological—and it is those wider coordinates of early American history that are now becoming obscured. Early American history is too broad and diverse to be squeezed into a single master narrative—the time of Turnerian epics is irrevocably in the past—but it is possible to widen the lens and interweave local and regional tales into larger *American* stories that transcend places, boundaries, and periods. This essay is an attempt to uncover such broader patterns—larger stories mined from the smaller ones. It asks how we might reconcile the multidirectional messiness of local contingencies with broader structural developments, and it probes how the many pieces of the American mosaic might coalesce to form an early American history that is greater than the sum of its parts.

A short essay can only point—not illustrate—how the new early American history might look like; it needs a lens that is at once broad and selective. Here that lens is power, the ability of human groups to control space and resources, to create dependencies and neutralize rivals, to influence the behaviors and perceptions of others, and to initiate and resist change. This essay places power at the front and center of analysis; it is, in a sense, a very short biography of power in North America at a time when the continent was contested by many and controlled by none. It charts how power was amassed, expressed, shared, deflected, and lost during the three centuries from the establishment of the first permanent European outposts to the consolidation of colonial conquest in the West in the late nineteenth century. It looks at how different forms of power intersected to shape the fates of human societies across the continent, and it traces how power dynamics varied from place to place and changed over time, constellating into broad spatial configurations around which different social worlds formed. These were distinctive worlds—in mood and in terms of social cohesion and stability—but they were not isolated. They emerged and evolved in interaction and they collapsed into one another at the edges. They were entangled worlds, and in their linkages can be found the sinews of new, multifaceted continental narratives.[5]

To understand these worlds and their distinctions, it is necessary to ask what counted as power in a volatile setting where drastically different peoples collided and somehow had to come to terms with another. The answers are not obvious. Traditional sources and forms of power—population, technology, wealth, military might, organizational efficiency, literacy—mattered greatly in shaping intergroup relations in early America, but they mattered less than one might think. Europeans often disagreed over the ends and meanings of their colonial projects, and Indians soon gained access to new technologies. Many Native societies suffered devastating losses in the new disease environment, but many others expanded in numbers. And when such things happened, other types of power grew more critical: kinship networks, moral authority through cultural knowledge, capacity to forge loyalties through persuasion, ability to play off rival powers against one another. These forms of power were often more readily available to the Natives rather than the newcomers, and Indians held sway over much of the continental interior during the so-called colonial era. In the plains and mountains of the American West that control did not break until the late nineteenth century when the United States turned itself into a continental empire through raw military and material might.

On the surface, North America appears to have been a soft target for European colonialism. Its long east- and south-facing coastline, studded with broad-mouthed rivers, seemed to invite in the major western European maritime powers that were racing to plant colonies across the Atlantic littoral. Its southwest corner was linked to Spanish Mexico, Europe's strongest New World colony, through a widening landmass that funneled people and pathogens northward. And even its rugged, subarctic northern cap had a welcoming dent—Hudson Bay—that anchored a fan-shaped river system extending deep into the interior. Europeans soon discovered these many entryways, building outposts from New Mexico to New England and from Florida to the St. Lawrence Valley, but the actual colonization of North America was slow and halting. Apart from infiltrations—French and British trading posts in the Great Lakes region and the Canadian Shield, the Franciscan mission belt in northern Florida—interior America remained beyond colonial reach well into the eighteenth century.

Traditional explanations for North America's slow colonization stress geopolitics, topography, and European disinterest. Because of their rich sugar plantations and silver mines, the Caribbean and central Mexico remained the focal point of colonial ambitions, while North American staples—fish, furs, and, slowly, tobacco—stirred fainter passions. And despite its outward openness, North America could be geographically forbidding: many of its inviting entryways turned into dead ends. Most rivers of the coastal plains offered but short penetrations, and the Appalachians beyond them repulsed the Atlantic empires that were not prepared to expand vertically. California's rough coast, the Southwest's rugged mountains, and the Great Plains' aridity and vastness deterred the expansion of agro-ranching frontiers from Mexico, while harsh winters in the north dissuaded settlers who had migrated latitudinally across the Atlantic. And when the long search for the Northwest Passage proved futile, making it plain that there would be no equivalent of the continent-spanning Spanish Mexico, both France and England devoted a growing portion of their resources to securing outposts in Africa and Asia.[6]

But there is another dimension to the riddle of a continent that seemed to at once invite and repel colonialism: the people living on it. If traditional explanations of North America's distinctive colonial trajectory neglected Native Americans, it was largely because historians, just like colonial agents, were blind to indigenous forms of territoriality. They saw Indians as prepolitical actors who had homelands but not boundaries. Native Americans, the thinking went, may have had deep historical and spiritual attachments to specific places, but geopolitically they just occupied space. Lacking maps, treaties, armies, and fences, they lacked both the mental and material tools to conceive borders and impose them on others. It is only recently that historians have begun to unearth indigenous conceptions of territoriality underneath such assumptions. Native notions of land, claims, and sovereignty differed drastically from European ones, but indigenous societies knew precisely where their domains began and others' ended. They abided by a complex array of principles and practices that guided how societies could share resources and how territories could overlap and merge at the edges. Behavior and tradition rather than contracts or nationality defined indigenous borders, making them difficult for Europeans to recognize. Yet, in the end, recognize them they did.[7]

From one bridgehead to another and across the continent's edge, European pretensions to empire crashed against indigenous territoriality. In New Mexico and Texas, Spanish colonists had to adjust their political ambitions and, eventually, their borders to varied and overlapping indigenous territorial practices. On the coastal lowlands, the nomadic Coahuilteco speakers steered clear of Spanish settlements but incorporated Spanish missions into their seasonal cycle as resource depots. Farther north, the Hasinai Confederacy kept its urbanized village world inviolate through surveillance and ceremonial protocols that amounted to a kind of passport system. On the short-grass plains north and west of the Hasinais, the Apaches and Comanches relied on raiding and nomadic mobility to protect and then expand their territories in regions that were claimed by Spain. The French Louisiana within French maps extended hundreds of miles west of the Mississippi Valley but was in reality boxed in by powerful indigenous confederacies and numerous *petites nations* whose collective presence reduced the colony to a marginal political player that often seemed to operate under Native control. In the eastern woodlands where colonial pressure was greater, Indians marked boundaries with painted trees, stones, graves, and stories; when those boundaries were violated, they killed European cattle, sheep, and pigs and littered the frontiers with mutilated carcasses, thus targeting the practice of livestock husbandry that both sustained and symbolized English colonization. In New England, the colonists began fencing their landholdings not only to separate fields and domesticates but also to contain the Indians whose claims to territorial sovereignty and wide-ranging hunting and gathering activities posed a threat to Puritan betterment and identity. There, by simply refusing to leave or die, Indians forced settlers to confine their domains.[8]

Violence, claims, and markers thus imposed indigenous territoriality on colonial powers, but Native Americans employed subtler methods as well. Around 1721, a Catawba Indian headman gave Francis Nicholson, the governor of South Carolina, a skin map that depicted a large section of the Southeast. Less a cartographic representation of space than a social manual for proper behavior on the frontier, the map made a series of political claims and demands. Native groups were marked with circles, and the Nasaws, the dominant members of the Catawba Confederacy, occupied the largest one near the map center. The colonies of Virginia and South Carolina lay in the periphery at opposite sides of the map, marked with rectangular borders and grid patterns that set them apart from the indigenous landscape of round shapes. Cross-cultural communication was to flow through the Nasaws, the only Native group with connective pathways to both colonies. Drawn after more than a century of colonization, the map acknowledged British presence in the Southeast but placed it within narrow confines: it taught the colonists how to behave in a world where Indians were still powerful enough to influence who belonged where and on what terms. The Catawbas, a relatively small confederacy, stayed in the same territory in the North Carolina Piedmont through the colonial era, imposing on Europeans—whom they called "nothings"—the conditions under which they could enter the region. Such a pattern of indigenous boundary enforcing ran the length of the Eastern Seaboard, demarcating limits for English colonialism.[9]

And so, through force and lessons, a sweeping geographical pattern took shape: indigenous societies across the continent limited colonial control to relatively small coastal and riverine outposts. These outposts were pockets of concentrated colonial power, whose influence radiated deep into the continent through commerce, diplomacy, and biological exchanges, but the great interior remained closed to European settlement. For generations, English settlers huddled close to the Atlantic. They expanded north- and southward on the coastal lowlands, dispossessing numerous Native societies and absorbing Dutch colonies in the process, but western advances remained incremental. Only in the Hudson, Connecticut, and James valleys did settlers push inland early on, and the backcountry, a distinct region separated from the coastal colonies by space and culture, took decades to emerge. Spanish colonialism leapt in the eighteenth century from Florida, New Mexico, and Texas to the lower Mississippi Valley and California, but Spanish dreams of a continuous North American empire remained elusive. French traders ventured far and wide, but French settlement never left the St. Lawrence and Mississippi valleys. Much of North America was still unknown to Europeans in the 1760s, and as late as the 1780s more than three-quarters of the continent remained under Native control.[10]

Thwarted by indigenous territoriality, the would-be colonists had to adjust to unexpected spatial and political realities. Legalistic denials of indigenous titles by way of *terra nullius* and other colonial doctrines remained dead letters, meaningful only in European diplomatic circuits, and vast imperial claims turned into imaginary—and often blind—paper claims. Spearheads of colonial expansion morphed into defensive ethnic enclaves, and imperial frontiers softened into borderlands where indigenous forms of social control not only prevailed but often dominated. North America's first settler colonies became awkwardly suspended between two cores—one of them European, the other Native American—and much of the continent remained for generations a fluid and open field where the nature of Indian-European relations varied widely and where numerous power configurations and social worlds were possible.[11]

THE great interior may have remained beyond their grasp, but the colonists clustered on North America's edges were neither demoralized nor powerless. Being confined to the margins did not quench their colonizing ambitions; rather, it focused and then differentiated them spatially. Unable to build expanding realms of domination and extraction, the colonists conceived other ways to access the things—pelts, converts, laborers, slaves, allies—they had come for. Gradually, and often in ad hoc fashion, the Spaniards, French, and English began a process of turning their fringe enclaves into composite systems of power and control: there would be relatively small, tightly regulated core areas of settlement beyond which there would be blurrier, outward-fanning outer spheres of political and commercial influence. The colonists would also formulate two distinctive Indian policies: one for the distant independent nations who were to be cajoled and co-opted, the other for near Native neighbors who were to be, depending on circumstances, eliminated, subjugated, or incorporated. If the former policy would ultimately become the key to European success in North America, the latter was, in the short run, more critical.

For the first two and a half centuries, Spanish colonialism in the Americas hinged on the conversion and incorporation of indigenous populations. There were unauthorized local improvisations and brief experiments with other policies, but assimilation—through conversion, disciplining, and eradication of Native ways—remained the cornerstone of the Spanish imperial project. Throughout Spanish North America, Franciscan missions became the principal vehicles for incorporation, backed in Florida and California by presidios and in New Mexico by a secular colonial government seated in Santa Fe. Spanish colonization involved substantial settlement in New Mexico only, where Hispanic peasants and elite *encomenderos* settled near Native villages along the upper Rio Grande Valley to exploit the labor of the Pueblo Indians, the province's only source of revenue. Yet New Mexico, too, was essentially a missionary enterprise through its first century of existence.[12]

Across Spanish North America, large numbers of Indians moved into missions, responding to various pressures and possibilities. Some were forced in by Spanish soldiers and some were drawn in by promises of gifts and spiritual largesse, but many more came to rebuild communities ravaged by the reverberations of colonial invasion: diseases, disintegration of traditional economies, hunger, and escalating intra-Native violence. Regardless of their motives, North American Indians entered a system that had been refined over generations to transform pagans into Catholics, nomads into farmers, polygamists into monogamists, and tribal leaders into colonial proxies. This Franciscan agenda of sociocultural uplift was, on the surface, a success comparable to the galvanizing feats of conversion and pacification by Franciscan, Dominican, and Augustinian friars in sixteenth-century Mexico and Peru. By 1630, Franciscans boasted having baptized eighty-six thousand Natives in New Mexico, and in mid-seventeenth-century Florida seventy friars ministered to twenty-six thousand converts. In 1821, California had twenty missions with more than twenty-one thousand Indians attached to them.

Such reports of missionary triumph conceal a more complex reality, however. Indians embraced Christian doctrine selectively, incorporating elements of it into their traditions while shielding an inner core of indigenous religiosity. Elected Indian *alcaldes* continued to draw their authority from both Spaniards and their own people, and many of them maneuvered to mitigate Spanish efforts to stamp out Native ways. Mission Indians toiled on fields, gardens, and kitchens, but often their labor was contracted rather than coerced. And yet, even if the level of Christianization and Hispanicization fell short of what the official reports suggest, the accounts capture an essential truth. In Spanish North America tens of thousands of Indians lived in colonial spaces where their actions—especially in the realms of marriage and sexuality—were closely monitored and where the boundaries of acceptable behavior were defined by imposed legal codes, public corporal punishments, rigid daily routines, and the compartmentalized architecture of mission complexes themselves.[13]

Spain's and England's American empires have often been presented as a study in contrasts: Spain, a land-based empire of conquest suffused by bureaucratic centralism, militant Catholicism, and racial tolerance juxtaposed with England, a market-driven maritime empire defined by political decentralization, religious pluralism, racial prejudice, and guarded engagements with indigenous populations. In the early stages of North American colonization, however, similarities between Spanish and English colonial projects were often more pronounced than their differences—especially when viewed from a Native perspective. Both had to come to terms with enduring indigenous societies in their midst, both saw in Indians lost souls worthy of saving, and both were alive with conquistador fantasies of ruling over submissive Natives. And, eventually, both incorporated Native peoples into their realms, although their motives for doing so were strikingly different.[14]

For Spaniards, the incorporation of Natives was an end in itself, the raison d'être of colonialism. They sought territorial control through social control and targeted the largest and richest Native societies on top of which they could insert themselves as masters. In English America, by contrast, conquest came first, and incorporation followed nearly as an afterthought. There were early attempts at mutual incorporation across the English seashore—most notably in the Chesapeake Bay where Powhatan Indians tried to turn the newcomers into kin even as Virginians tried to integrate the Indians as vassals and laborers—but such efforts did not last. Spurred by dreams of landed power—kindled in Virginia by a tightening land-labor-power nexus and in New England by a mixture of political localism and hot Protestantism—settlers began entering and claiming the territories of their Indian allies. Disputes and violence became routine, disease epidemics broke out, and Native societies splintered and coalesced into new hybrid formations. The colonists closed ranks in the face of indigenous power. In 1643 New England colonies formed an alliance against the local Indians and in 1646 Virginians delivered a crushing blow to the Powhatan Confederacy, thereby eliminating effective resistance in roughly two generations. By the 1680s, in the aftermath of Metacom's War and Bacon's Rebellion, English colonists controlled almost all of the coastal plain in New England and the Chesapeake Bay. Many Native groups withdrew to the interior, and those who stayed soon found themselves enveloped by farms, plantations, and towns. Remnants of much larger groups, they had to find ways to carve out niches among colonists who never really had planned to incorporate them.[15]

Their options were limited and became more so over time, for English colonies were developing into fully fledged settler societies that were self-reliant, agricultural, land-hungry, and impatient with indigenous presence. Some of the encapsulated Indians entered praying towns—the prime manifestation of New England's missionary impulse—in which, under the tutelage of ministers and pastors and in isolation from the corrupting influences of the larger colonial society, they were to be immersed in Christianity and Western civility. Others became attached to less insular missions and colonial schools that sprang up from Martha's Vineyard to Virginia. Like the thousands of Indians concentrated into *reducciones* throughout Spanish America, these Indians adapted and changed without ceasing to be Indians. Some accepted Christianity as a protective sheen against further abuse, and some refitted parts of the gospel to their needs. Some became genuine converts, responding to offerings of spiritual and communal support in a rapidly changing world.[16]

But only a portion of the resident Indians could or would adapt enough to win acceptance into English societies, which expected incorporated Natives to shed their Nativeness and yet often shunned those who seemed to assimilate too successfully. Most Indians living among colonists maneuvered at the social margins, blending in selectively while struggling to preserve their identity. They dressed, drank, and cursed like the English to avert attention and, putting old skills to new uses, sold their labor as hunters, sailors, soldiers, potters, woodworkers, farmhands, day laborers, interpreters, and healers. Some relied on poor relief and some became vagrants to escape colonial control. Some Native women married African men to rebuild families. For many, traditional kinship obligations of reciprocity—which evolved into a kind of informal welfare network—formed the last line against destitution.

Many, then, survived as Indians among Europeans, but the colonial world weighed heavily on them. If they settled into distinctive communities, they were expected to build English-style houses, erect fences, raise livestock, and practice plow farming. But too much adaptive acumen could be risky, prompting colonists to see Indians less as charges than as competitors. If Indians managed to register their land tracts, they faced the threat of being classified as "blacks" and have their claims nullified. For each resident Indian who managed to scrape by as a wage laborer, there were many more who slipped into bound servitude and de facto slavery. In the early seventeenth century, resident Indians had enjoyed limited legal rights in English colonies, sitting on juries and giving testimony, but those rights crumbled as the century wore on. Convictions favoring Indians over colonists grew rare, and discriminatory laws regarding Natives multiplied. Various disciplinary measures ranging from curfews to restrictions on assembly to prohibitions of firearms and alcohol shrank the Indians' public sphere. Between the 1690s and 1720s, across the Eastern Seaboard, white settlers created a legal and physical color line by prohibiting Indians from owning real estate, marrying whites, and walking at night without having passports or lanterns. In Virginia and the Carolinas, this racial segregation coincided, not coincidentally, with a rapid expansion of Indian slavery. In the closing decades of the seventeenth century, both colonies imported, either through raids or trade with Native traffickers, thousands of Indian captives who labored on rice and tobacco fields along with African slaves.[17]

If Spanish and English North Americas have sometimes been seen as a pair of contrasts, then French North America—a vast, amorphous interior empire of fur trade and Indian alliances—has stood apart. But this diffuse, crescent-shaped network was anchored at both ends to colonial nodes that had more in common with English and Spanish imperial enclaves than with the interior New France. The St. Lawrence Valley (Canada) and Louisiana linked La Nouvelle-France to the Atlantic supply lines and became points of hard and immediate colonial power. The climate, the seigneurial system, and a certain cultural aversion toward emigration thwarted mass migration to French North America; however, thousands came—*engagés*, soldiers, Jesuits—because they were drawn by fantasies of "La Nouvelle Jérusalem" among Indians and were sponsored by the French government, which assumed direct control of New France in 1663. By the early eighteenth century, the lower St. Lawrence Valley was lined with a continuous strip of small farms that stretched for more than two hundred miles on both sides of the river. In the lower Mississippi Valley, a similar, if patchier, riverfront settlement belt extended dozens of miles north and south of New Orleans.[18]

This expansion of French settlement brought death and dispossession for the indigenous habitants. Reflecting developments across the continent's colonial rim, burgeoning settlements sparked disease epidemics that killed tens of thousands of Indians and wrecked existing social formations. As in New England and the Chesapeake Bay, thousands of Indians fled the colonial encroachment, sometimes seeking refuge among more distant Native groups, sometimes clashing with them. But Canada and Louisiana did not become colonies without Indians. Some of the resident Indians stayed put to live among the French, and many more entered Canada and Louisiana involuntarily—as slaves purchased from Indian raiders, as captives ceremonially offered by Indian allies, as war captives taken from enemy tribes. Slave or free, these incorporated Indians mingled with French settlers at markets, streets, churches, and frontier posts, carving out social micro niches as field hands, domestics, dock loaders, millers, wives, and concubines. Yet, mirroring the developments in Spanish New Mexico and Florida, they also fell under piercing colonial surveillance and religious indoctrination. Exposed to lethal microbes and cut off from ancestral lands and kinship networks, they died in staggering numbers. In Canada, Indian slaves entering the colony were often no older than ten; they were dead, on the average, by eighteen.[19]

And so, at various points around the edge, European colonists planted themselves on and among Native communities, entrenching themselves in the continent. But while these violent impositions secured the viability of Old World colonial ventures in North America, they also accentuated how completely beyond European control the great Native nations of the interior were. Toward the end of the seventeenth century, European views of Indians were crystallizing into a polarity. There were subjugated Indians who were melting—or thought to be melting—into colonial domains, and there were independent Indians (*indios bárbaros*, *sauvages*, savages) whose territories and power extended unimaginable lengths toward the interior. From the former, Europeans wanted their land, labor, and souls. The latter they saw as potential allies and trading partners, conduits through which European influence could be extended beyond the small enclaves. But these independent Indians had political and economic ambitions of their own and, increasingly, the means to have them realized.[20]

BEHIND the indigenous territoriality that had closed most of North America to European settlement was indigenous agency, the ability of Native Americans to shape the creation and meaning of colonial America. The forces that defeated and destroyed indigenous groups near European outposts grew weaker with distance from the colonial rim. In the interior, the Columbian exchange did not simply wreak havoc; it could also work for Indians' advantage. Deadly pathogens made inroads but their impact remained local and limited, while new military technology—guns, metal, horses—became available through border markets and Native trade networks. The groups best positioned to take advantage of such circuits grew in numbers and power, and they then confronted European colonialism on their own terms.

Dynamic, domineering indigenous political formations rose across a broad transitional belt where Native societies were neither too close to European settlements to fall under their geo-biological shadow nor too far not to reap the technological and economic benefits that came with European presence. There were many such geographically privileged Native societies—the Osages and Quapaws west of the lower Mississippi Valley or the Muscogulges (Creeks) in the Southeast, to name just a few—but three large confederacies stand out: the Haudenosaunee, or the Iroquois League, in the interior Northeast; the Comanches in the Southwest; and the Lakota Sioux in the northern Great Plains. These three Native confederacies became dominant regional powers that extended their influence far beyond their core regions, growing more assertive, prosperous, and ethnically heterogeneous in the process. Did they become imperial? The Iroquois, Comanches, and Lakotas may not have understood themselves as unified empires, and they lacked centralized bureaucracies, standing armies, and other traditional hallmarks of empires. Yet, for a long while, and more successfully than the Europeans around them, they did what empires do. Like many domineering regimes in history, theirs were unintended ones, built and run by people who were busy doing something else: securing lives and livelihoods, reacting to external threats, protecting political interests and prestige.[21]

While European colonization of North America evolved with a kind of backward momentum—unbound by centralized control, the English expanded up and down the coastal plains through independent and largely ad hoc colonial ventures that seemed to fragment their realm as much as broaden it—the additions of Texas and Louisiana revealed the geopolitical anxieties of Spanish colonists rather than allayed them. The Iroquois, Comanches, and Lakotas built vast territorial domains through protracted, if episodic, conquests. The Comanches, newcomers to the Southwest from the Great Basin, relied on overpowering equestrian mobility to colonize the southern Great Plains—a quarter-million-square-mile expanse of vast bison herds, ancient commercial circuits, and protective river valleys—in a five-decade-long guerrilla war with the Apaches, who retreated into southern Texas and northern Mexico in order to build new lives from the fragments of the old one. Gradually, as the Apache lands of the southern Plains became *Comanchería*, a new *Apachería* emerged in the deserts and scrublands on both sides of the Rio Grande.[22]

The Lakotas penetrated the grasslands from the opposite side in the late eighteenth century, and theirs was an offshoot of a larger Dakota Sioux expansion that had already rearranged indigenous geographies in the western Great Lakes region during the previous century. While most Dakotas stayed east of the Mississippi River, vying to control the burgeoning fur trade, the Lakotas gravitated westward, drawn by the possibilities of equestrian bison hunting on the open Plains. On their way stood a belt of village farmers (the Mandans, Hidatsas, and Arikaras on the middle Missouri

River) and a zone of hunter-nomads (the Kiowas, Arapahos, Cheyennes, and Crows between the Missouri Valley and the Black Hills). Gradually, the Lakotas pushed through both barriers, capitalizing on their position at the intersection of two expanding technological frontiers: a northward-moving horse frontier and a southwestward-moving gun frontier. It was a powerful dynamic that drew the Lakotas, one band at a time, out onto the Plains where horses and guns came together. The Lakota expansion, like the Comanche expansion before it, was a sum of countless little invasions—autonomous bands inching their way westward, reacting to changing local circumstances rather than any overarching political agenda.[23]

The agricultural, village-dwelling Iroquois lacked the conquering reach of the equestrian Comanches and Lakotas, but they, too, carved out a vast domain through a series of small conquests. The consolidation of the Great League of Peace and Power in the sixteenth century stabilized relations among the five Iroquois nations—the Mohawks, Oneidas, Onondagas, Cayugas, and Senecas—and committed them to a vision of an integrated landscape of peace and belonging that enveloped Iroquoia and stretched beyond it. Colonial entrenchment in the early seventeenth century gave that vision new urgency and then militarized it. The Iroquois made a concerted bid to win access to the interior fur trade, which increasingly revolved around a French-Huron axis in the St. Lawrence–Great Lakes area, and to redirect the flow of furs, goods, knowledge, and power southward into their own villages. But even more than trade, the Iroquois wanted people: their campaigns were driven by a need to replenish disease-ravaged populations with war captives, a need that over time thickened into a military-cultural complex known as "mourning wars." These wars—which coincided with constant, often centrifugal relocations of Iroquois communities—extended the sixteenth-century Iroquoia between the Hudson and Genesee rivers into the northern and western shores of Lake Ontario. By the 1670s, the Iroquois League was the dominant territorial power in the eastern woodlands, its mobile villages covering a realm that dwarfed the French and English possessions around it. And like Comanche expansion within the southern Plains, Iroquois expansion left in its wake a shatter belt of destruction and displacement. Native confederacies collapsed, Huronia disintegrated, and refugees dispersed in all directions.[24]

The Iroquois, Comanches, and Lakotas carved out vast domains by projecting overwhelming violence, but as their expansions gradually slowed down, they fashioned more nuanced foreign policies. Conquests that were more improvised than planned solidified into realms that were more structured than shapeless. All three developed composite political economies that balanced warfare with diplomacy, coercion with commerce, and exploitation with conciliation.

In the 1670s, the Haudenosaunee and the English in New York forged a supple, long-standing coalition, the Covenant Chain, under which the two sides acknowledged their mutual dependence, conducted trade, defined the means to resolve conflict, and established a political partnership to manage the relationships between colonists and Natives from Virginia to Massachusetts. The Covenant Chain gave the Iroquois secure access to English markets and political support but, contrary to English claims, it did not lock them within an English orbit. Instead, the Covenant Chain bestowed the Iroquois with unparalleled political clout, which they leveraged on other fronts to pacify their borders and reduce rivals to security buffers. They absorbed thousands of captives as slaves and adoptees and embraced weakened enemies as metaphorical "women" or "nephews"—dependents whose ability to practice independent diplomacy was severely compromised and who were obliged to provide warriors for Iroquois campaigns. If the Iroquois never came to possess a cohesive empire, they did have, in the seventeenth century, a series of imperial moments, periods of political and economic ascendancy punctuated by temporary crises and reversals. A massive French army invaded Mohawk country in 1666 and destroyed several villages, but for the most part violence resided outside of Iroquoia: Haudenosaunee war parties raided pelts and captives from the Ottawa Valley to the upper Great Lakes, Ohio Country, the Mississippi Valley, and the Carolina Piedmont, creating protective, semideserted zones on their borders. The Iroquois shared power with the English in the East, jointly controlling smaller Native societies in their midst, and they dominated trade routes between the Hudson River and the Great Lakes. Their realm was an ever-shifting, multiethnic melting pot where Iroquois, Hurons, Eries, and Susquehannocks lived together and side by side, their old, often conflicting loyalties fomenting tension within the League without fracturing it. And while their many external entanglements seemed at times to overwhelm the Five Nations, village leaders managed to forge unprecedented unity of purpose and action through confederacy-wide political councils.[25]

Mirroring Iroquois policies, the Comanches forged in the course of the late eighteenth and early nineteenth centuries a far-flung power complex that consisted of three major components: a trading network that reached, through Native middlemen, from the Southwest to the Rocky Mountains, the northern Great Plains, and the lower South; a shifting raiding hinterland that extended from New Mexico and Texas to interior Mexico and served to funnel horses into Comanche commercial circuits; and a flexible frontier policy that allowed the Comanches to bring neighboring groups, Native and European alike, into their orbit as dependents and tributary vassals. Power and people concentrated into *Comanchería*, and like the Iroquois, the Comanches built a burgeoning slave system in which captivity, servitude, and adoption shaded into one another.[26]

Iroquois and Comanche foreign policies were a complex mixture of self-interest, coercion, kinship obligations, and accommodation. Outsiders may have entered Iroquois and Comanche worlds as symbolic women or junior allies, but their submission opened access to inclusive circuits of affinity, sharing, and protection. Just as within the domestic sphere, kinship-grounded bonds in the international sphere could be at once mutually supportive and hierarchical. This cultural logic baffled European colonists, who struggled with the emotion-laced metaphors of love and generosity and compliance. The colonists in New York won access to Iroquois networks by embracing, even if superficially, the symbols and rituals of the Covenant Chain, which allowed the marginalized middle colonies to claim imperial control on their borderlands by proxy. In contrast, Spanish attempts to approach the Comanches were more heavy-handed—a limitation of imperial vision that eventually turned Spain's expansionist project into a defensive one. Spanish agents failed to placate the Comanches with gifts and goods during much of the eighteenth century, shutting themselves off from *Comanchería*'s burgeoning alliance network that came to dominate social life in the lower midcontinent. Spaniards' status as outsiders rendered them vulnerable to violence, and Texas became a captive territory where Comanches plundered, traded, and collected tribute virtually at will. New Mexico, sliding toward economic collapse under Comanche raiding in the 1770s, saved itself by attaching itself to *Comanchería* through an alliance that outwardly resembled the Covenant Chain: Comanches and Spaniards established trade, joined forces against common rivals, and engaged in ceremonial gift exchanges and personal diplomacy that sustained the relationship. But Spanish agents also envisioned the alliance as an instrument to co-opt the Comanches and expand Spanish control to the interior through them. They failed to recognize the pull of the Comanche political economy and soon found the dynamic reversed. New Mexico grew dependent on

Comanche exports, and its multiethnic eastern villages gravitated politically and culturally toward the Comanches, inciting fears in Santa Fe that the colony was dissolving into *Comanchería*.[27]

Nestled deep in the continental interior, the Lakotas had fewer and less intensive contacts with Europeans, and they built their dominance on the exploitation of indigenous resources. When U.S. government officials and traders began to probe the Missouri River after the Louisiana Purchase, Lakotas drew them into a loose but mutually beneficial partnership that allowed both to expand their interests. Backed by U.S. weapons, troops, and vaccines, Lakotas expanded their hunting territories, and Americans followed in their wake with new trading posts. The Lakotas raided the Crows, Blackfeet, and Pawnees for horses and then traded those horses, along with bison products, for guns and manufactured goods with their Yankton Dakota relatives on the James River who in turn had access to European trading posts in the western Great Lakes. They formed a lasting alliance with the remaining Cheyennes and Arapahos and, through that alliance, dominated the political and economic life on the northern and central Plains, ranging from the Rocky Mountains to the Missouri Valley. The Arikaras, once-dominant traders who resisted the expansion of U.S. commerce, were reduced to tributary vassals who supplied Lakotas with corn and bought their meat and hides for greatly inflated prices. Mirroring the asymmetrical relations between the Iroquois and their Native neighbors in the Northeast, the Lakotas, according to European observers, "claim[ed] the country around them," treating the Arikaras as "tenants at will," "a certain kind of serf, who cultivates for them and who, as they say, takes, for them, the place of women."[28]

The Iroquois, Comanches, and Lakotas rose to power by forging fluid structures of inequality—they dominated and exploited others without formally ruling over them—and that rendered them vulnerable. Their extraterritorial ambitions were chronically contested and they faced threats that ranged from ecological degradation to internal schisms. Political splintering remained an ever-present problem for societies who were absorbing large numbers of foreign ethnicities and whose political entanglements dispersed them across vast spaces. But composite foreign policies gave the three groups tremendous staying power. Wrought by internal factionalism and defeated on the battlefield in the late 1680s and early 1690s, the Iroquois nevertheless remained a major regional power into the mid-eighteenth century by recalibrating their foreign policy. They incorporated the Tuscaroras into the League and made peace with New France without alienating the British. They adopted neutrality as a common policy in the Grand Settlement of 1701 and, capitalizing on their central location and influence over other Native societies, continued to shape the course of imperial rivalries in the Northwest. And while contriving to preserve peace on their immediate borders—where European colonists traded, worked, and worshipped with them, sometimes as their tenants—the Iroquois extended their hunting operations deep into the Great Lakes and shifted their slave raids far to the south, targeting Catawbas, Cherokees, Creeks, Choctaws, and others.[29]

On the Great Plains, the Comanche and Lakota equestrian regimes boomed well into the late nineteenth century, creating a startling disconnect between the industrializing East and the nomadic West. The Comanches suffered devastating losses of population and power during a deep, fifteen-year dry spell in the 1840s and 1850s, but they mounted a dramatic comeback in the 1860s by combining long-distance raiding with intensive pastoralism and clandestine trade across the new national borders. The Lakotas continued their expansion on the northern Plains well into the late nineteenth century, seizing new hunting grounds and pastoral niches. They defeated the U.S. Army—now assisted by the Crows, Pawnees, and other ancient enemies of the Lakotas—in a series of battles, humiliating a nation that was on the brink of becoming the world's largest economic power.[30]

The Iroquois, Comanche, and Lakota regimes were separated by centuries and vast distances: when the Lakotas pushed into the northern Plains, Iroquois dominance in the Northeast had already broken; the Comanches and Lakotas were both Plains societies, but the Comanche sphere of operations—Greater *Comanchería*—extended far beyond the grasslands into the Mexican tropics. Yet there were compelling parallels that point to key factors that explain why some Native societies were able to amass disproportionate power and dominate the colonial situation. The most elemental of those factors was location: the Iroquois, Comanches, and Lakotas were all beneficiaries of geography. They were removed—though not too far—from the colonial rim, which gave a measure of protection against European diseases without isolating them from European markets. Another critical factor was mobility. All three built what might be called kinetic regimes, which were networks of power and support that revolved around mobile activities—long-distance raids, wide-ranging diplomatic missions, shifting trade fairs, seasonal political meetings, itinerant villages—and all three maneuvered into positions where they had links to multiple colonial outposts, which in turn allowed them to control information conduits, play off rival colonial powers against each another, and build deep and varied import economies. The Iroquois, Comanches, and Lakotas were also remarkably adaptive societies, capable of incorporating new technologies and peoples and willing to modify their economic and political structures to meet the ever-changing external challenges. They developed composite political organizations that balanced factionalism with centralizing bodies in ways that allowed coordinated decision making on the community-wide level without compromising strategic flexibility on the local level. These were network societies in which power worked horizontally rather than vertically, binding people together through clans, societies, and kinship; from those attachments arose burgeoning confederacies that held the local particles in orbit. The key agents of these confederacies—grand councils, prominent local chiefs, wise elders—diffused internal strife, preserved shared identities, and periodically mobilized the collective power of the autonomous political units into concerted foreign political action. A tension between central initiatives and local inertia persisted, and yet this action proved time and again more coherent and effective than the imperial policies the major colonial powers were able to muster in North America.[31]

The Iroquois, Comanches, and Lakotas outlasted several colonial regimes around them, and they remained viable, independent powers until the United States' westward expansion caught up with them. And, as it turns out, even that final collision was more contingent than it might first appear.

THE expanding Native-dominated worlds of the Iroquois, Comanches, and Lakotas may push the historiographical envelope—they were something that was not supposed to exist in the historical space that became known as "colonial America"—but they are also conventional. Traditional historical roles may have been reversed, but the primal logic of colonial worlds lurks underneath: someone expands, others retreat, and history is a zero-sum game in which only one can prosper. In some ways a more radical departure from tradition is the discovery of shared cross-cultural worlds that emerged across North America, which around 1650 was becoming hardwired for violence. These common Indian-European worlds stood in stark contrast to Native-dominated worlds. The latter, undergirded by persisting power asymmetries, were places where contestation and coercion reasserted, time and again, the social distance between peoples. Shared worlds, by contrast, emerged from persisting attempts to narrow, even if artificially, the gap between societies and cultures. But how common were the common worlds, and what made them possible in the first place?

We tend to associate historical change almost automatically with agency and power, the capacity of people and peoples to make things happen, to bend others to their will. The shared worlds of early America reveal a different kind of process of historical change: rather than of power, they were borne out of weakness. When Indians and Europeans came in close contact, one often had an advantage over the other, and almost invariably the more powerful capitalized on that advantage to determine the terms of the relationship. But there were also pockets where a rough balance of power existed between the protagonists, forcing them to compromise and coexist. Both sides lacked the force to dictate to the other, and neither possessed the ability—or the will—to drive the other off its borders, so mediation became the principal means of cross-cultural interaction. But if mutual weakness was the key to common worlds—conciliation prevailed because coercion was not an option—mutual dependency was their underlying condition. The logic of colonial America was such that no group could survive alone without connections. Indians and Europeans both needed things the other possessed—food, furs, technology, information, allies, sexual partners—and these were things that were easier to acquire through persuasion than by force.

Such an intersection of wants and weaknesses engendered a long history of accommodation that saw Europeans and Indians adjusting their practices to the expectations of others and integrating themselves into alien social networks. But not all instances of mutual weakness and dependency led to enduring shared worlds, and not all shared worlds were the same. In some places nascent adaptations faltered, sometimes repeatedly, in the face of distrust and intolerance. People struggled to educate one another and, disliking what they saw, rejected one another as too brutish, conceited, or strange. Elsewhere power relations were too erratic for compelling cross-cultural practices to emerge. Violence and conciliation existed in a precarious balance, and nascent face-to-face arrangements were constantly disrupted by one group's attempt to dominate the situation. In such places the cohesive pull simply remained too weak to produce more than ephemeral reconciliation. People met and mingled, but cultural fault lines persisted, limiting accommodations to rough, shallow arrangements.[32]

But then, under particular circumstances, there emerged more enduring shared worlds marked by deep-rooted spatial arrangements and mature accommodations that moved cross-cultural relations beyond simple coexistence. These were places beyond the controlling reach of larger political entities—be they colonial regimes or indigenous confederacies—and they were places where different peoples adjusted to one another's expectations, forging new sets of practices that, as a whole, were distinctive from their own practices. Several North American places witnessed such processes of mutual reinvention, but only rarely did those processes consolidate into enduring historical spaces. The most dramatic example of sweeping mutual reinvention took place in the late seventeenth-century Great Lakes region, where French colonists and various Algonquian- and Iroquoian-speaking Indians forged a common world that lasted, in different forms, for generations.

The beginning was not promising. When French explorers and *coureurs de bois* pushed into the Great Lakes—the *pays d'en haut* (or "the upper country")—in the mid-seventeenth century, they discovered what seemed a shattered and disjointed world. Iroquois expansion in the Northeast had triggered chain migrations that dispersed thousands of newcomers—Hurons, Sauks, Foxes, Miamis, Potawatomis, Kickapoos, Ottawas—across the lands between Lakes Michigan and Superior. But contrary to French beliefs, this was not a broken world. The *pays d'en haut* had been a crossroads of indigenous migrations since the fifteenth century when Algonquian-speaking Anishinaabeg peoples had moved in from the east, gradually spreading throughout the region. Over generations, the emigrant and resident Indians mingled and merged, building on far-reaching kinship networks (*nindoodemag*) that fostered political alliances and collective identities. The seventeenth-century refugees of Iroquois expansion capitalized on this long tradition of ethnic coalescing by slipping into the semipermanent mixed villages dotting the landscape. French newcomers found this shifting, seemingly atomistic world confusing and declared it defunct. They saw only chaos, blamed the Iroquois for it, and dismissed the multiethnic villages as broken-down refuge centers. They failed to see the cohering indigenous world that was forming in the *pays d'en haut* and therefore remained strangers at its margins. This is how most incipient accommodations in early America dissipated: violence would ensue, but first there was a failure to understand, to cross the cultural crevasse.[33]

But the *pays d'en haut* would be different. By the late seventeenth century, the French had embedded themselves into its indigenous networks—not because they were so powerful but because they were so weak. Few in numbers and in need of allies against the English and Iroquois, the French encountered a cluster of equally weak Native refugee villages in the lands around Green Bay. Unable to dominate one another, the French and the refugee Indians found it necessary to accommodate one another in ways that became mutually beneficial. While across the continent cross-cultural dialogue often led to frustration, contempt, and violence, here it generated new practices that helped bridge the divide. Probing, cajoling, and eventually reinventing one another, the Indians and French formed an alliance that rested on carefully balanced mutual compromises. Indian "children" pledged loyalty to a French "father," Onontio, but this was a relationship that constrained rather than empowered the colonists. Indians expected Onontio and his many representatives to be caring, forgiving, and weak; they expected gifts, not orders. Most important, the Indians expected Onontio not to control Indian nations but to mediate disputes among them—a crucial service in the *pays d'en haut* where the continuous inflow of Native refugees encumbered Indian-Indian relations. This was the genesis of the hybrid world that Richard White called "the middle ground."[34]

The Great Lakes middle ground was inseparable from its cultural politics—it was first and last a diplomatic construction revolving around patriarchal metaphors—but mediation also manifested itself in a series of everyday arrangements. From economic to legal to sexual encounters, the Indians and French fashioned compromises that both sustained and symbolized their frail but enduring coexistence. Much of the accommodation consisted of ritualistic performances with intricate behavioral codes, but those performances produced tangible results: disputes were solved, political ties endured, and goods exchanged hands.[35]

The Great Lakes middle ground was an extraordinary, perhaps unique, phenomenon in early America; nowhere else, it seems, did cross-cultural accommodations cut so deep, involve so many peoples, and cohere into such enduring spatial arrangements.[36] If indeed there was only one early American middle ground, it was because its creation required daunting behavioral compromises: to enter a middle ground was in many ways an unnatural act. It meant not imposing one's own cultural norms on others; rather, it meant appealing to the perceived meanings and practices of others—practices that often seemed strange, absurd, and outright repulsive. To build a lasting common world meant finding something in an alien culture that one could recognize, manipulate, and, perhaps, absorb. And it meant doing that in a disorienting social environment where it was often less useful to be clearly understood than to be creatively misunderstood. Europeans and Indians studied, poached, and misconstrued—often deliberatively—each other's practices and beliefs to use them to their own purposes, but out of those distortions emerged novel meanings and protocols, which became the cultural sinews of the middle ground. The middle ground, at its core, was a mutual fiction whose artificiality could be perceived but not acknowledged. The new practices existed in a social limbo—they were invented by both yet internalized by neither—but they had to be obeyed for the accommodation to work. Both sides knew that real mutual understanding remained elusive, but both chose to ignore the disconnect and simply act as the fabricated protocols demanded.[37]

The closest comparable development to the Great Lakes middle ground—in terms of scope and resilience, if not of intensity and depth—took place in the eighteenth-century upper Rio Grande Valley and its adjacent regions; there, too, cross-cultural accommodations enmeshed numerous peoples for generations, accruing layered complexity over time. The process, however, could have hardly been more different. In the Great Lakes, imperial power, so to speak, dissolved into a multicultural matrix that was the middle ground. Coercive imperial authority was all but absent, replaced by persuasion and arbitration: French colonial officials mediated differences between Indians and French subjects and among the region's many Native societies, providing "what amounted to an imported imperial glue to reconstruct a village world."[38] In the upper Rio Grande Valley, by contrast, cross-cultural accommodations developed within and around Spanish New Mexico, a fully fledged colonial society. Seventeenth-century New Mexico was defined by a rigid division into Spanish masters and Pueblo subjects, but gradually in the eighteenth century, in the aftermath of the Pueblo Revolt, the colonial rule loosened, giving way to social niches where the colonist-subject dichotomy softened and to borderland spaces where Spaniards and independent Indians compromised rather than collided. If in the *pays d'en haut* imperial institutions penetrated only selectively a region that remained beyond the effective reach of the French empire, in the Rio Grande Valley a common world developed in the cracks and shadows of an enduring but evolving colonial world.

Eighteenth-century New Mexico was not a middle ground—it was too colonial in mood and too hierarchical in character—but like the Great Lakes middle ground, it was a distinctive and remarkably enduring social construction and as such something that requires explanation. What exactly was it that compelled so many people to accommodate one another, and for so long, in the Great Lakes and in the Rio Grande Valley? Mutual weakness and mutual dependency were critical factors, but the Great Lakes and the Rio Grande Valley were not the only places in early America where such conditions existed. Across the continent, Indians and Europeans encountered one another on nondominant frontiers, but more often than not nondominance remained but a fleeting condition. Sometimes, as on the French-Indian borderlands along the Mississippi Valley, potential common grounds evolved into Native grounds, where indigenous forms prevailed over European ones, and sometimes, as on the Anglo-Indian borderlands, contact zones were shifting and short-lived, dissolving time after time into bloodshed and hatred. Clearly, something else was involved.[39]

The common worlds of the Great Lakes and the upper Rio Grande Valley were exceptional historical phenomena that arose from specific historical circumstances, where military weakness and economic interdependency intersected with geopolitical vulnerability and domestic intimacy. The usual public actors of contact zones—traders, missionaries, chiefs, petty colonial officials—were almost invariably men, and they could take cultural mixing only so far. A key institution that helped move intercultural relations deeper was intermarriage between European men and Native women. Mixed households were, in a sense, common grounds in microcosm, sites where the social distance separating Europeans and Natives could be shortened fastest and most completely. A critical number of mixed households could turn ordinary meeting places into miniature common grounds, which in turn could become nuclei for far-reaching exchange networks, drawing diverse peoples together and changing the social chemistry of entire regions.[40]

Such a development is clearly visible in the *pays d'en haut*, where intermarriage *à la façon du pays* (after the custom of the country) became an established practice. Cross-cultural marriages opened indigenous social networks to French voyageurs and traders, and they secured Native societies' access to European markets and to the colonial administrative bodies that supported those markets. They created lateral alliances among peoples and spawned expanding kinship networks that cut across ethnic lines and territorial boundaries. Marriage *à la façon du pays* did not become a monolithic institution—its forms and frequency varied from locale to locale—but it did spread across the upper Great Lakes, hitching Indians and French into widening networks of kinship, exchange, and diplomacy.[41]

But perhaps the decisive element that pushed different people—indeed entire societies—to accommodate one another was fear: fear of a more powerful common enemy, or fear of being left alone in an unpredictable colonial world where the odds of group survival without allies were slim. People did not so much gravitate toward shared worlds as they were pushed into them. Large, enduring common worlds were predicated on a profound and shared sense of vulnerability and terror that compelled vastly different groups to seek protection in numbers and to embrace one another despite their in-built reluctance to do so.

The transformative power of fear is palpable in the Great Lakes region where the French and the refugee Indians accommodated one another because both felt threatened by the allied Iroquois and Anglo-Americans to the east and expanding indigenous coalitions to the west. The fear manifested itself as heightened insecurity over loyalties—nervous French fathers lavishing their Native children with gifts to negate the pull of British markets—but perhaps too much weight has been given to such imperial play-off dynamics in the making of the middle ground. Great Lakes Indians seldom threatened to side with the British to force concessions from the French, and when they tried in the 1740s, the resulting tension nearly destroyed the alliance.[42]

A more consistent factor than balance-of-power politics in sustaining the cross-cultural accommodation was the fear that the conciliatory impulse itself might evaporate in the tangled and shifting political milieu of interior America. The nascent middle ground that had emerged around Green Bay was flanked by hostile and unreceptive indigenous fronts throughout its existence, which both threatened and sustained the survival of the middle ground. In the East, Iroquois warfare consumed its very essence—people themselves—until the Great Peace of 1701 stabilized relations between New France and the Haudenosaunee. But as the Iroquois threat waned, weakening the accommodative impulse in the eastern Great Lakes and Ohio Country, a new threat emerged to the west, where the powerful Anishinaabe peoples forged an alliance with the Dakota Sioux, distanced themselves from the rights and obligations of the French alliance, and then, with the Dakotas, attacked French posts and allies across the western Great Lakes. Those Frenchmen who stayed among them had to conform to Anishinaabe and Dakota expectations, and mutual accommodation gave way to indigenous dominance. Then, between 1712 and 1734, violence washed over much of the *pays d'en haut* when the French sided with the Hurons, Illinois, Ottawas, Peorias, Potawatomis, and Saulteaux against the Fox, nearly demolishing the nation that they had tried for decades to integrate into the alliance. But even as the middle ground crumbled at its edges, it grew denser at its core where, under pressure, people tightened their bonds. It was here, in Native villages and French posts on the shores of Lakes Michigan and Erie, that the middle ground reached maturity and survived.[43]

A similar brew of fear, vacillation, rejection, and conciliation characterized cross-cultural relations in the eighteenth-century upper Rio Grande Valley, where—as in the *pays d'en haut*—cautious, often ambivalent accommodations arose from shared geopolitical vulnerability and nascent intimate ties. Spaniards reinstated colonial rule in New Mexico after the Pueblo revolts of 1680 and 1696, but this was not the colonial regime of old. Fearful of new uprisings, Spaniards accepted smaller landholdings and replaced the *encomienda* system with a less onerous *repartimiento* system. They established new legal practices that secured Pueblo holdings and appointed a public defender to protect Pueblo rights against colonial abuse. Franciscan friars—who would number only a few dozen by the late eighteenth century—allowed previously demonized Pueblo ceremonies, and Pueblos accepted Catholic sacraments while quietly conducting sacred rituals in underground *kivas*.

This new, more flexible colonial regime involved more than economic and legal accommodations: it had an undercurrent of ethnic mixing and democratization that cut against elite New Mexicans' attempts to isolate themselves at the top of the social hierarchy. Seventeenth-century New Mexico had been divided into only partially overlapping Spanish and Native enclaves, but the social distance between different groups narrowed significantly during the next century. Spaniards and Pueblos forged quasi-kinship relationships through a *compadrazgo* (co-godparenthood) institution, mixed settlements developed around *vecindàd* (community) ties, cross-cultural intimacies and intermarriages became more common, and *mestizaje* deepened. Spanish and indigenous customs and values toward sexuality and love blended into one another, and the Hispanic nobility grew increasingly anxious about its standing in a colony where racial divides of status and privilege were becoming blurred. Intermarriage remained an exploitative institution in eighteenth-century New Mexico where the persistence of colonial administration meant that Spanish men could exercise disproportional power over their Native wives, and their unions had an undercurrent of violence and exploitation. Yet, on a societal level, such relationships did help narrow the distance between Spaniards and Pueblos.[44]

That incipient narrowing of cultural distance was accelerated by an acute and shared sense of vulnerability. Spaniards and Pueblos closed ties in the eighteenth century because the destruction of the Pueblo rebellions had left both reeling: neither wanted another violent outburst, so both found ways to coexist and compromise. But the two groups accommodated one another also because Comanche ascendancy on the Great Plains was starting to threaten their very existence. Comanche raiding in New Mexico continued, with only brief respites, for most of the eighteenth century, claiming lives, depleting animal reserves, and obliterating entire communities. In such an environment of terror and uncertainty, Spaniards and Pueblos began to see in one another allies who deserved to be embraced rather than aliens who needed to be resisted or repressed. They launched joint military expeditions into *Comanchería*, dying—and occasionally claiming stunning victories—if not as equals then at least as collaborators. By the 1750s, the Spaniards and the Pueblos numbered around ten thousand each, living in close proximity in dozens of villages that often appeared more as nodes of cross-cultural confluence than as colonial outposts.[45]

Mirroring the extension of the Great Lakes middle ground from its Green Bay cradle, the Rio Grande–based Spanish-Indian network expanded to adjacent regions in a sprawling sequence that was driven and framed by indigenous expansions. Around the mid-eighteenth century, the Spaniards and the Ute Indians of the Colorado Plateau formed a political accord that over time deepened to include intimate personal ties that melded the two groups together. Utes raided New Mexico with Comanches until the partnership unraveled in the 1750s, after which they approached the Spaniards. The two forged a lasting alliance. As in the Great Lakes region, the alliance matured to include formal rituals for diplomacy, exchange, and redress, but it was held together by the Spaniards and Utes' shared fear of the Comanches, whose power politics had rendered them in a roughly equal state of weakness. The Comanches made peace with New Mexico in a momentous round of diplomacy between 1785 and 1786, but the fear of Comanche violence was so ingrained that it kept Spaniards and Utes on a common orbit even during peacetime. Fearful of a renewed Comanche war that could have ruined them both, Spaniards and Utes nurtured their alliance into the nineteenth century through commerce, gift and captive exchanges, and careful diplomacy.[46]

At the same time, the Spanish-Indian network was also spreading among the Apaches on the southern Great Plains, where Comanche expansion was rearranging the political landscape. Just as Iroquois warfare had pushed Indian refugees into an alliance with the French, so, too, did Comanche invasion push dispossessed Apaches into the Spanish fold. As the Comanches colonized the southern Plains, numerous Apache groups sought—and often received—shelter near Spanish settlements. Desperate to stop the Comanches, the Spaniards built short-lived walled missions at the outskirts of the expanding *Comanchería* to protect the Apaches, who welcomed the structures' military function while rejecting the religious one. More lasting arrangements developed in New Mexico. The colony took in several bands of Apache refugees who settled near Taos, Picurís, Pecos, and Galisteo, adding another dimension to New Mexico's ethnic mix. The attempts at coexistence were guarded and halting—the hatred and mistrust arising from generations of violence could not be easily erased—but for a while, in small niches, Apaches and Spaniards explored the possibility of shared existence.[47]

The cautious, mutually opportunistic movement of Apaches and Spaniards toward one another culminated in the 1780s and 1790s, when the Spaniards and Comanches, now allied in peace, launched a series of joint military campaigns against the many Apache groups living on both sides of the Rio Grande. Viceroy Bernardo de Gálvez had authorized the war with a genocidal urgency. "In the voluntary or forced submission of the Apaches, or in their total extermination," he wrote in 1786, "lies the happiness" of northern New Spain. Those Apaches who did not retreat or die sought refuge in newly established reservations in New Mexico, Sonora, and Nueva Vizcaya. As with missions, Spanish officials envisioned these reservations as sites of one-way cultural engineering where heathen nomads would transform into town-dwelling Catholic farmers, but in reality they became sites for two-way negotiation. Apaches—Gileños, Mimbreños, and Mescaleros—maneuvered carefully to protect their privacy and customs within the reservations, leaving and entering them as their economic and political needs dictated, and Spaniards, content with having some two thousand Apaches nominally pacified, eased the pressure. Over time, intimate bonds developed between Spanish and Apache families, and the accommodation that had sprung from Bourbon Spain's exterminationist policy prevailed for nearly two generations.[48]

These structural linkages between the rise of expansionist Native powers and shared worlds of Indian-European coexistence point to larger truths:

they illuminate the complex linkages among violence, expansion, and accommodation and the ways in which those linkages engendered transcending historical developments that melded the many parts of early America into an interconnected whole. The concentration of geopolitical power in Iroquoia and *Comanchería* reverberated far and wide, altering cross-cultural dynamics in places never visited by Iroquois or Comanches. The Great Lakes and the Rio Grande borderlands may have been beyond the effective controlling grip of European empires, colonialism, and capitalism; they were, as several prominent studies have shown, intensely localized places where intimate political and personal relations took precedence over the abstract market-driven dynamics of the Atlantic world. But they were not self-contained worlds evolving in isolation; neither would have existed, not at least in the form they did, without the rise of the Iroquois and Comanches, the two most successful expansionist powers in pre-1800 North America, whose oversized presences fundamentally shaped vast segments of the continent.[49]

THE interconnected realms of Native dominance and Indian-European coexistence covered much of the continental landmass, but in their midst there were different kinds of spaces: politically fragmented, intensely contested, and chronically unstable lands where power was persistently up for grabs and where intergroup relations became grounded in violence. Several places—seventeenth-century Ohio Country, mid-eighteenth-century Pennsylvania backcountry, and early nineteenth-century south Texas—bore elements of such violent fraction zones, but two large regions epitomize them: the Southeast and the Great Basin. The former fell into political flux with the collapse of the Mississippian chiefdoms in the fifteenth and sixteenth centuries, only to experience unforeseen instability and violence in the late seventeenth and early eighteenth centuries, when European colonial powers entered the region. In the Great Basin, violence escalated sporadically through the seventeenth and early eighteenth centuries until, in the late eighteenth century, it washed over the region.[50]

If the worlds of indigenous dominance and the worlds of Indian-European coexistence were the mountaintops of the early American geopolitical landscape, fraction zones were its valleys: concealed in shadows and more difficult to appreciate. Indeed, setting them apart in the first place may seem like a false distinction, for there was no early American region free of instability, contestation, or violence. And yet, even if the distinctions were a matter of degree, not of kind, those degrees made all the difference, because they had to do with life's fundamentals. Measured by the raw parameters of human existence—level of political autonomy, chances of survival, predictability of future—early American worlds were altogether different.

The key differentiating element was the violence itself, which in the Southeast and the Great Basin became endemic and profoundly destructive. In the realms of Native dominance, by contrast, violence was often a means to political ends and was interlaced with trade and tribute payments. The Iroquois, Comanches, and Lakotas raided their neighbors systematically and for decades, but the devastation of those raids was tempered by the fact that the aggressors never ceased to see potential allies or vassals in their victims. The contrast is even more pronounced with the realms of coexistence, where violence was often a periodic condition—less a reality than an ever-present threat that required constant conciliation. In the Great Lakes, for example, the specter of violence forced the protagonists to carefully placate one another, inching them ever closer together.[51]

It is one thing to differentiate regions by gauging levels and forms of violence, but it is quite another to explain why those differences emerged in the first place. Indeed, this is a question from which the historians of early America have often recoiled. They have realized that in early America there were places where violence prevailed and places where accommodation did, but they have rarely ventured to ask why. This has obscured one of the elemental questions in early American history: what were the human impulses and structural conditions under which societies relied on coercion, accommodation, or violence when facing others?[52]

Answering that question must begin with an exploration of how power works in different kinds of geopolitical settings. A crude but useful starting point is to distinguish among unipolar, apolar, and multipolar domains. Unipolarity can foster intergroup stability, for although often powered by violence, dominant societies can also pacify large regions by pulling other groups into their political orbit or by simply rendering them economically dependent. Apolarity, too, can harmonize relations among societies. On nondominant frontiers where no one has a monopoly on violence and where all feel insecure, people are often inclined to make far-reaching concessions with societies they otherwise might reject as too alien. A shared sense of weakness, combined with an acute sense of vulnerability from without, renders people more willing to embrace others across seemingly insurmountable cultural divides.

Applied to early America, such a differentiation by polarity can bring its regions into sharper focus. If the realms of dominance were unipolar worlds and the realms of coexistence apolar worlds, the Southeast and the Great Basin were multipolar worlds. Both regions hosted a number of societies that felt powerful enough to try to subjugate others—thus precluding developments toward wide-ranging accommodation—but none of those groups were strong enough to establish the kind of sweeping dominance that can stabilize intergroup relations over large areas.

In the Southeast, four militarized Native confederacies (the Creeks, Cherokees, Choctaws, and Chickasaws), four disorderly English colonies (Virginia, South Carolina, North Carolina, and Georgia), and two Caribbean-based colonies (Spanish Florida and French Louisiana) were locked in an unforgiving contest over boundaries, markets, allies, and prestige. In the Great Basin, the Utes, Navajos, Shoshones, and Paiutes all vied for power, resources, and trading privileges with New Mexico, the region's only European colony. In terms of power distribution, the Southeast and the Great Basin were thus conspicuously different from the worlds of Native dominance. They were imperial blind spots, places where power remained fragmented among numerous societies that were too weak to subjugate one another and yet too powerful to feel the need to accommodate one another. Boundaries, intergroup practices, and power relations remained chronically undecided and subject to contestation, priming these places for violence.[53]

Yet the absence of imperial power was but a precondition for violence. The crucial element that, in a sense, unleashed the in-built social potential for violence was slavery. In imperial blind spots violence fueled—and was in turn fueled by—large-scale trafficking in Indian slaves, which thrived within landscapes of fragmented power. Unstable geopolitical settings offered ample opportunities for raiding and slaving for various protagonists—both Indian and European—while the often unruly and chronically labor-hungry colonial outposts offered ready markets for human merchandise. Captive taking and slavery had existed in North America before European contact, but colonialism introduced a powerful materialist dimension. When one observer lamented in 1708 that South Carolina traders "excite them [Indians] to make War amongst themselves to get Slaves which they give for our European Goods," he captured an essential truth: colonial markets altered the meaning of captivity and slavery in Native societies and multiplied the scale of violence among them. New Mexico, Virginia, and the Carolinas became the largest Indian slave markets in North America, each importing thousands of captives that were either incorporated into local labor regimes or sold to the mining and sugar districts in tropical America. As the colonial slave markets boomed, Indians became their primary feeders, raiding other Native groups with the express purpose of securing captives that could be traded for various consumer goods, manufactures, and livestock.[54]

However, colonial markets not only incited violence but also provided tools for violence: flintlock muskets, powder, bullets, and metal weapons, often sold and even pushed to Native customers on credit. An indigenous arms race developed in the Southeast and the Great Basin, and competition over trading privileges became vicious. New technologies of war increased the death toll, demanding ever-bloodier retaliations, and slave raids escalated into slave wars. Seventeenth- and early eighteenth-century New Mexico, Virginia, and the Carolinas may have been small outposts at the edges of vast indigenous worlds, but they cast long shadows. They were conduits for Europe's capitalist penetration that, across the globe, created dependencies, rearranged social relations, and fueled violent rivalries on colonial frontiers. The Southeast and the Great Basin were such places of external disruption and escalating violence.[55]

Yet, paradoxically, the most striking feature of these volatile worlds was not their violence but their longevity and propensity to expand. Rather than collapsing into themselves, they ruptured outward. When weaker groups eventually disintegrated in the vortex of violence, stronger groups extended their raiding and slaving activities farther, seeking out new groups in adjacent lands—just as the Iroquois did in the Great Lakes and as the Comanches did in northern Mexico.

In the Great Basin, virtually all Native peoples raided other Native peoples for captives whom they either incorporated as laborers or sold to New Mexico, but Utes and Navajos did so more successfully than others. In the course of the eighteenth century, Ute raiders extended their range to the northern Rocky Mountains and California, targeting Paiutes and Shoshones. In the 1830s and 1840s, the Navajos carried the violence back to its source in New Mexico through a reciprocal cycle that saw mutual captive raids and killings hardening into collective grievances. Long-standing rituals of peacemaking dissolved into corrosive hatred, and violence enveloped much of the Great Basin.[56]

A similar sequence unfolded in the Southeast, where an expanding slave-raiding sphere stretched out from English colonies, gradually covering the entire region from the Chesapeake Bay to the Mississippi Valley and northern Florida (where the raids dismantled the 150-year-old Spanish mission network). The traffic in Indian slaves collapsed in the 1720s, when the factious Carolinians united to build a planter society on black slavery, but by that time as many as fifty thousand Indians—23 to 40 percent of the Southeast's total indigenous population—had been fed to colonial slave markets. And many more died from the disease epidemics that erupted in the wake of the slave traffic, which helped create an entirely new disease environment in the Native Southeast: when previously isolated groups came into violent contact, old buffer zones and subsistence systems crumbled, providing Old World germs multiple avenues from which to spread and kill.[57]

The slave trade engendered unprecedented violence in the Southeast, but its collapse did not end the carnage. As the slave traffic faded during the 1720s, another institution—colonial proxy wars—emerged to keep the Southeast in turmoil for three more decades. The global wars among Britain, France, and Spain inevitably involved the Southeast—the only place in North America where the three global behemoths vied for control of the same region—but the colonists there were too weak to inflict serious damage on their rivals. Unable to neutralize one another by force, the British, French, and Spaniards moved to fight one another through Indians. They orchestrated strategic gift distributions to create attachments and supplied loyal Indians with firearms, inciting them to attack rival colonists and *their* Indians. To keep the Indians divided and fighting—nothing frightened Europeans more than the prospect of large indigenous coalitions—the colonists meddled with both the domestic and foreign politics of the Southwest Indians. They paid for Indian scalps—French governors in Louisiana procured at least one thousand scalps between 1732 and 1752—and staged public executions of Native captives, a practice that Indians abhorred and that deepened animosities. To create internal factions, Europeans channeled presents into Native societies that were attached to rival colonies. The proxy wars intensified the simmering hostilities originating from the slave trade and ensnared the Native Southeast in escalating violence. The Choctaws waged, at French instigation, a nearly constant war against the Chickasaws during the first half of the eighteenth century and then, in 1748, fell into a two-year civil war. The Chickasaw population collapsed by half between 1730 and 1760.[58]

The Native Southeast was a "tribal zone," a militarized landscape where lethal microbes, new technologies of killing, and colliding colonial interests fueled wars that were only seemingly local. But Southeastern Indians kept fighting and killing one another not only because they were so vulnerable to external forces, but also because they remained so powerful. Although many Native groups dissolved into violence, in the early eighteenth century there were still four dynamic confederacies with expansionist, even hegemonic pretensions. Each of them—the Choctaws, Chickasaws, Cherokees, and Creeks—felt powerful enough to contain and even dominate others, but none of them possessed the capacity to realize those ambitions. Power relations and boundaries remained contested, perpetuating cycles of violence. Only toward the mid-eighteenth century did a modicum of stability set in when the Creeks, buoyed by a burgeoning deerskin trade with the British, emerged as a domineering military and economic power. Members from Alabama, Natchez, Shawnee, Yamasee, Seminole, and other nations attached themselves to an expanding and increasingly multiethnic Creek Confederacy, which capitalized on its diversity—and even its deepening factionalism—to conduct a three-way balance-of-power diplomacy that kept the surrounding colonial powers at bay. The Creeks and Cherokees, key rivals, forged a series of peace treaties in the late 1740s and 1750s, and the Southeast seemed to be on the verge of a new era of concentrated power and regional reconciliation—something akin to the pacification of Indian–Indian relations in the Comanche-dominated Great Plains in the early nineteenth century. But that development was crushed under the needs, ambitions, and anxieties of a new rising power in the East.[59]

CONTRARY to the persisting popular view, Americans did not have a sudden imperial awakening on the battlefields of Cuba and the Philippines; their nation became imperial gradually and over time. The United States was conceived both as a republic and an empire—it was at once postcolonial and neoimperial and within it brewed a potent mixture of exceptionalism and expansionism—and it evolved into a fully fledged imperial power in the crucible of westward expansion. The unprecedented use of state violence in the more than 1,600 official military engagements between the United States and Native Americans, the creation of a legal framework for an expanding federal realm with the Northwest Ordinance, the Louisiana Purchase and the Jeffersonian resurrection of the Doctrine of Discovery, the struggles with Spain for strategic frontiers and the acquisition of the Far West in the 1840s, the rise of the Cotton Kingdom and the Indian Removal, the building of transcontinental railroads, the growth of federal power in the West, and the consolidation of the segregationist reservation system in the 1870s and 1880s: all these key events and processes of continental expansion were also acts of empire building. They were driven by a settler ideology that dated back to the colonial era and they were geared toward opening the entire lower half of North America for agro-industrialism and capitalism.[60]

The emergence of the United States as a continental power washed aside the many early American social worlds, closing many alternate historical possibilities. But the arrows of influence did not point in one way only. The rise of the U.S. empire did not simply erase worlds that had been before; it was also made possible by them. The preexisting social worlds may have crumbled in the face of U.S. expansion, but they did not vanish without leaving a mark. They channeled, constrained, and sustained the emergence of the very empire that consumed them, shaping what came later.

From the Appalachian Mountains to the Great Lakes, the United States expanded westward on a path that was both unlocked and obstructed by older, still evolving histories. A myth of an overpowering Iroquois empire and Iroquois cessions of "conquered" western lands to British colonies had buttressed Britain's claims to a vast trans-Appalachian empire when nothing of the sort existed on the ground, and the United States inherited that paper empire in the Treaty of Paris, which extended its western border to the Mississippi Valley. Denouncing the treaty as a land usurpation, several Native nations joined forces in the late 1780s to make the Ohio River the permanent border between Indian Country and the upstart republic, but the alliance lacked the military strength to back its political ambition: disease epidemics and generations of warfare with the Iroquois had melted away much of Ohio Country's indigenous population. Once the pan-Indian military coalition disintegrated at Fallen Timbers in 1794, Americans began to push into the Great Lakes region, settling on both sides of the U.S.-Canada border and pulling the United States on a course of northward expansion. The United States made a bid to annex Canada in the War of 1812 but was repelled by an alliance of British and Native Americans, who resurrected a frailer version of the once-collapsed middle ground and together kept the Americans from extending their border beyond the St. Lawrence Valley and the Great Lakes.[61]

Intersections between U.S. expansion and older histories were even more pronounced on the continent's southern tier. In the Southeast, the traffic in Indian slaves and the ensuing slave and scalp wars energized

English colonies and weakened Native societies, preparing the ground for an Anglo takeover. The slave trade sustained Virginia and the Carolinas during the critical early decades of colonization when plantation economies were still fragile, and it later financed their shift to African slavery. In Indian Country, however, the traffic unleashed a demographic catastrophe. Slave raiders—who were mostly Indians—moved constantly between colonial outposts and Native villages, carrying pathogens from one to the other. The slave trade was a double disaster for the victim societies—it moved people out of them and lethal microbes into them—and this violent dynamic destroyed much of the region's Native population by 1776, decades before the cotton boom would launch large-scale Anglo expansion into the Gulf Coastal Plain.[62]

In what would become the American Southwest, U.S. expansion intertwined with Comanche expansion. Comanche power politics had driven several defeated and displaced Native groups to embrace Spanish protection, which changed the social makeup of northern New Spain: from deepening *mestizaje* in eighteenth-century New Mexico to the late Bourbon-era Apache reservation experiment, the Spanish imperial project bore a distinctive mark of Comanche influence. But Comanche imperialism also critically weakened Hispanic rule in the far north. It reduced large sections of northern New Spain to underdeveloped captive territories and then nearly broke the nascent Mexican Republic. Mexico City's inability to suppress Comanche violence sparked secessionist movements across northern Mexico, critically weakening the ties between the republic's center and its far northern periphery and inadvertently preparing the ground for the U.S. triumph in the Mexican War.[63]

These are just a few of many examples of how the modern map of North America reflects the power configurations and social worlds that had existed before. Contrary to contemporary pretensions, U.S. westward expansion was not an act of filling a politically raw and historically shallow continent with geopolitical order and substance. From the Northeast to the Great Lakes, from the Deep South to the Rio Grande Valley, it was a process of Anglo-Americans, either opportunistically or blindly, stepping into deep historical currents that carried them westward across the continent.

This, of course, was not how contemporary Americans saw things. They saw themselves as chosen people, destined to take over the continent from people who had failed to do anything historically impressive with it. Rushing to their divinely mandated date with a Western future, Americans stopped only to contemplate how much of the continent they should take, and they almost never stopped to think of the people whom they were pushing aside, disregarding them as mere frontier irritants. They saw North America as a politically naive landscape, short on historical content and free for the taking, and they ignored the fact that the continent they took over was encrusted with historical layers but broken in all the right places for their nation to take the shape it did.

CHAPTER 2

Dispossession in a Commercial Idiom: From Indian Deeds to Land Cession Treaties

Allan Greer

When Juan de Oñate came in 1598 to annex New Mexico to Spain's empire, he did not conclude treaties with the Pueblo peoples, nor did he ask them to surrender title to their lands; rather, he summoned them to acknowledge themselves as obedient subjects of King Philip II. On the king's behalf, he laid claim to the entire country, New Mexico as well as unspecified adjacent provinces, "without limitations, including the mountains, rivers, valleys, meadows, pastures, and waters." Oñate's act of possession—written, sealed, notarized, and read out to the assembled Indians and Spanish soldiers—enumerated all sorts of minerals and other resources, adding, significantly, "together with the native Indians in each and every one of the provinces, with civil and criminal jurisdiction, power of life and death, over high and low, from the stones and sands of the river to the leaves in the forests." The conqueror and his monarch claimed the country not *instead* of the indigenous peoples who currently occupied and possessed it, but *including* them. This was an assertion of *dominium*, of authority over and power to exploit a populated landscape of natural resources and productive communities. The Pueblos were not ordered to vacate their fields and villages; their land tenure was not really altered. From the point of view of property, less was demanded of the Natives of New Mexico than the document's rhetoric of voracity might suggest.[1]

Oñate's words and actions were meaningful in light of the long-standing Hispanic tradition of conquest; even though the term had been banished in favor of "pacification" by the terms of the royal ordinance of 1573, the culture of "conquest" remained fundamental to empire building. Oñate's takeover of New Mexico may have lacked the dramatic military confrontations that characterized the Spanish conquests of Mexico and Peru, but even if many Pueblos surrendered without a fight, it was a conquest all the same in its violence, its intimidation, and its general reliance on armed force.[2] In the wake of the conquest, indeed as an integral part of the conquest, came exactions of tribute and labor service, as well as irresistible pressures to convert to Christianity. Official policy directed conquerors like Oñate to respect Indian property rights even as they forcibly integrated Natives into a subordinated and exploited position in the colonial formation.[3] To some extent, settlers violated this rule in taking over lands for their own farms and ranches, but they had no interest in a wholesale displacement of Indians because the latter served as their reservoir of labor; they wanted Pueblos to be nearby and they wanted those Pueblos to be in possession of land to support themselves from the fruits of their own harvests.

Two and a half centuries later, the United States took over much of the Southwest borderlands, bringing a different model of colonial appropriation. Like the Spaniards before them, the Americans came bearing arms and were determined to overcome indigenous opposition, but their cultural construction of colonial expansion was much less centered on the concept of subjugation through "conquest"; instead, they tended to focus on the appropriation of Native territory rather than on the integration of Indians and their lands into an imperial hierarchy. At least that is the impression given by the treaties that were the favored legal instrument for formalizing relations between the state and indigenous peoples. In actual practice, the U.S. occupation of the Southwest had every appearance of a conquest. The Muache Utes of the San Luis Valley were among those who felt the painful consequences of defying the new colonial power. They were "chastised" in 1849 (that is, attacked by the military, resulting in the loss of ten Ute lives); an uneasy peace followed, marked by privation and deadly disease and then further violence ensued. "U.S. army colonel Thomas Fauntleroy pursued Muache, Capote, and Jicarilla bands throughout 1855, destroying lodges, capturing more than fifty women and children, and burning tons of Ute saddles, robes, and matériel."[4] Weakened and desperate, the Utes, along with several harried bands of Apaches, sat down on September 11, 1855, with David Merriwether, the governor of New Mexico Territory, to negotiate a surrender. The treaty they signed, though it provided for a cessation of hostilities and return of captives, mostly revolved around questions of land and money. The crucial clauses suggest not so much a conquest as a real estate transfer.

> The Mohuache Utahs hereby cede and forever relinquish to the United States all title or claim whatsoever which they have to lands within the Territory of New Mexico, except so much as is hereinafter reserved to them . . . In consideration of, and full payment for, the country ceded, and the removal of the Mohuache Utahs, the United States agree to pay to them the following sums, without interest, to wit: . . . during the years 1856, 1857, and 1858, pay to the Mohuaches five thousand dollars each year. [Annuities continue, at a reduced rate, until 1882.][5]

The language seems to imply a voluntary contract between Indians and whites, agreeing, as formal equals, to exchange valuable goods; in this respect the New Mexico treaties are typical of those concluded by the United States across the continent during the century following Independence. "The land cessions and payments for them were at the heart of the treaty system," writes the leading expert on this subject.[6] Great importance was attached to the treaty as artifact and object, complete with "signatures" recording the adherence of both government representatives and Indian leaders. The nearest analogue in Spanish America was the *capitulación*, but that was not a transaction between Natives and whites, but rather an advance agreement between the Crown and a prospective conquistador such as Oñate setting out the scope of his conquests. The king of Spain did not treat with Indians on a formal level of equality.

Of course, the actual relationship between the federal state and the Utes at the time of the 1855 treaty was not exactly the polar opposite of the Spanish "pacification" of the Pueblos. This was hardly a matter of sellers looking for a good price for their land and then signing off when they found the best deal; like so many other Indians before and after them, the Muache Utes took the treaty only when they had run out of options. Moreover, the treaty process (as opposed to the manifest content of the text) entailed Indian subjection to the increasingly severe reservation system of the day. In certain respects an empire is an empire and the colonized peoples of the Southwest suffered marginalization and dispossession, whether at the hands of Juan de Oñate or of David Merriwether. At another level, divergences in the style of dispossession and in the legal formulation of the colonial relationship seem consequential and worthy of sustained analysis. The treaty/land surrender system seems a curious foundation for colonialism. It is not altogether obvious why colonized peoples should be treated as protagonists in a business deal or why the forced surrender of territory should be formalized as though it were a voluntary contract; also for that matter it is not obvious why an arrangement between peoples that was really about relations of power should focus on a nonhuman object: land. The frankly imperious languages and formalities of Spanish imperialism, which were all about subjection and rule, seem more in keeping with the realities of colonial expansion.

Moreover, from the vantage point of Ute and other Native American cultures, the idea that intercultural relations should be cemented by the sale of land seems absurd. It is dangerous to generalize about the extremely diverse cultures of pre-Columbian North America, but it is safe to say that none of them treated land as a merchantable asset. Certainly, there was trade in material goods. The archaeological evidence is overwhelming: long-distance commerce, in, for example, native copper, shell beads, and foodstuffs, had connected distant peoples of different languages and cultures. When European explorers appeared on the coast, Native Americans, who were already accustomed to intercultural trade, frequently pressed forward to offer furs and food for mirrors, caps, and knives.[7] But nowhere do we find indications that land was treated as an object of commerce. Blades, furs, and foodstuffs are naturally tradable commodities in a way that land is not; the latter cannot be passed from hand to hand, nor can it be displayed on a rock and retrieved if the price is not right. For land to be bought and sold, it has to be surrounded by a particular kind of legal-institutional framework that defines ownership and establishes procedures for transferring title. Nowhere is that a straightforward matter and nowhere is the business of selling land truly equivalent to the intuitively simple and legally free-standing process of giving an axe for two beaver pelts.

Only to a limited extent could one speak of a market in land in sixteenth-century Europe,[8] still less so in indigenous North America. Property, trade, and land tenure were certainly features of pre-Columbian America. Nations laid claim to territory and individuals or families typically controlled the resources of specified zones. Goods might be demanded of outsiders for certain kinds of access: payment of a share of the catch in exchange for the right to fish or hunt in someone else's domain, or a presentation of goods for the right to travel across another's territory for commercial purposes. While there are numerous indications that payments resembling rents or tolls predated European contact, there is no evidence that land could be "sold" in a sense that would give the buyer a permanent and exclusive right to all the resources of a given tract while entirely eliminating the seller's stake. One simply could not alienate a portion of the earth in the way that one could turn over a canoe or a gold nugget.

And, yet, a recent work on Native dispossession in the United States and its colonial antecedents, *How the Indians Lost Their Land*, presents this extended process as essentially a series of business transactions. Writing of the formative colonial period, Stuart Banner declares, "The English, who had plenty of goods, wanted Indian land, while the Indians, who had plenty of land, wanted English goods. There were enormous gains to be had from trade." The author readily concedes that these "gains" accrued disproportionately to one side, but he points out that even on a level playing field there are bound to be winners and losers. "Two societies converged in a marketplace," Banner concludes, "and the better organized took wealth from the poorly organized."[9] But was there really a "marketplace" for land when Natives and settlers first converged? Or should we see this momentous encounter and the treaty/land surrender formalities that ensued as prior to, indeed as a founding act in, the establishment of a market in land? More generally, what are we to make of these strange documents that translate colonization into the language of the marketplace?

Transactions in a commercial vein have come to be seen as the normal and proper way to make Indian land available to settlers in not only the United States but also throughout the English-speaking world. Enshrined in the Royal Proclamation of 1763, the notion that formal, documented negotiations resembling a bargain and sale ought to form part of any legitimate transfer of territory from Natives, via the state, to settlers soon spread into British-ruled Canada, New Zealand, and other zones of colonization subject to English common law. Here it came to be naturalized as the proper standard by which to judge the justice and rectitude of state treatment of indigenous peoples.[10] Treaty rights and land rights are the prime terrain on which many Native leaders have struggled to defend indigenous interests down to the present day, because that is one of the few areas where the law provides them with some recourse. For non-aboriginal scholars, on the other hand, the voluntary, contractual form of treaty arrangements sometimes serves as an occasion for Anglophone-world self-congratulation;

some emphasize the land acquisition aspect of the procedure, others the extension of sovereignty. Paul G. McHugh writes that

> colonial practice in North America varied with the different contexts but the treaty-making pattern was fixed very early in the seventeenth century, indicating that whatever *imperium* was asserted over Indians rested on their agreement rather than the fact of their forced submission. British practice strove here, as in Ireland and the East Indies, to base any governance over non-British people on their consent or (less usually, conquest).[11]

Consent versus conquest, purchase as opposed to theft: Anglo-American colonization at least made an effort to do right by Natives.

ONE of the most striking expressions of this ideology of Anglo-American superiority in dealings with indigenous peoples is Benjamin West's 1771 painting, *William Penn's Treaty with the Indians When he Founded the Province of Pennsylvania in North America*.[12] This image depicts a benevolent Quaker colonizer presiding over a scene in which Lenni Lenape (Delawares) were being offered textiles and other valuable goods in an atmosphere suggestive of peace and mutual respect. Whereas William Penn had actually negotiated a series of local purchase agreements soon after the establishment of Pennsylvania, the artist's conceit was that these scattered transactions could be represented as a single treaty concluded on the shores of the Delaware River in 1682. The founder's son, John Penn, commissioned the original picture almost a century after the "event," at a time when the Penn family's proprietorship was under attack; it therefore has to be understood, in the context of 1770s Pennsylvania politics, as a highly partisan stratagem. However, Benjamin West's original composition was repeatedly copied and widely reproduced in later years, as lithographs and later photographic reproductions allowed the image of Penn and the Lenni Lenape to circulate far and wide. Bursting through the limits of its original provincial setting, *William Penn's Treaty* became "an allegory of Colonial America," as one art historian puts it,[13] an iconic image of idealized fair treatment of Indians that has resonated with the American public to the present day. This vision of a founding moment of peaceful negotiation and mutually beneficial exchange—cloth and other valuable products for land—held great appeal in a settler society with an uneasy conscience.

FIGURE 2.1. Benjamin West's famous painting of William Penn's treaty with the Lenni Lenape presents a seemingly fair bargain of trade goods for land. Indian understanding was otherwise, and a long history of dispossession by fraud and force was to follow.

Courtesy of the John Carter Brown Library at Brown University.

Like any iconic historical image, the West painting highlights some aspects of the past, hints at others, and conceals a great deal. Penn's justice is on view, but his ambivalent attitude to Native rights remains invisible (he was convinced that he already owned Pennsylvania by virtue of a grant from Charles II; payments to the Lenni Lenape were partly a courtesy, partly a matter of securing a quit claim).[14] More fundamentally, the painting gives no inkling of the history of dispossession that occurred, in Pennsylvania as well as in the other British colonies, during the ninety-one years that intervened between the Penn "treaty" and its artistic apotheosis. The "sordid transaction known as the 'Walking Purchase' [1737]," in which the founder's sons "swindled the Delawares out of a tract of land almost as big as Rhode Island,"[15] is only the most notorious episode in that history. Frontier skirmishes, violent expulsions, and the massacre of unarmed Conestogas perpetrated by the Paxton Boys in 1763 also featured prominently in the history that the painting points away from.[16] Insofar as the painter and the viewer may be expected to have had some notion of this other reality, the message of the canvas might be read as follows: "Even if natives were often cheated in practice, Penn's fair and honest exchange represents good intentions and an ideal to which we aspire."

If Benjamin West's tableau excludes much, it also hints at a broader international background, present but not seen, in the world beyond its frame. Other colonies and other empires, empires where Indians never received fair compensation for their lands, form a ghostly point of comparison that makes Penn's generous gesture meaningful. In texts of the seventeenth and eighteenth centuries, much was made of the contrast between the violent conquests of the Iberian powers and the French and the gentler practices of the British and Americans. English-speaking colonizers may not have been completely fair to Natives, goes the underlying narrative, but at least they appropriated territory with *consent* and in return for *compensation*; the Spaniards took land by violence and coercion and they gave Indians nothing in return. This is a story that draws on the Black Legend and harks back to the earliest English (and Dutch) discourses justifying intrusion into the New World: Catholics were cruel despoilers, whereas the English (or Dutch) approached America as benevolent and law-abiding colonizers.[17] In the eighteenth century the French joined the Spaniards as the object of Anglo-American polemics in a similar vein. During the War of Austrian Succession, a New England pamphleteer wrote of the French colonies of New France and Louisiana, "They have scarce any other title to the country than what they obtained by usurpation, or a lawless force, very seldom asking leave of the natives to settle in their country; which alone can give a foreigner a just right to the dominion of it."[18] Without putting it quite so bluntly, modern scholarship in the English language still tends to carry faint echoes of this flattering contrast between "good" (or at least well-intentioned) colonizers and "bad" colonizers when it asks whether Indians "lost their land" by sale or by conquest and when it proceeds to show that the United States was built on land sold by, rather than stolen from, Natives.[19] It is a shadow comparative claim that, like the West painting, implies a basic polarity without ever spelling things out, much less examining inter-imperial differences in the appropriation of Native lands.

In place of these shadow comparisons hearkening back to the imperial propaganda of earlier centuries, we need to introduce some genuine comparative analysis based on current historical scholarship in order to gain a better understanding of the meaning and purposes of dispossession-by-purchase as one style of appropriation among many possibilities. To say this is not to suggest that comparative analysis has been missing from the history of land and colonization. In fact, that field has seen a proliferation of comparative work in recent decades. Legal scholars and historians have contributed illuminating studies of land rights, treaties, and the modalities of appropriation by comparing developments in the United States, English Canada, Australia, New Zealand, South Africa, and other settler colonies and states.[20] However, these comparative ventures, valuable though they are in many respects, are not well adapted to addressing the questions raised here. For one thing, they tend overwhelmingly to focus on the nineteenth century, a time when some basic traditions and laws had already become firmly established in the area of aboriginal affairs. More important, most comparative legal-historical studies remain confined within a scholarly echo chamber, their gazes fixed on the English-speaking common-law world where (with the significant exception of Australia) treaties in a commercial idiom were the accepted norm.

If we go back to the sixteenth- and seventeenth-century origins of European New World empires, we discover some interesting divergences along a Catholic-Protestant fault line, differences that constitute the kernel of truth underpinning the Black Legend ideology of Anglophone superiority. To put the contrast very starkly, whereas the English, the Dutch, and even the Swedes (in New Sweden on the Delaware) were wont to establish relations with Native Americans on the basis of an exchange of goods for land, the Spanish, Portuguese, and French did no such thing. Occasionally an individual Spaniard purchased a piece of property from a Native owner, but such transactions occurred in areas already subject to colonial jurisdiction; moreover, they were quasi-illegitimate in light of legislation in New Spain intended to protect Indians from predatory Spanish land purchasers.[21] In these Catholic empires, territories and peoples were incorporated, and *dominium* established, without recourse to the language of commerce. On the whole, Spanish, Portuguese, and French imperialisms were not interested in separating Indians from the land, by purchase or by any other means. In a colonial formation where Indians were to work for Spaniards but support themselves from the products of their own holdings, the Spanish Crown repeatedly proclaimed Native landed property to be inviolable. Portuguese settlers in Brazil pushed Natives aside to create enclaves for themselves without recourse to formalities or land purchases, while leaving most of the country in Native possession; here, too, "Indian relations" revolved mainly around the colonists' appetite for labor.[22] The French, for their part, instituted seigneurial property forms in the St. Lawrence Valley; without acknowledging, denying, or eliminating existing indigenous property, they simply laid down colonial fiefs over the land. The layered and fragmented attributes of ownership characteristic of feudal tenure left ample room for Native possession in most areas. Unlike the English, the French did not need to extinguish Native tenure in order to institute European-colonial tenure.

In French, Portuguese, and Spanish America the accent was on inclusion, on incorporating indigenous peoples and their lands into a variegated and visibly hierarchical colonial polity. Indigenous peoples could be, and frequently were, displaced, slaughtered, or exploited, but this was done rarely for the purpose of gaining ownership of their lands. And yet Natives did indeed suffer dispossession in these Catholic empires. Over time, European settlers and their creole progeny gradually deepened and extended colonial tenures, developing colonial forms of property that reduced the scope of Indian control over land. Official Spanish policy protecting Indian lands did not prevent large-scale appropriation, for example, at the hands of *hacendados* in Mexico, nor did the seigneurs of New France shrink from placing land originally reserved for Natives into the hands of rent-paying French-Canadian peasants. However, one looks in vain in these colonies for a clear-cut boundary, resembling the one separating zones of settler tenure and zones of Native tenure that developed in the English colonies.

Moreover, Natives retained significant degrees of control over extensive territories even by the end of the colonial period in Mexico and French Canada. Thus, to imply that the Spanish, Portuguese, and French failed to live up to the high standards of the English and Dutch, that the former groups stole land by force whereas the latter bought it, is to be doubly misleading. Not only was it the case that Protestant colonizers also failed to live up to their own ideals, force frequently functioning as a determining factor in colonial purchases, but also the Spanish, French, and Portuguese were not pursuing the same objectives as their English and Dutch counterparts did. Territory construed as property did not play the same role in the colonial ventures of the former as it did in those of the latter.[23]

Carving out a space for the exclusive use of settlers, while keeping Indians at bay, was a procedure characteristic of the Protestant imperial powers. For the English, Dutch, and Swedes, much more than for the Catholic empires, landownership was a central issue in defining relations between colonizers and Natives. Overseas possessions were more likely to be seen as "plantations" or "colonies" in the Roman sense (that is, as enclaves in a foreign country that were occupied by emigrants from the mother country).[24] Natives were liable to appear as an impediment or an irrelevance when colonization was understood in these terms. In the Catholic empires, on the other hand, Indian labor, Indian souls, and Indian trade were the main targets. In this light, it makes sense that transactions in the form of land purchases would have a place in Protestant-style and not in Catholic-style colonial formations. Indeed, there is an intuitive appeal to the notion that English Puritans and Quakers of the seventeenth century, as well as Dutch Calvinists, would be particularly inclined to evaluate the justice of dealings with Natives in terms of "covenants" and in light of Old Testament accounts of the Israelites' struggles to secure a place for themselves in a populated land.[25]

To speak of contrasting Protestant and Catholic styles is to offer the beginnings of an explanation for the emergence of the land-purchase approach to colonization. In a general sense, the trappings of voluntary contract and fair compensation served ideological purposes, their particular form inflected by religious traditions. From the earliest Indian deeds, through William Penn's purchases and their later pictorial commemoration, and right up to some modern currents in historiography and memory, a basically consistent underlying impulse to depict colonization as fair dealing can be detected. Ideology is quite distinct from conscious deception or manipulation; it refers in this instance to a basically sincere desire to do right by Natives, to blunt the sharp edges of dispossession without actually preventing dispossession. This ideological function does go some distance toward explaining the prevalence of the commercial idiom in Protestant empires, but it hardly constitutes a complete explanation for the popularity of a set of practices that actually developed quite unevenly and that responded, in different historical settings, to a variety of political and legal considerations. These practical purposes become evident when we look back beyond William Penn's time to the early seventeenth-century origins of the land-purchase treaty.

Kuttattauamish aûke.	*I would buy land of you.*
Tou Nùckquaque?	*How much?*
Wuche wuttotânick.	*For a Towne, or, Plantation.*
Nissékineam.	*I have no mind to sell.*
Indiánsuck sekineámwock.	*The Indians are not willing.*
Noonapúock naûgum.	*They want roome themselves.*
Cowetompátimmin.	*We are friends.*
Cummaugakéamish.	*I will give you land.*
Aquíe chenawaûsish.	*Be not churlish.*[26]

Land and the buying thereof occupy an important place in Roger Williams's rough and ready Narragansett phrase book, and the brief dialogue quoted here is revealing at several levels. Modern linguistic experts point out that the English phrase "to buy land" is actually untranslatable in this context: the author can get no closer in the Algonquian tongue than a phrase suggestive of access to territory.[27] As usual with colonial guides to native languages, this one says more about the colonizers—what mattered to them, how they grouped topics and associated various concepts—than it does about the preoccupations of the indigenous people. While Williams stretches Native vocabulary to serve the purposes of land-sale negotiations, French Jesuit dictionaries and phrase books of the period make no such attempt; instead, they struggle to find terms in which to discuss religion, political authority, war, and trade (trade in furs and other concrete objects, that is, not purchases of land).[28] The different colonizers try to adapt indigenous languages to their particular purposes. And, yet, while documents like the *Key into the Language of America* may be seen as testimony to the preoccupations of the Europeans who drew them up, they also display the influence of the Native linguistic informants. From the quoted passage, it does appear that, in Roger Williams's experience, Indians were not always willing to sell their land. And as negotiations intensified, it seems that issues came to the fore that had little to do with price: questions of personal relations ("We are friends"), generosity ("I will give you land") and its opposite ("churlish"). The *Key* may not provide a perfectly transparent table of linguistic equivalences, but it does provide testimony of a sort about the way in which land came up in the Anglo-Algonquian encounter in early New England.

The first English settlers of the Chesapeake and New England did not leave written deeds or treaties; their authorized spokesmen also did not seem to feel obligated to buy land from indigenous peoples.[29] For Governor John Winthrop of the Massachusetts Bay Colony, all land but the small fields actually cultivated by Indians was *vacuum domicilium* and therefore claimable without formality.[30] Be that as it may as a matter of principle, in practice many early settlers found it necessary or expedient to come to terms with local Indians so that they could build houses and till the soil in peace. At an initial stage, when colonists were few in number at a given location, there was scope for a mutually beneficial relationship: this was not simply of the manufactured-goods-for-land variety, but rather one that encompassed various forms of cooperation such as military alliance, fur trading, and mutual support in times of dearth. During this brief "middleground" phase, Native custom predominated to a significant degree. Settlers promised friendship, and they offered gifts of metal tools, cloth, and wampum; Natives allowed them to live in their country and make use of its resources. From the Indian point of view, the payments may have represented a form of tribute, like that exacted from lower-ranking neighbors by a preeminent sachem.[31] Colonists, when they were not in a position of overwhelming power, had to accept the ways of people whose country consisted of a set of use rights that were inextricably bound to collective identities and personal relationships. Thus Roger Williams, looking back late in life and not without some idealizing, recalled that he had obtained possession of Providence and other lands thanks to the bonds of friendship and virtual kinship that united him with the Narragansett sachems who dominated the region, Canonicus and his nephew, Miantonomo. God moved the latter, he wrote, "to love me as his son to his last gasp" and to grant me "whatsoever I desire[d] of him." Williams adds that he reciprocated Canonicus's kindness: "And I never denyed him nor Miantonomy whatever they desired of me as to goods or gifts, or use of my boats or pinnace and the travels of my own person day and night."[32] Though the transaction was reconstructed later as a "land purchase," Roger Williams here describes it as being about the establishment and nurturing of a relationship, a constellation of ceremonies, services, and material exchanges that extended over time, not a single act concerning "land" abstracted from its social and ecological context. Such an agreement seems to correspond to what some consider the basic Native American approach to treaties as living agreements that, over time, establish and maintain peace and friendship.[33]

Of course, Roger Williams, usually regarded as occupying the "pro-Indian" pole of New England colonial opinion, can hardly be taken as a typical case. Williams may have been a doctrinaire proponent of Native "land rights," committed to a "Protestant" version of colonial justice and locked in conflict with Massachusetts's Governor Winthrop, who denied these same land rights, but Williams was also a hands-on colonizer who expressed views shaped by practical experience dealing with Indians. Led by Winthrop, Puritans had arrived on the shores of Massachusetts Bay in overwhelming numbers and they had little difficulty claiming lands whose indigenous populations had already been depleted by deadly epidemics. Williams, on the other hand, led settlers into Narragansett Bay, the home in the 1630s of a still-powerful nation that had somehow escaped the worst effects of Old World disease. He had to come to terms with Natives in a way that Winthrop did not. Other early New England colonists who found themselves in similar circumstances—that is to say, few in numbers and unable to count with certainty on the backing of a strong colonial state—seem to have followed a similar strategy of adapting to the expectations of their Native neighbors. Examples that come to mind include the early settlers of Martha's Vineyard, under the uncertain manorial jurisdiction of Thomas Mayhew, as well as those who set themselves up on Long Island in an area in dispute between the Dutch and the British.[34] Likely there were many other pockets on the edges of European-controlled territory where colonists, for one reason or another, could not dictate terms to the Natives of the place. We have to assume that settlers in such situations of rough parity of power must have negotiated agreements that responded to indigenous expectations, even if those agreements were not always recorded on paper.[35]

Even when the form of an agreement suggests that the object was a plot of ground abstracted from any social and ecological context, indications of a more complex reality can still be detected. By a deed signed on March 24, 1637, William Coddington bought Aquidneck Island (the current site of Newport, Rhode Island) for forty fathoms of white beads from the same duo of Canonicus and Miantonomo that Roger Williams dealt with. If the deed contained no further clauses, it would have the appearance of a simple transfer of ownership of a neatly defined territory, but other parties and additional considerations inserted themselves into the document. Wanamatraunemit, the leader of the Narragansetts actually residing on the island, signed a clause acknowledging that he had accepted five fathoms of wampum for agreeing to move away. Additionally, Coddington purchased the right to harvest hay from particular marshes and riverbanks on the mainland, paying Canonicus and Miantonomo, as regionally preeminent sachems, for the privilege, but also giving their Wampanoag tributary, Massasoit, five fathoms of wampum for these same use rights. Massasoit took the opportunity to "promise loveinge and just carriage of myselfe and all my men to the said Mr. Coddington and English his friends united to him."[36] Coddington's willingness to adapt his agreement to the layered tributary hierarchy of the Narragansetts is noteworthy, but more to the point is what this settlement leader indicated he was acquiring through his outlay of wampum: ownership of an island, use rights over some vaguely delineated mainland territory, the eviction of current residents of the island, and the friendship of Massasoit and his people. What were Coddington and his people purchasing for their strings of beads and their coats and knives? To say they bought "land" is too simple: quite apart from the fact that real estate in fee simple is not something Natives had for sale, the settlers themselves seemed to want both more (e.g., a particular demeanor on the part of the sellers) and less (e.g., mowing and grazing rights) than exclusive control of the soil.

Whereas Indian deeds tended to be deployed within the colonial sphere as though they conferred unconditional ownership, the wording of many such documents betrays a more qualified and uncertain territorial claim, reflective of the deeds' origins in cross-cultural negotiations. Boundaries tend to be rather indistinct and it is not always clear what particular "bundle of rights" is being purchased within the tract at issue. Early New Netherlands deeds could be quite vague on all these scores. In the specific case of the Connecticut River outpost that became a hot spot for conflict with the English, the Dutch deed referred to payment consisting of duffel, axes, kettles, knives, toys, and shears for a locality where a fur trading post would stand. The Native signatories undertook to allow other Indian groups access to the post, both friends and enemies, and agreed not to molest them within the territory purchased. This was not really a purchase of "land" for cultivation; it was payment for permission to conduct trade with distant nations and, as such, the agreement was quite compatible with established indigenous usages.[37]

Middle-ground relations did not last long in southern New England as a tidal wave of overseas migration quickly and decisively shifted the balance of numbers and of power in favor of the newcomers. Desperate for ever more land to establish their growing and multiplying settler families, the English had less and less patience with Native territorial claims and Native cultural sensibilities. When they did bother to "treat with the Indians," Puritans were more likely to impose their own ways of proceeding, which meant a greater emphasis on obtaining exclusive control over land; it also meant a single, once-and-for-all agreement rather than an ongoing exchange. Finally, it implied an emphasis on written documents, composed in the English language and incorporating tenets of English law, and therefore triply alien to the Algonquians. But just because the English gained the upper hand does not mean that the Natives instantly abandoned their own approach to coexistence on the land or that the settlers refused to accommodate them in any respect. Lastingly, and for obvious reasons, Native Americans continued to set stock by verbal negotiations and agreements rather than written documents. Moreover, whenever possible, they perpetuated a sense of shared use of the resources of a given territory. Consequently, deeds from the period of English ascendancy still frequently contained "reservations," clauses by which the Native signatories insisted on retaining space to plant, access to particular fishing resources, or the right to hunt over lands not yet under settler cultivation. To take one example, the Massachusetts town of Andover bought land in 1646 from a sachem named Cutshamekin for six pounds plus a coat, but with a proviso in the deed, "reserving to an Indian named Roger & his company the right to fish for alewives."[38]

To the ceremonies surrounding agreements on Indian-settler coexistence, the English attached a device, the signed written document or deed, that acquired great importance outside the realm of intercultural relations. Though they grew out of and claimed to commemorate a relationship with Natives, these papers, covered in words and marked with signatures and totemic symbols, took on a life of their own in the colonial world of relations among Europeans and Euro-Americans.[39]

It was actually the Dutch, Francis Jennings notes, who first introduced documented land purchases to North America, having learned during territorial disputes with the English in the East Indies the value of deeds signed by local inhabitants. The founders of New Netherlands were instructed in 1625 to secure written deeds from the Natives specifically for the purpose of reinforcing Dutch *dominium* vis-à-vis rival European claimants. Before many years had passed, they were brandishing Indian deeds for just that purpose when challenged by the English on the Connecticut River and by the Swedes on the Delaware.[40] The initial English response to Dutch claims based on purchase was to dismiss the notion that Indians of the Connecticut Valley had any ownership rights to sell, "their residences being unsettled and uncertain." The English claimed the country instead, "by first discovery, occupation and the possession which they have taken thereof, and by the concessions and letters patent they have had from our Sovereigns."[41] Before long, some English were following the Dutch lead and securing deeds of sale from Natives in certain New England localities. Connecticut was an early site of formal purchases precisely because it was a disputed zone. Already acquainted with the advantages of "buying" Indian goodwill, the English learned from the Dutch the value of inserting a deed of cession into negotiations over the terms of coexistence.

Never universal, Indian deeds tended to proliferate in the seventeenth century more in New England than in the Chesapeake colonies, partly because of territorial disputes between the English and the Dutch but also between rival English claimants. There was much contestation in the early colonial geography of New England, especially in Maine and New Hampshire, as well as along the uncertain boundaries between Rhode Island and Connecticut and between Rhode Island and Plymouth Colony. In some instances, contention between individuals over ownership and conflicts over jurisdiction between neighboring colonies produced a tangled web. In such circumstances, a document marked by one or several sachems could help bolster the case both of the party that had purchased it and of the colony that backed them.[42] When, in the 1680s, Governor Edmund Andros of the Dominion of New England challenged the legality of township grants, many towns hastily and belatedly paid local Indians to sign deeds ceding their property rights to the lands of the purchasing township. The object of the exercise was to provide a foundation for settler property rights independent of direct grant from the Crown.[43] In the context of rivalries between empires, or between colonies within a given empire, or between colonial and imperial interests, documents recording a purchase from Natives could play a role in deciding which Euro-Americans were entitled to which territories.

Individuals, companies, and townships all could be found among those seeking and paying for Indian deeds in seventeenth-century New England. The fact that the Puritan settlers of Southampton on Long Island had no governmental authority to turn to for an official grant of land did not stop them from improvising a property regime grounded on bases that seemed to them perfectly legitimate. "Wee purchased ye land wee now possess of the natives, the then proper owners," one of them wrote, "and . . . with long and hard labor, subdue . . . these lands with the peril of our lives."[44] Even in the least contested parts of the region, it was always useful to have an official document on hand should the need arise to brandish it in court and, given the rather improvised and informal procedures by which land was distributed first to towns and, through them, to settlers, a paper signed by Natives was often the most likely candidate. At the head of many a New England property's chain of title stood an Indian deed. So in addition to the "political" uses of deeds in the context of competing territorial jurisdictions, we see a more specifically "legal" function they played in anchoring property claims.

Private property claims and state jurisdictions reinforced one another to a degree, but there were also basic tensions between the "private" purposes of those who bought land from Natives and the "public" purposes of colonial and imperial governments. The Massachusetts General Court encouraged townships to negotiate with local Natives to extinguish any claims on land within their boundaries, but it required them to do so only with the specific approval of the court. By an order issued in 1633 it decreed that "noe pson whatsoever shall buy any land of any Indean without leave from the court."[45] Other New England colonies followed suit with similar legislation.[46] The colonial legislatures could see that issues of sovereignty and jurisdiction were at stake whenever settlers acquired title to Native land. Indigenous peoples occupied an uncertain position in the colonial body politic, because they were simultaneously outsiders and potential subjects. When individuals committed acts of theft or violence, it was not at all clear that their actions were to be treated as criminal offenses, as opposed to possible acts of war.[47] In a similar vein, colonial officials wanted to treat the acquisition of Indian land as a nation-to-nation affair, not as a purely personal transaction. When disputes arose in the wake of some early purchases, Plymouth Colony refused to hear complaints from any individual Wampanoag; only "theire cheife sachem, Phillip," was authorized to represent the entire nation.[48] New England governments of the seventeenth century saw Indian tenure and settler tenure as separate realms, and when land passed from Native to colonial ownership, that transfer was properly an act of state.

Although they repeatedly asserted authority in this area, the colonies themselves took few concrete steps in the early period to negotiate directly with Native nations: that would become the norm for governments seeking to extinguish aboriginal title in later centuries. For now, towns and individuals had to take the initiative while the colonies' General Courts struggled to maintain at least the appearance of official oversight. They did not succeed fully in suppressing unauthorized Indian purchases in spite of repeated proclamations, and when illegal purchases did come to the attention of the authorities, there was a reluctance simply to nullify them. William Nicarson of Yarmouth was fined one hundred pounds by the General Court of Plymouth Colony for unauthorized buying of land from Natives; he did get to keep the land, however.[49] Reliant on towns and individuals for a crucial part of the process of transforming Native land into colonial real estate, New England governments did their best to wrap the operation within their jurisdiction.

The insistence on keeping Indian deeds at least nominally within the context of nation-to-nation relations highlights the fact that when land was bought from Natives the transaction took place outside the emergent colonial real-estate market. By helping to build a paper edifice of title, Indian deeds in fact functioned as a vital element out of which that market in land was being constructed. As if to underline the point that this market was being built for settlers, colonial governments showed great reluctance to treat Natives, even those who lived under their jurisdiction and in the midst of their settlements, as landowners like other (i.e., white) landowners. Inhabitants of the "praying-Indian" towns set up in Massachusetts for Christian converts did not enjoy the same ownership rights as the English colonists who surrounded them. Their land grants came with various restrictions, notably regarding selling land.[50] A 1647 law in Connecticut prohibited even the renting of land to Natives, "forasmuch as divers inconveniences fall out by letting land to the Indeans, whereby they mixe themselves in theire labours with the Inglishe, and therby the manners of many young men are lyable to be corrupted." Indians were not completely cut off from access to the soil, however: the Connecticut law added that "such natyves as have caried themselves peacebly, and which will subjecte themselves to be ordered by the Inglishe, shall have permission for planting uppon reasonable terms sette forth for them."[51] Submissive Indians might be allowed to use land in the settler zone, but they could not be recognized as owners or lessees.

The thrust of these rules and regulations points toward another function of Indian deeds: they tended to effect a radical separation between Natives and property. Indians might occupy and possess territory—indeed much of southern New England remained under Native control as of the eve of King Philip's War in 1675—and they might, on sufferance, make use of the earth's resources within colonial jurisdictions, but they were generally ineligible to own property as property in land was coming to be defined in settler-controlled New England. Pockets of Native land survived colonization, but they were regarded as a legal anomaly. Thus a Rhode Island tax assessment of 1672 made a point of exempting Indians, "as persons not lyable to be rated in any places to be payd to the said assessment."[52] Originally associated with attempts to share the land of New England, Indian deeds were soon deployed for purposes of exclusion, playing a major role in the construction of tenures that were for settlers, not for Natives.

Given their value in the colonial sphere, many settlers succumbed to the temptation to procure Indian deeds by hook or by crook. One device, favored by William Pynchon in the Springfield, Massachusetts, area, was to make use of the fur trade, granting credit to Native hunters, parlaying debts into mortgages, and then seizing control of great tracts of land.[53] Divide-and-conquer techniques were also useful, exploiting ambiguities in Algonquian political organization in order to find a pliable leader willing to sell out his people's interests, particularly when he could be under the influence of alcohol. Various forms of deceit and coercion came to characterize land negotiations in circumstances where settlers were in a comparatively strong position. Natives complained loudly about such trickery and resisted fraudulent cessions to the best of their ability, but they often faced an overwhelming disparity of power that forced them to capitulate. The question then arises: if force, or at least the potential to use force, underpinned so many Indian deeds, why did New England settlers bother to maintain the pretense of a voluntary contract? Why not just take land from vulnerable

Natives as settlers of Virginia were inclined to do? The answer lies in not only the ideological realm—concerns to perform a "Protestant" version of justice—but also the legal realm. Deeds had their uses in establishing and documenting settler property.

OUT of the seventeenth-century precedents outlined above, a new "treaty system" emerged on the borderlands of British North America in the aftermath of the Seven Years' War,[54] setting a basic pattern that would prevail for a century in the United States, as well as in other settler states spawned by the British Empire. The Royal Proclamation, promulgated in 1763 in an attempt to secure peace with western Indian nations, set down some basic guidelines regarding settlement, property, and jurisdiction. The Proclamation reserved all lands west of the Appalachians to Indians, barring settlers from the region and prohibiting any private purchases from the Natives. It provided for land cessions but these could only be negotiated in the name of the Crown and only at a public meeting of Indians called for that purpose.[55] Peace through partition, keeping settlers and Natives geographically separate, was the initial objective of the Royal Proclamation, but because there was no practical way to police a boundary line thousands of miles in length, the decree proceeded by way of regulation of property rights.

In many respects, including the naive hope that the culturally intertwined societies of the contact zone could be neatly dissected into settler and Native sectors, the Proclamation represents continuity with the English American past.[56] Its commitment to upholding the ideal of land cession by voluntary contract also hearkens back to the days of Roger Williams and William Penn. Furthermore, the assertion of a state monopoly over Native purchases recalls the seventeenth-century General Courts' attempts to regulate such purchases, though now government was to take the initiative in negotiating cessions through its own agents. Much about the Royal Proclamation represents a new departure, however. To begin with, it was an imperial enactment boldly asserting centralized imperial control over "Indian affairs" and therefore over frontier lands. After the Revolution, the federal government would claim, as heir to the British, a similar dominant authority in this area, struggling for many years to fend off state challenges to its monopoly.[57] Implicit in the Proclamation's provision for future cessions of western lands is the concept of a public domain as a zone of proto-property: land cleared of aboriginal title and held by the state but not yet owned by individuals. In approaching relations between Natives and non-Natives as a problem of territories and boundaries, one that revolved around processes devised for transforming land into settler property, the Royal Proclamation appears as a culmination of sorts in the history of colonial-era dispossession.

This intervention from the empire's center did not sit well with colonists, particularly with those who hoped to make money from Indian lands. The authorities could do little to stem the swelling flow of settlers moving into the trans-Appalachian West; in an often violent version of the "middle ground," squatters were carving out space for their farms in Shawnee, Delaware, and Cherokee country.[58] These unauthorized settlers depended less immediately on legal formalities than the eastern speculators who also coveted Native lands, purely for the purpose of making money as opposed to pursuing an agricultural livelihood. Of course, American land had long been a source of profit for privileged proprietors like William Penn and for astute entrepreneurs like William and John Pynchon, but these landowners managed their holdings as *estates*, seeking to develop the regional economy and generally maintaining a continuing personal interest in its affairs. Land speculation had entered a new phase as of the mid-eighteenth century. Men with access to capital and political influence were organizing themselves into associations such as the Ohio Company, which accumulated, through grants and purchases, claims to vast tracts with the sole purpose of extracting a profit from future settlers.[59] Virginia was a center of speculation in western lands, and future revolutionary heroes such as Patrick Henry, George Washington, and Thomas Jefferson were among the most active speculators. They bided their time during the French and Indian Wars when western expansion was unavoidably blocked, eagerly anticipating spectacular profits once peace returned and rustic hordes streamed across the mountains ready to buy land. The Royal Proclamation frustrated the speculators' designs for they, more than the settlers, required clear legal title; that really was all they would have to sell.[60] In so many words, Jefferson and Benjamin Franklin accused the British administration of stealing land from Americans; the speculators' grievances on this point merged with other issues and eventually found expression in the Declaration of Independence.[61]

Though the Royal Proclamation had a deep and lasting effect on procedures for dispossessing Natives and establishing settler property, the line it laid down along the Appalachian ridges had never been intended as an immoveable boundary. Breached from the start by settlers, its location was soon adjusted to give wider scope to speculation. It is helpful in understanding this outcome to bear in mind that the categories "speculators" and "government agents" overlapped considerably. New York's foremost dealer in lands, Sir William Johnson, also represented the Crown as the superintendent for Indian affairs for all the northern colonies. Making good use of his official position, as well as his close personal connections with the Iroquois nations, Johnson engineered the first major land cession under the terms of the Royal Proclamation. At Fort Stanwix in 1768, at a conference dominated by Iroquois delegates, he secured the surrender of thousands of square miles, most of it south of the Ohio River, including "the southwestern quarter of Pennsylvania, all of present-day West Virginia, and most of Kentucky." The Native nations that lived in these regions, notably the Shawnee, Cherokee, and Delaware, felt, quite rightly, that they had been sold out by the Iroquois and they resisted implementation of the treaty's terms. Nevertheless, a new boundary had been established; in place of the "Proclamation Line," people began to refer to a "Line of Property," which now extended into the Mississippi Valley; that phrase speaks volumes for the centrality of property making in defining relations between indigenous peoples and the British-American empire, soon to become the United States.[62]

We know the sequel: a succession of treaties moved the Line of Property ever farther across the continent, encompassing what was becoming anglophone North America and extending beyond the seas to other British settler colonies. Survey lines would be traced, fields cleared and farms built, deeds registered, resources extracted; land would be an ownable, mortgageable, alienable commodity. Except where Native peoples lived, that is: the reservations set aside for them would remain as islands of quasi-property surrounded by a sea of real estate. Obviously, there was much more to the history of nineteenth-century dispossession than what this schematic formula conveys: in reality, peoples and places were never neatly bounded, legal regimes never uncontested, contentions and contradictions never resolved. Yet there was a kind of underlying logic to the treaty system established in the wake of the Royal Proclamation of 1763 that tended toward the creation, under the auspices of the imperial/federal state, of property in land for non-Natives.

By way of conclusion, let me return to the interimperial comparative perspective for a brief update on Spanish America. The Age of Conquest that loomed so large in British imperial ideology was of limited duration.

By the eighteenth century, Spanish authorities on the borderlands of North and South America where empire met independent aboriginal nations were concerned with mainly stabilizing relations while countering any threats posed by rival empires. It is in this context, and at about the time the treaty system was developing in British North America, that treaties of a different sort came to play an important part in building and consolidating alliances at the edges of Spanish America. In *Bárbaros*, David Weber surveys the various agreements by which Enlightenment-era Spain secured peace with and asserted dominion over Apaches, Navajos, Mocobíes, and others, noting that none of these entailed a cession of land.[63] As in the past (though with far less brutality), Spaniards still sought to incorporate peoples into their fold and under their monarchy, not to buy land or recast property. Recalling this point of comparison serves to remind us of a basic fact about the British-American treaty system: under procedural formalities cast in the language of voluntary contract and value-for-value, it concealed a drastic and absolutist ambition to clear Indians from the field of property.

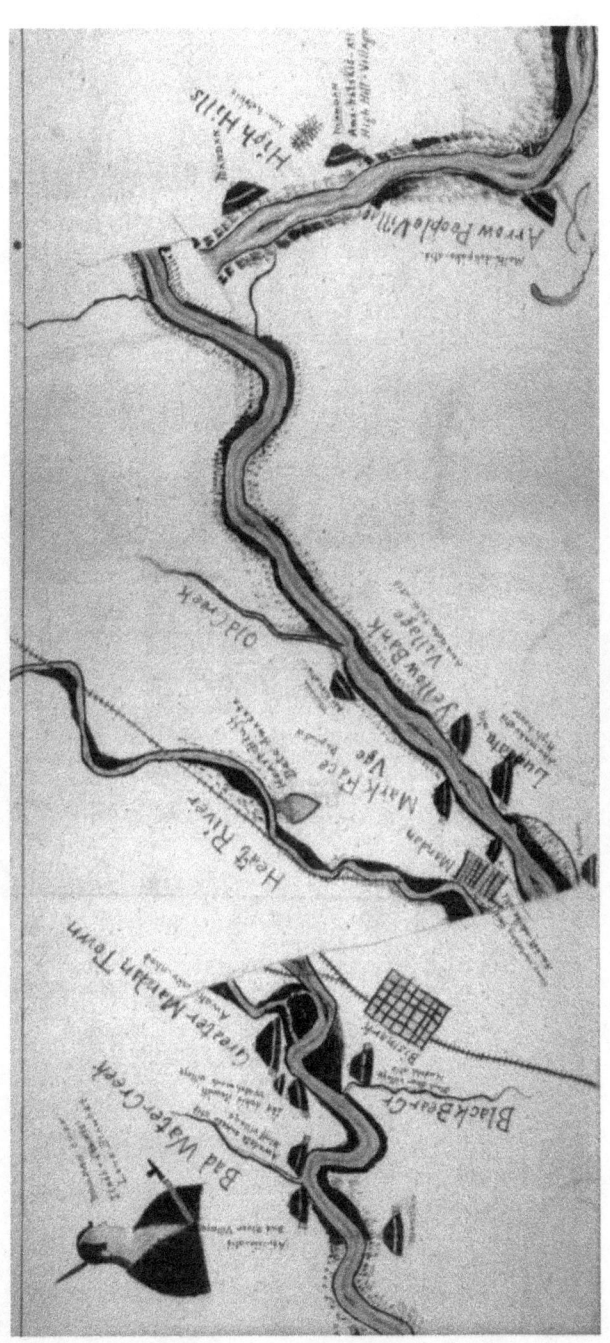

PLATE 1. Detail from the Sitting Rabbit map that shows three different segments of the Missouri River; a hash-marked line for the Great Northern Railroad, running through Bismarck, which appears as a rectilinear grid at the left; and Mandan, North Dakota, which appears as a similar but smaller grid on the other side of the river.

Reproduced by permission of the State Historical Society of North Dakota.

PLATE 2. "When there was water the prisoners were taken to wash and bathe."
From Doanmoe's manuscript, p. 11.
Courtesy of the Yale University Beinecke Rare Books and Manuscript Library

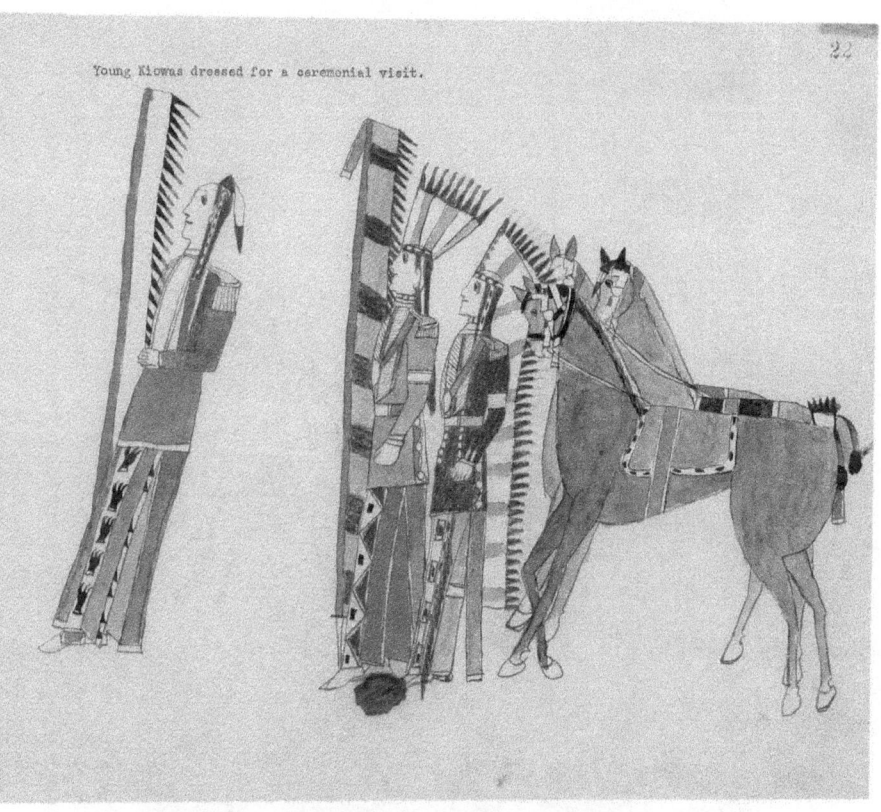

PLATE 3. "Young Kiowas dressed for a ceremonial visit."
From Doanmoe's manuscript, p. 22.
Courtesy of the Yale University Beinecke Rare Books and Manuscript Library.

PLATE 4. With its depiction of New Mexican equestrian militia, circa the 1720s, Segesser I provides the first visual record of new forms of armor, weaponry, and equestrian enslavement engulfing Native peoples across the Southwest.

Courtesy of the Palace of the Governors Photo Archives,
New Mexico History Museum, Santa Fe, Negative Number 152690.

PART II

Spaces and Landscapes

CHAPTER 3

The Mandans: Ecology, Population, and Adaptation on the Northern Plains

Elizabeth Fenn

In 1906–1907, a Mandan Indian man named Sitting Rabbit (also known as Little Owl) created a map illustrating more than six hundred years of his people's spatial and spiritual history.[1] In a segment-by-segment progression, Sitting Rabbit's painting portrays the sweeping, three-hundred-mile arc of the Missouri River in what we now know as western North Dakota. The work is so big—twenty-three feet long and eighteen inches wide—that only a small portion can be reproduced here (see Plate 1).[2]

Size and provenance are just two of the map's salient features. Also of note are the iconic earth lodges—domed, log-and-earth Indian homes—that line the circuitous turns of the Missouri River. The lodges indicate towns that were occupied by the Mandans or their Hidatsa and Arikara neighbors in both real and spiritual time. Some designate places where foundational events and origin stories unfolded. Eagle Nose Village, for example, was where Lone Man, the Mandan culture hero, once barricaded the Mandans against rising floodwaters.[3] And Village Where Turtle Went Back—possibly the fourteenth-century site called Shermer by archaeologists today—was where the Mandans got the "turtle" drums used in their most sacred ceremony.[4] Other settlements on the map include Yellow Bank Village, known famously as Double Ditch today, part of an impressive cluster of towns near where the Heart River flows into the Missouri from the west. Some distance upstream, the map portrays a side-by-side array of "Five Villages"—two Mandan and three Hidatsa—at the mouth of the Knife River, which enters the Missouri from the same direction. So, too, we see communities still farther north and west, including one labeled "Fishhook house." There are other symbols as well: rectilinear grids for non-earth-lodge settlements; a log cabin for a trading post; a knife indicating the Knife River (leading to flint quarries upstream); even hunters and a herd of bison representing a buffalo surround.

Everything about the map is compelling. It is a striking portrayal of Mandan space—or at least a significant part of it—in a collapsed chronological frame. Indeed, the conflation of time and space suited Sitting Rabbit's purposes. But for readers unfamiliar with the landscape, its features, and its meaning, there is something missing. The Mandan story, compressed so economically in Sitting Rabbit's images, fairly begs to be told.

In the years between 1500 and 1838, the Mandan people—Plains horticulturalists on the upper Missouri River—confronted a series of ecological challenges. First and foremost were the challenges of the land they occupied. In a region characterized by short growing seasons, sparse rain, and cruel winters, the Mandans built a horticultural and commercial juggernaut, with bountiful gardens and specialized craft production that supplied themselves and others through far-reaching trade connections.[5] But in the late 1500s and the centuries that followed, changing conditions undermined their success. Drought tested the horticultural skill of Mandan women, and population densities may have tested the sustainability of Mandan settlement patterns. Foreign peoples and species created new difficulties and opportunities that highlighted the extent and limits of Mandan social, cultural, and horticultural adaptability. During three centuries of contestation with human and environmental variables, the Mandans rearranged the villages they occupied and the physical spaces they claimed. They also reorganized clan configurations, craft production, and the bundle lines that governed ceremonial and spiritual powers. By allowing the Mandans to stay put, these changes reinforced the horticultural sedentism that brought their early success.

The Mandans and their ancestors had made their homes near the confluence of the Heart and Missouri rivers since approximately 1300 CE.[6] The location is roughly one hundred and fifty miles south of the present Canadian border, in the area where Bismarck and Mandan, North Dakota, sit today. Like the modern-day residents of those towns, the Mandans occupied large, permanent villages on the banks of the Missouri River. They also occupied a distinctive ecological niche. They grew corn in tremendous quantities despite living at the northern limit of maize cultivation and beyond the hundredth meridian, the widely accepted western boundary of nonirrigated agriculture.[7]

The Mandans also harvested meat—especially bison—to complement the grain and vegetable yield of their gardens. In the summer, they killed the animals on the prairies that extended in all directions around their villages.[8] In the winter, when weather drove people and bison alike into sheltered river bottoms, the Mandans hunted in the riparian forest, from which the animals barely budged before temperatures warmed.[9] Then, in the spring, the Mandans harvested delectable float bison—seasoned, drowned animals that drifted by their towns when the ice broke up.[10] The villagers also acquired bison products by trading with itinerant visitors and offering them handicrafts, farmstuffs, and other items in return.[11]

The Mandans' reliance on horticulture in such an unforgiving environment might seem like a tenuous choice. But the villagers found security, or at least food security, through diversification. To accommodate rogue frosts and a growing season typically fewer than a hundred and thirty days long, Mandan women cultivated at least nine varieties of maize.[12] The varieties served different culinary, nutritional, and ceremonial purposes. They also matured in different conditions and at different speeds, typically taking sixty to seventy days.[13] By making successive plantings to take advantage of specific varietal traits, Indian women ensured that an errant frost did not destroy the whole crop. Succulent green ears were edible in early August.[14] The women often sowed another, smaller round of green-corn varieties in July, in the oft-disappointed hope that they could enjoy another harvest of sweet, green ears before frost settled in.[15]

Drought also posed a challenge. In the 1950s, federal authorities forcibly removed Mandan, Hidatsa, and Arikara residents of the Fort Berthold Indian Reservation from their Missouri River valley towns to accommodate the water rising behind the newly constructed Garrison Dam. On the dry, thatch-laden grasslands above the river, irrigation was essential but unavailable, and wells could not keep up with demand. The relocated Indians struggled for their very survival, as did white farmers nearby. They found "it impossible to grow their own food or feed themselves," explains the author Paul VanDevelder, who wrote a book on the episode.[16]

How had their ancestors coped for generations before? Mandan women did not make their fields on the elevated prairie. Instead, they made them in the river bottoms, close to the water table, where capillary action pulled moisture upward to thirsty roots in all but the driest of seasons.[17]

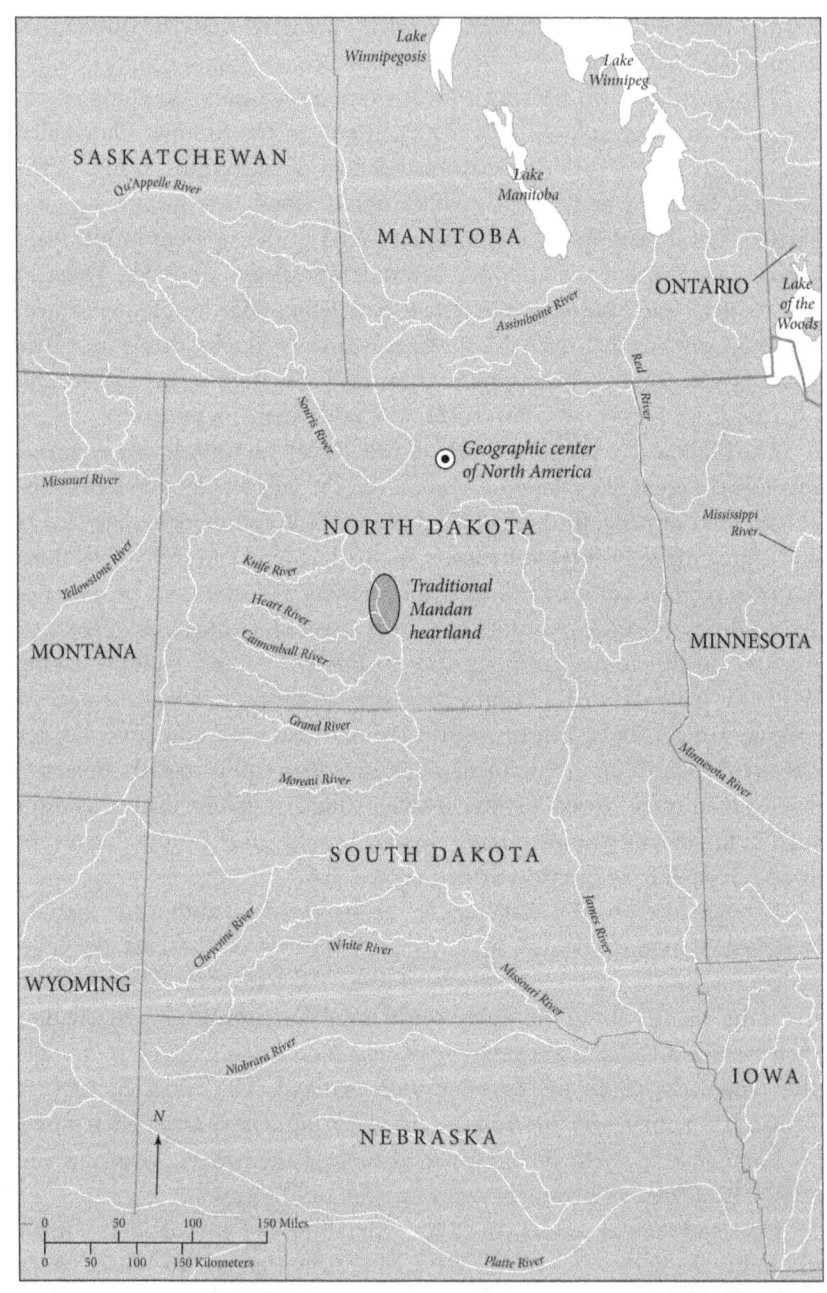

FIGURE 3.1. Midcontinent North America and the traditional Mandan heartland.

That is not to say that Mandan fields were entirely safe from drought. They were not. There were times when rains failed, and ears of corn shriveled on the stalk.[18] But the villagers—more particularly the women—had a backup plan. They turned to vast stores of dried maize, beans, squash, and sunflower seeds kept on hand for such emergencies. Archaeologists have tallied up 69,500 bushels of underground storage capacity in the cache pits of one early Mandan town. The villagers may not have used all this capacity at once. But the extent of their stores—for consumption and trade alike—remains mindboggling.[19]

So adept were the Mandans at managing their food supply that they rarely experienced serious famine. They knew periods of hardship, in which meat in particular was hard to come by. But full-fledged famine was rare. It was so rare that a Mandan winter-count keeper named Butterfly recalled the winter of 1866 as "our first famine. This was the first time our people ever went hungry, having neither corn nor meat." Evidence suggests this was not correct. But Butterfly's point is well taken. The Mandan lifeway accommodated the vicissitudes of North Dakota's climate in all but the most exigent circumstances.

Twenty-first-century archaeology is beginning to reveal the extent of the Mandans' success. High-tech imaging of sites in the area of the Heart River confluence has shown that several towns were substantial population centers. Double Ditch village, just north of Bismarck, may be the most spectacular and accessible example. The town's name reflects its most striking feature: two clearly discernible fortification trenches that still delineate its former boundaries. Indeed, the site impresses modern-day visitors on this basis alone.

But it turns out that the name Double Ditch is misleading. What appears to be the outermost trench does not mark the outermost boundary of the town. Scans completed in 2002 revealed at least two additional trenches beyond the two visible ones, for a total of four.[20] In its spatial dimensions, Double Ditch was once much larger than scholars had recognized. The two visible ditches represent only the town's smaller size as it pulled back in successive contractions. Surveys suggest that another nearby town, Larson, also had two additional fortification ditches detectable only through modern scanning techniques. Here, too, the passage of time had obscured the settlement's former size.[21]

Patterns of expansion and contraction differ from village to village, and scholars of the future will surely add surprising new discoveries to our

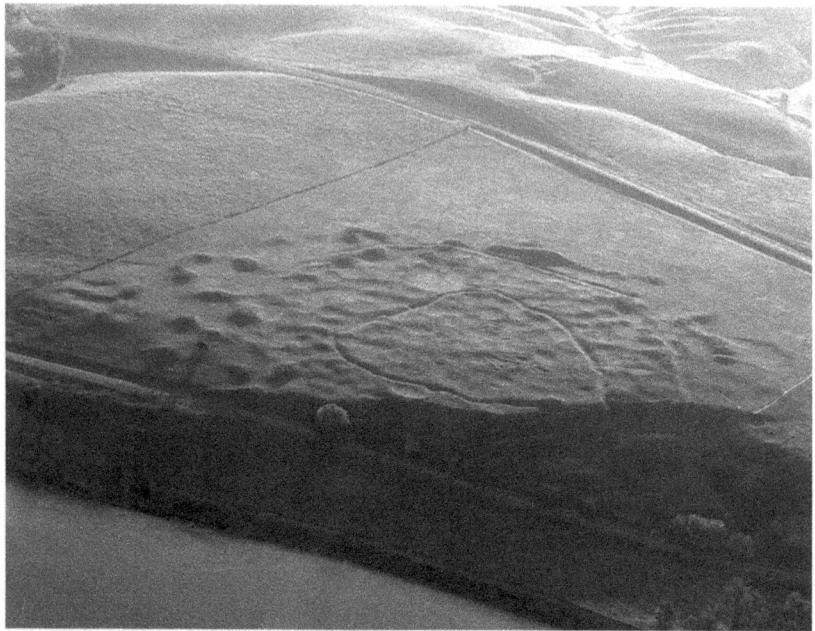

FIGURE 3.2. The Double Ditch site as seen from the air in June 2008. The town is named for its two visible fortification ditches, yet twenty-first-century remote-sensing technology has revealed the presence of two additional ditches beyond the ones visible to the naked eye, suggesting that the town was once much larger than a visual survey might indicate.

Photograph by Michael Frohlich. Reproduced by permission of the State Historical Society of North Dakota.

knowledge. But for now, it seems clear that the Mandans in their heyday lived in six or more settlements, mostly north of the confluence of the Missouri and Heart rivers. How many lived in these towns? The question looms large. It is complicated by several factors: radiocarbon dating is imperfect and limited in usefulness after 1650; towns did not shrink and grow in unison; and identification of sites as distinctively Mandan can be difficult. Some settlements appear to have housed not just Mandans but also Hidatsas, a neighboring people with a nearly identical lifeway.[22] Nevertheless, it seems possible that the Mandan population at the Missouri River–Heart River confluence numbered as many as twelve to fifteen thousand at its pinnacle, sometime between 1500 and the late sixteenth century.[23]

Then something happened.

IF archaeology sheds light on the Mandans' success, so it also reveals their collapse. Archaeologists think the outermost trench at Double Ditch is the oldest, representing the town's size—some nineteen acres—at its founding, around the time Columbus sailed.[24] By the late 1500s, however, the villagers had abandoned the outer two ditches. Their town shrank to fifteen acres, roughly a 20 percent reduction in size.[25]

Did the contraction take place sequentially or all at once? Archaeologists don't know for sure, but their working assumption is that the villagers dug ditch three, the inside ditch, after they dug ditch four. And likewise they dug ditches two and one—the innermost trenches—even later.[26] This suggests multiple phases of contraction. While surprises are possible, it seems likely that further study will confirm this sequence.

Will further study also reveal why the town shrank? This is a tougher problem. What caused Double Ditch—as well as Larson and perhaps other nearby towns—to dwindle in size and contract from ditch four to ditches three and then two in the late sixteenth century? The possibilities are manifold. They include overpopulation, drought, violent conflict, and epidemic disease—or some combination of these and other forces.

Overpopulation is an intriguing proposition. Around 1500, the upper Missouri towns constituted one of the most densely peopled areas north of Mexico. They did not measure up to the Pueblos of the American Southwest, but in numbers and density they were probably comparable to both the Hurons and the Iroquois in the Great Lakes area.[27] Beyond these, it seems unlikely that other regions could compare. Crowding often comes hand in hand with pollution and sanitation problems, as modern city dwellers well know. Jammed together cheek by jowl, the residents of Double Ditch and Larson may have faced just such challenges.[28] Or they may have found that their numbers overwhelmed the carrying capacity of the lands they occupied. Perhaps some died or left as a consequence. Perhaps birth rates dropped.

Ecologists of the late twentieth and early twenty-first centuries have recognized that carrying capacities are fluid, hinging on variables that change over time.[29] What if climate change or pests undermined the ability of the Mandans to sustain themselves in their traditional fashion? Drought was ubiquitous during the 1500s, when a recently recognized megadrought afflicted much of North America with conditions far more severe than those of the 1930s Dust Bowl. It hit the upper Missouri with particular force between 1574 and 1609.[30] Paleoclimatologists believe "the human impact" of this event "must have been substantial across much of North America."[31]

Even if the Mandans were able to sustain themselves through these hard years, drought-related pressures may have come to bear as nearby tribes found their own livelihoods threatened. Permanent villages, with their ready food supplies, were easy targets for raiders. Indeed, the fortifications that surrounded Mandan towns indicate that some kind of external threat existed. Pressed for resources, Arikara neighbors from the south may have borne down on them. Or other unnamed peoples could have done the same. Similar violence had unfolded among Missouri River peoples in drought episodes centuries earlier, long before Europeans or Africans set foot on the continent.[32]

It is possible, of course, that warfare had nothing to do with the Mandan contraction at Double Ditch. Referring to the destruction of his cotton crop by the boll weevil in 1923, the African American sharecropper Nate Shaw famously observed that "all God's dangers aint a white man."[33] So, too, the Mandans may have learned that the hazards of drought were not just desiccated crops and human enemies. Grasshoppers—still the bane of prairie farmers today—proliferate in dry conditions. One twenty-first-century appraisal warns that grasshopper populations "can double, triple, or quadruple with each successive year of drought."[34]

Another possibility has to do not with enemy peoples or pests but with pestilence. Wave after wave of sickness swept Mexico in the aftermath of Hernán Cortés's smallpox-assisted conquest of 1521. The years 1531, 1532, 1538, 1545–1548, 1550, 1559–1560, 1563–1564, 1576–1580, 1587, and 1595 all witnessed significant illness and mortality.[35] Scholars still struggle to identify the plagues involved. But there is no doubt that smallpox and measles—two Old World ailments new to the Americas—were among them. Other possibilities include typhus, plague, mumps, influenza, diphtheria, and an indigenous, drought-assisted hemorrhagic fever.[36] Along the Atlantic seaboard, imported diseases appear to have accompanied European explorers in 1535 and perhaps even earlier.[37] Indeed, Southeastern Indians endured a stunning population decline in the late 1500s—a decline plausibly caused by such plagues.[38]

Could the new contagions have reached the very center of the continent during the sixteenth century? Archaeology yields clues. The first European trade items reached the Mandans right around 1600.[39] The remnants are tiny—a few glass beads and bits of iron—but the implications are large.[40]

Barely a century after Columbus, the accoutrements of European colonization had penetrated to the very center of the continent. Indeed, the little town of Rugby, North Dakota, a hundred and twenty miles northwest of the Missouri River–Heart River confluence, touts its status as the "Geographical Center of North America" to draw tourists today.

If novel trade items reached the upper Missouri around 1600, foreign infections could have done the same. But the population of Double Ditch appears to have collapsed shortly *before* the novel trade goods arrived.[41] Imported disease may thus have moved across the landscape even faster than the wares that today mark the beginning of indirect contact with colonial interlopers. This may seem unlikely, but the possibility is real, especially for infections like measles and smallpox that have long incubation periods. An extended incubation period facilitates the spread of contagion by allowing infected individuals to travel substantial distances before falling sick.[42] One need only think of the global spread of HIV in the twentieth century to understand the mechanism at work.[43]

Whether or not the arrival of new diseases and new merchandise coincided on the upper Missouri, the trade items uncovered by archaeologists show how thoroughly indigenous networks connected the Mandans to far-flung areas of the North American landmass. In 1600, the closest permanent European settlement was New Mexico, some nine hundred miles away. The French had penetrated the continent as far as Lake Michigan. The English had explored the fjord-riven Labrador shoreline and had built a short-lived colony on the North Carolina coast. And the Spanish had probed the Midwest as far as present-day Kansas. But the beads, iron awls, and knife blades that marked their presence had moved far ahead of them.[44] Indigenous commerce was as vibrant and vital as the time-honored pictographs invoked by the Kiowa captive Etahdleuh Doanmoe in his 1877 sketchbook. (See Birgit Brander Rasmussen's essay in this volume.) Both were indigenous forms that took on new trappings with the onset of colonization.

UNCERTAINTY dissipates with the passage of time. By the early 1700s, Plains life was in upheaval, due in large part to the adoption of horses by Natives on the southern grasslands. The animals had evolved on the North American continent, migrating across the Bering land bridge, entering Asia, and establishing themselves there before becoming extinct in their ancestral homeland around 10,000 BCE. Thus when Spaniards reintroduced them in the fifteenth century, horses were foreign to Native Americans.

Plains peoples embraced the new creatures, especially after New Mexico's great Pueblo Revolt of 1680 made them more widely accessible. The animals flourished on the American steppe and spread northward in the early 1700s. The Mandans had seen horses by 1738, when the Frenchman Pierre de la Vérendrye trekked overland to visit them from what is today southern Saskatchewan.[45] In the next three years, the villagers got mounts of their own.[46]

Itinerant equestrianism did not become a way of life for the Mandans as it did for so many Plains peoples. But the adoption of horses still changed many things. It altered Mandan bison hunting, wealth patterns, gender roles, warfare, and domestic space.[47] It also changed the commerce so fundamental to Mandan existence. Horses became objects of trade in their own right. But beyond this, the animals stepped up the pace of trading traffic; they increased the frequency and number of contacts among people; and they hauled much more weight than dogs or humans ever did.[48]

What did horses haul? Most obviously, they transported people, food, tipis, household goods, and trade items. In 1739, two Frenchmen who stayed among the Mandans after La Vérendrye left reported that huge groups of mounted Indians crossed the Plains to visit the upper Missouri towns in the spring. They brought "white buffalo-skins" and "dressed skins trimmed and ornamented with plumage and porcupine quills, painted in various colors" to trade with the Mandans. They departed with "grain and beans," which "the Mandan give them in exchange." As horses invigorated Plains transit, so, too, they invigorated Plains trade.[49]

But the animals carried invisible cargoes as well: news, ideas, information, and—sometimes—microbes. La Vérendrye's men reported that one of the visiting chiefs spoke Spanish and described Spaniards in detail. "They prayed to the Great Master of Life in books which they described as made of leaves of Indian corn," he said. And "they sang holding their books in great houses where they assembled for prayer."[50] (The Kiowa captive Etahdleuh Doanmoe compiled his own book of sketches just 136 years later.) The horse-borne chief showed the Mandans and their French guests a Spanish-style bridle, a cotton shirt, and a cotton quilt "embroidered on the edges with silk" and "coloured wool."[51] He even imitated "the movements" of playing "the harpsichord and the bass viol."[52]

Information was a coveted commodity. But microbes were not. Whether or not the imported plagues of the eastern hemisphere had struck the Mandans in the pedestrian days of the sixteenth and seventeenth centuries, they did so in the equestrian days of the eighteenth century. Horses helped almost everything travel across the grasslands.

Smallpox or some other infection afflicted northern Plains peoples in the 1730s. Among those who suffered were the Sioux, while raiding and trading among the upper Missouri villagers. A Lakota winter count, or calendar, recalls 1734–1735 as "used them up with belly ache winter" and marks its passage with a figure bearing two distinctive features: first, a midsection spiral indicating abdominal distress; second, an overlay of red dots like those used to designate a smallpox rash. Because vomiting is a classic early symptom of smallpox, the two symptoms combined make it likely that this was in fact the pestilence of the 1730s.[53]

Additional evidence comes from the Arikaras, the Mandans' southerly neighbors who lived in what is now South Dakota. In 1795, the Arikaras told the fur trader Jean Baptiste Truteau that they had already endured three separate smallpox epidemics.[54] The 1730s outbreak may well have been one of them.

If the infection reached the Arikaras and Sioux, did it also reach the Mandans? No written or oral accounts of such an outbreak survive. La Vérendrye's 1738–1739 report is especially disappointing in this regard. It is worth remembering, however, that the only surviving record of the Frenchman's journey is in an abridged account presumably drawn from a long-lost full-length journal.

Where else can we look? The telltale evidence may well lie buried in ghost towns like Larson and Double Ditch.[55] By 1600 or so, the Mandans at Double Ditch had ensconced themselves behind ditch two, a trench still visible in the early twenty-first century. At some point, the villagers contracted again, taking shelter behind the innermost ditch and palisade. Was this in the 1730s? Was epidemic disease the cause? Or did something else, like warfare, reduce Mandan numbers? Radiocarbon dating poses problems in the eighteenth century. But at some point in the future, archaeologists may find other means to narrow the range of possibilities.

Dating aside, another finding at Double Ditch may shed light on what unfolded there. Town residents appear to have scraped their village clean before rebuilding it within the innermost ditch. According to archaeologists who worked on the site, the Mandans built their new homes "directly on a sterile surface," removing topsoil, refuse, and old house floors before construction began. The "entire area" was "planed off and borrowed away," writes the archaeologist Stanley Ahler. The villagers left one feature intact: a high section in their ceremonial plaza that may mark the location of the sacred shrine that invoked their history and their emergence as a people.[56]

Today no one knows why the Double Ditch Mandans scraped the earth from their town. Because they dumped much of the dirt into large fortification mounds beyond the inner ditch, it is clear they had concerns about defense. The Sioux, invigorated by equestrian life, posed a growing threat over the course of the eighteenth century. But the earth removal may have served two purposes at once. Ahler and a fellow archaeologist, Philip Geib, speculated in 2006 that it "may also have functioned as a village-wide cleansing and renewal mechanism triggered by repeated and horrendous smallpox epidemics."[57]

Mandan towns like Double Ditch and Larson—and probably the west-bank town of Boley as well—had suffered stunning population loss by the mid-eighteenth century.[58] At its founding, Double Ditch had contained one hundred and sixty homes and two thousand people. Three centuries later, it was 80 percent smaller, with thirty-two homes and no more than four hundred people hunkered down inside the smallest of four fortification ditches.[59]

Then disaster struck again. In 1781, smallpox made its way to the upper Missouri from Spanish settlements to the south. The precise route it followed is not clear. But fleet-footed horses made its transit easy. Comanches, Pawnees, Arikaras, Shoshones, Dakotas, Blackfeet, Assiniboines, Crees, Hidatsas, Mandans—all contracted the infection.[60] The pestilence infested the towns at the Heart River confluence with suffering, death, and despair. It undermined families, age-group societies, and bundle lines. Of thirteen clans, only six survived.[61] The Mandans reeled, and the Sioux closed in, seeking to control the fur trade and prime bison territory themselves. In a clash over space among Natives, the Mandans struggled to survive.[62]

At a village called On-a-Slant, a venerable chief named Good Boy rallied the Mandans who lived on the west bank of the Missouri River.[63] All of the west-side towns consolidated into a single new one, upstream from their former location. The east-bank Mandans, including those at Double Ditch and Larson, did the same, building a new settlement upstream on their own side of the river.

The Heart River villages, once home to thousands, became ghost towns. Meriwether Lewis and William Clark, who passed the Heart River confluence twenty-three years after the epidemic, indicated the empty former settlements on their maps: "Old Mandan Village" was designated On-A-Slant. "Old Indian Village killed by the Soux" marked Double Ditch. And "Old Mandan Village destroyed by the Soux and Small Pox" denoted a site known as Chief Looking's town.[64] Some of the sites stand silent and still to the present, mutely testifying to the ravages of 1781.

The quest for safety drove the Mandans' consolidation and move upstream. By 1797, they lived in two Missouri River towns—one on the east bank, one on the west—near the mouth of the Knife River. Here they joined forces with the Hidatsas, who lived in three villages of their own less than six miles away.[65] The two peoples shared a lifeway and a common enemy in the Sioux, who now controlled the trade and the bison range in the Mandans' Heart River homeland fifty miles below.[66] The Mandans by this time numbered no more than 1,520 persons in all.[67]

It was only at the Knife River that the Mandans entered the documentary mainstream. At the Heart River, they may have hosted European guests as early as 1688.[68] But the first reliable account is La Vérendrye's brief 1738 report. By contrast, the Mandans' arrival at the Knife River coincided with a growing Anglo-American presence on the northern Plains. With it came a burgeoning written record as travelers such as David Thompson, Lewis and Clark, George Catlin, and Prince Maximilian and scores of less famous tourists and traders spent time in the Knife River towns.

Their writings reveal much of what followed. Foreign diseases—now easier to identify—swirled across the Plains. Whooping cough coursed through the villages in the summer of 1806, filling the air with hacking coughs and the whistlelike wheezing that gives the infection its name. The fur trader Charles McKenzie reported that in "less than a months time," it took the lives of one hundred and thirty Mandans and Hidatsas. Particularly vulnerable were "children [who] had not strength enough to resist its violence" and "the old men & women whose constitution was worn out."[69]

Thirteen years later, the whooping cough struck again, this time in tandem with measles.[70] The twin infections, according to the governor of the Hudson's Bay Company, "first shewed themselves at the Mandan villages and have from them spread all over the Country." The "rapidity" with which they circulated was "almost beyond belief."[71] As focal points of commerce, the Knife River villages were also focal points of contagion. Reports of infection are abundant for the Assiniboines, the Sioux, and other nearby peoples.[72]

The impact of the dual scourges on the Mandans is not clear. During and immediately after the War of 1812, the Euro-American presence in the villages subsided. Hence no eyewitness accounts survive. Measles is extremely contagious and probably did much damage. By way of comparison, when measles erupted among previously unexposed Natives of Fiji in 1875, it swept away 25 percent of the population.[73] But whooping cough, in this instance, may not have had such dire effects. The disease leaves survivors with a modicum of immunity, and many of the Mandans present in 1819 had lived through the 1806 outbreak.

More challenges came quickly, as the St. Louis fur trade extended its reach northward. In 1826 or 1827, a fur company keelboat brought the first Norway rats to the Mandan village of Mih-Tutta-Hangkusch.[74] The new species lacked the imposing physical presence of the horse. But in some respects it was even more impressive. "Litters can be as large as fourteen, but generally average between six and eight," writes the rat scholar Jonathan Burt. "Females can be ready to mate as soon as eighteen hours after giving birth and offspring are sexually mature by three months."[75] Norway rats are assiduous burrowers, building nests, storing food, and living much of their lives beneath the surface of the earth.[76] This aspect of rat ecology combined with their prodigious reproductive rate to have dreadful consequences.

Mandan grain caches were formidable constructions. Dug by women and lined with protective grass and willows, they were sometimes deeper than their builders were tall. Ladders enabled users to reach their deepest recesses.[77] But rats had easier access, since they chewed through cache linings with ease.

With a seemingly bottomless storehouse of maize to consume, the rats burrowed and multiplied. The artist-ethnographer George Catlin observed that within six years of their arrival at Mih-Tutta-Hangkusch, the animals had infested "every wigwam," and the Indians' "caches, where they bury their corn and other provisions, were robbed and sacked." So voracious were the rats that earth-lodge floors buckled and collapsed, no longer supported by stores of grain below.[78] Twentieth- and twenty-first-century archaeologists report that rat bones constituted 54 percent of all microanimal remains at Fort Clark, the American Fur Company post that sat beside Mih-Tutta-Hangkusch.[79]

In 1832, as the rats ran amuck, a steamboat named *Yellow Stone* churned up the Missouri River, docking below Mih-Tutta-Hangkusch in order to service Fort Clark.[80] The *Yellow Stone* was the first steamer to reach the Mandans. But like the other boats that followed, it had a voracious appetite of its own—not for maize but for wood.

The Mandans and the fur traders who lived beside them consumed plenty of wood on their own. They used it for fires, homes, and fortifications. They also used trees—especially saplings, small branches, and bark—as forage for the horses now ensconced in their lives.[81] The charcoal-fired blacksmithing operation at Fort Clark took its own cut of the riparian forest, the main source of timber in the grass-dominated plains.[82] Then steamboats arrived. A small steamer like the *Yellow Stone* needed twelve cords of wood—the equivalent of sixty ten-inch trees—for each day of travel.[83] The boats reloaded with wood at Mih-Tutta-Hangkusch.[84]

The German Prince Alexander Maximilian of Wied noted the cumulative effects in the winter of 1833–1834. In the nearby forests, he observed, "only a very small quantity of useful timber is found."[85] In 1836, fur company woodcutters "walked Several Miles down the river in search of a Suitable point to cut wood for the Steam Boat," noted the head trader Francis Chardon. Their quest failed. Stymied along the Missouri, where the steamboat could easily load its fuel, Chardon had to send his men four miles overland to Mandan Lake to cut trees.[86]

The dwindling forests had far-reaching effects.[87] Each winter, the Mandans and the bison herds both migrated to the Missouri River's forested bottomlands to escape the full force of the weather. For the Indians, this made for easy hunting and abundant meat in an otherwise difficult season. But the river bottom now offered little shelter, and the winter herds went elsewhere. "Mandans starveing, the Fort full of Men, Women & Children a begging Meat," wrote Francis Chardon on December 3, 1836. Hunters returned with some fresh meat later in the day, but it did not go far.[88] Despairing entries fill his journal in the weeks that followed: "Cattle scarce," "Cattle far off," and "Prospects of starvation, No Cattle."[89]

Occasional animals drew near and fell to Mandan hunters. But for the most part, the herds stayed away, primarily to the north. Chardon reported "plenty" of bison "30 Miles off" on February 4.[90] Ten days later, the same situation prevailed. "Mandans all starveing," he wrote, "although cattle are [with]in 30 miles of the Fort." This time, however, the trader added a key bit of information: "Fear," he said, caused the Mandans to "Keep at home."[91]

Fear? All winter long, the Sioux had hung close to Mih-Tutta-Hangkusch. Sightings of "enemies" came in regularly and sent ripples of panic through the Mandan towns.[92] The Sioux presence, in fact, added to hunting pressure and frightened bison and villagers alike. The Mandans thus faced a three-dimensional problem in the winter of 1836–1837: Their corn was too meager, the Sioux were too close, and the bison were too distant.[93]

In April, two additional pressures came to bear. The first is a mystery: For some reason, the thawing Missouri River ice failed to yield its annual supply of prized float bison, an important source of nourishment in the leanest of seasons. "The Mandans have lost all hope of catching the drownded Buffaloe," said Chardon, "as Not One has passed this year."[94] Second, the entire Arikara nation sought shelter with the Mandans after abandoning villages downriver and testing nomadic life for a year.[95] Despite similar, town-centered lifeways, the two tribes were traditional enemies. But the Mandans offered the Arikaras temporary quarters, perhaps hoping that combined they might ward off the Sioux. The net effect was still more strain on the Mandans' paltry food stores.[96] Indeed, at two hundred and fifty lodges—two thousand or more people—the Arikaras surely outnumbered the Mandans.[97]

The decisive blow came two months later. On June 18, 1837, the fur company steamer *St. Peter's* landed at Mih-Tutta-Hangkusch.[98] Onboard were passengers, supplies, and the smallpox virus. What followed is one of the most calamitous and oft-repeated episodes in the history of the American West, documented day by day in Francis Chardon's journal.[99]

Fifty-six years had passed since 1781, when the last smallpox epidemic had struck the Mandans. None but the elderly had acquired immunity. "A young Mandan died to day of the Small Pox," Chardon wrote on July 14; "several others has caught it."[100] Thereafter, the pox ripped through both Mih-Tutta-Hangkusch and Ruptare, a smaller Mandan town close by.[101] The Hidatsas and Arikaras also suffered terrible mortality, but circumstances spared them the near-annihilation that afflicted the Mandans.[102]

Chardon reported deaths not just by smallpox but also by suicide and mercy killing.[103] "I Keep no a/c of the dead, as they die so fast that it is impossible," wrote the trader on Friday, August 11. On the same day, the Mandans who could do so abandoned Mih-Tutta-Hangkusch. They left "all that were sick in the Village" to heal or die on their own.[104] Five weeks later, a Mandan from the "little Village" of Ruptare told him there were "but 14 of them living" at that town.[105]

When the 1837 epidemic struck, the Mandans probably numbered between one and two thousand.[106] When it ended, fewer than one hundred and fifty remained.[107] Chardon's estimate that the smallpox carried away "seven eights of the Mandans" was close to the mark.[108]

THE Mandans were the canary in the northern Plains coal mine. No other people experienced a collapse of such scale between 1500 and 1838. Their experience is therefore telling. It shows the perils of living on the ecological cusp, however thoroughly adapted. It suggests how fully and quickly the effects of the European colonial presence extended to the center of the continent. It shows how devastating these effects could be even in the absence of violence between the Mandans and colonial powers. And it highlights the hazards of large-scale sedentism, a lifeway in which concentrated populations lived in permanent settlements.

The Mandans were not the only corn-growing farmers on the upper Missouri. Their Hidatsa neighbors pursued a way of life so similar that archaeologists struggle to distinguish between the two cultures. Indeed, the hazards that challenged the Mandans necessarily challenged the Hidatsas as well. But knowledgeable observers have noted that the Hidatsas were more devoted to war and the hunt than the Mandans, who, according to the fur trader Alexander Henry, were "not so enterpriseing" as their neighbors in this regard. Among the Hidatsas, Henry said, "seldom the village is to be found without a party are absent on an excursion" of war.[109] When contagion struck village centers, absent hunters and warriors were more likely to escape it and survive. Parties abroad could also pick up microbes and carry them home, but even then, other absentees might escape unscathed. The pursuit of animals and enemies may thus have saved Hidatsa lives when infections circulated.

In 1837–1838, the Hidatsas escaped the full wrath of smallpox through a mixture of luck, dispersal, and semi-effective quarantine. They were lucky because the distance from Fort Clark meant the disease erupted later among them.[110] Both Mandans and Hidatsas went out on bison hunts as the pox made its appearance in July 1837. But the Mandans, among whom the virus already circulated, carried it with them to their meat camp. The Hidatsas did not. In fact, the hunt sequestered them from the contagion.[111] Those left behind at Big Hidatsa Village took protective measures as the danger became clear. They "made a quarantine," reported Francis Chardon, and allowed "no one from this place to come near them."[112] The virus did infect the town eventually, but the quarantine and the dispersal of the population checked its impact.[113] Eyewitnesses estimated that while the Mandans lost around 90 percent of their numbers, the Hidatsas lost a lower but still galling 50 percent.[114]

The Arikaras also suffered lower mortality than the Mandans. They, too, were villager-horticulturalists, but like the Hidatsas, they may have ventured abroad with some frequency. Indeed, their arrival at Mih-tutta-hangkusch came after a period in which the entire tribe had taken up nomadism, and it was not the first time they had done so. In 1803, a flood had destroyed the entire Arikara corn crop and this forced the villagers to turn to the hunt. They were "obliged to hunt at a distance," reported the trader-explorer Pierre Antoine Tabeau, so their life "became a wandering one up to the time of the maturity of the corn the next year."[115] If such accounts exist for the Mandans, they remain to be discovered. Tabeau makes it clear that the Arikaras did suffer terrible losses in eighteenth-century infectious outbreaks. But even so, their more varied lifeway may have mitigated the damage.[116]

Other circumstances also conspired against the Mandans. Some infections, such as smallpox and measles, confer immunity to those who survive them. Those who suffer through these diseases can live secure in the knowledge that they will never endure such agonies again. Neither the Mandans nor the Hidatsas had encountered smallpox since the epidemic of 1781. This meant that when the pestilence struck again in 1837, only elderly survivors of the earlier plague were immune to its renewed ravages. Indeed, Francis Chardon confirmed that the pestilence spared just "a few Old Ones, that had it in Old times."[117] The relative absence of acquired immunity in the population at large—what epidemiologists call "herd immunity"—had at least two consequences. First, it meant the pox could spread readily, even explosively. Second, it meant that as more and more people fell sick, nursing care—necessarily the domain of the pockmarked 1781 survivors—was unsustainable. When the Mandans fled Mih-tutta-hangkusch, they left sick loved ones behind, and some who might otherwise have survived surely died from dehydration and lack of care.

Other tribes faced the 1837 scourge from somewhat better positions. In 1801, smallpox had found its way into many Plains nations but somehow did not reach the Mandans and Hidatsas. North of them, it infected the Blackfeet and Atsinas.[118] South of them, it infected the Osages, Otoes, Omahas, Sioux, Poncas, Pawnees, and Arapahoes.[119] It may have hit the Arikaras too.[120] Because it came just twenty years after the epidemic of 1781, which probably affected the same tribes, herd immunity was still high. This meant lower rates of infection and mortality. Another outbreak in 1831 also spared the Mandans and Hidatsas but spread among the Pawnees, Poncas, Arikaras, Lakotas, and possibly Crows.[121] It seems perverse to suggest that any smallpox epidemic had benefits. But the 1801 and 1831 contagions inevitably left behind pock-scarred cohorts with acquired immunity. When the affected tribes faced the outbreak of 1837, they had higher levels of herd immunity than the Mandans and Hidatsas, whose last exposure had been in 1781.

Prior exposure is not the only route to acquired immunity. As twenty-first-century readers well know, vaccination yields a similar result.[122] In the aftermath of the 1831 scourge, Congress had passed a "vaccination act" to extend "the Benefits of Vaccination, as a Preventative of the Smallpox, to the Indian Tribes, and Thereby as far as Possible, to Save Them from the Destructive Ravages of that Disease."[123] A federally funded vaccination campaign got under way in the late summer of 1832, immunizing Plains peoples at posts and villages as far north as Fort Pierre, South Dakota. Some, skeptical of the procedure, refused to undergo it. Others did not have the luck to be in the right place at the right time, when the vaccinators arrived. But in all, some three thousand Indians appear to have garnered the benefits of the procedure.[124] The Mandans and Hidatsas were not among them. Nor were their northern Plains neighbors. Deeming the upper Missouri peoples economically marginal and in some cases militarily problematic, officials deliberately left them out of their immunization campaign.[125]

IN the spring of 1838, as the smallpox expired, the Mandans were refugees. The little band of survivors watched from the far side of the Missouri River as the Arikaras took possession of Mih-Tutta-Hangkusch.[126] Then, for a period, the Mandans scattered. A few tried to live with the Arikaras.[127] A handful stayed at the tiny Ruptare settlement above Mih-Tutta-Hangkusch. Others took to nomadic life for the first time. Winter counts from 1839 to 1845 put them on the Yellowstone River and in the Black Hills.[128] Then in the summer of 1845, at the invitation of the Hidatsas, the itinerant Mandans returned to the upper Missouri River. Some thirty miles above Mih-Tutta-Hangkusch and Fort Clark, the two tribes built a new town together.[129] The Arikaras joined them in 1862.[130] The town's name was Like-a-Fishhook, a name derived from its location on a distinctively shaped bend of the Missouri River. Like-a-Fishhook was the last earth-lodge village on the upper Missouri.

On the giant map that Sitting Rabbit created in 1906–1907, the earth lodge representing Like-a-Fishhook appears over three labels: The first, in Sitting Rabbit's large, bold hand, says "Fort Berthold." (Fort Berthold was the American trading post beside Like-a-Fishhook.) Beneath it, in smaller letters—apparently the hand of the Congregationalist missionary Charles Hall—are the words "Búa-idútskupe hísa átiś," Hidatsa for Like-a-Fishhook Village. And beneath this, also in Hall's hand, are the words "Fishhook house."[131] With its chock-a-block appearance and different Arikara and Mandan-Hidatsa sections, Like-a-Fishhook may seem to represent the nadir of the Mandan story, a dismal counterpoint to the cosmopolitan array at the Heart River three centuries before. But in fact, the nadir had come a few years earlier, in the post-smallpox wandering period, before the Mandans returned home to the Missouri River and the lifeway that defined them. There were signs of hope and self-possession at Like-a-Fishhook, including a medicine lodge, central plaza, and shrine that staked out Mandan spiritual terrain. All captured the essence of Mandan identity, and all were signs of resilience. In the years that followed, the villagers faced new tests as authorities circumscribed religious life, federal mandates imposed new living patterns, and engineers flooded precious bottomlands. But again and again they bounced back, drawing on a deep well of tradition and proving that the very challenges that weakened them could also make them strong. For the Mandans, Like-a-Fishhook was both an end and a beginning.

CHAPTER 4

Colonial Spaces in the Fragmented Communities of Northern New Spain

CYNTHIA RADDING

The province of San Ildefonso de Ostimuri, nestled in the foothills and cordilleras of the Sierra Madre Occidental, first emerged in colonial documentation during the mid-seventeenth century. The history of settlement in Ostimuri, with its webs of migration, commerce, and points of exchange, illustrates the production of space and the different meanings ascribed to human geography in the diverse colonial settings of northern New Spain. Ostimuri filtered into colonial nomenclature from indigenous place-names, and Spanish settlements there appeared on maps as small islets surrounded by Yoreme, Tegüima, Rarámuri, and Nevome villages and *rancherías* with deep histories of horticulture, territorial rivalries, and chiefly governance. Colonial mining enterprises and missionary *entradas* produced new social spaces, adding layers of complexity to indigenous ethnic patterns and bringing new populations to the region. Centered on mining, ranching, and agriculture, Ostimuri exemplified the mosaics of different communities that were integrated unevenly into the commercial and migratory networks that clustered around numerous *reales de minas* throughout northern New Spain.

Ostimuri constitutes an internal borderland within New Spain distant from the centers of viceregal governance and colonial society. Located in the Mexican north, Ostimuri was firmly part of the Spanish imperial sphere of North America through the commercial and labor corridors that connected it with Nueva Vizcaya, as shown by Chantal Cramaussel in this volume. Borderlands, like all regions, are produced historically through human labor and social practices, with specific ecological, cultural, economic, and political components; furthermore, their boundaries and distinguishing features change over time. Borderlands encompass contested spaces where different cultural traditions and living peoples meet and at times clash.

Two principal questions guide our discussion: How did indigenous and colonial societies intersect with one another in Ostimuri? In what ways did Ostimuri emerge as a province of multiple borderlands through both indigenous and Hispanic patterns of settlement and conflict? In order to respond to these questions, this chapter will focus on the migrations and displacements arising from advancing European colonists, agricultural villages, commercial enterprises, and seminomadic peoples, leading to resettlement in new places and the formation of mixed communities. Colonial documents, including mundane correspondence, formal reports, and maps, provide different temporal and spatial lenses through which to view the mixed populations of indigenous, African, and Hispanic descent in the colonial towns and cities of Mexico's *gran septentrión*. These vast northern arid lands of New Spain became strategic for colonial administration because of their mineral wealth and the challenges they presented for territorial defense. This study anchors the discussion of contested spaces in several localities through their historical and geographical linkages. It focuses on the changing boundaries and regional networks of the province of Ostimuri, thus questioning the definition of a given region solely in terms of its geographical features or administrative conventions. This historical portrait focuses on the distinct populations that produced Ostimuri, pluralizing it into *spaces* with different material uses and symbolic meanings.[1]

Following the conceptual framework developed by Henri Lefebvre for the social production of space through labor and the representations of space through cultural artifacts, this chapter illustrates the ways in which Ostimuri became a region with ecological, cultural, and historical roots and meanings. The narrative comprehends a broad chronological span from the earliest Spanish encounters with the indigenous peoples to the establishment of the mature colonial economy, but I concentrate on the late seventeenth and early eighteenth centuries. The chapter begins with the territorial conflicts among indigenous peoples and relates this human geography to the major ecological features of the area. It then highlights the early *entradas* and reversals of Spanish missionaries, militias, and colonist-entrepreneurs, and it proceeds to show how the colonial identities and institutions of

Ostimuri developed in this region and linked it to the other major provinces of northern New Spain. It concludes by arguing that the indigenous communities both shaped and contested the colonial missions and, in parallel processes, their labor sustained the migratory and commercial networks that produced these borderlands regions.

ANDRÉS Pérez de Ribas, a Jesuit, began book 4 of his *Historia de los triunfos de nuestra santa fé* with the following explanation of spatial boundaries in reference to the Mayo peoples: "The word *mayo*, in their language, means *limit* or *boundary*, because this river valley is located between two others with peoples who are enemies [of the Mayos] and continually at war with them, thus confining them within their boundaries. The first of these are the war-like Hiaquis . . . and the others are the Teguecos and other peoples living along the Río Grande of Çuaque."[2]

Ethnic territories, constituted through constellations of villages, smaller shifting settlements (*rancherías*), and migratory routes, described a mosaic of tribal spaces long before Europeans entered the complex geography of Ostimuri. In these borderlands of chieftaincies and bands, ethnic nomenclatures and boundaries shifted within changing networks of alliances and conflicts. Colonial cartographies and administrative jurisdictions defined the provinces of northwestern New Spain along the series of river valleys that flowed from the barrancas of the Sierra Madre to the Gulf of California, in a south-to-north progression. These same Spanish sources followed the contours of indigenous contested spaces in their construction of territorial divisions from the valley of Culiacán northward through fluvial drainages of Mocorito, Petatlán (later named Sinaloa), Çuaque (or Zuaque), Mayo, and Hiaqui (Yaqui). Cartographers uniformly set the lower Yaqui River (roughly from Cumuripa to the Gulf Coast) as the geographic and political border between Ostimuri and Sonora. To the south, the Zuaque River, later named El Río Fuerte after the establishment of the presidio of Montesclaros in 1610, marked the division between Ostimuri and Sinaloa. Thus, Ostimuri constituted a transitional space between the Sonoran Desert and the subtropical river valleys and foothills leading southward to the geographical features and cultural traditions of Mesoamerica.[3]

These river valleys and their peoples shared common patterns of material subsistence and political affiliation that distinguished them from the urbanized settlements of the Culiacán Valley to the south and from the tribal peoples to the north.[4] Notwithstanding their rivalries and numerous

FIGURE 4.1. Colonial provinces of Sinaloa, Ostimuri, and Sonora, identifying the major indigenous pueblos, *reales de minas*, missions, and presidios of these three provinces of northwestern New Spain.

Map originally drawn by Jeffrey A. Erbig, Jr., 2012.

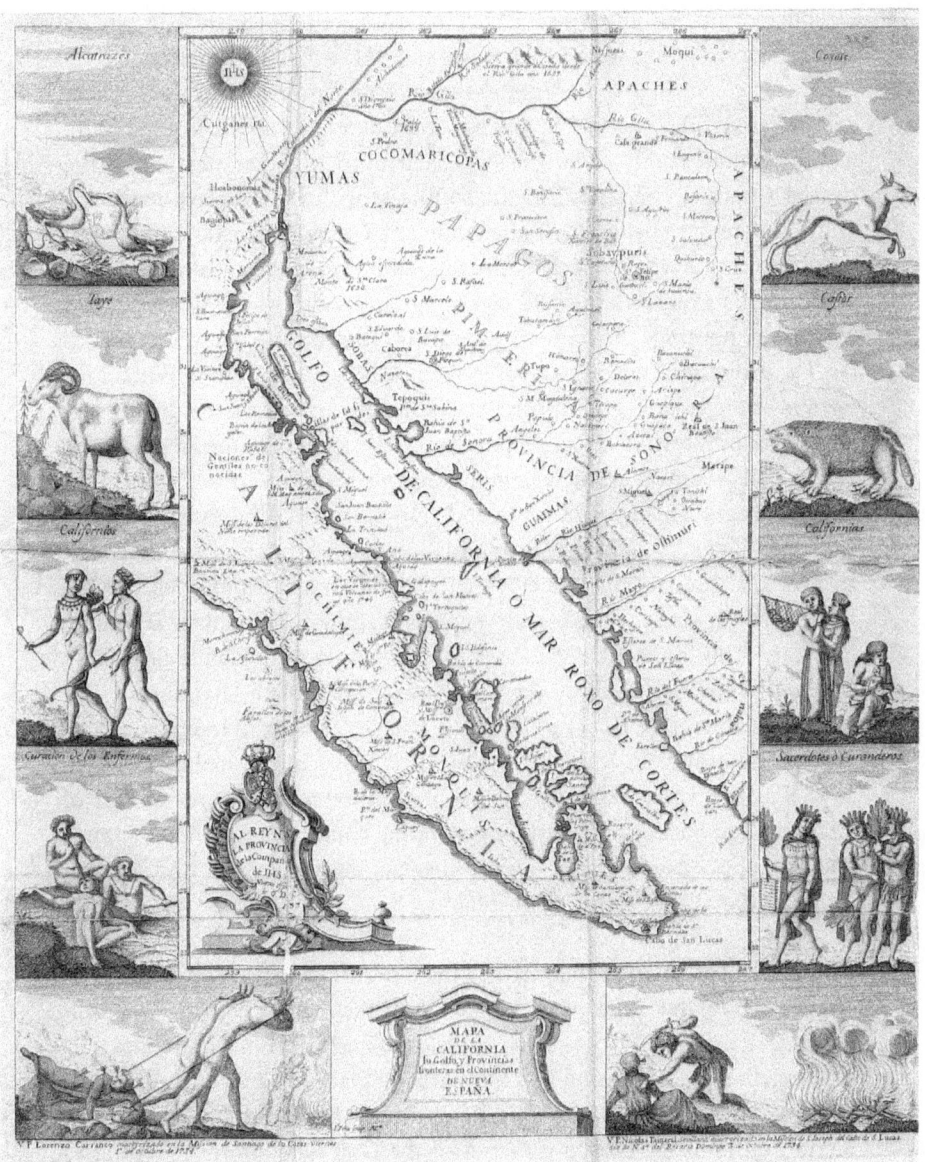

FIGURE 4.2. "Mapa de la California, su Golfo, y Provincias Fronteras en el Continente de Nueva España, 1739, 1757" includes place-names for the Sonoran river valleys; locates the province of Ostimuri; depicts regional fauna, indigenous persons, and shamans along its sides; and shows the uprising of 1734–1735 in the southern portion of Baja California at the bottom.

Courtesy of DeGolyer Library, Southern Methodist University, Dallas, Texas, Vault F864.V3.

episodes of open warfare—in which sixteenth-century Spanish explorers and military captains found themselves obliged to assume the diverse roles of allies, antagonists, and arbiters—the cultural similarities of the lowland *rancherías* became codified in the historical and anthropological literature as the Cahitan family of languages.[5] Their borders to the north with the coastal Cunca'ac (Seri) and to the southeast with the Guasave marked a cultural boundary between Uto-Aztecan and Yuman linguistic clusters and between peoples whose subsistence centered on agriculture, with important supplements from hunting and gathering, and those whose lives centered on fishing, hunting, and gathering, and who traded for harvested grains.

These divisions were less clearly defined, however, in the mountainous terrain of the middle and upper river drainages among the piedmont and barrancas, progressing in height toward the escarpment of the Sierra Madre Occidental, where Spaniards would confront a multiplicity of territories and languages. In the cordilleras and *serranías* of the interior, upstream from the alluvial valleys that Spaniards found densely populated and cultivated, the Cahitan chieftaincies shared and disputed numerous borderlands with Chínipas, Guazapares, Teguecos, Varohíos (Guarijíos), Tepahues, Conicaris, and other tribal groups whose languages were identified as Nevome and Tepehuán (Tepima or O'odham), Tarahumara (Rarámuri), and Tegüima (southern Ópata and Eudeve). The multiplicity of indigenous languages and groups in highland Ostimuri recorded in colonial documents, as well as the Acaxée and Xiximé peoples on the southeastern borders of Ostimuri and Sinaloa, signaled long-standing contacts among these groups and complicated missionary advancement along the eastern and western slopes of the Sierra Madre Occidental.[6]

THE cultural boundaries that marked the indigenous societies of northwestern Mexico followed the natural contours of the region, shaped by ancient volcanic activity, soil deposits, river systems, and climate. Nature and culture together created a dynamic morphology that produced anthropogenic landscapes in discrete spaces extending from the barrancas and peaks of the Sierra Madre to the coastal estuaries of the Gulf of California. Central to the production of space are the river systems that molded the land, descending from the forested piedmont and creating the floodplains that nurtured the agricultural communities of Ostimuri.

The Mayo headwaters flow from multiple streams and tributaries that began in the western sierras of Chihuahua. The major tributaries, made of innumerable streams and arroyos, include the Río Cedros, the Arroyo Guajaráy, the Arroyo San Bernardo, and the Río Batopilillas. During the period of early historical contacts most of the highland streams were perennial, flowing year-round, while on the coastal plain, the current of the Mayo River flowed partially underground.[7] The highland tributaries of the Mayo River cut deeply into the escarpment of the Sierra Madre and shaped the contours of the barrancas and piedmont hills and basins, laying the deposits of sand, gravel, and alluvial soils that sustained floodplain farming.

The lower foothills and coastal plains extending from the Sierra Madre to the sea widen considerably north of the Mocorito and Sinaloa river channels, thus extending the landmass westward into the Gulf of California. While the Mayo River is exceeded in length and stream flow by the Yaqui and Zuaque (Fuerte) rivers, bordering it to the north and south, all three river systems traverse different ecological zones and drain separate portions of the cordillera, flowing roughly from northeast to southwest. Their currents pass through a number of microclimates, marking different points of transition between tropical and temperate zones. From their headwaters six thousand feet above sea level, the streams that flow into the Mayo River carry the silt and debris of pine and live oak forests and oak savannas, short-tree forests in the piedmont, thorn forests on the coastal plain, and riparian vegetation with shrubbery and thickets growing along the arroyos in the lowlands.[8]

Each of these forest biomes encompasses dozens of species whose boundaries are not neatly demarcated into discrete zones; rather their distribution varies along hill slopes and mesas, in canyons, on coastal plains, and in the margins of streams and arroyos. Elevation and topography together influence the length of rainy seasons and drought and the occurrence of frost. Thorn-forest vegetation is adapted to the distinct periods of rainfall (winter and summer) and drought (spring and fall) of the lowlands and piedmont, alternating stages of dormancy and growth. Characteristic species from arid lands, like mesquite, acacia, cholla, nopal, pitahaya, and sahuaro, grow together with plants from the northern desert and the piedmont. Furthermore, a number of species, notably the torote, hecho, and agave, cross the thorn and short-tree forests and appear even in the higher elevations as different varieties of trees, shrubs, and cacti.[9]

This patchwork pattern of vegetational borderlands, bringing together elements of tropical, temperate, and arid lands, evolved from the highly varied conditions of climate, topography, and soils within the region as well as from the imprint of human geography through cultural practices of cultivation and appropriation. Cycles of clearing forests to plant milpas, and then leaving the milpas to fallow, in the piedmont and highland areas opened spaces for the redistribution of herbaceous plants as well as trees and shrubs, both restoring and changing the composition of the forest. Horticulture in this region, as throughout northwestern Mexico, adapted the techniques for planting and harvesting Mesoamerican cultigens centered on the trilogy of maize, cucurbits, and beans to develop local varieties of these staples as well as of chiles, gourds, amaranthus, tobacco, and peanuts. Numerous plant species were gathered and cultivated, thus generating new varieties, as observed in the Guarijíos' use of chapote (*achras zapota*) and the widespread plantings of maguey (*agave americana*); the Guarijíos also harvested several wild species of agave, like the amole (*agave mayoensis*) and the mescal (*agave yaquiana*) from the *monte*.[10] Setting grass fires at the height of the dry season (May through June)—whether for hunting, planting, or (in the postconquest era) renewing pasture land for grazing—helped to fertilize the soil, stimulated the germination of new plants, eliminated desiccated weeds and annuals, and selectively favored the spread of certain forest species. All Native peoples in the region gathered the roots, stems, seeds, trunks, and seasonal fruit of wild plants for fuel, building materials, and food and medicines. Cutting, gathering, transporting, grinding, and roasting plants, as well as their consumption and human wastes, all contributed immeasurably to spreading the genetic material of plants and to renewing the heterogeneous forests of these transitional borderlands between the tropics and the desert.

The vegetational mosaics of the coastal plains and uplands reflected in nature the cultural boundaries that were created, defended, and—at times—transgressed by the peoples whose settlements drew their livelihood from the rivers and whom the Spaniards learned to designate by different tribal names and geographic locations. The apparent fixity of the ethnic boundaries indicated by colonial sources and reproduced in well-documented studies of cultural geography and ethnography for this region should be interpreted with caution, however, when we approach the contested spaces of indigenous societies.[11] Native settlements, whether constructed of woven palm leaf and thatch (*petates*) or puddled adobe (*casas de terrado*),[12] defended certain territorial claims, to be sure, but the seasonal movements of diverse tribal groups through coastal estuaries, river valleys, and the *monte*—from desert lowlands to pine-forested cordilleras—made those territorial spaces fluid and unstable. The successive phases of Spanish colonization, beginning in the late sixteenth century, added new layers of contention to the ecological and cultural borderlands of this Native world.

THE earliest Spanish explorations of the piedmont and coastal lands west of the Sierra Madre were inspired by the combined European and Mesoamerican legends of Cíbola, in which explorers searched for fabled cities with wealth and urban populations that could emulate Tenochtitlan.[13] The violent conquests of the Totorame and Tahue peoples of the Culiacán Valley, the extraordinary odyssey of Álvar Núñez Cabeza de Vaca, and the fabled (and failed) expeditions of fray Marcos de Niza and Francisco Vázquez de Coronado all sought "other Mexicos" in which to harness the labor of the Native populations to serve an aspiring nobility, produce wealth for the Crown, and deliver souls for the Church. Yet, by the late sixteenth century, no lasting Spanish settlements had endured north of Culiacán, and the legend of Cíbola had faded into memory as an attainable goal of conquest.[14] Indigenous communities endured, despite devastating epidemic contagion, and Spaniards could not impose forced labor or tribute payment among the riverine villagers of Sinaloa and Ostimuri.

The search for wealth and the evangelical zeal to bring Native peoples into the Christian fold remained strong, but this pursuit took a different turn and shifted the geography of colonial expansion, spanning the Sierra Madre Occidental and linking the province of Sinaloa with the governorship of Nueva Vizcaya. The discovery of extensive silver lodes as well as many smaller mines in Zacatecas (1546) and, subsequently, in Fresnillo, Sombrerete, Indé, and Santa Bárbara channeled Spanish ambitions toward the direct production of silver. Over the second half of the sixteenth century successive silver strikes led to the founding of *reales de minas*, with the development of assaying and ore processing through smelting and mercury amalgamation.[15] These mining centers developed unevenly as complex industrial spaces; each center's nucleus constituted settled communities, with judicial and administrative authorities, but surrounded by ephemeral mining camps and stock-raising and agricultural ranches. Mineral lodes produced precious metals of gold and silver, and when the finest ores played out, they were mined for lead, litharge (lead oxide), and salt, to be exploited in the region or sent by mule train to the mines of Zacatecas and southern New Spain.[16]

The growth of mining, livestock ranching, and agriculture set in motion new demands for labor and widespread migration across northern, western, and central Mexico, bringing a mixed population of Spaniards, Indians from central Mexico, and African descendant laborers to the arid central plateau east of the Sierra Madre through enslavement, *repartimiento*, and contractual labor. Over three-quarters of a century, the province of Santa Bárbara, spanning numerous tributaries that fed into the river systems of the Río Conchos and the Río Florido, yielded a series of *reales de minas*, haciendas, and missions. The province's history was linked to sources of entrepreneurial capital in Zacatecas, and, in turn, the colonial spaces that took root in Santa Bárbara fueled the expanding webs of Spanish dominion in the western provinces of Sinaloa and Ostimuri.

The explorations of Francisco de Ibarra northward from Zacatecas led to the founding of the Real y Minas de Santa Bárbara in the 1560s by Rodrigo del Río. The initially promising veins of precious metals were quickly exhausted, but the *vecinos* and indigenous laborers who had sought wealth in Santa Bárbara fanned out to make new discoveries in San Juan and Todos Santos. During the four decades following the establishment of Santa Bárbara, despite its relatively meager output, Spanish ranchers and Franciscan missionaries brought cattle into the region and established maize and wheat farms along irrigable floodplains in the valleys of San Bartolomé and San Gregorio, overtaking lands occupied and worked by Tepehuán villagers. By the early seventeenth century Franciscans had established missions at San Bartolomé, Atotonilco, and San Francisco de Conchos, intermingled with Spanish ranching and mining settlements. Northwest of Santa Bárbara, in the San Pablo basin, the Jesuit Order established a mission at San Pablo Tepehuanes (1611) and, in the 1630s, it placed the missions of Huejotitlán and Santa Cruz Tarahumara at the confluence of the San Pablo and Conchos rivers.[17] Jesuit missionary *entradas* in the valley of San Pedro paralleled their northward advancement from the Villa de Sinaloa on the western piedmont of the Sierra Madre and opened a passage between the western and central corridors of the colonial invasions into the borderlands.

Santa Bárbara served as a military outpost against nomadic groups to the northeast and as an important supply node on the Camino Real de Tierra Adentro leading across the Chihuahua Desert to New Mexico. In the 1630s, however, new silver strikes at La Prieta and Minas Nuevas made the province of Santa Bárbara one of the principal mining districts of northern New Spain centered on the Real de San Joseph del Parral, established at the bonanza (a new mining strike) of La Prieta. With a third strike at San Francisco del Oro, Parral overtook the Villa de Santa Bárbara as the center for mineral production in the province, with smelters, amalgation patios, municipal offices, and merchant houses that were supported by increased agriculture and stock raising, salt mining, timber, and charcoal production in the surrounding area.[18] Ore processing at Parral through both smelting and amalgamation demanded shipments of reagents, lead oxides, copper pyrite, and salt, supplied from New Mexico, Mapimí, and Nuevo León, in addition to the mercury that was imported through royal monopolies and controlled via transshipments from Mexico.

Parral cast a long shadow over northern New Spain for its consumption of fuel, reagents, livestock, and grains and for its ever-expanding networks of labor recruitment, extending westward across the Sierra Madre Occidental and as far south as the Tarascan (Purépecha), Otomí, and Nahua peoples of Nueva Galicia and the central provinces of the viceroyalty. From the northwest, Ópata, Cahitan, Acaxée, and Xiximé workers entered the mines and refineries of Parral. Enslaved nomadic laborers captured from the campaigns against Toboso, Salinero, Guachichil, Apache, and other groups, and "rebellious" Rarámuri, Tepehuán, Concho, and other villagers, worked alongside *repartimiento* Indians and free workers, the latter paid in pesos (*reales de plata*), unminted silver, and cloth. The Real de San Joseph del Parral defined the regional contours of Sinaloa, Ostimuri, and Sonora in important ways, as prospectors moved westward in search of new mineral deposits, as merchant houses and muleteers freighted supplies to the Real from the western provinces, and as labor channels sent indigenous workers from the western corridor to Parral through *repartimiento* and voluntary migration.[19]

The colonial history of Ostimuri, then, took shape in the seventeenth century through its linkages to the mining and ranching economy of Nueva Vizcaya. Spanish settlement and colonial governance were not merely grafted onto the natural and cultural features of Ostimuri; instead they were shaped by and molded the physical environment and the indigenous landscapes of this regional space.

Jesuit Missions, Indigenous Territories, and Colonial Conflicts in Sinaloa and Ostimuri

Spanish *entradas* in the western corridor north of the Mocorito Valley were tenuous during most of the sixteenth century. The explorations undertaken by Francisco de Ibarra and his followers in Nueva Vizcaya led to the ephemeral outpost of San Juan Carapoa on the upper Zuaque River valley, founded in 1564, but this was soon abandoned when the beleaguered handful of *vecinos* retreated to Culiacán. Two decades later, Carapoa was refounded briefly on the Zuaque, but then relocated southwest to the middle Petatlán where it was renamed the Villa de San Felipe y Santiago de Sinaloa. This settlement became an anchor of Spanish military and missionary advancement to the northwest, especially after the founding of a Jesuit college there in 1591. The Jesuits Gonzalo de Tapia and Martín Pérez began their labors among the villages and *rancherías* of the piedmont and coastal valleys, and, within the decade, they succeeded in establishing missions in Ocoroni, Bamoa, and Mocorito.[20]

The Jesuits established the foundations for what would become an enduring network of mission districts and *rectorados* during the following three decades, extending through Sinaloa, Ostimuri, and Sonora. Three important circumstances paved the way for this initial period of missionary advancement: indigenous military alliances and overtures to the Jesuits in Sinaloa; a formal request extended by Governor Rodrigo del Río de Loza of Nueva Vizcaya to the Society of Jesus to send missionaries to the provinces north of Culiacán, thus assuring viceregal support for the endeavor; and the partnership forged between Jesuit missionaries and the military commander of Sinaloa, Captain Diego Martínez de Hurdaide. Contemporaries and historians alike have credited Hurdaide with a sagacity that evolved over his years of service in the region.[21] Well acquainted with the land and its peoples, Hurdaide developed the art of negotiation as skillfully as he did the strategies of warfare. He exploited the divisions within and among different tribal groups and forged alliances with bands of indigenous warriors. Thus, the descriptions of his armed forays against rebellious factions, like the Tegueco, Guazapare, and Warohío mountainous peoples, and—most famously—the *entradas* that he organized into the Hiaqui Valley enumerated a few hundred armed and mounted Spanish militias deployed together with thousands of indigenous allies. Hurdaide depended on these alliances, and he cultivated friendships with select *caciques* from his base in Sinaloa with gifts and the rituals of hospitality.

The missions of the northwestern provinces are richly documented by the Jesuit *cartas anuas*, preserved from as early as 1593, and chronicled by Pérez de Ribas's monumental *Historia de los triunfos de nuestra santa fé*. Published in Madrid in 1645, Pérez de Ribas's *Historia* combined firsthand accounts from the author's memory, having served in the missions of the Zuaque and Yaqui valleys, with his synthesis of the Jesuit *cartas anuas* and other reports to which he had access in his subsequent offices as secretary to the provincial, rector of the Colegio Máximo, and provincial of the province of New Spain. In addition, Pérez de Ribas embellished his own narrative with excerpts from contemporary published histories—most notably, the *Décadas* of Antonio Herrera y Tordesillas.[22] As the mission network of northwestern New Spain grew, its historical documentation included letters, reports, ledgers, and periodic visitations that were directed within the Order and to colonial authorities.

In a process parallel to the gradual advance of the Spanish colonial frontier in Nueva Vizcaya, but different in its rhythm and principal components, the slow and uneven growth of the Jesuit mission *reducciones* and Spanish military ascendancy along the western corridor of the Sierra Madre Occidental engaged both Indians and Spaniards in the production of space and the reconfiguration of ethnic territories. Yet this was a process fraught with conflicts and marked by advances and retreats. Even as new baptisms ostensibly brought thousands of souls into Christendom, the Jesuits' sacramental accounts were troubled by disease, massive population losses, flight, and rebellions that subtracted whole clusters of villages from the rosters of *indios cristianos*. The mission regime took root and endured through a fragile colonial pact that combined distinct rationales based on the quest for spiritual power, material gain, and tribal political realignment. It provided a thread of continuity for Indians and Spaniards alike even as it was tested repeatedly by skirmishes, subsistence crises, violence, and the overweening ambition of military commanders and private entrepreneurs. As a tentative agreement of reciprocal, if uneven, claims to negotiation, the colonial pact anchored the missions in these provinces by drawing the indigenous peoples into networks of borderland exchanges that crossed the Sierra Madre and extended from the southern tropics to the northern deserts.

Let us return to the valley of Ostimuri to consider the drama of mixed encounters among the Cahitan and upland tribal peoples of this region with Jesuit and military *entradas*. The early seventeenth century opened with natural calamities, even as the missionaries claimed new souls through baptism, doctrinal preaching, and the rituals of the liturgical year. In 1604, heavy rains caused flooding throughout the Sinaloa Valley, washing out planted fields and razing houses, extending the damage to the Villa de Sinaloa. Hunger followed, and rebellious Indians from Topia persuaded some of the recently Christianized *Çinaloas* to flee the pueblos and return to the scrub forests in the *monte*, where they would be free from the watchful eyes and discipline of the Jesuit priests. During these same years (1604–1606), however, Zuaque, Tegueco, Sinaloa, and Ahome delegations traveled to the Villa to request missionaries.

In response, Captain Hurdaide journeyed to the viceregal capital with a number of indigenous *caciques* to request new supplies and missionaries. They returned with the Jesuits Cristóbal de Villalta and Andrés Pérez de Ribas, who were armed with royal authorization and material support from both the Jesuit padre provincial and the archbishop of Mexico. Pérez de Ribas took up his mission to the Ahome and Zuaque *rancherías* in 1605; yet this same year Hurdaide led a punitive expedition against rebellious bands of Tepahue, Bacoburitu, Ocoroni, and other mountainous tribes.[23] The military arm of colonial expansion through the river valleys north of Culiacán received further reinforcement with the construction of the Fuerte (presidio) de Montescaros in 1610, in the heart of the Tegueco tribal territories. The fort was built on a hilltop with an ample view of the river and savannas for grazing cattle; the horses were quartered within its walls, "because, in times of war, the Indians first attack the horse herds with their bows and arrows, knowing that without their horses, the Spaniards would be lost."[24] Indeed, the presidio provided a base of colonial advancement, but it also became a site of contestation.

The rhythm of advance and retreat marked a pattern of relationships and reciprocal actions, in which Spaniards and Indians tested one another. First, the indigenous *rancherías* of different river valleys, although often at war or allied in different combinations, traveled from one valley to another; they observed, consulted, and reported back to their home villages what they discerned of the mission towns and the military strengths and weaknesses of these new strangers who had invaded their lands. Second, Spanish missionaries and military officers alike dealt with the indigenous peoples through their *caciques*. The principal leaders and, occasionally, their wives, whom the Spaniards learned to distinguish by their clothing and bearing, entered into negotiations with Captain Hurdaide or the Jesuits and brought their people to baptism; conversely, the *caciques* carried their *rancherías* into flight during episodes of rebellion. These tribal leaders seemed to represent segments of the linguistic and territorial *naciones* that the Jesuit *reducciones* began to group with collective names like Sinaloa, Ahome, Zuaque, and Mayo.[25] Their overtures to the Jesuits and military stationed in the Villa de Sinaloa and in the Fuerte de Montesclaros suggest strategies for seeking alliances in the rivalries for influence and territory that so complicated the ethnic mapping of the region. For their part, the tiny minority of missionaries and Spanish militias, stretched thin from Culiacán to El Fuerte, actively sought indigenous allies among both *cristianos* and *gentiles*.[26] In their efforts to attract new converts, recover fugitive *rancherías*, and put down rebellions, the Spaniards worked to retain the *caciques*' loyalty and rewarded them with gifts of clothing, tools, and horses, which *caciques* had come to value as coveted possessions and symbols of prestige.[27] Third, the subsistence crises due to flooding or drought, as alluded to above, were magnified with repeated disease episodes that spread through the entire region even prior to the chronicled Spanish *entradas* and missionization. Thus, the *caciques*' strategies for seeking political alliances seem to have been motivated by their positioning for influence as well as their pressing needs for new means of survival for their communities. What Pérez de Ribas and his co-religionists interpreted as an epic struggle between the devil and his minions, the tribal shamans, and God and his saints, may have signified for the Indians a crossroads of alternative paths to spiritual power in order to meet the extraordinary circumstances of their world.

The Mayo communities' cautious acceptance of mission life illustrates this crossroads. Mayo *caciques* began to visit the Zuaque pueblos, resettled in missions, as early as 1605.[28] The Mayos were sufficiently impressed with their own peaceful entry into Zuaque territory, the material security of their villages, and the pageantry of their new rituals that they requested missionaries to preach to them in their own land. Mayo emissaries received return visits from "Christian" Indians and persevered in their requests for missionaries. They voluntarily supplied laborers to help build the Fuerte de Montesclaros and, when Captain Hurdaide put out a call for allied warriors, the Mayos—while yet *gentiles*—willingly swelled the ranks of his forces sent on punitive expeditions against rebellious Teguecos and Tepahues in 1612.

Nine years after their initial exploration of the missionized towns of the Zuaque Valley, the Mayo *caciques* were rewarded with the arrival of the aging but venerated Padre Pedro Méndez, who had served in the Sinaloa missions and been retired to Mexico City. In January 1614, when failed harvests and hunger had dispersed the Mayo population, the head *caciques* and fifteen *principales* brought together more than four hundred adult men, with their families, to welcome Captain Hurdaide and Padre Méndez. The

Indians had decorated their own heads with plumage, according to their custom, and they had erected crosses and arches along the foot paths, as they had surely observed in the Zuaque and Sinaloa missions. They built temporary *ramadas* to serve as chapels for baptism, greeting their missionary on horseback and on foot and arranging themselves in rows by age and sex in order to be counted. Méndez declared that with the watchful assistance of Captain Hurdaide and the active direction of the *caciques*, from the "first pueblo" and proceeding downstream, twenty thousand Mayos were gathered in seven mission towns. This roster of souls for Christendom did not include "many others," who had remained in the forested *monte* to search for food or coastal groups who lived by fishing, but whose *caciques* promised they would later gather into settled villages provided they could remain near their fishing grounds.[29]

Hunger and disease took their toll on this labor of evangelization. Modern historical debates over the causes and extent of indigenous depopulation following European contact and missionization emphasize the impacts of epidemic and endemic diseases, Spanish labor demands, and the apparent "loss" of population through migration away from the missions where periodic censuses were taken.[30] It is interesting to note, in this vein, that Pérez de Ribas, while engaged in presenting his order's mission in the best light, acknowledged openly that the mission towns that he helped to found did not become permanent settlements; rather they may have opened new directions for indigenous short-term and long-term migration across ethnic boundaries and through Spanish towns, haciendas, and *reales de minas*.

The villagers of the lower Mayo floodplain had watched, waited, and negotiated the terms of their collaboration with Hurdaide and the Jesuits. Their embrace of Christianity and resettlement in seven mission towns kindled different responses among the tribes of the headwaters of the Fuerte and Mayo drainages. The Tepague and Conicari communities followed the lowland Mayos' example, requesting missionaries and, it would seem, obtaining favorable land on which to establish their pueblos.[31] During the following two decades, however, portions of the Chínipa, Guaçapari, Temori, Ihío, and Varohío *rancherías*, located deeper in the sierra to the southeast, rebelled against the Spanish presence in their midst, leading to the deaths of the Jesuits Julio Pascual and Manuel Martínez in 1632. In the aftermath of these armed encounters, both the rebellious bands of Guazapares and Varohíos and the loyal Chínipas lost their territorial base. Under threat of renewed attacks, the Chínipas left their lands and dwellings and were absorbed into the missions of the Sinaloa Valley. Following the punitive expedition against the Guazapares and Varohíos, led by Captain Pedro de Perea and reinforced with Indian allies, an estimated eight hundred warriors were killed, and the remaining families were absorbed into the Sinaloa missions.[32] All the piedmont communities involved in the violent encounters of 1632 suffered severe and perhaps irreversible consequences in the difficult conjuncture of "loyalty" and "rebellion."

The historical accounts of these events establish a number of themes that illustrate the segmentary nature of political alliances and enmities among the indigenous peoples. The uprising of the Guazapares and their allies did not encompass all of their kinsmen, for individuals and families among the Chínipas and Varohíos remained loyal to the Jesuits. Motivations for the rebellion stemmed from the Jesuits' insistence that the Christianized Indians abandon polygyny, and these resentments may have fueled the rituals of warfare that had signaled prestige among the highland *caciques*.[33] Undeniably the cultural divide between indigenous and Catholic lifeways and values remained a potent counterforce to the spiritual inroads that Jesuits made among their new converts, assisted by Christian Indians; yet, behind these accusations, rebellion simmered in the shrinking of Native territories as mining and ranching settlements moved westward from Nueva Vizcaya and—slowly, but perceptively—advanced northward from Culiacán and Sinaloa.

The territorial integrity of indigenous identities, countered by the fragmentation of tribal political alliances, frames the dramatic history of military encounters between the Yaqui *rancherías* and the Spanish and allied invading forces. As many as eighty *rancherías*, representing an estimated thirty thousand inhabitants, raised two harvests in normal years from the rich alluvial floodplain of the lower Yaqui River valley.[34] All the Yaqui *rancherías* were dedicated to agriculture, like the Mayos to the south and the Nevome and Tegüima to the north, and they supplemented their crops with hunting, gathering, and fishing. Thus, the Yoreme communities combined diverse ecosystems, extending from the delta and estuaries of the Gulf Coast to the scrub and oak forests of the piedmont.

In the opening decade of the seventeenth century, Captain Diego Martínez de Hurdaide avowed that the Yaqui warriors were among the "most valiant"—that is, unrelenting in warfare—of all New Spain. The incident that impelled Hurdaide to lead a military force into the Yaqui Valley stemmed from the flight of Ocoronis from the missions of the upper

Sinaloa Valley, seeking refuge among the Yaqui, who apparently welcomed them into their *rancherías*. The Ocoronis' rejection of Christianity and the mission regime put the military garrison of Sinaloa and the Jesuits on alert, because it occurred simultaneously with the Jesuits' entry into the Zuaque Valley and with separate uprisings in the eastern piedmont of the Sierra Madre. Spanish forces saw such episodes of defiance not as isolated occurrences but as part of a pattern that threatened their precarious hold on the northwestern corridor of the colonial frontier.

Hurdaide determined to eliminate these zones of refuge by employing a combination of negotiation and force. Hurdaide made three entries into the Yaqui Valley between 1607 and 1609, mounting and provisioning a mixed force of Spanish militias and indigenous allies. The first *entrada* ended in a standoff; Hurdaide retreated to the Villa de Sinaloa to send messengers with the demand that the Yaquis turn over to him the fugitive Ocoronis. If they complied, there would be peace and commerce between the Yaquis and the Spaniards. In reply, the Yaquis appeared to accept Hurdaide's terms, and they sent one of their *caciques* to parlay with the captain in the Villa de Sinaloa. Accepting the Yaqui leader's feigned agreement to return the Ocoronis to Spanish custody, Hurdaide sent with him on his return trip to the valley several Christian Teguecos and two Yaqui women, who had been taken captive during the first expedition and baptized, in the belief that they could help to cement the peace. On their arrival in the Yaqui *rancherías*, however, the Yaquis took the women and killed the male messengers, seizing the horses and clothing they had brought with them as gifts from Hurdaide.

Faced with this provocation, Hurdaide led an army of forty armored horses and mounted soldiers, accompanied by two thousand allies, to challenge the Yaquis in their territory. Yaqui warriors opened battle, and while losses were heavy on both sides, Hurdaide was forced to retreat to Sinaloa. In preparation for the third encounter, Hurdaide recruited fifty armed soldiers and horses from the garrison in Sinaloa and the Villa de Culiacán as well as four thousand Indian allies—principally Tehuecos and Mayos—and gathered supplies from a wide range of Christian and *gentil* nations. The Yaquis, for their part, had united all eighty of their *rancherías* in their enlarged ranks of armed warriors, whom the Spaniards had estimated to number eight thousand. Hurdaide established his camp in the Yaqui Valley and sent new messages of peace, demanding the return of the Ocoroni fugitives, but he was rebuffed. At dawn the combined Yaqui force attacked the Spanish camp; casualties were high on both sides, but the Yaquis persisted unabated and used the river, swollen with summer rains, to their advantage. Yaqui warriors crossed and recrossed the river far more ably than could the Spaniards on horseback. Hurdaide's indigenous allies wavered, and the captain again saw that he was in danger and gave the order to retreat; Yaqui forces tried a number of stratagems to frustrate Hurdaide's escape, but the wounded captain and a small squadron of soldiers managed to return to the Villa de San Felipe de Sinaloa.[35]

In the aftermath of this third armed encounter, when Hurdaide seemed to have run out of options, discussions among the Yaqui *caciques* changed course. Several influential *caciques* began to prepare overtures of peace. They could not simply open bilateral discussions with the Spanish officers, however, because their warfare had cost many lives among their indigenous enemies, and these losses needed to be acknowledged and avenged. The Yaquis sought help among the Mayos, and they sent a woman with a message of reconciliation. Two Mayo *caciques* heard her entreaty favorably, but they demanded to see additional proof of the Yaquis' peaceful intentions. The Yaquis sent a second delegation of three to meet with the Mayo leaders; the Mayos then sent a delegation to the Villa de Sinaloa to inform Hurdaide of the Yaquis' intentions. Gifted with horses and clothing, the women and their small entourage returned to the Yaqui Valley, carrying Hurdaide's message that the Yaqui *caciques* themselves should travel to Sinaloa, under his safe conduct, to negotiate the terms of peace. Yaqui counsels were not yet unanimous in their opinions; discussions ensued between those who clamored for renewed war and those who favored peace. In the end, the latter prevailed, and Yaqui leaders did appear before Hurdaide, returning part of the booty they had taken in the last battle and offering their sons to serve as "pledges" (hostages) and remain in the College of San Felipe to learn Christian doctrine. The Yaqui youths would later accompany Tomás Basilio and Andrés Pérez de Ribas, who began organizing mission *reducciones* in the Yaqui Valley in 1617. To cement their alliance with the Spaniards, the Yaquis turned over the Ocoronis to Hurdaide, who submitted them to judgment and execution.[36]

Out of the crucible of violence for more than a decade, it appeared that the principal Yaqui *caciques* had concluded that while they were winning separate battles they were losing the war. As the Spaniards formed alliances with groups of both Christian and *gentil* tribal groups, the Yaquis saw their territorial and political spaces shrinking. In negotiating their terms for the colonial pact, the *caciques* created the framework for resettling the *rancherías* of their valley into enduring villages and retaining control over the fertile floodplain of the lower Yaqui Valley and the surrounding piedmont forests. Their missions became a centerpiece for the entire Jesuit enterprise in northwestern New Spain, opening linkages to mission districts and *reales de minas* in Sinaloa, Sonora, Baja California, and Nueva Vizcaya. The sacred geography of the *ocho pueblos* emerged from the mission towns, Catholic ritual, and their institutions of internal governance. It provided the foundations of Yoreme ethnic space, manifested in both the peaceful development of the pueblos for over a century and in the rebellion of 1739–1741, a provincewide uprising that erupted from the pressures of the mission system and the colonial economy, seeking to renegotiate the terms of village autonomy.[37] The territorial integrity of the Yoreme villages, a colonial construction resting on the deep roots of ecological and cultural development, illustrates vividly the contested spaces of the mixed colonial fabric of northwestern New Spain.[38]

The Yoreme cultural stronghold in the heart of the Yaqui Valley and their ethnic frontier with the Nevome villagers upstream, in the vicinity of Cumuripa, constituted the northern border of what would become the province of Ostimuri. Following the peaceful resolution of the military conflicts between the indigenous warriors of the Yaqui Valley and the allied forces led by Hurdaide, a number of *caciques* representing the northern and inland tribes approached the Villa de Sinaloa to ask for missionaries.[39] In subsequent years, segments of these and other tribal entities would accept baptism and enter into Jesuit *reducciones*, but not infrequently they left mission life and returned to the *monte*.

Martínez de Hurdaide's successor, Pedro de Perea, submitted his *memorial* of military service and merit in 1637, in which he gave a rough count of his efforts to "reduce" and baptize both adults and children of different tribal affiliations.[40] Table 4.1 does not present an accurate count of population; rather, it shows the uneven and partial extent of missionization, reflecting a mosaic of tribal groups that Spanish officials could only imperfectly identify across Sinaloa and Ostimuri.

In the following decade Perea claimed to have recovered for "the holy faith and royal obedience" many "non-Christian and fugitive Indians" (*indios naturales e infieles y cristianos fugitivos*) through military forays accompanied by indigenous allies and missionaries. His exploits coincided

Table 4.1. Territories and Partial Counts of Tribal Groups (1626–1630)

River Valleys	Pueblos	Baptisms	
		Adults	Children
Mocorito			484
Pitlatán (Petatlán/ Sinaloa)	San Lorenzo, Aguero, Taburcava, Moa, Guaçave	75	1,173
Zuaque (Fuerte)	Taguero, Toro, Vaca, Coes, Guiches, Acoratos	200	1,914
Mayo	Tepagüe, Canicarito, Níos Piecachinipa, Guazapares	2,984	4,590
Yaqui	Guaymas	350	3,986
Nevome *nación*	Saguaritas, Sisigueraris, Batucos, Ayguinos	1,169	2,599

Source: Don Pedro de Perea, *Gouernador y capitan a guerra de la Prouincia de Sinaloa y la Nueua Andaluzia* (Mexico, 1637), from the *Catálogo Colectivo de Impresos Latinamericanos hasta 1851*, accessed through http://cbsrdb.ucr.edu.

with the Guazapare rebellion of 1632 and, two years later, Perea reported widespread hunger in the province (*hambre general en aquella tierra*).

Pedro de Perea sent expeditions northward through the Bavispe, Sonora, and San Miguel rivers in search of new mineral deposits, calling this region Nueva Andalucía. In 1637 Perea's troops founded a cattle ranch near the Eudeve village of Tuape and, in 1640, they reported finding several ore deposits, but their exploitation awaited assaying and authorization in order to establish a *real*. Empowered with the title of *alcalde mayor*, Pedro de Perea recruited settlers and Franciscan missionaries for Nueva Andalucía from New Mexico, and he attempted to open a road from Sinaloa through the valley of San Pablo to Parral. Perea's violent means of recruiting labor, bordering on enslavement, and his repeated skirmishes with Eudeve, Nevome, and Tegüima villagers, however, undermined his effective governance of the province.

Mining and the Formation of a Province: San Ildefonso de Ostimuri

The mid-seventeenth century signaled a turning point in the production of space in the western provinces of the Sierra Madre Occidental. At this time the frontiers of missionization advancing northward unevenly from the Villa de Sinaloa met the mining frontier proceeding westward from Parral and Santa Bárbara. Mining effectively began in Sonora and Ostimuri after Pedro de Perea's death (1645), with silver strikes on the San Miguel tributary of the Sonora River, San Juan Bautista between the Sonora and Oposura valleys, San Miguel Arcángel on the headwaters of the Yaqui River, and San Ignacio and San Ildefonso de Ostimuri deep in the sierra between the Yaqui and Mayo drainages.[41] From the 1660s to the early eighteenth century, new mining *reales* developed in parallel sequences in both provinces: Nacozari, Nacatóbari, and Bacanuche in Sonora, and Real de los Alamos, Río Chico, Tacupeto, and Baroyeca in Ostimuri. The silver veins that supported Alamos and its sister *real* La Aduana came into production beginning in 1683.[42] Located in the sierras that separated the Mayo and Fuerte river systems, Alamos belonged administratively to the province of Sinaloa. Socially, and economically, however, Alamos constituted an important node in the southern boundary of Ostimuri, with San Miguel Arcángel marking its northwestern border and San Ildefonso marking the northeast.

As had occurred in Santa Bárbara, ore extraction in Sonora and Ostimuri first exploited the rich surface deposits and outcroppings of gold, silver, lead, and copper minerals; digging pits and excavating shallow shafts sufficed in the early years of a silver strike to amass precious metals. When the surface deposits were depleted or shafts became flooded, however, miners typically abandoned these works and moved on in search of new bonanzas. Smelting was the preferred method for processing ore, due to the high price and uncertainty of mercury shipments, until the latter eighteenth century. Mine workers at Ostimuri and Sonora crushed the ore by hand or with mule-powered stampmills, then smelted the crushed ore in stone furnaces, using lead or litharge as reagents and burning charcoal as fuel. In the amalgamation process documented for Nacatóbari, San Miguel Arcáncel, and Alamos, crushed ore was ground to a powder in the mule-drawn *arrastre* and mixed with mercury, salt, and magistral (copper sulfate). The coastal salines of Ostimuri supplied salt, and regional mines yielded the copper sulfate ores.[43]

Table 4.2. Estimated Indigenous Populations of Sinaloa, Ostimuri, and Sonora

Province	Date					
	1530	1625	1660	1720	1760	1790
Sinaloa	220,000	70,000	20,000	14,600	16,000	15,000
Ostimuri	103,000	70,000	18,000	12,000	22,000	20,000
Sonora	85,000	79,000	40,500	18,200	17,000	9,300

Source: Peter Gerhard, *The North Frontier of New Spain* (Norman: University of Oklahoma Press, 1993), 249.

The smelting and amalgamation processes in Ostimuri produced *planchas de plata*, flat bars of ore, that were shipped to Parral and other centers in Nueva Vizcaya for further refinement and assessment of the royal tax. Smaller bits of silver, called *tepusques*, circulated in Ostimuri and Sonora in lieu of coin for purchases among merchants, missionaries, and Indians. A number of trails crossed the Sierra Madre, linking Alamos, San Miguel Arcángel, and Ostimuri to the northern plateau and the *camino real* communicating the western provinces with Parral. These same trails linked the mission districts with local mining centers and Nueva Vizcaya. Mineral production in Ostimuri and Sonora contributed significantly to the wealth garnered from northern New Spain. During the last third of the seventeenth century, silver production from Ostimuri and Sonora constituted one-third of the ore mined in all of Nueva Vizcaya.[44]

The estimated indigenous populations of Sinaloa, Ostimuri, and Sonora declined precipitously over the sixteenth and seventeenth centuries through the subsistence crises and migratory labor recruitment alluded to above, as indicated in Table 4.2. Even at its nadir, possibly in 1720, the combined indigenous populations of Cahitan, Nevome, and other groups who were either native to Ostimuri or had migrated there to work in the mines and ranches or as temporary laborers in the missions easily surpassed the Hispanic and mixed-race settlers by two-thirds.

In sequence, San Miguel Arcángel, San Ildefonso de Ostimuri, and Real de los Alamos represented centers of mining assaying and merchant capital, regional markets, and the nuclei of a small elite of propertied *vecinos* and a plebeian population of African and mulatto slaves and freed persons as well as indigenous and *mestizo* peones, servants, and day laborers.[45] Scattered archival and published references to sermons and military service records provide glimpses of the entwined relations among mission communities and Spanish settlements. For example, the Jesuit Pedro Quiles de Cuéllar, long established in the Eudeve mission district of Sahuaripa, preached the titular sermon in honor of the Purísima Concepción in the Real de San Juan Bautista in 1667.[46] José de Tapia, a Jesuit who had served for more than twenty years as the missionary of San José de Toro (on the upper Río Zuaque [Fuerte]), preached the sermon for the saint's day celebration in Real de los Alamos in 1691.[47]

Captain Pedro de Perea had established his household in the area he claimed as Nueva Andalucía with his wife and five children; it appears that following his death, his widow, Doña María de Ibarra, had remained in the Ópata (Tegüima) pueblo of Banámichi in the upper Sonora River valley.[48] Nearly half a century later, a similar career path characterized Don Joseph Fernández de la Canal. He submitted his *relación de servicios* in 1684, in which he summarized the offices he had held in the provinces of Sinaloa and Ostimuri, including the title of *alcalde mayor* and *capitán a guerra* of the Real de San Ildefonso de Ostimuri. His career traced the route of mining and commercial centers that developed in the western corridor from Rosario in the south to Ostimuri in the north.[49]

Behind the colonial officials whose signatures punctuate the documents, Ostimuri emerged from the mixed labor force that coalesced around the *reales de minas*. Alamos, San Ildefonso, San Miguel Arcángel, Baroyeca, Río Chico, and the mining centers farther north recruited *indios de repartimiento* and free, migratory indigenous laborers, African slaves, and, in greater numbers, free *mulatos libres*. Mine laborers worked in organized *cuadrillas* for both ore extraction and processing; Yaquis and Mayos gained formidable reputations as skilled workers, with talents for prospecting as well as for different tasks in the mines, smelters, and *haciendas de beneficio*. Labor hierarchies were based on skills and on the distinction between slave and free status, but not necessarily on race or ethnicity. While men constituted overwhelmingly the mine labor force itself, both male and female workers toiled in domestic service and on rural haciendas by raising cattle and gathering crops.[50]

Mule trails and wagon roads linked mission districts with *reales de minas* as well as with Nueva Vizcaya. Missionaries and indigenous producers actively traded food supplies (grains), molasses, tallow, soap, and livestock to the mining centers in return for silver bars (*tepusques* valued in *marcos de plata*), cloth, and other merchandise shipped from central

Mexico through the merchants established in the *reales*.⁵¹ More controversially, however, the missions became repositories of labor for the mines through the supply of *tapisques* (work gangs) under the rules of *repartimiento*. As codified in 1609, forced recruitment of Indian workers for specific places and periods of time should have been overseen by the local magistrates (*justicias* or *alcaldes mayores*), and the workers should have received payment for their labor and travel time to and from their villages of origin. In practice, the indigenous councils in the missions intervened directly in the supply of laborers to specific miners or *hacendados*, upon receiving a *sello* (work order) stipulating the number of workers and their destination. The language of the *sellos* commanded indigenous governors to comply with the work order on pain of punishment should they not supply the laborers. All too often the number of workers demanded and the time they spent in the mines away from their home villages exceeded the legal limits stated in the regulations. The *repartimiento* became an important conduit of labor to the mines in Sonora and Ostimuri during the late seventeenth and early eighteenth centuries, with a significant impact on the missions as the forced recruitment of laborers exacerbated the effects of epidemic disease in removing adults in their productive years from the villages.⁵² In Ostimuri, the Real de los Alamos drew heavily from the Mayo pueblos; moreover Yaquis, Mayos, and other indigenous groups from the western provinces worked in the mines of Nueva Vizcaya. The labor demands for mining centers created webs of itinerant laborers that were set in motion by *repartimiento* and led to the continued circulation of free laborers during the eighteenth century.⁵³

CONTESTED spaces evolved in the borderlands of Ostimuri, shaped by their physical geography and the production of landscapes and settlements. The histories condensed in this chapter underscore the conflictive *and* interdependent movements of village-dwelling chieftancies, seminomadic bands, and colonial seekers of mineral wealth and souls. These layered territories do not fit neatly on one map, and their histories do not constitute an unbroken narrative; rather, they reveal overlapping communities with reciprocal and competing claims to resources, spheres of power, and religious authority. This view of the making of a province, beginning with the physical geography and proceeding through the indigenous and colonial productions of landscapes and claims to territoriality, tempers constructivist approaches to ethnic labels with historical sensitivities to regional and cultural identities. While attentive to the importance of discursive analysis of colonial textual and visual documents, the presentation offered here has attempted to show that colonial social and ethnic identities developed not only in the minds and pens of the colonizers but also through the material objectives and symbolic meanings that indigenous communities and the heterogeneous populations of colonial society negotiated as conditions for their labor, religious observation, and access to land and water.

The colonial pact, however tenuous and fragile, created webs of interdependency and contestation in the production of borderlands as fluctuating, hybrid spaces. San Ildefonso de Ostimuri emerged in colonial cartography from the *real de minas* that gave its name to an administrative province. Its significance derived not so much from the authority of its *alcaldía mayor* as from the natural contours of its river valleys and the labor networks and political alliances of its indigenous and colonial inhabitants. This chapter has traced the multiple borderlands of Ostimuri through the ecological transitions from the desert to the subtropics, the initial encounters of indigenous peoples and Spanish military officers and missionaries, and the development of an extensive mining economy. The history of contested spaces recounted here has emphasized the uneven and tenuous character of Spanish colonialism in this borderland, subject to negotiation and made possible through only the transitory alliances of indigenous leaders, military and ecclesiastical officers, colonial settlers, and a mixed population of both free and unfree laborers.

Ostimuri entered the historical record as a distinct administrative province in the late seventeenth century, but the name did not endure after Mexican Independence. Its history, then, invites us to question how regions come into being and how they either persist or meld into other territorial units as—in this case—Ostimuri was divided between the early republican states of Sonora and Sinaloa. Nonetheless, the pueblos, villas, and *reales de minas* that gave Ostimuri its historical identity and through which the province was peopled have endured as villages and ranches to the present day. The Yoreme strongholds of the Yaqui and Mayo valleys and in northern Sinaloa have persisted as ethnic territories distinguished by their language, ritual complex, and communal landscapes. During the period under study Yoreme spatial identity encompassed both the villages of the lower river floodplains and the mining *reales* of Río Chico, Baroyeca, Ostimuri, and Alamos. Highland and lowland indigenous and mestizo rural communities of Ostimuri developed historically through the changing production of social space, modified through technology, commercial investment, and migration. In dialogue with the contributors of this volume, the present chapter argues that borderlands describe not only territories controlled by indigenous nations beyond the sway of colonial powers but also the contested spaces of heterogeneous populations, forged in the land itself by both indigenous and colonial peoples through their economies, religious practices, and constructions of meaning.

CHAPTER 5

Transformations: The Rio de la Plata During the Bourbon Era

RAÚL JOSÉ MANDRINI

The year 1740 was a difficult one for Buenos Aires, a small town lost in the vastness of the southern plains of the Spanish domains in the Americas, and for the relatively small number of settlers living in the surrounding rural areas. That year, between October and November, the Indians had assaulted the districts (known as *pagos*) of Arrecifes, Luján, and Matanzas,[1] but the worst was yet to come. The most violent attack began on the night of November 25, when the southern Indian chiefs (*caciques*) Cacapol and his son Cangapol commanded a terrible and surprising uprising (or *malón*) to revenge a cruel massacre of Indians ordered by a Spanish military official, Juan de San Martin, during an incursion (*entrada*) into Indian territory a few weeks earlier.[2]

Encountering no resistance from the Spaniards, the Indians raided the borderlands, in particular the Magdalena district located in the south of Buenos Aires, ravaging the surrounding rural areas and creating panic for the small town's population. The careful planning of the attack and the violence with which it was carried out disturbed the witnesses, who were not accustomed to these sorts of situations because, as we will see, from the time of its foundation in 1580 the relationship that Buenos Aires had with the Pampean Indians had been relatively peaceful.

The Jesuit missionary Thomas Falkner recalled those dramatic episodes many years later. He wrote, "Cacapol . . . took field at the head of a thousand men (some say four thousand) . . . fell upon the District of the Magdalena . . . and divided his troops with so much judgment, that he scoured and dispeopled, in one day and a night, above twelve leagues of a most populous and plentiful country in these parts. They killed many Spaniards, and took a great number of women and children captives, with above twenty thousand head of cattle, besides horses, etc."[3] The number of assailants was truly very high if one takes into account the low population density on the plain, and only an alliance of different groups, as Falkner mentioned, made it possible. This fact indicates that a chief like Cacapol had great authority and the capacity, beyond the reaches of a band or tribe, to mobilize warriors.

Another contemporary witness was Miguel Antonio de Merlo, the procurator of the *cabildo* (a town council in Spanish American cities). He pointed out in a report presented to the authorities that the Indians had "so fiercely attacked the settlers who looked after the crops of the countryside that they came within five leagues of [the] city, killing everyone they encountered."[4]

The news spread quickly through the town, and it was feared that the Indians would attack it.[5] But the enemy did not enter into the town because the *caciques* preferred to withdraw with their captured booty, with the Spanish forces being incapable of doing anything about it. The attack showed the weakness in the defense system and its effect was engraved in the memory of the inhabitants of Buenos Aires for a long time. Almost three months later, the members of the *cabildo* remembered the ravages that such heathens inflicted on the Magdalena district "had never seen nor experienced . . . with a great death toll for the vecinos of this district, capturing many women and children and plundering many haciendas."[6]

This episode calls up images of other Indian attacks along the colonial Spanish borderlands, especially the uprising carried out by the Comanches and a group of Wichita allies against the San Sabá Mission in Texas in March 1758, when Indians formed a force of nearly two thousand warriors, who were well equipped with firearms in order to attack and destroy the mission. The garrison of the near presidio could do nothing to protect the mission.[7]

In Buenos Aires these outbreaks of frontier violence had begun a few years earlier, during the middle of the 1730s, and would be repeated in the following decades, until the middle of the 1780s, alternating with periods of relative peace. In spite of these peaceful intervals, the Indian menace was a problem that was always present after the first attack, and colonial authorities had to confront it. The periods of open conflict did not entirely interrupt the older links between both societies, especially commercial exchanges. Starting from 1784 to 1785, it became possible to articulate an effective system to be able to support pacific relationships with southern Indians. This system continued until the last year of the first revolutionary decade.[8]

A preliminary analysis of these episodes suggests that some affirmations that had been defended in Argentina by historians for a long time must be questioned. Influenced by nineteenth-century nationalism, older historians only considered the frontier as a limit, as a line that separated different and opposite worlds or spaces—"us" from the "others"—whose relationships essentially were competitive, conflictive, and violent.[9] As a result, the analysis of the frontier history was solely reduced to the war against the Indians or to the occupation of their lands. It is obvious that war and violence took place in the borderlands, but the commotion that the events of 1740 provoked for the Buenos Aires settlers suggests that this situation was not so common. On the contrary, as we will see, war seems to have been significant in only specific periods.

Moreover, this situation also suggests that the relationships between Spaniards and Native peoples living behind the frontier—the savages or barbarians, as they are frequently named in the sources—were more complex, involved all the levels of social life, and deeply changed during the course of the colonial period.[10] Finally, we will need to consider the situation of the Native peoples in the same period, the changes that Indian societies experienced, and the role that these peoples and their chiefs played in the frontier history.

With these questions in mind I attempt in this essay to summarize the history of the Pampean borderlands during the colonial epoch, according to the more recent advances of our knowledge. In this history I recognize at least three periods: the first contacts (around 1580 to 1730); the intensification of Indian-Spaniard relationships and the alternation of war and peace (around 1730 to 1785); and the stabilization of peaceful relationships on the borders (around 1785 to 1820).

In the Rio de la Plata the situation of the region had been different from that of other Spanish American frontiers, and the upswing in violence that began around 1740 lacked any local antecedents. In large terms, borderland conflicts were nothing new for the Iberian population that had settled on the American continent since the beginning of the sixteenth century. They had been a permanent fixture in the farther lands of the Spanish Empire: the north of New Spain, the eastern slopes of the Andes, and Araucanía in the central-south region of Chile, during the sixteenth century. In spite of the stabilization of the borders in the following century, the conflicts never disappeared altogether.[11] But in the area of Buenos Aires, that had not been the case.

The particular situation of Buenos Aires and its hinterland was related to the characteristics that the conquest of the territory and the European settlement had, as well as to the particular way of life of the Native people who lived there, especially the initial objective that the foundation of Buenos Aires by Juan de Garay in 1580 had in the context of colonial politics.[12]

To the colonial government, the occupation of the Rio de la Plata littoral area responded to the need to find a quick and easy way out to the productions of Paraguay, and especially as a way to access silver from Potosí, the main and most valuable resource in the southern lands of the empire in Upper Peru.[13]

At the time of its founding, Buenos Aires was a lonely outpost in the extreme south of the Iberian colonial world. It was the final point of the terrestrial route that connected Asuncion and Potosí to Atlantic commerce, especially toward the port of Seville in Spain. The union of the Crowns of Spain and Portugal (1581–1640) also opened up the possibility of commerce with the Portuguese colonies in Brazil. This trade, both legal and illegal, was the main interest of Buenos Aires' inhabitants and the most important source of their wealth.

The small town, with its precarious port and weak garrison, survived for over a century, despite vagaries and continuous changes in the Crown's commercial policy and even the entrenchment of its monopoly on commerce. Eventually, Buenos Aires was able to assert its position toward the end of the century and become the main urban center in the territories that stretched south from Potosí to the Atlantic coast, with a population of between six thousand and seven thousand inhabitants in addition to about two thousand that lived in the surrounding countryside.[14]

Besides its position as a port, Buenos Aires survived with the products of surrounding farms and ranches—*chacras* and *estancias*—and the resources of the neighboring plains. Precisely the bases for future prosperity of the town already were there, in effect, when in 1541 the first settlement of Buenos Aires, founded by Pedro de Mendoza five years earlier, was abandoned and some horses and mares were set free and abandoned to their fate. A favorable environment and lack of competitive species favored the reproduction of these animals so that they reverted to a wild status—*cimarrones*, as they were then called—and constituted an abundant resource as early as at the end of the sixteenth century. Some domesticated bulls and cows also expanded in the pampas where they also reverted to wildness. In this way, at the moment of the second founding of Buenos Aires in 1580 these wild cattle and horses were the most important and attractive of the region's resources.[15]

An account of the situation in 1582 was written by Juan de Garay in a letter sent to the Council of the Indies after his voyage of exploration into the territories of modern-day southwest Buenos Aires.[16] This *entrada*, which reached the immediate area around the modern-day city of Mar del Plata, demolished the initial conqueror's illusions: in the vast prairies, the land was plentiful, but there was no mineral wealth, there was no dense Indian population to subdue and exploit, and there were none of the fabulous cities that the conquerors' imaginations dreamed up. These legends never entirely disappeared: in the periphery of the colonial world, fantastic cities and fabulous wealth retreated farther and farther as new territories were explored, as happened in the remote northern frontier of New Spain. The legend of the Seven Cities of Cíbola has its counterpart in the Pampean borderlands with the legend of the City of the Caesars.[17]

The reduced needs of the early population of Buenos Aires did not encourage an important occupation of the space or provoke significant conflicts with Native people who lived in the neighboring plains.[18] For a long time, each group seemed to ignore the other and the relations between them were few and relatively peaceful. The vastness of the territory, the low population density of both Spaniards and Indians, and the abundance of wild cattle and horses allowed both societies to coexist without major confrontations. In the lands beyond the Andes, on the contrary, wars and violence disturbed relationships, especially during the decades after the insurrection of the *reches* and their victory in Curalaba in 1598.[19]

In this context, the main preoccupation of the Buenos Aires authorities was the relationship that the Pampas Indians had with their counterparts in Araucanía, because the Pampas provided the *reches* with ever-increasing numbers of horses (as well as men) for their wars against colonial authorities.[20] In 1678, Bishop Antonio of Buenos Aires informed the king that horses and mules were being transported by Pampas Indians to Chile and sold to enemy Indians.[21]

The situation began to change only in the first decades of the eighteenth century. It was then that Buenos Aires, which until then had been reduced to the role of being the guardian of the South Atlantic side of the empire, started to acquire the trappings of a true frontier society.[22] Its settlers turned their gazes to the vast plains and their resources. Relations with the Indians of the south became increasingly intense, conflicts escalated, and the colonial authorities were forced to apply, with some difficulty, different types of measures in order to assert control and protect the settlers. These changes were responses not only to more profound transformations in the colonial world but also to changes within and among Indian societies.

From the beginning of the eighteenth century a new dynasty, the Bourbons, governed Spain. Ensconced on the Spanish throne after a long struggle (the War of the Spanish Succession), the new kings and their ministers began to introduce a series of reforms in the colonial organization to restructure imperial commerce and governance.[23]

These measures, the most important of which were introduced during the reign of Carlos III (1763–1788), did not represent a coherent body of laws and regulations; they were answers to specific situations raised by the new political realities. Sometimes referred to as Bourbon Reforms, these measures sought to reactivate the economy of the American possessions to the benefit of the Crown and to reposition the imperial economy in a new international context in which Great Britain had become the dominant sea power. These reforms also sought to centralize the government of the colonies in the hands of the Crown and its functionaries, and they re-created for this purpose a bureaucracy that was loyal to royal interests. The bureaucracy, in turn, which sought to limit further accumulation of power for local elites, was already composed for the most part by *criollos* (that is, Spaniards born in the Americas). To grow the economy, the Bourbon kings encouraged economic activities by, among other things, relaxing the regulations of the commercial monopoly put in place by the Habsburgs. To this end, the reforms introduced into the imperial economy included opening ports and commercial routes that had been heavily regulated or even restricting as well as stimulating regional production of items that were valuable in Europe but did not compete with the industries established in Spain.

These measures were important for the region of Rio de la Plata and especially for Buenos Aires because they slowly developed the regional economy. Early in this process, at the very end of the War of the Spanish

Succession in 1713, a Spanish concession to the British allowed for the establishment of a small settlement, or *asiento*, in Buenos Aires that would introduce African slaves and some commodities. During the following years, commerce continued to grow, especially when the route to Cape Horn was reopened to commercial traffic. This route linked ports in the Atlantic coast with those in the Pacific, and it was crucial for growth in traffic and commercial exchanges. This commercial expansion was based on making valuable local products, such as leather and tallow obtained from cattle, and ñandu feathers (*Rhea americana*), into commodities for the Atlantic trade. Silver continued to be the main export item for Buenos Aires, but these and other "products of the land" began to have an increasing presence in its economic life.

During the 1730s, on the other hand, the demand for livestock in the interior provinces (Cuyo, Paraguay, el Tucumán, and Chile) grew just as the supply of wild cattle around the Banda Oriental (modern-day Uruguay), which had supplied the *vecinos* of Buenos Aires, was becoming exhausted. These simultaneous processes forced a search for alternative cattle resources from the Pampas even though here they had to compete with Indians for these resources. It is not a coincidence that conflicts with the southern Indians surged around the middle of the decade, starting a cycle of frontier violence that, as we have seen, had its highpoint in 1740.[24]

By this time, Indian societies had been fundamentally transformed by the long century of contact with the colonial world. Their economy had changed and they began to show the first effects of the changes in their social structure, in political organization and functioning, and in their ideological system.[25] There had also been a rise in the demand for goods and cattle among the Indians, especially those of European origin. As a result, relations with the colonial world intensified during the eighteenth century and the first two decades of the nineteenth.

HOWEVER, this intensification of relations with the colonial world was not linear or uniform. War, a relatively new phenomenon in the Buenos Aires borderlands, constituted a significant aspect of these relations and had come about from friction caused by increased proximity and a growing competition for cattle resources. The most conflicting moments took place when Indian chiefs organized violent raids over the borderlands, or *malónes*, to revenge actions that they considered injuries and damages caused by the Spaniards or when the colonial authorities ordered military campaigns to punish Indian attacks. These peaks of violence happened during the 1740s and 1750s and in the first half of the 1780s.[26]

In order to deal with this new situation, colonial authorities attempted to put into practice, with uneven results, the various options that the Spanish colonial tradition put at their disposal. Above all else, what was intended was to strengthen the frontier's defenses through the creation of a more stable and efficient military organization in order to replace the meager, ill-prepared, and underequipped military presence of the first militias.[27] The new system, which was implemented in 1745 after the raids carried out by the Indians brought the founding of a few *fortines* (or *presidisos*, small military outposts) along with more permanent militia garrisons, but these soon failed. Within five years, as Indian attacks intensified, the *fortines* were empty, in large part because the militiamen had deserted them. In 1752 the *cabildo* created a rural militia with a salaried corps of light cavalry (known as *blandengues*) in Luján, Salto, and Magdalena. Its efficacy depended, however, on how reliable and punctual the payments of salaries were; if payments were regularly delayed, the militiamen left the guards.

As the 1770s began, colonial authorities planned with renewed vigor a more efficient defense system. Different measures taken allowed for the creation of a series of forts and *fortines* with improvements in their physical layout and construction. There was also a reorganization of the *blandengues* corps and an increase in the number of enlisted men. Juan José de Vértiz, first as governor then as viceroy, played an important role in implementing these measures. As a consequence, by 1781 the southern border of Buenos Aires was established at the Salado River, some 130 kilometers south-southwest from the town proper.

This defensive system's main source of funding was the *cabildo* and the contributions of the Buenos Aires *vecinos*, but a lack of appropriate funding was always an obstacle to the proper functioning of the defenses. When analyzing the efficacy of different frontier policies, the various vested interests have to be weighed. Local interests must be taken into account, as well as conflict between these interests and those of the Crown and other groups linked to the frontier.[28] Thus, some of those who opposed most strongly the plan for the advancement of the military frontier proposed by Viceroy Pedro de Cevallos in 1777 were local: the military chiefs of the frontier, whose interests merged with those of merchants linked to Indian trade, a very profitable endeavor.[29]

In the following years, the demographic and social situation in the borderlands became more complex when new settlers arrived in Buenos Aires' rural area, which had previously been thinly settled. They were principally migrants from the northern provinces whose economies had been affected by measures of the Crown because some imports, such as textiles, competed with local production. Attracted by the growing development of Buenos Aires, these migrants especially settled the southern districts of Buenos Aires, and some of them spontaneously exceeded the Salado boundary and settled in Indian territories by means of negotiations or agreements with some *caciques*.[30]

At the same time, colonial authorities tried to use another means of control available since the start of the conquest: missions. Frontier missions had a dual role in the borderlands of Spanish America: in addition to their religious role, they played a fundamental part in the territorial occupation and social control of the local Indian population throughout the empire's frontiers. In the borderlands to the south of Buenos Aires, this role was assigned to the Jesuits. Their first and only missionary experience took place between 1740 and 1753, in a climate of violence that characterized frontier life during those turbulent years. The conflict had led to the signing of treaties with colonial authorities. Through these treaties, some *caciques* near Buenos Aires asked for missionaries to be sent to them, surely with the intention of obtaining Spanish support in confronting rival *caciques* and of eventually being recognized as chiefs and receiving more gifts of prestige goods.[31]

Three Jesuit missions were founded on this frontier. The first (in 1740) was Purísima Concepción de las Pampas, near the mouth of the Rio Salado. The others, both founded in 1747, were Nuestra Señora del Pilar de los Serranos and Virgen de los Desesperados de los Tehuelches, both on the northern slopes of the eastern Tandilia mountain range. The names show that each mission was destined for one of the main Indian nations that Europeans recognized as living in those territories: the Pampas, Serranos, and Tehuelches. But ethnic realities were much more complex than that.[32]

The missions failed in their intended role of reducing tensions by pacifying the local Indians and instilling in them a sedentary lifestyle. In a few years, the situation became unsustainable: the Desamparados mission never really got off the ground, and those of Pilar and Concepción were abandoned not long afterward, in 1751 and 1753, respectively. The failure of the mission strategy was due to different factors. Above all, the missions had to bear the hostility of the *cabildo*, and the Jesuits found almost no economic support from the elite of Buenos Aires.³³ The missions only survived for as long as they did through the Jesuits' own funds. In addition, the missionaries could not establish stable population centers around their missions and they could not organize Indians as productive units to make the missions have a stable economic base (though in Concepción an *estancia* existed that at one time had more than six thousand animals). Lastly, the missions had to endure the hostilities of the local Indian groups and the presence of some powerful *caciques* little disposed to surrendering their authority to the missionaries.

Other practices destined to neutralize the hostility of Native groups were of increasing importance due to a series of difficulties. Among these was the impossibility of establishing a defensive military system; the failure of the Jesuit missionary enterprise; and the lack of a truly offensive vision with a project destined to occupy those spaces beyond the frontier.³⁴ Among the practices used to blunt the effects of these difficulties was the attempt to win over through gifts and offerings of friendship those *caciques* considered more inclined to strike a deal with colonial authorities. This policy was used in the pampas of Buenos Aires starting in 1717 when the *cabildo* named two *caciques*, Mayupilquiyan and Yati, as Major Guards of the Countryside (*guardas mayores de la campaña*). But in this case, the treaty depended on those Indians opposing the incursions of the Spanish concessionaries of *vaquerías* from other provinces, in particular those from Córdoba. This policy of making deals with Indians intensified as the century progressed and such deals many times culminated in more formal treaties with *caciques*, as happened with the signing of the treaty with Callfilque o Callpisqui in 1790.³⁵ However, in other occasions, it was the *caciques* themselves who asked for the signing of a peace treaty, because through these treaties they would obtain gifts and economic and military aid for their internal conflicts.³⁶

The internal situation of the Native societies favored such policy because conflicts and internecine struggles increased during the last decades of the eighteenth century. This in turn led to a long and bitter cycle of wars, even as a new economic system was being consolidated within Native societies and as socioeconomic changes deepened, disrupting previous ways of living in economic and political terms.³⁷ These internecine wars were associated with ancient ethnic rivalries, such as those that faced Pehuenches and Huilliches, but were also due to the increasing struggle and competition for control of lands, animals, and commercial routes.

Complicating the situation further, the pampas attracted young warriors, or *conas,* from Araucanía. These young Indians crossed the mountains seeking fortune and prestige, which were essential for their future political careers back in their native lands.[38] On the plains, these young warriors made a name for themselves by attacking Spanish outposts and rival groups and taking booty. This in turn attracted other young men who aspired to follow in their path so that one day they, too, could go back to Araucanía and dispute power to the old chiefs (*ulmenes*).[39] The best-known case of these young warriors seeking their fortune in the southern borderlands was Llanketruz, who was active during the 1770s and 1780s.[40]

Other chiefs, especially Pehuenche, preferred a closer relationship with the colonial authorities because they benefited more from the commerce, gifts, and aid that they received than from hostile relationships. That was, for example, the case with the *caciques* Carrilipi and Ancán Amún, who played a crucial role in the death of the aforementioned Llanketruz. The case of Ancán Amún was important because he at first raided Spanish settlements but later signed a deal and became an ally of the colonial authorities in their common battle against Llanketruz. Colonial officials were not blameless in the upsurge of violence because they encouraged conflicts and skirmishes among different Indian groups; for example, they supported Pehuenche chiefs with resources, weapons, and men in their struggle against the Huilliches. The colonial government tried to shift the frontier violence from the areas under its control toward the interior of the indigenous zone of control.

These policies seemed to work. Conflict between Indian and Spanish societies was reduced, open war disappeared, and peace was consolidated over the next few years, especially after the treaty signed in 1790 by Viceroy Loreto and the Indian chief Callpisqui, after long and difficult negotiations.[41] Argentine historiography has traditionally assumed that this peace was the result of the successful policies implemented by Viceroys Vértiz and Loreto, especially the establishment of a more efficient defensive system, a successful policy of alliances, and an economic stimulus for the Indians.

However, recent research has shown that the *caciques* had a very important role in the gestation of a peace that also benefited them. They were interested in peace because peaceful relations helped their economic interests, especially with regards to commerce.[42] According to Crivelli Montero, the attacks from the beginning of the 1780s sought to force the colonial government to put an end to the commercial restrictions imposed by Viceroy Vértiz.[43]

THE next few decades were ones of relative peace for the southern frontiers of the Spanish Empire. The Bío Bío frontier in Araucanía seemed to be pacified; in neighboring Cuyo the alliance with the Pehuenche was working well, and the situation in this area calmed down considerably after the death of Llanketruz in 1788. On the Buenos Aires frontier, after the violent *malónes* of the early years of the 1780s, peace was kept for the most part without major violent incidents until close to the year 1820.

Some contemporary eyewitnesses to these events—men like Miguel Lastarría, Félix de Azara, and Pedro Andrés García—underlined the importance in the growth of commerce for establishing peaceful relations with the Indians. In a petition written to the king in 1804, Lastarría, the personal secretary of Viceroy Avilés (1799–1801), highlighted the importance of commerce for establishing peace, and he referred to the Indians of the south as "savage merchants" (*salvajes comerciantes*). Félix de Azara, a notable colonial official who knew the lands around the Rio de la Plata region very well, described the broad circuit of exchanges embedded in the commerce between Spaniards and the Indians of the Pampas. García in 1822 referred explicitly to these commercial networks and explained how they had developed since 1790 in response to the prevailing peace.[44]

These and other colonial officials from the time considered commerce to be a fundamental tool for pacifying and integrating the Native populations of the American peripheries into the empire, reflecting the ideas of the Enlightenment then common in the imperial bureaucracy. It is impossible to quantify this commerce, but surviving sources show that its importance grew throughout the second half of the eighteenth century, reaching its highest point in the two decades before the start of the struggle for Independence in the 1810s.[45]

However, it is necessary to point out that, contrary to some eyewitnesses' accounts and what many contemporary historians still maintain, this commerce had started well before the peace of 1790. A large file full of eyewitness accounts from 1752 proves that commerce with Indians was important for the Buenos Aires of that era. Wool *ponchos*, taken to Buenos Aires to trade there by Indians from the southern missions (especially Concepción) were an important item of commerce. These *ponchos* were produced in Araucanía and taken to the pampas by other Indians that arrived there from the western lands. Throughout the same decade, other documents also refer to this type of transaction.[46]

From a strictly economic perspective, this intensification in commercial exchanges—a phenomenon also happening in other borderlands of the empire—benefited both Indian groups and colonial society. For the latter, the Indian world was a source of supply of goods meant for local consumption as well as for export. Commerce included items such as salt, leather and animal hides, and *ñandú* feathers, among others. Indian trade also constituted an important market for colonial merchants, who did not hesitate to venture into territories controlled by Indians with carts loaded with merchandise, sometimes challenging the orders of local colonial authorities. The profitability of this commerce generated strong conflicts among the merchants of Buenos Aires, particularly those who hosted the Indian trading parties when they came to the town to trade.[47]

Indian commerce was furthermore encouraged for political reasons by the colonial state itself. Indeed, many of its functionaries considered commercial exchange an activity that, by introducing among the Indian population tastes and necessities that could be satisfied with only European products, would attract Indians into a peace deal with the Spaniards. Practical experience seemed to support this, since from the middle of the 1780s, the continuous growth in trading with the Indians from the south had been accompanied in the Rio de la Plata by a strengthening of other sorts of peaceful interactions.[48]

Commerce took place, above all, in Buenos Aires, where numerous Indian parties arrived to trade. The frequency of these parties—almost always consisting of a *cacique*, with a few warriors and some women—was documented in numerous entries written by the captain of the forts. They recorded the name of the *cacique*, how many members were in his party, and the motive for the visit. Sometimes these chiefs came to pay their respects to the governor or viceroy, but they mostly came to trade.[49] There were times when the presence of a great number of Indian trading parties seriously worried the colonial authorities, who saw them as a potential danger to the security of the town. In 1760, the governor of Buenos Aires reminded the commander of La Matanza of the existing policy seeking peaceful relations with Indians, and he upbraided him for not implementing it. Years later in 1785 Viceroy Loreto wrote to the Commandant of Monte, ordering him to take the necessary precautions so that there were never too many Indian trading parties in the capital at the same time.[50]

Commercial exchanges also took place outside of the boundaries of Buenos Aires. In effect, there was a large amount of commercial transactions taking place in the frontier outposts when the Indian parties arrived: *pulperos* (storekeepers), colonial officials, and commanders of the forts as well as enlisted soldiers played a fundamental role in this part of the commerce. But these exchanges were also very important in the remote fort of El Carmen, located on the banks of the Rio Negro. This fort survived, in great measure, thanks to commerce with neighboring Indians that supplied it with cattle. In this area, cattle trading seems to have been more important than was previously believed.[51]

Other opportunities for exchanges between Indians and Spaniards, according to the testimonies of the military commanders, were the periodic expeditions to the Salinas Grandes, where the town supplied the demand for salt.[52] Lastly, many small merchants and peddlers (*mercachifles* and *buhoneros*) ventured with their wares all the way to the *tolderías* (Indian campsites) in order to conduct their transactions. There were many of them, and their presence was readily accepted by the Indians.[53]

This commerce was also convenient for the Indians, especially those who lived in the lands south of Buenos Aires, because it involved them in the transport of cattle to the lands in the foothills of the Andes and beyond. These Indian groups had changed their means of production during the seventeenth and eighteenth centuries. When the Europeans arrived in the Rio de la Plata, these Indian groups were mostly hunter-gatherers who traveled on foot. They especially hunted guanacos but also a large number of smaller animals. From the beginning of the seventeenth century they adopted an equestrian lifestyle and culture, transforming their societies into groups of mounted hunters of wild cattle herds. Later, when wild cattle herds became scarce, they moved on to attacking frontier outposts.[54] However, in the second half of the eighteenth century, these same groups developed herding as an important economic activity that soon reached a high degree of specialization and whose geographical center was located in the lands between the Tandil and Ventana mountain ranges, a zone rich in water and pasture. By the end of the century, this area had become the privileged supplier of cattle for the commercial networks going west.[55]

As is common with all economies of this type that we know of, the strengthening and survival of this specialized cattle geographical center was only possible insofar as it supplied other items for trade, especially agricultural products and handicrafts.[56] In this case, Indian access to these goods, which were largely produced by Spanish colonial society, could be accomplished through different means. One of these was commerce and exchanges; another was as booty from attacks on frontier outposts or trading parties that circulated near the frontier, in particular those that traveled through the Camino Real that stretched from Buenos Aires to Mendoza (these attacks provided the *caciques* with a rich bounty that included wine and liquor, European manufactures such as weapons and clothing, and captives).[57] Lastly, European goods could also be obtained as gifts made by colonial authorities or as ransom for the freedom of Spaniards and *criollos* captured during raids.

In this wider context, both the establishment of a system of regular trade in the Buenos Aires borderlands and the strengthening of peaceful relations seem to have been the most economic and profitable solutions. And if this peace implied to the chiefs a diminution in the booty that they obtained through warfare, it also meant an increase in the gifts and presents that colonial authorities gave them to preserve this peace. These gifts given to the main Indian chiefs increased their prestige and strengthened their authority.[58] To judge from descriptions in our sources such conditions—both environmental advantages and the place that they played in the exchange system—were most likely on the basis of the prosperity those Native groups seemed to have experienced during the last decades of the colonial era.[59]

The *caciques* of the south knew very well what the situation was. On December 22, 1806, a few months after the English invasion of Buenos Aires, ten chiefs from the Pampas came before the *cabildo* to offer twenty thousand well-armed warriors for the purpose of confronting the new English invasion (*colorados*, as they called them); the number of warriors was impossibly large, even though these chiefs could usually summon several hundred men each. It was not the first time the Buenos Aires *cabildo* had received such offers of assistance: in September, and then in December, other chiefs also offered numerous warriors to fight against the English.

Members of the *cabildo* worried that a high number of Indians so near the town was potentially dangerous. Thanking the *caciques* for their offer, the *cabildo* treated them to meals and gifts and asked them to watch the Atlantic coast and maintain peace throughout the frontier. But even more interesting is the rationale the *caciques* gave to explain their offer. One of them said that they did it "for the good reception that you give to our goods and your permission to take anything we need."[60]

As we have seen, Argentine historiography was dominated until about three decades ago by a strong tendency to reduce the analysis of frontier history solely to war against the Indians or to the occupation of their lands. Other types of relationships between Native peoples and Europeans were not taken in account by historians; also, historians did not attempt to understand the history, organization, or functioning of the Native societies. These societies were considered as very simple ones in their functioning and organization: their economy was considered as predatory and essentially based on hunting, gathering, and uprising, and their society was qualified as nomadic bands. Indian territories were thought to be the true barriers that separated the spaces controlled by the Spaniards.

These perspectives have begun to change. Old historians were influenced by nineteenth-century nationalism, and they considered the frontier as a limit. Many scholars today consider the frontiers as borderlands, as social spaces or areas of contact between different societies, and as historically constructed, where specific historical processes operated. Other historians, as it is in my case, are more and more interested in the Indian world, traditionally considered a subject that only concerned anthropologists. We also have learned that Native peoples deeply changed after the European invasion in the sixteenth century and that these changes affected all aspects of their social life.

According to these advances we need to reconsider the traditional perspectives. Thus, we know today, first, that war was only one aspect of the rich and complex relationships between both societies. Some level of violence never was lacking along the borders, but true wars only happened in some moments and places. In the colonial Rio de la Plata borderlands, genuine wars with the nearby Native peoples were only important from 1735 to 1785 and even during these years war was not permanent.

Second, we can establish that the Pampean Indian economy was complex, diversified, and specialized in obtaining and/or producing goods for interchange. In the second half of the eighteenth century, for example, Indian peoples who settled in the southern Buenos Aires province developed an important specialized pastoral activity, and they became the privileged providers of cattle to the commercial networks that connected the eastern pampas, the Andes, the Araucanía, and Chile. But to survive, this pastoral nucleus needed to guarantee the supplies of other goods, especially cereal crops and manufactures that mainly were produced in the colonial world. Indian chiefs had to accommodate their political and economic strategies to meet these needs.

Third, Indian societies played an important role in forming the main commercial circuits in America. By means of their trading activities, these societies linked their economies to the colonial ones—and indirectly to the European World—and contributed to articulating different colonial spaces. Along the southern borders of the Hispanic colonial world an extensive net of routes and a complex interchange system linked the Indian peoples of the pampas, Patagonia, Cordillera, and Araucanía with the colonial spaces of Rio de la Plata, Cuyo, Chile, and their hinterlands. The growing intensification of these interchanges between 1750 and 1820 was successful because it benefited both Native peoples and colonial society.

Fourth, we need to revise the traditional assumptions that Native societies were passive peoples unable to change and in consequence were peoples "without history," with their economies dependent on the colonial economy, and Indian chiefs accommodating their decisions and behaviors to defer to Spanish policies. A serious analysis of the documentary evidence reveals that Indian peoples truly were active participants in their history. The most important Indian chiefs made their own decisions and they played a significant role in the definition of the frontier policies: sometimes they put limits and successfully confronted initiatives of the colonial government; other times, using force or negotiation, they took their own initiatives and encouraged policies that they considered convenient. Remember, for example, the decisive role that southern chiefs played in the establishment of peaceful relationships at the end of the colonial period, or how some Pehuenche chiefs manipulated the friendship of the Spanish authorities to obtain men, weapons, and aid in their wars against the Huilliche.

So, in my analysis, the *caciques* were in some moments the persons who "established the *agenda*." Here, I agree with Kathleen DuVal regarding her writing about the Mississippi Valley: the traditional view implies sometimes unconsciously a misuse of dependency theory.[61] Indian societies did not sink into mere dependency, and they used different strategies to interact with the colonial world. They rearranged their own economies and social structures; they adopted and selected goods, practices, and ideas of "the other" and reevaluated them in the context of their own cultures, as happened, for example, during the ceremonies of the Holy Week among the Rarámuri in northern Mexico.[62]

Finally, some processes seemed to be similar—in spite of the specificity of each of them—to other processes that operated in different colonial borderlands, including the Araucanía, the eastern border of the Andes and the near lowlands (the Upper Amazonas, Upper Parana, and Paraguay rivers), northern New Spain, and the extensive central Plains and the Southwest in North America. As already suggested, the violent uprising of Cacapol and Cangapol in 1740, for example, reminds us of the Comanche raid against the San Sabá Mission in Texas in 1758. In both cases, the high number of warriors mobilized (surely one thousand or more), the careful campaigns, and the violence and easiness with which both actions were carried out revealed the weakness of the Spanish defenses, as well as the authority and power of the chiefs that organized the raids and their capacity to organize warriors within an alliance of different ethnic groups. Moreover, these Indian peoples controlled and participated in extensive commercial nets.

In the same way, the great navigable rivers in Chaco and Amazonia were used for active commercial movements that connected the Andean colonial space with the Atlantic settlements, including Portuguese colonies in Brazil. In these areas, the riverside Indian communities moved in their canoes along the rivers, and the missions located on the fringes of the eastern Andes jungles were fundamental to the building of such trade networks.[63] The wars between Guaykurú peoples in the Paraguayan north in the middle decades of the eighteenth century reveal complex relationships between Spanish ranchers (*hacendados*), Portuguese miners who exploited the gold in Guayra, and the Payaguá and Nbayá Indian communities (*parcialidades*, of which both groups were Guaykurú speakers and allies of the Spanish and Portuguese, respectively). But the war among these Indian communities was in fact a way to trade secretly—trading gold for cattle, for instance—which was otherwise prohibited by both monarchies.[64]

Indian societies played a similar role in northern New Spain and on the central Plains of North America, although their situations were more complex because of the diversity and mobility of the Native peoples and the presence of other powerful rival empires: France, Great Britain, and eventually the United States. Pekka Hämäläinen demonstrates that from roughly 1750 to 1850 the Comanches built an extensive cultural, economic, and political unity that involved other Native communities as well as developing relationships with different European settlements. We can also find this with the Native peoples of the Arkansas Valley during the same period, according to Kathleen DuVal.[65]

These Indian groups and their chiefs also manipulated their relationships with the European colonists. The Comanches did so within the outposts of New Mexico, Texas, Louisiana, and northern Mexico. Indians in the Arkansas Valley were able to determine the character of the intercultural relationships in their territory, thus DuVal rejects the concept of a middle ground (elaborated by Richard White) in preference for a "native ground" to designate the space where the Native peoples preserved their sovereignty and identity and where they were able to make independent decisions.[66]

Advances in our understanding of Spanish American frontier history and Indian societies have not only challenged some stereotypes long held in the field but also opened up other issues that must be considered going forward. Among these various issues, it is first and foremost necessary to more clearly define the character of frontier relationships and the changes that operated at the borderlands. Second, we must analyze the impact that these relationships had on both Spanish and Indian societies. Finally we need to define a more adequate chronology and to determine periods in order to build the history of that frontier. We have the questions; now we need to find the answers.

PART III

Spaces and Resettlements

CHAPTER 6

Blurred Borders: North America's Forgotten Apache Reservations

Matthew Babcock

On October 29, 1790, Lieutenant Ventura Montes's Spanish patrol escorted Chief Volante's group of Mescaleros off their protected reservation at Presidio del Norte (modern Ojinaga, Chihuahua, Mexico, across the river from Presidio, Texas) and onto the open and exposed southern Plains to hunt buffalo. Volante knew this territory well because Mescaleros had once controlled it, and he hoped that Spanish troops might help them reclaim it from their Comanche archenemies. Upon making camp south of San Antonio along the Nueces River in late November, Volante and his people breathed a sigh of relief. Six Mescalero women, held captive in Coahuila and recently released by Commander-in-Chief of the Interior Provinces Jacobo Ugarte, had arrived to help prepare the hides and meat. But their reconciliation was short-lived. The women explained that "a party of Comanches" had killed their escort, the interpreter Francisco Pérez, in a driving "snow and hail storm." Incensed at this unprovoked violent act and unbeknownst to Lt. Montes and his troops, Volante and the Mescaleros ambushed a Comanche *ranchería* (camp) the following day, "which they attacked repeatedly, killing three and taking various captives of both sexes" before returning to their reservation.[1]

This chaotic series of events highlights the complicated nature of Indian relations on early North American frontiers, and reveals the blurred cultural and spatial borders between Apaches, Comanches, and Spaniards in the colonial Southwest. As the historian David J. Weber has argued, through the acquisition of new values, skills, sensibilities, and technologies, enlightened Bourbon officials and powerful independent Indians were relating to each other in new ways across the frontiers of the Americas in the late eighteenth century.[2] Yet what was transpiring between Spaniards, Apaches, and Comanches on the ground in the fall of 1790 was not what any of the parties, especially Bourbon policy makers, intended. Several key questions come to mind: Why were freedom-loving Mescalero Apaches, who had warred successfully with Spaniards for decades, residing on a Spanish-run reservation? Why were Spaniards, who had negotiated peace treaties with Comanches in Texas and New Mexico, escorting Mescaleros into the *Comanchería* (Comanche homeland) to hunt buffalo? And what efforts, if any, would these groups make to reconcile relations?

Between 1786 and 1793 increased military pressure from Spaniards and Indian allies influenced thousands of Mescalero, Chiricahua, and Western Apaches to resettle in eight reservation-like *establecimientos* (establishments or settlements), which stretched from Presidio del Norte, in the east, to Tucson, in the west (see Figure 6.1). These so-called peaceful Apaches (*Apaches de paz*), who comprised more than 30 percent of all Mescaleros and Chiricahuas and less than 5 percent of all Western Apaches, shared similar reasons for choosing a more sedentary life under Spanish protection.[3] By 1790, they had faced four straight years of sustained and coordinated military campaigns from Spaniards and their Comanche, Navajo, and Ópata Indian allies amid an extended drought.[4] These offensives were the culmination of a prolonged war, which Apaches and Spaniards had been waging with varying levels of intensity since at least the 1660s.[5] Apache families who settled in the *establecimientos*, then, sought protection from military attacks, especially for women and children. They also hoped to recover their captured kinsmen; to receive gifts, rations, and trading privileges; to obtain information about Spanish troop movements; and to gain closer proximity to Spanish livestock for small-scale raids.[6]

Just as Apaches had their own reasons for making peace, Spanish officers had specific motives for offering it to them. Carrying out the enlightened Indian policies of Viceroy Bernardo de Gálvez and Commander-in-Chief Pedro de Nava, presidial commanders conducted a dual strategy of peace and war to pacify Apaches.[7] On the one hand, they offered gifts, rations, protection, and plots of "fertile land" to those Apache bands who requested peace in the hope of curbing their livestock raids and turning them into productive sedentary farmers subject to the Crown authority. At the same time, however, Spanish troops and their Indian allies, including

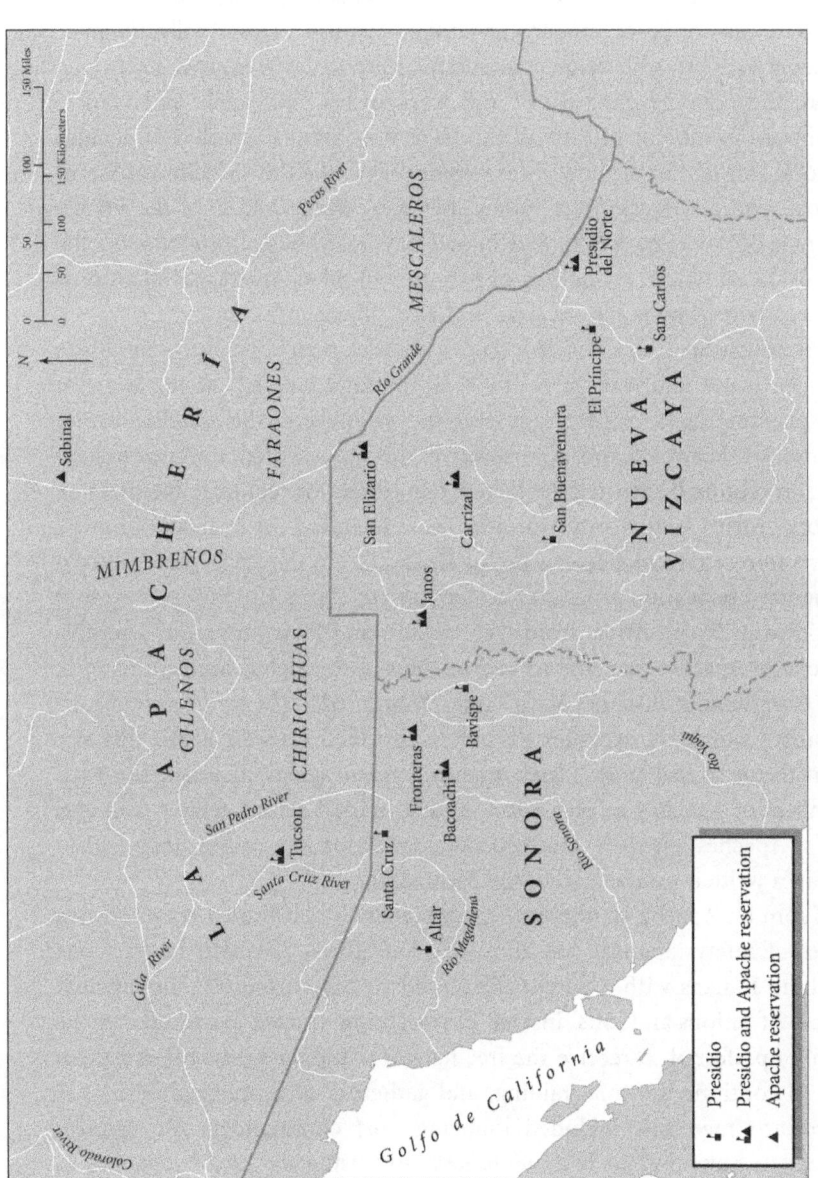

FIGURE 6.1. A map of the Spanish-Apache frontier, 1786–1793, originally drawn by Scott Cassingham, Foscue Map Library, Southern Methodist University, Dallas, Texas.

Apache auxiliaries, were to wage incessant offensive campaigns into the *Apachería* (Apache homeland) to compel the remaining independent Apache bands to "sue for peace" under standardized Spanish terms. Finally, the most resistant Apaches who refused to submit were to be "removed from land where they can be dangerous" and transported "humanely and gently" southward to interior Mexico and Cuba as prisoners.[8] Regardless of Spanish rhetoric, this part of the policy was reminiscent of the British exiling of Wampanoag captives to the West Indies after King Philip's War, of the French shipping of Fox deportees to Martinique and Guadeloupe from 1660 to 1760, and of the American extraditing of Apache and other American Indian prisoners to Fort Marion and Alcatraz in the late nineteenth century.[9]

Although Spanish officials intended to offer Apaches a clear-cut choice between peace and war, in reality these options merged. At the heart of this blending lay a contestation over the meaning of the *establecimientos* themselves. From a Spanish perspective, they constituted a unified system of reservations built on established precedents on colonial frontiers in Europe, Africa, and North America. These included the Spanish military's efforts to resettle Chichimecas in "peace camps" in the 1580s, their seldom-recognized relocation program for *moros de paz* ("peaceful Moors") around presidios in North Africa from 1739 to 1803, and their numerous attempts to resettle Apaches in missions and pueblos in the eighteenth century.[10] In 1791 Commander-in-Chief Nava explicitly ordered, "The territory that each [Apache] ranchería occupies should be specified, as well as the distance from the principal post." Each month, Indian agents recorded the total numbers of Apaches in each band, noting marital status, gender, and age, and if Apaches left their specified boundaries for any reason, they had to obtain a written passport from the commander.[11]

From an Apache standpoint, *establecimientos* constituted resource-rich zones of safety. Spanish presidios, like U.S. forts, provided reservation-dwelling Indians with a potentially abundant but chronically inconsistent supply of rations and gifts. Instead of remaining in fixed locations, Apache families preferred to receive the free handouts Indian agents offered them and to continue hunting, raiding, and gathering on a seasonal basis. For Mescalero men this included lobbying post commanders for Spanish escorts to hunt buffalo in *Comanchería* and using the *establecimientos* as bases for small-scale livestock raids into Spanish territory, which were both clear-cut violations of imperial Bourbon policy. Never content to be exclusively farmers, Apache women also sought to harvest mescal and raise their children without fear of military attack from Spaniards or Indian enemies.[12] Rather than a radical first step toward civilization, then, from an Apache perspective, settlement on protected reserves represented an opportunity to fulfill temporary needs, rebuild their population, and circumvent the overambitious incorporation efforts of Spanish and Mexican officials.

In recent years some borderlands specialists have characterized this and similar more short-lived Spanish efforts to turn equestrian Indians into farmers as failures. Taking Spanish policy as the starting point, they have concluded that since most Apaches, Navajos, and Comanches did not become self-sufficient farmers as authorities had hoped, these experiments could not be considered successes.[13] Even though the peace fell short of Spanish officials' expectations, however, Spaniards and a core group of Apaches benefited from the reservation system by adapting its provisions to suit their own interests. Taking advantage of the reduction in Apache raiding, Spaniards Hispanicized a select group of Apaches by employing, baptizing, adopting, and educating them. At the same time, laborers and entrepreneurs from interior New Spain moved north to the frontier, fueling demographic and economic expansion across the region. Meanwhile, the vast majority of reservation-dwelling Apaches used Spanish protection, rations, and gifts to rebuild their war-ravaged culture and reassert their independence.

Highlighting these patterns of amalgamation and differentiation provides a corrective to scholars of American Indian history who contend that cycles of violence and indigenous trauma are the most important trends in North America before U.S. expansion.[14] Violent warfare was the norm between Apaches and Spaniards for most of the eighteenth century and between Apaches and Mexicans from the 1830s onward. But even prior to 1786 Spaniards and Apaches sometimes negotiated peace accords, even if they tended to be temporary localized agreements.[15] What is significant about the period from 1786 to 1831 is the extent that Spaniards and reservation-dwelling Apaches across the colonial Southwest worked together to reduce reciprocal treachery and violence and to overcome deep-seated mutual distrust, even though those practices never entirely disappeared.[16]

The Chiricahuas who negotiated peace at the garrisoned Ópata pueblo of Bacoachi provide a good case in point. Although inadequate rations and attacks from independent kinsmen influenced some of the Indians to return to *Apachería* prior to 1790, at least nineteen families remained there continuously from December 1786 onward, and an average of sixty families received weekly rations there through January 1790.[17] Looking back on the Chiricahua experience at Bacoachi from the fall of 1786 to the spring of 1789, Commander-in-Chief Ugarte suggested that a small degree of Hispanicization had already occurred. At first the *Chiricahuas de paz* camped a league outside of Bacoachi and entered it daily; then they settled on a mountaintop on the outskirts of the town; and, finally, they lived in houses inside the town. "Some families," Ugarte noted, "work hard at sowing small plots of land."[18] Bacoachi, then, was the most immediate successful precedent for the developing larger system of reservations, a point numerous scholars have overlooked.

EVEN though most peaceful Apaches never farmed, hundreds of Apaches and redeemed captives of Christian parents served Spanish interests as scouts, interpreters, and auxiliaries, and a handful of these allies and an untold number of Apache children became productive laborers in Spanish society. Three beneficial results of the Apache peace from a Spanish perspective, then, were Hispanicization, demographic expansion, and economic growth.

Spanish documents reveal that at least some of the "Apache" men who agreed to serve as scouts, interpreters, and auxiliaries were former captive Spaniards who voluntarily surrendered to Spanish troops in the field in an effort to avoid being shipped southward to Mexico City or Havana as "hostiles." An Agua Verde soldier named Joaquín Gutiérrez, for instance, was captured by the Mescaleros in the Santa Rosa Valley when he was six or seven years old, and he spent roughly twelve years in captivity before escaping from them in 1779. He then agreed to employ his language skills and geographical knowledge as an interpreter and scout for Governor Juan de Ugalde in Coahuila and loyally served his interests for more than a decade.[19]

Apache women also offered to serve as scouts for Spaniards and their Indian allies.[20] Some of these women were daughters of prominent chiefs and others, like the men, were former captive Spaniards. Proving just as resourceful as their male counterparts, female scouts not only revealed the locations of enemy camps but also described the military strength of enemy *rancherías* to Spanish officers and informed them of Apache movements, thus directly influencing Spanish military strategy in the field.[21]

Spaniards rewarded those redeemed captive men who served most effectively as scouts and auxiliaries, such as the Sonoran-born ex-Apache captive José María González, by making them paid presidial soldiers. After González killed several independent Apache men in battle, Commander-in-Chief Ugarte rewarded González for his "excellent courage" by making him a salaried soldier in the Bacoachi company of Ópatas.[22] At the same time, Chiricahuas continued to respect González because he understood them and knew their territory. Within a year, González had risen to the rank of ensign and had led a group of fifteen to twenty Chiricahua scouts who punished independent Apache bands with increasing efficiency.[23] Military service was one of the most valuable assets that captive men offered Spaniards in the *establecimiento* system. At the same time captives themselves benefited from their rise in social status.

The most Hispanicized Apaches at peace were not all necessarily captives, however. The most favored Apaches, such as the Chiricahua chief El Compá, were not only excellent soldiers but also savvy politicians. Like many other Apache scouts, El Compá began serving Spanish interests after voluntarily surrendering to Spanish troops in 1788 so that he could be reunited with one of his wives and his children, whom Spaniards had captured and held as a bargaining chip. He and his family settled first at Bacoachi and then moved to Janos in 1790, where some of them would remain for more than thirty years.[24] Prior to dying from natural causes at age fifty-two in July 1794, the Chiricahua chief was the most loyal and trusted Apache scout, informant, and cultural broker on any reservation. He launched repeated military campaigns into *Apachería* with Spanish troops and independently with Chiricahua auxiliaries, and he used his diplomatic prowess in peace proceedings with independent Chiricahua chiefs to bolster the numbers of peaceful Apaches in Nueva Vizcaya and Sonora.[25] For such efforts, Spaniards rewarded El Compá and several of the most loyal first-generation, peaceful Apache headmen with adobe homes outside of the presidio.[26] In addition, in August 1791 Lieutenant Colonel Antonio Cordero increased El Compá's political authority by naming him "principal chief of the Apaches at Peace" at Janos and further distinguished him by calling him *El Capitán* Compá in contrast to other Apache headmen who were merely *capitancillos* (chiefs).[27] In exchange for his continued loyal service, Spaniards offered him horses, clothing, playing cards, liquor, cows for stock raising, and additional daily rations of half a sheep for his three wives. Perhaps most significantly of all, by June 1793 El Compá's Chiricahua band moved inside the walls of the Janos presidio: this was the only Apache band known to have done so after 1786.²⁸

El Compá's two sons, Juan Diego (Nayulchi) and Juan José, who lived at Janos for decades, offer further evidence of Hispanicization and accommodation. Juan Diego, who was twenty-two years old and married when his father died in 1794, took over his father's band and continued to live inside the presidio. Meanwhile, in the same year El Compá's seven-year-old son Juan José began attending the presidio school for sons of Spanish soldiers, the only Apache known to have done so. By the early nineteenth century both Compá brothers were fluent in Spanish and Juan José was also fully literate. In the summer of 1804 Commander-in-Chief Nemesio Salcedo even issued him a one-peso reward for having the best handwriting at the presidio school and expressed interest in having Juan José serve Spanish interests as a scribe. Because of their language skills and demonstrated loyalty, the Compá brothers, like their father, often served unofficially as interpreters, spies, and cultural brokers between Apaches and Spaniards, which further distinguished them from their kinsmen. As a result, some independent Apaches distrusted these peaceful Apaches and may have even questioned their Athapaskan identity. Nevertheless, Spaniards and Mexicans referred to the Compás as Apaches at the time, and in their twentieth-century interviews with Eve Ball, Chiricahua Apaches did as well.²⁹

Apache baptisms, while infrequent, demonstrate that a small group of Apaches and frontier Spaniards adapted and reached an accommodation in the 1790s. In May 1792, Commander-in-Chief Nava ordered that the Janos chaplain Francisco Atanasio Domínguez cease baptizing Apache children for the sole purpose of "pleasing their parents" because of the "risk of profaning the sacraments."³⁰ The only exceptions were Apache children who voluntarily accepted Catholicism and whose parents permitted them to be "reared and educated" among the Spaniards.³¹ Domínguez, however, continued to defy the orders of his superior officers by complying with the requests of numerous favored Apache chiefs to baptize their *parbulos* (young children) without Captain Manuel de Casanova's knowledge.³²

In spite of the general policy discouraging baptism, then, post chaplains baptized the most favored Apache men on a discretionary basis and, most commonly, Apache children.³³ One anthropologist has pointed out that the number of recorded Apache baptisms at Janos is so small that Apache Christianization can only be considered on an individual basis.³⁴ Even so, it still seems worth examining the motives behind the practice and pointing out that some Apaches did become Catholic, Spanish-speaking subjects of the Crown after all.

A predominant trend, especially in the late 1780s, was that Apaches sought baptism when suffering from illness. A Franciscan friar, Antonio Rafael Benites, the *ministro doctrinero* at the mission of San Miguel de Bacoachi, baptized six Apaches who were "feeling ill" and "at risk" (three women, a young girl, and a young boy) from the fall of 1785 through the winter of 1787, and all of them died.[35] What did Apaches gain from seeking baptism on the verge of death? It may have been an attempt to acquire supernatural healing power to fight off illness, which Apaches believed could be caused by witchcraft, an angry god, or an offended force of nature. In contrast to the Algonquian-speaking Montagnais who perceived French Jesuit priests as shamans with the power to cure them, young Apache warriors preferred to harness the power of God and the Christian saints themselves to enhance their spiritual and political prestige among their kinsmen.[36]

In addition to seeking baptism as a last resort, small numbers of Apache parents asked for their healthy children to be baptized at the *establecimientos*, and some of them were incorporated into Spanish frontier society as mission Indians or as adopted children in Spanish households.[37] At Janos eleven of the fifteen recorded Apaches baptized from 1799 to 1802 were babies and young children that reservation-dwelling Apache parents "voluntarily" sold to Spanish military and civilian families in exchange for a horse, a calf, a scarf and a blanket, or a small sum of four to ten pesos. The other four were young girls between the ages of four and seven whom Spaniards captured on military campaigns in *Apachería*. In this situation, the Spanish post commander either adopted the orphaned girls himself or gifted or sold them to Spanish officers. After Domínguez baptized the children, he gave them Christian names, usually José and María, and he advised the godparents of their obligation to raise and educate their Apache children as Catholics. Not surprisingly, the majority of Spanish godfathers (ten of fifteen, or two-thirds) were enlisted and retired officers and soldiers. The remaining third consisted of Spanish settlers who were on good terms with the post commander.[38] The fates of these fifteen Apache adoptees are unknown. Presumably, if they did not die prematurely from disease, the boys became presidial soldiers and the girls became servants in their godparents' households.

Not all Apaches whom Spaniards attempted to incorporate into the workforce had the privilege of remaining on the frontier. In the 1790s

Spanish soldiers routinely extradited the most bellicose and recalcitrant Apache male and female *prisioneros* (prisoners) southward to Mexico City and Cuba.[39] In October 1789, the second Conde de Revillagigedo, who succeeded Manuel Antonio Flores as viceroy, ordered all prisoners, from Indians to vagabonds, including those already in Mexico City, to be sent to Veracruz and shipped to Havana for forced labor.[40] Commander-in-Chief Nava's frontier Apache policy, however, only called for "childless adult women and the adult males" to be removed from the frontier because of their tendency "to flee," and evidence indicates that he did his best to follow this in practice.[41] When an Apache *collera* (chain gang) of prisoners arrived in Chihuahua from San Elizario (along the Rio Grande south of El Paso) in August 1794, for example, Nava fulfilled Casanova's request that the Apache woman Can-slude and her three sons be separated and returned to Janos to be reunited with her sister María, the widow of the deceased chief El Compá.[42]

A small number of exiled Apache women worked as laborers in Spanish households and businesses from Chihuahua to Mexico City, and some of the men worked on fortifications in Havana, Cuba, alongside Spanish convicts. The vast majority of Apache prisoners, however, either escaped and fled back to *Apachería* or died from malnutrition, fatigue, and disease and thus remained unincorporated into Spanish society. Based on my own calculations, Spaniards exiled at least 979 Apache men, women, and children to interior Mexico and Havana from 1739 to 1805. After peaking at 300 in 1788, the number of Apache prisoners dropped to between fifty and one hundred as the reservation system solidified in the 1790s. Of the 371 who are identifiable by age, more than 80 percent were adults. Of the 214 adults identifiable by gender, 67 percent were women. Of the 247 whose fate is identifiable, 59 percent escaped and returned to *Apachería*, 23 percent remained in interior Mexico and Cuba, and 17 percent either died en route or soon after arrival. Of the 23 percent who remained in the interior, 81 percent worked in Mexico City or Havana and 19 percent were distributed in private homes north of Mexico City.[43]

Were any of these Apaches slaves? Although Spanish officers sometimes referred to captured Apaches as *piezas* (slaves), given their wide range of fates they are better understood as war captives or prisoners until they actually began forced labor.[44] Just like so-called *genízaros* in New Mexico, a minority of removed Apache women did work as slaves in Spanish households and businesses such as *obrajes* (textile workshops) from Chihuahua to Mexico City, and a minority of the men worked as criminalized slaves on fortifications in Havana.[45]

As a matter of policy, Spaniards tried to divorce the forced removal and enslavement of "hostile" Apaches from the admittance of "peaceful" Apaches at presidios. According to Cordero, the reservation system "does not aspire to the destruction or slavery" of the Apaches, but instead "it seeks their happiness by the most efficacious means."[46] In practice, however, peaceful and exiled Apaches were members of the same Apache groups, *rancherías*, and families, and they shared common interests. One of the most important reasons that independent Apaches chose to resettle in *establecimientos* was to recover their captured kinsmen whom Spanish soldiers and their Indian allies had captured on military campaigns. At the same time, a "peaceful" Apache who committed a serious crime such as murder could find himself quickly extradited to Mexico City, as was the case when the Chiricahua chief Tidaya turned himself in at Janos after killing a *vecino* in 1793. Yet he was lucky enough to return two years later.[47]

Despite the high number of Apache fatalities and escapes, Spaniards still garnered clear-cut benefits from the *establecimiento* system, although many were unintended. At its height in the early 1790s, approximately 2,000 Apaches resided on eight reservations across the frontiers of Nueva Vizcaya, New Mexico, and Sonora, with 782 Chiricahuas at Janos alone in 1795 (see Figure 6.1).[48] As a result, the Crown spent increasing amounts on rations and gifts in these years. Annual expenditures at Janos rose from 1,100 pesos between 1787 and 1790 to 13,011 pesos in 1796, which comprised about a quarter of the presidio's annual budget.[49] In spite of these high costs, the experiment clearly paid off for Spaniards economically. The system was still much cheaper than the combined cost of waging an all-out war and paying for lost resources from retaliatory raids.

Another way that the reservations benefited Spaniards is that they gave the most competent post commanders, whether Spanish- or American-born, the opportunity to showcase their administrative skills as higher officials. The Presidio del Norte commander Manuel Muñoz served as the governor of Texas from 1790 to 1798 and the Fronteras commander Antonio Narbona, a native of Mobile, Alabama, was promoted to Commander of Arms of Sonora and then served as governor of New Mexico from 1825 to 1827. Most notable of all, the Janos commander Antonio Cordero served as governor of Coahuila from 1797 to 1817, including a three-year term as acting governor of Coahuila y Texas from 1805 to 1808.

Cordero was subsequently appointed Commander-in-Chief of the Western Interior Provinces in 1822 and was ultimately promoted to field marshal general, a position he held until his death in Durango, Colorado, in the spring of 1823.[50]

More importantly, as a result of the overall reduction in raiding and warfare, New Spain's northwestern frontier began to expand economically. Farming, mining, church building, and especially ranching all flourished in Sonora in the mid-1790s.[51] The Franciscans, who criticized the army's reservation system because they thought they could do a better job themselves, benefited from the completion of beautiful missions at Tumacácori and San Xavier del Bac at Tucson, and Spanish-language oral tradition and a single Spanish document indicate that Apaches helped perform the work.[52] Spanish and Mexican *rancheros* pushed into the San Pedro, Sonoita, and Santa Cruz valleys into the 1820s, reoccupying many of the same sites where missionaries had previously established *visitas* and missions in the eighteenth century before surrendering them to the Apaches. This sustained growth demonstrates that Apache raiding from Janos to Tucson did not pick up immediately with the onset of the war for Mexican Independence in the 1810s, as some scholars have mistakenly assumed.[53] *Rancheros* would not have chosen to move their herds northward into Apache territory, if they expected to be attacked by them.[54]

As ranchers moved northward from Sonora, so did miners from Nueva Vizcaya. In 1803 and 1804 Spaniards founded the copper-mining community of Santa Rita del Cobre (fifteen miles east of today's Silver City, New Mexico) and began extracting copper from the surrounding Santa Rita Mountains, which lay just south of the Mogollon range in *Apachería*. Operations lasted until 1838. Just as with the Chichimecas at Zacatecas two centuries earlier, folk history holds that Apaches discovered the deposits. Whatever the case, Spanish documents tell us that the highly literate Chiricahua Juan Diego Compá wrote a petition in Spanish asking permission to explore for gold and copper ore along the San Francisco River, which lay west of Santa Rita del Cobre in Gila Apache (Mogollon) territory. The mining settlements of Corralitos and El Barranco followed in the 1830s, and Mexicans even began extracting salt from a mine in the Mogollon Mountains.[55] While one might imagine that the Mogollon band of Chiricahuas would have immediately responded to this encroachment with intensified raiding and warfare, they instead ratified a peace agreement with

Spanish troops in 1816, and a portion of their tribe opted to receive weekly rations at Janos from 1818 until at least 1822.[56]

With the increased economic opportunity on a less violent frontier came demographic expansion. From 1800 to 1830 northern New Spain's population grew at three times the rate as the rest of New Spain.[57] At Janos this same pattern of growth is evident from 1792 until at least 1822, when the Hispanic population more than tripled. Further evidence of stable relations between soldiers, settlers, and the Apaches at peace there is that census takers included the Apaches in the overall numbers in four consecutive censuses from 1812 to 1822.[58]

By adopting a wider geographical lens, we can connect the economic benefits of the Apache peace in Sonora and Nueva Vizcaya with that of the Comanche and Navajo alliance in New Mexico. One scholar has emphasized the importance of the Comanche alliance in fueling New Mexico's economic expansion. Although the Comanche peace did play a significant role, without securing simultaneous peace agreements with Navajos and Apaches, Athapaskan raiders would have continued to disrupt regional trade and little economic growth would have been possible. Although the Comanche peace enabled *vecinos* to apply for land grants and to found new villages on the outskirts of Taos, Abiquíu, and the Mora Valley, the expansion south and west of Albuquerque, including Sabinal, stemmed directly from Apache peace accords.[59]

Finally, Tucson itself merits special attention because of its sustained growth during and after Mexican Independence. Although most reservations either destabilized or continued to function at a low level of effectiveness during the transition from Spanish to Mexican rule, the Tucson reservation appeared to grow stronger. Peaceful Apaches there continued to serve royalist forces loyally during the Hidalgo revolt and helped ease the impact of troop depletion in Sonora. Moreover, in 1819 the program expanded when Chief Chilitipagé and 236 Western Apaches from the Pinal band settled at Tucson and apparently managed to coexist peaceably with the Arivaipas already in residence. Although the reservation's numbers were reduced during a general Apache rebellion from 1832 to 1834, by 1835 the numbers had rebounded. Chief Antuna remained in residence with 488 Apache men, women, and children, all of whom received weekly rations of wheat.[60] Apache bands continued to reside at Tucson and Tubac through the 1840s, despite increased raiding from independent Apaches. Some of those still at Tucson in the 1860s become scouts at Fort Goodwin, where they intermarried with White Mountain Apache women on an American-run reservation.[61]

THE trends of Hispanicization and Christianization described so far were pronounced only among a minority of Apaches during this time period. Although scholars in multiple disciplines have defined acculturation as a unidirectional linear process in which a colonized culture adopts the traits of the colonizer, it is in fact a dynamic reciprocal process.[62] Apaches and Spaniards both adapted and modified their cultures as they came into contact with one another, demonstrating processes of mutual adaptation and acculturation, and the overall direction of culture change was never fixed. Most independent Apaches had only limited contact with Spaniards, and most *Apaches de paz* continued to subsist on their own procured fruits, nuts, and game, while receiving weekly rations of Spanish corn, meat, and tobacco simply as dietary supplements. In general, supposedly "peaceful" Apaches typically exhibited mixed loyalties, sometimes serving Spanish interests and at other times subverting them.[63]

Reservation-dwelling headmen and interpreters frequently started rumors. Sometimes they tried to incite their people to revolt by claiming that the Spaniards wanted to kill all of the Apaches.[64] Most often, however, they reversed the tactic and warned of pending revolts or attacks from their kinsmen in order to strike fear in the hearts of Spanish troops and frontier settlers.[65] Even Juan Diego Compá, despite living inside the Janos presidio with his people, spread so many unsettling rumors at Janos that Commander-in-Chief Salcedo tried to move him permanently to another reservation in 1803.[66] Although his motives are unclear, he may have been voicing his displeasure at not being named principal chief like his father.

Operating out of their bases at *establecimientos*, the most influential peaceful Apache leaders served their people's interest by negotiating for the release of Apache war captives. Sometimes they even traveled to Spanish provincial capitals to meet with Spanish officials. In 1790 El Compá met with Commander-in-Chief Nava in Chihuahua and convinced him to keep several Apache relatives from being shipped to Mexico City.[67] Similarly, in 1819, after making peace at Tucson, the Western Apache chief Chilitipagé traveled to Arizpe and successfully negotiated the release of an Apache woman and a boy imprisoned at Fronteras.[68] Spaniards did not return every prisoner the Apaches requested. When officers refused, peaceful Apache leaders used several ways to express their displeasure and convince Spaniards to change their minds, including refusing to serve as scouts or deserting their reservation.[69] At the same time, reservation-dwelling Apaches were under no obligation to give up their most acculturated "Christian captives ... who were raised in their way and who remain with them as Apaches."[70] By recovering their incarcerated relatives and retaining their most indoctrinated captives, Apaches reunited their families and began rebuilding their population at the *establecimientos*.

Apaches at peace also used Spanish rations and gifts for their own purposes. In the early 1790s Spanish officials gave Apaches livestock for breeding in an effort to reduce the costs of rations and promote self-sufficiency. But the Apaches simply consumed all of the animals.[71] Year after year peaceful Apaches confounded Spanish officials by devouring their entire weekly food rations on the first day of issue, or selling, trading, or gambling their food rations and clothing away to Spanish settlers.[72] Such allegedly gluttonous behavior prompted numerous Spanish priests and military officers to question whether they could ever transform seminomadic Apaches into sedentary Spaniards.[73]

Apaches, however, had good reasons for butchering and eating breeding animals quickly. Because of droughts, floods, and Indian raids, Spanish mule trains did not always arrive on schedule with adequate rations. Apache men attempted to compensate for the shortage and demonstrate their anger by eating whatever was available, whether breeding animals or in some cases even soldiers' own horses.[74] Moreover, just as when hunting deer and buffalo in *Apachería*, headmen sought to enhance their political status by slaughtering animals on the spot and redistributing meat among as many of their kinsmen as possible. When the often volatile Mimbreño chief Yagonxli (Ojos Colorados) repeatedly complained that he was not receiving enough rations at Janos because Spanish officers only issued rations to his immediate family members, he spoke the truth.[75]

In spite of some Apaches' legitimate need for more rations, their overall tendency to demand a wider range of rations and gifts than delineated in Spanish policy quickly drove up the costs of the system. At Janos in 1795 these not only included soldiers' abandoned mounts but also "deer hides, money, sheep, bull-hide shields, [and] corn cobs."[76] Clearly, Spanish officials' fanciful hope that post commanders could economize by giving Apaches gifts "of little value" that were "highly esteemed" was not coming to fruition.[77] Instead, Apaches were pressuring Spaniards into giving them items that they could actually use, while retaining their cultural identity. Apaches preferred horse meat to beef, and acquiring tanned deer hides saved them precious time and labor and eliminated the risk of off-reservation attacks from their enemies.[78]

Another way that Apaches adapted to Spanish reservations was by allegedly adopting and building on the vices of frontier Spaniards and mission Indians. One of the best examples of this is gambling. Rather than becoming sedentary agriculturalists or pious Catholics, Chiricahuas at Bacoachi preferred to play cards with "Christians," which included both Spanish settlers and Ópata mission Indians.[79] They made their own painted-leather card decks and developed their own card games, which they incorporated into their already large repertoire of games of chance.[80] Another favorite Apache pastime was betting on foot racing. When the peaceful Apaches repeatedly outpaced Tucson settlers in an off-duty contest in 1825, Spanish residents complained that the Apaches had "fixed" the races and demanded the return of their bets.[81] Other "Spanish" vices Apaches reportedly adopted included dancing, swearing, and concubinage. According to one Franciscan friar, Apaches exhibited all three of these evils at frequent fandangos in Bacoachi "in which a thousand improprieties are sung and the most evil movements are made."[82] From a Franciscan perspective, then, Spanish subjects simply corrupted Apaches rather than helping them to Hispanicize in any morally acceptable way. But in reality this may have been a case of reciprocal acculturation—of Spaniards Apacheanizing (adopting Apache cultural traits). Gambling, especially horse racing, was a serious Apache enterprise, dancing held spiritual significance, and acquiring more than one wife was a way for Apache men to raise their social rank.[83]

Not surprisingly, the most important way in which Apaches adapted to living on reservations was by moving off of them. Like missions, close quarters on reservations fostered the transmission of infectious disease, and, whenever an epidemic struck, Apaches tried to ensure their survival by moving to other reservations or back to *Apachería* to avoid contracting it. In the spring of 1801, for example, Juan Diego and thirty-six kinsmen moved from Janos to Fronteras in Sonora because of a smallpox outbreak. Others went to Bavispe or returned to *Apachería*. A subsequent smallpox outbreak in 1816 and a measles outbreak in 1826 caused further "restlessness" among Apaches.[84]

At other times peaceful Apaches returned to their homeland because of political instability. Sometimes they did this peaceably, such as in August

1794 at Janos. Within three weeks of El Compá's death, 40 percent of the nearly five hundred peaceful Apaches left the presidio. Although one scholar has suggested that the Apaches may have been following their custom of abandoning a camp after a kinsman's death, the fact that El Compá's entire family and band remained in residence inside the presidio points against that interpretation.[85] What more likely happened, as one of El Compá's wives, María, personally attested was that new Apache leaders vying for influence tried to incite a general rebellion among the *Apaches de paz* in the midst of the power vacuum.[86]

In addition to internal political instability, peaceful Apaches also left the presidios because of political disagreements with independent Apache groups. *Nantan* (chief) Chiganstegé's independent Chiricahuas killed Spaniards' imposed "peaceful" Apache Chief Isosé at Bacoachi in February 1788. Four years later, Gila Apache bands launched a second attack in the same month, which prompted nearly 90 percent of the five hundred peaceful Apaches to leave the reservation.[87]

Apaches sometimes deserted their reservations to seek revenge against Spanish troops for launching punitive expeditions into *Apachería*. In March 1794, the Mescaleros left San Elizario after Spanish troops had launched several campaigns against independent Mescaleros. When a Spanish patrol tried to punish them for their insubordination, the once peaceful Mescaleros ambushed the Spaniards in the Organ Mountains, killing fourteen soldiers and settlers, including the post commander Manuel Vidal de Lorca.[88] The following July, the Mescaleros at El Paso del Norte followed suit, killing fifty-seven Spanish soldiers and three officials in two days with only twenty-one losses of their own.[89]

In the aftermath of this revolt, the former *Mescaleros de paz* reunited with their kinsmen and formed an alliance with independent Mimbreño and Gileño Chiricahua bands. Such coordinated defense efforts reveal that distinct Apache tribes were fully capable of working together and posed a significant obstacle to Spanish troops and their Indian allies, who continued to wage war against Mescaleros until at least 1799.[90] This prolonged conflict indicates that the Spanish-Mescalero peace was unstable long before Mexican Independence. The Mescaleros, it seems, were the first pacified Apache group to permanently abandon a reservation and reassert their cultural independence.

Most frequently, Apaches moved because of shortages of rations. From the reservation system's inception, Apaches had convinced Spanish officers to let them leave the presidios to hunt when rations were in short supply.[91] As a means of distinguishing these Apaches on furlough from their independent kinsmen, post commanders issued passports to Apaches to hunt for ten to twenty days in their own territory. As a Franciscan friar, Antonio Barbastro, reported in 1795, passports were "the main stumbling block" to a stable peace with the Apaches because they permitted supposedly loyal *Apaches de paz* "to roam about and steal under the pretext of going hunting."[92] Thus, Mescaleros at peace in eastern Nueva Vizcaya often raided for horses in Coahuila, and Chiricahuas at peace in western Nueva Vizcaya did the same in Sonora, often with their relatives on other reservations or with independent kinsmen. If a Spanish or Mexican patrol confronted them, the Apaches simply showed the soldiers their passports, blamed the raids on independent Apaches, and gambled that they would be left alone. Once they had a sizeable number of Spanish horses, peaceful Apaches either traded them to independent Apaches or back to Spanish settlers near their reservation.[93] Most frontier Spaniards were willing to tolerate such small-scale raids and illicit exchanges in the 1790s. The system began to rupture, however, in the 1810s as Spaniards diverted troops and money from the frontier during the war for Mexican Independence. It would deteriorate further when Mexican officials tried to cut costs by eliminating meat rations in 1822 and rations *in absentia* in 1824 and Apaches responded by raising the frequency and intensity of their raids.[94]

HISPANIC economic growth and demographic expansion in these years were real. They were uneven processes, however, and need to be understood in the context of Comanche southward expansion and Spain's own monetary and supply problems. Comanches' ongoing wars with Mescaleros and Lipanes meant that the peace on the southern Plains periphery of eastern Nueva Vizcaya and Coahuila was less enduring than in western Nueva Vizcaya and Sonora, and the demographic and economic benefits were less pronounced.[95] At the same time Spain's war with France from 1793 to 1795 meant that the Spanish Crown diverted money and troops from the Apache frontier. As a result, Spanish officials were left in the unenviable position of reducing rations to peaceful Apaches and asking them to return to their homeland just as the program was stabilizing. Spanish officers hoped that Apaches would remain at peace but had little to offer in exchange. Shortages of rations and troops seem to have influenced the Chiricahuas and Mescaleros to desert Sabinal in 1794, and this may have helped precipitate three Mescalero revolts at El Paso, San Elizario, and Presidio del Norte from 1794 to 1795.[96] These same problems also likely prompted close to 70 percent of the Chiricahuas to leave Janos in mid-1796. Although some of them came back, the numbers at Janos never again approached the more than eight hundred that lived near the presidio in 1795. Instead, Janos averaged around 234 individuals for the next three decades.[97]

Without question, in practice the *Apaches de paz* program turned out to be far more complicated and volatile than Spanish policy makers envisioned at the outset. These reservations had costs for both sides. The heightened violence from independent Apaches and Spanish troops between 1786 and 1790 nearly prevented the system from being fully implemented. Even after its implementation, they were expensive to run and were incubators for disease; few Apaches ever farmed or even became sedentary Spaniards. From an Apache perspective, as long as Spaniards failed to distinguish between neutral and hostile Apaches in *Apachería* and continued to ship their men and women southward, this was not peace at all. Indeed, the vast majority of Apaches who settled at Spanish reservations did so only to fulfill temporary needs. Demonstrating minimal signs of Hispanicization, Christianization, and incorporation, they instead found ways to creatively adapt to maintain their cultural independence and retain dominion over the full extent of their territory.

This did not mean the system failed, however. After 1790 the number of extraditions declined, and by 1800 the military attacks became more localized and infrequent. This more controlled violence enabled a core group of Apaches and Hispanics, including Chief Volante's Mescaleros and Spanish troops at Presidio del Norte, to work together to remake frontier colonial society in the Southwestern borderlands after 1790. When Chief Volante's Mescaleros returned to Presidio del Norte with their Comanche captives, the post commander Domingo Diaz nearly destroyed their relationship by callously proposing to invite the Comanches to conduct a revenge raid on the *Mescaleros de paz* in order to maintain the Spanish-Comanche alliance. But cooler heads prevailed. Commander-in-Chief Nava vetoed Diaz's suggestion and restored twelve Spanish and Mescalero-held Comanche captives, including Chief Ecueracapa's daughter, to the Comanches. At the same time the Mescaleros remained on their reservation, retaining a Comanche woman and several babies to raise as Apaches.[98]

What, then, is the legacy of the *establecimientos*? Given the prolonged cycle of reciprocal violence that erupted after 1831, it is tempting to conclude that the reciprocal benefits that Spaniards and Apaches had once achieved through peaceful exchange and political negotiation were a forgotten memory. True enough, the vast majority of Mexicans and Apaches chose war over peace in this period and forgot the lessons they had previously learned from one another. Vestiges of that era still remained, however. Mexican and American officials in the 1840s and 1850s recognized Chiricahua bands formerly at peace at Janos and Carrizal by calling them Janeros and Carrizaleños in their reports.[99] In addition, some Apaches opted to serve Mexican interests as scouts from Janos to Tucson, as they had since Spanish times and they would do again for Anglo-Americans in the 1880s. One of the most notable of these scouts, Gervacio Compá, served at Janos in the 1850s and may have been Juan José Compá's son.[100] Finally, a minority of Mexican officers did employ Spanish diplomatic measures, including holding Apache prisoners as bargaining chips, issuing rations, and even reserving specific tracts of land, as a means of convincing war-weary Apache groups to make peace agreements at the local level.[101] Echoing the sound logic of Spanish Viceroy Gálvez, Chihuahua's governor, Francisco García Conde, believed that even if a peace treaty produced a mere "truce" it was still worth it because it reduced hostilities, was far cheaper than war, and allowed Mexicans and Apaches to make friendships and better understand each other. "Exterminating their race," García Conde wrote, "is neither convenient, nor just, nor possible."[102]

Perhaps the most important and least-recognized legacy of the *establecimientos* is that they helped familiarize Apaches with a system that was remarkably similar to the reservations the U.S. military established for Apaches at posts in New Mexico in the 1850s.[103] Specialists have long known of the peaceful relations between Apaches and Anglo-Americans in the decades preceding the discovery of gold at Pinos Altos, New Mexico, in 1860.[104] But recognizing that the first group of Apaches who agreed to settle on U.S.-run reservations were Mimbreños or eastern Chiricahuas who had previously resided on Hispanic reservations helps us better understand the political dynamics of this period from a Native perspective and to connect the histories of the Indian, Hispanic, and American Southwest.[105]

When a U.S. Indian agent, Michael Steck, met with Mangas Coloradas (Red Sleeves) and other Chiricahua Apache leaders at the Apache agency near Fort Thorn in the fall of 1854, the peace terms Steck offered them must have seemed strangely familiar. Much like Spaniards, Steck wanted to turn Apache raiders into farmers and issue their families monthly rations of corn, mutton, and beef. Just as they had with Spaniards and Mexicans, the Chiricahuas helped shape the terms of peace. Whenever possible, Chiricahuas employed male and female interpreters who were fluent in Spanish. In this case, two Mimbreño women, Monica and Refugia, participated in the negotiations, and Monica was fully literate in Spanish, having learned to read and write from Catholic nuns.[106] Although Congress never ratified the treaty, Mimbreños and Americans still reached an accommodation at the local level that reflected both of their interests.

The principal achievement of the Apaches who made peace at Fort Thorn was farming, but historians have not properly understood it. Mimbreño families, including that of Mangas Coloradas and numerous others who had previously settled at the *establecimientos*, raised hundreds of acres of corn along the Mimbres and Gila rivers in 1855–1856 and 1858–1859.[107] If we recognize that the Apaches were doing this in their own territory, where they had farmed for centuries prior to monthly coordinated military offensives by Spaniards, this accomplishment looks much more like a "return to normalcy" than a "rise of civilization." Apaches did not need Steck or U.S. soldiers to teach them how to farm, but they did appreciate the protection that Americans offered them from Mexican troops and scalp hunters.

Accommodation, then, not just conflict, characterized Apache relations with Anglo-Americans during these years. Relying on their previous experience at the *establecimientos* and their long-established ability to work peace terms in their favor, Apaches once again raided for Mexican horses and livestock, while unseasoned troops naively tried to teach them how to farm in the desert.

CHAPTER 7

The Forced Transfer of Indians in Nueva Vizcaya and Sinaloa: A Hispanic Method of Colonization

CHANTAL CRAMAUSSEL

In the last two decades a great deal of research has been done in Mexico on the history of northern New Spain.[1] This flourishing period opened different perspectives from the ones generated by scholars of American borderlands studies, where missions, presidios, and mines as separate institutions dominated the historiography. New books published in Mexico gave birth to a more integral research. Northern New Spain became less exceptional and less "peripheral" than it appeared in former works. Imperial institutions and social Spanish life did not differ much from those farther south. Indians took a broader importance in colonial enclaves, which are no longer considered as mainly settled by Europeans and mixed-blood persons. The labor systems and the general interaction between conquerors and Indians must be considered in this perspective.

In the north of New Spain, there was no "frontier" similar to that conceptualized in the nineteenth-century American West. Colonial borderlands were made out of scattered settlements in a huge territory mainly controlled by unsubmitted Indians. In the case of the mining centers, the maintenance and growth of the Spanish enclaves depended on Indian labor and Indian crops. Both societies negotiated their mutual relations but the dependence of Spaniards on Indian resources generated continuous violence that increased during droughts and epidemics. Spaniards took advantage of these disasters and expanded as local societies became weaker.[2] The presence of enough peaceful Indians was surely more important than silver as many permanent agricultural settlements like Parras, Saltillo, Valle de San Bartolomé, or Durango in Nueva Vizcaya show. The supply of the Indian labor force made the difference but it was not a free labor system as is usually adduced.[3]

THE colonization of Nueva Vizcaya (nowadays north-central Mexico, containing the states of Chihuahua, Durango, and southwestern Coahuila) and northwestern New Spain (which included the provinces of Sinaloa, Sonora, and California)[4] began in the sixteenth century and reached its peak with the discovery of the mines in Chihuahua two centuries later. The history of this region is similar to the colonial past of New Mexico, which goes back to the beginning of the seventeenth century. Both Spanish jurisdictions were made up of Spanish enclaves located in the middle of unconquered territories. Land was plentiful but the Spaniards lacked Indian workers and could not completely utilize the large estates that they officially owned. The numerous and industrious Natives generated the wealth of New Mexico but it took a long time until Indian or mixed-blood servants raised in the colonial society were numerous enough to guarantee food and labor supplies for the Spanish haciendas. In any case, this process was quicker in New Mexico where no mining center had been discovered. In Nueva Vizcaya, on the contrary, the density of the Indian population was lower; violence to obtain food and workers from missions and military raids on Indian villages became frequent during mining booms. Spaniards used all legal means in order to get food and labor. In the eighteenth century the stress was put on already-Christianized mission Indians, although most of them lived far away from the haciendas where they were required. The ravages caused by expeditions to round up Indian workers were so harsh that entire villages were soon abandoned.

Many scholars have compared Spanish colonization in northern New Spain—the borderlands of the northern hemisphere—with the European invasion of central Argentina, where most of the Indians were not sedentary. But in fact the process was completely different in Buenos Aires and the Pampas, because Spanish conquerors were even fewer, they settled only on the coast, and no silver strike occurred. Local Indian communities had genuine chieftains, a social feature that did not exist even among the agricultural societies of northwest New Spain, and they were divided in numerous and politically independent villages. No treaty was signed in northern New Spain in the eighteenth century between Spaniards and Indians; when military fights there were finished, Spanish authorities forced every village to surrender, one by one. After the 1680 rebellion in New Mexico no further uprising was able to threaten Spanish colonization. On the northern borderlands, peace was always ephemeral and even at the end of the eighteenth century, outside the *establecimientos de paz*,[5] violence could arise at any time. As Matthew Babcock reports, between 1739 and 1805 one thousand "true" Apache enemies were exiled southward to New Spain and to Cuba, and the remaining tribes could not offer open resistance; instead a guerrilla war continued until the 1880s. Rebels killed many people in the countryside and haciendas sometimes disappeared during the conflicts, but the main colonial settlements asserted their positions. From an Indian perspective, former uprisings by the Tepehuanes, Tarahumaras, Mayos, Yaquis, and other Cahitan Indians had the same poor results. More and more Indians were reared in colonial society and incorporated into the haciendas while the indigenous populations in missions and outside of Spanish settlements was decreasing.

In any case, these general demographic trends must be reconsidered. As I will discuss, population studies based on parish records and censuses reveal that for non-Spaniards, the gaps between *calidades* (social status groups) were almost nonexistent in the eighteenth century. Indians could easily become mulattos or mestizos to take advantage of this change, from which other social groups also benefited. On the other hand, multiethnic families could be found everywhere in New Spain: between 20 and 60 percent of all married couples had children with different *calidades*, depending on their phenotype.[6] In northern New Spain these shifting categories have to be related to labor regimes, as will be explained in this essay.

In the immediate region north and east of Nueva Vizcaya, in the Great Basin and what is now western Texas, except for some precarious enclaves that survived to a large extent thanks to slaving raids,[7] the European conquest was very late. When thousands of Old World immigrants moved westward at the end of the eighteenth century they were eager for lands, but they did not need a Native workforce to build settlements. Instead of incorporating Indians as had occurred in Nueva Vizcaya and in the provinces of Sinaloa and Sonora, here they removed them from the best tillable lands and established themselves there, although indigenous agency was part of the process. There was a link between Apaches[8] in this region and population transfers farther south in Nueva Vizcaya when mounted Indians from the north crossed the Rio Grande to steal horses from colonial settlements. As Salvador Álvarez explains,[9] new Apache incursions from the north began at the end of the seventeenth century. In the south of New Mexico, there were no wild herds, and most horses and mules were branded because they had to be raised in haciendas near lakes or rivers. When nonsedentary Indians began to ride in Nueva Vizcaya, they also became dependent on appropriating horses from haciendas, and then a new cycle of violence began. Conflicts over horses were added to the continuous necessity for labor in Spanish settlements. The European colonizers took advantage of the situation to enslave as many Indians as they could, and the most reluctant ones were simply exterminated during wars *a sangre y fuego* (by blood and fire).[10] Although the population size of Apaches in Parral and Chihuahua was significant during specific periods, they were never numerous enough to satisfy Spanish labor needs. Many other Indian societies were involved in those transfers to the haciendas. In fact, the history of Indian transfers started at the beginning of the conquest in northern New Spain.

The best-known and well-documented transfer of a population is that of the Tlaxcaltecans, who migrated mostly to the northeast frontier at the end of the sixteenth century. We also know of Otomís, Tarascans, and "Mexicans" (Nahuatl-speaking groups) that also migrated as part of the whole enterprise that was the Spanish conquest of the north and the advancement of the colonial frontier. These population transfers from the center and western parts of the viceroyalty to the northern borderlands, though sanctioned by the Crown, soon ceased because of the demographic catastrophe of the sixteenth century, though this did not mean a complete interruption in the flow of Indians from the more populous areas of the viceroyalty toward the north. Once this flow from the south decreased, areas with a higher demographic density in the plains of the Pacific and the upper Rio Grande were the ones that supplied Indian labor for the Spanish haciendas in the more prosperous *reales de minas* (mining centers) of the region. During the seventeenth and eighteenth centuries, among the most important of these were El Rosario and Álamos in the northeast coastal region and Parral and Chihuahua in the north-central region.[11]

These four mining centers had in common the benefit of a continuous supply of Indians coming sometimes from very remote regions, as shown in the sacramental and marriage records of their parish archives. These parish books often list the origins of foreign Indians (*indios foráneos,* or Indians whose places of origin were not the areas around the *reales de minas*) in order to distinguish them from the mission Indians from surrounding areas. This sort of bookkeeping was important because parish priests imparted the sacraments to foreign Indians, and the owners of haciendas in which these Indians toiled paid the corresponding fees; it became the rule in the mining centers of northern New Spain that the diocesan clergy ministered to those Indians together with the rest of the servants. Meanwhile the local Indians, unless they had been reduced to personal service, were spiritually ministered to at no cost by Jesuit or Franciscan missionaries who received an annual royal stipend. Both diocesan and regular priests were very protective of their jurisdictions, so the documentation used had to be trustworthy.

San José del Parral (hereafter Parral) has been the subject of detailed studies that allow us to plot the evolution of the various labor systems under which the Indians of Nueva Vizcaya were exploited during the colonial era. In Nuestra Señora del Rosario (hereafter El Rosario), these systems were implemented during the seventeenth century and this implied a resettlement of Indians very far from their places of origin in order to force them to work in the haciendas of the colonizers. It is difficult to imagine that Spaniards appropriated the Native structure of seasonal migrations because these transfers were not voluntary and were circumscribed to Spanish jurisdictions, as I discuss later. When mineral ores were discovered in the district of Nuestra Señora de Álamos (hereafter Álamos) in 1683, the miners of El Rosario had to share with the new *real de minas* part of the workforce from Culiacán and Sinaloa that had been assigned to them decades earlier. The same thing happened in central Nueva Vizcaya with the *hacendados* and miners of Parral, who had to accept the fact that the flow of Indian labor had to move north, toward the Chuviscar Basin, where several *reales* emerged to give birth to the mining district of Villa de San Felipe El Real de Chihuahua (hereafter Chihuahua) at the start of the eighteenth century.

Because Indians were scarce, they had to be employed in the most prosperous mining centers. This did not mean that an organized space emerged in the north of Nueva Vizcaya or on the Pacific coast where most of the land remained outside of Spanish control during colonial times. An analysis of parish records and other colonial documents shows that even in the eighteenth century Indian transfers were forced and had little to do with movements of free Indian workers. The cases of Parral, El Rosario, Álamos, and Chihuahua are emblematic.

OF the four *reales de minas* studied here, Parral was the oldest. During its apogee in the middle of the seventeenth century (1631–1680), Indians from all of Nueva Vizcaya were forcibly transferred to the Santa Bárbara district to work in response to wars and uprisings.[12] As they did elsewhere, Spaniards used local Indians as a labor force during the first years immediately after striking silver. It was from Nueva Galicia, the province south of Nueva Vizcaya, that several of the most important miners came, and they brought with them many of the Indians the Spaniards had used as laborers back there.[13]

The first foreign Indians to arrive thereafter in large numbers to Parral were mainly from two areas: Sinaloa, a province that until 1640 included all the Pacific coast (that year Sonora was founded to the north),[14] and Culiacán, from where many members of the local oligarchy came from, including Juan Rangel de Biesma, who had discovered the Negrita vein, the main source of wealth for the entire *real*. These Indians were transferred to Parral via the Topia road, a natural mountain pass used when crossing the Sierra Madre Occidental and an important exchange route going back to prehispanic times. By using this route, Culiacán was a week's travel from Parral.[15]

In the northern borderlands, all labor systems that were used by the Spaniards implied some geographical transfer of Indians, whether in *encomienda*, *repartimiento*, wage work, or personal servitude.[16] During the sixteenth and seventeenth centuries, the Spaniards of Parral had in *encomienda* the Concho and Tepehuan Indians of the province of Santa Bárbara, as well as those of the Sierra Tarahumara and the desert *altiplano*. These *encomiendas* were different from others in other areas of the viceroyalty because they were for personal service to Spaniards. In these *encomiendas* Indians paid tribute through their labor, whether in mines or agricultural haciendas. After 1582, each Indian head of household had to leave his home once a year to work at a hacienda for three weeks. But under the pretext that they were fulfilling their legal obligation of evangelizing them, the *encomenderos* (the Spaniards who held title to the *encomiendas*) would unilaterally "aggregate" the allotted Indians onto a property and then simply go searching for them with an armed posse each time they were needed. In fact, the governor of Nueva Vizcaya rewarded those settlers who had uprooted Indians from their pueblos and forced them to live besides their *estancias* (inchoate haciendas) with these *encomiendas*. This arrangement was known as a "war *encomienda*" because the Crown gave rights over Indians yet to be conquered in geographical areas far removed from the haciendas in which they were assigned. Relocating unbaptized Indians by force was one of the war *encomienda*'s main characteristics. Thus *encomienda* in Nueva Vizcaya usually implied the long physical transfer of Indians from their homelands to Spanish enclaves, and it is possible that these colonizing techniques resulted in the disappearance of ancient Indian settlements. In fact, this labor system was not very different from enslavement although *encomienda* Indians could not be sold. Runaway Indians ventured into regions inhospitable to Spanish colonization, such as the desert *altiplano* and the steep canyons of the Sierra Madre Occidental, where Europeans could not reach them easily.[17]

Encomiendas of Indians from the Rio Florido basin did not last long. In 1632, each hacienda in the Parral area had a nearby *ranchería* (Indian ranch) from which its *encomienda* Indians came,[18] though there is not a single mention of these Indians in the following decades. On the other hand, by midcentury there are numerous references to *encomiendas* of Indians from the Conchos and Norte (Grande) rivers farther north. These were probably war *encomiendas*, and Spaniards had already integrated these Indians into their haciendas as well as others that no longer had their own *rancherías*. Although the *encomienda* was abolished in 1670, the descendants of the Nueva Vizcaya *encomenderos* were granted royal extensions of this privilege for several more decades.[19]

Every single Indian in the province that had not been assigned to an *encomienda* was subjected to the *repartimiento*. This included non-Christianized Indians, too, though those from Tarahumara Alta and Pimería Alta were exempt for twenty years. The length of the *repartimiento* was established in 1600 but Spaniards never managed to implement it in all of northern New Spain because Indians resisted and ran away. It consisted of two months of labor per person per year, with the caveat that the number of Indians that would perform this service should never exceed one-sixth of the inhabitants of the same pueblo. Sometimes Indian leaders were the beneficiaries of the *repartimiento*, as they colluded with the armed minions of *encomenderos* to forcibly draft into service the tributary Indians of their own pueblos. As was the case for the *encomienda*, the *repartimiento* also caused the long-range forcible relocations of Indians. The law allowed for transfers of up to sixty to eighty leagues from the Indians' homeland (approximately three hundred kilometers).[20] As time progressed, Indian intermediaries played an increasingly important role in the *repartimiento* system. By the second half of the seventeenth century, the task of recruiting

Indians for this type of work fell to the Indian governor of each mission or the Indian captain of a *ranchería*, who were themselves exempt from tribute and furthermore received a reward in exchange for turning over *repartimiento* Indians to *hacendados* that needed their labor. How these people of Indian origin were recruited is unknown. They probably were born under Spanish rule and were therefore part of the colonial society. Governors and captains of *rancherías* were not always willing to cooperate with the colonizers, but if they refused to join the military expeditions, they were considered outlaws and threatened with death; they complained that when entering unconquered territories their lives were in danger because the Indians were reluctant to leave their homes.[21]

By 1645, records show that there were about thirteen hundred *repartimiento* Indians living around Parral, including non-Christianized Indians. When all the *encomienda* and *repartimiento* Indians of the area around Parral died or ran away, Spaniards were forced to increase their radius of operations for obtaining the labor force they needed until it reached over a thousand kilometers. In 1777 a new prohibition took effect forbidding *alcaldes mayores* (governors of a district with civilian and military duties) from promulgating orders for Indians to fulfill *repartimiento* duties.[22] However, the governor of Nueva Vizcaya retained this prerogative, and royal authorities ratified the system throughout the viceroyalty in 1783 when new laws regulating mining were passed.[23] Despite this, there were never enough hands to fulfill the demand for labor, even though there are repeated instances of missionaries complaining to the authorities that *encomienda* and *repartimiento* Indians were being kept in haciendas beyond their legal duty. Other tactics besides the use of force were also employed, such as tying the Indians to *hacendados* by debts, but the amount of Indian labor these tactics provided was not enough. The *repartimiento* lasted all through the colonial era in agricultural zones such as San Bartolomé; in contrast, several reports indicate that the *repartimiento* of local Indians assigned to work in mining haciendas around the mining center had ceased by the 1670s.[24]

The demographic situation in the Santa Bárbara district made the *repartimiento* restrictions difficult to comply with, and this forced settlers to improvise new networks for the supply of Indian labor. This was the case, for example, in the middle of the seventeenth century, when a combination of Indian uprisings, drought, and epidemics disrupted the labor supply coming from the nearby Sierra Tarahumara (1648–1652), the Concho Indian homeland in the nearby valleys, and the plains Indians (1644–1645). In order to make up for this loss in the labor supply, settlers looked to New Mexico and the recently colonized province of Sonora, whose founders included some Parral Spaniards. These regions supplied most of the Indian labor that worked in Parral for the rest of the century. These population movements were larger during the Indian rebellions in northwest New Spain and New Mexico, and thus it is very likely that Indians working in the mines of Parral during this time were at least to some degree reduced to personal service to a particular Spaniard and not by means of *repartimiento*. Despite legal restrictions to the contrary, this type of labor was almost the same as slavery, though it was limited to a specific number of years.[25] Furthermore, after 1680 the *real* of Parral experienced a decline in output and it became very difficult to entice a sufficient amount of wage laborers; it was then that Indians from Sonora came to represent over half of the *indios foráneos* working there.

Parish records show that during the second half of the seventeenth century more than half of the foreign baptized Indians in Parral were categorized as *expósitos* (orphans) captured during punitive expeditions. Priests would record these Indians' places of origin even when they did not know who the parents were. After the Pueblo Revolt of 1680 there was a marked increase in slave raids in the upper Rio Grande Valley, and the captives were taken for the most part to Parral, the nearest and wealthiest mining center. Among the baptismal records of San José Parish were some familiar places of origin from New Mexico, including Santo Domingo, Alameda, and Taos. The exact locations of other names mentioned in the sources (Tenen, Tiguex, Puaray) remain a mystery but are probably also from the same province. These records also show that between 1680 and 1689, half of the entries mention the age, and of these most are children or adolescents, and over 70 percent were women, who were mostly destined for domestic labor. Adult men were most likely killed or sold as slaves in distant regions. During these years, when Spaniards were expelled from New Mexico, most Indian captives were Apaches but among them were also some Julimes, Chizos (from the desert *altiplano*), and Quiviras (from the Great Plains). They were either booty from punitive parties (*piezas de campaña*) or so-called rescue Indians (*indios de rescate*) who had been taken captive by other Indians and then sold to the Spaniards. Almost a century later in 1777 both parish and census records frequently mention "free Indians" (*indios libre*), which therefore suggests that most of the others were not.[26]

From 1680 to 1689 there are no entries for foreign Indians from Sonora in the parish records. Nevertheless, the governor of Nueva Vizcaya confessed in 1691 that "most of the Indians now in Parral and Cusihuirachi were Sonorans that had run away from their pueblos."[27] It is difficult to know whether these Indians had been captured by Spaniards under the pretext that they had abandoned their missions of origin, or if they had moved there voluntarily to avoid the yearly *repartimiento* transfers and therefore chose to settle in a *real de minas* where they would stay year-round. However, the coincidence of Indian uprisings with the arrival of foreign Indian laborers shows once again that war allowed for the imprisonment of a large number of Indians destined for agricultural labor in haciendas and that, generally speaking, migration flows into Parral were not voluntary in nature. As the information only relies on Spanish sources it is difficult to know the true origin of the uprisings; at least some of them could have been provoked or misrepresented by the Spaniards themselves in order to gain more captives to work in the haciendas.

Indians from Sonora came mostly from the Ópata[28] homeland in the upper Yaqui River Valley and also from Pima settlements in valleys of its tributaries farther upstream in the Sierra Madre, like the Matape and Tecoripa rivers. In more than half of these cases, the settlements of Sahuaripa, Batuco, and Bacanora are mentioned. These Indian settlements were located along the road connecting Nueva Vizcaya with the Pacific provinces of Sonora and Ostimuri and in fact were part of these jurisdictions. There are also references to the Yaqui pueblos of Potam, Vicam, and Torim[29] and to pueblos from the missions of the Mayo Indians from the Fuerte River. The Sinaloa Indians came from the area around the river of the same name and from the town of Mocorito.

There is, however, an important caveat. During the seventeenth century, parish archives record sacraments being performed on "Sonoras" and "Sinaloas"; in other types of documents from the same period, as well as those from the eighteenth century, the main reference is to Yaqui Indians. By the end of the seventeenth century there are references to a "Yaqui pueblo" in Parral that lasted until the eighteenth century. The Yaquis were a case apart. No other group had its own settlement within Parral as the Yaquis did, which reveals special treatment by the Spaniards of this particular ethnic group. This sort of village might have emerged when a group of runaway Indians gathered in Parral and sought the protection of the Spanish authorities to avoid being sent back to their missions. They were allowed to have their own settlement. Yet those Yaquis also worked for Spaniards like all the other *repartimiento* Indians.[30] In order to be able to leave their homes, these Yaquis, like all the other Indians in Parral, needed the permission of the governor of Nueva Vizcaya, of the *alcalde mayor* or his lieutenant, the missionary who ministered to them, or of the Yaqui governor.

The Yaquis of Parral had their own political authorities but their legal status was different from other Indians living in the mining center or the surrounding Indian villages. They were considered to be only residents of the "Yaqui *barrio* of Parral" and not members of a particular *pueblo de indios* because they "had no land of their own nor communal property."[31] A description of the unique situation of the Yaquis in Parral is recorded in the census of 1777: "the Yaqui *pueblo* living in the outskirts of this *real* is made up of 29 families, [including] 50 Indians, 33 married, 17 single or widowers, natives of the Rio Yaqui [and] each one working on mining and the harvest of wheat and corn, and there are also 65 Indians, including 20 [Yaqui] boys and 13 girls that were born in this *real* or that of Aguacaliente."[32] The following year another census was taken, and the Yaquis are described as living "in the lands of the Sanctuary of Nuestra Señora del Rayo"; it also lists the inhabitants of the Yaqui pueblo: the Indian governor Don Alejo, his wife and two sons, a captain, a soldier, an *alferez*, a sheriff, and thirty-four families. Most of the Yaqui male adults were married and had children. The parish priest admitted that the census was only a snapshot of the situation in that year but claimed that there was no way to accurately monitor or control the Yaqui population because they were not very stable:

> With respect to the Yaqui Indians living in the *real* of Parral, even though they live in the surroundings of the Sanctuary of Nuestra Señora del Rayo, they are not legally organized as a pueblo and are merely called such, though it is only a voluntary congregation of such Indians and being inclined towards mining work, they are as home here as they are in other *real* and are frequently found wherever there is a mining boom. It is difficult to record here the increase or decrease in the numbers of this nation, but in spite of this during this year I notice there are a few more of them than there were last year, and I am witness to this as the parish priest of this church in the *real* of Parral on December 22 of 1778.[33]

This gives us a good idea of the size of the Yaqui pueblo in Parral, which was a little above a hundred persons. Most of these Yaquis had been born in the *real* or its surrounding area, and not all of them toiled in mining. Those who did not work in the mines were dispersed throughout the region's haciendas but the Spaniards were unable to control them. Unfortunately, it is not possible to know how long they kept their identity because the information about Yaquis is poor; in most of the documents indigeneous people are just called "Indians." They also might have mixed with other Natives and lost their ancestral identity.

Nuestra Señora del Rosario

This *real de minas* was located within the coastal region that bordered Nueva Galicia to the south. During the sixteenth century its Native population was distributed in *encomiendas* and ordered to serve in *repartimientos* at the haciendas of local Spaniards. But as was the case in Parral, these *hacendados* had many difficulties exercising their rights over local Indians. Many *encomiendas* existed only on paper. In addition, Spanish colonization was not continuous but instead had to be abandoned twice before a more permanent presence was achieved. The first Spanish settlement was called Villa del Espíritu Santo and was founded after the military campaign of Nuño de Guzmán, but it was abandoned in 1536. The second settlement was deserted after the rebellion of the Indians of the province of Chiametla in the 1580s.[34]

Half a century later, the situation had changed dramatically, and by 1655 El Rosario—as it was called—became the most dynamic *real de minas* in the plains of the Pacific. This coastal region had a catastrophic decline in population[35] and a particularly brutal and violent conquest, so finding an ample supply of labor was an especially difficult problem that was nevertheless solved in the same way as it was in other *reales de minas* throughout the colonial period: by the forced transfer of Indians from their homelands to other areas for mining and agricultural labor. The first mining boom was short, but there was a much larger strike in the second half of the eighteenth century. El Rosario had a royal exchequer where silver could be stamped and royal tax assessed by 1775, after the one in Álamos was closed.[36]

Baptismal records for the parish of El Rosario begin in 1677, and among the various Cahitan Indian nations recorded are Mayos, Sinaloas, Guasabes, and Bacoreguis.[37] During the eighteenth century foreign Indians living in El Rosario came mostly from the province of Culiacán, more than four hundred kilometers to the north. Many of the baptized Indians are referred to as Tahues, which was also the name of a language spoken by Indian groups living around Culiacán.[38] In addition to Culiacán, the most common name in these baptismal records is "Sinaloa." To a lesser degree there are also references to various other Indian groups such as Bamoa, Tamazula, and Mocorito, all located to the north of Culiacán. There is also an isolated reference to Tepahui (south of the Ostimuri province). What is very notable is the small number of Indians from the missions near the Presidio and Piaxtla rivers or from the neighboring *alcaldía mayor* of Copala, which bordered El Rosario to the north.[39] Indians knew that missionaries did not always have good relations with the civil government; open conflicts between them in the Northwest allowed the Natives to choose where they preferred to live and to negotiate their *calidad* in colonial society.

It is surprising that there are no references to Indians from the Sierra Madre in the mine records for El Rosario. This is especially puzzling considering that there are numerous references in the archives to Indians from the Tepehuan areas of the Sierra Madre who worked farther away in haciendas near the city of Durango and the jurisdiction of Nombre de Dios, which were several hundred miles from their homeland.[40] This was most likely because the Sierra region did not belong to the Sonora and Sinaloa jurisdiction that was created by an administrative reorganization in 1733. In fact, with the exception of administrative enclaves like Culiacán and Nombre de Dios, the transfer of Indians for labor was organized in the capitals of each province throughout the Spanish Empire, which means again that these movements were far from voluntary.[41] This is one issue in which apparently the Crown made no exceptions. For example, in the Tepehuan areas of the Sierra, not very far from El Rosario and the Pacific coast, a *real* was discovered in San Diego del Río, and the *repartimiento* Indians who were taken there to work in the mines were Tepehuanes and Xiximés. These Indians were originally from pueblos that were very distant but within the Nueva Vizcaya jurisdiction and not from the nearer coastal provinces of Sonora or Sinaloa.[42]

During the eighteenth century El Rosario also had its own Yaqui population nucleus, called the "Yaqui pueblo" or "*ranchería* of Yaqui Indians." This settlement appears to have had its own governor from at least 1736.[43] This "pueblo" was similar to the Yaqui settlement in Parral, though in this case it had its own authorities. Even so, in reality it was more like a *barrio* than a traditional Indian pueblo with its own communal lands, and it was probably small in size. It is very likely that among the Yaquis of this settlement there were some *barreteros* (mine workers who specialized in locating mineral veins). This skill allowed these Indians to be free laborers and to contract their services to any miner willing to pay; this in turn gave them an unusual amount of mobility that few other Indians had. The use of the term *pueblo* to describe the settlement also suggests that it was more stable than others of a similar nature such as the one in Parral, even considering that some of its inhabitants often moved to other places. Suffice it to say that the *Yaquimi* (the Yaqui name for their homeland) was by far the most populous Indian region in the whole of the northern parts of the viceroyalty at the end of the colonial period; hence it was unique. By 1765 there were about forty thousand Yaquis dispersed from Nueva Vizcaya to California, though only about fourteen thousand of them lived in their ancestral homelands.[44] The demographic decline caused by the spread of European disease during the sixteenth century that so devastated the population of the viceroyalty's northern borderlands seems not to have had as much of an impact on the population of Indian groups living in the river valleys located between Culiacán and Ostimuri. Or it may be that the populations in these valleys recovered much more quickly than the coastal population did. Throughout the northern borderlands, this was without a doubt the most densely populated region during the colonial era. Few early baptismal and death records have been conserved in the old missions and the current state of demographic history does not permit us to explain this strange phenomenon. At least in Álamos as elsewhere during the eighteenth century, Indians still seemed to be more affected by epidemics than the rest of colonial society.[45]

During the eighteenth century, the entries in the parish records of the northern parts of the viceroyalty generally make no distinction between Mayo and Yaqui Indians. In the surviving documents for the parish of El Rosario there are only two references to Yaqui pueblos. The first reference is from the town of Torim and concerns an Indian that served as a traveling mailman and wanted to get married in El Rosario. The second reference is an entry for an Indian from Cocorim (nowadays Cocorit) who worked as an *indio de cuadrilla* (mine worker).[46] However, different records also show that Yaqui Indians were part of the *repartimiento* for El Rosario as late as the eighteenth century.[47] If there are so few early references to Yaquis, on the other hand there are many references to Indians from Mayo pueblos:

Santa Cruz de Mayo, Mochicagua, Charay, and others. These Mayo Indians could have been recorded by the parish priest as Yaquis because the distinction between both groups was made only after the colonial era. This systematic distinction between Yaquis and Mayos was based on political and mission divisions in the region, not on cultural origin. In fact both groups not only lived as neighbors but also shared the same language.[48]

A reference from 1749 located the towns of Bachigualato and Otameto[49] somewhere in the area around the estuary of the Culiacán River, and it referred to them as Yaqui pueblos. This shows that Yaquis did not just migrate to mining centers. The Jesuits also had a role in these population transfers, as was the case when in 1678 they settled seventeen families of Sinaloa and Sonora Indians in their mission of San José del Tizonazo (close to Indé in central Nueva Vizcaya). This mission had been depopulated after the rebellion of the local Salinero Indians.[50] A century later, the Society of Jesus also proposed to repopulate their Pima missions with Yaquis.[51] Viceroys Fuenclara and Francisco Güermes complained in 1746 that Yaquis and Mayos were spreading into *reales de minas* where they were accepted but were not being properly indoctrinated because there were no priests that spoke their language.[52] They recommended to civil and ecclesiastical authorities that new pueblos be created and populated by those Indians that had been taken from the missions; they asked for wandering Yaquis and Mayos (*vagabundos*) to work on the haciendas.[53] From this reference it is obvious that by the middle of the eighteenth century Yaquis were considered to be mission runaways and that there was a considerable number of them being branded as vagabonds and were therefore susceptible to be reduced to personal service within Spanish haciendas.

It is very difficult to ascertain the exact provenance of the Indians of El Rosario for the second half of the eighteenth century. References to Indians tend to disappear from the entries, and many were probably being registered as Spaniards, mulattoes, or other *castas*.[54] This was a common occurrence throughout the northern borderlands and is a phenomenon that I discuss later in this essay.

Nuestra Señora de la Purísima Concepción de Álamos

It is believed that the *reales de minas* of Promontorios, La Aduana, and La Purísima Concepción de los Álamos[55] (this last one is also known as Los

Frailes) emerged at approximately the same time. Around 1683, miners coming from San Ildefonso de Ostimuri to the north struck an important vein of silver. There was another short-term boom in the area in the 1760s that lasted until 1782; at that time Álamos had three thousand inhabitants. This second boom was so promising that Álamos had its own royal exchequer between 1769 and 1775.[56]

The first recorded baptism in the parish archive of Álamos was of a Yaqui Indian on May 12, 1685. The baptismal document was signed by Francisco Saenz de Carriosa, the parish's first resident priest. The same book that contains this record also contains all the baptismal entries for the nearby *real* La Aduana. All three mining centers from the area (Álamos, La Aduana, and Promotorios) were able to supply their labor demands through the numerous Yaqui and Mayo pueblos nearby that, by the time of the mining boom, had been ministered to by the Jesuits for more than half a century. Most mine workers in the Álamos mining district originally came from Jesuit missions.[57]

The relatively high demographic density of the local Indian population allowed the Spaniards of this region to maintain a dispersed settlement pattern, in which *estancias* and haciendas were placed next to the missions and *rancherías*. The main silver strike was that of Cerro de Nuestra Señora de la Concepción de los Frailes, but the parish seat was actually originally established in the *real* of Nuestra Señora de Guadalupe y Santo Tomás de Paredes near the Mayo River. It was located between Concocari and Camoa, but the settlement there was ephemeral. The parish seat was eventually moved to Álamos, which became the main population center of the region, despite the fact that water and tillable lands were in lower supply there than on other nearby settlements.[58] This was perhaps due to an abundance of caution, as a settlement with few Spaniards surrounded by Mayos many times their number was in constant danger of being overrun. Besides, Álamos was a shorter distance from Promotorios and La Aduana, the two other mining centers in the region. However, three of the main haciendas that had their own chapels were located near the Mayo River.[59]

Indian *rancherías* alternated with Spanish *estancias* where mineral ore was processed throughout the valleys of the Álamos, Cuchujaqui, and Guirocoba rivers and those of some lesser tributaries of the Mayo River. South of Álamos, near where the hacienda of San Antonio de Basiroa and the *estancia* of San José del Maquipo were located, there was a high number of Indians.[60] In fact, the establishment of the Basiroa hacienda and the neighboring *estancia* of Tapizulas preceded the emergence of *reales de minas* in this region.[61] Contrary to what occurred in central Nueva Vizcaya, there are numerous *rancherías* around the area of Álamos that had no missionaries to indoctrinate the Indians, as seen in the records that refer to them with their Cahita names. These *rancherías* were ministered to by the diocesan clergy and not the Jesuits, because from south of the Mayo River all the way to the Fuerte River there were no missions. In contrast, the prehispanic toponymy around Parral and Chihuahua disappeared along with the indigeneous *rancherías*.

During the first decades of existence for Álamos there is evidence for the constant presence of Pima Indians around the mining centers. These Pima Indians were probably taken there by the first miners or were taken prisoner during the uprisings at the end of the seventeenth century. However, parish records have many more references to the local Mayos and Yaquis and fewer from Sinaloa than to Pimas. Unlike the *reales* of Parral, El Rosario, or Chihuahua, where the radius for supplying the labor needs expanded through the decades, in Álamos most of the labor force was made up of local Indians who only increased in relative numbers as time progressed. Indians coming from the missions on the Mayo River represent about half of the baptized Indians. Furthermore, the haciendas did not absorb all the nearby Indian labor, as many Indians remained in their *rancherías*. On the other hand, there is an almost total lack of references to Apaches, even though Álamos was close to the frontier areas where unsubdued Indians continuously harassed the missions and settlements of the province of Sonora. It was not necessary then to resort to Indian slave labor in Álamos as was the case in other areas because there was enough Indian labor supply in this region.

There was considerable continuity in the place of origin of the Álamos labor force throughout the eighteenth century. The places of origin for the grooms in the marriage entries from the early part of the century (March 30, 1716, to December 24, 1757)[62] match closely the same entries for more than ninety marriage records[63] taken from the parish archive after the expulsion of the Jesuits (from October 28, 1788, to January 27, 1798). Information gleaned from these marriage records gives a picture of Indian mobility at the end of the colonial era.[64] During the first part of the century there are more references to pueblos located along the banks of the Fuerte and Sinaloa rivers (for the former, Charay, Ahome, and Carapoa; for the latter, Bamoa and Guasave). There are isolated references to places in the

Pima and Ópata homelands (Sahuaripa, Mátape, and San Juan). Toward the end of the century, Indians settled around Álamos came from pueblos located on the banks of the different rivers from the area.[65] There are some references to an individual from Binapa in the province of Culiacán, a man from Témoris, and a woman from Batopilas in the Sierra Tarahumara.[66] *Indios foráneos* usually married local Indian women in order to be accepted as residents. Mixed marriages between different Indian groups tended to increase for this reason but in the available documents it is impossible to see its consequences for the identity of the people involved.

Many Indians who had moved to El Rosario and Álamos came from the Fuerte and Sinaloa river valleys. This exodus depopulated those regions. In 1784 a Franciscan missionary from El Fuerte lamented the "pitiful state" of the pueblos of Charay, Mochicahui, and San Miguel Ahome, caused by the *repartimiento* that took Indians from these pueblos and transported them to mining centers. Esteban Gutiérrez de Gandarilla, the captain and *alcalde mayor* of the area, forced the Indians to work in the mines, which is why Santiago de Quitu, another *real de minas*, was abandoned (the location of this mining center is unknown).[67] The titular head of the Bamoa parish, *Bachiller* Manuel María de Aviles, asked the bishop to assign him to a non-Indian parish because, according to him, priests could not survive near the Yaqui and Sinaloa rivers because "most of the Indians are roaming around *reales de minas*, ranches, and the tidal swamps of the coast" instead of staying in those areas.[68]

Yaqui and Mayo Indians in Álamos wishing to marry had either been or had attempted to be incorporated into the population of local Spanish haciendas as *indios laboríos*.[69] They claimed to have been raised in the region or to have been living in it for a long time. When they first arrived in the area, they would usually tell their places of origin and marital status to the Spanish owners of the mining haciendas where they wanted to work. Others would claim to be "servants" of the pueblo. By doing this they could avoid being sent back to their places of birth as the law demanded.

In the sacramental entries for the parish of Álamos there are few references to Tarahumara Indians, in spite of the relative closeness of the settlement to their homeland in the Sierra Madre Occidental. This is despite the fact that the governor of Nueva Vizcaya accused some Tarahumaras of hiding out in the Pacific flank of the Sierra. In 1803 Bernardo Bonavia complained that the Indians missing from all the missions had ended up in the pueblo of Huites[70] and a *ranchería* named Guara[71] in the *alcaldía mayor* of

Fuerte in the province of Sinaloa. The Indians would also hide in the Taymuco and Gecopaco ranches in the *alcaldía mayor* of Álamos[72] or would take refuge in the pueblos of Macoyagui[73] and Nuri,[74] as well as the remote canyons of the *alcaldía mayores* of Ostimuri and the Batopilas area.[75]

There are other references to this effect. In the sacramental entries from Álamos that have been consulted, an entry from 1782 indicated that "Juan Tarahumar and María Catalina Matus, Indians from this parish," married.[76] Other marriages of Indians from the sierra in Álamos include one from the Chínipas mission (1791), one from San Miguel Tubares (1794), and a woman from Témoris (1796). Burial records indicate that in 1780 "a Tarahumara Indian from the Sierra that lived in Tecorahui whose name was not known" was buried in the parish cemetery. Two years later "a Tarahumara from Bocoina" died. Thus although the references to Tarahumaras are relatively scarce, it is possible that many of them were simply registered as "Indians" without specifying their places of origin if they had already been permanently settled in Álamos.

The demographic situation in Álamos changed toward the end of the century. After smallpox devastated the local population in 1782 there was a period of catastrophic drought and epidemics between 1784 and 1787. But after these events the birthrate surged (a typical phenomenon in old demographic patterns), and there was also an influx of Indians migrating toward Álamos made up in great part by mission Indians. The population movement coming from mission pueblos was difficult to control, and this seems to have caused considerable worry to the colonial authorities. Commandant General Jacobo de Ugarte urged the Álamos parish priest on September 15, 1786, "that no Indian, mestizo, or any other *casta* could leave his residence . . . to go and establish himself somewhere else without the appropriate permission from his parish priest." A *real cédula* promulgated by the king on March 14, 1786, ordered that "in no hacienda or ranch can there be Indians living permanently there, though the Spanish owners could host them for specific tasks or services with the obligation of returning them to their place of origin once these chores had been completed." It was a concession by the Spanish Crown to the missionaries that was not respected, as local authorities made no allowances for Indians who were not living in a mission or mining camp. Commander Ugarte ordered on July 2, 1790, that any Indians found by a representative of the law without their passports or written permission to move around would be taken "and considered to be a vagrant and sent to the town where he came from." (Each written permit had to include the dates of departure and arrival, along with any stopovers the Indian may have taken during the trip.) Penalties for those Indians that did not have these official documents included lashes for the first two offenses; a third offense would automatically condemn the Indian to be placed in chains and do a year of forced labor, though others could be condemned to serve ten years in a presidio or two to work in a *mortero* (mining mill).[77]

With the passage of time, the Indians of Álamos, like their counterparts from El Rosario and many other places in the northern frontier, came to be categorized as mulattoes.[78] The African slave trade with Portugal practically came to an end for the Spanish empire after Portugal achieved its independence in 1640. Yet the number of mulattoes in the northern borderlands increased significantly so that by the second half of the eighteenth century mulattoes made up over half of the permanent population of Durango and Parral, among many other locations.[79] In Álamos mulattoes accounted for about 40 percent of the baptisms in the last two decades of the eighteenth century. This large presence of mulattoes cannot be explained by rates of illegitimacy or abandonment, nor can it be attributed to the presence of multiethnic families.[80] Intermarriage among members of different social classes did not happen often enough to fully explain this phenomenon.

The transformation of Indians into mulattoes happened in Álamos as it did in other Spanish settlements because everybody seems to have had some benefit from this arrangement: the Indians who wanted to flee their missions in order to avoid *repartimiento*; the *hacendados* that wanted to keep as many labor hands as possible by not allowing them to go back to their pueblos; priests who wanted to charge the *hacendados* for their sacramental services to their servants. It should also be noted that in northwest New Spain mulattoes were not subject to any sort of tribute as they were in the rest of New Spain. As for the missionaries, they seldom received any answer from the authorities to their complaints about the drain of Indians from their missions because the Crown was mostly interested in increasing the income for the *Real Hacienda* and the more that Indians worked in the mines instead of in missions, the more minerals that were mined and minted. But it must be pointed out that there were also people referred to as mulattoes in the missions themselves, and it is possible that these may have also been Indians classified as such to avoid *repartimiento*. This was probably done with the knowledge, indeed the help, of the missionaries themselves because in this way they kept these Indians under their care in the mission.[81]

La Villa de San Felipe El Real de Chihuahua

San Felipe El Real de Chihuahua would become the de facto capital of Nueva Vizcaya when the governor of the province moved to this mining center during the second decade of the eighteenth century. The governors in turn would remain there until 1761, even though the mining boom in Chihuahua was relatively short, having been exhausted by the middle of the century.[82]

As was the case for the other *reales de minas*, during the initial stages of the mining boom most Indians working in the mines of Chihuahua were from the surrounding region and from the provinces of Santa Bárbara and Cusihuirachi, which had experienced an earlier mining boom. Many of the Spaniards and their Indian servants that settled in the Chuviscar river basin came from these two locations. According to the parish records, at first, from 1709 to 1718, Sonora and Yaqui Indians were twice as numerous as the Tarahumaras and three times as numerous as the Apaches.[83] But as was the case for Parral, the records of the Jesuit and Franciscan missions did not survive, and it is difficult to properly evaluate how many of the local Indians were redistributed to the local haciendas from the nearby missions, which were depopulated over the next few decades.[84]

Most of the foreign labor in Chihuahua came from Sonora, in particular the Yaqui homeland. Here, as was also the case in El Rosario and Álamos, the Yaquis formed their own pueblo with their own chapel dedicated to Nuestra Señora de Guadalupe, located on the outskirts of the Spanish settlement. But it is not possible to know how often the Yaquis established in Guadalupe mixed with the other Yaqui workers, because there are not enough marriage records concerning them. As occurred in Parral, the number of baptized Yaquis living in Chihuahua varied through time, but, judging from the baptismal records, these Indians arrived *after* the mining boom (1725–1745). From 1736 to 1746, the parish priest baptized a total of 8 Yaquis; during the next decade this number increased to 131, with an average of 11 Yaqui children being baptized every year between 1747 and 1760.[85] Yaquis were not as numerous as the "Sonoras" of Parral had been a century before, and they seemed to have replaced Apaches. There are ninety-eight listed for this group between 1736 and 1748, but only eighteen Apaches between 1749 and 1760.

It was also possible to discern for Chihuahua, unlike other *reales de minas*, more information about the places of origin of the Yaquis living there. As in the case of El Rosario, Indians born on Mayo pueblos were also registered as Yaquis. In the references in the Chihuahua parish archive to the places of origin for the Indians named as "Yaquis," most had come from pueblos in the area between the Fuerte and Yaqui rivers. The largest number were from towns on the banks of the Yaqui River, with most of the references coming from Torim, but there are also numerous references to Vicam, Huiribis, Potam, Rahum, Bacum, and Belén (which were mostly inhabited by Pima Indians). There are references to some pueblos near the Fuerte River and to Tesia, Echeojoa, and Santa Cruz, which were located on the Mayo River.[86] There are two references to Yaqui Indians born in Nueva Vizcaya in 1753 and 1754: one in Carichi and the other in Satevó, both pueblos from the Tarahumara missions. As was the case for the Yaquis of Parral, some of them worked in mining and kept a certain amount of independence and had settled in small ranches around the villa.[87] Among the other references there are also a few Pima Indians (also called Sonoras or *Sonoreños*, as well as two Yutas from the 1739 to 1746 time period; the latter were probably adult Indians, or small children taken captive from heathen *rancherías* because there is no mention of their parents).

Yaquis used to be considered quite autonomous and resistant against colonization but as shown in the case of mining centers during colonial times they were the ones who most suffered from Indian transfers. Nobody would be willing to work in colonial mines. The *barreteros* who localized the richest veins were very few. Most of the mine workers were *tenateros* and had to go up and down carrying on their shoulders the heavy metal stones. In the narrow galleries, there was no proper ventilation and the difference between the interior and outside temperature was unhealthy. Those who worked outside were in contact with mercury, which is a powerful poison, and they were therefore sentenced to a slow death. In the mines and in the mining mills, dust also destroyed the workers' lungs. Nonetheless, scholars thought that Yaquis voluntarily went to the mining centers because they belonged to the so-called free workers who were attracted by high wages (*asalariados libres*). Spaniards claimed that all servants unless enslaved were free; they received a salary in goods (food and clothes) but they were not allowed to leave the hacienda where they had been hired without the owner's permit. As most of the workers, Yaquis were tied to owners by debts. If an indebted worker left the hacienda where he had been incorporated, local justice officers would sue him. "Free workers" and "wage workers" in colonial times had completely different meanings.[88]

The Apache case is different from all others; free Apache workers were even fewer. Among the most salient differences are that most were adults and there were barely any children. The few references to Apache minors were the result of military raids of un-Christianized Indians; others were probably those known as *indios de rescate*, who were captive Indians sold to Spaniards by other Indians who had presumably made them into slaves. An important difference between the various *reales* concerning Apaches was that in Parral during the seventeenth century there are numerous references to Indians coming from the Franciscan missions in the upper Rio Grande Valley, whereas there are no such references for San Felipe El Real de Chihuahua. It would seem that all Apaches were war captives. This is suggested by several facts: there are only references to group baptisms; no parents are listed; and they are children of single mothers (a common occurrence for women reduced to slavery).

A detailed analysis of parish records regarding the places of origin for *indios foráneos* in the main *reales de minas* for northern New Spain shows that mining centers did not exert a spontaneous pull for Indians from their surrounding areas as earlier historiography has stated. In the cases of Parral, Álamos, El Rosario, and Chihuahua, the places of origin for the Indians working in them were mostly from within the boundaries of their own civil jurisdictions. Indians were not inclined to try their luck in the nearby *reales de minas*, and their arrival there did not correspond to the boom times, as was proven by the cases of Parral and Chihuahua. There were, however, voluntary movements to the *reales de minas* when Indians were fleeing their missions where they had been settled, but it is problematic to correctly identify these fugitives because they tended to merge with the local population and in many instances passed themselves off as mulattoes in order to avoid being drafted or recaptured.

A special and particularly interesting case is that of the Yaqui and Mayo Indians. These could be located throughout Nueva Vizcaya, from El Rosario all the way to Sonora to the north and to Parral and Chihuahua to the east. However, there are no Yaquis in the jurisdiction of Durango (where work was mostly done by Tepehuan Indians) or to the south of Zape.[89] Apparently, a good number of the Yaquis and Mayos (as well as some Indians from New Mexico) were taken prisoner by Spaniards when they ran away from their mission pueblos, and they were transported along with their families to the mining centers; in contrast, most of the captive Indians from New Mexico generally remained single.

The necessary long-distance transfers of Indians in Nueva Vizcaya and Sinaloa oblige researchers to consider a very wide region in order to fully understand Spanish colonization in northern New Spain. The geographical scale, generally based on colonial provinces or current modern state limits, must be modified. Both Yaquis and the Indians of New Mexico supplied labor in the main *reales de minas* when the local Indian population decreased, as has been shown for Parral, El Rosario, and Chihuahua. For this very reason, foreign Indians became more numerous once the first mining boom faded (these booms were usually short-lived). It is therefore difficult to believe that these Indians were free wage laborers being attracted to mining activities. Further research in historical demography is needed to find out more about indigenous population flows during colonial times.[90]

CHAPTER 8

Remaking Americans: Louisiana, Upper Canada, and Texas

ALAN TAYLOR

In the wake of the American Revolution, the new republic alarmed its imperial neighbors: the British to the north in Canada and the Spanish to the west in Louisiana. The imperial officials especially feared the great and growing number of Americans, who expanded their settlements with a remarkable rapidity. About 3.7 million in 1790, the American population would double during the next twenty-five years. And the population was shifting westward. From just 12,000 in 1783, Kentucky's population exploded to 73,000 in 1790 and to 221,000 in 1800. In 1793 the Spanish governor of Louisiana, Baron de Carondelet, warned his superiors in Spain to beware of

> the unmeasured ambition of a new people, who are vigorous, hostile to all subjection, and who have been uniting and multiplying . . . with a remarkable rapidity from the time of the recognized independence of the United States. . . . This vast and restless population, driving the Indian tribes continually before them and upon us, is endeavoring to gain all the vast continent occupied by the Indians between the Ohio and Misisipi [sic] Rivers, the Gulf of Mexico, and the Appalachian Mountains.[1]

Another Spanish official regarded the settlers as "distinguished from savages only in their color, language, and the superiority of their depraved cunning and untrustworthiness." The Spanish worried that the American frontier folk would sweep across the Mississippi River into Louisiana—and on across the Great Plains to take New Mexico and eventually Mexico, the silver-rich heart of the Spanish Empire.[2]

The British and Spanish colonies were especially vulnerable because they were so vast and so thinly populated by colonists. Sprawled along the entire western side of the Mississippi River, Louisiana stretched westward across the Great Plains to the Rocky Mountains to include about 828,000 square miles, but Louisiana had only about forty thousand colonists in 1790. Almost all of them lived in two clusters on the colony's eastern margin in the Mississippi Valley. The main cluster lay along the lower river around the capital and seaport at New Orleans. In Upper Louisiana, a secondary, and more dispersed, set of settlements stretched along the Mississippi River near the confluence of the Missouri and Ohio rivers (in the future state of Missouri). At one thousand inhabitants, St. Louis was the primary Euroamerican settlement in Upper Louisiana and second only to New Orleans in the colony. Most of the Louisiana colonists descended from French settlers who came before the colony's 1763 transfer from French to Spanish rule. Enslaved Africans made up the second largest group. A few Spanish high officials governed a small French population (and their slaves), while struggling to cope with the many Indian nations who dominated the continental interior. No wonder the governors dreaded the looming prospect of American intrusions and invasions.[3]

The British colony of Upper Canada was equally immense and thinly populated. In 1790 the fourteen thousand colonists lived in new settlements straggled along the St. Lawrence, Niagara, and Detroit rivers and the northern shores of Lake Erie and Lake Ontario. Most of the colonists were newly arrived Loyalists, refugees from the civil war known as the American Revolution. As in Louisiana, Upper Canada had more Indians than colonists.[4]

To strengthen their colonies, British and Spanish officials sought emigrants who could provide a militia and develop the agricultural economy. Florida's Spanish governor, Vicente Manuel de Zespedes, explained, "The best fortification would be a living wall of industrious citizens." Imperial officials preferred to recruit Europeans, deeming them more tractable to authority and less prone to revolutionary republicanism. But Europeans lacked the experience and skills needed to dispossess Indians and to transform forests into farms. They were also expensive to ship across the Atlantic and to subsidize during their first two years, when they would struggle to subsist in a new land. During the 1780s and 1790s, Britain and Spain could not afford those additional costs because they were burdened by the massive military establishments demanded by their global wars. Already reeling from crushing debts inflicted during the American Revolution, the empires faced renewed war in 1793.[5]

For want of European settlers, the British and the Spanish enticed Indians to leave the United States. Greatly outnumbered by the Americans, the British counted on Indian warriors to defend Canada. Noting the loss of the populous colonies on the Atlantic seaboard, a British agent explained, "We are no longer the first landed power in North America. Therefore [we] cannot have too many Indians under our protection and countenance." The British drew their Mohawk allies across the border to settle in reserves at Grand River and Tyendinaga. They also sought to nullify that border by arming the Indians who dwelled south of it but north and west of the American settlements. By bestowing arms and ammunition, the British helped them resist American expansion. The British hoped that their Indian allies could constitute a buffer zone between Canada and the republic.[6]

In the Mississippi Valley, the Spanish also sought to bolster a broad buffer zone by building Indian alliances and by persuading eastern Natives to settle within Louisiana. In the Southeast, the Spanish gave generous presents to build alliances with the Creek, Choctaw, and Chickasaw nations. Dwelling east of the Mississippi River, those Natives shared the Spanish interest in slowing American expansion. In Upper Louisiana, the Spanish attracted Indians from the Ohio Valley by setting aside a tract of about 750 square miles located near Cape Girardeau. In addition to fending off the Americans, the Indian newcomers were supposed to protect the colonial settlements from the Osage nations of the interior. The Osages had long intimidated and plundered the colonists with impunity because of the small and weak Spanish garrisons: one thousand men for the entire colony. By the mid-1790s, six new villages sustained twelve hundred Shawnees and six hundred Delawares along Apple Creek. But those Indian numbers fell short of Spanish hopes.[7]

When both Europeans and eastern Indians proved to be in short supply, British and Spanish officials explored a desperate alternative: recruiting American settlers. By rewarding them with generous grants of land at rock-bottom prices, the empires hoped to convert the American settlers from menace to asset. Grateful for their land, they would embrace the culture of their new patrons and defend their colonies against other Americans bent on invasion (or so the officials gambled).[8]

The imperial officials took hope from the instability of the American union and the discontent of western settlers during the 1780s and early 1790s. Britons and Spaniards insisted that no republic could long survive given the volatility of common people, particularly when dispersed over a vast country that stretched across the Appalachian Mountains into the Mississippi watershed. The imperial officials astutely noted the contingency and fluidity of political allegiance among western settlers devoted primarily to the pursuit of self-interest. In the wake of the Revolution, the settlers distrusted the eastern leaders as indifferent to their conflicts with Indians and to their right to trade down the Mississippi River to New Orleans. In 1789 the Americans established a more coherent union under a new federal constitution, but the new government's taxes alienated many westerners. The imperial officials sought to exploit the frontier troubles of the unstable new republic.[9]

Nationalist American historians have long dismissed the British and Spanish programs regarding the assimilation of Americans as naive and futile—as incapable of overriding an innate and cohesive American nationalism. But a closer examination of the three experiments in converting Americans reveals less nationalism and more opportunism among settlers who sought to acquire property under any flag of convenience. Fluid and contingent, national identities along the frontier persuaded officials that they could convert Americans into loyal subjects of their empires.[10]

ALTHOUGH underdeveloped and weak when compared to the United States, Louisiana had immense long-term economic potential, thanks to vast tracts of fertile land linked to oceanic trade by the vast internal system of rivers dominated by the Mississippi. The Spanish possessed the richest part of the continent for agricultural settlement, so they desperately needed to obtain settlers of reliable loyalty. Success would convert Louisiana from a vulnerable buffer zone into a rich and powerful colony. To that end, the Spanish sought to attract American settlers to become loyal subjects within Louisiana.

In 1784, the Spanish tried to stifle American western settlements by closing the mouth of the Mississippi to downriver trade. To move their grain and lumber to market, the western Americans needed access by riverboats to the port at New Orleans, near the mouth of the Mississippi. If denied that access, their frontier economy would stagnate, which promised to discourage Americans from crossing the Appalachian Mountains to settle the west. Or the bleak economy might persuade the western settlers to secede from the United States and seek some dependent association with the Spanish Empire. In a third scenario, the settlers would move peaceably into Louisiana to accept Spanish land grants and authority. As Spanish subjects in Louisiana, they could freely trade down the river to New Orleans.[11]

But the Spanish played a tricky and dangerous game, for, in a fourth scenario, the settlers might descend in armed force to open the trade by capturing New Orleans. The same powerful river that could carry their trade would also swiftly propel southward the boats of an attacking expedition, surprising and overwhelming the flimsy Spanish defenses at New Orleans long before reinforcements could arrive from Cuba or Florida. Moreover, the Spanish colonies needed provisions imported from the American settlements.[12]

To reduce their risk (and increase their food supply), in 1787 the Spanish opened the Mississippi to American boat trade but demanded heavy customs duties: 25 percent (reduced to 15 percent a year later). The governors also cultivated leading men in the western territories. By offering cash and special licenses to trade at New Orleans, the governors tried to "interest" prominent men in promoting either secession by western territories or defection by western settlers. At a minimum, the governors expected their prominent friends to discourage filibustering attacks on New Orleans—or to provide timely warnings of their launch. In particular, the Spanish cultivated James Wilkinson, a former (and future) American general who had become a land speculator, trader, and politician in Kentucky.[13]

In 1787, the Spanish opened up Louisiana to American settlers but only under restrictions meant to promote their assimilation. Governor Esteban Rodriguez Miro confessed that "at first glance it seems dangerous to settle foreigners in Luisiana," but he considered them less menacing within his colony than on its margins. He reasoned that, as subjects holding and improving Spanish land grants, they would defend the colony, for "once they have emigrated and sworn vassalage, anyone who takes part in a revolution will risk a great deal." Unable to keep out all Americans, Miro preferred to convert some to rebuff the rest: "circumstances force us to take this risk." The Spanish sought to activate the newcomers as a militia to fend off hostile interlopers from the United States. Miro explained, "We ought not to lose an instant and populate Luisiana with individuals who will swear a solemn oath to take up arms against any invasion attempted by Kentucky."[14]

The Spanish preferred Catholics as subjects, but few could be had from the United States, so the officials accepted Protestant emigrants, provided they brought no clergy. In Louisiana, only Catholic priests could perform baptisms and marriages, and the newcomers had to commit to the Catholic education of their children. To facilitate conversions, the Spanish recruited English-speaking Irish priests to serve in Louisiana. Catholicism remained the sole legal and public form of worship.[15]

During the 1780s, the American emigrants usually settled around Natchez, on the east bank of the lower Mississippi within a region claimed by the United States but clung to by the Spanish. The fertile lands along the river sustained prosperous tobacco plantations, which attracted an English-speaking majority. In return for generous land grants, the newcomers swore allegiance to the Spanish Crown. "May God keep us Spanish," wrote one settler who feared higher taxes and less secure land titles if the American state of Georgia obtained the Natchez district.[16]

While welcoming common settlers, the Spanish distrusted leading men of means and ambition who sought to leverage their influence with immigrants into power within the colony. Imperial officials worried that such leading men eventually would rally their common clients to wreak a republican upheaval. If, however, only common settlers came, they would have to accept the leadership of the Crown officials, who would hold a local monopoly in education, property, and connections. Consequently, the Spanish declined to make large land grants for speculative resale by leading Americans. The Crown set the maximum legal land grant at 800 arpents (about 680 acres).[17]

In 1788, the Spanish minister to the United States, Diego de Gardoqui, proposed to make an exception for George Morgan, a former Ohio Valley trader and colonel in the American army with great ambitions as a frontier land speculator. Charmed by Morgan's enthusiasm, Gardoqui provisionally granted Morgan fifteen million acres at the confluence of the Mississippi and Ohio rivers in Louisiana. In addition, Gardoqui promised Morgan that he could conduct a colony within the colony by appointing his own magistrates, establishing a representative assembly, and tolerating Protestant diversity. Those three concessions violated long-standing Spanish policies—as did the vast land grant to a foreigner. But Morgan insisted that only his leadership and those concessions could quickly draw thousands of Americans to settle in Upper Louisiana.[18]

Without waiting for ratification by the Spanish Crown, Morgan founded a settlement at New Madrid and offered lands for sale to settlers.

Morgan's presumption (and Gardoqui's naivete) infuriated Governor Miro, who refused to recognize the land grant. Undercut, Morgan returned to the United States in a snit, blasting "an avaricious, ignorant, indolent, rash, imprudent, or despotic Governor." Neglected by Morgan, his little colony withered at New Madrid. By 1790 only 293 Americans had emigrated to Upper Louisiana, and 106 of them were enslaved African Americans. By frustrating Morgan's colony within the colony, Miro demonstrated the Spanish determination to avoid American middle management of the settlement process.[19]

THE British adopted a similar settler policy in Upper Canada, a newly organized colony beside the Great Lakes north of the United States. During the 1780s, the region had drawn in about six thousand Loyalist refugees fleeing from defeat in the American Revolution. To govern that frontier colony, in 1791 the British selected John Graves Simcoe, a veteran officer who had commanded a Loyalist regiment during the American Revolution. Refusing to accept the British defeat as final, Simcoe saw Upper Canada as ideally positioned to revive the empire by sapping people from the adjoining republic. Simcoe believed that Americans would sooner return to their proper allegiance if they could look north to see the fruits of empire in a prosperous and orderly Upper Canada.[20]

To resist and roll back the American republic, Simcoe needed to accelerate Upper Canada's development by recruiting thousands of settlers. Unable to procure enough from Britain, he sought settlers from the nearby republic. On the plus side, American settlers were nearby and experienced at farm building. They could emigrate cheaply at their own expense and would quickly support themselves as frontier farmers. And Simcoe reasoned that every settler drawn into Upper Canada subtracted from the republic's resources as it added to the empire's strength.[21]

He devoutly believed that the American states remained filled with closet Loyalists who longed to escape republicanism by returning to the empire. To attract them, Simcoe promised lower taxes and cheaper land grants than those that prevailed in the United States. On February 7, 1792, Simcoe issued a proclamation inviting Americans into Upper Canada to receive virtually gratis at least two hundred acres of land per family. To obtain a land grant, a settler needed only to take an oath of allegiance and to pay some official fees. During the mid-1790s those fees amounted to only six pence per acre—which rendered land in Upper Canada dirt-cheap relative to the one to three dollars per acre charged by the United States government in Ohio and by private land speculators in New York and Pennsylvania.[22]

Simcoe's land proclamation increased American immigration to Upper Canada. In March 1792, John Munro reported, "I have the pleasure to inform Your Excellency that Emigrants are flocking in from the States with all their property." During the four years, 1792–1796, Simcoe's administration fielded four thousand applications for land, about three-quarters from newcomers, euphemistically known as "the Late Loyalists." Primarily from the mid-Atlantic states of New York, New Jersey, and Pennsylvania, the newcomers opened new settlements along the north shore of Lake Ontario and to the west in the Grand River and Thames valleys.[23]

Like the Spanish, the British discouraged ambitious Americans from immigrating to become local leaders within Upper Canada. In 1794, John Cosens Ogden observed: "The object of the British nation is to people and cultivate this country, and to make it as perfect a part of the Empire as possible. Dreading revolutions, they are cautious in receiving republicans from the States, and wish to encourage husbandmen and labourers only. Clergymen, lawyers, physicians, and schoolmasters from the States are not the first characters who would be fostered." An Anglican minister from New Hampshire, Ogden spoke from experience. Despite flaunting his loyalty—and despite the shortage of Anglican clergy in the colony—Ogden received neither a land grant nor any parish appointment in Upper Canada.[24]

Upper Canada attracted common, rather than genteel, Americans by offering cheap access to two-hundred-acre plots of land—each perfect for a small farm—while restricting larger grants to British officials and their friends. One of those settlers, Michael Smith, explained that Upper Canada enticed "many thousands of my fellow-citizens of the United States, who were without land, and [without any] prospect of obtaining any in the United States upon such easy terms as they might in Upper Canada." Two hundred acres was as much as they could manage in Canada *and* more than they could afford to buy in the United States. In Upper Canada, American settlers could more easily and cheaply obtain farms, but they faced poorer prospects for speculating their way to greater prosperity.[25]

Upper Canada did attract some prosperous families who belonged to pietist denominations with pacifist convictions: German-speaking Mennonites and Dunkers (or Tunkers), as well as English-speaking Quakers.

During the American Revolution, they had suffered persecution for their pacifism, reaping arrests and heavy fines from Patriots who treated them as Loyalists. After the war, the pietists continued to suffer fines for their absence from mandatory militia musters. Those with large families and small farms sought new lands, but they wanted to avoid the American frontier because of the Indian war that raged in the Ohio Valley until 1795. They preferred Upper Canada, where the British kept the peace by treating the Natives more generously than did the Americans. The British welcomed the pietists as especially hardworking and orderly farmers who would not challenge authority—and would not speculate in land.[26]

IN 1793 both Britain and Spain became embroiled in a massive new war against the revolutionary new republic in France. After initially allying with the British, the Spanish changed sides under French pressure in 1795. Both empires had to give higher priority to waging the massive and expensive war in Europe and the West Indies, eclipsing their interests in North America. At the same time, the United States became stronger in 1794 with the consolidation of a new federal government that defeated the Indians of the Ohio country and suppressed a western tax resistance. In Europe, the imperial governments backed away from their confrontational policies in North America as dangerous and expensive distractions. In the Jay Treaty of late 1794, the British reconciled with the United States by withdrawing from the border posts along the southern shores of the Great Lakes. The reconciliation dismayed Simcoe, who returned to England before the forts passed into American hands.[27]

In 1795, the Spanish also sought better relations with the United States. Facing a war with the British, the Spanish wanted to head off American assistance to an attack on New Orleans. In the Treaty of San Lorenzo, the Spanish appeased the United States by withdrawing within a constricting border, the 31st parallel. They abandoned their fort and settlements in the Natchez District and forsook their Indian allies east of the Mississippi. The Spanish also opened up the Mississippi River to free American trade. In the short term, the concessions avoided an American war, but they killed any Spanish prospects of promoting western secession or a Native buffer zone. In sum, the United States benefited from the European entanglements of their imperial rivals.[28]

As the British and French abandoned their containment policy, the Americans could expand more freely and rapidly to and beyond their borders into Louisiana and Upper Canada. The colonial officials preferred to hope for the best rather than risk the humiliating futility of resisting the settler flow. Between 1796 and 1804, about six thousand Americans settled in Upper Louisiana. The officials welcomed them in hopes of strengthening the frontier militia to repel an anticipated attack from British Canada. The Spanish officials even made their peace with American land speculation by bestowing larger land grants on more ambitious men, including the lead-mining entrepreneur Moses Austin and the celebrated Daniel Boone with his family.[29]

In Upper Canada, Simcoe's successors also continued to grant lands to American emigrants who vowed loyalty. Through 1811 American emigration persisted at the rate of about five hundred families (or about twenty-five hundred persons) per year. Thanks primarily to American immigration, Upper Canada's population swelled from fourteen thousand in 1791 to seventy-five thousand by 1812, when the Late Loyalists comprised at least three-fifths of Upper Canada's inhabitants, outnumbering both the original, true Loyalists, who had arrived during the 1780s, and the still small number of immigrants from Great Britain.[30]

THE loyalty of Louisiana's American-born subjects was never put to the test of an invasion because the Spanish betrayed their own colony by retroceding it to the French. Weary of the large administrative costs and scant revenues, in a secret treaty of October 1, 1800, the Spanish government restored the colony to the French in exchange for a part of Tuscany in Italy. The dictator Napoleon Bonaparte dreamed of reviving the French empire in the Americas, and the Spanish hoped that he could provide a more formidable barrier between the Americans and precious Mexico. To that end, Napoleon promised never to transfer the territory to the United States. Within three years, however, Napoleon soured on his acquisition for want of an army to occupy Louisiana. He had dispatched across the Atlantic a large army, but it had collapsed when first sent to crush a slave rebellion in Saint Domingue (the future Haiti) in the West Indies. Too few soldiers survived the violence and yellow fever to proceed on to New Orleans, so Napoleon cut his losses. Betraying the Spanish, Napoleon sold Louisiana for $15 million to the American administration of Thomas Jefferson. In March 1804, the American officials and troops occupied St. Louis, completing the transfer.[31]

Initially, Jefferson meant to withdraw the settlers from Upper Louisiana, relocating them east of the river to create a vast reservation for Indians on the west bank of the Mississippi. Jefferson then hoped to push into it all of the Indian nations that remained to the east of that river. Preferring consolidated over dispersed settlements, Jefferson planned fully to settle the lands east of the Mississippi before allowing Americans to proceed further west. He expected that process of infill to take fifty years. Meanwhile, in their trans-Mississippi reserve, the Indians would have time to assimilate to American "civilization."[32]

The plan revealed Jefferson's weakness for utopian schemes that defied the messy realities of the frontier. In fact, most of the eastern Indians wanted no part of moving west to fight the Osage and other western nations for land. And the settlers of Missouri clung to their farms and villages. In addition, thousands of Americans despised any restriction on their migration westward in search of prized locations. Rufus King, a U.S. senator, scoffed, "Nothing but a cordon of troops will restrain our people from going over the [Mississippi] River and settling themselves down upon the western bank." Dependent on elections, the American leaders lacked both the troops and the will to use force against fellow citizens, so Congress tabled Jefferson's scheme. The president organized a territorial government, and the federal government began selling lands to newcomers, who flocked into Upper Louisiana. If the empires could not stop American settler expansion, neither could the United States.[33]

IN Upper Canada, the British did face an American invasion during the war that began in 1812. Unlike the Spanish in Louisiana, the British fought to keep Upper Canada. In that war, the British and the Americans regarded the allegiance of the Late Loyalists as pivotal, for they were a strong majority in the colony. If they assisted the invasion, the Americans would probably conquer the colony. But the British expected to prevail if the newcomers helped to defend the colony that had so generously treated them with land.

Attracted by the cheap land and low taxes, the Late Loyalists cared little about their political regime, so long as it demanded little from them. In 1805 near Buffalo, a traveler saw American emigrants preparing to cross the border: "I believe that, were they to learn that even in Hell there were lands producing excellent wheat and corn and at six cents an acre, despite all the flames and all the torments, they would give up their *liberty and equality* to go and settle there." In 1808, Michael Smith agreed that he had emigrated from Pennsylvania into Upper Canada, "in order to obtain land upon easy terms (as did most of the inhabitants now there) and for no other reason."[34]

Simcoe had enticed immigrants who did not particularly care for the republic, but he had not attracted people who cared deeply for the empire. Although most Upper Canadians lacked both the motives and the means to challenge their rulers, the diverse settlers also lacked the common purpose and patriotic passion actively to support their colony. The pacifists certainly could not be counted upon to bear arms to defend Upper Canada—and the other Late Loyalists balked at the hardships and dangers of militia service. In 1807 an American agent assessed the Americans in Upper Canada, concluding that it was "of no consequence to them who governs, if they have good land, light taxes, and can raise a plenty of wheat." Designed to remain politically inert, Upper Canada had attracted a population averse to mobilizing for war.[35]

During the War of 1812, the Late Loyalists disappointed both sides. Loyal enough when left alone, most balked when called into military service. Hundreds fled back across the border to the United States. The majority stayed with their hard-earned farms in Upper Canada but did their best to avoid the militia drafts. But fewer still rallied to help the American troops, who lost credibility as they bungled their invasion. Worse still, the invaders plundered Canadian farms and burned some villages, alienating the inhabitants. By 1814, most of the Late Loyalists concluded that defending the colony was the best means to protect their farms and to hasten an end to the war. But the militia was an auxiliary in a war primarily fought and won by British regulars and their Indian allies. The frustrated American government made a peace treaty that preserved the border and the British colony of Upper Canada.[36]

After narrowly surviving the invasion, the British decided that the Late Loyalist support had been too little and too late. Anticipating another war with the Americans, the British sought to reduce their security risk by reversing their immigration policy. In 1815, the British discouraged American settlement by denying further Crown land grants to immigrants from the United States. At the same time, the British subsidized immigration from Scotland and Ireland. Between 1815 and 1842, the colony attracted 78,000 Irish, 41,000 English and Welsh, and 40,000 Scots. During that period, the 159,000 emigrants from Britain outnumbered the 32,000 from America by nearly 5 to 1. Thanks to the immigration, and to the growing number born in the colony, the American-born share of the population fell to 7 percent by 1842. A majority in 1812, the American-born had become a small minority thirty years later.[37]

THE third act of this continental play took place in Texas, on the northeastern frontier of the new republic of Mexico. In 1821 Mexico won independence from Spain and inherited the border problem posed by all those reproducing and expanding Anglo-Americans. By 1820, the United States had 9.6 million people compared to 6.2 million in Mexico. Having swept across the Mississippi into the Louisiana country, the Americans began to press into Texas on the northeastern frontier of Mexico. In 1820, Texas consisted of a few settlements within a Native world of some thirty-one nations, principally the Comanches who dominated the southern Great Plains. The forty thousand Natives outnumbered the region's twenty-five hundred Hispanics (known as *Tejanos*) by sixteen to one.[38]

During the 1810s and 1820s, the Native numbers grew as ten thousand eastern Indians immigrated into northeast Texas. The newcomers included Cherokees, Chickasaws, Choctaws, Creeks, Kickapoos, Seminoles, and Shawnees. Although pushed west by American settlers, the "immigrant Indians" had also adopted many settler ways, including the keeping of domesticated livestock. Some of the newcomers distrusted and fought the settlers of Texas, but others sought to collaborate with them against the mounted Indians of the Plains.[39]

The *Tejano* population had been impoverished and reduced by the destructive wars for Mexican independence. The survivors primarily clustered in the towns of San Antonio and Goliad. A third presidio and town, Nacogdoches, lay to the northeast, near the Louisiana border, but it already had more Anglo-Americans than *Tejanos*. Meant to guard the border and suppress smuggling, Nacogdoches instead functioned as an open gateway into Texas for American trade, people, and influence. By 1823 about three thousand Americans had squatted illegally in Texas.[40]

Like their Spanish predecessors in Louisiana, the Mexican officials in Texas concluded that the Americans (known as *extranjeros*) should be recruited and converted to Mexican citizenship, if they could not be kept from crossing the border. In 1822, Antonio Martinez, the chief Mexican official in Texas, explained that the *Tejano* population was "too small, and yet it is absolutely essential to settle Texas, so the easiest and least costly way to accomplish this is by admitting *extranjeros*." Another leading San Antonioan declared that Mexico should welcome "honest, hard-working people, regardless of what country they come from . . . even hell itself." And so they welcomed emigrants from the American South.[41]

The pro-immigration policy reflected the liberalism of the early republic in Mexico. The liberals sought to tear down the central bureaucratic institutions and the economic restrictions of the Spanish Empire. Crediting liberal principles for the dramatic economic and demographic growth of the United States, the Mexican republicans also sought elected legislatures, civic equality, entrepreneurial commerce, a decentralized federal system, and an open immigration policy. The Mexican liberals also proposed to go beyond the American example by outlawing slavery in their constitution. The liberals treated Texas as a test case to influence the development of the entire nation. But the liberals faced fierce opposition from conservatives who favored the Catholic Church establishment and a centralized and authoritarian government as essential to avoid anarchy. Compelled to compromise, the liberals had to accept the enduring primacy of the Catholic faith and special privileges for military officers.[42]

In 1824, Mexico adopted a decentralized federal system that turned immigration policy over to its states. A year later, the northeastern state of Coahuila y Tejas passed a colonization law that welcomed foreign settlers who would adopt the Catholic faith and embrace Mexican citizenship. As in Spanish Louisiana, the Mexican lawmakers expected the newcomers to assimilate by mixing with at least equal numbers of *Tejanos* and European immigrants. The Mexican officials wanted the newcomers to live in compact villages along the Hispanic model and to pay an annual fee to support a local Catholic church.[43]

To accelerate settlement, the Coahuila y Tejas government awarded large grants to immigration agents, known as *empresarios*, who received a bonus of twenty-two thousand acres for every one hundred settler families introduced to Texas. Exempt from taxes for six years, the settlers also could bring in tools and implements duty free. In contrast to Louisiana and Upper Canada, the Mexican state counted on American entrepreneurs to manage the settlement process by screening out immoral and disorderly men and by supervising the rest of the newcomers. Seventeen of the twenty-four *empresario* contracts went to Americans, who recruited their countrymen as settlers. Most of the settlers came from Kentucky, Arkansas, and Louisiana.[44]

The premier *empresario* was Stephen F. Austin, a lawyer and banker from Missouri. He followed the lead of his father, Moses Austin, who had colonized Upper Louisiana as a Spanish client. Bankrupted by the banking crisis in 1819, Moses rolled the Spanish dice a second time by procuring a

Crown land grant to settle three hundred families in Texas. In 1821, the death of Moses and Mexican Independence threatened to cancel the contract. So Stephen went to Mexico City, where he persuaded the new regime to sustain his *empresario* located along the Brazos, Colorado, and Bernard rivers. He subsequently secured three more contracts to settle another twelve hundred families next to his original colony.⁴⁵

Austin offered especially large farms at remarkably low prices. In return for just $60 in fees, a married couple received 960 acres plus another one hundred acres for each child and eighty acres for each slave. By comparison, the United States government charged $100 for a farm of just eighty acres, with no bonus for children and slaves. Ruined by the depression of 1819, many of the settlers sought to rebuild their fortunes on cheap and fertile land in Texas.⁴⁶

Austin advised malcontents to shed their "foolish republican obstinancy" by submission to the government of Mexico. But Austin lacked authority over the border area around Nacogdoches, where hundreds of Americans had intruded as squatters. In late 1826 the squatters rallied to the reckless leadership of the brothers Haden and Benjamin Edwards, rogue *empresarios* who had been disavowed by the Mexican government. The brothers also won the support of the Cherokees who had emigrated from the east and had been frustrated in their bid for a government land grant. Shortly before Christmas, the squatters and Cherokees arrested the local Mexican officials and declared the independence of the Republic of Fredonia, which they divided into two zones: the southern two-thirds of Texas for "the White People" and the northern third for "the Red People."⁴⁷

But the Fredonia revolt was the exception that proved the rule of *extranjeros'* adaptation to Mexican authority. In early 1827, Mexican troops suppressed the rebels with the aid of American volunteers rallied by Austin and other *empresarios*. Austin accused the rebels of "jeopardising the prospects of hundreds of innocent families who wish to live in peace and quietness in the country." Austin also played to the anti-Indian sentiments of the settlers, denouncing the Fredonians for seeking an "unnatural and bloody alliance with Indians." Outnumbered, the leading rebels, including the Edwards brothers, fled across the border to Louisiana, while the Cherokees executed their chief, Richard Fields, who had supported Fredonia. Mexican clemency toward those who remained at Nacogdoches helped to consolidate support for the government. The loyal majority of the colonists seemed to vindicate the *empresario* system as safe means for developing Texas.⁴⁸

But Mexican officials worried as the *extranjero* population grew far faster than the Hispanic populations, reaching twelve thousand in 1829 to outnumber the region's *Tejanos* by four to one. Rather than cluster in Hispanic villages, the newcomers spread out on dispersed ranches and farms. Few converted to Catholicism and fewer still paid any fee to sustain that church. Contrary to Mexican law, the newcomers continued to import slaves, and many settled within twenty leagues of the American border, violating a regulation meant to separate the settlers from their American neighbors. The military commander responsible for the northeastern frontier, General Manuel de Mier y Teran, concluded, "If it is bad for a nation to have vacant lands and wilderness, it is worse without a doubt to have settlers who cannot abide by some of its laws."[49]

The settlers developed Texas as an economic satellite of the United States with only a tenuous political tie to Mexico. They exported their cotton and cattle to the United States, and they consumed American goods and brought in American slaves and paid no customs duties or taxes to Mexico. Weakened by deep inequality, pervasive poverty, and violent political upheavals, the government could afford only sporadic attention, a few officials, and a mere two hundred soldiers in Texas.[50]

On April 6, 1830, the Mexican Congress adopted a new settlement policy, which banned further immigration from the United States, barred slave imports, and rescinded all *empresario* contracts that had not yet been fulfilled. The Mexican government also sought to increase the non-American population in Texas by offering cash advances to Mexican families and European immigrants. The new policy outraged the *extranjeros*, who dreaded restrictions on immigration and slavery as a threat to economic development. Without a continued flow of new settlers and slaves, they feared that Texas would lapse into a backwater chronically threatened by its Indian neighbors. But Austin also saw the new policy as self-defeating, deeming any effort "to dam out the North Americans" as like "trying to stop the Mississippi with a dam of straw."[51]

Indeed, despite the law, the number of Anglo-Americans in Texas more than doubled in the four years after 1830. Emboldened by growing numbers, armed Texans drove out the Mexican garrison at Anahuac, near Galveston, in June 1832. Later that summer, the government withdrew almost all of its troops from Texas to deal with a new political crisis in Mexico City. General Mier y Teran sadly concluded, "There is no physical force that can stop the entrance of the *norteamericanos*, who are exclusive owners of the coast and the border of Texas." In despair over the failed policy, and renewed political upheaval at Mexico City, Teran put on his dress uniform before plunging a sword through his heart on July 3, 1832.[52]

During the spring of 1834, General Antonio Lopez de Santa Anna seized power in Mexico City, dissolved the Congress, and, a year later, abolished the state governments. Although the Texans had long disliked their subordination within Coahuila y Tejas, they expected far worse from a centralized dictatorship. On a lobbying trip to Mexico City, Austin was seized and jailed, which weakened moderation in Texas. In his absence, the common white men of Texas rallied to populist firebrands who denounced the *empresarios* as elitists who monopolized land and served the Mexicans. In 1835, the malcontents in Texas rose up in armed rebellion and, a year later, declared independence, legalized slavery, and announced that free blacks had no rights and could be sold back into slavery. Most in the *Tejano* minority supported the revolution rather than risk losing their lives and property to the aggressive majority of Texans.[53]

During the spring of 1836, Santa Anna invaded Texas, but the rebels routed and captured him at San Jacinto, winning their independence. Austin had returned to Texas and ran to become the first president of the new republic, but he lost in a landslide, for most Texans considered him too soft on Mexico for far too long. At the end of 1836, Austin died, aged only forty-three. In 1845, Texas joined the United States, provoking a war with Mexico. Crushed after a war of two years, Mexico lost her entire northern tier, including New Mexico and California, to the triumphant United States. Far from securing the northeastern frontier, the American settlers in Texas had become a wedge that blew open Mexico, allowing the United States to sweep to the Pacific.[54]

WHY did American settlement compromise Louisiana and overwhelm Texas—but not Upper Canada? Comparing the three regions reveals the diversity that belies our usual practice of lumping Americans together as a category. Coming from the Mid-Atlantic region, the Late Loyalists belonged to a very different migration stream from the southerners who moved to Louisiana and Texas. The Canadian immigrants lacked slaves and accommodated easily to the antislavery policies of their new home—in stark contrast to the Texans who ignored and violated Mexico's antislavery constitution. The short growing season of a northern climate also precluded the development of a plantation system worked by slave labor. Upper Canada attracted many pacifist pietists because the British kept peace with the Indians by treating them with relative generosity and restraint. Texas, by comparison, held no appeal for Quakers. While Texan men prided themselves on their firearms, few Upper Canadians possessed any in 1812 when war broke out. In sum, British Canada attracted a population inclined to accept foreign rule, but Texas did not.

Differences in the three political regimes also mattered. Assimilation was easier in a British colony, where the American immigrants already knew the language, the legal system, the settlement practices, and the Protestant faith of their governors. American immigrants showed far more cultural resistance when told to learn another language, adopt a new faith, live in villages, and adapt to a Roman legal code.

Upper Canada also belonged to the world's most powerful and prosperous empire. Britain could better afford to subsidize a colony and to defend it from invaders than Spain or Mexico could. After suffering defeat in the War of 1812, the United States never again invaded Canada—and most Upper Canadians nurtured a new nationalism bred by bitterness against the invaders. By contrast Louisiana lay on the distant and poorly defended margins of a weaker empire under great distress during the Napoleonic wars. That distress led to the loss of Louisiana and to the Latin American wars for independence. Ravaged by those wars, Mexico became a republic but could never muster the resources needed to govern and to defend its distant northeastern frontier.

Finally, varying Indian relations played a pivotal role in the three settings. In Upper Canada, the British paid generously to sustain an alliance of Native peoples that kept the peace. The British also enjoyed extensive influence because their traders could entice Indians with the highest quality manufactured goods at modest prices. And the Indians and the British found a common cause in resisting American expansion. During the War of 1812, the Indians intimidated dissident colonists, which helped to minimize support for the invaders. In peace, good relations with Indians helped to draw American immigrants. In war, the newcomers sought to keep in the good graces of those Native allies.

By comparison, the Spanish could never compete with the British traders and could ill afford enough presents to sustain the goodwill of the many Indian nations that surrounded their small frontier settlements. In Upper Louisiana, the Spanish lost credibility as rulers when they failed to protect their colonists or their Native allies from Osage raids. The liberal project in Mexico had rejected the paternalistic presents and diplomacy that had bought some peace for the Spanish frontier during the late eighteenth century. And Mexico was too impoverished and distant to help the Texans dispossess their Indians. Committed to white supremacy, the Texans regarded the Mexicans as a mongrel race ill-suited to help them exterminate the Indians. By seeking independence, the Texans sought a freer hand to deal violently with their frontier foes. The Mexicans underestimated the racial dominion demanded by the American immigrants in Texas.[55]

In the end, the British enjoyed better success at remaking Americans into reasonably loyal subjects. Comparing British Upper Canada, Spanish Louisiana, and Mexican Texas reveals that the British tapped a more tractable and less bellicose stream of emigrants. Those newcomers also adapted more easily to the more familiar culture in Upper Canada than they did in the Hispanic West. And the British Empire could bring more military power to defend their colony and to manage relations with Native peoples. That British success helped to ensure that the republic would expand westward rather than northward across the continent. But that expansion would receive a jolt in 1861, when Texas seceded from the United States, reaffirming the contingency of frontier allegiances and the instability of the American union.

PART IV

Spaces and Memory

CHAPTER 9

Blood Talk: Violence and Belonging in the Navajo–New Mexican Borderland

Brian DeLay

It's a few hours before daylight, somewhere, and there's a commotion outside. You bolt upright out of your blankets, heart pounding in the darkness. Men are yelling to each other in a language you don't understand. A familiar voice cries out. You grab a weapon and stumble into the freezing night, just in time to see most of the animals being driven out of your corral. In the darkness you see the outline of a young man (your nephew?) lying face down on the other side of the fence. You shout and two men on horseback wheel 'round and glare. You raise your weapon but hear a familiar wind-whistle sound and then something buries itself in your shoulder. The riders watch you slump to the ground, then say something to one another. One dismounts, strides past you into your home, and then emerges with a terrified girl—your daughter. He heaves the child onto a horse, climbs up behind her, and in ten seconds you can't even hear the hoofbeats over the howling wind.

Who did this? Had the attack happened yesterday in, say, Nebraska—that is, somewhere inside a sovereign nation-state capable of enforcing its laws—authorities would pose the question with a particular, individualistic aim in mind. They would set about trying to discern the personal identities of the assailants, locate and apprehend them, and punish them, as individuals. But in borderlands, places defined precisely by their plural sovereignties, the question *who did this* is more complicated and more perilous. In contested spaces, individuals always imply collectives in ways that confer power even as they invite danger.¹

When personal injuries threaten collective violence, to ask *by whom* something was done is also to ask *for whom* it was done. There may be an objective answer to the first question, but this is rarely the case for the second. Instead, acts of cross-cultural violence usually spark rival discourses of culpability. These take place both across the divide, between the societies involved, and also within each society as factions vie with one another through statements about alienation and belonging. The perpetrators acted on our behalf, championing our rage and our interests. They acted alone, for selfish, base reasons. The perpetrators belong to us. They don't belong to us. Such statements seek to frame the original injury in a particular light, and in so doing to stop, manage, or encourage escalation and war. Sometimes they are conveyed through words. But they can also be registered through further actions—acts of communicative violence meant to punish and terrify through demonstrations of unity as much as through wounds. Violence and community are mutually constitutive in contested borderlands. Residents of these volatile places are compelled to engage in what I call "blood talk": dialogues about belonging performed not only through words but also through acts of violence and their attendant, urgent statements about who belongs to whom.²

There are few places better suited to an analysis of blood talk than the region between Diné (Navajos) and New Mexicans—the most enduring colonial borderland in all of North America. Navajos and New Mexicans interacted regularly with each other as members of independent polities in the same region for more than two hundred and fifty years. The relationship's durability depended on several things, including the absence of imperial rivals, isolated New Mexico's relatively small colonial population, a dearth of precious metals, and the fact that most of the land between the two societies was unsuited for agriculture. Few North American borderlands fit this profile. In all of Spanish North America, only certain groups of Apaches and Utes could be said to have comparable stories, and neither interacted as regularly with a fixed colonial center as Navajos. Nothing as durable can be found in French North America, if for no other reason than the simple fact that New France only lasted about one hundred and fifty years. British North American interactions with the great Iroquois, Cherokee, and Creek confederations come closer, but even these iconic borderland relationships start later and end (in forced removal) far earlier than the one forged by Diné and New Mexicans. The unique longevity of this borderland makes it possible to discern the practices and protocols these peoples developed to build and maintain community and to manage the explosive dangers of borderland violence over the long term.

What follows is a tour of those practices and protocols: of how they emerged and matured in the eighteenth and early nineteenth centuries to structure disputes within an unequal colonial relationship; of the changes that undermined their efficacy in the generation after Mexican Independence; and of their sorry, brutal dissolution on the eve of the American invasion. The narrative contrasts with much of what we now think we know about North American borderlands. West of the Mississippi, recent historiography has traced interethnic conflict to raw material ambition (for animals, slaves, territory, or trade goods). East of the river, the most appalling and therefore the most dazzling stories have been about borderland violence as an economic and annihilationist enterprise (e.g., the Beaver Wars, Metacom's War, and the Southeastern Slave Wars, all conflicts with economic engines powering mass expulsions and ethnocides).

But sometimes borderland peoples were more or less stuck with each other, unable or unwilling to extinguish the relationship through destruction or expulsion. The Navajo–New Mexican borderland fit that description for a quarter millennium. Over generations, distinctive regional traditions of discourse and violence helped ensure a collective response to individual trauma and grievance, as well as collective answers to the inevitable, essential question—*who did this*? In so doing, blood talk made wars terrible but intelligible and therefore brief, rare, and useful in settling grievances immune to peaceful negotiation. The slow collapse of these shared traditions inaugurated an unsustainable period of endemic violence that would culminate in the defeat and incarceration of most Diné in the 1860s. In the aftermath of that searing experience, Navajos and non-Native historians trying to make sense of its origins emphasized narratives of individuals and alienation that obscured the collective nature of the region's historic conflicts. That collective story is worth recovering. In the Navajo–New Mexican borderland, and in contested spaces generally, most understood that violence between individual people threatened violence between peoples. And that was often the best hope anybody had for peace.

DURING the seventeenth century the subjects of New Mexico (colonists, deracinated Indians, and colonized Pueblo peoples) came into frequent contact with the "Apaches del Nabajú" living in the San Juan Basin to their west. It is often difficult to disentangle Navajos from Apaches in Spanish sources from this century, but a pattern of frequent conflict is clear enough. Confrontations sometimes emerged from conspiracies (real and imagined) between Navajos and various western pueblos, especially Jémez. As they would be throughout the Spanish and Mexican periods, Navajo relations with Pueblos during the seventeenth century were, in one expert's phrase, "confusingly variable." Through attacking certain Pueblos, "illicitly" trading with others, harboring apostates from still others, or doing all three with the same Pueblos at different times, Diné gave New Mexican authorities reasons, or at least pretexts, for several offensive campaigns in the decades prior to the Pueblo Revolt. All the while, Spanish slavers preyed upon Navajos as they did on all the region's free peoples. Following the Pueblo Revolt, conflicts resumed throughout the long reconquest in the 1690s and into the second decade of the next century, in large part because so many Pueblo refugees fled to live with Navajos in these years. Spaniards seem to have launched their last military campaign against Diné in 1716, and thereafter generations would pass before the two peoples next went to war.[3]

To make sense of blood talk and the connection between violence and belonging in this borderland during the chaotic nineteenth century, we have to understand the asymmetries of power that crystallized during this long eighteenth-century peace. Colonial and early national New Mexico is sometimes referred to as a "non-dominant frontier."[4] It was certainly true that neither Navajo leaders nor Spanish-speaking authorities in Santa Fe could mobilize the necessary power to destroy, dominate, or permanently displace one another. But that fact ought not mask potent and mutually recognized inequalities in power hovering in between the poles of perfect equality and dominion. At its most basic this was a matter of raw demography. Historic Navajo population estimates are necessarily speculative, but it is unlikely that there were ten thousand Diné at any point prior to the U.S. takeover in 1846. The province of New Mexico encompassed at least twice as many people, eighteen to twenty thousand Spanish subjects, in the late eighteenth century. That figure would double by Mexican Independence in 1821 and then surpass sixty thousand by 1846.[5] Despite very real fissures dividing the diverse Pueblos, *genízaros*, and Spanish colonists in the province—fissures often widened by economic and institutional rivalries within and between church and state—fractious New Mexico could nonetheless assume a terrifying coherence in time of war. Governors could and did compel men from all the province's towns and villages to march against adversaries. Drawing upon two, four, or six times the manpower of their Diné neighbors, New Mexican governors projected real force against enemy Indians.

The asymmetries in the New Mexican–Navajo relationship structured the long peace. Diné endured New Mexican intrusions into their culture, economy, and politics that seldom if ever happened in reverse. From the 1730s through the 1770s, for example, Franciscans launched an ambitious if ultimately doomed missionary program among Navajos. Many hundreds submitted to baptism, and still others experimented with cultural and religious compromises that Spanish counterparts would have found unthinkable outside of captivity. New Mexican authorities regularly intervened in Navajos' external relations, and in the 1780s they even enlisted newly aligned Comanches to compel Diné to go to war with Gileño Apaches, their linguistic kin and historic allies. Officials in Santa Fe often felt secure enough in their superior position to meddle directly in Navajo politics. As they did with many Native polities, Spaniards bestowed medals and various insignia of rule upon Navajo leaders they wished to strengthen while they schemed to undermine others. Spanish and Mexican authorities would have thought absurd the notion that they could be subject to detention and imprisonment by Diné counterparts in the course of diplomatic wrangling. Yet late in the century Spanish authorities twice "arrested" a prominent Navajo headman, Antonio el Pinto, for advocating policies contrary to Spanish interests.[6]

The verb is telling. New Mexican authorities understood themselves to be administrators of a legal regime that in certain vital matters encompassed the Diné. This understanding followed from predictable cultural chauvinism, certainly, but also from a realistic assessment of relative power. Authorities in Santa Fe knew they couldn't police daily life among Navajos as they did in their own villas or among the Rio Grande Pueblos. But when frictions arose on the borderland, as they inevitably did over land, trade, security, property, and so on, Spaniards insisted on mediating relations through their own judicial values and processes. And they believed, correctly, that they usually had the power to do so.

Consider tensions over land. New Mexicans and Navajos alike needed new lands for farming and grazing. In search of new pasture and perhaps fleeing Ute attacks and drought in the mid-eighteenth century, many Navajo families moved out of their traditional homeland, the Dinétah, and emigrated west to the Canyon de Chelly or south into the area surrounding the sacred mountain they called Tsoodzil (Cebolleta to the Spanish; today's Mt. Taylor).[7] The southern branch of this migration soon encountered newly arrived *pobladores* (settlers) from New Mexico, who had also come to pasture their growing flocks and to plant fields between the Ríos Puerco and San Juan. When the *pobladores* sought formal land grants in this region, Spanish officials endeavored to incorporate the Diné into their legal process. Grants were contingent upon the *pobladores* causing no "injury to the Apaches of the Navajo country," and Diné with nearby claims were to be invited along with any other neighbors to raise objections prior to finalization. Spanish officials took these matters seriously and insisted that individual Navajos with grievances could obtain justice through law (they would not have thought to qualify the term as "Spanish" law). Some Diné seemed willing to be convinced. In 1808, for instance, the headmen Delgadito and Segundo complained that *pobladores* from the settlements at Cebolleta and Alameda had encroached on their farms and grazing land. Upon review the governor found in favor of the plaintiffs and sent an officer to "place the Navajos in possession."[8]

Surely there is no more sensitive barometer of relative power on a borderland than the judicial mechanisms that neighboring peoples employ to settle serious disputes, and in the Navajo–New Mexican borderlands these processes had a decidedly Spanish aspect. Peace treaties consistently prescribe Spanish law as the prevailing judicial framework. If a New Mexican killed or injured Navajos, he was to be tried and punished by Spanish authority. If a Diné killed a New Mexican, he, too, was to be tried and punished by Spanish authority. Should headmen refuse to cooperate, to answer the question *who did this* by naming and surrendering an individual, the homicide would be considered an act of war rather than a murder and Diné would be attacked collectively in their country.[9]

There is a difference, of course, between proscription and practice. Even signed treaties required further approval at higher levels in both societies. And no doubt private disputes in the borderland were sometimes mediated by hybrid traditions and the influence of key local personalities. There are even glimpses of Diné invoking their own judicial traditions at the highest levels of negotiation. In 1799 a Navajo killed a New Mexican trader who had refused to sell him a gun. Two headmen came in to assure the governor that this was a regrettable accident and not an act of war. They offered to right the wrong by paying a price for the dead man. While he dropped his insistence that the headmen deliver the killer, the governor would not "condescend" to cover the dead with presents. Instead, framing the matter as a collective rather than an individual crime, he "said that it would be enough that they recognize guilt and his forgiveness would be a sign of his friendship so that they would not commit similar insults."[10]

On some other borderlands, high-level compromises such as these abounded and settled into novel diplomatic and judicial protocols based on "shared misunderstandings" that helped mediate the relationship.[11] But when dealing with Navajos, New Mexican authorities consistently resisted this. Throughout the eighteenth and early nineteenth centuries they retained the conceits—colonial par excellence—that they posed no threat to core Diné interests and that all disputes could be managed equitably and peacefully through Spanish law. In the Navajo–New Mexican borderland, novelties in shared ritual rarely defined the asymmetric peace, at least not at the highest levels. But they did come to define a pattern of asymmetric wars.

THANKS to the careful work of several anthropologists and historians who have labored over Spanish and Mexican records, we know a good deal about these wars. There are inconsistencies, distortions, deliberate omissions, and archival gaps in the records, and these shortcomings are compounded by the fact that Navajos did none of the writing. Still, the archives are full of official letters and military dispatches that conveyed basic practical information to superiors in wartime: dates and locations of particular confrontations, numbers of men in this or that engagement, numbers of people killed or captured, kinds of property seized or stolen, and so on. Drawing on these sources, scholars have produced detailed chronicles of the relationship over the long term. Rendered into quantitative data, these chronicles reveal striking patterns (see Figure 9.1). Rather than the undulating foothills one might expect with an interminable "cycle" of raid and counterraid, the pattern of killings and captures looks like buttes and valleys. Until the 1810s, it's almost all valleys. During the century following the end of hostilities in 1716, these peoples seem to have gone to war only twice, in 1774–1775 and again in 1804–1805. As one would expect in such an asymmetric relationship (and as the data illustrate), these conflicts extracted a far higher price from Diné than New Mexicans.[12] During these two destructive conflicts Navajos lost eight people for every enemy they killed or captured.

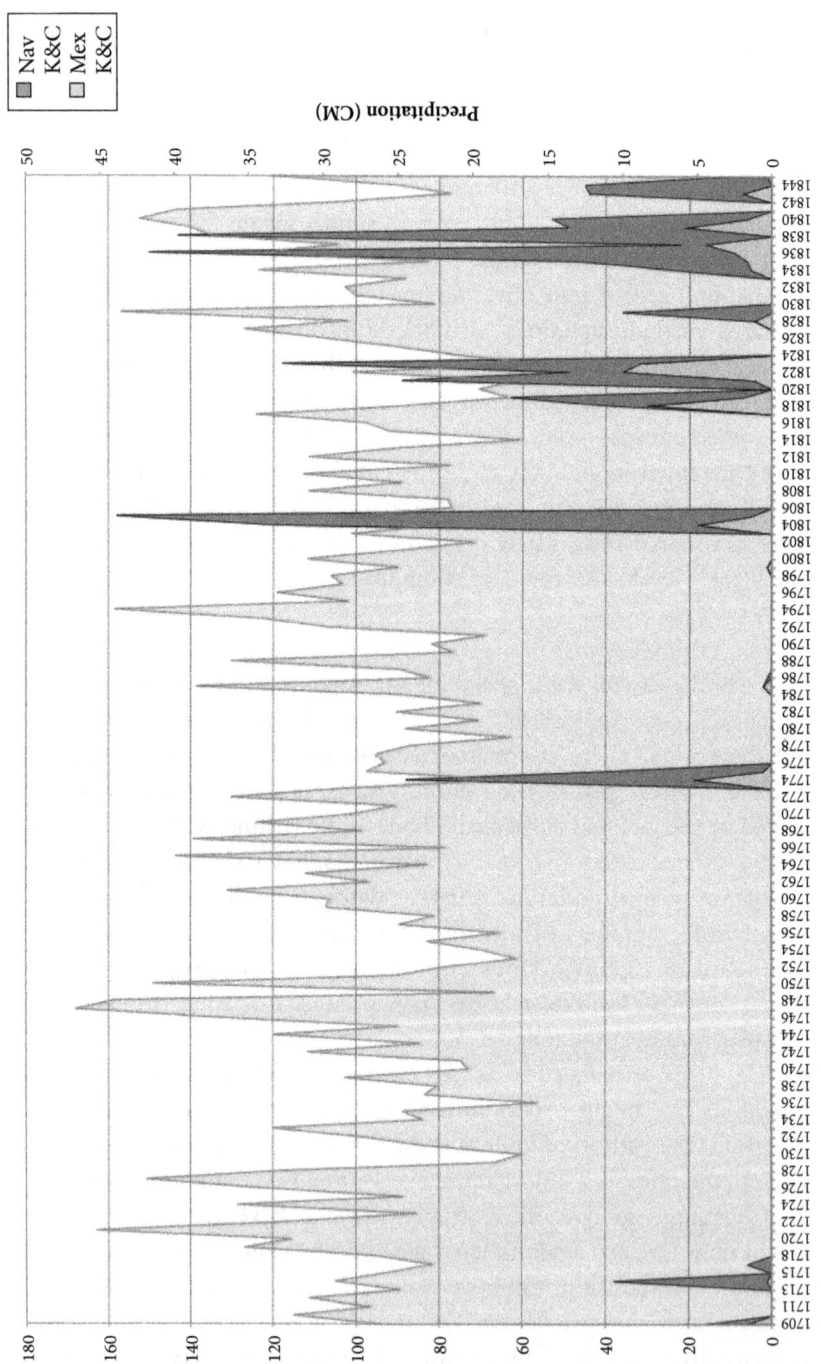

FIGURE 9.1. Navajos and New Mexicans killed and captured by one another, 1709–1845, with precipitation data.

These very imbalanced wars served an important purpose: they were waged to continue conversations that had become stalled within the confines of peace. War served to lodge collective grievances and force a restructuring of peace through an acceptable or at least definitive settlement of these grievances. This worked because both sides were in agreement over the predictability and appropriateness of responses to particular statements—in other words, collective violence had its own rules, and they had to be followed by both sides if violence was to be useful and brief. The origins, course, and conclusions of this pair of brief, brutal quarrels reward attention because they helped establish the expectations that made blood talk mutually intelligible.

Historians debate the origins of these conflicts. Drought probably aggravated regional tensions prior to the violence in 1774, but, as Figure 9.1 demonstrates, precipitation is an uneven predictor for warfare between Navajos and New Mexicans.[13] Perhaps, as has been suggested, the Diné raids that sparked these conflicts were attacks of opportunity, launched by ambitious men wanting sheep and horses. But both episodes began with targeted homicides. The long peace had depended first and foremost upon restraining killings—and they had in fact become exceedingly rare over the previous half century. Partly this may be attributed to Navajo belief. All Diné held corpses in dread, and they associated killing with profound supernatural danger. A late nineteenth-century Navajo informant reported that "one who killed an enemy by striking him in the chest would get disease in the chest, one who killed an enemy by striking him in the head would get disease in the head." Diné could be protected from the malevolence of alien ghosts through proper ceremonial magic, the intricate Enemy Way ceremony in particular. But in sharp contrast to Spaniards, Comanches, and some other neighboring peoples, Navajos had reason not to revel in wartime killing. It seems unlikely that the initial casualties of these wars—several *pobladores* and Pueblos struck down in their fields and pastures—can be attributed to aggressive stock rustlers.[14]

It is more likely that a critical mass of Navajos became aggrieved because of some specific, collective injury and decided to kill Spanish subjects in protest, in spite of homicide's supernatural and earthly dangers. Spanish records provide suggestive clues as to the nature of these injuries. In 1774 Navajos correctly surmised that the governor had been encouraging Ute attacks on Diné *rancherías* (in hopes, the governor told a superior, of making Navajos more dependent on Spaniards and hence more tractable).

Such a gross breach of the colonial relationship may well have been what finally wrecked the long-lived peace.[15] The killings in 1804 followed several years of fruitless Navajo protests over the new Spanish settlement of Cebolleta, the site of one of the Franciscans' stillborn missionary efforts and a place Diné had long occupied seasonally.[16] Both bouts of killing, in other words, seem to have been deliberate provocations on behalf of Navajos aggrieved with particular Spanish policies.

In this sense, there is a disciplined, collective character to Navajo interactions with New Mexicans evidenced both by the extraordinary durability of peace and the cooperative character of war. However punishing, Ute raids directly touched relatively few, and only a minority of Navajo families laid claim upon Cebolleta. That the majority would accept war in order to protest the grievances of relatively few suggests the power and depth of the connections binding these people together. Diné recognized distinct and interlocking levels of social and political organization. Most decisions fell to individual families or to collections of families within residence groups. But on important matters such as war and peace Navajos relied on a complex and far-flung kinship system to help them coordinate at higher levels. Matrilocal and organized into exogamous clans, most Diné would have been seen as family by multiple clans and therefore had broad and diverse networks through which to lodge complaints, seek help, and argue for policy. They also held an elaborate tribal council known as *naach'id*, wherein nearly all Navajos would come together to listen to speeches, to negotiate, and to seek unanimity in policies toward outsiders. During the *naach'id*, as one anthropologist explains, "a single individual acted as a patient to be cured by the ceremonies, but it seems that the real patient was the entire tribe, gathered to find a solution to some problem of great importance." Thus, as with the exposed Spanish-speaking boys and men tending flocks in the shadow of Tsoodzil, individual Diné were never really alone. No matter how few, or how spare and vulnerable they might seem in the flesh, unseen legions stood behind them.[17]

Proof of this came when, as they almost always did, New Mexicans gave Navajos an opportunity to claim or renounce the killer. As soon as news of homicides broke, officials in Santa Fe scrambled to confirm the meaning of the violence by asking the only question that mattered: *Who did this?* Was the murder the crime of a deviant individual? Or was it a killing on behalf of some significant Diné faction and hence an act of war? Go-betweens, often allied Indians, went out to get answers to these questions and to discern Navajo intentions. Had the killings been the work of alienated individuals or a rogue minority, this would have been the opportunity for prominent Diné to wash their hands of them or at least to make excuses and apologies as they had in 1799 with the murdered trader. But they didn't. In the 1770s and again in the 1800s, go-betweens returned to report that the Navajos "had risen up," "were at war," or had "become . . . declared enemies again." Lest any doubt remain, Diné reiterated their answers through more violence. Who did this? *The Navajos* did this.[18]

That, at least, was what the governor concluded, so he and his subordinates drew upon their own social and political mechanisms to begin organizing offensive campaigns. Consider the machinery that began to sputter to life in New Mexico as soon as a handful of impoverished shepherds turned up dead in April 1804. Within days local leaders sent letters to a man in Santa Fe (Governor Fernando de Chacón) who probably had no personal connection to the victims whatever. Commissioned with authority by representatives of another man (King Charles IV) whom no one in New Mexico had ever laid eyes on, the governor began writing his own letters. Governor Chacón believed that the Navajos had to endure decisive collective punishment before a lasting peace could be established. He reasoned that conciliation would only "confirm their feeling that we are afraid of them and that they are superior to us because they are united." Only continual campaigns, he insisted, would allow him to "dictate the manner in which I contract peace when [the Navajo] seek it."[19] He ordered his subordinates in villages and pueblos up and down the Rio Grande to gather their neighbors (and other men with little or no connection to the deceased), equip and provision militias, and prepare for weeks or even months of campaigns of killing, enslaving, and plundering in the distant west. Drawing on the value of his province's trade and diplomatic largess—funded in complex ways by people and communities elsewhere in New Spain—the governor was also able to recruit Ute and Jicarilla warriors for the cause. And, most crucially as it turned out, Chacón appealed to a faraway superior who ordered Sonoran Lt. Antonio Narbona to march hundreds of men—including sedentary Ópata Indians—hundreds of miles north into territory they had probably never seen in order to attack Indians few of them had ever heard of. Directed by Zuni guides, Narbona and his men killed 118 Navajo men, women, and children, and they took 36 as captives.[20] In light of recent scholarship stressing the weakness or incoherence of Spanish power in the far north relative to mighty Indian peoples, it is instructive to reflect upon the crackling institutional wires running from those luckless shepherds to the governor's palace, the militias, the Ópata farmers, and the many dozens of lives shattered inside the rust-red walls of the Canyon de Chelly that January in 1805.

Such campaigns aimed to make Diné afraid, individually and as a people, and through fear thereby turn every Navajo into an advocate for peace. In this sense the Spanish made their own claims about Navajo solidarity. Blood talk involved more than fraught statements about alienation and belonging within one's own community. Just as important, it always and inevitably provoked statements about who did and didn't belong to your adversary. One would have been hard-pressed to find a more zealous believer in Navajo unity than the governor of New Mexico in wartime. All Navajos were culpable and fit targets for retribution. And as the invaders grew increasingly familiar with their neighbors' vast, diverse territory and with locally specific patterns of transhumance, campaigns could often be conducted with increasing precision. With everyone suffering, so the logic went, popular support for peace would force reluctant headmen and enable cooperative headmen to come in and negotiate a comprehensive agreement. The campaigns were thus meant to make Diné talk, as a people, but of course they were mostly meant to make them listen. Along with animals and captives, New Mexican campaigners brought other trophies back to their capital. As if to emphasize their superior position in the dialogue, the returning New Mexicans nailed the severed ears of dead Navajos on the outer wall of the governor's palace—dozens and even (as in the aftermath of Narbona's pitiless campaign) hundreds of mismatched ears listening silently to the governor's arguments for peace.[21]

Navajos had to decide how to respond to the devastating campaigns in their homeland. Doubtless forging consensus across families and bands was all the more difficult in time of war, but crisis could inspire remarkable displays of unity. In 1804, for example, panicked Spanish officials reported one thousand Navajos marching on Cebolleta. More commonly Spanish campaigns provoked more small and medium-sized raids, and these raids provoked still more Mexican campaigns. Violence had diminishing political value as conflicts wore on, and in relatively short order Navajos began internal discussions about peace.[22]

Once headmen agreed that the conditions were right or timely for peace talks, they opened negotiations to bring the blood talk to a conclusion. Representative leaders would travel to one of the pueblos or settlements

FIGURE 9.2. A Navajo woman with infant, photographed by John Gaw Meem c. 1864–1868.
Library of Congress, LC-USZ62–98366.

west of the Rio Grande, usually Jémez, bearing symbols of peace—crosses and New Mexican captives—and would inquire about the governor's views. This was a critical moment. If properly managed by New Mexican authorities, these advances led to treaty negotiations, usually in Santa Fe. Spanish and Mexican officials staged these culminating events to remind Diné of their subordinate position in the relationship, mostly through the macabre humiliation of negotiating in the governor's palace, a ghastly building one observer described as "festooned with Indian ears."[23]

But there was no hiding the fact that the governor dearly wanted peace restored. He had little to gain and much to lose through war. Like most colonial authorities the world over, officials in Santa Fe much preferred to get what they wanted without costly wars. From Diné they wanted land around Tsoodzil for their expanding population and flocks, orderly commerce, and submission to Spanish law in the event of quarrels. Compared to these goals, the spoils of war looked paltry indeed. New Mexicans owned perhaps three million sheep by the middle of the nineteenth century, and they annually exported as many as five hundred thousand. Returning from a campaign with several hundred or even several thousand Navajo sheep (especially given the fact that many and sometimes most had been recently stolen from New Mexicans in the course of the war) contributed little to the colony's overall animal wealth. Much the same applied to captives in the late colonial period. New Mexicans had for centuries relied upon deracinated Indian captives as domestic servants. But most colonists found it safer and less costly to buy these slaves from other Indians than to go slave raiding themselves. Regional captive markets presented a far more efficient and reliable method of obtaining Indian servants than organized warfare, and Diné historically comprised a small proportion of a captive pool consisting mostly of Apaches, Comanches, Paiutes, and Utes.[24]

War, meanwhile, imposed severe costs on New Mexicans. Bouts of violence with Navajos repeatedly hounded *pobladores* from the Tsoodzil region and discouraged the economic and territorial expansion Spanish and Mexican officials so prized.[25] The complex offensive campaigns intended to end war placed most of the burden on the poor majority. Militiamen endured compulsory service and usually had to supply their own mounts, provisions, arms, and ammunition. "This extremely heavy and unbearable burden," wrote one commentator in 1812,

> is the cause in New Mexico of evils that are more easily experienced than narrated. Suffice it to say that many of those unfortunate men

are ruined by one single campaign; they have to sell their own clothing and that of their family in order to equip themselves with ammunition and supplies. This evil reaches such an extreme condition that it often becomes necessary for residents to sacrifice the liberty of their children in order to fulfill their duty as settlers.

Overwrought, surely, but the observation captures widespread resentment felt by men compelled to leave their fields, flocks, and families in order to fight Diné at their own expense. Local officials tasked with enforcing this unpopular service sometimes buckled under the collective resentment it engendered. "Señor," a weary *alcalde* of Laguna sighed to the governor, "I am the dust upon which everyone treads." No doubt some men within both societies welcomed war as opportunities to acquire animals and captives and to improve their own and their immediate families' fortunes. But this wasn't how war worked for the large majority of Navajos and New Mexicans, which is why, overall, both peoples usually managed to restrain mutual violence. Once violence did erupt, each side relied upon mutually recognized signs and shared protocols to bring it to an end as quickly as possible.[26]

Much depended, therefore, on the visits to western pueblos of men with crosses in their hands and captives in their train, on the speedy relay of their intentions to Santa Fe, on the haggling over preliminary terms, and on the formal negotiations that culminated in treaties. In these moments leaders on both sides tried to capitalize on the dead and vanished, on the traumas and transformations of the past months in healing the breach: by granting concessions, by refusing concessions in light of success in war, or, more often, by doing both.

Some clarity emerged out of the anguish and wreckage of 1774–1775 and 1804–1805, and it brought two facts into focus. First, individual or local grievances on the Diné–New Mexican borderland easily metastasized into collective war. Violence between people usually escalated into violence between peoples. Indeed, it was supposed to. The promise of collective war powerfully discouraged casual offense and violence on the borderland. Second, when war did erupt, it could be useful and brief so long as both sides adhered to a few basic protocols. If these were followed, war could address grievances immune to nonviolent diplomacy and could be brought to conclusion with relative dispatch.

Such were the expectations that the conflicts of 1774–1775 and 1804–1805 established on both sides, expectations very much in evidence in the late 1810s when Navajos and New Mexicans fell to quarreling again. The trouble began in the summer of 1816 when Comanche raiders fell upon Navajo families on the south side of Tsoodzil. Diné observed Spaniards driving their sheep to distant pastures just before the raids, and they sensibly concluded that their erstwhile patrons knew the Comanche plans in advance.[27] New Mexican denials didn't convince, and by 1818 the pattern began all over again. Navajos started killing country-folk. Ever optimistic, Spanish authorities sent out various runners, even two obliging Utes, to urge the Diné to call it murder and surrender the killers to Spanish justice. With emissaries rebuffed and news of more killings in the countryside, the governor dispatched militia campaigns to the west. As in 1805, these included professional soldiers from Sonora and, as always, Spanish forces killed and kidnapped out of all proportion to Navajo raids. Before long Diné representatives arrived at Jémez bearing a cross and four captives. Talks began and then culminated with a new treaty in the summer of 1819. Everyone had been here before.[28]

THE regional custom of blood talk served Navajos and New Mexicans relatively well for several decades. It helped to keep wars brief and unusual throughout the Bourbon era, and by channeling individual grievances into collective violence it facilitated the constitution of peoplehood on both sides of the borderland. For this reason, core traditions of violence held throughout the 1820s and early 1830s, following Mexican Independence. Most important, both sides continued in their expectations of how wars began. Killings—not theft—endured as the unique and inevitable opening statement in war. Diné and New Mexicans stole animals from each other frequently. Into the 1830s certain western *pobladores* agitated for war, complaining that while Diné "respect the lives of the inhabitants of the territory, they destroy the property that the people depend upon for survival."[29] Despite the thefts, officials in Santa Fe grudgingly respected the regional precedent that Navajos decided when wars began and ended (that homicide, not robbery, signaled the end of peace). Killings were still met by inquiries about culpability. Failure to surrender killers prompted retaliatory campaigns, and violence was expected to cease once Navajos began the dialogue of peace and initiated formal treaty talks.[30]

But as Figure 9.1 makes clear, peace became more fleeting and violence more common as the nineteenth century progressed. War proved less and less effective at quieting grievances by the 1830s, and by the 1840s the regional blood talk shattered into incoherence. This transformation depended on three developments. First, wounds inflicted in war left some in the region nursing hatred and willing to violate traditional protocols. The most breathtaking of these violations came in early 1822, following several months of war. After the usual cycle of raids and campaigns, thirteen Diné headmen followed the well-established script and traveled to Jémez bearing signs of peace. The residents welcomed them in but were then all beaten to death.[31] By the time of this massacre, the people of Jémez and its environs had probably suffered more from Navajo raids than anyone else in New Mexico. And surely the word *peace* sounded cheaper to their ears in 1822, with the previous war ended only two years prior, than it had in 1775 or 1805 when peace was something expected to last decades. Moreover, Navajos had long maintained a close, complex, and often contradictory relationship with the people of Jémez; the term for Navajo in the Tewa language spoken in several pueblos means "Jémez Apache." No doubt there were deep communal and personal dynamics at work in the pueblo that day, dynamics mostly irrecoverable now. But one can only marvel at the animosity necessary to deliberately dismantle the mechanisms of peace this way, to waste so useful a thing as an enemy's trust. This unprecedented violation of the rules that structured violence between Diné and New Mexicans had dire consequences, despite the governor's purported outrage and the temporary imprisonment of the culprits. Navajos killed more New Mexicans in the next two years than in any other two-year, five-year, or even ten-year period, ever. New Mexicans responded with more campaigns, more corpses, more wailing slaves. The fighting finally ended two years after the massacre with a fourteen-point treaty, signed, remarkably, in Jémez. The ghosts made their way into point thirteen, appropriately, which admonished the signatories to remember that "the nature of peace is to quiet old grievances originating in time of war."[32]

In fact, for Diné and New Mexicans the reverse had always been true: the nature of war had always been to quiet grievances arising in time of peace. New Mexico had much to lose in outright war and little interest in initiating it. Navajos stood to lose even more. Yet they occasionally appealed to war precisely because it had the power to quiet grievances, either by forcing a change in Spanish policy or by proving to supplicants and discontents that their complaints could not be satisfied through violence and would have to be endured. The obvious trouble, as the treaty suggests and as the passions at Jémez made plain, is that wars always generate new grievances. If war is a tool to fix a broken peace, what tools exist to fix a broken war?

The second major factor in worsening post-Independence violence was increasing fragmentation within Diné society. To the inevitable, essential question asked over the bodies of slain *pobladores* in the 1770s, 1800s, 1810s, and 1820s—*who did this?*—Diné had time and again answered collectively: *we* did. Violence constituted community, and community constituted violence. But after the 1820s the answer became more equivocal. As early as 1818, a Diné headman that Spaniards called Joaquin came to Jémez with several stolen horses he had recovered from his raiding countrymen. He had advocated for peace, he explained, but since "his efforts to dissuade the Navajos proved useless, he had separated his band from the rest of the tribe." As proof of his sincerity, he pledged that "he and his warriors would accompany and aid the Spanish troops" campaigning in Navajo country. In later years Joaquin's band, called the Diné Ana'aii (the *enemy* or *alien Navajo*) by others of their people, would be led by men like the mixed-descent Francisco Baca and Cebolla Sandoval who not only allied with New Mexicans in time of war but also seem to have launched their own private slave raids among fellow Navajo. And yet on other occasions Joaquin and his successors would fight as Diné against New Mexicans, participate in integrative ceremonies such as the *naach'id*, and join other headmen in formal treaty negotiations.[33]

The Diné Ana'aii, in other words, seem not to have been a schismatic band so much as an extreme example of the political fragmentation spreading across Navajo country generally by the 1820s and 1830s. Obligations and allegiances increasingly depended on context and could shift from situation to situation. Older social and political mechanisms that facilitated tribal consensus in times of crisis stopped working like before. Scholars estimate that Navajos possessed a half million sheep and goats by the end of the Mexican era, and that the richest 7 percent of Diné families owned 40 percent of this animal wealth. The same families owned 75 percent of all horses. As Lynn Bailey and James Brooks have shown so powerfully, this mounting inequality does much to explain fracturing opinions about war and peace. Wealthy Navajos had much to lose in times of war, and they often emerged in this period as the advocates for peace. By 1825, Mexican sources begin to reflect an emerging discourse among Navajos pitting *los ricos* (the rich) against *los ladrones* (the thieves). Increasingly conflicts would be attributed by some prominent headmen to thieves seeking to enrich themselves in wars that were ruinous to the peacefully inclined majority. By the 1830s New Mexican authorities were convinced enough of the import and authenticity of Diné factionalism that they occasionally broke with their tradition of collective punishment, ordering campaigning militia to avoid the *rancherías* of headmen thought to be hostile to the pro-war "dissidents of their nation." Selective aggression was easier to order than execute, and the animal-rich *rancherías* of conciliatory headmen sometimes proved too tempting for New Mexican militia to resist. But by fighting Diné selectively, authorities in Santa Fe lent momentum to forces pulling the Navajo community apart from the inside out.[34]

Third, and most consequentially, war became more common in the Navajo–New Mexican borderland because of transformations in New Mexico's culture of Indian slavery. Prior to the 1820s, diplomatic protocols and formal treaties nearly always called for a mutual exchange of captives at the conclusion of war. Diné leaders seem to have had the ability to turn over New Mexican captives when obliged to by treaty stipulations, mainly because they held so few. Both peoples kept each other as captives, certainly, but the mutuality of this activity is easy to overstate. There is little evidence that captive acquisition was a major objective of Navajo raids upon New Mexico in the first half of the nineteenth century. Indeed, the data from 1774 to 1846 suggest that Diné probably took fewer than twenty New Mexicans captive during all of these years. Surrendering most of the captives they did have from time to time seemed a small sacrifice for peace.[35] Spaniards captured far more Navajos in war than vice versa. Some they baptized and quietly put to work in New Mexican households. Occasionally Diné captives went to Ute or Apache auxiliaries or else marched out of the province altogether, as in 1805 when Narbona and his men took twelve enslaved Navajos to Sonora. Some of these may have gone on to labor as "Apaches" in the mines that Chantal Cramaussel discusses elsewhere in this volume. But, despite such episodes, in principle and usually in practice Spanish officials assumed mutual captive exchange to be a precondition to peace with Navajos.[36] Consequently, while imperfect and as imbalanced as most things were in the Diné–New Mexican relationship, captive redemption presented few obstacles to peace in the eighteenth and early nineteenth centuries.[37]

Santa Fe celebrated Mexico's independence from Spain only a few months before the massacre at Jémez, and independence created complex economic, institutional, and attitudinal changes in New Mexico's culture of Indian slavery. Slave raiding became a more pronounced goal of formal and informal New Mexican raiding campaigns after 1821, and this transition leaps out from the baptismal records of the era. Whereas there were only fourteen Navajo baptisms recorded for the last thirty years of Spanish rule (1790–1819), over the next thirty years (1820–1849) New Mexico's priests baptized 408.[38] David Brugge's seminal work in examining nineteenth-century baptismal records reveals that these captives lived scattered throughout New Mexico's households. More than six hundred New Mexican households had one Diné captive during the century, but only eleven households had five or more Diné captives. Thus hundreds of captured Navajos lived scattered throughout the state, toiling along a continuum of postures from cherished adopted kin to terrorized sex slaves. Spanish law nominally regulated when slaves could be acquired, under what circumstances, and for how long. But captors grew adept at evading the spirit of such laws, especially after Independence. At a time when thousands of African American slaves toiled as chattel in cotton fields a few hundred miles to the east in the Mexican state of Texas y Coahuila, New Mexican families with Indian slaves had little incentive to honor laws concerning slaves.[39]

On the contrary, by the 1820s New Mexicans had a powerful incentive to seek more Navajo slaves and hold them in bondage as long as possible. Independence opened the province to the huge and hungry American market, via the overland trade to Missouri. New Mexicans consequently enjoyed previously unthinkable opportunities for trade, and this dramatically boosted the value of household labor. Diné slaves had particular appeal in the new context, for by the 1820s and 1830s Navajo blankets had acquired continental renown for their beauty, durability, and watertight weave. Josiah Gregg, America's chief chronicler of the Santa Fe Trail, noted that a fine example of one of these blankets sold for as much as $60; another cautious observer claimed the blankets sold from $50 to $100 each. There is little doubt that market opportunities made New Mexican families increasingly reluctant to part with Diné slaves.[40]

New Mexican officials found it not only unpopular but also culturally difficult to secure the return of Navajo captives to their families after 1821. Spaniards and Mexicans had long justified their slaving through the notion of spiritual salvation: better that Indians be slaves redeemed to Christ than that they go free for a life of idolatry and damnation after death. The culmination of this convenient idea was baptism, after which it became much more complicated to release Diné captives back to their people. Independence resulted in benign neglect of New Mexico, enabling local officials to do things that superiors farther south may have countermanded in earlier years. Indeed, the increasingly rapacious approach to Navajo captives ought to be seen as part of a broader post-Independence process whereby New Mexico's Indian policies diverged from those of the Mexican state. Apaches had constituted the majority of New Mexico's captive baptisms in the mid-eighteenth century, and Comanches became most prominent between the 1760s and 1790s. These trends roughly correspond to decades in which Apaches and then Comanches were considered the key strategic threats across northern New Spain. Though undoubtedly opportunistic, New Mexico's slave markets harmonized with broader imperial policy in these years. After Independence the territory's slaving practices became more provincial, unmoored from northern Mexico's strategic imperatives. Apaches and Comanches nearly drop out of the territory's baptismal records after the 1820s, an era in which Apache and Comanche raiders became the great scourges of the other northern Mexican states. Post-Independence New Mexicans trafficked with Apaches and feted Comanche leaders in Santa Fe, but they sought household slaves among Utes and especially Navajos, peoples with little or no quarrel with Mexicans in other states.[41]

José Antonio Vizcarra emerged as the great exponent of this newly independent posture regarding Indian policy in the 1820s. Vizcarra became military commander at the close of 1822, several months after the massacre at Jémez prompted the most violent year of Navajo raiding in New Mexican memory. He spent much of 1823 campaigning zealously in Diné country.[42] When headmen made peace overtures that fall, the ranking political figure in New Mexico, Bartolomé Baca, ordered local authorities to assemble all the Navajo captured during Vizcarra's raiding campaign in advance of an anticipated captive exchange. Vizcarra sent a furious letter to Baca protesting any plan to surrender the captives and framing his argument in the language of independence. "If a liberal government like this one we have adopted were to hand over to infidels individuals who have entered our society, all or most of whom have received the health-giving waters of holy baptism, we might as well go on supporting the despotic government of which we are now free." Vizcarra complained to the central government, and he managed to insert his views into the long-awaited peace treaty, signed in January 1824. He clouded an otherwise straightforward promise to return Diné captives with this ambiguous phrase: "provided they wish to go, since to send back those who received baptism or intended to was unchristian."[43]

In future treaties the New Mexicans would go further and consistently refuse to surrender all but a few captives, even in the interest of peace. Because these terms were virtually impossible for Navajos to accept, New Mexican authorities experimented with various clauses meant to obscure the brazen audacity of their captive policy. A treaty from 1829, for example, stipulated that while captive exchanges would be one-sided, any Navajo managing to escape on his or her own would be left at liberty.[44] In 1839, following another war and another treaty with lopsided captive terms, the military commander of Jémez wrote an open letter to the people of New Mexico imploring them to contribute to finance the liberation of Diné captives, "according to their consciences."[45] Little came of this, and war resumed soon after. A treaty in 1844 reiterated the imbalanced captive policy but encouraged Navajos to ransom enslaved loved ones from their masters. Sometimes authorities quietly released the kin of key headmen, hoping to pry them away from the war camp. None of these cynical moves obscured the profound change that had taken place since Independence. Navajos captured in war would toil their lives away as slaves in enemy homes. In times of invasion, this certainty could lead to scenes of wild terror and despair—as in 1840 when a group of Navajos flung themselves off a mesa rather than be taken alive by New Mexican forces. Such was the permanence and horror of captivity in Diné imaginations.[46]

The three post-Independence changes—violations of protocol borne of war-weariness and hatred, Navajo economic and political fragmentation, and, especially, New Mexico's increasingly rapacious culture of Indian slavery—combined to make peace all but impossible and blood talk all but unintelligible by the early 1840s. There emerged an unprecedented pattern where the rituals of war coexisted with the rituals of peace.

Consider the mixed messages, contradictory policies, and unintelligible signs that prevailed in the three years prior to the U.S. invasion. In February 1843, the governor regaled Navajo leaders in Santa Fe, and in June a prominent headman stole five hundred cows near Belen and fifty horses near Jémez. Several other leading Diné moved their families and denounced the thieves, promising even to help New Mexicans campaign against them.[47]

Raiding continued into July, and headmen were again regaled in the capital in August. One month later, New Mexicans campaigned in Navajo territory, killing fifteen, capturing twenty-two, and stealing fifteen thousand sheep. In November, several Diné received presents at Santa Fe while other Navajos killed five *pobladores* at San Miguel del Bado.[48]

Amid the confusion it was little wonder that individual Mexican towns and villages tried to conclude their own peace agreements with Navajos. Officials in Santa Fe furiously declared such agreements illegitimate.[49] But their own policy had become hopelessly confused by 1844. In January, the Comandante General sent out messengers to try and bring Diné negotiators into Santa Fe, and, in a gesture of goodwill, insisted several animals stolen from Navajos be returned. At the end of the month he even directed local officials to discover the culprits who participated in a private campaign that had lately attacked Diné. Peace with the Indians had become all the more difficult because of these actions, and he ordered that those involved in the campaign be dealt with "to destroy suspicions." But only two weeks later, he approved another private campaign that killed and captured nearly forty Navajos.[50]

For their part, Diné headmen tried to resume the dialogue of peace in February of 1844. They released a number of captives and signed yet another treaty in March.[51] The terms were unrealistic and contradictory, a reflection of the times. Peace and commerce would resume, providing that the Diné return New Mexican captives. As had by this point become customary, any Navajo who managed to escape would remain free. In New Mexico's continuing efforts to find innovative ways to retain their slaves but satisfy Navajo demands, they conceded that Navajos could try and recapture their kin from their individual New Mexican owners. But the treaty seemed to make this a practical impossibility by stating that if the Diné committed even one hostile act, the peace would then be broken "and constant war will be made against them."[52]

New Mexicans had by now realized that some captives would have to be returned if the peace were to take hold, no matter the treaty terms. And if any were to be released, better that they be kin to prominent headmen. The Commandant General withdrew funds from the depleted treasury to pay for the return of three captives, and Navajo headmen received presents in the capital in April. Still, when Navajo raids resumed in the summer, Governor Armijo apparently took a cue from his counterparts in Chihuahua and recruited foreign scalp hunters to hunt Diné like animals. The bewildering combination of mutual violence and diplomatic ritual continued throughout the year.[53]

It would be no different in 1845 and 1846. Raids and campaigns continued alongside diplomacy. Both sides sent out messengers to try and discern the others' intentions while the contradictions multiplied. A massive Diné raiding party turned back one hundred New Mexican militiamen in April. In May, other raiders were pursued and two killed. Days later, a prominent headman arrived in Jémez demanding compensation for the dead men, under the pretext that the peace was still intact. Both sides continued to raid and send out signals for peace through the rest of the year.[54] In March 1846, Armijo notified subordinates that "the Navajos have declared war, committing murders and carrying off a number of sheep." Soon after he began explicitly authorizing private raiding campaigns. "The war with the Navajos is slowly consuming the department," he wrote, "reducing to very obvious misery the district of the southwest."[55] Four months later American troops marched into this exhausted little world and were unopposed.

In 1933 the ethnographer Willard Williams Hill interviewed older Navajo about warfare. These men had been children or hadn't yet been born when Diné suffered the great tragedy of their history. In 1863, following seventeen years of American frustration over interminable borderland violence, Kit Carson helped guide U.S. army troops, New Mexican militia, and allied Indians into Navajo country. The invaders slaughtered stock, burned fields, chopped down orchards, and waited. Before long thousands of starving Diné poured out of the mountains and canyons. The army forced them on the Long Walk, a 450-mile forced march to a wretched, pestilential internment camp near Ft. Sumner on the plains of New Mexico. Only in 1868, after much trauma and the abject failure of the government's planned reservation there did U.S. authorities relent and allow the captives to return to a confirmed reservation in their own homeland. Thereafter relations with the people of New Mexico were as quiet as they had been for most of the eighteenth century.

When Hill asked his informants about the history of the long feud with New Mexicans, therefore, none could answer from firsthand experience. But they still had stories to tell, narratives of alienation and belonging that reprised the old blood talk. These were stories about schisms small and large, about individual, ungovernable Navajo or rogue factions who bore responsibility for the endemic warfare that had become the norm by the mid-nineteenth century. Hill learned that "the desire for plunder was the motivating force" behind Navajo raids, that "the majority were opposed to these expeditions and the local headmen did all in their power to suppress them." One informant told him that Diné and New Mexicans had a history of amicable trade until "some of the Navajo learned Spanish and prevailed on the Mexicans to raid the Navajo for horses," whereupon all the trouble started. Another tradition, "the most popular," began with wealthy Mountain Navajo stealing beautiful women, descendants from seventeenth-century Pueblo refugees, from their impoverished Navajo kin in the canyons. Canyon men reacted by raiding "the Pueblos, then the Ute, and finally the Mexicans. This drew attention to the Navajo, and raids in retaliation were sent into Navajo country." Other variations on the theme blamed ungovernable, self-interested Navajo men for provoking New Mexican reprisals and insisted that "that is why the Navajo were ruined at the time of Fort Sumner."[56]

The strain of oral tradition conveyed to Hill provides one answer to the question *who did this?* Who bore responsibility for the conflict with New Mexico that had become so entrenched and unmanageable by the mid-nineteenth century? Perhaps, as Hill's informants believed and scholars have often since claimed, most of the violence should be attributed to ambitious men eager to obtain animals and captives and indifferent to the horror and heartbreak their actions called down upon other Diné.[57]

But I am more convinced by another scenario, one more in continuity with the practices and values of previous decades. Navajos and New Mexicans alike had long possessed the personal and collective restraint necessary to avoid killing one another over animals. When it came to stock, people in this borderland did seem to be *people*—individuals or families who mostly had to struggle alone to protect their animals. Not so when it came to corpses. Destruction of people almost invariably meant war between peoples. This made killing momentous and extraordinarily dangerous. Hard experience had shown that the New Mexicans could inflict orders of magnitude more damage upon Navajos than Navajos inflicted upon them. Killing was therefore something to undertake only out of deeply held, communal grievance, out of a profound and agreed-upon need to change something intolerable—not out of atomized, personal, or familial ambition.

By the 1830s and 1840s the Diné with the keenest grievances against New Mexicans were the kin of the hundreds of women, children, and men held as slaves in New Mexican homes. Navajos traveled widely, and the Rio

Grande was not that far away. Surely many knew or thought they knew what town or even what house their loved ones labored in. I suspect that these grieving kin bore the primary responsibility for provoking war again and again in the generation prior to the U.S. invasion. There is every reason to believe that such people would have begun with appeals to their own extended families, bands, and clans: they would have invoked obligation, sought pity, implored their people to fight together, to bloody New Mexicans and make them eager for peace, and then endeavor to redeem their captive people as part of treaty talks as had previously been the norm. There was no question that men sought animals and even captives in wartime. But the previous century of collective behavior suggests that this was never at the center of things, that even into the 1830s and 1840s appeals for war had far more to do with families than with sheep, goats, and horses. War was waged in order to redeem captives, not acquire new ones.

Perhaps such appeals failed to secure broad consensus for war because the injury seemed too personal and narrow. Or perhaps they failed because Diné society had become too fractured by lines of wealth and poverty. Whatever the reason, the fact remains that many decades of practice had bequeathed upon the weak and aggrieved a way to force their people into consensus, whether powerful headmen wanted it or not. All they need do was to begin killing New Mexicans. Once corpses started turning up, New Mexican authorities gave Diné leaders a chance to avoid war. Tell us *who did this*: call it murder and surrender the culprit. But no matter the fault lines widening in their society, this was something headmen found culturally and politically impossible.

Homicide ignited war, and war turned people into peoples—or at least it used to. By the 1840s, the old protocols no longer worked as they had in years before. Unable to surrender other Diné to New Mexican justice and retain political credibility among their own people, some of the more prominent, wealthy headmen nonetheless could and did separate from war advocates and denounce them in Jémez and Santa Fe. When they did so, these men whose families had so much to lose in wartime blamed the homicides not on heartbroken people trying to ignite wars in hopes of regaining their mothers, fathers, daughters, sons, sisters, and brothers. They blamed the violence on *thieves*.

This narrative sought to shape the future, not objectively describe the past. It may have been the case that plunder came to dominate regional events in the chaotic period between the American conquest and the internment at Ft. Sumner, and that disorganized thieving led to incidental killings and cycles of reprisal. But this was not what was happening in the twenty years prior to the U.S. invasion, when wealthy Navajos first began talking about uncontrollable *ladrones*. Externally, such talk aimed to dissuade New Mexicans from their long-standing practice of collective punishment—to disrupt the very protocols through which killers provoked war. Internally, the argument about thieves highlighted a ubiquitous but secondary aspect of war—plunder—in order to trivialize and obscure the deeper motivations of those who waged it. It is perhaps unsurprising that this story would prevail over others following the traumas of the Long Walk and captivity at Ft. Sumner. That tragedy did nothing if not prove the danger and folly of warring upon New Mexicans and retroactively vindicate those headmen who had so long urged restraint. Little wonder then that the *ricos*' narrative could have evolved from political argument to inherited tradition by the time of Hall's research. Indeed, by the early twentieth century the Navajos that Hill interviewed seemed to blame alienated Diné—rather than colonialism—for their people's historic catastrophe.[58]

And yet the long quantitative record of peace and war on the Navajo–New Mexican borderland recommends an alternative version of blood talk: a rival narrative of alienation and belonging, one about loved ones alienated from those to whom they belonged. It attributed the quickening and momentous violence of the day not to individual material ambition but to collective grief. A U.S. Indian agent recorded its essence in an interview with a headman called Armijo in January 1852. The agent had come to ask variations on the essential, inevitable question. Why won't the violence cease? Who is to blame? Why are these injuries continually inflicted, and in whose name? Though it would have less traction upon the future than the tale about thieves, I think the narrative Armijo gave in response does much more to illuminate the past.

> Question: "The people living in the Rio Abajo complain that the Navajos have captured their children—stolen their stock—that their fields have to be idle for they cannot work them for fear of your people—Is this not so?"
>
> Answer: "*My people are all crying in the same way* three of our Chiefs now sitting before you mourn for their children—who have

been taken from their homes by the Mexicans—More than 200 of our children have been carried off and we know not where they are—The Mexicans have lost but few children in comparison with what they have stolen from us. . . . Eleven times have we given up our Captives—only once have they given us ours—My people are yet crying for the children they have lost."[59]

CHAPTER 10

Toward a New Literary History of the West: Etahdleuh Doanmoe's Captivity Narrative

BIRGIT BRANDER RASMUSSEN

On May 21, 1875, seventy-two young Cheyenne, Kiowa, Arapaho, Caddo, and Comanche men from the southern Plains arrived in St. Augustine, Florida. They were prisoners of war, exiled far away from their tribal homelands in order to prevent them from fighting the United States. Exhausted from a one-thousand-mile journey east via wagon, train, steamboat, and horse-drawn cart, they were brought to Fort Marion for indefinite detention.[1]

Within months of their arrival, some of these young men acquired paper and pencils and began to produce images depicting their captivity, as well as their journey to Fort Marion and their pre-captivity life on the Plains. Of the seventy-two captives, twenty-six of them are known to have produced well over fourteen hundred pages, an archive that constitutes an important and thus far understudied contribution to nineteenth-century American literature and cultural history. Although the Fort Marion corpus is well known to scholars of Native American art, culture, and history, I am interested in reading these materials as literature informed by Plains literacy practices brought to Fort Marion by the captives.

Scholars of the colonial period in America have increasingly become aware that indigenous Americans in many regions possessed their own distinct literary practices, rooted in non-alphabetic forms of literacy.[2] We are only slowly beginning to develop the methodology to take account of this literary legacy and to understand how indigenous and European forms of literacy intersected across America. This chapter will contribute to that effort by analyzing a non-alphabetic captivity narrative by a young Kiowa warrior that has recently been recovered and published for the first time by Philip Earenfight under the title *A Kiowa's Odyssey*.³ The manuscript at the heart of this publication is a collection of thirty-one pages that is presumed to have been a single book produced by a young Kiowa named Etahdleuh Doanmoe, sometime between 1875 and 1878. This book is intriguing to a literary scholar because it appears to be a coherent, chronological narrative, contained within the pages of a single sketchbook, and it bears the traces of subsequent intervention by Doanmoe's captor and likely interlocutor, Richard Pratt, as well as by Pratt's son, Mason.

Sometime after Doanmoe completed the manuscript, it was taken apart by Pratt so that his own captions could be typed onto the pages. Mason, to whom Pratt gifted the book, also made alterations. It was Mason who entitled the re-bound book *A Kiowa's Journey*. Eventually, this bound book was disassembled in order to matte and exhibit the individual pages. At this point, Doanmoe's pages were apparently mixed up with pages produced by Bear's Heart, a fellow prisoner at Fort Marion. This collection, incorrectly attributed to only Doanmoe, was subsequently divided between Dickinson College and Yale University.⁴

A specialist in manuscript studies, Earenfight was able to reconstruct Doanmoe's book by using the methodological tools of his field, including analysis of visual style as well as careful examination of physical evidence such as binding edges and matching binding marks.⁵ His critical edition is particularly useful because it includes scholarship that traces the complex material history of the original manuscript and the ways in which it has been overwritten, disassembled, and reassembled by various colonial agents. This publication provides us with high-quality reproductions of the original manuscript in its entirety, making Doanmoe's narrative available for general study and, potentially, classroom use. The book now stands poised to gain recognition as an important piece of nineteenth-century American literature.

Along with Howling Wolf, Bear's Heart, Making Medicine, and Zotom, Etahdleuh Doanmoe is one of the most prolific and best known of the warrior-artist-author-captives at Fort Marion. By the time he reached the Florida coast fort, he was nineteen years old. Doanmoe was a child of the southern Plains and of the violent history of the borderlands. His father was a Kiowa warrior, and his mother was a Mexican captive brought north as the result of raids to the South. Doanmoe was raised, then, by someone intimately familiar with what it meant to negotiate the space between captive and captor. In addition, he was shaped by the warrior, hunter, and raider culture of the southern Plains.[6] His name, which means Boy Hunting, references his first successful buffalo kill at age fifteen, an act that is crucial to his identity and also figures significantly in the manuscript. As conflict escalated on the Plains following the conclusion of the American Civil War, Etahdleuh Doanmoe joined a band of warriors led by Lone Wolf. This group included a number of his fellow prisoners at Fort Marion.[7]

As they began to fill the blank pages of sketchbooks supplied by their jailor, Captain Richard Henry Pratt, these young men became part of a cohort attempting to adapt the conventions of Plains pictography to the circumstance of captivity that had not traditionally formed the basis of pictographic records on the Plains. Because these narratives were produced for Anglo-Americans, they must also have thought about how to best tell the story they wanted to tell across linguistic and cultural barriers. At the same time, they were being educated by their captors in literacy practices that were radically different from those familiar to them from the Plains. For that reason, texts like Etahdleuh Doanmoe's book reveal to us how these young Kiowa and Cheyenne men theorized the intersection between different narrative conventions, different forms of literacy, and different ways of communicating with pen and paper in a space organized by colonial power relations.

SHORTLY after arriving at Fort Marion, Doanmoe earned the trust of Richard Pratt, who came to consider him a protégé. Although Doanmoe was part of a failed plot to escape from Fort Marion, uncovered by Pratt in the spring of 1876, the two maintained a special relationship throughout his time in captivity. Pratt appointed Doanmoe as the quartermaster sergeant. When the Fort Marion prisoners were released after three years, Doanmoe was one of a few who stayed behind to acquire further education before returning to Kiowa territory (Paul Zotom was another). Pratt helped finance that education. For the rest of his rather brief life, Doanmoe would travel back and forth between the Plains and the East Coast, between Kiowa and Anglo-American worlds.[8]

Reading his manuscript from 1877 confronts us with a number of difficulties. In addition to the methodological challenge of how to "read" the narrative, we are also confronted with the sediments of colonial interference that compete with Doanmoe's own narrative. Earenfight's edition does not attempt to produce an "authentic" version of Doanmoe's work but rather presents it as the product of multiple, often competing, narrative processes that affect not only our understanding of Doanmoe's work but also our ability to recognize it as literature.

As Doanmoe's work comes to us as a reconstructed manuscript, it is hard to see it as anything but a collection of, admittedly wonderful, images. Not surprisingly, it is an art historian, Janet Catherine Berlo, who provides page-by-page guidance for how to interpret the images, aided by Pratt's captions, his diary, and other historical sources. My readings build on and add another disciplinary layer of analysis to the information and interpretations provided by Berlo.

In the reconstructed form of the book, the images that make up the narrative seem to form a whole that illustrates the journey from the Plains to St. Augustine, disrupted by a few pages of what seems like unrelated, nostalgic Plains imagery. And this is indeed how Pratt asks us to read the book. On the inside of the front cover, Pratt penned the following inscription: "Drawn by E-tah-dle-uh/Kiowa prisoner/Fort Marion, Fla./April 26 1877/A present to Mason from Papa." These words tell us that the images in the book are made by Etahdleuh Doanmoe, name the circumstance of captivity, and provide the date we presume the book was finished. The inscription also marks the book as a prized possession passed down to Pratt's son, Mason. Finally, these words situate the book in the realm of the visual, rather than the literary: the very first word we encounter is "drawn."

This injunction to see "drawings" in the pages that follow is the first of several gestures by which Pratt directs our interpretation of the book and its contents. While we can only speculate about the ways in which Pratt shaped the production of the book, either directly or indirectly, we can trace some of those interventions and their consequences for subsequent reception of the manuscript. The manuscript tells us Doanmoe's story of captivity, and it also provides a textual record of Pratt's subsequent efforts to seize control of that narrative. Indeed, reading *A Kiowa's Odyssey* is a process of tracing multiple narrative voices and desires and mapping their intersections and contradictions.

The most obvious evidence of Pratt's interference is the presence of typed captions. The captions appear to simply explicate the images, as if they represent Doanmoe's absent voice. However, these are not Doanmoe's words. The captions were composed by Pratt and added years later, a process that required him to take the manuscript apart. Given that Doanmoe learned to read and write English at Fort Marion, we may wonder why Pratt didn't simply ask him to provide brief captions if he felt the images needed elaboration. Such captions appear on many of the images produced at Fort Marion, and their absence in this particular book may indicate that Pratt explicitly asked Doanmoe *not* to write on the pages. But this we cannot know. We may also wonder why, when Pratt decided to add his own words to the manuscript, he didn't simply write in longhand on the pages. His willingness to essentially destroy the original manuscript in order to put the pages into a typewriter indicates that it was very important to Pratt that the captions be typed.

Two things distinguish typed captions from longhand text: their permanence and their visual authority. Both must have been important to Pratt. Conversely, his willingness to take the manuscript apart (it was only reassembled years later by Mason) suggests that he did not place a high value on the coherence of Doanmoe's work or the chronology of the narrative. Indeed, his decision to destroy the original manuscript removes it even further from the realm of the literary. What he passed down to his son was neither a narrative nor a book but a collection of drawings. More than one hundred years would pass before a manuscript scholar with the skills to reconstruct Doanmoe's manuscript would, simultaneously, restore it to the status of narrative. The typed captions, however, cannot be undone.

Pratt's captions and Earenfight's story of recovery serve as important reminders of the colonial violence that had shaped Doanmoe's manuscript from its initial production to its contemporary reception. Any effort to study the non-alphabetic literatures of America's Native people confronts this legacy of violence, rooted in colonial conflict, which accounts for the paucity of extant documents, their dispersal, and our difficulty in reading them appropriately.

THE process of reading the manuscript in Earenfight's edition must attend simultaneously to at least three distinct elements: Doanmoe's story, how that story is told, and how Pratt attempts to colonize the story. After reading Pratt's inscription on the inside cover of the sketchbook, we can move on to the narrative that Doanmoe authored. The first page facing Pratt's inscription depicts two rows of soldiers facing out toward the reader. Two other soldiers face the group and have their backs to the reader. The soldiers look identical in their U.S. military uniforms. On the top of the page, Pratt explicates the image for us: "The younger prisoners were organized as a company and drilled in military movements, and then were used as guards over the Fort and for two and a half years guarded themselves and the Fort without serious breech of orders during that whole period. Their drill movements were so excellent as to elicit warm praise from General Hancock who commanded the Department."[9]

These captions cast the prisoners as the perfect fulfillment of Pratt's mission: they have been disciplined, converted into U.S. soldiers, and were so obedient that they were guarding both the fort and themselves. Looking at the page, one might conclude that Pratt has indeed succeeded in his famous mission to "save the man" and "kill the Indian"; the insurgent Native American warriors have become dutiful U.S. soldiers.

This narrative of conversion and assimilation is reinforced by Mason Pratt's addition of two photographs when he had the sketchbook rebound and embossed with the title *A Kiowa's Odyssey*. The first photograph has been glued to the inside of the new front cover, making it the first thing a reader would see. It shows five of the Fort Marion prisoners, including Doanmoe, wearing military uniforms. Their hair is short and they are in a photographer's studio. This image provides a stunning contrast to a photograph Mason glued to the inside back cover. Widely published, this is a picture of the prisoners taken inside Fort Marion shortly after their arrival. The men have long hair and wear their own clothes. The practice of pairing "before" and "after" pictures like this was pioneered by Pratt, Sr., and used to make a visual argument about the success of his mission to "civilize" Native prisoners in Fort Marion and Native students at Carlisle Indian School.

A careful reading of the manuscript reveals, however, that Doanmoe tells a different story. We are alerted to this discrepancy by a small number on the top left corner of the page. The page we have been reading as the first is numbered "31." This is not the first but the last page of Doanmoe's story, which follows reading-direction conventions seen in other Plains sketchbooks. Unlike an alphabetically written text, this narrative should be read from the back to the front and from the right to the left. Although Doanmoe had learned about Western reading directions in the Fort Marion jail school, he organized the manuscript according to indigenous conventions familiar to him from the Plains. This assertion of indigenous literacy practices is not only respected but also reinforced by Pratt who added the page numbers to the unpaginated sketchbook pages. We can only speculate about Pratt's rationale: perhaps he felt that it added authenticity.

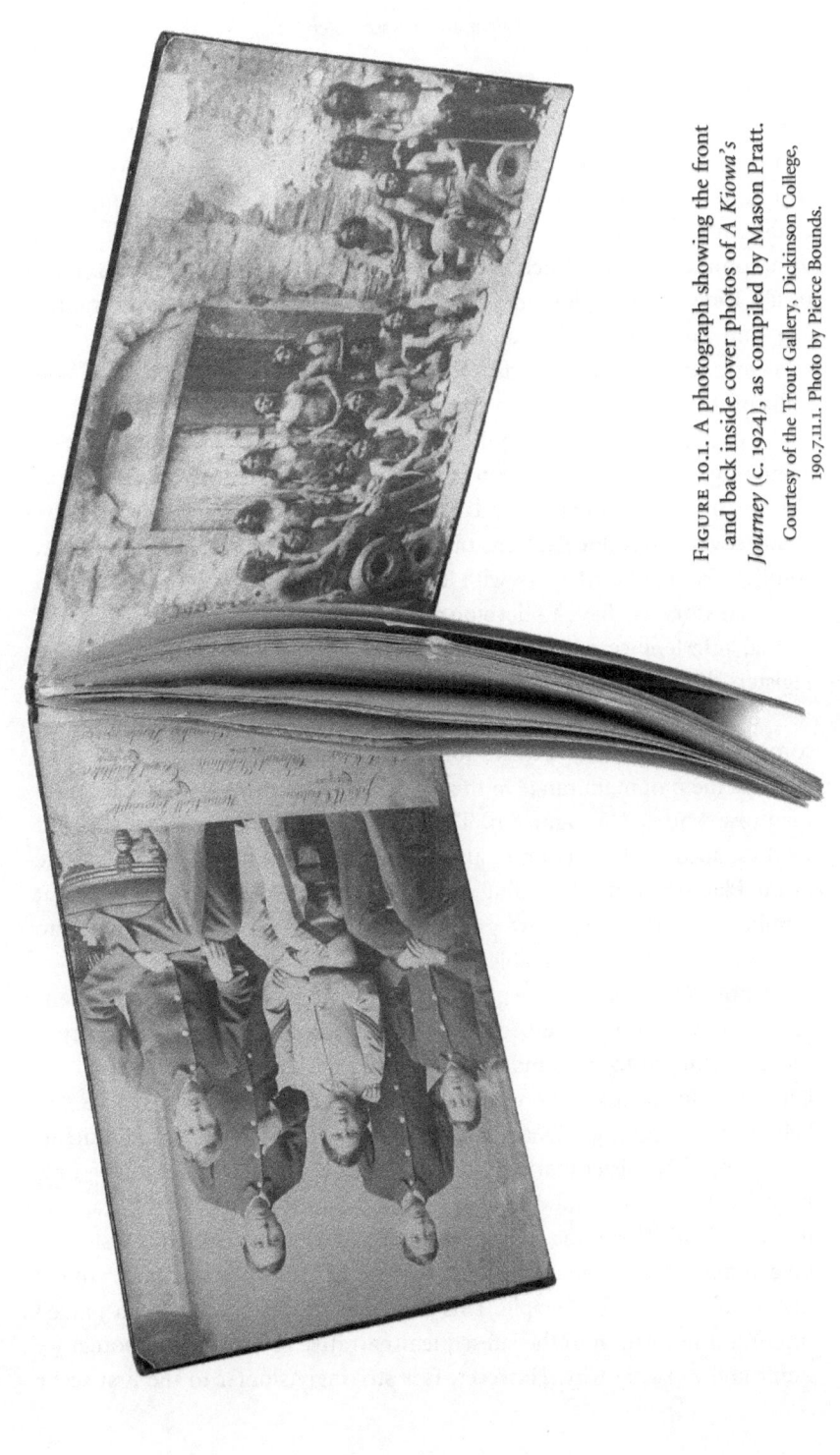

FIGURE 10.1. A photograph showing the front and back inside cover photos of *A Kiowa's Journey* (c. 1924), as compiled by Mason Pratt. Courtesy of the Trout Gallery, Dickinson College, 190.7.11.1. Photo by Pierce Bounds.

Whatever the reason, the result is that once we turn to the "real" page 1, at the end of the manuscript, we are drawn into a narrative universe that is organized at least in some measure by indigenous literary conventions. In this way, Doanmoe foregrounds the existence of multiple, competing traditions of literacy and narrative. Furthermore, he asks his interlocutors to accommodate this difference and change their reading practices. As a result, Kiowa and Anglo-American forms of literacy are marked as contingent and culturally specific rather than universal.

As we turn to the page marked "1," we see a world beyond the prison walls of the fort. This is where Doanmoe's narrative begins, facing a blank back-cover page unmarked by Richard Pratt. The book then contains two beginnings, which correspond to two competing narratives. Pratt's narrative of military dominance and prisoner submission is inscribed on the inside cover and in the captions throughout the book. This story, however, conflicts in significant ways with Doanmoe's own narrative. In order to read that story, we have to develop a reading practice that can resist Pratt's textual interference while recognizing the relevant semiotic and cultural registers that shape Doanmoe's work.

The narrative begins with an image of a camp with numerous tipis, some of them painted. The location seems to be somewhere on the Plains. Perhaps the mountain range in the background identifies a precise location for those who can recognize it. The American flags indicate that this is a world shaped by the encounter and conflict between the indigenous people of the Plains and the expanding settler state. Inside a circle of tipis, a great number of Native people are present. Despite the two American flags, no U.S. military officers are visible.

Among the tipis, four are painted, indicating the presence of tribal leaders. Two of the tipis have been identified: the second decorated tipi from the left belonged to the family of Never Got Shot, while the third from the left (with blue bands at the top and bottom) is the Tail Picture Tipi. It had belonged to Carrying a Quarter of Meat, a well-known warrior and medicine man, whose sister married Big Bow. A leader of the resistance, Big Bow negotiated his own amnesty in return for the surrender of young warriors like Etahdleuh Doanmoe. It is likely that all four tipis reference historical objects and people. The image then locates the reader on the Plains, among historically identifiable people. This page references a specific event judged important in relation to the subsequent narrative of captivity, although we don't know exactly why. However, it is strikingly similar to the first scene in another narrative by a captive named Zotom.[10] This fact suggests that there may have been some agreement on its significance among the Kiowa captives at Fort Marion—and that the narratives reflect prior discussion and some collective agreement about what story to tell.

The opening scene in Doanmoe's book draws the reader from the Fort Marion prison into the world of the Kiowa where the narrative begins in a time and space prior to captivity. In the pages that follow, Doanmoe documents the surrender of the group, the journey of the captives from Kiowa territory to St. Augustine, and life at Fort Marion. In doing so, he depicts subject matter that is outside the range of standard genres on the Plains where history and heroic exploits formed the primary subjects of pictographic records. Art historians have commented extensively on the representation of landscape, trains, and so on, in the various known Fort Marion sketchbooks. This analysis will focus briefly on the representation of the captives and what it might tell us about how Doanmoe, Zotom, and their fellow captives conceived of their experience.

In the early pages of the book, the Kiowa warriors are wearing regalia that mark them as members of a tribal community and, possibly, identified specific individuals (3). From the moment the captives enter Fort Sill as prisoners (7), however, they are stripped of individual markers. Throughout the journey, and as they arrive at the fort, the captives are depicted as small, anonymous figures in red, white, and blue. This color scheme matches the colors of the American flag (see Plate 2).

It is maintained on subsequent pages as the group moves from a train to a steamer boat to horse-drawn carriages (19). The figures are minuscule against the landscape and buildings. The manner in which Doanmoe depicts the group of captives is consistent with pictographic conventions on the Plains and in the eastern woodlands. It is a reminder that Doanmoe's visual narrative is rooted in an indigenous scriptural tradition that predates the arrival of Europeans on the continent.

In striking contrast to the small and anonymous captives, the reader is suddenly confronted on page 22 with a completely different image that seems out of place in the chronology: three huge figures, brightly colored, with horses and detailed regalia. Pratt and Janet Catherine Berlo (she explicates the images in Earenfight's edition) both see this image as an interruption in the narrative chronology. Pratt's caption reads "Young Kiowas dressed for a ceremonial visit" (see Plate 3), while Berlo notes that "to modern eyes, it seems surprising that Etahdleuh would break up his sequential narrative by inserting large-scale scenes referring back to life on the Plains."[11] Perhaps, Berlo muses, exact sequencing was only important to Doanmoe in relating the journey to St. Augustine.

However, it is possible to read the image of the three warriors as an important part of Doanmoe's chronology. The three warriors, filling up the space in the manner of traditional Plains exploit narratives, appear right after a scene in which the young men successfully fight and capture sharks, which they call "water buffalo," at the entrance to the harbor. In captions on page 21, which depicts that exploit, Pratt notes that they caught five sharks that day, each weighing from six hundred to twelve hundred pounds. In the narrative, this heroic feat is linked directly to the reemergence of Kiowa warriors and more traditional Plains iconography.

Importantly, the warriors on page 22 are not idealized or nostalgic representations of the past.[12] Their regalia combine tailored military jackets, gold epaulets, and U.S. government military peace metals of the sort worn by Lone Wolf and Big Bow with beaded buckskin leggings, lances, and feathered headdresses. They are, as Berlo notes, "high-ranking warriors" of the late nineteenth century.[13] The men may have been contemporary leaders or they may represent the leaders that Doanmoe and his cohort hoped to become.

The progression of the narrative suggests that the group of captives eventually began to conceive of themselves not simply as defeated prisoners but as individuals with the capacity to perform feats of the kind that affirmed (and constituted) masculine identity on the Plains. Pratt's unusual penal experiment gave the men latitude to practice certain aspects of Kiowa and Cheyenne warrior culture, adapted to the confines of captivity. They were able to hunt ("water buffalo"), they taught archery, and they exhibited their skills as hunters and marksmen in contests. On a few occasions they were able to sing and dance wearing regalia, and they were permitted to make (and sell) their "drawings."

In Doanmoe's narrative, the despondency of the prisoners upon arrival in St. Augustine is evident in the anonymity and diminutive scale of the captives "inside Fort Marion" where they are dwarfed by, and contained within, the imposing structure of the fort (20). However, that page faces the depiction of their successful hunt of water buffalo, which, in turn, precedes the visually stunning reemergence of Kiowa warriors. Unlike the opening scene, which we also see in Zotom's narrative, this scene is unique to Doanmoe's narrative both in terms of the subject and the return to more traditional Plains iconography. These figures, men of status and dignity, fill up the page in a manner reminiscent of the visual style of Plains exploit narratives. On this page, the three warriors are not performing any feats unless we count their survival and reemergence as exploits in themselves. On the page facing the warriors, Doanmoe depicts another scene of relative freedom on Anastasia Island where the prisoners sometimes went during the brutal heat of summer. Only three figures are visible, all of them wearing U.S. military uniforms. The anonymous captive figures of the earlier pages are nowhere to be seen.

This camp is contrasted, on the following page, with a scene from beyond St. Augustine. Pratt's caption reads "A Kiowa banquet in the good old days back home" (24). As in most of Plains pictography, the geographic location is unclear. There is no landscape or architecture, features that seem to be associated with Anglo-America in the sketchbook. So we are likely on the Plains and outside the control of the U.S. military. The absence of landscape and architecture can be read as markers of the absence of direct colonial domination. Five Native people with their backs to the reader face a row of other Native people, all seated under a beautifully decorated "tarp." Behind them we see a single tipi with details that likely identify it (and its owners) to people who share Doanmoe's cultural references. On the left of the page, a woman is cooking a meal. While I have not been able to identify the tipi and thus can offer no theory about what Doanmoe is depicting, the scene does not strike me as an image of nostalgia. Perhaps the five men with their backs to the reader are Fort Marion captives who have returned to share their knowledge of the world back east? This is speculative at best. The page facing this one, however, is easier to interpret.

As we read from right to left, we move to a depiction of a "dance" held inside the fort where the young warriors are dressed in traditional regalia, holding what Berlo calls "war implements" such as axes, feathered lances, and bows. Pratt permitted such events to entertain local audiences, and his caption presents it as "amusement." However, to the captives it likely marked a very meaningful, if carefully circumscribed, connection to their identities as warriors and tribal members.

Upon their arrival at Fort Marion, the young warriors had been forced to shed all markers of tribal identity. Their long hair was cut and they were forced to wear U.S. military uniforms. We know that his braids meant a great deal to Doanmoe, because he kept them and wore them when he performed at a great public event toward the end of his captivity in Fort

FIGURE 10.2. "Inside Fort Marion," from Doanmoe's manuscript, p. 20. Courtesy of the Yale University Beinecke Rare Books and Manuscript Library.

Marion.[14] For the warriors, the moment of arrival in St. Augustine marked the end of bloody military engagement, defeat, an arduous journey, and the beginning of an unknown destiny inside musty jail cells in the walls of the fort. It marked enormous loss: of the captives' freedom, of their clothes and hair, of their proximity to their families and homelands. Several warriors died en route or at Fort Marion. As the months passed, however, it appears that the captives came to see new ways in which to inhabit and reclaim their identity as Plains warriors. The Omaha or Ohoma dance that Doanmoe depicts on page 25 of the sketchbook was, in Berlo's words, "traditionally a victory dance after a successful war expedition."[15]

The reemergence of traditional Plains iconography in the narrative can be read as a defiant statement of cultural survival: the man *and* the Indian survive. The image that follows supports this interpretation. Here, Doanmoe returns to traditional Plains iconography in both style and subject. Two men on horseback are nearing two buffalo. The action fills the page, and the scene is dynamic and organized by movement: this is typical of more traditional pictographic exploit narratives from the Plains. The image of the two men hunting buffalo is not a nostalgic invocation of a precolonial past, because one holds a bow and the other a rifle. This is the kind of scene a distinguished warrior might include in an autobiographical narrative to record a heroic exploit. It is particularly significant in Doanmoe's narrative, because the killing of a buffalo at age fifteen was foundational to his identity; this is the deed that earned him his name. Doanmoe's narrative thus reveals that he eventually comes to see himself as something more than a defeated captive; he reclaims the name that marked his entry into manhood.

This aspect of Doanmoe's text differs from other, comparable narratives like the one authored by Zotom. This is particularly striking because so many of the scenes, and the chronology itself, are so similar as to indicate agreement and some kind of collaborative process. But whereas Zotom provides us with a narrative that focuses on only the journey and experiences of the group, Doanmoe's text is both a collective and an individual story of survival. It may be that Doanmoe's closer association with Pratt accounts for Doanmoe's more defiant "tone." Zotom's narrative does depict a staged exhibition "buffalo hunt" that took place at the fort. For this event, however, Zotom uses the same panoramic perspective he uses throughout the narrative, a visual perspective influenced by the captives' exposure to European artistic conventions. Doanmoe's decision to depict the buffalo hunt in more individualistic terms that also return to the narrative and visual conventions of exploit narratives from the Plains is thus striking and unique to his narrative. Perhaps what we have before us is instead the autobiography of a new kind of warrior, one who is fighting with pen and paper. On the Plains, autobiographical narratives documented heroic exploits and often focused on one individual. But these narratives were not simply records of past events, nor were they mnemonic aids. They functioned as texts. The production of such narratives enabled their authors to shape memory of their deeds, to claim them as significant, and to use them to constitute their own identity. The young Kiowa and Cheyenne men in Fort Marion probably had many reasons for putting pen to paper. Pratt encouraged it, the men were allowed to sell their work, and perhaps they were bored. In addition, the making of narratives about their captivity helped them shape understanding of this experience and, possibly, the historical record. These sketchbooks were acts of textual self making.

Two dynamics intersect in Doanmoe's narrative, quite apart from Pratt's interference: the effort to recoup a tribal and warrior identity within the confines of captivity, and the effort to imagine and represent the self as a worthy subject of a narrative. At the same time, however, Doanmoe's sketchbook is also a historical record of a more collective nature. The sketchbooks in Fort Marion combine, as Joyce M. Szabo notes, attributes of winter counts and exploit narratives. Szabo argues that the Kiowa excelled at winter counts, that exploit narratives constituted the most common form of pictographic narratives among the Cheyenne, and that Fort Marion became a site of cross-fertilization between these groups and these genres.[16]

Sketchbooks like Doanmoe's record the history of the group of captives as they traveled from the Plains to the coast and, in the process, can create a particular narrative about that experience and its meaning. In that sense, it embodies some of the logic of the winter counts, particularly if we consider the striking similarities of Doanmoe's and Zotom's narratives. In contrast to the individualism of autobiographical coup tales on buffalo robes and tipis, winter counts represent a communal vision of a collective identity formed around significant events strung together into a coherent whole that reached into the past and into the future.[17] Taken collectively, the pictographs in a given winter-count mark the progression of time and the collectivity of the community. At the same time, a winter count functions as a textual site wherein the community imagines itself as stable and continuous. That sense of collectivity, stability, and continuity may have been particularly important to the captives at Fort Marion.

In Doanmoe's sketchbook, the story of this community of warriors becomes a story of heroism rather than defeat. On page 3 of the manuscript, for example, Doanmoe depicts an encounter between the U.S. military and a group of warriors. At the front, or bottom, of the page, we see a number of mounted warriors. Behind a line of trees, we see wagons, U.S. soldiers, and an officer negotiating with a warrior. According to Pratt's captions, this image "represents what came near to being a battle." In his memoir, *Battlefield and Classroom,* Pratt writes that "in the summer of 1870 a very large portion of the Kiowas were off their reservations, west of the Wichita Mountains."[18] General Grierson, the commander at the fort, "took a portion of the Fort Sill Cavalry and went after them . . . they were off their reservation in violation of their treaty and plainly defiant. Why not charge at once and punish them for their insolence?"[19] At some point, the military group spotted a number of warriors seemingly inviting a fight. Suddenly, they waved a white flag and requested a conference. Only afterward did the military discover that "the Indian demonstration had been made to hold our command back while the women moved their camp across a stream (the Sweet Water) and onto their reservation where we dare not attack them. It was our duty to attack and destroy them off their reservations, which we would have done but for the moving of their camp.[20]

This page then refers to historical events that took place in the summer of 1870. Avoiding what could have been a massacre of the entire community, the group outwitted the military. It records not just a particular historical event but a victory by the Kiowa. It is an important moment in the history of the group, and it was a heroic act where the warriors put their lives on the line and thereby enabled the entire community to survive.

Although the warriors were later taken into captivity, this scene records their heroic deeds and frames them as fitting subjects for a pictographic narrative. It is a kind of collective coup on their captors that also foreshadows the terms in which Doanmoe will represent journey into captivity: not as a defeat but as a heroic act of engagement with the enemy for the benefit of the larger community.

On the Plains, the production of winter counts was a communal effort. A council of elders would determine the most important events of the year.

These would be recorded by a tribal historian with one or more pictographs. The striking similarity between the images and the chronology in Doanmoe's and Zotom's texts is evidence of a similar process at Fort Marion. Like Doanmoe, Zotom opens his narrative with a Kiowa camp by the Wichita mountains.[21] This fact suggests that it was not only an important event but also an event that both Zotom and Doanmoe considered the "beginning" of their stories of captivity and exile.

Like Doanmoe, Zotom proceeds with depictions of Fort Sill, the "almost . . . battle" at Sweet Water, Big Bow's surrender, and the transport to and arrival at Fort Marion. Art historians have used this consistency to compare and contrast their artistic abilities, with most finding Zotom the more accomplished artist and Doanmoe perhaps derivative. The degree of realism, perspective, and accurate detail in various images speak to the level of mastery the men attained in Western modes of representation. Such skill may have increased Anglo-American appreciation for the images, and it likely reinforces our perception that these are artistic, rather than literary, efforts. Discussions about who was the better artist, however, obscure an important issue. These striking similarities provide evidence that the Fort Marion narratives were produced in the context of some communal discussion and consultation. Comparative close readings of different extant Fort Marion narratives would then provide important clues about the nature of this process and the formal features of the narratives.

Such analysis is possible because of the survival of a document produced by Zotom—a kind of missing link between the Fort Marion books and the Plains winter-count tradition. On a piece of paper torn from a ledgerbook, someone made thirteen small images. Below them is the following caption: "Zotom is busy drawing a book."[22]

Each image corresponds to an event in the journey, and collectively the drawings provide a chronology of the passage from the Plains to St. Augustine. As Szabo notes, "Such a schematic rendering is unique among Fort Marion drawings currently known and suggests the kinds of icons employed by Kiowa calendar keepers for the twice-yearly entries they made on hide, canvas, or paper surfaces. . . . Zotom used these cryptic icons as a guide in creating many drawings in Florida that detail, apparently in chronological order, the events that affected the lives of the Florida prisoners."

Each of the small images then corresponds to particular pages in the narrative. Indeed, each page can be seen as an elaboration of the miniature image that contains what Zotom must have considered the most crucial element of the page. One of the small images is a representation of the icehouse where the captives were kept before being sent on their journey to Fort Marion. This icehouse appears at the center of page 9 in Doanmoe's manuscript when the prisoners leave Fort Sill and also at the center of Zotom's depiction of the same event.[23] This relationship is made explicit in one version of Zotom's narrative, which is housed in the National Cowboy and Western Heritage Museum in Oklahoma.

Instead of numbered pages, this collection of "drawings" has the pictographic images in the top corners where page numbers would be. We can only speculate about whether Zotom made this chronology on his own, in collaboration with a council of fellow captives, or at the direction of some of the elders in the group. Either way, this document provides clear evidence that Fort Marion captivity narratives like Doanmoe's are one end of a formal spectrum rooted in Plains pictography where the narrative conventions of the Plains have been translated for Anglo-American interlocutors into largely visual terms. The visual elaboration in the sketchbooks and ledgerbooks might be seen to replace what, in a tribal context, would have been verbal elaboration.[24]

Read collectively, Fort Marion books and other extant documents reveal to us how the men theorized the intersections between different semiotic registers and the process of translation for non-indigenous interlocutors. The images in their sketchbooks can be seen as visually elaborated pictographs that narrate the history of the warriors and their captivity. The pictographs from Zotom's master chronology are essentially embedded within the images on the page, made to speak to an Anglo-American reader. The visual elaboration takes the place of verbal explication by the author who would be separated from the narrative and unable to explicate its meaning to readers unfamiliar with any non-alphabetic forms of literacy.

Some scriptural elements from Plains pictography, such as name-symbols, survive in the Fort Marion corpus. But they are often transformed or recede in favor of the visual. This development obscures the literary roots of the narratives, a problem that is compounded by the fragmented nature of the archive and by the interference of Pratt and others. A fuller understanding of the sketchbooks requires not only recovery and restoration of the material objects but also recovery of the literary history of pictography and, for that matter, its standing as a form of writing.

SCHOLARS of writing have historically excluded pictography from the realm of writing, which has been defined as recorded speech.[25] However, the term "writing" is deeply entangled with colonial history. The European conquest of the Americas brought not only different peoples but also diverse forms of writing into contact and conflict. As I have argued elsewhere, the way we understand and define writing is a consequence of that history.[26] European and American scholars of writing have traditionally placed great emphasis on phoneticism, but as this manuscript reveals, it is precisely the phonetic elements of pictography that are least likely to be understood and recognized by non-Native readers and, therefore, the least effective means by which Native authors like Etahdleuh Doanmoe can transmit narrative to Anglo-American audiences.

The visual elements are dominant in a narrative like Doanmoe's, and the scriptural elements of pictography have effectively disappeared in the transition for an Anglo-American reader. This makes it easy to misinterpret the narrative as simply a collection of images. Furthermore, the circumstances of its production led in many, if not most, cases to a fragmentation that obscures the whole and leaves us only with parts. In fact, Doanmoe's narrative is one of a few that comes to us as a coherent whole, and this is only because of the remarkable recovery work of Earenfight.

Without recognizing these texts' relationship to indigenous forms of literacy, we are doomed to fundamentally misread them. Furthermore, we will fail to recognize that it is the colonial context, not the absence of an indigenous tradition of literacy, that accounts for the predominance of the visual over the scriptural. *A Kiowa's Journey* is what we might, via Mary Louise Pratt and Galen Brokaw, call a "textual conflict zone," a material space in which "disparate cultural modes and conventions of representation meet, clash, and grapple with each other, often in highly asymmetrical relations of domination and subordination."[27] Only when the whole is reconstituted can we begin to recognize that such manuscripts are not just a collection of "drawings"; they are narratives rooted in a centuries-old tradition of pictographic writing on birch bark and buffalo hide. Recovering the literary history of Native American pictography is one of the more difficult aspects of reading these narratives. The Fort Marion sketchbooks are crucial for this process because here, authors like Doanmoe and Zotom meet us more than halfway.

Given the rich complexity of a book like *A Kiowa's Journey*, and the many issues it raises, even a lengthy essay like this is only a beginning. This analysis is meant to serve as a literary introduction to this rich text and as a model for a new kind of American literary studies. The books from Fort

Marion deserve careful further study by literary scholars, particularly those with tribal affiliations, who can take account of their multiple formal antecedents in order to unlock their narrative power. Comparative study of different narratives from Fort Marion, like Doanmoe's and Zotom's, can further flesh out the achievements of this remarkable group of authors. Their books, the specificity of what they say and the specificity of how they say it, are of great significance for scholars of American literature, history, and culture, as well as for scholars of writing, colonialism, and Native American studies.

In the pages of their sketchbooks, Fort Marion captives like Etahdleuh Doanmoe contest Pratt's narrative of subjugation and inscribe their own story of resistance and survival. Their work represents a landmark in American literary history and reminds us that the textual is itself an important contested space in the borderlands of the American west.

CHAPTER 11

Toward an Indigenous Art History of the West:
The Segesser Hide Paintings

NED BLACKHAWK

Few have ever pronounced the history of the Americas to be, first and foremost, a history of the indigenous peoples of the western hemisphere. Certainly, the national histories of the nation-states of North and South America do not support such a contention, but the growing prominence of Native Americans within narratives of borderlands history invites such consideration. As a generation of scholarship has now demonstrated, across multiple imperial realms, throughout centuries of historical change, and amid massive economic and demographic transformations, the Native peoples of North America not only endured the brunt of European colonization but also directed the processes of the continent's historical development. They did so moreover following millennia of autonomous social and cultural developments. Indeed, as Brian DeLay writes, "By the early 1820s, more than a dozen generations after Columbus, indigenous polities still controlled between half and three-quarters of the continental landmass claimed by the hemisphere's remaining colonies and newly independent states."[1] Surely, such indigenous histories compose an enduring and central feature of the hemisphere's historical landscape.

Unlike virtually all other fields of North American historical inquiry, borderlands histories have explored such developments, lodging new places, people, and paradigms within the vocabulary of particularly early American history.[2] While the general contours of such historiographic transformations are increasingly coming into focus, the institutional structures that have guided such scholarly developments remain less apparent.

As in any field of historical inquiry, the countless archivists, bibliographers, translators, and related scholars fueling the production of work are often recognized solely within the acknowledgments of monographs, grants, and specialized journals. The field's recent ascendency stands on the shoulders of so many.

Few developments in borderlands historiography are as surprising as those associated with the discovery by the Swiss ethnographer Gottfried Hotz after World War II of a set of extraordinary paintings. Notified about the presence of two extensive wall hangings within the Lucerne castle of the venerable Segesser family, Hotz initiated a decades-long inquiry to discern the origins and ultimate meanings of these "Segesser hide paintings," as they would eventually become known. Hotz's research would identify the distant family member, Philip von Segesser, who sent these remarkable items from the northern reaches of New Spain back to Switzerland as well as the likely motivations fueling their production. Hotz would also publish the classic work about these "Indian skin paintings," leading eventually to their return to New Mexico on March 11, 1986, over two and a half centuries after their creation.[3] They currently reside in Santa Fe at the Palace of the Governors Museum, where, according to the former museum director Thomas E. Chávez, they "are viewed at home by some one hundred thousand annually."[4] (See Plate 4.)

Much like the emergence of borderlands history as a leading feature of twenty-first-century American historical inquiry, these paintings provide alternative conceptual and spatial perspectives on North America's eighteenth-century past. As borderlands histories have questioned the teleological narrative of an American history that has equated early America with exclusively British North America, numerous studies have made the study of economic, social, and political relations within and between imperial and American Indian communities an increasingly recognizable feature of early American history. Military affairs and violent social relations have received particular attention, and historicizing the adaptations of indigenous peoples to varying cycles of colonial expansion has provided methods for assessing the extent and forms of colonialism's multiple, disruptive influences across Indian homelands.

Colonial violence, however, belies summation and comprehension, as the transmission and receipt of pain remains one of the least communicable sensory experiences. As Karl Jacoby has suggested, "Unlike almost any other object of historical study, violence simultaneously destroys and creates history.... One of the most immediate manifestations of violence is thus a terrifying silence that no testimony of the past can fathom in its entirety."[5] Moreover, throughout the course of American history, internecine relations of indigenous violence have largely occurred outside of the immediate spheres of colonial observation and documentation. The Segesser hide paintings allow us simultaneously to assess such processes and to recognize such "terrifying silences."

Borderlands and U.S. western historians have, for generations, assessed the histories of indigenous and equestrian warfare in the American West, but, while related, warfare and violence are not synonymous. One implies organized and concerted strategic combative actions; the other, a range of painful and potentially disabling material as well as immaterial practices. Within the recent nomenclature of borderlands Indian history, "raiding" has become a preferred heuristic, one that bridges economic and military realms and escapes the often prejudiced and static location of indigenous aggression within culture.[6]

While instructive, studies of indigenous raiding require continued historicization as well as conceptualization. Viewing raiding either episodically, as moments rather than processes of violent attack, or reactively, as responses to accumulated sets of aggrieved communal injury, can limit engagement with the broader forces of colonialism remaking the early American landscape. In the American West, indigenous raiding not only accelerated after European settlement but also became for many Native peoples strategies of adaptation and survival in response to the incalculable pressures being wrought by European colonization.[7] As James Scott has suggested, indigenous subsistence patterns that "are pliable and fugitive" both inherently challenge the effective sovereignty of state-building practices and reveal concerted attempts by "nonstate actors" to "avoid incorporation in state structures."[8]

Viewing indigenous raiding and the history of the early American West accordingly, this essay revisits the historical context behind the creation of the Segesser paintings and also examines their materiality, doing so in order to discern broader connections between borderlands and indigenous histories. Moreover, these paintings provide windows into, according to Scott, the "symbiotic history" of empires and imperial peripheries, one that exposes fundamental dialectics animating the strategic choices made by "self-governing peoples."[9] Throughout the history of the American West, indigenous communities have maintained self-governing and autonomous spaces "outside the realm of the state," and such spaces have remained inescapably shaped by the establishment of colonial spheres around them. To write a coherent history of either process, as Scott contends, is not possible.[10] Returning to the middle of the American continent in the early 1700s provides insights into how waves of imperial-initiated disruption crashed upon one another as well as cast a multiplicity of indigenous communities into its turbulent wake.

The study of western indigenous raiding and warfare intersects with the history of equestrianism. Spreading across New Spain's northern colonial footholds, equestrianism transformed the eighteenth-century American West, and the history of Spanish-Indian relations provides opportunities for considering the dialectics of indigenous adaptation and colonial formation across broad swaths of time and space. Such analysis also offers counterpoints to commonplace, static visions of American Indian peoples commonly found within U.S. historical analyses. Not only was North America's oldest permanent colony—New Mexico—first chartered in the 1500s, but it also bore little resemblance to many of the canonical features of Anglo-American colonial history, especially in the area of Indian affairs. Rather than seeing New Mexico, or New Spain for that matter, as peripheral to the early American experience, U.S. historians would be well served considering northern New Spain—particularly the Hispano and Pueblo communities along the northern Rio Grande River—as the epicenter of larger historical dynamics that remade the American continent. Scholars additionally would profit from historicizing the spread of equestrianism and viewing its expansion across indigenous communities as both violent and political processes.

The Segesser hide paintings expose such violent transformations. The set's origins and genealogies lie not only in military encounters upon the American continent but also in the subsequent circulation of such representations to, and more recently from, Europe. The images hail from the early 1720s and concern groups of largely unidentifiable combatants on the distant peripheries of colonial New Mexico. Roughly of equal size, each measures roughly four and a half feet wide and between seventeen and nineteen feet long. While each is referred to as a single hide painting, the set comprises several individual hides that are sewn together to form a larger painting.[11]

As Hotz first revealed, Jesuit Father Philipp von Segesser sent at least three hide paintings to his family from his mission in northern Mexico. He did so in 1758 and they resided thereafter in his family's possession until Hotz initiated his inquiry. The two surviving hides now carry the Segesser family name, known as Segesser I and Segesser II, while of "the third of the three paintings Father Philipp mentioned . . . nothing has survived." Like many borderlands documentary materials, each hide painting remained unstudied for generations and has only recently been examined.[12]

Each painting offers incomparable insight into select moments in borderlands history, while collectively they expose broader dynamics that reshaped much of the eighteenth-century West. Chávez—who figured centrally in their acquisition during his tenure as museum director—calls them "the most novel and important artifacts of Spain's colonial history in New Mexico and the Great Plains."[13] Their influence has been particularly apparent in studies of the indigenous West. First utilized in George Hyde's *Indians of the High Plains* from 1959, many scholars have included images of them in their works. Hyde, James F. Brooks, and John L. Kessell, for example, have each adorned the covers of their respective works with scenes from each.[14]

Hotz first published his remarkable study in German in 1960, and it was translated and reissued in 1970 within the University of Oklahoma Press's "Civilization of the American Indian Series." Reissued in 1991 by the Museum of New Mexico Press, this latter printing provided at its time the only detailed color reproductions of each, notwithstanding a full-scale reproduction of Segesser II in the 1976 Time-Life Books Series, *The Old West*.[15] This reissued and illustrated 1991 volume provides, then, the only color reproductions of both paintings.

Segesser I details an attack by unspecified Indian raiders on an overmatched Indian community. With a substantial portion of the painting missing due to a wide cut and without any clearly identifiable individuals, communities, or geographic features, scholars have offered contrasting assessments of this critical document, in which the identities of both sides remain unrecoverable.[16]

By contrast, Segesser II details the well-known defeat of New Mexico's lieutenant general, Pedro de Villasur, from 1720. Ordered to travel north to monitor suspected French inroads among northern Indian communities, Villasur and his Pueblo Indian auxiliaries were routed by a joint Pawnee-French ambush near the confluence of the Platte and Loup rivers in eastern Nebraska. As Hyde relays, "Villasur fell with thirty-five of his forty-two Spaniards, of sixty Pueblos, twelve or thirteen died. . . . It was the worst

FIGURE 11.1. Segesser II depicts an epic battle between French and allied Indians from Canada and Spanish and Indian allies from New Mexico, which ended with the death and defeat of Pedro de Villasur (featured at the center).

Courtesy of the Palace of the Governors Photo Archives, New Mexico History Museum, Santa Fe, negative number 152690.

defeat Spain ever suffered in battle against Plains Indians, and in the fight fell nearly all of the best and most experienced Spanish soldiers of New Mexico." As he also notes, "With the men were lost all the best firearms and other military equipment in the province."[17]

As the survivors retreated back to Santa Fe, they informed Governor Antonio Valverde Cosio of the defeat. Valverde, according to Hotz, figures centrally in the origins of the hides, as he or someone close to him eventually enlisted the survivors' participation in the making of Segesser II, the structure, size, and composition of which so clearly resembles Segesser I that their joint authorship is universally recognized.[18] According to Hotz, Valverde had Segesser II crafted at some point to exonerate his administration, one that had suffered the colony's greatest debacle since the 1680 Pueblo Revolt.

Leaving office in 1722, Valverde faced subsequent administrative inquiries and eventual trial. In 1727, he "was ordered to pay 50 pesos for masses for the fallen soldiers and to pay 150 pesos to the church, but was otherwise acquitted." Such nominal tribute hardly impacted his coffers.[19] Having developed near El Paso the hacienda de San Antonio de Padua—"New Mexico's most lucrative farming, wine-producing, and stockraising property"—his estate was "valued in the tens of thousands of pesos" upon his death. Notwithstanding such minor duties, in a colonial realm structured by forms of patriarchal authority and masculine codes of honor, Villasur's defeat colored Valverde's leadership, character, and legacy.[20]

More than any event, Villasur's defeat both clouded Valverde's governorship and shaped New Mexico in the 1720s. As scholars from Alfred Barnaby Thomas to Pekka Hämäläinen have suggested, the defeat contributed not only to the failed missionization of horticultural Apache villages on the Plains but also to the subsequent Apache diaspora, one set in motion by the newest equestrian arrivals in the region, the Comanches. Having led an expedition of nearly a thousand in 1719 aimed at crushing the Comanches and their Ute allies, Valverde had visited and camped alongside Apache villagers. He knew well of their suffering at the hands of equestrian raiders and had offered endless assurances of anticipated Spanish missionization. According to Hämäläinen, the subsequent failure to missionize *Apachería* not only foreclosed the expansion of Spanish "authority to the plains" as well as the creation of "a barrier against the Comanches" but also contributed to the transformation of the fertile watersheds of *Apachería* into the staging grounds for equestrian raiding into New Mexico. The consequences of such transformations would reverberate throughout the eighteenth- and nineteenth-century West.[21]

Segesser II thus provides the earliest known visual representations of Indian-imperial conflict from the American West and does so prior to the rise both of equestrianism and of several of North America's most powerful indigenous peoples, most notably the Comanches. It highlights the contingency as well as unforeseen paradoxes emanating from the Villasur defeat, and it does so in laboriously rendered form. In the recently rewritten history of the early American West, it is becoming iconic. Similar to the battle scenes from Samuel de Champlain's narrative of Algonquian-Iroquoian warfare on the banks of Lake Champlain or to John Underhill's account of the 1637 Pequot War and Mystic River Massacre, Segesser II communicates essential borderlands truths rooted in the collision of multiple imperial and indigenous peoples.[22]

Within the scene itself, the conflict clearly involves both indigenous and imperial communities—Scott's "state actors" and "nonstate actors." However, the heterogeneity of each side challenges such terminology. For example, in contrast to the relatively identifiable European and indigenous combatants in either Champlain's or Underhill's seventeenth-century narratives, the composition of each opposing side in Segesser II belies ethnographic precision. With Francophone soldiers and indigenous allies from the central Plains as well as the western reaches of New France, the victorious French forces were a multicultural polyglot. Largely composed of Pawnee allies, they also hail from and resemble the bewildering constellation of *petite nations* that characterize "the middle ground" and potentially include combatants who had previously served or would continue to serve in the Fox Wars in the Illinois country.[23] As Brett Rushforth illustrates, Francophone-indigenous expeditions from the early 1700s onto the Plains included Mississippian Osage, Oto, and Illinois combatants, all of whom were engaged in various conflicts spiraling across the *pays d'en haut*. The prevalence of French-incited campaigns of captivity, Rushforth suggests, hindered French expansion farther onto the Plains, as the demographically small colony of New France sought to acquire indigenous captives from various western wars, most notably in conflicts with the Fox and Dakotas from the early 1700s. French inability to sustain peace with such far western communities prevented the formation of alliances that "would have drawn colonial settlement and trade deep onto the North American plains."[24]

Fought on the central Plains, moreover, the encounter occurred far beyond the boundaries of New France where, according to Michael Witgen, seventeenth-century French ethnographic classifications in the western Great Lakes subsumed an infinite "family of nations" into fixed and unstable political designations.[25] French officials, traders, and missionaries attempted to classify as singular peoples Algonquian-speaking villagers whose kinship, village, and seasonal attachments rarely resembled the stable political classifications the French aspired for as well as attached to them. Such ambiguous, often fleeting, and unstable "situational identities," Witgen relays, formed the "heart" of the "relationship between the French and their native allies."[26]

Such imperial-initiated ethnographic classifications thus failed to make sense of the lived realities of Algonquian village life *and* potentially missed, or were shaped by, the deliberate, political efforts of Great Lakes villagers to live outside of such forms of imperial inscription. The social identities of the Indian allies fighting alongside the French in Segesser II are thus fully discernible and also may represent deliberate strategies of unintelligibility.

As Scott suggests, the politics of retaining, deploying, and/or developing unintelligible "ethnic" or "tribal" identities—claiming in essence to be many things—has historically frustrated imperial and state-centered projects. Moreover, the historic "incoherence of tribe and ethnicity" as well as the strategic deployments of such social and political categories remain a product of imperial expansion.[27] Accordingly, communal and ritual ceremonial practices, in this case in preparation for warfare, become political features within such processes of inscription. Just as decisions to name or not name oneself become intentional acts of resistance by self-governing peoples, the ceremonially act of rendering oneself in explicit and unintelligible forms both draws on long-standing communal cosmological practices and also articulates the autonomous purposes of indigenous authority vis-à-vis imperial designs. While crafted by New Mexicans, the inescapable dialectics of cultural retention and production within a sphere of expanding French colonial influences are exposed in Segesser II, as the innumerable motivations animating these French allies—their decisions to fight alongside the French, to render themselves accordingly—belie easy summation. The traumatic cycles of transformation that forged the *pays d'en haut* in the early 1700s brought indigenous allies into service with French officials and deepened their attachments to preserving communal autonomy, particularly within overlapping zones of imperial expansion. Rendering oneself distinctive before battle potentially communicated then multiple lessons and meanings to imperial as well as other self-governing, indigenous peoples.

While less spectrally positioned as well as portrayed, the diversity of the New Mexican forces parallels that of their Plains Indian and French combatants. It is easy to forget that Segesser II was composed either by the survivors themselves—including some of the Pueblo Indian auxiliaries who hailed from Pueblo communities long known for their artisanal traditions—or by other indigenous artisans potentially supervised by surviving Spanish soldiers.[28] The vibrant and lurid coloring of the Plains Indian combatants potentially communicates recognizable forms of cultural difference circulating throughout eighteenth-century northern New Spain. The levels of detail rendered to each character retain intentional if no longer decipherable meanings, and the alterity of the French and Indian forces might indeed remain not only radical but also purposeful.

If the western reaches of New France remained a world on the margins of French ethnographic classifications, New Mexico confronted to its north a social universe undergoing similarly rapid and often undecipherable transformations. Its northern borderlands in many ways mirrored the far western boundaries of "the middle ground," where Algonquian villagers who had been pushed west by Iroquois raiders throughout the seventeenth century in turn began displacing Siouian-speaking peoples from the woodlands onto the Plains.[29] Villasur was sent north to monitor such changing imperial and indigenous fortunes, and his defeat came just as Plains Indian communities were beginning to harness the potential of Spanish-introduced equestrianism, a process that Apache missionization had intended to curb. Notably, all of the attacking French forces and their indigenous allies were on foot. They possessed no horses. It was their superiority in numbers, their use of firearms, and their reported surprise attack that carried the field against the unsuspecting New Mexicans. The painting's only group of horses appears in the corner where six Indian guards and three New Mexican soldiers protect the Villasur herd, while several of their compatriots vainly attempt on horseback to rescue the expedition's outnumbered and surrounded nucleus who, tellingly, have been cut off from their horses.

In the early 1700s, New Mexican governors not only confronted raids from northern peoples desperate to seek horses but also had to deal with a colony still coming to terms with the aftermath of the 1694 Reconquista. As

John Kessell has suggested, "The 1690s were prologue," a decade when New Mexico began to shed its century-long isolation and began contending with broader imperial influences emanating from imperial spheres across the continent. The region's escalating equestrian raids, the growing fissures between Pueblo communities, and the arrival of new indigenous communities on the colony's borders increasingly differentiated the eighteenth-century colony from its pre-Reconquista form.[30]

Such shifting social relations as well as increased hybridity are reflected within Segesser II. The New Mexican forces include not only Villasur and resident Spanish citizen-soldiers but also Pueblo and potentially other indigenous auxiliaries drawn from across northern New Spain. As Oakah Jones has detailed, Pueblo military service with Spanish soldiers paradoxically increased after the Pueblo Revolt, as the crisis of equestrian raiding increasingly prompted joint Pueblo-Spanish expeditions. Of course, such strategic alliances highlight rather than limit the dialectics of colonialism wherein imposed state authority and assertions of indigenous self-autonomy remain intertwined. As Scott and Clifford Geertz have both suggested for Southeast Asia, for example, imperial-centered political struggles have often centered "more for men than land" and across numerous imperial realms the "overwhelming concern for obtaining and holding population at the core is shot through every aspect of precolonial statecraft."[31]

Spanish-Pueblo relations from the early 1700s highlight such theorization. A generation after their reconquest, Pueblo allies joined forces with Spanish officers and together moved to counter threats emanating from the overlapping zones of the Spanish and French empires in North America. Their motivations were manifold and help expose important dimensions in the crafting of each painting, because, as Thomas Chávez has suggested, Segesser II is not only an exoneration but also a memorialization. It commemorates fallen Spanish as well as Pueblo fathers, friends, and relatives. Much scholarly reconstruction has in fact been done in an attempt to identify each of the fallen Spanish soldiers.[32] In the aftermath of the Reconquista and within the growing crisis of equestrian raiding, the painting reveals emergent and shared sensibilities—New Mexican "situational identities"—binding recently reconquered Pueblo communities with their imperial rulers. In this distinctively New Mexican tapestry and within New Mexico's distinctive set of colonial relations, indigenous peoples retain a valued if inequitable place within the colony, as Pueblo heroism is both communicated and commemorated in Segesser II.[33]

Analysis of the Villasur defeat and its representation in Segesser II thus challenge fixed ethnographic as well as political categories of analysis while highlighting the webs of imperial mutuality enmeshing nonstate peoples throughout the early West. At a time when Anglophone settlement in the Carolinas had only recently been secured following the Yamasee War, the center of the continent witnessed borderland conflicts between indigenous and imperial combatants drawn from across the hemisphere.[34]

Most important, such borderlands remained contested spaces not only by distant French and Spanish leaders but also by indigenous communities coping with the broader cycles of colonial disruption reshaping their homelands. The site of the Villasur defeat would in fact remain unincorporated for over a century into any imperial or national polity and would become transformed by hosts of emergent indigenous powers in the decades ahead. As the study of early America has come to include multiple as well as competing "American colonies," consideration as well of competing "indigenous autonomies" can help deepen appreciation of larger historical forces. As James Tully has suggested, within such forms of indigenous cultural articulation, "strange multiplicities" can be found, fluid social positions that provide alternative formulations to the colonial prescriptions of normative subjectivity within liberal democratic societies. Such articulations of difference expose historic forms of mutualism that, while inherent in the construction of settler societies, have often been overshadowed by "the imperial features of modern constitutionalism." Recognition of such mutualism, Tully contends, "is more than a civic awareness that citizens of other cultures exist in one's polity. One's own identity as a citizen is inseparable from a *shared history* with other citizens who are irreducibly different; whose cultures have interacted with and enriched one's own."[35]

Historicizing, then, the evolution of such expressions by North America's many self-governing peoples provides heuristic and philosophical assistance in rethinking the legacies of colonialism. Deep historicization, in particular, reorients linear histories away from imperial or metropolitan cores and highlights centuries-old dynamics that refashioned indigenous communities often before the arrival of Europeans within their homelands. For example, the transformation of pedestrian, horticultural homelands across the northern, central, and southern Plains remains one of the defining and underdocumented features of the eighteenth-century West. Increased patterns of indigenous warfare, growing networks and forms of captivity, and a shifting dependence to horse and bison economies characterize the transformation of pedestrian and semihorticultural worlds. As Juliana Barr has suggested, such "Native polities" came not to "resemble those of Europeans. Nevertheless the fluid categories of familiar, cultural, and linguistic affinity by which Indians configured their polities were by no means at odds with structural integrity and clear geographic domain."[36]

Equestrianism thus entered into and reorganized the history of Indian power across the early West. Reconfigured due to imperial-introduced technologies, equestrianism recalibrated indigenous autonomies, eroding many while increasing others. From the bend of the Missouri in the north to the Rio Grande in the south and from the headwaters of the Arkansas in the west to the Mississippi in the east, the heart of the American continent underwent an ecological and indigenous revolution of still-undetermined proportions.[37]

While commonplace within Spanish correspondence, the seemingly inevitable and ubiquitous nature of equestrianism's rise must not mask the violent processes that attended its spread. As with guns, metals, furs, and the motivations to acquire them in eastern North America, horses accelerated the displacement of colonial violence across western societies. Borderlands historians have helped identify the violence inherent to such reconfigured indigenous autonomies and can provide additional insights. The equestrian revolution precipitated pandemic cycles of indigenous warfare that included the forced removal of countless horticultural communities and the militarization of social and economic relations across innumerable "nonstate spaces."[38] Borne out of borderlands encounters, such indigenous histories characterize the history of the eighteenth- and nineteenth-century North American West, as competition over resources, retention of autonomous spaces away from expanding colonial forces, and growing control over access to centers of trade shaped generations of indigenous relations.

Tantalizingly implicit in Segesser II, the displacement of violence remains centrally identifiable within Segesser I. While less exact than its more familiar twin, Segesser I carries equally valuable insights, particularly when viewed in the context of equestrianism's violent spread. Many have written about the painting and have offered similarly hesitant suggestions about the identities of the combatants involved.[39] Because Segesser I is an anonymous text of an unspecified encounter, it invites interpretive and even speculative claims. Thomas Chávez's recent analysis of Segesser I, for example, provocatively suggests that the cherub-faced women and children behind the pedestrian defenders are New Mexican captives, specifically Pueblo Indians taken by Apache raiders who are in the process of being rescued by New Mexican forces. The large missing section of Segesser I, he suggests, includes additional members of the attacking party and even potentially features more clearly identifiable Spanish commanders or soldiers.[40]

Given that Segesser I and II share the same authorship, there are potential limitations to such an "Apache" interpretation. Leaving office in 1722 and residing in El Paso until his 1726 trial, Valverde, according to Hotz, had the paintings commissioned as administrative inquiries were brewing in Mexico City. Hotz suggests that resident mission Indians in and around his hacienda at San Antonio de Padua may have continued working on them following his departure from Santa Fe.

Hotz is much less familiar with the history of the Plains during Valverde's tenure than he is with the hides themselves, and he repeatedly refers to unidentifiable pedestrian defenders as "Apaches," a suggestion that Chávez and others have followed.[41] Valverde, however, largely attempted to missionize Apache communities during his tenure and treated Apache leaders, such as Jicarilla Chief Carlana, as respected diplomats and warriors. Carlana, for instance, shared with the Iberian-born governor a deep and abiding amity against the Utes and Comanches, adding dozens of his warriors to the governor's unsuccessful 1719 campaign into Colorado. If made by the same artist or artists, the hides invariably also describe events from the same period, at a time when Apaches not only maintained close diplomatic relations with New Mexico but also anticipated "reduction . . . to our holy faith," as Pedro de Rivera, the visitor-general of the region's northern presidios, described Apache religiosity. It was in fact Valverde's successor, Carlos de Bustamante, who was forced to deliver the final verdict to these loyal allies and hopeful converts that Viceroy Marqués de Casa Fuerte had decided not to extend the mission system outside of the colony. With no identifiable battles or captive raids between New Mexico and its Apache allies during Valverde's tenure, the suggestion that the defenders are Apaches who have captured Pueblo women and children invites further consideration.[42]

The clear and potential motivations behind Segesser II—to exonerate an embattled governor, to venerate fallen family members or kinsmen, and/or to narrate the spectacular western American chapter of the larger war of which it was a part—have left scholars searching for comparable reasons behind Segesser I. With a large piece missing and a third potentially related painting unaccounted for, the uncertainty behind this crucial document will continue.

A primary concern in revisiting Segesser I is to encourage such engagement as well as cautious speculation, but to do so with additional suggestions. Notably, the materiality of the document invites consideration along several fronts. The intentional utilization of the distinctive coloring for the European metal technologies highlights the instinctive recognition the artist(s) had when purposefully distinguishing between the attacking and defending parties. The attacking warriors are all equipped with Spanish weaponry, horses, and armor for both themselves and their horses. All of the attackers employ distinctly blue-colored metal weapons (e.g., swords, axes, and metal-tipped lances), while only one of the defenders possesses such weaponry. A single defender has a strip of colored metal attached to his shield. The attackers are most likely Pueblo or other Indian auxiliaries of the Spanish. Like Carlana's Apaches or the Pueblo allies of Villasur, they may have been allied with either Valverde or other Spanish leaders who may actually be potentially profiled in the painting's missing section.[43]

Given that this hide painting has been reproduced almost exclusively in black and white, analysis of the actual coloring of Segesser I remains warranted. Like the thousands of northern Indians who came to New Mexico to trade, the anonymous artist(s) of Segesser I instinctively recognized the importance of Spanish-introduced weaponry when creating this image. The artist(s) differentiated between such metals when composing these documents and understood that such distinctions mattered. As everyone in the region either understood or came to violently understand, the possession of metals, horses, and guns determined the outcomes of borderlands conflicts. The defenders are potentially Athabaskan-speaking Apaches or Navajos in close proximity to New Mexico or more distant nonequestrians who are portrayed as undergoing the processes of violent incorporation that the displacement of colonial violence produced. In fact, such "nonstate actors" often sustained their first direct encounters with the violence of colonialism at the hands of recently recalibrated and militarized indigenous powers, themselves struggling for autonomy in a world now saturated with imperial violence. As in Southeast Asia as well as the American Southeast, indigenous peoples lived within overlapping zones of imperial influences that were created by the dialectical processes of European expansion and indigenous autonomous responses. Unlike in other colonial theaters, however,

European horses, metals, and diseases represented recently introduced colonial technologies that devastated non-equestrian and epidemiologically nonresistant American populations.[44]

Moreover, such technologies of violence circulated beyond the region and deep into the recesses of the continent. Such eighteenth-century borderlands conflicts thus remained largely outside the purview of Spanish and other imperial chroniclers and also occurred largely between indigenous communities. Within such a perspective, Villasur's defeat at the hands of distant French-allied Indians remains an exception within the context of not only constant equestrian raids upon New Mexico but also escalating conflicts between indigenous communities. As such, Segesser I sketches a far more common and ubiquitous scene than Segesser II, one involving exclusively indigenous combatants. The defending *ranchería* stands little chance against the intruders, as the underequipped were undoubtedly overrun and their women and children, at best, were captured and transported to one of the region's growing captive markets.

The content of Segesser I thus illuminates central themes in eighteenth-century western history. While the identities of those featured in Segesser I may never be fully identified, their clash illustrates how indigenous people equipped with superior technologies of violence incorporated distant and underequipped peoples into the disruptive folds of empire and often did so prior to their communities' encounters with Europeans. But what of its form? What might the motivations behind its creation similarly reveal?

As in so many recorded conflicts between equestrian and non-equestrian societies, in Segesser I equestrian raiders target Indian women and children. Within the pandemic relations of violence occurring across the expanses of the eighteenth-century West, gendered forms of violence and captive taking exacerbated the many difficulties of life on the margins of empire. Moreover, the incorporation of nonstate actors into the colonial economy yielded new social relations and subject positions, as well as creative imaginings within settler communities. Indigenous captives in sum provided many of the social ties within and between overlapping borderlands communities across the American continent.[45]

Historians have largely failed to contend with such anterior histories of violent transformation within and between indigenous peoples. Narratives of U.S. history often mitigate the presence of diverse and recalibrated indigenous communities as well as fail to see how indigenous communities maintained autonomous self-governing societies longer than most of the continent has been under the political jurisdiction of states or empire. As Scott comparatively suggests, "The huge literature on state-making... pays virtually no attention to its obverse: the history of deliberate and reactive statelessness."[46] In North America the largest portion of such autonomous spaces were governed by equestrians, and Segesser II and I provide insights into the long "century of equestrianism" as the early 1700s to mid-1800s may someday be termed.

The enslavement and forced incorporation of indigenous women and children into colonial society by equestrian raiders established new social communities across the West. In New Mexico, such communities eventually came to be known as *genízaros*, as throughout the 1700s, new coalescent communities of de-tribalized exiles from Pueblo nations, unrecognized children by Spanish masters and fathers, and other stigmatized social groups increasingly comprised semiautonomous *genízaro* villages across the perimeters of the colony.

In 1733, the earliest *genízaro* petition for land within the colony was rejected, but by the end of the 1740s, *genízaros* began receiving recognized authority over village communities, eventually constituting recognizable social communities within the colony. Over time such villagers became valued guides, traders, and members of the most outlying regions of the realm, and they enlisted with colonial forces to defend the colony.[47] Rooted in Moorish expansion into the Iberian Peninsula, the term *genízaro* is derived, according to Fray Angelico Chavez, "ultimately from Turkish *yeniçeri*, 'select guard', 'janissary', a term applied to auxiliary troops." As with their history in New Mexico, the etymology of *genízaro* evokes the utilization of nonstate peoples on behalf of imperial projects.[48]

While those incorporated by equestrian raiders and subsequently trafficked to colonial markets made up such *genízaro* communities, before 1750 their histories remain unclear. Beforehand, captives generally found their way into New Mexican households, colonial workshops (*obrajes*), or Spanish mining districts to the South.[49] Rendered shortly after 1720, then, what might Segesser I tell us about these networks of captivity prior to the establishment of clearly identifiable captive or *genízaro* communities?

As the pain and anguish of Villasur's defeat spread back to Santa Fe, Valverde confronted a reconfigured world. Despite the assurances that he and shortly Bustamante would relay, Apache missionization was now imperiled. The crisis of equestrian raiding would continue to grow, and the loss of so many soldiers, auxiliaries, and matérial crippled his and subsequent administrations. News of the debacle circulated throughout the settler, church, and Pueblo communities. Preparations for religious and ceremonial burial now linked the colony together in shared loss. The decision to exonerate and commemorate those fallen eventually led to the unprecedented translation of the Villasur massacre into visual form, and rendering the battle into the visual conventions of Baroque tapestries mirrored the forms of artistic authority so widely commemorated across Catholic and Iberian tapestries in the seventeenth century.[50] As Valverde ordered the few Spanish survivors and their Pueblo auxiliaries to participate in the construction of this monumental rendition, he also prepared for his anticipated testimonies regarding the events of that fateful summer.

Unlike Segesser II, Segesser I's place in such commemoration and exoneration remains undetermined. Whereas Valverde likely ordered the creation of Segesser II to assist his exoneration, Segesser I has no visible or now attributable colonial intentions. Its service in the project of colonial governmentality is ambiguous. It features indigenous auxiliaries and non-equestrian actors and was crafted *at some point* along with its more famous twin. Segesser I thus lacks any clearly identifiable motivation within the administrative world other than potentially highlighting the crisis of sedentary life outside the protective folds of the colony. It may potentially communicate the plight of New Mexico's Apache allies subjected to not New Mexican raids but those by the growing Ute and Comanche alliance members to the north. Such grievances filled the pages of Valverde's communications with Spanish authorities and were recounted by Apache delegations throughout the 1710s and 1720s.[51]

Such sequential production and rendering of an intra-indigenous conflict invite such imaginative, historicized readings. Segesser I's content provides a window into the violent patterns of incorporation occurring outside the colony, but its production, form, and ultimate purposes remain unclear. Read in concert with the history of equestrianism and Spanish-Indian relations from this time, might Segesser I's origins intersect with the processes of commemoration that similarly animate Segesser II?

While one reading of such motivations might be to highlight the masculine achievements of the raiders involved—seeing the tapestry as a commemoration of their military prowess and virility—such auxiliaries on their own would not have held positions of authority within the colony itself. Indigenous equestrian allies remained not only comparatively less powerful than they would become in the decades ahead but also within the lower castes of New Mexico's racial order.⁵² Their potential hold on the governor's time and authority was hardly coeval. Why, then, would the governor authorize the rendering of a commonplace battle between pedestrians and his Indian auxiliaries and then keep the documents together for display before the viceroyalty? Moreover, militarized indigenous combatants would not have stayed within the borders of the colony for the extended duration required to oversee such production or travel with Valverde to El Paso after their creation. The governor likely carried his new possessions with him as he fled Santa Fe, awaiting his upcoming trial with representatives of the viceroy.

Of their many potential origins, Segesser I and II were likely crafted at one of the *obrajes* in Santa Fe, where Apache, Navajo, and other servile Indian laborers carried out the menial tasks of leather making, saddle repair, and other technical forms of metal needlework. Such leather making remained a growing feature of colonial economic and artistic exchange. As E. Boyd has noted, "soon after the reconquest . . . a few resourceful Franciscans painted religious subjects on buffalo, elk, and deer hides . . . apparently as much to help in the instructions of the Indians as to adorn the walls of new chapels and churches."⁵³ In contrast to such theological purposes, *obraje* workers fashioned domestic and regional trade goods; they may have potentially crafted the leather armor of the horses and attackers in Segesser I. Ordered to assist in the production of the Villasur texts, such workers organized their sharpest needles, cleanest hides, and sets of dyes needed for this uncommon undertaking. Some may have potentially worked alongside Franciscan leaders in previous projects, and now they accompanied and assisted the more technically trained artisans who began rendering the hundreds of distinct characters in Segesser II. Their detailed visages, weaponry, and wear clearly differentiated this painting from subsequent ones, and despite their naming, Segesser II was most likely commissioned as well as commenced first.

Obraje workers cleaned the brushes, resupplied needed paints and materials, and filled in portions of the painting as needed. Over time, they, too, shared their understandings of these northern peoples and also came to share in the fear that the survivors still carried. Such spectrally positioned masses of unknown peoples working with distant and encroaching French imperialists not only terrified but also galvanized New Mexicans, and upon its completion, Governor Valverde, Spanish clergy, and leading families convened to remember their fallen family and friends. Franciscans, accustomed to making their own "paintings on tanned animal hides," likely marveled at the majestic creation and the craftsmanship of their former neophytes. New Mexicans from every walk of life invariably learned similar lessons when seeing this public text, whose display may have occurred prominently within the few colonial offices in the city, perhaps even the Palace of the Governors.[54]

With so many materials gathered for this uncommon purpose and with additional tanned hides lining the stores of the colony, an unspecified group, family, or individual approached the governor to order the creation of additional hides. Segesser I's origins lie at this moment. Done sequentially after the first but without the comparable labor and cast of characters, this painting would tell a different tale, a more intimate one. Allow us, the artist(s) asked Valverde, to similarly construct a tapestry relaying essential elements within our family and community's heritage. Show it as well to the viceroy as evidence of our abiding faith and fidelity and utilize it to recognize our achievements during such perilous times.

Consenting to contract Santa Fe's *obraje* for such purposes, Valverde allowed for the additional paintings to be made. Whether Segesser I was thereafter drafted in Santa Fe, El Paso, or even farther south remains unclear; because of its resemblance to northern Mexican pictography and even central Mexican codices, Hotz suggests that "one is strongly tempted to place, if not the locale then at least the origin of the painting, within the boundaries of present-day Mexico."[55] The joint authorship of the hides and authorizations from Valverde, however, locate the painting's origins in New Mexico. As the completed Villasur hide we call Segesser II enjoyed reception within the colony, the artist(s) of Segesser I focused on rendering this additional painting.

This was done for related but different purposes. The construction of Segesser I commemorated a recent conquest of an outlying Indian community. The missing cut of the document potentially includes, as Hotz suggests, New Mexican forces, and tellingly at the far left-hand margins of Segesser I is a lone archer, clothed in leather armor, carrying his shield on his back. He appears to be leaving the painting—as opposed to joining in the conflict—but his pedestrian, armored rendering both distinguishes him from the armored equestrians and suggests the presence of a larger military force between him and the horseman in the front phalanx. Whether Spanish New Mexicans are featured in this attacking party remains, of course, a mystery.

If Segesser I commemorates New Mexican military achievement, then it correspondingly provides a narrative of success at a time when Villasur's defeat gripped the colony. One of its purposes then is to draw attention away from Villasur and to showcase the allegiance and capabilities of New Mexico's growing cadre of indigenous allies. With potential Pueblo or Apache auxiliaries featured on horseback, their respective places within the colony now received attention, lending support, for example, for either Apache missionization or increased Pueblo religious or communal autonomy. The painting suggests that the duty and loyalty of those on horses merit recognition. But what of those who are defending their community and homes? What might be their place in the makings of this incomparable text?

Of those attacked, their expected place in the empire's expanding spheres remains known. As "peoples without reason" and "savage Indians," they are by definition justifiable targets for military incorporation. While troubled by the place of such nonstate peoples within the empire, by the 1720s, Spanish leaders had long confronted the challenge of incorporating self-governing peoples and had developed elaborate ideologies justifying their continued enslavement and subjugation. As Ilona Katzew has suggested, such *indios bárbaros* figure prominently in Mexican "caste paintings" of the eighteenth century. Nominally clad in hides or non-European clothing and usually carrying indigenous forms of weaponry, such "barbarous Indians" both stand in contradistinction to the evolving racial hierarchies within the "Spanish body politic" and illuminate the domesticity of other, normative racial positions. "Although the threat of heathen Indians in the colony was tangible," Katzew writes, "their visual representation was carefully constructed . . . and has little to do with their actual appearance." By rendering autonomous indigenous communities as inherently unassimilative, caste painters both figured self-governing peoples as antithetical to colonial subjectivity and reinforced the construction of new colonial social positions or communities, such as *genízaros*, who first appeared in caste paintings in the 1780s.[56]

Tellingly, according to Katzew, the first caste paintings featured "heathen" or "barbarous" Indians who hailed from San José del Parral in the 1710s.[57] Central to the booming mining districts of northern Mexico, Parral became an epicenter in the evolving traffic of captive indigenous laborers across northern New Spain, receiving after the Pueblo Revolt, according to Chantal Cramaussel, "a marked increase" in slaves from the upper Rio Grande. Authored in 1711 by Manuel Arellano, two *casta* renditions of a "Chichimeco" and "Chichimeca" reveal an Indian warrior and disrobed

Indian mother and child, respectively. Both stand in an unidentifiable landscape, clearly outside the domestic spheres of colonial households, village streets, or urban structures found throughout the caste-painting genre. By contrast, even the first known *genízaro casta* from 1786 features subjects on a village street, surrounded by adobe structures.[58]

As with representations of *indios bárbaros*, the pedestrian defenders in Segesser I wear rudimentary clothes. They stand in opposition then not only to the equestrian dexterity of the attackers but also to the forms of social incorporation that the attackers have obtained. They do not possess horses, metals, or forms of leather armor or clothing. They also fight with inferior weaponry and show only nominal traces of interactions with New Mexicans. Their single, blue metal strip, for example, is placed on a shield and has not been transformed into offensive military technologies, such as arrowheads, spear tips, or swords. Their pedestrian, defensive passivity provokes little concern.

They also stand in front of women and children. According to Chávez, the women and children may be Pueblo captives awaiting reunification with their families.[59] Their comparatively larger numbers vis-à-vis the male defenders, potential hair and blanket styles, and most notably expectant visages communicate familiar, hopeful meanings. Such an interpretation identifies additional layers of motivation behind Segesser I, because if the painting not only commemorates the military prowess of New Mexican forces but also serves to memorialize the reunification of captives with their families, then the text provides multiple windows into colonial history. In such a perspective, loyal Pueblo or Apache warriors are defeating "heathen" enemies in a noble pursuit to reunite their families.

Ultimately, we may never know either the identities of those featured in this painting or the motivations animating its creation. Interpreting the origins and forms exposed in Segesser I does, however, provide essential opportunities for revisiting the earliest decades of the century of equestrianism, and the presence of captives—whether Pueblo or not—links the painting with the history of the displacement of colonial violence. In Segesser I, the inherently violent nature of the life outside the colony's borders remains communicated as well as implied, because the fate of the women and children remains clear in one sense. They were either taken from their pedestrian village as captives trafficked by the featured equestrians or they were returned to New Mexico to rejoin family and friends. Regardless, their experiences as either previous or eventual captives remain clear. Captivity in short either awaits or has already visited them. Their smiling visages confirm, according to Chávez, the latter. Such cheerful dispositions cannot, however, mask the former.

In Segesser I then one can see not only the displacement of violence but also the patterns of captivity emanating across the Spanish borderlands. Such violent and captive networks fueled the creation of new social communities within the colony's borders as well as new cultural practices and imaginative longings in their aftermath. By considering the servile and potentially captive authorship underlying its creation, Segesser I may in fact draw on such creative imaginings, evoking a lost but not forgotten world. It might ultimately relay a lost homeland as well as lost but not forgotten loved ones.

Whether the neophyte or captive artists who rendered Segesser I were related to those featured in its content is an unanswerable suggestion. It is more likely that they had experiences in the captive-taking networks that forged the Spanish borderlands, and few scholars have fully considered the imaginative, creative, and ultimately diasporic sensibilities animating New Mexico's *genízaro* as well as captive communities. Segesser I provides a faint but nonetheless potentially revealing glimpse into such evolving social formations and highlights the violent processes of incorporation that beleaguered thousands of indigenous peoples as well as the potential memorialization of such displacement. The *obraje* artists who rendered the scene of equestrian raiders stealing captive women and children invariably knew of such processes. They potentially had suffered the same as children or had seen and lived among captives who had. Shuttled through networks of equestrian trafficking, captives soon found their way into New Mexico and entered its labor systems among Spanish families, New Mexican parishes, and herding communities. Potentially seeing other community members selectively throughout the year or at annual northern trade fairs, these young captives grew up amid and between similarly displaced peoples, developing diasporic sensibilities rooted in the shared experiences of traffic, enslavement, and loss. When crafting or even viewing Segesser I mournful sentiments washed over them.

Segesser I then provides a narrative of enslavement and displacement. Done to showcase imperial power and accomplishment, the text also memorializes the existence of anterior indigenous autonomies. It provides a latent but nonetheless potential mechanism for the mourning or grieving of lost families and homelands. Crafted by servile laborers, the women and children's cheerful visages may represent intentional self-representations—the imagined joy of either rescue from captivity or a yearning for the life before it.

By reading Segesser I historically and in Scott's formulation dialectically, an inherent relationality between the colony and its expanding hinterlands becomes exposed, one that conjoins autonomous Indian homelands with expanding spheres of colonial influence. Segesser I exposes not only this shared history of violence but also the growing forms of cultural transmission linking imperial centers with nonstate actors. Ultimately, while providing potential new strategies of remembrance, such visual production still concerns the destruction of autonomous indigenous communities. Within this document, the strategies and technologies of imperial inscription serve commemorative purposes and do so potentially for the evolving diasporic sensibilities of New Mexico's growing captive population.

CHAPTER 12

~

The Borderlands and Lost Worlds of Early America

Samuel Truett

In traditional frontier histories, America stretched east to west across continental bones. Pioneers threaded high mountain passes, crossed prairies and deserts, facing the setting sun—paying scarce attention to the deeper America that had accumulated underfoot. Frontier mythologies suppressed these lost worlds. At best, they viewed their shattered remains as curiosities and relics: fragments of a long-forgotten past that heaved up periodically from below to lend color to, at times haunt, but rarely shape our imperial, national, or regional histories.[1]

Yet frontier histories buried America far less deeply than one might expect. For it was often at the frontier—that archetypal new world, virgin land, space of new beginnings—that newcomers were most deeply haunted by American loss and antiquity. At the front lines of expansion west and south across the continent, they found an older America peering stone white and adobe brown from overgrown fields, freshly cut jungles, and sun-parched cliffs. These encounters confounded dreams of youth and immortality, evoked nostalgia for worlds that empire had unmade, and compelled U.S. Americans to think in new ways about their place in the world and in history.

America's lost worlds surfaced most visibly in the Southwestern borderlands with Mexico, a land of ancient cliff palaces, crumbling Spanish missions, and, ultimately, the architectural ghosts of the western frontier. Few visitors to this region imagined the emptiness, virginity, and novelty that myth makers ascribed to the frontiers of early America. And yet the differences between early and later borderlands were never that clear-cut. In this essay, I reconstruct some of the cultural threads that linked these spaces. Visions of antiquity and loss that became Southwestern hallmarks, I argue, had their roots in earlier American borderlands. Part of my argument is that Kentucky and Arizona had more in common than we think. But I am also interested in tracing the obsession with America's lost worlds beyond the borders of national history, by showing how much of what we now consider to be a peculiarly *national* obsession with American antiquity and loss was connected to—and drew on—prior British, French, and Spanish colonial histories.[2]

By examining this obsession across the *longue durée*, I hope to suggest new ways of thinking across borderlands histories in North America. Early Americanists often see borderlands as spaces that *end* with the coming of modern nation-states—the same event that *initiates* those relationships so central to later borderlands histories. The result is a bifurcated field, divided between those who study the borderlands among European empires and Indians and those who study the borderlands between modern American nations. The fascination with America's lost worlds crosses this divide. It is not just that earlier travelers to the imperial borderlands wrote about these spaces in ways that informed later visions of national borderlands. It is also that by engaging America's ghosts, travelers were placing temporal border crossings front and center, by imagining what their own empires and nations had in common with the various "civilizations" that came before.[3]

This was not merely a search for continuity. Ruins, relics, and histories of lost worlds, more often than not, also marked perceived points of disjuncture. While they offered a bridge to a deeper past, they also marked what made *this* America different. It is this matrix of tensions—between old and new, between continuity and difference—that I am most interested in interrogating. For only by charting these complex dynamics can we begin to fully comprehend the borderlands and contested spaces that entangled earlier and later Americas.

To understand how America's new world became old—how virgin lands yielded visions of antiquity and loss—we might begin with the prototypical U.S. frontier myth. We might begin with the rise of the American nation and the man who introduced the story of Daniel Boone to the world in 1784, a frontier promoter named John Filson. Born in Wilmington, Delaware, Filson was one of thousands caught in the fever of westward expansion following the American Revolution. In 1783, he boarded a barge at

Pittsburgh and sailed down the Ohio River to Kentucky, which was then part of western Virginia. He acquired more than twelve thousand acres of land north of the town of Lexington, and he then sat down to write an account of Kentucky to attract other settlers west.[4]

As a backcountry booster, Filson built on a tradition extending back to the end of the French and Indian War in 1763. What made his account different was its historical sensibility, his effort to write Kentucky into a new American narrative. He traveled from settlement to settlement, locating old-timers and writing down their stories. Eventually he met an entrepreneur named Daniel Boone, a man who had moved to Kentucky in the 1760s, braved Indian wars and captivity, suffered the loss of family and friends, and was now dreaming of prosperity in the wake of the late war. Through the tale of one man, packaged as "The Adventures of Col. Daniel Boone," Filson wove a yarn worthy of a new nation. The tale began in hardship on the British backcountry, and it pointed to a future in which Kentucky would become "one of the most opulent and powerful states on the continent." In Filson's telling, men like Boone started the historical clock. "The first white man [was] one James McBride," Filson wrote, "who in the company with some others landed at the mouth of the Kentucke river, and there marked a tree, with the first letters of his name and the date." McBride was a sojourner—he scrawled his name and moved on— but, as a first white man, he set in motion that progressive story that Daniel Boone continued in 1769.[5]

Boone's West was a "howling wilderness," wrote Filson, a land of "savages and wild beasts." It was also "a second paradise," a tabula rasa lifted from nature, and engraved with the dreams of a new agrarian nation. But this view of American surfaces—the skin of a tree, the skin of a land—was haunted by a deeper history. Near Lexington are "curious sepulchers, full of human skeletons," and farther north lay numerous ancient fortifications, unlike anything seen in eighteenth-century Native villages. "Pieces of earthen vessels have also been plowed up," Filson added, of "a manufacture with which the Indians were never acquainted." If these graves, fortifications, and implements were not Indian-made, then whose were they? To whom did this history pertain? Filson had his theories. "It may perhaps be worthy of enquiry," he wrote, "whether these repositories of the dead do not bear a considerable resemblance to the ancient British remains."[6]

As odd as Filson's query might seem today, it would have resonated deeply with many of his readers in the 1780s. For years, the backcountry had been rife with tales of lost tribes, claiming—of all things—Welsh ancestry. Rumors spread in the 1740s after a Boston newspaper retold the story of Morgan Jones—a Welshman captured by Tuscaroras in South Carolina in 1660, who was released when their leader recognized similarities in their languages. Another traveler said he had stumbled upon a tribe of Welsh-speaking Indians who were "better cloathed than other tribes" and who inhabited "ruinous buildings," one appearing like "an old Welch castle" and "another like a ruined church." In 1766, a former white captive, Benjamin Sutton, claimed that he had visited a town of "tawny-skinned Indians" near New Orleans who spoke Welsh and had in their possession an old "Welch bible, which they carefully kept wrapped up in a skin, but that they could not read."[7]

These rumors built on a story of a Welsh prince named Madoc, a story that Richard Hakluyt had circulated years earlier in his 1584 *Discourse of Western Planting*. Hakluyt drew on a history of Wales compiled by the antiquarian Humffrey Llwyd and enlarged by the English minister David Powel. According to their history, Madoc had sailed west to America with his retinue to America in 1170, a fact corroborated by Aztec tales of descent from a "strange nation" to the north. Similarities between Nahua and Welsh words, Llwyd and Powel added, further proved Aztec descent from this European colony. Hakluyt used these claims to counter Spanish claims of prior discovery, claiming that Wales (and thus, the British) reached America first. Although few took his sleight of hand to heart, the tale lived on, eventually moving from the realm of metropolitan propaganda to that of provincial rumor. And so it was that by the eighteenth century, settlers began to see the ghosts of medieval Welshmen everywhere in the American interior.[8]

The retelling of the Madoc legend on the early U.S. frontier pushed the first white man trope farther back in time, but it did more. The search for lost civilizations tugged the curious toward the West. "The day is not far distant," offered Filson, "when the farthest recesses of this continent will be explored, and the accounts of the Welsh established beyond the possibility of a doubt." Indeed, as newcomers followed Filson down the Ohio and beyond, visions of ancient Welsh America retreated, always just beyond reach. The search for lost Welshmen led up the Missouri River and across the Plains, to the western edges of Louisiana. Rumors of blue eyes and Welsh grammar abounded. This was a land of uncanny vestiges: words buried in Native vocabularies, ancient European blood flowing under dark

American skin, the remains of a forgotten civilization overgrown by a savage land.⁹

IN some versions of the Welsh Indian tale, the lost tribes are white. In others they are mixed-race—building on anxieties of racial loss and tropes of the white Indian, both of which were invoked years earlier in the story of Roanoke and its lost colony. In the Roanoke story, as in Filson's tale of Boone, the peregrinations of white America are carved upon a tree. The word *Croatan*, read by Europeans revisiting Roanoke in 1590, pointed to pioneer migrations—but into spaces of degeneracy, not regeneration. On Roanoke, "the Ruins of a Fort are to be seen to this day," noted the naturalist John Lawson in 1709. The Indians of nearby Cape Hatteras "tell us, that several of their Ancestors were white people, and could talk in a Book as we do," he wrote, "the Truth of which is confirm'd by gray Eyes being found frequently amongst these Indians and no others." And so, Lawson added, "we see, how apt Humane Nature is to degenerate."¹⁰

John Lawson, a naturalist and surveyor who came to the Carolinas three generations before John Filson reached Kentucky, hailed from a cohort whose interest in America's ghosts was tied to a parallel interest in American nature. One distinguished member of this cohort was Sir Hans Sloane. Sloane grew up in the 1660s and 1670s with an interest in natural history, and by his early twenties he had found his place with other like-minded souls in the newly formed Royal Society of London. In 1687, he sailed to Jamaica where he traveled incessantly, recording the island's plants, animals, resources, and natural phenomena. He returned with a collection of plants and curiosities that later became a foundation for the British Museum. He also drew on his collections and travel journals for essays in the *Philosophical Transactions of the Royal Society*, and his *Voyage to the Islands*, which he published in two parts in 1707 and 1725.¹¹

Spain had claimed Jamaica in the 1490s but had lost it to England in 1655. Sloane therefore encountered a land similar to the U.S. Southwest two centuries later, a land haunted by prior waves of European colonization. It would have been easy enough to do what readers did with the myth of Boone in Kentucky, to declare this lost world a virgin land. But Sloane's curiosity takes the lead. He recovers a deeper history among the Native relics of Jamaica's cave, while aboveground vestiges of a lost golden age seize his imagination. It is strange to see how quickly "a Plantation formerly clear'd of Trees and Shrubs, will grow foul," he observes. "The Settlements

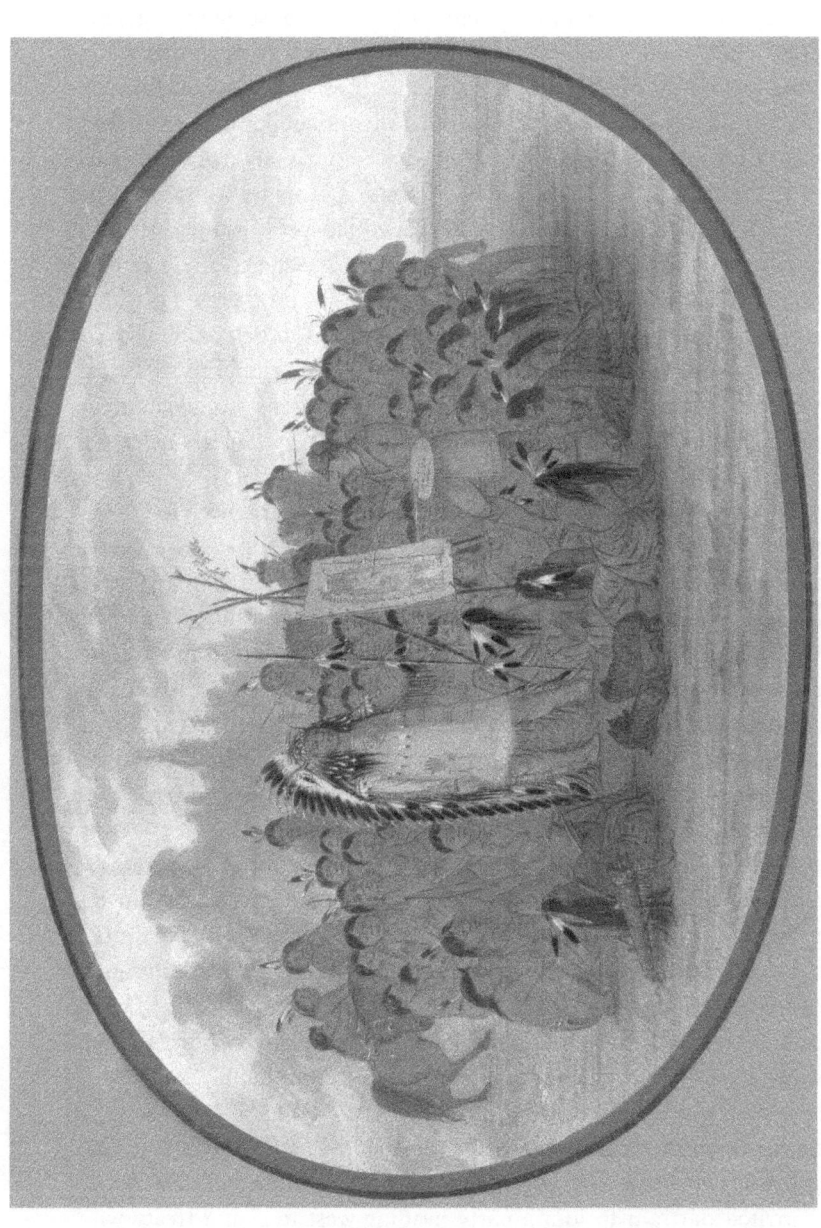

FIGURE 12.1. In the 1830s, the artist George Catlin imagined the Mandan Indians of North Dakota as the descendants of Madoc's Welsh colonists. *Catlin Painting the Portrait of Mah-to-toh-pa—Mandan, 1861–16.* Paul Mellon Collection, National Gallery of Art, Washington, DC.

and Plantations, not only of the *Indians* but even the *Spaniards*," are "overgrown with tall Trees, so that there were no Footsteps of such a thing left," he adds, "were it not for old Palisades, Buildings, [and] Orange-Walks."[12]

Sloane passed on his obsession with America's ghosts, often through Royal Society channels, to other naturalists. I mentioned John Lawson, who traveled to Carolina in part to collect plants for Sloane's circle of apothecaries and naturalists. After Lawson came Bernard Romans, whose *Concise Natural History of East and West Florida* echoed Sloane's vision of Spanish loss in 1763, after Spain lost Florida to England. Then there was John Bartram. Raised on a farm near Philadelphia in 1699, Bartram grew up with a love of Native plants. In the 1730s, he was introduced to Peter Collinson, a London merchant with similar interests. Collinson knew English collectors who wanted to import American exotics into their gardens. Collinson made Bartram a proposition. If Bartram would ship new specimens from the American backcountry, Collinson would not only find buyers but also send European strains west for Bartram's own Philadelphia garden.[13]

Bartram traveled extensively in his search for seeds and plants. Clients were also interested in American curiosities, so Collinson urged Bartram to keep an eye out for fossils, birds, insects, and the like, as subscriber tastes dictated. By 1760, Bartram had walked and ridden from Nova Scotia to Georgia, sending his finds to such men as an aging Hans Sloane, who cultivated Bartram's interest in America's buried antiquity. In 1742, Sloane thanked him for the "triangular arrow-head" and stone hatchet-head—the latter also found in Jamaica, he added. He sent Bartram his *Voyage to the Islands*, which set the collector's mind afire. "When I read . . . of thy extraordinary collection of curiosities," he replied, "I thought it would be difficult to send thee anything . . . that would be new." He selected for his patron "an Indian Tobacco Pipe of stone . . . dug by chance out of an old Indian grave." In this way, an older passion set root in new frontier venues. Tellingly, when Bartram sent a similar box of pottery remains to the Dutch botanist Jan Frederick Grovonius two years later, Grovonius confessed that he had not seen such things since Sloane returned from Jamaica.[14]

If Bartram was encouraged by metropolitan antiquarians and natural historians, his interest in arrowheads, stone pipes, and graves was also shaped by his experiences on the frontier. In 1743, a fellow botanist, James Logan, invited Bartram to join a party heading west to sign a treaty with the Iroquois Confederacy. For Bartram, it was a new world: he saw plants unlike any he'd seen before, he scrambled over the hills after fossils, and it was probably here that he unearthed the pots that he sent to Grovonius. "In this journey into the heart of a country, still in the possession of its original inhabitants," he wrote, "I could not help sometimes but to conjecture at their origin." His European clients sent him west in search of novelty, but the West reset his compass. As the century unfolded, Bartram found himself increasingly drawn to America's buried past.[15]

Bartram's wanderings were soon curtailed by the French and Indian War, but the end of the war opened new horizons. What lay in wait, Bartram and Collinson wondered, in the land acquired from France? Bartram traveled to the Ohio country in 1761, where he heard stories of an enigmatic beast downriver. It is "a shame to the learned curiosos," he wrote Collinson, of what became known as the American mastodon, "that they don't send some person that will take pains to measure every bone exactly, before they are broken and carried away . . . by ignorant and careless people." No less intriguing was the newly acquired terra incognita of Florida. "Oh if I could but spend six months on the Ohio, Mississippi, and Florida," Bartram scribbled feverishly, "I could find more curiosities than the English, French, and Spaniards have done in six score of years."[16]

And so it was, in 1765, that Bartram and his son, William, headed south into Florida. Sailing up the St. John's, they found themselves in paradise. "Is this not, dear Peter, the very palace garden of old Madam *Flora*?" Bartram wrote Collinson. And yet on all sides were the signs of humankind's fall. Deserted cornfields, crumbling Spanish walls, and fragments of pottery embedded in the river banks unsettled any notions these botanical explorers may have entertained of being the first white men in the American wilderness. Forty miles south of St. Augustine, at a place called Mount-Royal, a twenty-foot-high mound threw them off their plant-collecting game for a day. They paced around the structure, took measurements, and scratched their heads, much as Filson's cohort did years later in Kentucky. "It must be very ancient," was all John Bartram could say. That, and "What a prodigious multitude of Indians must have laboured to raise it."[17]

The differences between Bartram's and Filson's backcountries are worth noting. As curious as the mound at Mount-Royal was, Bartram needed little conjecture to put it in context. He and his son were satisfied that they had reached a land formerly inhabited by Indians, not wandering tribes of lost Welshmen. The St. John's was haunted by lost indigenous and European worlds—crumbling entrenchments, overgrown orchards, vacant fields—but centuries of British-Spanish rivalry and the devastating campaigns waged by the British and their Native allies in Florida made this loss easy to comprehend. The connection between antiquities and Indians was easy for the Bartrams to see for another reason: it drove their business. Patrons like Sloane and Grovonius collected pots and pipes because British collectors were developing a new romantic passion for Native America. What might have been harder for John and William Bartram to grasp were efforts *after* the American Revolution to reimagine ancient America—and its lost worlds—as non-Native places.[18]

To be fair, not everyone emerging from the shadow of British rule felt the need to populate the new national backcountry with lost white Indians. The romance of these tales—like the romances of lost French and Spanish America—stoked imaginations on the frontier. But at the emerging intellectual centers of the United States, those looking to the West were more apt to follow the lead of Sloane and Bartram, who saw American antiquity and loss in much the same way as they saw novelty and opportunity: with the eyes of Enlightenment science. Such was the case with Thomas Jefferson. In the 1780s, as John Filson drifted westward, Jefferson wrote his own frontier tract in response to questions posed by French statesmen. The French were curious about America's history in the light of Buffon's arguments that American nature and people had degenerated over time in an inferior environment. As Filson wove frontier yarns against the backdrop of a lost white antiquity, Jefferson penned his *Notes on the State of Virginia* to refute parallel visions of natural loss and degeneration.[19]

Like Filson, Jefferson peeled back the American skin and peered beneath the surface. From an early age he had been intrigued by Indian burial mounds. A large one lay near Monticello, and as a youth he watched as Indians went out of their way to visit it and commemorate their dead. By the 1780s, frontiersmen had dug into the mounds, possibly out of curiosity or seeking lost treasure; stories in U.S. newspapers of wealth found across the Atlantic in the barrows and tumuli of the Old World were common. Jefferson soon joined their ranks. At some point in the early 1780s, he had the mound near his childhood home excavated—an effort described in gruesome detail in his *Notes on the State of Virginia*. He made his slaves cut through the middle of the mound, creating a passage wide enough to walk through and inspect the strata on both sides. He was content to read these as pages in a deeper Indian history. For one thing, it lacked the monumentality of Old World antiquity. "I know of no such thing as an Indian monument," Jefferson noted, "for I would not honour with that name arrow points, stone hatchets, stone pipes, and half-shapen images."[20]

However, Jefferson was far from dismissive of America's deeper history. If anything, he was frustrated at his inability to transcend the mortal remains of this corner of Virginia. There had to be more: the question was where. He lamented the fact that Europeans had destroyed Native peoples without having "collected and deposited in the records of literature, the general rudiments at least of the languages they spoke." Like those who scoured Native vocabularies for vestiges of medieval Welsh, Jefferson was convinced that these linguistic relics, more than bones or stones, would reveal America's place in the world. By gathering and comparing New World languages to their Old World cousins, he felt, one might turn relics into road markers, connecting America to the global matrix of historical relationships that gave rise to older empires and civilizations.[21]

If Jefferson was concerned about America's historical depth, he was also anxious to disprove Buffon's theory of American degeneracy. If Native antiquities lacked the monumentality of Europe, other backcountry ghosts told a different tale. Like Bartram, Jefferson was intrigued by tales of the American mastodon. Long before the American Revolution, shipments of mastodon tusks and teeth from the Ohio River country had reached London, creating a buzz in Royal Society meetings. Here, as with American languages, the curious sought to map out a global antiquity: what was the beast's relationship to the recently discovered mammoth of Siberia? Were these animals still living, or had they vanished? And what did all of this say about America? At the very least, Jefferson argued, this beast rebutted Buffon. Not only was it enormous, he argued, but its highly ridged molars indicated that it was a carnivore, a true king of beasts.[22]

A sticking point was that the beast had been reduced to relics. If the American environment had not weakened the beast, then where was a living specimen to prove it? Jefferson held out hope. According to Native tradition, he proposed, the beast survived somewhere in the American interior, beyond the U.S. frontier.[23] This vision of the American mastodon, reduced to its tusks, molars, and bones in the trans-Appalachian West (but possibly alive beyond the edges of U.S. empire), echoed visions of lost white Indians. But this was more than just the recovery of a deeper history.

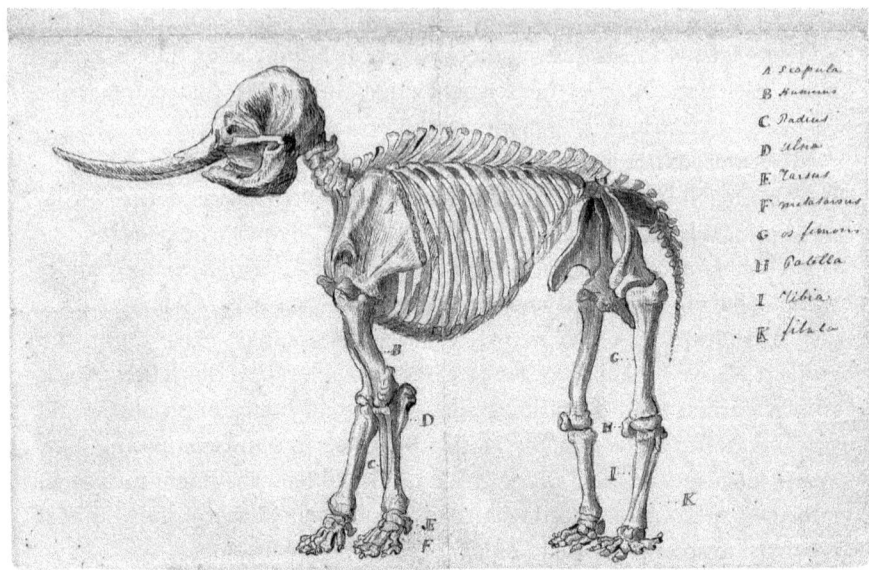

FIGURE 12.2. Sketch of a mastodon skeleton exhumed in New York in 1801 and reassembled as evidence of American monumentality. Rembrandt Peale, 1801.
Courtesy of the American Philosophical Society.

Ancient bones and fortifications also served as road markers, pointing west to a lost America that was ripe for *territorial* recovery. Filson and Jefferson wrote for a generation in which England had expanded its North American claims to the Mississippi and had then yielded to a new nation that seemed ready to push even farther west. Vestiges of ancient America confounded the notion of a young America, but they also played into the hands of empire by orienting tales of American loss and recovery west into a mythical terrain of once and future kings, princes, and civilizations.[24]

This is where Jefferson's similarities to Sloane, Bartram, and Filson stand out most. All four men wrote about history and loss in ways that set powerful narrative coordinates for expansion. In Jamaica and Florida, Sloane and Bartram went to the edges of empire looking for novelty—whether for botanical markets (apothecaries, gardeners) or for the curious—and were increasingly drawn in by the past. Of course, part of the story is that these *were* haunted lands, places unmade by imperial conquests and contests. But timing was also key: Sloane's and Bartram's obsessions with antiquity and loss coincided with bursts of imperial expansion. In these visions, it was not simply the decline of others but also the subsequent *reclamation* of frontier space that made ruins meaningful. Youth and progress were not merely juxtaposed to antiquity and loss on America's frontiers. One created the conditions for the other. It was a familiar tale: the rise and fall of empire, the phoenix emerging from the ashes. Sloane and Bartram might have even invoked a botanical metaphor. Like fruit that had aged on the vine, these old new worlds were ripe for the picking.

Likewise, in Filson and Jefferson, visions of a new nation's expansion were energized in part by earlier lost worlds. Filson recrafted a myth of Anglo migration, tied to English appropriations of the Welsh, in which ancient wanderers reached forward across what Mikhail Bakhtin would call the "epic distance" between heroes and poets, beckoning to a nation in formation.[25] Similarly, down the Ohio and west across the Mississippi, Jefferson imaginatively chased the American mastodon out of extinction and into vigorous new western frontiers. In each of these tales, America's ghosts created a narrative tension—an imperial *telos*—in which heroic or monumental beginnings point to equally heroic, monumental ends. It was a classically epic tale, in which expansion seemed not only natural and inevitable but even, to some extent, circular. It was a story in which national subjects moved into the void created by lost civilizations and imagined this as a sort of homecoming, coming into a territorially preordained inheritance.

IF America's ghosts found new form in age-old tales of epic and empire, they also entered the British and Anglo-American imagination through other imperial histories of North America. As U.S. settler-colonists began to follow the Ohio west to the Mississippi after the American Revolution, obsessions with American antiquity grew. In places like Cahokia, and the Natchez area of southern Mississippi, one found platform mounds and pyramidlike structures unlike anything in the trans-Appalachian West. Continuing west along the Missouri River, and southwest to New Mexico after 1821, the ruins and relics of a lost precolonial America became characteristic features of the landscape. And as the British and Anglo-Americans pushed the French and Spanish into the West, reimagining their Americas also as lost (and backward) Americas, they increasingly turned to the tales these empires left behind in an attempt to make sense of older worlds beyond the Appalachians.[26]

Some of these tales had already begun to migrate east, through usual backcountry channels of rumor and hearsay, by the 1780s. Like the tales of the Welsh Indians, these moved only unevenly to the emerging cultural centers of British and U.S. America, often tucked away in the pages of early American newspapers, and only then by the early nineteenth century. More commonly, British and Anglo-Americans turned to published texts that circulated from the Americas to Europe and back to America—tracing metropolitan networks across the Atlantic that were more familiar to those who devoted their attention and ink to American antiquities. One such border-crossing text appeared in North America at the conclusion of the French and Indian War. As colonial gentlemen-collectors of the elder Bartram's cohort looked west to new frontiers, some added to their libraries the recently translated *History of Louisiana*, by the French colonist Antoine-Simon Le Page du Pratz.[27]

Le Page du Pratz, a self-described engineer-mathematician with botanical interests, came to Louisiana with a group of French settlers in 1718. He set up a plantation near New Orleans, entered into an intimate relationship with a Chitimacha woman (who started out as his slave), and, in 1720, acquired a land grant upstream with the Compagnie d'Occident (John Law's "Company of the West"), adjoining the villages of the Natchez Indians. Using his Chitimacha companion as a cultural broker, he nurtured close ties with Natchez leaders and historians, and he began to record their traditions. He eventually returned to France in 1734 and published an account of Louisiana in twelve parts in the *Journal Oeconomique* in the early 1750s. Le Page du Pratz then elaborated on this foundation in his *Histoire de la Louisiane*, published in Paris in 1758 and then translated, abridged, and republished in London just after the French and Indian War ended in 1763.[28]

Le Page du Pratz wrote his *Histoire* with French settlement in mind, focusing not only on the history of the colony but also on agriculture, trade, and the management of slaves. But it ended up being of much greater importance to the British, who used the book to begin imagining their newly won possessions in the West. The translation's title, *The History of Louisiana, or of the Western Parts of Virginia and Carolina*, marked a clear imperial *telos*: French America found historical significance as a proto-West. It is hoped that the British "may now reap some advantages from these countries," its preface read, "by learning from the experience of others." In translation, then, Le Page du Pratz's history, much like Sloane's and Bartram's ruins and relics, became meaningful primarily by way of a future *reclamation* of frontier space.²⁹

And yet the relationship was more complicated than this. The *History* may have bequeathed to the British a vision of frontier abundance—the resources and trade opportunities that Le Page du Pratz had described for France—but Anglo-American readers seemed more powerfully drawn to its tales of antiquity and loss. As early as 1754, a section of the serialized account in *Journal Oeconomique* appeared in the *Boston News-Letter*. Le Page du Pratz, explained the newspaper, was obsessed with the question of Native origins and "was continually enquiring of the Old Indians concerning it." One day he met an elder of the Yazoo tribe named Moncacht-Apé, who, "having been possessed with the same Curiosity as himself," had made an epic journey north and west beyond the Mississippi, to the origin place of his people. He walked and walked, Le Page du Pratz said, until he reached the "Great Water." There, he met an old man, who remembered another old man, "who had seen this Tract of land, before the Sea broke thro' . . . [what] had formerly been dry Land." As for further clues, added the old man, the traveler was unlikely to find anything to the north except a "cold and desart" land. He "joined to dissuade me from traveling any farther," Moncacht-Apé told Le Page du Pratz. And so "[I] returned by the Way that I came."³⁰

What made Le Page du Pratz's account of Moncacht-Apé's travels even more intriguing to an audience in 1754 were its resonances with shifting colonial understandings of American geography. Not long after reaching the coast, the Yazoo came across a group of men who lived "concealed in the Woods for fear of the bearded Men" who came from "where the Sun sets" in a "great Canoe." These men, they said, carried weapons that "made a great Noise, and a great fire." They invited the Yazoo to go with them to the coast, where they ambushed several of these men, and they gave Moncacht-Apé a chance to inspect their bodies. "Upon examining the Dead, I found them to be less than we are, and very white," he told Le Page du Pratz. They wrapped their heads "with some sort of stuff," wore soft and fine cloth of assorted colors ("Silk without Doubt" wrote the Frenchman), and came to the coast in search of "yellow wood."³¹

A *Boston News-Letter* reader had to sort through multiple layers: a Frenchman in the 1750s, remembering a tale from the 1720s, told by a Native traveler who, in his seventeenth-century youth, examined white, bearded bodies near a "Great Water" out west. For all they knew, Le Page du Pratz had made the whole thing up. But it was intriguing nevertheless. The British were still thirty years away from the detailed knowledge of the Pacific Northwest (and the appetite for expansion into this region) that emerged from Captain James Cook's third voyage, but they already know something of the maritime networks that extended east into the Pacific from Asia. Perhaps Le Page du Pratz had the Javanese or Chinese in mind (silk, sandalwood), but British readers by the 1750s also knew that Russian explorers and fur trappers had begun to make their way east across Siberia into this part of the world. Indeed, "the Conformity of this Account with the late Discoveries of the Russians," noted the *Boston News-Letter*, should give readers little room to doubt the tale.[32]

What mattered in the early 1750s—and in the 1760s, when the story appeared again within the newly translated *History of Louisiana*—was not so much the truth or the precise spatial-cultural coordinates of Moncacht-Apé's travels. What mattered more was the fact that stories of lost worlds (whether populated by ancient Native populations crossing long-vanished land bridges, or by white wanderers from other places) found their place at the acquisitive edges of empire. Le Page du Pratz interwove stories of frontier loss and antiquity with visions of American fertility and opportunity, a juxtaposition that would have resonated with the likes of Filson or Jefferson. And, not surprisingly, it translated perfectly after Louisiana became the new British West after 1763. England was poised to expand into new maritime realms (young James Cook would soon make his first ocean voyage), a context in which the *Pacific* coordinates of Moncacht-Apé's lost worlds were most apropos. Le Page du Pratz most likely found his way into Thomas Jefferson's library at Monticello around this time as well. It is worth noting that the epic of Moncacht-Apé became one of a series of tales (along with tales of white Indians and majestic mastodons) that Meriwether Lewis and William Clark took with them in the early 1800s, when they approached this same region by land.[33]

Part of what distinguishes the Moncacht-Apé tale are its complex circulations. What began as a tale of the search for Native origins—a voyage imagined as a *Native* homecoming—became first a French, then a British, and, ultimately, an American imperial tale. Although this final tale was not a homecoming narrative of the sort activated by the Welsh Indians (where American travelers, like Moncacht-Apé, came into a land formerly peopled by their own), it clearly set coordinates for future journeys to the West. Scholars began to call Moncacht-Apé the "Native" Lewis and Clark—and even if they doubted the veracity of the Frenchman's tale, they rarely hesitated to connect Lewis and Clark to its prior (historical or mythological) horizons. This entanglement of tales was far from innocent. Even Jefferson and Lewis and Clark knew something about the ideological pull of journey narratives. U.S. readers typically forgot that the Corps of Discovery reached the Pacific only by trespassing on lands beyond the pale of the Louisiana Purchase. All one needed was an epic passage across this land—a tale of men progressing from beginning to middle to end—to make the U.S. possession of the Pacific Northwest seem natural and inevitable.[34]

Le Page du Pratz was also aware of the power embodied in stories of travel, whether in tales of discovery or tales of past cultural peregrinations. Take the stories he extracted from the Natchez. This group oriented their culture around temples and platform mounds, something that for Le Page du Pratz made them seem as out of place as Kentucky's ancient mounds later seemed to Filson. He told a Natchez temple-keeper "that from the little resemblance I observed between the *Natches* and the neighboring nations, I was inclined to believe they were not originally of that country." In reply, the temple-keeper recounted an epic tale of migration, pointing "nearly south west" to their land of origin, which Le Page du Pratz took to be Mexico. "Warriors of fire who made the earth to tremble, had arrived in our old country," he told the Frenchman, and their ancestors, refusing to be enslaved, went north. Le Page du Pratz inquired about the warriors of fire. "They were bearded white men, somewhat of a brownish colour, who carried arms that darted out fire with a great noise," explained the temple-keeper. And they "came from the sun-rising in floating villages."[35]

As with the Frenchman's tale of Moncacht-Apé's epic westward voyage, it is difficult to tease apart fact from fiction here. These two stories have a suspicious amount in common, not least being their prehistories of violent contact with white outsiders from beyond the pale. Collectively, they limn a greater American space connected by tales of origin and migrations to the banks of the Mississippi: tales that speak of worlds lost (to natural catastrophe, to conquest) and of worlds to be recovered. In the years leading to the French and Indian War, French traders along the Mississippi River saw both the Missouri River and the borderlands with New Spain as potential areas of commercial (if not also imperial) expansion. And after 1763, Britain—and, later, the United States—gazed out across these same horizons, west into Indian Country and southwest toward Mexico. Yazoo and Natchez epic tales of travel and migration, filtered through Le Page du

Pratz, coincided with imperial visions of American space long before Lewis and Clark added their own epic journey to the mix.

TAKEN individually, tales of Yazoo travelers and Natchez migrants (and their respective lost worlds) may seem only coincidentally linked to later imperial or national visions of expansion. The old and new here may seem as curiously juxtaposed as, say, Kentucky's burial mounds were to the forward-looking frontier tale of Daniel Boone. It is when we read these imperial tracts and their antiquarian insets in the aggregate that larger patterns emerge—and these patterns become even more evident as the United States pushed farther west to the Mississippi, across the new Louisiana country and into its new borderlands with Mexico. On these new frontiers, one encountered familiar juxtapositions of older and younger epics. And nowhere did imperial pathfinders and ancient wanderers more powerfully entangle than on the turn-of-the-century borderlands with Spanish America.

In 1787, Benjamin Smith Barton, a botanist and naturalist of William Bartram's circle, gazed out over the mounds and fortifications of the Ohio River valley. Like William's father, John Bartram, Barton's interest in antiquities had been piqued in part by the frontier while he was on a journey with his uncle, the astronomer David Rittenhouse, to map Pennsylvania's western border. Yet, more than the elder Bartram, Barton faced in the 1780s an unprecedented accumulation of ideas about ancient America, most of which had emerged in the early years of the American republic. To help him make sense of the Ohio country, he had before him Jefferson's published notes on the Indian burial mound that he had excavated at Monticello, along with the "rude and conjectural" theories—revived by John Filson and countless others—regarding Madoc and his lost tribes.[36]

But Barton also had something else in mind, an American history published in Italy in 1781 by Francisco Javier Clavijero, an exiled, Mexican-born Jesuit. Like Jefferson, Clavijero had turned to America's antiquity to counter Buffon's theory of American degeneracy. Yet whereas Jefferson had harnessed the fledgling U.S. nation to a monumental *natural* history, Clavijero focused on the robust *cultural* foundations of American history—particularly those connected to Mexico's Nahua peoples. Even though he wrote a full generation before Mexico's battles for independence, this Mexican-born cleric saw America's lost worlds through a quasi-nationalist lens. Anticipating Mexico's embrace of its indigenous roots, Clavijero began

FIGURE 12.3. An 1848 lithograph of the Grave Creek mound, a well-known landmark for travelers on the Ohio River in the early nineteenth century.

From Ephraim George Squier and Edwin Hamilton Davis, *Ancient Monuments of the Mississippi Valley: Comprising the Results of Extensive Original Surveys and Explorations* (Washington, DC: Smithsonian Institution, 1848), 169.

not with the first white man but with a much deeper history of Native migrations derived from Native codices and colonial compilations of Native histories, some of which extended back a thousand years before the Spanish conquest. He published the result, *Storia di Messico*, in exile in Italy in 1781, and an English-language translation was published in London in 1787. Almost immediately, the *History of Mexico* crossed the Atlantic and began to circulate among a new generation of U.S. intellectuals.[37]

The differences between Clavijero's antiquity and that of his U.S.-American counterparts are worth repeating. If Jefferson claimed to "know of no such thing as an Indian monument," Clavijero's indigenous antiquity was of the most monumental kind. And where Filson imagined the lost worlds of ancient America as fundamentally *white* worlds, whose vestiges stood apart from those of Native America, Clavijero embraced and incorporated the indigenous past, grafting it as an epic precursor to the story of *criollo* Mexico. And yet the distinctions between nations who incorporated the Native past and those who did not were already starting to blur. Clavijero had a lot to do with this—and not because his historical insights were new. To a certain extent, he simply compiled histories that had been in circulation among European readers for years. Clavijero mattered to the early United States because his history coincided with U.S. independence from England and Anglo-Americans' resulting desire for new American tales. And with Clavijero's *History of Mexico* as a guide, Anglo-Americans began turning to indigenous migration stories like never before.

They were particularly drawn to Clavijero's narratives of ancient Native migrations from the north into the central basin of Mexico. Barton pointed his readers to what Clavijero considered the first of these migrations, that of the ancient Toltecs. All one needed to do was compare the ruins of Kentucky or Ohio to those of Mexico, Barton proposed, to understand how the U.S. backcountry had, at one time, been a homeland to these wanderers. Even if the fortifications on the banks of the Ohio were not quite as impressive as those of central Mexico, the United States could lay claim to that monumental tradition by claiming its cultural hearth. Its Mexican antiquity had come first, and thus it embodied that same notion of *precedence* that Madoc arguably had over Columbus. And yet, like Filson, Barton seemed unwilling to embrace a full-blown tale of indigenous origins. The Toltecs were Kentuckians first, he wrote, but their true place of origin must have been to the east, possibly ancient Denmark—a conjecture that echoed

Llwyd and Powel's sixteenth-century Welsh-Aztec genealogy. If they were ancestral Mexicans, they were also, nevertheless, America's first white men.[38]

Barton used Clavijero conservatively, but his incorporation of ancient Mexican histories was relatively new. Llwyd and Powel had commingled Welsh and Aztec histories, but these coordinates had dropped away by the early seventeenth century. It was only in the late 1780s, as the United States began to look west, that Mexico began to matter once again. And the fact that Mexican history came to the U.S. frontier by way of New Spain added a new layer of entanglement, in which prior appropriations at the borderlands of one empire found new significance at the acquisitive edges of another. By the early nineteenth century, one particular cultural feature of New Spain's northern borderlands—the colonial obsession with tales and ruins of former Indian civilizations—would capture the American imagination like no other. And perhaps the most palpable of all these obsessions was the search for ancient road markers to Aztlán, the ancient homeland of those Nahua migrants from the north who later founded the so-called Aztec Empire.

Spaniards learned about Aztlán soon after the conquest of Tenochtitlan through the Mexica, who passed on stories of their migrations by word of mouth and in codices. These stories appeared later in Spanish compilations of Nahua histories. But the tale of Aztlán, like the stories of travel and cultural origin retold by Le Page du Pratz in the eighteenth century, became even more significant in contexts of imperial expansion. When the Jesuit missionary Eusebio Francisco Kino attempted to push Spanish settlement north into what is now Arizona in the 1690s, he rode out of his way to visit what his Native and Spanish guides called Casa Grande ("great house"), an ancient Native American site near the Gila River. "It is said that the ancestors of Moctezuma deserted and depopulated it," he wrote, most likely drawing from traditions carried north from the basin of Mexico by Spaniards and their indigenous allies. In the 1770s, as the Spaniards Juan Bautista de Anza and Pedro Font passed by with settlers for the new imperial outpost of California, they also visited the site. By then, "Casa Grande de Moctezuma" had taken a generic name that Spaniards also applied to multistoried ruins across the sierras, in Casas Grandes, Chihuahua. The epic journey from Aztlán to Tenochtitlan was thus fully inscribed on the northern frontier by the time of New Spain's final consolidation of its far north in the late eighteenth century.[39]

It is worth remembering in all of this that the Aztlán of Nahua tradition was never so clearly situated (its north was indeterminate, something akin to the east of Eden). And yet for the Spanish newcomers, the effort to *place* Aztlán and its sites of peregrination became an obsession. Nowhere was this effort to "fix" precolonial antiquity more evident than in accounts of military and religious expansion—and in eighteenth-century efforts to map the frontier for the Crown. Imperial efforts to claim territory and make the frontier legible went hand-in-hand with ancient pioneering tales and their associated remains. Histories of earlier Mexican empires set the coordinates for new Mexican empires. The Spanish appropriation of Nahua histories was, in this sense, similar to British and U.S. appropriations of Welsh histories: by pointing the future of empire toward monumental spaces of imperial origin, European-Americans could imagine expansion as a kind of homecoming—a natural *ending* to their epic encounter with America.[40]

This effort to appropriate indigenous origin stories and to amplify and naturalize European-American imperial tales began to move in two different directions in the 1780s. Clavijero wrote his *Storia di Messico* in 1781 as what David Brading calls a "creole patriot," producing a Native story for a Mexican-born creole elite (even if not for a full-blown Mexican nation). After Mexican Independence, stories of Native origins resonated deeply with efforts to roll indigenous and colonial elements into a larger national identity. Meanwhile, in the United States, intellectuals like Barton took a translated *History of Mexico* in hand as they tried to create a different nation-centered history of origins. It was harder for U.S. intellectuals to embrace a *mestizo* identity: thus, Barton assimilated ancient Toltecs to older tales of white Indians. And yet as nineteenth-century U.S. readers begin to follow these tales west—and, eventually, to the earlier Spanish frontiers of Arizona, New Mexico, and California—they began to embrace the indigenous grounding of Nahua migration narratives, anchoring their new frontiers, just as the Spanish had anchored theirs, in epic tales of pioneering Indians.[41]

If Clavijero opened the door to this new vision of America, the Prussian naturalist Alexander von Humboldt took the United States more decisively through it. Humboldt traveled through Mexico in 1803 and 1804, visiting New Spain's archives, libraries, and botanical gardens and learning from Spanish fellow-intellectuals about Mexican antiquities. After sharing insights with Jefferson in Washington, DC, on the eve of Lewis and Clark's journey, he continued to Paris where he published the results of his

American voyages. U.S. readers were drawn in 1814 to his *Institutions and Monuments of the Ancient Inhabitants of America*, which reenvisioned monumental Mexico and its ancient migrations for a new era. Just as Clavijero's history coincided with U.S. expansion west into Ohio and Kentucky, Humboldt captured the next generation as it continued to the Mississippi and beyond. If Le Page du Pratz had the Natchez to make sense of lost Mississippian worlds, U.S. newcomers in the 1820s and 1830s had Humboldt—not to mention Humboldt's Mexico, now a new trade partner and a potential addition to the land-hungry United States—to help them find their bearings.⁴²

And so it was in 1837, when white settlers of Milwaukee, Wisconsin, moving west into lands recently dispossessed from local Indian tribes, stumbled across a series of ancient platform mounds and pyramid-shaped structures. This place, announced a Milwaukee doctor named Nathaniel Hyer, "we have taken the liberty to call Aztalan." Hyer and his well-read companions took the name, based on Aztlán, straight from the tattered pages of Humboldt. The Aztec "usurpers" had migrated to Mexico from the north, from a land called "Aztalan," Hyer told the editor of the *Milwaukee Advertiser*. And since Humboldt had clearly placed this ancient land somewhere above the forty-second parallel, might it not be here in the wilds of Wisconsin? Might this not be the place where America's most monumental imperial narrative began? Another writer, Stephen Taylor, saw the story in a slightly different way in 1842, as he gazed over the frontier village of Aztalan. The ruins showed this to be a formerly "flourishing region," he wrote, one "destined . . . to have in a few years as dense and powerful a population as we have reason to believe flourished there in former times."⁴³

When he first visited the Aztalan ruins in 1850, the Wisconsin naturalist Increase A. Lapham perhaps shrugged part of this off—as readers shrugged off Welsh Indians in Filson's Kentucky three generations earlier—as backwoods propaganda. If some found it easy to weave American antiquity and American prophecy into a larger frontier cloth, Lapham found the temporal juxtapositions a bit less enlightening. "A modern city lies above the ancient, and its streets are named after the ancient as Azteck Street, etc.," he told his wife in a letter, not knowing whether to laugh or cry. "Many of the mounds have been partially opened [and] the south part of the citadel is in a cultivated field." Yet it was difficult for him to discount the similarities between the platform mounds in Aztalan and those to the south on the Mississippi. Even if one might be hard-pressed to connect the antiquities of this isolated frontier village to the monumental speculations of Humboldt, it was difficult for him—as it would be for others—to ignore what seemed to be an ancient trail of architectural ghosts stretching south from Aztalan, along the banks of the Mississippi River to the Gulf of Mexico, and from there to the ancient landscapes of Mexico. Even though Lapham and others would increasingly turn to field methods (rather than to histories and travelers' tales) to place antiquities, it proved harder to shake the spatial coordinates of these earlier narratives than they might have anticipated.[44]

Most inhabitants of Aztalan today are of German and Norwegian immigrant stock. The idea of finding Aztecs here seems almost like a bad joke. But in the 1830s it made sense. Few westward-moving Americans knew at the time about the precolonial antiquities of Arizona and New Mexico. And Aztalan did, after all, have pyramid-shaped platforms, and it was at the northern fringes of a vast Mississippian system that seemed to point—no less clearly than Le Page du Pratz's Native historian had—toward Mexico. It had not been so long since pioneers plowed up vestiges of lost Welshmen in Kentucky, proving that the old tales might be true after all. It hadn't been that long since Thomas Jefferson—a pioneer of American archaeology—had taken such narratives seriously, whether they be stories of modern mastodons, white Indians, or epic voyages. It wasn't just that the stories were possible. It was that they were *compelling*, especially for a nation that had devoted so much energy to frontier mythologies that buried the American past. All of this suppression had made the frontier an uncanny place, where ruins and relics haunted the nation in both unexpected and uncomfortably familiar ways. A nation that suppressed history had become a nation in particular need of stories—of meaningful connections between past and future, loss and rebirth, beginnings and endings—that might help the nation put these frontier ghosts to rest.[45]

Soon the nation would be on the move again, marking out new borderlands west into North America, south across Mexico. Soon the antiquities of Wisconsin, like those of Kentucky and Ohio, would began to gather dust in local frontier cabinets, as monumentality and antiquity and places of origin migrated to the nation's expanding edge, where they always seemed to belong. By the 1850s, U.S. travelers seemed to be more generally convinced that they had finally caught up with Aztlán, or at least the cultural and material vestiges of the Nahua journey south. Newcomers like Josiah

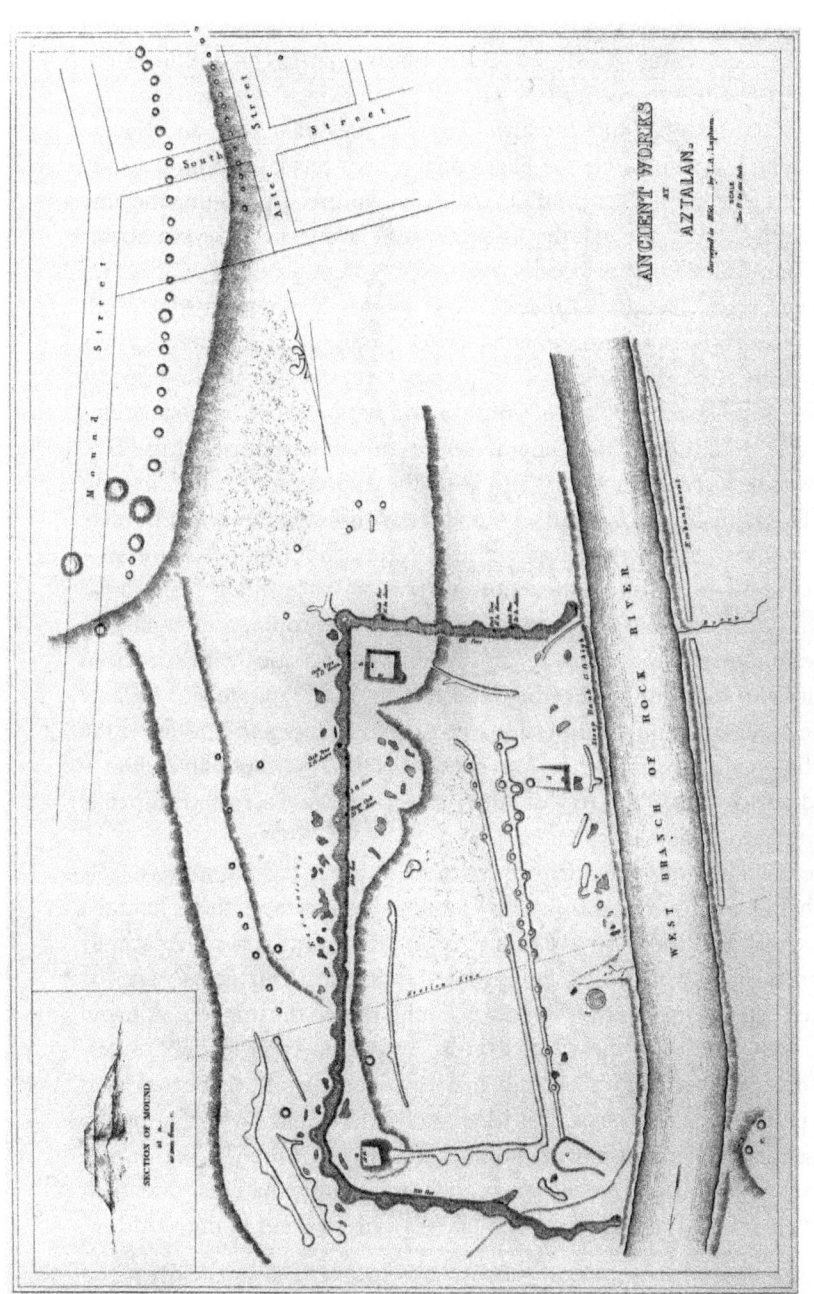

FIGURE 12.4. An 1850 sketch of the Mississippian site of Aztalan, by Increase A. Lapham, juxtaposed with the "Mound" and "Aztec" streets of the modern town of Aztalan, Wisconsin.

From *The Antiquities of Wisconsin: As Surveyed and Described.* By I. A. Lapham, *Civil Engineer, Etc., on Behalf of the American Antiquarian Society* (Washington, DC: Smithsonian Institution, 1855), plate XXXIV.

Gregg and James H. Simpson imagined that they had found the descendants of the original Mexica tribes or their cousins among the Navajos, and names like Montezuma's Castle and Aztec Ruins appeared on Southwestern maps, next to their respective lost worlds. Meanwhile, from the 1820s forward, familiar tales of white Indians migrated into Zuni, Hopi, and Navajo country and sometimes off the edges of the map in places bound to the nation, it seemed, only by rumor. As on earlier frontiers, it was the uncanny nature of these tales, the fact that they emerged in unexpected, yet uncomfortably familiar ways, that became their most salient feature.[46]

However one imagines America's lost worlds by the mid-nineteenth century—as vestiges of monumental civilizations, or as shadowy realms transected by ancient pioneers—it is impossible to disentangle these spaces from the acquisitive impulses of empires and nations. The appropriations of American antiquity that characterized the nineteenth-century U.S. Southwest proceeded hand in hand with the appropriation of American space. This dynamic, more than anything else, connected these later borderlands to those of earlier American empires. Although it later became easy—even natural—to imagine the Southwest as a space apart from prior American frontiers, this was because its historical appropriations came last. They were remembered long after prior frontier obsessions with American antiquity and loss had been buried and forgotten. The Southwest became the safety valve for our suppressions of American loss and antiquity: the land whose cultural confluences and contested spaces—whose *differences*—allowed us to stretch the rest of America east to west across continental bones, to ignore the history underfoot.

There is no better time than the present to begin digging more deeply beneath the surface—to more fully engage and reconnect these haunted spaces, to ask how the warp and weft of imperial America was systematically built on the lost worlds of other peoples and times. Our generation has rewritten the history of early America by pulling back the imperial skin and rewriting the stories of these lost worlds. But we have yet to fully understand those processes of uncovering and reburying the past that brought us to this point in the first place. It is time to revisit the narratives of antiquity and loss that created, unsettled, and then forgot early America. For only in this way can we begin to comprehend how empires, nations, and their storytellers found and then lost their places in history and in the world.

NOTES

Introduction

1. Consider a sequence of fairly recent collections and syntheses, beginning three decades ago with David G. Sweet and Gary B. Nash, eds., *Struggle and Survival in Colonial America* (Berkeley: University of California Press, 1980) and continuing through with the following publications: Peter H. Wood, Gregory A. Waselkov and M. Thomas Hatley, eds., *Powhatan's Mantle: Indians in the Colonial Southeast* (Lincoln: University of Nebraska Press, 1989); Stuart B. Schwartz, ed., *Implicit Understanding: Observing, Reporting, and Reflecting on the Encounters Between Europeans and Other Peoples in the Early Modern Era* (Cambridge: Cambridge University Press, 1994); David J. Weber and Jane M. Rausch, eds., *Where Cultures Meet: Frontiers in Latin American History* (Wilmington, DE: SR Books, 1994); Andrew R. L. Catton and Fredrika J. Teute, eds., *Contact Points: America Frontiers from the Mohawk Valley to the Mississippi, 1750–1830* (Chapel Hill: University of North Carolina Press, 1998); Donna J. Guy and Thomas E. Sheridan, eds., *Contested Ground: Comparative Frontiers on the Northern and Southern Edges of the Spanish Empire* (Tucson: University of Arizona Press, 1998); Alan Taylor, *American Colonies* (New York: Viking, 2001); Daniel Vickers, ed., *A Companion to Colonial America* (Malden, MA: Blackwell, 2003); the most recent edition of *Colonial America: Essays in Political and Social Development*, ed. Stanley Nider Katz, Douglas Greenberg, David J. Silverman, and Denver Brunsman (New York: Routledge, 2011); Daniel K. Richter, *Facing East from Indian Country* (Cambridge, MA: Harvard University Press, 2001), and *Before the Revolution: America's Ancient Pasts* (Cambridge, MA: Harvard University Press, 2011). To that list must be added David Weber's two magisterial late-career books, *The Spanish Frontier in North America* (New Haven, CT: Yale University Press, 1993), and *Bárbaros: Spaniards and Their Savages in the Age of Enlightenment* (New Haven, CT: Yale University Press, 2005). Ending the list at this point is an arbitrary choice. It could expand to include a long list of monographs and specialized articles, by many authors in addition to the ones who have contributed to this volume. Following Weber's lead, the essays here make the collective point that to really understand "colonial America" we need to understand not just North America but the whole hemisphere. That point already is clear in the study of the development of slavery. We extend it to the study of American space and the people who contested to control it.

2. David J. Weber, "Foreword," in *Continental Crossroads: Remapping U.S.-Mexico Borderlands History*, ed. Samuel Truett and Elliott Young (Durham, NC: Duke University Press, 2004), ix; Armando Cortesao, "António Pereira and His Map of Circa 1545: An Unknown Portuguese Cartographer and the Early Representation of Newfoundland, Lower California, the Amazon, and the Ladrones," *Geographical Review* 29, no. 2 (April 1939), 205–225; Jerry Brotton, *Trading Territories: Mapping the Early Modern World* (London: Reaktion, 1997), 82–83; Matthew H. Voss,

" 'In this sign you shall conquer': The Cross of the Order of Christ in Sixteenth-Century Portuguese Cartography," *Terrae Incognitae* 39 (January 2007), 24–37.

3. Barbara E. Mundy, *The Mapping of New Spain: Indigenous Cartography and the Maps of the Relaciones Geográficas* (Chicago: University of Chicago Press, 2000), 1–9; Raymond B. Craib, "Cartography and Power in the Conquest and Creation of New Spain," *Latin American Research Review* 35 (2000), 14 for "breathless progression"; Paul Carter, *The Road to Botany Bay: An Exploration of Landscape and History* (New York: Knopf, 1988), 349; J. Brian Harley, "Rereading the Maps of the Columbian Encounter," *Annals of the Association of American Geographers* 82 (1992), 530; J. B. Harley, "Silences and Secrecy: The Hidden Agenda of Cartography in Early Modern Europe," *Imago Mundi* 40 (1988), 57 for "political discourse," 59–61, 68; Brotton, *Trading Territories*; Monique Pelletier, "Cartography and Power in France During the Seventeenth and Eighteenth Centuries," *Cartographica* 35 (Autumn/Winter 1998), 41–53; J. B. Harley, *Maps and the Columbian Encounter* (Milwaukee: University of Wisconsin Press, 1990), 97 for "tools of imperialism"; Ricardo Padrón, *The Spacious Word: Cartography, Literature, and Empire in Early Modern Spain* (Chicago: University of Chicago Press, 2004); Paul Mapp, *The Elusive West and the Contest of Empire, 1713–1763* (Chapel Hill: University of North Carolina Press for the Omohundro Institute of Early American History and Culture, 2011).

4. Doreen Massey, *For Space* (London: Sage, 2005), 4, 5; Harley, "Silences and Secrecy," 66; Harley, "Rereading the Maps," 531 for "engulfing"; Brotton, *Trading Territories*, 46–86.

5. Barbara E. Mundy, "Mapping the Aztec Capital: The 1524 Nuremberg Map of Tenochtitlan, Its Sources and Meanings," *Imago Mundi* 50 (1998), 11–33; G. Malcolm Lewis, "Native North Americans' Cosmological Ideas and Geographical Awareness: Their Representation and Influence on Early European Exploration and Geographical Knowledge," in *North American Exploration, I: A New World Disclosed*, ed. John Logan Allen (Lincoln: University of Nebraska Press, 1997), 71–126, esp. 116–117; "Voyages of Father Jacques Marquette," Section 7, in *The Jesuit Relations and Allied Documents*, ed. Reuben G. Thwaites, vol. 29, http://puffin.creighton.edu/jesuit/relations/relations_59.html.

6. G. Malcolm Lewis, ed., *Cartographic Encounters: Perspectives on Native American Mapmaking and Map Use* (Chicago: University of Chicago Press, 1998); Mark Warhus, *Another America: Native American Maps and the History of Our Land* (New York: St. Martin's, 1997); Louis De Vorsey, Jr., "Silent Witnesses: Native American Maps," *The Georgia Review* 46 (Winter 1992), 709–726; Mundy, *Mapping of New Spain*; Renée Fossett, "Mapping Inuktut: Inuit Views of the Real World," in *Reading Beyond Words: Contexts for Native History*, ed. Jennifer S. H. Brown and Elizabeth Vibert (Orchard Park, NY: Broadview, 1996), 74–94; John C. Ewers, "The Making and Uses of Maps by Plains Indian Warriors," in *Plains Indian History and Culture: Essays on Continuity and Change* (Norman: University of Oklahoma Press, 1997), 180–190; F. Terry Norris and Timothy R. Pauketat, "A Pre-Columbian Map of the Mississippi?" *Southeastern Archaeology* 27 (Summer 2008), 78–92; Kent C. Ryden, *Mapping the Invisible Landscape: Folklore, Writing, and the Sense of Place* (Iowa City: University of Iowa Press, 1993).

7. For the Inca road system, see Mapp, *Elusive West*, 69, 94–95.

8. For El Turco's path aimed at Cahokia, see Richard Flint, *No Settlement, No Conquest: A History of the Coronado Entrada* (Albuquerque: University of New Mexico Press, 2008), 163–164. For Chaco, see Stephen H. Lekson, "Lords of the Great House: Pueblo Bonito as a Palace," in *Palaces and Power in the Americas: From Peru to the Northwest Coast*, ed. Jessica Joyce Christie and Patricia Joan Sarro (Austin: University of Texas Press, 2006), 110–111, and Stephen H. Lekson,

The Chaco Meridian Centers of Political Power in the Ancient Southwest (Walnut Creek, CA: Altamira, 1999).

9. Margot Beyersdorff, "Covering the Earth: Mapping the Walkabout in Andean *Pueblos de Indios,*" *Latin American Research Review* 42 (October 2007), 129–160; Amara L. Solari, "Circles of Creation: The Invention of Maya Cartography in Early Colonial Yucatan," *Art Bulletin* 92 (September 2010), 154–168; Jean O'Brien, *Dispossession by Degrees: Indian Land and Identity in Natick, Massachusetts, 1650–1790* (New York: Cambridge University Press, 1997); Margaret Wickens Pearce, "Native Mapping in Southern New England Indian Deeds," in Lewis, *Cartographic Encounters,* 154–186; José António Brandão and William A. Starna, "'Some things may slip out of your memory and be forgott': The 1701 Deed and Map of Iroquois Hunting Territory Revisited," *New York History* 86 (Fall 2005), 417–433; J. A. Brandão and William A. Starna, "The Treaties of 1701: A Triumph of Iroquois Diplomacy," *Ethnohistory* 43 (Spring 1996), 209–244; Jon Parmenter, *The Edge of the Woods: Iroquoia, 1534–1701* (East Lansing: Michigan State University Press, 2010); Alan Taylor, *The Divided Ground: Indians, Settlers and the Northern Borderland of the American Revolution* (New York: Knopf, 2006).

10. Guillaume de L'Isle, "Carte du Mexique et de la Floride des Terres Angloises et des Isles Antilles: Du cours et des environs de la Riviere de Mississipi [sic], dressée sur ungrand nombre de memoires principalemt. sur ceux de M.rs d'Iberville et le Sueur / par Guillaume Del'Isle; C. Simonneau, fecit." (1703), http://memory.loc.gov; Henry Popple, "A Map of the British Empire in America, with the French, Spanish, and the Dutch Settlements Adjacent Thereto" (Second State, 1741), http://memory.loc.gov.

11. Gregory A. Waselkov, "Indian Maps of the Colonial Southeast," in Wood, Waselkov, and Hatley, *Powhatan's Mantle,* 324–329; Warhus, *Another America,* 102–107.

12. Mundy, "Mapping the Aztec Capital," 13 for "cosmic linchpin," 16; Rolena Adorno, *Guaman Poma: Writing and Resistance in Colonial Peru,* 2nd ed. (Austin: University of Texas Press, 2000); Gordon Brotherston, *Image of the New World: The American Context Portrayed in Native Texts* (London: Thames and Hudson, 1979), 237–240.

13. Mundy, *Mapping of New Spain;* Dana Leibsohn, "Primers for Memory: Cartographic Histories and Nahua Identity," in *Writing Without Words: Alternative Literacies in Mesoamerica and the Andes,* ed. Elizabeth Hill Boone and Walter D. Mignolo (Durham, NC: Duke University Press, 1994), 161–187. For similar Mayan patterns, see Amara L. Solari, "Circles of Creation: The Invention of Maya Cartography in Early Colonial Yucatan," *Art Bulletin* 92 (September 2010), 154–168; Waselkov, "Indian Maps of the Colonial Southeast," 292–243; Patricia Galloway, "Debriefing Explorers: Amerindian Information in the Delisles' Mapping of the Southeast," in Lewis, *Cartographic Encounters,* 223–240.

14. See, in particular, Parmenter, *Edge of the Woods,* and Pekka Hämäläinen, *The Comanche Empire* (New Haven, CT: Yale University Press, 2008).

15. Harley, "Rereading the Maps," 522; Lewis, *Cartographic Encounters,* 18–19; G. Malcolm Lewis, "Indian Maps: Their Place in the History of Plains Cartography," *Great Plains Quarterly* 4 (Spring 1984), 101–102; Mapp, *Elusive West,* 76–79.

16. Juliana Barr, "Geographies of Power: Mapping Indian Borders in the 'Borderlands' of the Early Southwest," *William and Mary Quarterly* 3rd ser., 68 (January 2011), 5–46; Harley, *Maps and the Columbian Encounter,* 131–133; Michael Witgen, "The Rituals of Possession: Native Identity and the Invention of Empire in Seventeenth-Century Western North America," *Ethnohistory* 54 (Fall 2007), 641.

17. See particularly Parmenter, *Edge of the Woods*, and Mapp, *Elusive West*.

18. Harley, *Maps and the Columbian Encounter*, 135 for "declaration[s] of exclusion"; J. B. Harley, "New England Cartography and the Native Americans," in *American Beginnings: Exploration, Culture, and Cartography in the Land of Norumbega*, ed. Emerson W. Baker et al. (Lincoln: University of Nebraska Press, 1994), 287–313; John Locke, *Second Treatise of Civil Government* (1690), section 49, see http://www.gutenberg.org/files/7370/7370-h/7370-h.htm.

19. "A map of the British and French dominions in North America, with the roads, distances, limits, and extent of the settlements, humbly inscribed to the Right Honourable the Earl of Halifax, and the other Right Honourable the Lords Commissioners for Trade & Plantations, by their Lordships most obliged and very humble servant, Jno. Mitchell. Tho: Kitchin, sculp." (1st ed., third impression), http://memory.loc.gov.

20. Jean M. O'Brien, *Dispossession by Degrees: Indian Land and Identity in Natick, Massachusetts, 1650–1790* (Cambridge: Cambridge University Press, 1997); Philip J. Deloria, "From Nation to Neighborhood: Land, Policy, Culture, Colonialism, and Empire in U.S.-Indian Relations," in *The Cultural Turn in U.S. History*, ed. James W. Cook, Lawrence B. Glickman, and Michael O'Malley (Chicago: University of Chicago Press, 2008), 351 for "delineated," 358 for "concentration camp" and "reeducation camp"; Edward S. Casey, *The Fate of Place: A Philosophical History* (Berkeley: University of California Press, 1997), xii for "deplacialization"; James Taylor Carson, "Ethnogeography and the Native American Past," *Ethnohistory* 49 (Fall 2002), 769–788.

21. Raymond Craib, *Cartographic Mexico: A History of State Fixations and Fugitive Landscapes* (Durham, NC: Duke University Press, 2004); Jordana Dym and Karl Offen, eds., *Mapping Latin America: A Cartographic Reader* (Chicago: University of Chicago Press, 2011), 168–171, 181–185; Deloria, "From Nation to Neighborhood."

22. See, particularly, Donna Merwick, *Possessing Albany, 1630–1710: The Dutch and English Experiences, 1630–1710* (Cambridge: Cambridge University Press, 1990).

23. Mapp, *Elusive West*.

24. We paraphrase Colin G. Calloway from his 2008 presidential address, "Indian History from the End of the Alphabet; And What Now?" *Ethnohistory* 58 (Spring 2011), 200; Benjamin H. Johnson and Andrew R. Graybill, eds., *Bridging National Borders in North America: Transnational and Comparative Histories* (Durham, NC: Duke University Press, 2010), 2 for "inevitability" and "succumb."

25. Allan Greer, "National, Transnational, and Hypernational Historiographies: New France Meets Early American History," *Canadian Historical Review* 91, no. 4 (2010), 720 for "are at the starting point"; Weber, *Bárbaros*; Eric Hinderaker and Rebecca Horn, "Territorial Crossings: Histories and Historiographies of the Early Americas," *William and Mary Quarterly* 3d ser., 67 (July 2010), 414 for "tend to attribute," 429 for "wherever we analyze." For Latin American debates over a hemispheric history of America, see Herbert Eugene Bolton, "The Epic of Greater America," *American Historical Review* 38 (1933), 448–474; Silvio Zavala, "A General View of the Colonial History of the New World," *American Historical Review* 66 (July 1961), 913–929; Lewis Hanke, ed., *Do the Americas Have a Common History? A Critique of the Bolton Theory* (New York: Knopf, 1964); Felipe Fernández-Armesto, *The Americas: A Hemispheric History* (New York: Modern Library, 2003); J. H. Elliott, *Empires of the Atlantic World: Britain and Spain in America, 1492–1830* (New Haven, CT: Yale University Press, 2006).

26. Greer, "National, Transnational, and Hypernational Historiographies," 697 for "obfuscat[e]" and "ideological"; Carson, "Ethnogeography and the Native American Past," 772–775;

Paul Cohen, "Was There an Amerindian Atlantic? Reflections on the Limits of a Historiographical Concept," *History of European Ideas* 34 (2008), 402; Amy Turner Bushnell, "Indigenous America and the Limits of the Atlantic World, 1493–1825," in *Atlantic History: A Critical Appraisal*, ed. Jack P. Greene and Philip D. Morgan (New York: Oxford University Press, 2009), 191–221; Juliana Barr, "Beyond the Atlantic World: Early American History as Viewed from the West," *OAH Magazine of History* 25 (January 2011), 13–18.

27. Carson, "Ethnogeography and the Native American Past," 775 for "a place"; Massey, *For Space*, 9 for "sphere in which," 107 for "dynamic simultaneity."

28. Claudio Saunt, "The Indians' Old World," *William and Mary Quarterly* 3d ser., 68 (April 2011), 218.

29. For colonial and national history, see Deloria, "From Nation to Neighborhood," and Jack P. Greene, "Colonial History and National History: Reflections on a Continuing Problem," *William and Mary Quarterly* 64 (April 2007), 240, 243. For territorial sovereignty of Indian nations in 1800, see Weber, *Bárbaros*, 12; D. W. Meinig, *The Shaping of America: A Geographical Perspective on 500 Years of History*, 3 vols. (New Haven, CT: Yale University Press, 1993), II: 195. Keith Basso, *Wisdom Sits in Places: Landscape and Language Among the Western Apache* (Albuquerque: University of New Mexico Press, 1996), 144 for "what has accured."

30. Craib, "Cartography and Power in the Conquest and Creation of New Spain," 29.

31. For layered histories see Daniel K. Richter, *Before the Revolution: America's Ancient Pasts* (Cambridge, MA: Harvard University Press, 2011), and Edward Countryman, "The Layers of New York History: A Look Through Time at Rensselaer County," *New York History* 89, no. 1 (Winter 2008), 5–26. William Faulkner, *Requiem for a Nun* (1951; reprint, New York: Vintage, 2012), act I, scene 3, 73,

Chapter 1

1. Carl Bridenbaugh, "The Neglected First Half of American History," *American Historical Review* 53 (April 1948), 505–517; Peter Thompson, "Inventive Localism in the Seventeenth Century," *William and Mary Quarterly* 64 (July 2007), 523–548.

2. On the fragmented, disjointed makeup of American history, see Thomas Bender, "Wholes and Parts: The Need for Synthesis in American History," *Journal of American History* 73 (June 1986), 120–136; Matthew Dennis, *Cultivating a Landscape of Peace: Iroquois-European Encounters in Seventeenth-Century America* (Ithaca, NY: Cornell University Press, 1993), 2; Joyce E. Chaplin, "Expansion and Exceptionalism in Early American History," *Journal of American History* 89 (March 2003), 1433–1451; Daniel K. Richter, "Whose Indian History?" *William and Mary Quarterly* 50 (April 1993), 390–391; and Peter C. Mancall, "Pigs for Historians: Changes in the Land and Beyond," *William and Mary Quarterly* 67 (April 2010), 357.

3. Quotes are from Edward Countryman, "Respond," *William and Mary Quarterly* 53 (April 1996), 382; James H. Merrell, "Indian History During the English Colonial Era," in *Companion to Colonial America*, ed. Daniel Vickers (Malden, MA: Blackwell, 2003), 129; and Stephen Aron, "Pigs and Hunters: 'Rights in the Woods' on the Trans-Appalachian Frontier," in *Contact Points: American Frontiers from the Mohawk Valley to the Mississippi, 1750–1830*, ed. Andrew R. L. Cayton and Fredrika J. Teute (Chapel Hill: University of North Carolina Press, 1998), 175. Merrell, on page 120, also notes how, inspired by colonial community studies, "many of the works on Indians have been, essentially, studies of one community or tribe." Obviously, not all recent studies have

been consigned to the local-regional level. For a small sample of broadly conceived works, see Colin G. Calloway, *New Worlds for All: Indians, Europeans, and the Remaking of Early America* (Baltimore: Johns Hopkins University Press, 1997); Alan Taylor, *American Colonies: The Settling of North America* (New York: Viking, 2001); Colin G. Calloway, *One Vast Winter Count: The Native American West Before Lewis and Clark* (Lincoln: University of Nebraska Press, 2003); and Paul W. Mapp, *The Elusive West and the Contest for Empire* (Chapel Hill: University of North Carolina Press, 2011). For calls for continental approaches to early American history, see Elliott West, "A Longer, Grimmer but More Interesting Story," in *Trails: Toward a New Western History*, ed. Patricia Nelson Limerick, Clyde A. Milner II, and Charles E. Rankin (Lawrence: University Press of Kansas, 1991), 103–111; Claudio Saunt, "Go West: Mapping Early American Historiography," *William and Mary Quarterly* 65 (October 2008), 745–778; Peter H. Wood, "From Atlantic History to a Continental Approach," in *Atlantic History: A Critical Appraisal*, ed. Jack P. Greene and Philip D. Morgan (New York: Oxford University Press, 2009), 279–298; Juliana Barr, "Beyond the 'Atlantic World': Early American History as Viewed from the West," *OAH Magazine of History* 25 (2011), 13–18; and Andrew R. L. Cayton, "Writing North American History," Journal of the Early Republic 22 (Spring 2002), 105–111.

4. See, for example, Fred Anderson and Andrew Cayton, "The Problem of Authority in the Writing of Early American History," *William and Mary Quarterly* 66 (July 2009), 467–494; and Pekka Hämäläinen and Samuel Truett, "On Borderlands," *Journal of American History* 98 (September 2011), 338–361. For forceful endorsements of a microhistorical approach to early American history, see Darrett B. Rutman, "Assessing the Little Communities of Early America," *William and Mary Quarterly* 43 (April 1986), 163–178; James H. Merrell, "Some Thoughts on Colonial Historians and American Indians," *William and Mary Quarterly* 46 (January 1989), 117–118; and Joshua Piker, "Lying Together: The Imperial Implications of Cross-cultural Untruths," *American Historical Review* 116 (October 2011), 964–986.

5. There are some comparable studies. In 1999, in a landmark essay, Jeremy Adelman and Stephen Aron took a sweeping look at different early American places, but they identified only two kinds of social worlds: European imperial realms and contested "borderlands," where the exigencies of imperial rivalry allowed Indians to play colonial powers against one another to retain a level of political autonomy. In 2000, Daniel Richter provided a brief but nuanced analysis of the different indigenous worlds as they existed in the early eighteenth century in the lands that eventually became the eastern United States, but the developments he uncovered are only partially applicable to the rest of the continent. His 2011 synthesis brilliantly unearthed the complex historical substrata of early America, but the narrative focused mostly on that part of early America that became the United States and it made only sporadic plunges into other early American worlds. In 2008, François Furstenberg provided an illuminating wide-angle view of power struggles, imperial centers, and cross-cultural borderlands in eastern North America between the 1750s and 1815. Rather than on broader processes or social worlds, however, Furstenberg focused on "hot spots," shifting places of concentrated historical action that marked the process that eventually delivered the trans-Appalachian West to the U.S. fold. See Jeremy Adelman and Stephen Aron, "From Borderlands to Borders: Empires, Nation-States, and the Peoples in Between in North American History," *American Historical Review* 104 (October 1999), 814–841; Daniel K. Richter, *Facing East from Indian Country: A Native History of Early America* (Cambridge, MA: Harvard University Press, 2000), esp. 164–171; François Furstenberg, "The Significance of the Trans-Appalachian Frontier in Atlantic History," *American Historical Review* 113 (June 2008),

647–677; and Daniel K. Richter, *Before the Revolution: America's Ancient Pasts* (Cambridge, MA: Harvard University Press, 2011). On the notion of entangled histories, see Eliga H. Gould, "Entangled Histories, Entangled Worlds: The English-Speaking Atlantic as a Spanish Periphery," *American Historical Review* 112 (June 2007), 764–786.

6. D. W. Meinig, *The Shaping of America: A Geographic Perspective on 500 Years of History*, vol. 1, *Atlantic America, 1492–1800* (New Haven, CT: Yale University Press, 1986), 3–254; Mapp, *Elusive West*, 43–68. On the importance of the Appalachian Mountains in American history, see Furstenberg, "Significance."

7. As recently as 2009, a major university press brought out a book that presents European colonization of a seemingly borderless indigenous North America as a foregone conclusion: "The simple truth is that Indians and confederations of tribes, some of them sophisticated and others essentially Neolithic, really could do nothing to stop this march to the Pacific. . . . For the most part they did not really try; Indians were much more welcoming, or less resistant, to whites peopling the continent than most Americans imagine." See Bruce Cummings, *Dominion from Sea to Sea: Pacific Ascendancy and American Power* (New Haven, CT: Yale University Press, 2009), 29. For important openings toward retrieving indigenous territoriality, see Patricia Albers and Jeanne Kay, "Sharing the Land: A Study in American Indian Territoriality," in *A Cultural Geography of North American Indians*, ed. Thomas E. Ross and Tyrel G. Moore (Boulder, CO: Westview, 1987); Keith H. Basso, *Wisdom Sits in Places: Landscape and Language Among the Western Apache* (Albuquerque: University of New Mexico Press, 1996); and Juliana Barr, "Geographies of Power: Mapping Indian Borders in the 'Borderlands' of the Early Southwest," *William and Mary Quarterly* 67 (January 2011), 3–44.

8. On the Southwest and the Mississippi Valley, see Barr, "Geographies"; Mapp, *Elusive West*, 147–165; and Kathleen DuVal, "Interconnectedness and Diversity in 'French Louisiana,'" in *Powhatan's Mantle: Indians in the Colonial Southeast*, ed. Gregory A. Waselkov, Peter H. Wood, and Tom Hatley (Lincoln: University of Nebraska Press, 2006), 133–162. On the Eastern Seaboard, see Virginia DeJohn Anderson, "King Philip's Herds: Indians, Colonists, and the Problem of Livestock in Early New England," *William and Mary Quarterly* 51 (October 1994), 601–624; William Cronon, *Changes in the Land: Indians, Colonists, and the Ecology of New England* (New York: Hill and Wang, 1983), 35–81; Jill Lepore, *The Name of War: King Philip's War and the Origins of American Identity* (New York: Knopf, 1998), 81–83; and Nancy Shoemaker, *A Strange Likeness: Becoming Red and White in Eighteenth-Century North America* (New York: Oxford University Press, 2004), 13–34.

9. "A Map Describing the Situation of the Several Nations of Indians Between South Carolina and the Mississippi River," in *The Crown Collection of Photographs of American Maps*, Archer Butler Hulbert (Washington, 1873), ser. 3, vol. 1, plates 7–8, available at http://www.newberry.org/k12maps. Also see Gregory A. Waselkov, "Indian Maps of the Colonial Southeast," in Waselkov, Wood, and Hatley, *Powhatan's Mantle*, 439–445; Louis De Vorsey, Jr., "The Colonial Georgia Backcountry," in *Colonial Augusta: "Key to the Indian Countrey,"* ed. Edward J. Cashin (Macon, GA: Mercer University Press, 1986), 20; and April Lee Hatfield, "Spanish Colonization Literature, Powhatan Geographies, and English Perceptions of Tsenacommacah/Virginia," *Journal of Southern History* 69 (May 2003), 246–282. The quote is from James H. Merrell, "Racial Education of the Catawba Indians," *Journal of Southern History* 50 (August 1984), 365.

10. Meinig, *Shaping of America*, 91–160; Eric Hinderaker and Peter C. Mancall, *At the Edge of Empire: The Backcountry in British North America* (Baltimore: Johns Hopkins University Press,

2003), 8–45; J. H. Elliott, *Atlantic Empires: Britain and Spain in America, 1592–1800* (New Haven, CT: Yale University Press, 2006), 36, 47–48; David J. Weber, *The Spanish Frontier in North America* (New Haven, CT: Yale University Press, 1992), 236–270; David J. Weber, *Bárbaros: Spaniards and Their Savages in the Age of Enlightenment* (New Haven, CT: Yale University Press, 2005), 12; Mapp, *Elusive West*, 5–15; Saunt, "Go West," 767–771.

11. On the various doctrines and rites that European colonists employed to alienate indigenous lands, see Anthony Padgen, *Lords of All the World: Ideologies of Empire in Spain, Britain, and France, c. 1500–c. 1800* (New Haven, CT: Yale University Press, 1995); and Patricia Seed, *Ceremonies of Possession: Europe's Conquest of the New World, 1492–1640* (New York: Cambridge University Press, 1995).

12. Weber, *Spanish Frontier*, 87–91.

13. Elliott, *Atlantic Empires*, 68–71; Weber, *Spanish Frontier*, 92–121, 258–265; Paul E. Hoffman, *Florida's Frontiers* (Bloomington: Indiana University Press, 2002), 47–147; Jerald T. Milanich, *Laboring in the Fields of the Lord: Spanish Missions and Southeastern Indians* (Washington, DC: Smithsonian Institution Press, 1999); Amy Turner Bushnell, *Situado and Sabana: Spain's Support System for the Presidio and Mission Provinces of Florida* (Athens: University of Georgia Press, 1994); Robert Galgano, *Feast of Souls: Indians and Spaniards in Seventeenth-Century Missions of Florida and New Mexico* (Albuquerque: University of New Mexico Press, 1995); Steven W. Hackel, *Children of Coyote, Missionaries of Saint Francis: Indian-Spanish Relations in Colonial California, 1769–1850* (Chapel Hill: University of North Carolina Press, 2005); James A. Sandos, "Social Control Within Missionary Frontier Society: Alta California, 1769–1821," in *Choice, Persuasion, and Coercion: Social Control on Spain's North American Frontiers*, ed. Jesús F. de la Teja and Ross Frank (Albuquerque: University of New Mexico Press, 2005), 253–275.

14. For parallels between Spanish and English colonial ambitions and ideologies, see Jorge Cañizares-Esguerra, *Puritan Conquistadors: Iberianizing the Atlantic, 1550–1700* (Stanford, CA: Stanford University Press, 2006); and Elliott, *Atlantic Empires*, 3–28.

15. Edmund S. Morgan, *American Slavery, American Freedom: The Ordeal of Colonial Virginia* (New York: W. W. Norton, 1975), 71–91, 149; James H. Merrell, "Indians' New World: The Catawba Experience," *William and Mary Quarterly* 41 (October 1984), 539–549; James H. Merrell, "'The Customes of Our Country': Indians and Colonists in Early America," in *Strangers Within the Realm: Cultural Margins of the First British Empire*, ed. Bernard Bailyn and Philip D. Morgan (Chapel Hill: University of North Carolina Press, 1991), 121–124; and Michael Winship, *Making Heretics: Militant Protestantism and Free Grace in Massachusetts, 1636–41* (Princeton, NJ: Princeton University Press, 2002).

16. James P. Ronda, "Generations of Faith: The Christian Indians of Martha's Vineyard," *William and Mary Quarterly* 38 (July 1981), 369–394; James Axtell, *After Columbus: Essays in the Ethnohistory of Colonial North America* (New York: Oxford University Press, 1988), 100–123; Jean M. O'Brien, *Dispossession by Degrees: Indian Land and Identity in Natick, Massachusetts, 1650–1790* (New York: Cambridge University Press, 1997), 51–58; Robert James Naeher, "Dialogue in the Wilderness: John Eliot and the Indian Exploration of Puritanism as a Source of Meaning, Comfort, and Ethnic Survival," *New England Quarterly* 62 (1989), 346–368; Richard W. Cogley, *John Eliot's Mission to the Indians Before King Philip's War* (Cambridge, MA: Harvard University Press, 1999); Elliott, *Atlantic Empires*, 72–76; David J. Silverman, *Red Brethren: The Brothertown and Stockbridge Indians and the Problem of Race in Early America* (Ithaca, NY: Cornell University Press, 2010).

17. Merrell, "'Customes of Our Country,'" 135–156; Jean O'Brien, "Divorced from the Land: Accommodation Strategies of Indian Women in Eighteenth-Century New England," in *Gender, Kinship, and Power: A Comparative and Interdisciplinary History*, ed. Mary Jo Maynes, Ann Waltner, Brigitte Soland, and Ulrike Strasser (New York: Routledge, 1996), 319–333; Cronon, *Changes in the Land*, 159–170; Anderson, "King Philip's Herds"; Ruth Wallis Herndon and Ella Wilcox Sekatau, "The Right to a Name: The Narragansett People and Rhode Island Officials in the Revolutionary Era," *Ethnohistory* 44 (Summer 1997), 433–462; Morgan, *American Slavery*, 329–332; Alan Gallay, *The Indian Slave Trade: The Rise of the English Empire in the American South, 1670–1717* (New Haven, CT: Yale University Press, 2002), 288–314; Margaret Ellen Newell, "Indian Slavery in Colonial New England," in *Indian Slavery in Colonial America*, ed. Alan Gallay (Lincoln: University of Nebraska Press, 2009), 33–66.

18. Gilles Havard and Cécile Vidal, *Histoire de l'Amerique française* (Paris: Flammarion, 2003), 413–435; Richter, *Before the Revolution*, 131–136.

19. On population decline, see Daniel H. Usner, Jr., *American Indians in the Lower Mississippi Valley: Social and Economic Histories* (Lincoln: University of Nebraska Press, 1998), 33–55. On slaves, see Marcel Trudel, *L'esclavage au Canada français: Histoire et conditions de l'esclavage* (Quebec: Presses Universitaires Laval, 1960); Havard and Vidal, *Histoire de l'Amerique française*, 238–241; Gallay, *Indian Slave Trade*, 308; Brett Rushforth, "'A Little Flesh We Offer You': The Origins of Indian Slavery in New France," *William and Mary Quarterly* 60 (October 2003), 777–808; and Juliana Barr, "From Captives to Slaves: Commodifying Indian Women in the Borderlands," *Journal of American History* 92 (June 2005), 29–30.

20. Gordon M. Sayre, *Les Sauvages Américains: Representations of Native Americans in French and English Colonial Literature* (Chapel Hill: University of North Carolina Press, 1997); Weber, *Bárbaros*, 1–18; Havard and Vidal, *Histoire de l'Amerique française*, 276–284.

21. On the Osages and Quapaws, see Kathleen DuVal, *The Native Ground: Indians and Colonists in the Heart of the Continent* (Philadelphia: University of Pennsylvania Press, 2006). On the Creeks, see E. Holland Braund, *Deerskins and Duffels: Creek Indian Trade with Anglo-America, 1686–1815* (Lincoln: University of Nebraska Press, 1993), 3–25; and Steven C. Hahn, *The Invention of the Creek Nation, 1670–1763* (Lincoln: University of Nebraska Press, 2004).

22. On English colonies, see Bernard Bailyn, *The Origin of American Politics* (New York: Knopf, 1968); Richard R. Johnson, "Growth and Mastery: British North America, 1690–1748," in *The Oxford History of the British Empire: The Eighteenth Century*, ed. P. J. Marshall (Oxford: Oxford University Press, 1998), 276–282; Jack P. Greene, "The American Revolution," *American Historical Review* 195 (February 2000), 93–102; Taylor, *American Colonies*, 271–288; and Elliott, *Atlantic Empires*, 118–119, 139–143, 148–152, 221–223. On Spanish insecurities, see Weber, *Spanish Frontier*, 186–203, 279–285. On Comanche expansion, see Pekka Hämäläinen, *The Comanche Empire* (New Haven, CT: Yale University Press, 2008), 1–67.

23. On Lakota expansion, see Richard White, "The Winning of the West: The Expansion of the Western Sioux in the Eighteenth and Nineteenth Centuries," *Journal of American History* 65 (September 1978), 321–337; James O. Gump, *The Dust Rose Like Smoke: The Subjugation of the Zulu and the Sioux* (Lincoln: University of Nebraska Press, 1994), 28–32; and Calloway, *One Vast Winter Count*, 308–310. On Dakota politics in the western Great Lakes region, see Michael J. Witgen, *An Infinity of Nations: How the Native New World Shaped Modern North America* (Philadelphia: University of Pennsylvania Press, 2012), 157–211. On the intersecting gun and horse frontiers, see Frank Raymond Secoy, *Changing Military Patterns of the Great Plains Indians* (1953;

reprint, Lincoln: University of Nebraska Press, 1992); and Elliott West, *The Contested Plains: Indians, Goldseekers, and the Rush to Colorado* (Lawrence: University of Kansas Press, 1998), 44–71.

24. Dennis, *Cultivating a Landscape of Peace*; Bruce G. Trigger, *The Children of Aataentsic: A History of the Huron People to 1660*, 2 vols. (Montreal: McGill-Queen's University Press, 1976), 2: 725–825; Richard Aquila, *The Iroquois Restoration: Iroquois Diplomacy on the Colonial Frontier, 1701–1754* (1983; reprint, Lincoln: University of Nebraska Press, 1997), 29–42; Daniel K. Richter, *The Ordeal of the Longhouse: The Peoples of the Iroquois League in the Era of European Colonization* (Chapel Hill: University of North Carolina Press, 1992), 30–189; José António Brandão and William A. Starna, "The Treaties of 1701: A Triumph of Iroquois Diplomacy," *Ethnohistory* 43 (1996), 210–212; Jose Antonio Brandão, *"Your Fyre Shall Burn No More": Iroquois Policy Toward New France and Its Native Allies* (Lincoln: University of Nebraska Press, 1997), 31–116; Jon Parmenter, *The Edge of the Woods: Iroquoia, 1534–1701* (East Lansing: Michigan State University Press, 2010), 3–125.

25. Trigger, *Children of Aataentsic*, 2: 826–840; Francis Jennings, *The Ambiguous Iroquois Empire: The Covenant Chain Confederation of Indian Tribes with English Colonies from Its Beginnings to the Lancaster Treaty of 1744* (New York: W. W. Norton, 1984), 93–94; Aquila, *Iroquois Restoration*, 156–193; Richter, *Ordeal of the Longhouse*, 99–161; Daniel K. Richter, "Ordeals of the Longhouse: The Five Nations in Early American History," in *Beyond the Covenant Chain: The Iroquois and Their Neighbors in Indian North America, 1600–1800*, ed. Daniel K. Richter and James H. Merrell (University Park: Pennsylvania State University Press, 2006), 16–24; Mary Druke Becker, "Linking Arms: The Structure of Iroquois Intertribal Diplomacy," in Richter and Merrell, *Beyond the Covenant Chain*, 29–39; Richard L. Haan, "Covenant and Consensus: Iroquois and English, 1676–1760," in Richter and Merrell, *Beyond the Covenant Chain*, 41–57; James Merrell, "'Their Very Bones Shall Fight': The Catawba-Iroquois Wars," in Richter and Merrell, *Beyond the Covenant Chain*, 115–133; Gregory Evans Dowd, *War Under Heaven: Pontiac, the Indian Nations, and the British Empire* (Baltimore: Johns Hopkins University Press, 2002), 34–38, 158–159; William A. Starna and Ralph Watkins, "Northern Iroquoian Slavery," *Ethnohistory* 38 (Winter 1990), 32–57; Brandão and Starna, "Treaties of 1701," 212–215; William A. Fox, "Events as Seen from the North: The Iroquois and Colonial Slavery," in *Mapping the Mississippian Shatter Zone: The Colonial Indian Slave Trade and Regional Instability in the American South*, ed. Robbie Ethridge and Sheri M. Shuck-Hall (Lincoln: University of Nebraska Press, 2009), 63–80; Parmenter, *Edge of the Woods*, 127–179.

26. Gary Clayton Anderson, *The Indian Southwest, 1580–1830: Ethnogenesis and Reinvention* (Norman: University of Oklahoma Press, 1999); James F. Brooks, *Captives and Cousins: Slavery, Kinship, and Community in the Southwest Borderlands* (Chapel Hill: University of North Carolina Press, 2002), 180–197; Brian DeLay, *War of a Thousand Deserts: Indian Raids and the U.S.-Mexican War* (New Haven, CT: Yale University Press, 2008), 86–139; Hämäläinen, *Comanche Empire*, 141–238.

27. Jennings, *Ambiguous Iroquois Empire*, 148–206, 352–374; Richter, *Ordeal of the Longhouse*, 134–161; Becker, "Linking Arms"; Hämäläinen, *Comanche Empire*, 141–238; James F. Brooks, "'We Betray Our Own Nation': Indian Slavery and Multiethnic Communities in the Southwest Borderlands," in Gallay, *Indian Slavery in Colonial America*, 336–343.

28. White, "Winning," 328–339; Gump, *Dust Rose Like Smoke*, 41–44; Pekka Hämäläinen, "The Rise and Fall of Plains Indian Horse Cultures," *Journal of American History* 90 (December

2003), 854, 856, 859–862; Guy Gibbon, *The Sioux: The Dakota and Lakota Nations* (Malden, MA: Blackwell, 2003), 85–89. The quotes are from Gary E. Moulton, ed., *The Journals of the Lewis and Clark Expedition*, 13 vols. (Lincoln: University of Nebraska Press, 1983–2001), 3:401; and Pierre Antoine Tabeau, *Tabeau's Narrative of Loisel's Expedition to the Upper Missouri*, ed. Annie Heloise Abel (Norman: University of Oklahoma Press, 1968), 130.

29. Richard Haan, "The Problems of Iroquois Neutrality: Suggestions for Revision," *Ethnohistory* 27 (Autumn 1980), 317–330; Brandão and Starna, "Treaties of 1701," 215–232; Jon Parmenter, "After the Mourning Wars: The Iroquois and Their Allies in Colonial North American Campaigns, 1763–1760," *William and Mary Quarterly* 64 (January 2007), 39–82; Timothy J. Shannon, *Iroquois Diplomacy on the Early American Frontier* (New York: Viking, 2008), 47–133; David L. Preston, *Texture of Contact: European and Indian Settler Communities on the Frontiers of Iroquoia* (Lincoln: University of Nebraska Press, 2009), 61–146; Gail D. MacLeitch, *Imperial Entanglements: Iroquois Change and Persistence on the Frontiers of Empire* (Philadelphia: University of Pennsylvania Press, 2011), 45–112; Theda Perdue, "Cherokee Relations with the Iroquois in the Eighteenth Century," in Richter and Merrell, *Beyond the Covenant Chain*, 135–149; and Fox, "Events as Seen from the North," 75.

30. On the Comanches, see Hämäläinen, *Comanche Empire*, 292–330. On the Lakotas, see White, "Winning," 342–343.

31. Richter, *Ordeal of the Longhouse*, 2–3, 30–49; Cary C. Anderson, *Sitting Bull and the Paradox of Lakota Nationhood* (New York: Longman, 1996); Hämäläinen, *Comanche Empire*, 275–283, 345–349; Parmenter, *Edge of the Woods*; Kingsley M. Bray, "Before Sitting Bull: Interpreting Hunkpapa Political History, 1750–1867," *South Dakota History* 40 (Summer 2010), 97–135; James Macfarlane, "'Chief of All the Sioux': An Assessment of Sitting Bull and Lakota Unity, 1868–76," *American Nineteenth-Century History* 11 (September 2010), 299–310.

32. Richter, "Whose Indian History?" 390–392; Martin H. Quitt, "Trade and Acculturation at Jamestown, 1607–1609," *William and Mary Quarterly* 52 (April 1995), 227–258; James H. Merrell, "'Our Bond of Peace': Patterns of Intercultural Exchange in the Carolina Piedmont, 1650–1750," in Waselkov, Wood, and Hatley, *Powhatan's Mantle*, 274.

33. Richard White, *The Middle Ground: Indians, Empires, and Republics in the Great Lakes Region, 1650–1815* (New York: Cambridge University Press, 1991), 1–14; Heidi Bohaker, "*Nindoodemag*: The Significance of Algonquian Kinship Networks in the Eastern Great Lakes Region, 1600–1701," *William and Mary Quarterly* 63 (January 2006), 23–52; Witgen, *Infinity of Nations*, 29–68.

34. White, *Middle Ground*, 1–222. As Catherine M. Desbarats has shown, gifting to manage Indian alliances was extensive: "the costs of native alliances exceeded trade revenues flowing into the colonial coffers: from a mercantilist point of view Canada was thus not paying for itself, let alone yielding profits for the crown." See Desbarats, "The Cost of Early Canada's Native Alliances: Reality and Scarcity's Rhetoric," *William and Mary Quarterly* 62 (October 1995), 629.

35. White, *Middle Ground*, 5–185.

36. Analyzing sources through a specific lens and finding what they are looking for, historians generated in the 1990s and 2000s a veritable cottage industry of middle-ground studies. As a result, the concept of the middle ground was gradually stripped of meaning, its many dimensions flattened into a portable metaphor for cross-cultural mediation. This eagerness to see middle grounds anywhere where colonial expansion stalled coincided with a tendency to emphasize cooperation over contestation in early American history. On the overuse and consequent dilution of the middle-ground metaphor, see Susan Sleeper-Smith, "The Middle Ground Revisited Introduction," *William and Mary Quarterly* 63 (January 2006), 4–5; Philip J. Deloria, "What's the

Middle Ground, Anyway?" in Sleeper-Smith, "The Middle Ground Revisited," 15–16; and Hämäläinen and Truett, "On Borderlands," 349. For discussions on the balance between accommodation and violence in borderlands historiography, see Andrew R. L. Cayton and Fredrika J. Teute, "Introduction: On the Connection of Frontiers," in Cayton and Teute, *Contact Points*, 6–9; Brian Sandberg, "Beyond Encounters: Religion, Ethnicity, and Violence in the Early Modern Atlantic World, 1492–1700," *Journal of World History* 17 (March 2006), 1–25; and Claudio Saunt, "'Our Indians': European Empires and the History of the Native South," in *The Atlantic in Global History, 1500–2000*, ed. Jorge Cañizares-Esguerrea and Eric R. Seeman (Upper Saddle River, NJ: Pearson/Prentice Hall, 2007).

37. White, *Middle Ground*. Also see Richard White, "Creative Misunderstandings and New Understandings," *William and Mary Quarterly* 63 (January 2006), 9–14; Deloria, "What's the Middle Ground?"; Catherine Desbarats, "Following the Middle Ground," *William and Mary Quarterly* 63 (January 2006), 81–96; and Merrell, "Indian History During the English Colonial Era," 123–124, 130–132.

38. The quote is from White, *Middle Ground*, 2. For an argument that emphasizes the role of French imperial power in shaping the Great Lakes world, see Gilles Havard, *Empire and Métissages: Indiens et Français dans le Pays d'en Haut, 1660–1715* (Sillery, Quebec: Septentrion/Presses de l'Université Paris-Sorbonne, 2003).

39. On the lower Mississippi Valley and its borderlands, see Daniel H. Usner, Jr., *Indians, Settlers, and Slaves in a Frontier Exchange Economy: The Lower Mississippi Valley Before 1783* (Chapel Hill: University of North Carolina Press, 1992); DuVal, *Native Ground*; and DuVal, "Interconnectedness." On English-Indian borderlands, see James H. Merrell, *The Indians' New World: Catawbas and Their Neighbors from European Contact to the Era of Removal* (Chapel Hill: University of North Carolina Press, 1989); James H. Merrell, *Into the American Woods: Negotiators on the Pennsylvania Frontier* (New York: W. W. Norton, 1999); Merrell, "'Customes of Our Country'"; Stephen Aron, *How the West Was Lost: The Transformation of Kentucky from Daniel Boone to Henry Clay* (Baltimore: Johns Hopkins University Press, 1996); Gregory Evans Dowd, "'Insidious Friends': Gift Giving and the Cherokee-British Alliance in the Seven Years' War," in Cayton and Teute, *Contact Points*, 116–119; Karen Ordahl Kupperman, *Indians and English: Facing Off in Early America* (Ithaca, NY: Cornell University Press, 2000); Hinderaker and Mancall, *At the Edge of Empire*, 46–97; and Jane T. Merritt, *At the Crossroads: Indians and Empires on a Mid-Atlantic Frontier, 1700–1763* (Chapel Hill: University of North Carolina Press, 2003), 19–166.

40. On the importance of the role of women and multicultural families in stabilizing contact zones, see, for example, Sylvia Van Kirk, *Many Tender Ties: Women in Fur-Trade Society, 1670–1870* (Norman: University of Oklahoma Press, 1983); Tanis C. Thorne, *The Many Hands of My Relations: French and Indians on the Lower Missouri* (Columbia: University of Missouri Press, 1996); Ann Marie Plane, *Colonial Intimacies: Indian Marriage in Early New England* (Ithaca, NY: Cornell University Press, 2000); Brooks, *Captives and Cousins*; Juliana Barr, *Peace Came in the Form of a Woman: Indians and Spaniards in the Texas Borderlands* (Chapel Hill: University of North Carolina Press, 2007); and James C. Scott, *The Art of Not Being Governed: An Anarchist History of Upland Southeast Asia* (New Haven, CT: Yale University Press, 2009), esp. 36–39.

41. White, *Middle Ground*, 60–75; Susan Sleeper-Smith, *Indian Women and French Men: Rethinking Cultural Encounter in the Western Great Lakes* (Amherst: University of Massachusetts Press, 2004); Claiborne A. Skinner, *The Upper Country: French Enterprise in the Colonial Great Lakes* (Baltimore: Johns Hopkins University Press, 2008).

42. White, *Middle Ground*, 196–232. For a forceful argument of the significance that indigenous play-off politics performed in the Great Lakes region, see Adelman and Aron, "From Borderlands to Borders," 818–823. For a critique of Adelman and Aron's argument, see Evan Haefeli, "A Note on the Use of North American Borderlands," *American Historical Review* 104 (October 1999), 1222–1223.

43. White, *Middle Ground*, 29–34, 142–185; Witgen, *Infinity of Nations*, 116–297; Eric Hinderaker, *Elusive Empires: Constructing Colonialism in the Ohio Valley, 1673–1800* (New York: Cambridge University Press, 1997), 12–18, 32–45; Brett Rushforth, "Slavery, the Fox Wars, and the Limits of Alliance," *William and Mary Quarterly* 63 (January 2006), 53–80.

44. Oakah L. Jones, Jr., *Los Paisanos: Spanish Settlers on the Northern Frontier of New Spain* (Norman: University of Oklahoma Press, 1979), 163–165; Elizabeth A. H. John, *Storms Brewed in Other Men's Worlds: The Confrontation of Indians, Spanish, and French in the Southwest, 1640–1795* (Norman: University of Oklahoma Press, 1975), 143–152; Edward P. Dozier, *The Pueblo Indians of North America* (New York: Holt, Rinehart and Winston, 1970), 71–88; John L. Kessell, "Spaniards and Pueblos: From Crusading Intolerance to Pragmatic Accommodation," in *Columbian Consequences: Archaeological and Historical Perspectives on the Spanish Borderlands West*, ed. David Hurst Thomas (Washington, DC: Smithsonian Institution Press, 1989), 127–138; Ramón A. Gutiérrez, *When Jesus Came, the Corn Mothers Went Away: Marriage, Sexuality, and Power in New Mexico, 1500–1846* (Stanford, CA: Stanford University Press, 1991), 95–336; Weber, *Spanish Frontier*, 133–141; Margaret Szasz, *Between Indian and White Worlds: The Cultural Broker* (Norman: University of Oklahoma Press, 1994), 36–43; Ross Frank, *From Settler to Citizen: New Mexican Economic Development and the Creation of Vecino Society, 1750–1820* (Berkeley: University of California Press, 2000), 21–30, 177–181; Nan A. Rothschild, *Colonial Encounters in a Native American Landscape: The Spanish and Dutch in North America* (Washington, DC: Smithsonian Institution Press, 2003), 223–225; Dedra S. MacDonald, "Intimacy and Empire: Indian-African Interaction in Spanish Mexico, 1500–1800," in *Confounding the Color Line: The Indian-Black Experience in North America*, ed. James Brooks (Lincoln: University of Nebraska Press, 2002), 21–46.

45. Kessell, "Spaniards and Pueblos"; Dozier, *Pueblo Indians*, 78–83; Francisco Atanasio Domínguez, *The Missions of New Mexico, 1776: A Description by Fray Francisco Atanasio Domínguez*, trans. and ed. Eleanor B. Adams and Angelico Chavez (Albuquerque: University of New Mexico Press, 1956), 84, 89–91, 112–113, 119. The importance—at least for the Spaniards—of these joint military expeditions is captured in the Segesser hide paintings. See Ned Blackhawk, "Toward an Indigenous Art History of the West: The Segesser Hide Paintings," in this volume.

46. Ned Blackhawk, *Violence Over the Land: Indians and Empires in the Early American West* (Cambridge, MA: Harvard University Press, 2006), 55–118; Hämäläinen, *Comanche Empire*, 355–356; John R. Wunder, "'That No Thorn Will Pierce Our Friendship': The Ute-Comanche Treaty of 1786," *Western Historical Quarterly* 42 (Spring 2011), 7–19.

47. John, *Storms Brewed in Other Men's Worlds*, 248–257, 294–303; Anderson, *Indian Southwest*, 123–126; Barr, *Peace Came in the Form of a Woman*, 177–196; Hämäläinen, *Comanche Empire*, 35–36, 40, 58–61.

48. Hämäläinen, *Comanche Empire*, 128–130; Weber, *Bárbaros*, 193–194; Matthew Babcock, "Blurred Borders: North America's Forgotten Apache Reservations," in this volume. The quote is from Bernardo de Gálvez, *Instructions Governing the Interior Provinces of New Spain 1786*, ed. and trans. Donald E. Worcester (Berkeley, CA: Quivira Society, 1951), 43.

49. For a similar point, see Adelman and Aron, "From Borderlands to Borders," 6.

50. On Ohio Country, see Richter, *Facing East from Indian Country*, 168. On the Pennsylvania backcountry, see Merrell, *Into the American Woods*; Merritt, *At the Crossroads*; and Peter Silver, *Our Savage Neighbors: How Indian War Transformed Early America* (New York: W. W. Norton, 2007), 39–71. On south Texas, see Gary Clayton Anderson, *The Conquest of Texas: Ethnic Cleansing in the Promised Land, 1820–1875* (Norman: University of Oklahoma Press, 2005).

51. White, *Middle Ground*, 75–82.

52. Despite palpable possibilities, comparative studies of early American contact zones are few and far between. For notable examples, see Hinderaker, *Elusive Empires*; Donna J. Guy and Thomas E. Sheridan, eds., *Contested Ground: Comparative Frontiers on the Northern and Southern Edges of the Spanish Empire* (Tucson: University of Arizona Press, 1998); Clayton and Teute, *Contact Points*; Weber, *Bárbaros*; and Elliott, *Atlantic Empires*. Moreover, violence, perhaps surprisingly, has been an underdeveloped topic in early American historiography. Historians have written volumes about violent encounters in the colonial era, but except for few important recent studies, the scholarship has been descriptive rather than analytical. Many early Americanists have also focused their efforts on discursive rather than corporeal violence, examining how European colonists forged new identities in reaction to outbursts of indigenous brutality. The best recent studies on violence in the context of early American borderlands are a varied lot, which points to the vast empirical and theoretical possibilities in the field. See Brooks, *Captives and Cousins*; Blackhawk, *Violence over the Land*; Barr, *Peace Came in the Form of a Woman*; DeLay, *War of a Thousand Deserts*; and Karl Jacoby, *Shadows at Dawn: A Borderlands Massacre and the Violence of History* (New York: Penguin, 2008).

53. On the geopolitics in the Southeast and the Great Basin, see J. Leitch Wright, Jr., *Creeks and Seminoles: The Destruction and Regeneration of the Muscogulge People* (Lincoln: University of Nebraska Press, 1986), 1–20; Braund, *Deerskins and Duffels*, 26–80; Richter, *Facing East from Indian Country*, 169–170; Gallay, *Indian Slave Trade*; Brooks, *Captives and Cousins*, 108–116, 150–152; Blackhawk, *Violence over the Land*, 45–118; and Hämäläinen, *Comanche Empire*, 49–55, 88–90.

54. On the intersections of colonial markets, slavery, and intra-Indian violence in the Southeast and the Great Basin, see Gallay, *Indian Slave Trade*; Ethridge and Shuck-Hall, *Mapping the Mississippian Shatter Zone*; Christina Snyder, *Slavery in Indian Country: The Changing Face of Captivity in Early America* (Cambridge, MA: Harvard University Press, 2010); Gutiérrez, *When Jesus Came*, 101–105, 149–155, 180–190; Brooks, *Captives and Cousins*; and Blackhawk, *Violence over the Land*. The quote is from Francis Le Jau to the Secretary, September 15, 1708, in *The Carolina Chronicle of Dr. Francis Le Jau, 1706–1717*, ed. Frank J. Klingberg (Berkeley: University of California Press, 1956), 41.

55. Robbie Ethridge, "Introduction: Mapping the Mississippian Shatter Zone," in Ethridge and Shuck-Hall, *Mapping the Mississippian Shatter Zone*, 16–21; Blackhawk, *Violence over the Land*, 8–9.

56. Blackhawk, *Violence Over the Land*, 70–80, 102–121; Brooks, *Captives and Cousins*, 153–159, 300–301; Brian DeLay, "Blood Talk: Violence and Belonging in the Navajo-New Mexican Borderland," in this volume.

57. Gallay, *Indian Slave Trade*, 294–299; Daniel K. Richter, "Native Peoples of North America and the Eighteenth-century British Empire," in Marshall, *Oxford History of the British Empire*, 351–352; Paul Kelton, *Epidemics and Enslavement: Biological Catastrophe in the Native Southeast* (Lincoln: University of Nebraska Press, 2007); Robbie Ethridge, "The Making of a Militaristic Slaving Society: The Chickasaws and the Colonial Indian Slave Trade," in Gallay,

Indian Slavery in Colonial America, 251–276; Jon Bernard Marcoux, *Pox, Empire, Shackles, and Hides: The Townsend Site, 1670–1715* (Tuscaloosa: University of Alabama Press, 2010), 28–50.

58. Richard White, *The Roots of Dependency: Subsistence, Environment, and Social Change Among the Choctaws, Pawnees, and Navajos* (Lincoln: University of Nebraska Press, 1983), 34–68; Saunt, "'Our Indians,'" 61–71; Peter H. Wood, "The Changing Population of the Colonial South," in Waselkov, Wood, and Hatley, *Powhatan's Mantle*, 95.

59. For the concept of "tribal zone," see Brian R. Ferguson and Neil L. Whitehead, "The Violent Edge of Empire," in *War in the Tribal Zone: Expanding States and Indigenous Warfare*, ed. Brian R. Ferguson and Neil L. Whitehead (Santa Fe, NM: School of American Research, 1992), 1–30. On Creeks and Cherokees, see Braund, *Deerskins and Duffels*, 121–163; Hahn, *Invention of the Creek Nation*, 81–228; Joshua Piker, *Okfuskee: A Creek Indian Town in Colonial America* (Cambridge, MA: Harvard University Press, 2004), 15–74; and John Oliphant, *Peace and War on the Anglo-Cherokee Frontier, 1756–62* (Baton Rouge: Louisiana State University Press, 2001). Unlike other Southeastern native societies, the Creeks grew in numbers in the eighteenth century: their population nearly doubled between the 1710s and 1790s, from an estimated ten thousand to more than fifteen thousand. See Wood, "Changing Population," 85–86.

60. For traditional views, see, for example, Niall Ferguson, *Colossus: The Rise and Fall of the American Empire* (London: Penguin, 2004); and Charles Maier, *Among Empires: American Ascendancy and Its Predecessors* (Cambridge, MA: Harvard University Press, 2006). On the deep roots of the U.S. empire and of U.S.-Indian relations as a process of empire building, see Peter S. Onuf, *Statehood and Union: A History of the Northwest Ordinance* (Bloomington: Indiana University Press, 1987); Fred Anderson and Andrew Cayton, *The Dominion of War: Empire and Liberty in North America* (New York: Viking, 2005), 160–273; Robert J. Miller, *Native America, Discovered and Conquered: Thomas Jefferson, Lewis and Clark, and Manifest Destiny* (Westport, CT: Praeger, 2006); Jack P. Greene, "Colonial History and National History: Reflections on a Continuing Problem," *William and Mary Quarterly* 64 (April 2007), 235–250; Philip J. Deloria, "From Nation to Nationhood: Land, Policy, Culture, Colonialism, and Empire in U.S.-Indian Relations," in *The Cultural Turn in U.S. History: Past, Present, and Future*, ed. James W. Cook, Lawrence B. Glickman, and Michael O'Malley (Chicago: University of Chicago Press, 2008), 343–382; and Walter Nugent, *The Habits of Empire: A History of American Expansion* (New York: Knopf, 2008).

61. Jennings, *Ambiguous Iroquois Empire*, 223–365; Dowd, *War Under Heaven*, 153–158; Michael M. McConnell, "Peoples 'in Between': The Iroquois and the Ohio Indians, 1720–1768," in Richter and Merrell, *Beyond the Covenant Chain*, 93–112; White, *Middle Ground*, 351–353, 413–517; Patrick Griffin, *American Leviathan: Empire, Nation, and Revolutionary Frontier* (New York: Hill and Wang, 2007), 85, 297n66; Alan Taylor, *The Civil War of 1812: American Citizens, British Subjects, Irish Subjects, and Indian Allies* (New York: Knopf, 2010); Alan Taylor, "Remaking Americans: Louisiana, Upper Canada, and Texas," in this volume.

62. James Axtell, *The Indians' New South: Cultural Change in the Colonial Southeast* (Baton Rouge: Louisiana University Press, 1997), 42; Alan Gallay, "South Carolina's Entrance into the Indian Slave Trade," in Gallay, *Indian Slavery in Colonial America*, 109–145; C. S. Everett, "'They shalbe slaves for their lives': Indian Slavery in Colonial Virginia," in Gallay, *Indian Slavery in Colonial America*, 67–108; Ethridge, "Introduction," 16–19; Kelton, *Epidemics and Enslavement*, 101–159.

63. David J. Weber, *The Mexican Frontier, 1821–1846: The American Southwest Under Mexico* (Albuquerque: University of New Mexico Press, 1982); DeLay, *War of a Thousand Deserts*; Hämäläinen, *Comanche Empire*, 219–238, 353–358.

Chapter 2

The author wishes to thank Neal Salisbury and Kate Desbarats, as well as the volume editors, for their very helpful comments and suggestions.

1. "Act of Taking Possession of New Mexico, April 30, 1598," in *Don Juan de Oñate: Colonizer of New Mexico, 1595–1628*, 2 vols., ed. George Hammond and Agapito Rey (Albuquerque: University of New Mexico Press, 1953), 1: 329–336.

2. David Weber, *The Spanish Frontier in North America* (New Haven, CT: Yale University Press, 1992), 77–87.

3. "Ordenanzas de descubrimiento, nueva población y pacificación de las Indias dadas por Felipe II, el 13 de julio de 1573, en el bosque de Segovia," http://www.biblioteca.tv/artman2/publish/1573_382/Ordenanzas_de_Felipe_II_sobre_descubrimiento_nueva_1176.shtml; Marta Milagros del Vas Mingo, "Las ordenanzas de 1573, sus antecedentes y consecuencias," *Quinto Centenario* 8 (1985), 93; Weber, *Spanish Frontier*, 302.

4. Ned Blackhawk, *Violence over the Land: Indians and Empires in the Early American West* (Cambridge, MA: Harvard University Press, 2006), 191–200. The quote is from p. 199.

5. "Treaty with the Mohuache Band of the Utahs, in New Mexico, September 11, 1855," in Charles J. Kappler, comp., *Indian Affairs: Laws and Treaties*, 5 vols. (Washington, DC: Government Printing Office, 1904–1941), 5: 689–690. See also Francis Paul Prucha, *American Indian Treaties: The History of a Political Anomaly* (Berkeley: University of California Press, 1994), 258–259.

6. Prucha, *American Indian Treaties*, 234.

7. Neal Salisbury, "The Indians' Old World: Native Americans and the Coming of Europeans," *William and Mary Quarterly*, 3rd ser., 53 (1996), 435–458. For firsthand accounts of early commercial encounters, see Ramsay Cook, ed., *The Voyages of Jacques Cartier* (Toronto: University of Toronto Press, 1992), 21; [George Best], "A True Report of Such Things as Happened in the Second Voyage of Captaine Frobisher . . . 1577," in Richard Hakluyt, *The Voyages of the English Nation to America Before the Year 1600* [originally published 1598–1600], 3 vols. (Edinburgh: Goldsmid, 1889), 1: 73.

8. With feudal lords and expectant heirs claiming some control over the disposal of a given tract, transfers of ownership only became practical with the development in England of the legal concept of the "estate," an abstraction that treated an individual's stake in a plot as a saleable commodity. See William Searle Holdsworth, *An Historical Introduction to the Land Law* (Oxford: Clarendon, 1927), 102–110.

9. Stuart Banner, *How the Indians Lost Their Land: Law and Power on the Frontier* (Cambridge, MA: Harvard University Press, 2005), 51, 74.

10. See, for example, J. R. Miller, *Compact, Contract, Covenant: Aboriginal Treaty-Making in Canada* (Toronto: University of Toronto Press, 2009). James Tully proposes an interesting variant on this approach, arguing that the treaty process at its best embodies a mixture of aboriginal concepts of territoriality and English common-law traditions.

11. Paul G. McHugh, *Aboriginal Societies and the Common Law: A History of Sovereignty, Status, and Self-Determination* (Oxford: Oxford University Press, 2004), 103.

12. On the West painting, see Ann Uhry Abrams, "Benjamin West's Documentation of Colonial History: William Penn's Treaty with the Indians," *Art Bulletin* 64 (March 1982), 59–75; Colin G. Calloway, *First Peoples: A Documentary Survey of American Indian History* (Boston: Bedford/

St. Martin's, 1999), 205–206; and Beth Fowkes Tobin, "Native Land and Foreign Desire: *William Penn's Treaty with the Indians*," *American Indian Culture and Research Journal* 19 (1995), 87–119.

13. Abrams, "Benjamin West's Documentation," 60.

14. Francis Jennings, *The Ambiguous Iroquois Empire: The Covenant Chain Confederation of Indian Tribes with English Colonies from Its Beginnings to the Lancaster Treaty of 1744* (New York: W. W. Norton, 1984), 242–247.

15. Kevin Kenny, *Peaceable Kingdom Lost: The Paxton Boys and the Destruction of William Penn's Holy Experiment* (New York: Oxford University Press, 2009), 3. On the Walking Purchase, see Jennings, *The Ambiguous Iroquois Empire*, 333–346; Steven Craig Harper, *Promised Land: Penn's Holy Experiment, the Walking Purchase, and the Dispossession of Delawares, 1600–1763* (Bethlehem, PA: Lehigh University Press, 2006).

16. Kenny, *Peaceable Kingdom*; Peter Silver, *Our Savage Neighbors: How Indian War Transformed Early America* (New York: W. W. Norton, 2008).

17. See Carla Gardina Pestana, "Cruelty and Religious Justifications for Conquest in the Mid-Seventeenth-Century English Atlantic," in *Empires of God: Religious Encounters in the Early Modern Atlantic*, ed. Linda Gregerson and Susan Juster (Philadelphia: University of Pennsylvania Press, 2011), 37–57.

18. A Gentleman, *An Account of the French Settlements in North America* (Boston: Rogers and Fowle, 1746), 7. During and after the conquest of Canada, the British posed as liberators to the Indians, prepared, unlike the French, to offer just compensation for land. See Alain Beaulieu, "'An Equitable Right to Be Compensated': The Dispossession of the Aboriginal Peoples of Quebec and the Emergence of a New Legal Rationale (1760–1860)," unpublished paper in the author's possession.

19. Banner, *How the Indians Lost Their Land*. Banner quite sensibly notes that purchase and conquest are not antithetical terms (p. 3) and yet his whole book is organized on the assumption that the commercial form of treaties and purchases is what matters most, rather than the larger substantive factors (wars, epidemics, environmental change, intimidation, etc.), which together account for dispossession.

20. Some comparative studies on Native dispossession and related topics that exemplify this tendency are A. R. Buck, Nancy E. Wright, and John P. S. McLaren, *Land and Freedom: Law, Property Rights and the British Diaspora* (Aldershot, UK: Ashgate/Dartmouth, 2001); Peter Karsten, *Between Law and Custom: "High" and "Low" Legal Cultures in the Lands of the British Diaspora: The United States, Canada, Australia, and New Zealand, 1600–1990* (New York: Cambridge University Press, 2002); John C. Weaver, *The Great Land Rush and the Making of the Modern World, 1650–1900* (Montreal: McGill-Queen's University Press, 2003); John McLaren, ed., *Despotic Dominion: Property Rights in British Settler Societies* (Vancouver: UBC Press, 2005); Louis A. Knafla and Haijo Westra, eds., *Aboriginal Title and Indigenous Peoples: Canada, Australia, and New Zealand* (Vancouver: UBC Press, 2010); and Lisa Ford, *Settler Sovereignty: Jurisdiction and Indigenous People in America and Australia, 1788–1836* (Cambridge, MA: Harvard University Press, 2010).

21. Rebecca Horn, *Postconquest Coyoacan: Nahua-Spanish Relations in Central Mexico, 1519–1650* (Stanford, CA: Stanford University Press, 1997), 159–160, 207–209, 231–234. For the record, there were also some isolated purchases of Native lands in French Louisiana and Illinois country. Daniel Usner, *Indians, Settlers, and Slaves in a Frontier Exchange Economy: The Lower Mississippi Valley Before 1783* (Chapel Hill: University of North Carolina Press, 1992), 156; Gilles Havard and Cécile Vidal, *Histoire de l'Amérique française* (Paris: Flammarion, 2003), 212–213.

22. My thanks to Hal Langfur for his expert advice on this point.

23. See Patricia Seed, *American Pentimento: The Invention of Indians and the Pursuit of Riches* (Minneapolis: University of Minnesota Press, 2001), 12–39.

24. Anthony Pagden, "Law, Colonization, Legitimation, and the European Background," in *The Cambridge History of Law in America*, vol. 1, *Early America, 1580–1815*, ed. M. Grossberg and Christopher L. Tomlins (New York: Cambridge University Press, 2008), 1: 4; J. H. Elliott, *Empires of the Atlantic World: Britain and Spain in America* (New Haven, CT: Yale University Press, 2006), 9

25. In a sermon preached on the occasion of the departure of the first fleet of Massachusetts Bay settlers, John Cotton enumerated three ways in which "God makes room for a people." The first was by lawful war and the third was through the provision of empty, neglected land, but God's second means of making lands available to newcomers was "when hee gives a forreigne people favour in the eyes of any native people to come and sit downe with them either by way of purchase, as *Abraham* did obtaine the field of *Machpelah*; or else when they give it in courtesie, as *Pharoah* did the land of *Goshen* unto the sons of *Jacob*." John Cotton, *God's Promise to His Plantation* (London: William Jones, 1630), 4.

26. Roger Williams, *A Key into the Language of America* (London: Gregory Dexter, 1643), 157–158.

27. Blair A. Rudes, "Indian Land Deeds as Evidence for Indian History in Western Connecticut," *Northeast Anthropology* 70 (2005), 34.

28. See, for example, P-J-M. Chaumonot's French-Huron dictionary and vocabulary, Codex Ind 12, John Carter Brown Library, Brown University.

29. The important, but partial, exception to this pattern would be the agreement negotiated between the Plymouth pilgrims and Massasoit's Wampanoags in 1621. According to the terms, as recorded by Governor Bradford, this was a treaty of peace and friendship; land is not even mentioned. William Bradford, *Of Plymouth Plantation, 1620–1647: The Complete Text*, ed. S. E. Morison (New York: Knopf, 1952), 80–81.

30. Neal Salisbury, *Manitou and Providence: Indians, Europeans, and the Making of New England* (New York: Oxford University Press, 1982), 176–177; Christopher L. Tomlins, *Freedom Bound: Law, Labor, and Civic Identity in Colonizing English America, 1580–1865* (New York: Cambridge University Press, 2010), 149.

31. See Kathleen Bragdon, *Native People of Southern New England, 1500–1650* (Norman: University of Oklahoma Press, 1996), 137–139.

32. "Deposition of Roger Williams relative to this purchase from the Indians, 18 June 1682," in *Early American Indian Documents: Treaties and Laws, 1607–1789*, 20 vols., ed. Alden T. Vaughan (Washington, DC: University Publications of America, 1979–1985), 19: 45. In a contemporary report on his arrangements with the Narragansetts, Williams had written of "the frequent promise of Miantenomy my kind friend, that it should not be land that I should want about these bounds mentioned, provided that I satisfied the Indians there inhabiting, I having made covenantes of peaceable neighborhood with all the sachems and natives round about us" (ibid., 46).

33. Robert A. Williams, *Linking Arms Together: American Indian Treaty Visions of Law and Peace, 1600–1800* (New York: Oxford University Press, 1997).

34. David J. Silverman, *Faith and Boundaries: Colonists, Christianity, and Community Among the Wampanoag Indians of Martha's Vineyard, 1600–1871* (New York: Cambridge University Press,

2005); Faren Siminoff, *Crossing the Sound: The Rise of Atlantic American Communities in Seventeenth-Century Eastern Long Island* (New York: New York University Press, 2004).

35. It is in the nature of undocumented agreements that they are hard to verify. However, there are many indications in the record of colonists claiming to have purchased land from Natives without a written deed. See, for example, Vaughan, *Early American Indian Documents*, 19: 217.

36. "Narragansett and Wampanoag Deed for Aquidneck Island," in Vaughan, *Early American Indian Documents*, 19: 49–50.

37. "Purchase and Agreement Between Jacob Van Curler and Sickenames Chief for Land Along the Connecticut River [June 8, 1633]," in Vaughan, *Early American Indian Documents*, 7: 32–33.

38. Nathaniel Bradstreet Shurtleff, ed., *Records of the Governor and Company of the Massachusetts Bay*, 5 vols. (Boston: W. White, printer to the Commonwealth, 1853), 2: 159–160. In lightly populated Maine, land-sharing arrangements lasted through most of the seventeenth century. Emerson W. Baker, "A Scratch with a Bear's Paw: Anglo-Indian Land Deeds in Early Maine," *Ethnohistory* 36 (1989), 245.

39. Of course the "Native" and "Euro-American" spheres were not completely separate. Where Indian people had been living under colonial jurisdiction and in close proximity with settlers over the course of generations, they might have recourse to written deeds to formalize their own land transactions. The Wampanoag of eighteenth-century Martha's Vineyard produced numerous legal documents in their language. See Ives Goddard and Kathleen Bragdon, *Native Writings in Massachusetts*, 2 vols. (Philadelphia: American Philosophical Society, 1988), 1: 30, 45, 49, 97.

40. Francis Jennings, *The Invasion of America: Indians, Colonialism, and the Cant of Conquest* (Chapel Hill: University of North Carolina Press, 1975), 132–133. For a fuller account of the Dutch dispute with the English over the Connecticut Valley, see Donna Merwick, *The Shame and the Sorrow: Dutch-Amerindian Encounters in New Netherland* (Philadelphia: University of Pennsylvania Press, 2006), 77–86. See also Sabine Klein, "'They Have Invaded the Whole River': Boundary Negotiations in Anglo-Dutch Colonial Discourse," *Early American Studies: An Interdisciplinary Journal* 9 (2011), 332.

41. "English Answer to the Remonstrance of the Dutch Ambassadors," May 23, 1632, in Vaughan, *Early American Indian Documents*, 7: 31–32.

42. Jennings, *Invasion of America*, 139–143.

43. Viola Barnes, *The Dominion of New England, a Study in British Colonial Policy* (New Haven, CT: Yale University Press, 1923), 174–211; Sidney Perley, *The Indian Land Titles of Essex County, Massachusetts* (Salem, MA: Essex Book and Print Club, 1912), 64–92.

44. Quoted in Siminoff, *Crossing the Sound*, 112.

45. Shurtleff, *Records of Massachusetts Bay*, 1: 112.

46. Marshall Harris, *Origin of the Land Tenure System in the United States* (Ames: Iowa State College Press, 1953), 158; James Warren Springer, "American Indians and the Law of Real Property in Colonial New England Society, 1630–1790," *American Journal of Legal History* 30 (1986), 35–38; Vaughan, *Early American Indian Documents*, 17: 13, 423.

47. On this general topic, though in relation to a later period, see Ford, *Settler Sovereignty*.

48. Springer, "American Indians and the Law of Real Property," 40–41.

49. Nathaniel Bradstreet Shurtleff and David Pulsifer, eds., *Records of the Colony of New Plymouth, in New England*, 12 vols. (Boston: W. White, 1855–1861), 4: 58–59, 96–97.

50. Shurtleff, *Records of Massachusetts Bay*, 5: 486–487; Daniel Gookin, *Historical Collections of the Indians in New England* (Boston: Belknap and Hall, 1792), 179; Yasuhide Kawashima, *Puritan Justice and the Indian: White Man's Law in Massachusetts, 1630–1763* (Middletown, CT: Wesleyan University Press, 1986), 55.

51. Quoted in Vaughan, *Early American Indian Documents*, 17: 262.

52. Quoted in ibid., 17: 432.

53. Kawashima, *Puritan Justice and the Indian*, 61–62. For an example of a similar technique for acquiring lands along the Merrimack River, see Southern Essex County, Register of Deeds, vol. 1, fol. 13., February 17, 1652.

54. Dorothy V. Jones, *License for Empire: Colonialism by Treaty in Early America* (Chicago: University of Chicago Press, 1982); Banner, *How the Indians Lost Their Land*, 85–111.

55. Adam Shortt and Arthur G. Doughty, eds., *Documents Relating to the Constitutional History of Canada, 1759–1791* (Ottawa: King's Printer, 1918), 163–168; Colin Calloway, *The Scratch of a Pen: 1763 and the Transformation of North America* (New York: Oxford University Press, 2006), 92–100. John Borrows argues that, though it had the appearance of a unilateral act, the Royal Proclamation was actually part of a mutual agreement with the nations of the Great Lakes region; it needs to be understood in conjunction with a treaty negotiated at Fort Niagara in 1764. See Borrows, "Wampum at Niagara: The Royal Proclamation, Canadian Legal History, and Self-Government," in *Aboriginal and Treaty Rights in Canada: Essays on Law, Equality, and Respect for Difference*, ed. Michael Asch (Vancouver: UBC Press, 1997), 155–172.

56. See the Virginia Indian treaty of 1646, which established the York River as a boundary between Native and English territories (Vaughan, *Early American Indian Documents*, 4: 69).

57. On this topic, see Ford, *Settler Sovereignty*.

58. See Richard White, *The Middle Ground: Indians, Empires, and Republics in the Great Lakes Region, 1650–1815* (New York: Cambridge University Press, 1991), 339–351; Stephen Aron, "Pigs and Hunters: 'Rights in the Woods' on the Trans-Appalachian Frontier," in *Contact Points: American Frontiers from the Mohawk Valley to the Mississippi, 1750–1830*, ed. Andrew Cayton and Fredrika J. Teute (Chapel Hill: University of North Carolina Press, 1998), 175–204.

59. Bernard Bailyn, *Voyagers to the West: A Passage in the Peopling of America on the Eve of the Revolution* (New York: Knopf, 1986), 355–358.

60. Woody Holton, *Forced Founders: Indians, Debtors, Slaves, and the Making of the American Revolution in Virginia* (Chapel Hill: University of North Carolina Press, 1999), 3–38.

61. Holton, *Forced Founders*, 35; Banner, *How the Indians Lost Their Land*, 101.

62. Alan Taylor, *The Divided Ground: Indians, Settlers, and the Northern Borderland of the American Revolution* (New York: Knopf, 2006), 40–45.

63. David J. Weber, *Bárbaros: Spaniards and Their Savages in the Age of Enlightenment* (New Haven, CT: Yale University Press, 2005), 205–220.

Chapter 3

The author thanks Ann Carlos, Peter Wood, Edward Countryman, Juliana Barr, the anonymous reviewers, and her fellow writers in this volume for their helpful comments on earlier drafts of this essay.

1. The map's contents inevitably reflect the conditions of its creation. Sitting Rabbit painted it at the request of Orin Libby, the secretary of the State Historical Society of North Dakota, who promised him payment and provided him with canvas and supplies. But there were misunderstandings between the two men, disputes over money, and differences over the quality of the composition. Some villages do not appear, and some that do have no apparent correlation with known settlements. For a discussion, see Thomas D. Thiessen, Raymond Wood, and A. Wesley Jones, "The Sitting Rabbit 1907 Map of the Missouri River in North Dakota," *Plains Anthropologist* 24 (1979), 145–149.

2. Ibid., 145. This valuable essay contains an account of the map's production, a segment-by-segment reproduction, and a discussion of its notable features.

3. Alfred W. Bowers, *Mandan Social and Ceremonial Organization* (1950; reprint, Lincoln: University of Nebraska Press, 2004), 162–163, 197, 199.

4. Shermer was indeed known to the Mandans as "Village Where Turtle Went Back," but the west-bank location on the Sitting Rabbit map is confusing, because the town was in fact on the east bank of the river. Thiessen, Wood, and Jones, " Sitting Rabbit 1907 Map," 150–151, 154; Bowers, *Mandan Social and Ceremonial Organization*, 161, 353, 360. On the dating of Shermer, see Craig M. Johnson, *A Chronology of Middle Missouri Plains Village Sites*, Smithsonian Contributions to Anthropology 47 (Washington, DC: Smithsonian Institution Scholarly Press, 2007), 61, 178–179.

5. Mark D. Mitchell, "Community and Change in the Organization of Mandan Craft Production, 1400–1750" (Ph.D. diss., University of Colorado, 2010).

6. Johnson, *Chronology*, 178–185.

7. Waldo R. Wedel discusses the remarkable feat of upper Missouri horticulture in "Prehistory and Environment in the Central Great Plains," *Transactions of the Kansas Academy of Science* 50 (June 1947), 15.

8. Alexander Henry, *The Journal of Alexander Henry the Younger, 1799–1814*, 2 vols., ed. Barry M. Gough (Toronto: Champlain Society, 1988), 1: 227–228. Henry describes a Hidatsa bison hunt as well (274–275). See also Henry M. Brackenridge, *Views of Louisiana, Together with a Journal of a Voyage up the Missouri River in 1811* (1814; reprint, Chicago: Quadrangle Books, 1962), 260; and Prince Maximilian of Wied, *The North American Journals of Prince Maximilian of Wied*, 3 vols., ed. Stephen S. Witte and Marsha V. Gallagher (Norman: University of Oklahoma Press, 2012), 3: 198–199. It is worth noting that we have no accounts of these hunts in the pre-horse, pedestrian era.

9. Maximilian, *Journals*, 3: 198–199; Charles Mckenzie, "Some Account of the Mississouri Indians in the Years 1804, 5, 6 ,& 7," in W. Raymond Wood and Thomas D. Thiessen, eds., *Early Fur Trade on the Northern Plains: Canadian Traders Among the Mandan and Hidatsa Indians, 1738–1818, the Narratives of John Macdonnell, David Thompson, François-Antoine Larocque, and Charles McKenzie* (Norman: University of Oklahoma Press, 1985), 239.

10. There are many accounts of float bison. See Mckenzie, "Some Account," 239; Henry, *Journal of Alexander Henry*, 1: 231; and Maximilian, *Journals*, 3: 199. Maximilian also recorded a version of the Mandan origin story in which a girl's consumption of a float bison led to a sort of immaculate conception and the birth of a founding Mandan chief (3: 175). (Cf. Maximilian Alexander Philipp prinz von Wied-Neuwied, *Travels in the Interior of North America, 1832–1834*, ed. Reuben Gold Thwaites, Early Western Travels 22–24 [Cleveland: A. H. Clark, 1906], 23: 308.) Pierre Antoine Tabeau describes Arikaras harvesting float bison in *Tabeau's Narrative of Loisel's*

Expedition to the Upper Missouri, ed. Annie Heloise Abel (Norman: University of Oklahoma Press, 1939), 74–75.

11. Pierre de la Vérendrye, "Explorations of 1738–39 to the Missouri River: The La Vérendrye 'Journal,'" in G. Hubert Smith, *The Explorations of the La Vérendryes in the Northern Plains, 1738–1743*, ed. W. Raymond Wood (Lincoln: University of Nebraska Press, 1980), 49.

12. WPA, Project 65–73–215, "Maps and Graphs Prepared for the Water Resources Committee, North Dakota State Planning Board," supervisor Frederic W. Voedisch, *North Dakota Geological Survey Circular No. 3* (n.d.), 11. Average growing seasons along the Missouri River in North Dakota were probably a few days shorter in the years addressed here, as they have lengthened by approximately one day per decade since the Industrial Revolution. Ambika Badh, Adnan Akyuz, Gary Vocke, and Barbara Mullins, "Impact of Climate Change on the Growing Seasons in Select Cities of North Dakota, United States of America," *International Journal of Climate Change: Impacts and Responses* 1 (2009), 105–118.

13. While corn on the upper Missouri matured to an edible state in sixty to seventy days, it took ninety days or more to ripen to a hard state for storage. George F. Will and George E. Hyde, *Corn Among the Indians of the Upper Missouri* (1917; reprint, Lincoln: University of Nebraska Press, 1964), 73, 301–303.

14. Ibid., 117, 301; Buffalo Bird Woman, *Buffalo Bird Woman's Garden, as Told to Gilbert L. Wilson* (1917; reprint, St. Paul: Minnesota Historical Society Press, 1987), 36.

15. On the second planting, which "often got caught by the frost," see Buffalo Bird Woman, *Buffalo Bird Woman's Garden*, 37. Buffalo Bird Woman explained that the second planting took place "when June berries were ripe." In North Dakota this was typically July. The June berry (*Amelanchier alnifolia*) is also known as the Saskatoon berry, or service berry. On varieties of maize, see ibid., 58–67, and Will and Hyde, *Corn Among the Indians*, 301–303.

16. Paul VanDevelder, *Coyote Warrior: One Man, Three Tribes, and the Trial That Forged a Nation* (New York: Little Brown, 2004), 173, 176–177. See also Terri Berman, "For the Taking: The Garrison Dam and the Tribal Taking Area," *Critical Issues in Native North America*, International Work Group for Indigenous Affairs Document no. 68 (1991), 150–151. (The latter was originally published as Terri Berman, "For the Taking: The Garrison Dam and the Tribal Taking Area," *Cultural Survival Quarterly* 12 [June 1988], 5–8.)

17. Bob and Diane Askew describe this as "microclimate gardening" in "A Century of Gardening in America," *History of Agriculture* 3 (1992), 75–88; Henry, *Journal of Alexander Henry*, 1: 217. Mandan women also heaped up dirt around the base of each cornstalk so "the moisture has better access to them." See Maximilian, *Journals*, 3: 157. Henry Boller notes that cultivation patterns, specifically hoeing, were also drought-protective. Henry A. Boller, *Among the Indians; Eight Years in the Far West, 1858–1866*, ed. Milo Milton Quaife (Chicago: Lakeside Press, 1959), 123.

18. Maximilian, *Journals*, 2: 179, 3: 128, 218; George Catlin, *Letters and Notes on the North American Indians* (1844; North Dighton, MA: JG Press, 1995), 152. Will and Hyde note that Indian plantings rarely failed entirely (*Corn Among the Indians*, 40).

19. Stanley A. Ahler and Kenneth L. Kvamme, *New Geophysical and Archaeological Investigations at Huff Village State Historic Site (32MO11), Morton County, North Dakota*, report submitted to the State Historical Society of North Dakota, Bismarck (Flagstaff, AZ: PaleoCultural Research Group, 2000), 34; Kenneth L. Kvamme, "Multidimensional Prospecting in North American Great Plains Village Sites," *Archaeological Prospection* 10 (2003), 139. A woman interviewed by the anthropologist Gilbert Wilson in the early 1900s said Indian gardeners kept a two- to three-year

supply of seed corn on hand, selecting it carefully from the most robust and productive plants. Buffalo Bird Woman, *Buffalo Bird Woman's Garden*, 48.

20. Stanley A. Ahler and Fern E. Swenson, "Investigations During 2001," in *Archaeological Investigations During 2001 and 2002 at Double Ditch State Historic Site, North Dakota*, ed. Stanley A. Ahler (Flagstaff, AZ: PaleoCultural Research Group, 2003), 48; Stanley A. Ahler, "Research Design for 2002–2003," in Ahler and Swenson, *Archaeological Investigations*, 53–59; George T. Crawford and Stanley A. Ahler, "Fortification Trench Investigations," in Ahler and Swenson, *Archaeological Investigations*, 95–114. The findings are accessibly summarized in Stanley A. Ahler and Phil R. Geib, "Investigations at Double Ditch Village, a Traditional Mandan Earthlodge Settlement," in *Seeking Our Past: An Introduction to North American Archaeology*, ed. Sarah W. Neusius and G. Timothy Gross (New York: Oxford University Press, 2006), 442–451.

21. Mark D. Mitchell, "Abstract," in *Geophysical Survey and Test Excavation During 2006 at Larson Village, Burleigh County, North Dakota*, ed. Mark D. Mitchell (Flagstaff, AZ: PaleoCultural Research Group, 2007), iii; Kenneth L. Kvamme, "Geophysical Investigations," in Mitchell, *Geophysical Survey and Test Excavation*, 36–52; Kenneth L. Kvamme, "Geophysical Survey and Topographic Mapping," in *Archaeological and Geophysical Investigations During 2007 at Larson Village, Burleigh County, North Dakota*, ed. Mark D. Mitchell (Flagstaff, AZ: PaleoCultural Research Group, 2008), 28–34.

22. Scattered Village, on the west bank of the Missouri beneath the present city of Mandan, North Dakota, is an example of a site with features (and oral traditions) suggesting both Mandan and Hidatsa residence. The archaeological findings and the ethnographic literature are discussed in Stanley A. Ahler, "Site Description and Previous Investigations," in *Prehistory on First Street NE: The Archaeology of Scattered Village in Mandan, North Dakota*, ed. Stanley A. Ahler (Flagstaff, AZ: PaleoCultural Research Group, 2002), 1.1–1.17.

23. Early twenty-first-century estimates tentatively put the population of Double Ditch at two thousand. My estimate is based on this number. On Double Ditch, see Kenneth L. Kvamme and Stanley A. Ahler, "Integrated Remote Sensing and Excavation at Double Ditch State Historic Site, North Dakota," *American Antiquity* 72 (July 2007), 547; and Ahler and Geib, "Investigations at Double Ditch Village," 447. The population estimate reaches three thousand in Paul Thacker, "It Takes a Fortified Village," *Archaeology* (January–February 2003), 12.

24. Stanley A. Ahler, "Introduction and Background for 2004–2005 Studies," in *Archaeological Investigations During 2004 at Double Ditch State Historic Site, North Dakota*, ed. Stanley A. Ahler (Flagstaff, AZ: PaleoCultural Research Group, 2005), iii, 4; Stanley A. Ahler, "Summary and Conclusions, in Ahler, *Archaeological Investigations During 2004 at Double Ditch*, 332; Stanley A. Ahler, Kenneth L. Kvamme, Phil R. Geib, and W. Raymond Wood, "Settlement Change at Double Ditch Village, AD 1450–1785," paper presented at the 62nd Plains Anthropological Conference, October 13–16, 2004, Billings, MT, 1.

25. Ahler et al., "Settlement Change at Double Ditch Village, AD 1450–1785," 1–2.

26. Ibid.; Ahler, "Summary and Conclusions," 332.

27. For a summary of Pueblo population data, see Albert H. Schroeder, "Pueblos Abandoned in Historic Times," in *Southwest*, ed. Alfonso Ortiz, vol. 9 of *Handbook of North American Indians*, ed. William Sturtevant (Washington, DC: Smithsonian Institution, 1978–1983), 254. On Iroquois and Huron populations, see Bruce G. Trigger, *The Children of Aataentsic: A History of the Huron People to 1660* (1976; reprint, Kingston, Montreal: McGill-Queen's University Press, 1987), 31–32, 98; and Bruce Trigger, "Early Iroquoian Contacts with Europeans," in *Northeast*, ed.

Bruce Trigger, vol. 15 of *Handbook of North American Indians*, ed. William Sturtevant (Washington, DC: Smithsonian Institution, 1978), 352.

28. S. Ryan Johansson and Douglass Owsley have suggested that "pollution" problems may have afflicted the Arikaras, earth-lodge dwellers to the south of the Mandans whose lifeway was nearly identical. S. Ryan Johansson and Douglass Owsley, "Welfare History on the Great Plains: Mortality and Skeletal Health, 1650 to 1900," in *The Backbone of History: Health and Nutrition in the Western Hemisphere*, ed. Richard H. Steckel and Jerome Carl Rose (Cambridge,: Cambridge University Press, 2002), 537–539. I would like to thank Ann Carlos for raising this issue and making me aware of this volume.

29. Nathan F. Sayre, "The Genesis, History, and Limits of Carrying Capacity," *Annals of the Association of American Geographers* 98 (2008), 120–134.

30. Drought patterns can be reconstructed from the International Tree-Ring Data Bank maintained by the NOAA Paleoclimatology Program and World Data Center for Paleoclimatology. For the upper Missouri, the key data set is that developed in Edward R. Cook, Connie A. Woodhouse, C. Mark Eakin, David M. Meko, and David W. Stahle, "Long-Term Aridity Changes in the Western United States," *Science* 306 (November 2004), 1015–1018. The data are available online at two sites with somewhat different interfaces: the North American Drought Atlas (http://iridl.ldeo.columbia.edu/SOURCES/.LDEO/.TRL/.NADA2004/.pdsi-atlas.html) and the NOAA Paleoclimatology website (http://www.ncdc.noaa.gov/paleo/newpdsi.html). See data points 143 and 159.

31. David W. Stahle, Edward R. Cook, Malcolm K. Cleaveland, Matthew D. Therrell, David M. Meko, Henri D. Grissino-Mayer, Emma Watson, and Brian H. Luckman, "Tree-Ring Data Document 16th Century Megadrought Over North America," *Eos, Transactions, American Geophysical Union* 81 (March 2000), 121.

32. Douglas B. Bamforth, "Climate, Chronology, and the Course of War in the Middle Missouri Region of the North American Great Plains," in *The Archaeology of Warfare: Prehistories of Raiding and Conquest*, ed. Elizabeth Arkush and Mark W. Allen (Gainesville: University Press of Florida, 2006), 66–99.

33. Theodore Rosengarten, *All God's Dangers: The Life of Nate Shaw* (New York: Knopf, 1974), 223.

34. Resource Management Services, State of Montana Multi-Hazard Mitigation Plan and Statewide Hazard Assessment (October 2004), 3.3.8.2, http://montanadma.org/sites/default/files/Section_3_Part_10_Drought.pdf. On North Dakota in particular, see Phillip A. Glogoza and Michael J. Weiss, "Grasshopper Biology and Management," North Dakota State University Extension Circular E-272 (revised) (February 1997), http://www.ag.ndsu.edu/pubs/plantsci/pests/e272-1.htm.

35. Hans J. Prem, "Disease Outbreaks in Central Mexico During the Sixteenth Century," in *"Secret Judgments of God": Old World Disease in Colonial Spanish America*, ed. Noble David Cook and W. George Lovell (Norman: University of Oklahoma Press, 1992), 20–43.

36. Ibid., 21–48; Noble David Cook, *Born to Die: Disease and New World Conquest, 1492–1650* (New York: Cambridge University Press, 1998), 60–133, 137–140; Rodolfo Acuna-Soto, David W. Stahle, Malcolm K. Cleaveland, and Matthew D. Therrell, "Megadrought and Megadeath in 16th Century Mexico," *Emerging Infectious Diseases* 8 (April 2002), 360–362.

37. Jacques Cartier, *The Voyages of Jacques Cartier*, ed. Henry Percival Biggar (1924; reprint, Toronto: University of Toronto Press, 1993); xxxvi–xxxvii, 119. Henry Dobyns suggests that the

initial importation of Old World diseases to Florida may even have taken place as early as 1513–1514. He describes this episode and others from the sixteenth century in Henry F. Dobyns, with the assistance of William R. Swagerty, *Their Number Become Thinned: Native Population Dynamics in Eastern North America* (Knoxville: University of Tennessee Press, 1983), 254–278, 332.

38. Ann F. Ramenofsky, *Vectors of Death: The Archaeology of European Contact* (Albuquerque: University of New Mexico Press, 1987), 42–71.

39. Stanley A. Ahler, "Analytic Structure and Collection Chronology," in Ahler, *Archaeological Investigations During 2004 at Double Ditch*, 161, 167.

40. European trade goods and chronology at Double Ditch are discussed in three reports: Stanley A. Ahler, "Radiocarbon Dating and Site Chronology" and "Analysis of Trade Artifacts," in Ahler, *Archaeological Investigations During 2001 and 2002 at Double Ditch*, 133–140, 229–245; Stanley A. Ahler, "Analytic Structure and Collection Chronology" and "Analysis of Trade Artifacts," in Ahler, *Archaeological Investigations During 2003 at Double Ditch*, 133–150, 269–283; and Stanley A. Ahler, "Analytic Structure and Collection Chronology" and "Analysis of Trade Artifacts," in Ahler, *Archaeological Investigations During 2004 at Double Ditch*, 157–179, 295–312. I am excluding copper artifacts from my own discussion because archaeologists still need to ascertain the extent to which Native production contributed to the accrual of these items at Double Ditch.

41. Ahler et al., "Settlement Change at Double Ditch Village, AD 1450–1785," 1.

42. The typical incubation period for smallpox is twelve days. The disease is not contagious until symptoms set in at the end of this time. F. Fenner, D. A. Henderson, I. Arita, Z. Ježek, and I. D. Ladnyi, *Smallpox and Its Eradication* (Geneva: World Health Organization, 1988), 6, 41, 188–189. The typical incubation period for measles is ten to twelve days. It, too, is transmissible once symptoms appear. Centers for Disease Control and Prevention, *Epidemiology and Prevention of Vaccine-Preventable Diseases*, ed. William Atkinson, Charles Wolfe, Jennifer Hamborsky, and Lynne McIntyre, 11th ed. (Washington, DC: Public Health Foundation, 2009), 158, 162.

43. Unlike HIV, smallpox is not contagious during its incubation period. But the point that a prolonged incubation period facilitates human travel and thus more widespread disease dispersal remains valid.

44. Stanley A. Ahler and Chad Badorek, "Trade Artifact Analysis," in Ahler, *Prehistory on First Street NE*, 15.1.

45. For indications that the Mandans had seen horses by this time, see Charles Beauharnois, Report of Beauharnois, n.p. [Quebec?], September 28, 1733, in *Journals and Letters of Pierre Gaultier de Varennes de la Vérendrye*, ed. Lawrence J. Burpee (Toronto: Champlain Society, 1927), 107, 108.

46. Charles Beauharnois to Jean Frédéric Phélippaux Maurepas, Quebec, October 12, 1742, in ibid., 387. A Hidatsa oral tradition related by Wolf Chief suggests that the Cheyennes were the source of the first horses. While this is conceivable, it seems unlikely, as the migrating Cheyennes had not yet established regular occupancy of the western plains. For Wolf Chief's account, see Gilbert L. Wilson, *The Horse and the Dog in Hidatsa Culture*, Reprints in Anthropology 10 (1924; reprint, Lincoln, NE: J & L Reprint Co., 1978), 142. On Cheyenne migrations, see Elliot West, *The Contested Plains: Indians, Goldseekers, and the Rush to Colorado* (Lawrence: University Press of Kansas, 1998), 69.

47. Jeffrey Hanson describes the transformation wrought by the horse among the Hidatsas. Most if not all of his account also applies to the Mandans. Jeffrey R. Hanson, "Adjustment and Adaptation on the Northern Plains: The Case of Equestrianism Among the Hidatsa," *Plains Anthropologist* 31 (May 1986), 93–107. See also Wilson, *Horse and the Dog*, 141–195.

48. A fully loaded dog hauled one hundred pounds at about one half a mile per hour. A horse hauled four hundred pounds plus its rider at a much faster pace. Hanson, "Adjustment and Adaptation," 96.

49. "Extract from the Journal of La Vérendrye," in *Journals and Letters of la Vérendrye*, 366, 370–371.

50. Ibid., 369.

51. Ibid., 370.

52. Ibid., 371.

53. Candace S. Greene and Russell Thornton, *The Year the Stars Fell: Lakota Winter Counts at the Smithsonian* (Washington, DC: Smithsonian National Museum of Natural History, Smithsonian National Museum of the American Indian; Lincoln: University of Nebraska Press, 2007), 81. (See pp. 101–104 for comparison to known smallpox images.) On vomiting, see Fenner et al., *Smallpox and Its Eradication*, 5–6. It is worth noting that smallpox appears to have spread through northwest Mexico and Texas around this time. Gottfried Hotz, *Indian Skin Paintings from the Southwest: Two Representations of Border Conflicts Between Mexico and the Missouri in the Early Eighteenth Century*, trans. Johannes Malthaner (Norman: University of Oklahoma Press, 1970), 6; John C. Ewers, "The Influence of Epidemics on the Indian Populations and Cultures of Texas," *Plains Anthropologist* 18 (1973), 107, 108.

54. Jean Baptiste Truteau, "Journal of Truteau on the Missouri River, 1794–1795," in *Before Lewis and Clark: Documents Illustrating the History of the Missouri, 1785–1804*, 2 vols., ed. A. P. Nasatir (1952; reprint, Lincoln: University of Nebraska Press, 1990), 1: 299.

55. In addition to Double Ditch and Larson, both on the east bank of the Missouri, a town site named Boley on the west bank of the river has begun to reveal a complex of receding fortification lines. Unfortunately, the site is less well preserved than the others, and interpretation is difficult. Stanley A. Ahler, "Introduction and Project Overview," *Geophysical Survey and Test Excavation During 2005 at Boley Village (32MO37), North Dakota*, ed. Stanley A. Ahler (Flagstaff, AZ: PaleoCultural Research Group, 2006), 3–6; Mark D. Mitchell and Stanley A. Ahler, "The Excavation Program," in ibid., 62–75; Ahler et al., "Summary and Conclusions," in ibid., 223–226.

56. Fern E. Swenson, "Settlement Plans for Traditional Mandan Villages at Heart River," in *Plains Village Archaeology: Bison-Hunting Farmers in the Central and Northern Plains*, ed. Stanley A. Ahler, Marvin Kay, Society for American Archaeology, and Meeting (Salt Lake City: University of Utah Press, 2007), 255–256; Stanley A. Ahler and Fern Swenson, "Investigations during 2001," in Ahler, *Archaeological Investigations During 2001 and 2002 at Double Ditch*, 50–51; Ahler and Geib, "Investigations at Double Ditch Village," 449–450.

57. Ahler and Geib, "Investigations at Double Ditch Village," 450–451. It is also worth noting that "planar borrowing" may have taken place in several stages, perhaps representing a sequential alteration in defenses (or cleansing) as the village contracted. Stanley A. Ahler, Phil R. Geib, Fern E. Swenson, and W. Raymond Wood, "Moving Earth, Then and Now, at Double Ditch Village, North Dakota," paper presented at the 61st Plains Anthropological Conference, Fayetteville, AR, 2003.

58. Swenson, "Settlement Plans for Traditional Mandan Villages," 248–253; Mark D. Mitchell, "Project Overview," in Mitchell, *Archaeological and Geophysical Investigations During 2007 at Larson*, 8; and Mark D. Mitchell, "Summary and Recommendations," in Mitchell, *Archaeological and Geophysical Investigations During 2007 at Larson*, 98–99. Mitchell notes in his project overview that the "occupation history" of the Larson site "closely parallels that of Double Ditch,"

but because archaeologists have yet to date the inner two fortification ditches, they cannot be sure at present that the towns "contracted synchronously" (8).

59. Swenson, "Settlement Plans for Traditional Mandan Villages," 253.

60. Elizabeth A. Fenn, *Pox Americana: The Great Smallpox Epidemic of 1775–82* (New York: Hill and Wang, 2001), 196–223.

61. The epidemic may have destroyed some clans entirely, but others were subsumed by groups with more survivors. Bowers, *Mandan Social and Ceremonial Organization*, 113–114.

62. Adam R. Hodge, "Pestilence and Power: The Smallpox Epidemic of 1780–1782 and Intertribal Relations on the Northern Great Plains," *The Historian* 72 (Fall 2010), 563–565.

63. Bowers, *Mandan Social and Ceremonial Organization*, 36.

64. "Clark-Maximilian Sheet 17, Route about October 19–23, 1804," in *Atlas of the Lewis and Clark Expedition*, vol. 1, *The Journals of the Lewis and Clark Expedition*, ed. Gary E. Moulton (Lincoln: University of Nebraska Press, 1983), 28. See also William Clark, October 21 and 22, 1804, in *The Definitive Journals of Lewis and Clark*, ed. Gary E. Moulton (Lincoln: University of Nebraska Press, 2002), 3: 189–191; and Maximilian, *Journals*, 2: 186.

65. Heterogeneity may have been the norm at the Knife River villages. Although the Mandan and Hidatsa towns were readily distinguished from each other, the explorer David Thompson noted that in three of the five villages, the two peoples apparently mingled. See the editor W. Raymond Wood's discussion in David Thompson, "David Thompson at the Mandan-Hidatsa Villages, 1797–1798: The Original Journals," *Ethnohistory* 24 (Autumn 1977), 337–341.

66. Hodge, "Pestilence and Power," 563–565.

67. David Thompson, *The Writings of David Thompson*, vol. 1: *The Travels, 1850 Version*, ed. William Moreau (Toronto: Champlain Society, 2009), 211–212. Thompson's field notes and his *Travels* (sometimes called his *Narrative*) offer differing population tallies. Using both in combination, it can be said that the Mandans numbered between 1,216 and 1,520. W. Raymond Wood appraises the conflicting tallies in his "Editor's Discussion" in Thompson, "David Thompson at the Mandan-Hidatsa Villages," 337–339.

68. See the sixteenth letter of Louis Armand de Lom d'Arce Lahontan, in his *New Voyages to North-America*, 2 vols., ed. Reuben Gold Thwaites (1703; reprint, Chicago: A. C. McClurg, 1905), 1: 167–215. I am grateful to Peter H. Wood for bringing Lahontan to my attention. Wood first suggested that Lahontan may have visited the upper Missouri in "The Mysterious 1688 Journey of M. Lahontan," paper presented at the annual meeting of the Omohundro Institute of Early American History and Culture, Laval University, June 11, 2006, Quebec.

69. Charles McKenzie, "Charles McKenzie's Narratives," in Wood and Thiessen, *Early Fur Trade*, 270–271. The epidemic also appears in Henry, *Journal of Alexander Henry*, 1: 233.

70. It is conceivable that yet another whooping cough epidemic struck the Mandans in 1813–1814, when it wreaked havoc among the Sioux. On the one hand, the interconnectedness of Plains life makes it unlikely the Mandans were spared. But the fact that the disease confers some immunity to those who contract it makes it conceivable that they did indeed escape the infection. For evidence of this outbreak, see Greene and Thornton, *Year the Stars Fell*, 153–154.

71. William Williams, Hudson's Bay Company Archives, D.1/2:11d, quoted in Paul Hackett, *"A Very Remarkable Sickness": Epidemics in the Petit Nord, 1670 to 1846* (Winnipeg: University of Manitoba Press, 2002), 147. (The twin measles and whooping cough outbreaks are described thoroughly in Chapter 7 of Hackett's book.)

72. On the Assiniboines, see John West, *The Substance of a Journal During a Residence at the Red River Colony, British North America* (London: Printed for L. B. Seeley, 1824), 39. For the

Sioux, see Greene and Thornton, *Year the Stars Fell*, 163–165; Roger T. Grange, Jr., "The Garnier Oglala Winter Count," *Plains Anthropologist* 8 (May 1963), 76; "The No Ears, Short Man, and Iron Crow Winter Counts," in James R. Walker, *Lakota Society*, ed. Raymond J. DeMallie (Lincoln: University of Nebraska Press, 1982), 134; Edward S. Curtis, *The North American Indian*, 20 vols., ed. Frederick Webb Hodge (Cambridge, 1908), 3: 172; and Lucy Kramer Cohen, "Big Missouri's Winter Count," *Indians at Work* 6 (February 1939), 17.

73. It is important to note that these are not case-fatality rates but death rates based on total population. A. D. Cliff, Peter Haggett, and Matthew Smallman-Raynor, *Measles: An Historical Geography of a Major Human Viral Disease from Global Expansion to Local Retreat, 1840–1990* (Oxford: Blackwell, 1993), Table 2.7.

74. George Catlin, *The Manners, Customs and Condition of the North American Indians*, 2 vols. (London: Author, 1841), 1: 194–195. Henry Boller says it was a steamboat that carried the first rats to the Mandans, but given the timing, this seems impossible. Catlin's claim that it was a keelboat must therefore be correct. Boller, *Among the Indians*, 28–29.

75. Jonathan Burt, *Rat* (London: Reaktion, 2006), 32. See also John B. Calhoun, *The Ecology and Sociology of the Norway Rat*, Public Health Service Publication no. 1008 (Bethesda, MD: U.S. Department of Health, Education, and Welfare, Public Health Service, 1963), 152–160, 260–275. Twentieth- and twenty-first-century archaeologists report that rat bones constituted 54 percent of all microanimal remains at Fort Clark, the American Fur Company post that sat beside Mih-Tutta-Hangkusch. William J. Hunt, Jr., "Summary of Results and Conclusions," in *Archaeological Investigations at Fort Clark State Historic Site, North Dakota: 1968 through 2003 Studies at the Mandan/Arikara Village* (Flagstaff, AZ: PaleoCultural Research Group, 2003), 225.

76. John B. Calhoun describes the Norway rat's burrowing behavior in detail in *Ecology and Sociology of the Norway Rat*, 15–54.

77. Buffalo Bird Woman, *Buffalo Bird Woman's Garden*, 87–97.

78. Catlin, *Manners, Customs and Condition*, 1: 195.

79. Hunt, "Summary of Results and Conclusions," 225.

80. Catlin, *Manners, Customs and Condition*, 1: 135, 137.

81. Meriwether Lewis, February 12, 1805, in Moulton, *Definitive Journals*, 3: 292; John Bradbury, *Travels in the Interior of America* (1817; reprint, n.p.: Readex Microprint, 1966), 173; Maximilian, *Journals*, 3: 28, 122, 134, 154.

82. On blacksmithing, see Francis A. Chardon, *Chardon's Journal at Fort Clark, 1834–1839*, ed. Annie Heloise Abel (1932; reprint, Lincoln: University of Nebraska Press, 1997), 13, 15, 25, 172, 173.

83. "Each boat is presumed to consume one cord of wood, for every 12 tons, every 24 hours." Morgan Nevill, quoted in James Hall, *Statistics of the West, at the Close of the Year 1836* (Cincinnati, OH: J. A. James, 1836), 235. The *Yellow Stone* was rated at 144 tons. Louis C. Hunter, *Steamboats on the Western Rivers: An Economic and Technological History* (New York: Dover, 1993), 48. To convert trees to cords, see Scott DeWald, Scott Josiah, and Becky Erdkamp, "Heating with Wood: Producing, Harvesting, and Processing Firewood," *NebGuide* 164, University of Nebraska-Lincoln Extension, Institute of Agriculture and Natural Resources G1554 (March 2005), E-9.

84. Chardon, *Chardon's Journal*, 7, 13, 52, 245n173, 327 (Kennedy Journal).

85. Maximilian, *Journals*, 3: 134. The more recent edition of Maximilian's journals offers a different translation: "In the forests on the Missouri there are few kinds of timber." Maximilian, *Travels in the Interior*, 23: 245.

86. Chardon, *Chardon's Journal*, 52.

87. My analysis here has been deeply influenced by the work of Elliot West. See especially Elliot West, "Animals," in *The Way to the West: Essays on the Central Plains* (Albuquerque: University of New Mexico Press, 1995), 51–83.

88. Chardon, *Chardon's Journal*, 90.

89. Ibid., 90, 91.

90. The Hidatsas also came near starvation and had suffered for want of bison. But they did not share hunting territory with the Mandans, and their own location put them closer to the herds, if even by a few miles. Wildlife biologists have theorized that animal populations had always found safer territory north of the Mandan-Hidatsa towns, an intertribal "war zone" that could be dangerous for hunters. Chardon, *Chardon's Journal*, 96, 97; Paul S. Martin and Christine R. Szuter, "War Zones and Game Sinks in Lewis and Clark's West," *Conservation Biology* 13 (February 1999), 36–45; Andrea S. Laliberte and William J. Ripple, "Wildlife Encounters by Lewis and Clark: A Spatial Analysis of Interactions Between Native Americans and Wildlife," *Bioscience* 53 (October 2003), 994–1003. For a slightly different view of the ecological dynamics in play, see R. Lee Lyman and Steve Wolverton, "The Late Prehistoric-Early Historic Game Sink in the Northwestern United States," *Conservation Biology* 16 (February 2002), 73–85.

91. Chardon, *Chardon's Journal*, 99 (see also 102, 104).

92. Ibid., 85, 90, 92, 94–95, 98, 99.

93. On short corn supplies specifically, see ibid., 83, 111. References to starvation more generally can be found throughout the winter and spring of 1836–1837 in this source.

94. Ibid., 107.

95. The Arikaras had sent a delegation to the Mandans in fall 1836 that laid the groundwork for the tribe's arrival the next spring. Ibid., 109; Maximilian, *Journals*, 2: 169–170, 179, 3: 227–228; Jedediah Morse, *Report to the Secretary of War of the United States on Indian Affairs* (New Haven, CT: S. Converse, 1822), Appendix, 252; Henry Atkinson, *Expedition up the Missouri* (Washington, DC: Gales & Seaton, 1826), 10–11.

96. Michael K. Trimble, *An Ethnohistorical Interpretation of the Spread of Smallpox in the Northern Plains Utilizing Concepts of Disease Ecology*, Reprints in Anthropology 33 (1979; reprint, Lincoln, NE: J & L Reprint Co., 1986), 46–47.

97. Chardon put the Arikaras at two hundred and fifty lodges but did not say how many people lived in each. Maximilian described "three hundred earth lodges abandoned" and reported that they were "said to be 600 valiant men strong." It thus seems likely that the Arikaras numbered three to four thousand when they set out on their wandering year. Chardon, *Chardon's Journal*, 109; Maximilian, *Journals*, 2: 169–170, 179, 3: 228; Morse, *Report to the Secretary of War*, Appendix, 252; Atkinson, *Expedition up the Missouri*, 10–11.

98. Chardon, *Chardon's Journal*, 118.

99. The epidemic swept all of the Plains tribes, but the consequences were most devastating for the Mandans. These events are described in Michael K. Trimble, "Epidemiology on the Northern Plains: A Cultural Perspective" (Ph.D. diss., University of Missouri, Columbia, 1985); Trimble, *An Ethnohistorical Interpretation*; Michael K. Trimble, "The 1837–1838 Smallpox Epidemic on the Upper Missouri," in *Skeletal Biology in the Great Plains: Migration, Warfare, Health, and Subsistence*, ed. Douglas W. Owsley and Richard L. Jantz (Washington, DC: Smithsonian Institution Press, 1994), 81–89; and R. G. Robertson, *Rotting Face: Smallpox and the American Indian* (Caldwell, ID: Caxton, 2001), passim.

100. Chardon, *Chardon's Journal*, 121.

101. The pox erupted in Ruptare by July 27, 1837. Ibid., 123.

102. The Hidatsas implemented a quarantine at their meat-drying camp after the epidemic erupted. Although the virus eventually breached the cordon, the strategy did hinder the disease's spread. Some of the Arikaras also implemented a quarantine of sorts after the epidemic got under way, moving out of Mih-Tutta-Hangkusch and taking shelter downriver. The Arikaras may have had another advantage as well. Some may have contracted smallpox in outbreaks in 1801 and 1832, leaving them with a much higher level of herd immunity. Trimble, "Epidemiology on the Northern Plains," 223–225; Chardon, *Chardon's Journal*, 129–130. On 1801 and 1832, see Tabeau, *Tabeau's Narrative*, 123–124, and Edwin Thompson Denig, *Five Indian Tribes of the Upper Missouri: Sioux, Arickaras, Assiniboines, Crees, Crows*, ed. John C. Ewers (Norman: University of Oklahoma Press, 1961), 57–58.

103. Chardon, *Chardon's Journal*, 129, 130, 133.

104. Ibid., 126.

105. Ibid., 137.

106. Maximilian, *Journals*, 3: 144; Pierre-Jean de Smet, *Life, Letters and Travels of Father Pierre-Jean de Smet, S.J., 1801–1873*, 4 vols., ed. Hiram Martin Chittenden and Alfred Talbot Richardson (New York: Francis P. Harper, 1905), 3: 1135; Frederick Marryat, *Second Series of a Diary in America with Remarks on Its Institutions* (Philadelphia: T. K. & P. G. Collins, 1840), 271; Henry R. Schoolcraft, *Historical and Statistical Information Respecting the History, Condition, and Prospects of the Indian Tribes of the United States*, 6 vols. (Philadelphia: Lippincott, Grambo and Co., 1851–1857), 6: 486.

107. D. D. Mitchell, Superintendent of Indian Affairs, to Henry R. Schoolcraft, January 28, 1852, in Schoolcraft, *Historical and Statistical Information*, 3: 254, 6: 486.

108. Chardon, *Chardon's Journal*, 138.

109. Henry, *Journal of Alexander Henry*, 1: 227, 255–256. (Cf. 1: 234, where Henry describes the "Soulier" Hidatsas as "a stationary people the same as their neighbours the Mandans," suggesting a distinction from the other Hidatsas.) Samuel Parker, who did not visit the Mandans but heard about them at Council Bluffs, learned they were "a much more stationary people than almost any other tribe in this whole region of country." Samuel Parker, *Journal of an Exploring Tour Beyond the Rocky Mountains* (Minneapolis: Ross & Haines, 1967), 43. See also Alfred W. Bowers, *Hidatsa Social and Ceremonial Organization* (1963; reprint, Lincoln: University of Nebraska Press, 1992), 287.

110. Joshua Pilcher to William Clark, February 27, 1838, in Trimble, *Ethnohistorical Interpretation*, 74; Joshua Pilcher to William Clark, September 12, 1838, cited in Trimble, "Epidemiology," 278.

111. Trimble, "Epidemiology," 223–224.

112. Chardon, *Chardon's Journal*, 129.

113. Trimble, "Epidemiology," 246–266.

114. Joshua Pilcher to William Clark, February 27, 1838, in Trimble, *Ethnohistorical Interpretation*, 74; Trimble, "Epidemiology," 278–279; Chardon, *Chardon's Journal*, 138–139.

115. Tabeau, *Tabeau's Narrative*, 149–150.

116. Ibid., 123–124.

117. Chardon, *Chardon's Journal*, 138.

118. Archibald N. McLeod, "The Diary of Archibald N. McLeod," in *Five Fur Traders of the Northwest: Being the Narrative of Peter Pond and the Diaries of John Macdonnell, Archibald N.*

McLeod, Hugh Faries, and Thomas Connor, ed. Charles M. Gates (St. Paul: Minnesota Historical Society, 1965), 155; Peter Fidler, "Chesterfield House Journals 1800–1802," in *Saskatchewan Journals and Correspondence*, ed. Alice M. Johnson (London: Hudson's Bay Record Society, 1967), 294, 317n1.

119. On the Osages, see Willard H. Rollings, *The Osage: An Ethnohistorical Study of Hegemony on the Prairie-Plains* (Columbia: University of Missouri Press, 1992), 142, 183–184, 278–279. On the Omahas, see William Clark, August 14, 1804, in Moulton, *Definitive Journals*, 2: 478–479; John Ordway, August 13, 1804, and September 4, 1806, in *The Journals of the Lewis and Clark Expedition*, 13 vols., ed. Gary E. Moulton (Lincoln: University of Nebraska Press, 1995), 9: 38, 358; Charles Floyd, August 14, 1804, in Moulton, *Journals of the Lewis and Clark Expedition*, 9: 394; and François Marie Perrin du Lac, "Extract from the Travels of Perrin du Lac, 1802," in Nasatir, *Before Lewis and Clark*, 2: 710. On the Sioux, see Greene and Thornton, *Year the Stars Fell*, 129–131. On the Poncas, see Perrin du Lac, "Extract," 2: 710, and Tabeau, *Tabeau's Narrative*, 99–100. See also Trimble, "Epidemiology," 30 (Table 2). On the Pawnees, see Morse, *Report to the Secretary*, 91–92.

120. On the Arikaras, see Tabeau, *Tabeau's Narrative*, 123–124. Tabeau does not offer any dates for the smallpox he mentions.

121. On the 1831–1832 outbreak, see Helen Hornbeck Tanner, ed., *Atlas of Great Lakes Indian History* (Norman: University of Oklahoma Press for the Newberry Library, 1987), 173; *Daily National Intelligencer*, Washington, DC, Tuesday, November 15, 1831 (transcription), Dale Lowell Morgan Collection, Box 3, folder 19, Henry E. Huntington Library, San Marino, CA; Maximilian, *Journals*, 2: 104; Denig, *Five Indian Tribes*, 57–58; Trimble, "Epidemiology," 30 (Table 2); Michael K. Trimble, "The 1832 Inoculation Program on the Missouri River," in *Disease and Demography in the Americas*, ed. J. W. Verano and D. H. Ubelaker (Washington, DC: Smithsonian Institution Press, 1992), 260–261; and John F. Taylor, "Sociocultural Effects of Epidemics on the Northern Plains: 1734–1850," *Western Canada Journal of Anthropology* 7 (1977), 80.

122. In fairness, it should be noted that the comparison of acquired immunity by vaccination and acquired immunity by prior exposure is not perfect. For infections such as smallpox, immunity acquired by vaccination subsides over time, whereas immunity acquired by prior exposure does not.

123. Quoted in Trimble, "1832 Inoculation Program," 261.

124. Ibid., 263.

125. J. Diane Pearson, "Lewis Cass and the Politics of Disease: The Indian Vaccination Act of 1832," *Wicazo Sa Review* 18 (Fall 2003): 12, 19–23.

126. Chardon, *Chardon's Journal*, 153.

127. Ibid., 165.

128. Foolish Woman, "A Mandan Winter Count," in *Mandan and Hidatsa Tales*, ed. Martha Warren Beckwith, 3rd ser., Publications of the Folk-Lore Foundation, no. 14 (Poughkeepsie, NY: Vassar College, 1934), 310; James Howard, "Butterfly's Mandan Winter Count: 1833–1876," *Ethnohistory* 7 (Winter 1960), 30; Will Bagley, ed., "Lou Devon's Narrative: A Tale of the Mandan's Lost Years," *Montana: The Magazine of Western History* 43 (Winter 1993), 34–49. The Black Hills report is from a Sioux winter count. Greene and Thornton, *Year the Stars Fell*, 216.

129. The tribes had separate sections of the village, and the consolidation of Mandans at Like-a-Fishhook was incremental, taking place over the years to come. G. Hubert Smith, *Like-a-Fishhook Village and Fort Berthold, Garrison Reservoir, North Dakota* (Washington, DC: U.S. Government Printing Office, 1972), 6–9.

130. Smith, *Like-a-Fishhook*, 10.
131. Thiessen, Wood, and Jones, "Sitting Rabbit 1907 Map," 148, 149–150, 152.

Chapter 4

1. Henri Lefebvre, *The Production of Space* (Cambridge, MA: Blackwell, 1991), provides a framework for analyzing both the material production of space and the representations of social spaces by different groups of historical actors. Robert C. West, in *Sonora: Its Geographical Personality* (Austin: University of Texas Press, 1993), follows a parallel intellectual tradition from the nineteenth-century French geographer Paul Vidal de la Blache, *Tableau de la géographie de la France* (Paris: Table Ronde, 1994), and Carl O. Sauer, "The Personality of Mexico," *Geographical Review* 31 (July 1941), 353–364.

2. My translation from Andrés Pérez de Ribas, *Historia de los triunphos de nuestra santa fee entre gentes las más bárbaras y fieras del nuevo Orbe* (Madrid: Alonso de Paredes, 1645). In Spanish, it reads: "La palabra, Mayo, en su lengua significa, Término: por ventura, por estar este rio entre otros dos de gentes encontradas, y que traían guerras continuas con los Mayos, y no les davan lugar a salir de sus términos. La una era la belicossísima Hiaqui, de que se escribirá en el libro siguiente. Y la otra, de los Teguecos, y demás habitadores del rio grande, de que avemos hablado."

3. Patricia Carot and Marie-Areti Hers, "La gesta de los toltecas chichimecas y de los purépechas en las tierras de los antiguos pueblo ancestrales," in *Vías del noroeste I: Una macrorregión indígena americana*, ed. Carlo Bonfiglioli, Arturo Gutiérrez, and María Eugenia Olavarría (México: Universidad Nacional Autónoma de México, Instituto de Investigaciones Históricas, 2006), 47–82.

4. Carl O. Sauer, *Aboriginal Population of Northwestern Mexico* (Berkeley: University of California Press, 1935), insert map: "Tribes and Modes of Subsistence of the Aboriginal Population of Northwestern Mexico"; Ralph L. Beals, *The Comparative Ethnology of Northern Mexico Before 1750* (Berkeley: University of California Press, 1932), Map 1, "Ethnic Groups of Northern Mexico," facing p. 96.

5. The cultural geographers Carl Sauer, Ralph Beals, and Robert West, as well as the anthropologist Edward H. Spicer, have standardized the term "Cahita," associated particularly with the Yaqui and Mayo peoples of the historical period. See Carl Sauer, *The Distribution of Aboriginal Tribes and Languages in Northwestern Mexico* (Berkeley: University of California Press, 1934), 23–25 and the map facing p. 1. "Cahita" is not, however, a term used by present-day Yoreme to describe themselves or their language. Helena Simonett, personal communication, December 6, 2010.

6. Pérez de Ribas, *Historia*; *History of the Triumphs of our Holy Faith Amongst the Most Barbarous and Fierce Peoples of the New World*, trans. Daniel T. Reff, Maureen Ahern, and Richard K. Danford (Tucson: University of Arizona Press, 1999); Susan M. Deeds, *Defiance and Deference in Mexico's Colonial North: Indians Under Spanish Rule in Nueva Vizcaya* (Austin: University of Texas Press, 2003).

7. Howard Scott Gentry, *Río Mayo Plants: A Study of the Flora and Vegetation of the Valley of the Rio Mayo, Sonora* (Washington, DC: Carnegie Institution, 1942), 5–11, Map 1, "Contour Map of the Rio Mayo Basin," facing p. 18. The initial description of the Río Mayo in Howard Genry's classic study of 1942, based on fieldwork carried out during the 1930s, reflects remarkably the phrases penned in Pérez de Ribas's seventeenth-century history. The two texts are not identical

by any means, but they bear comparison for periods prior to the building of major dams in Sonora that altered the morphology of rivers and their tributary networks, beginning in the 1930s.

8. Gentry, *Río Mayo Plants*, 27–41, Map 2, "Vegetation Map of the Río Mayo Basin," 28.

9. Ibid., 42–50, 74, 279, and plates 5, 6, 10, 15, 19, 25. Gentry photographed the *agave bovicornuta* beneath the *quercus chihuahuensis*, and the common name for the torote corresponds to several species of the *bursera genus* and to the *fouquieria macdougalii* with widespread distribution among shrubs and low trees in the thorn and short-tree forests, along hill slopes, mesas, and arroyo rims.

10. Gentry, *Río Mayo Plants*, 51–72; Cynthia Radding, *Wandering Peoples: Colonialism, Ethnic Spaces, and Ecological Frontiers in Northwestern Mexico, 1700–1850* (Durham, NC: Duke University Press, 1997), 56–57. Pérez de Ribas observed "planted mescal" in the region of Tepague, northeast of the Río Mayo, in early spring (*Historia*, Libro III, Cap. XX, 186–189).

11. The legacies of Carl O. Sauer, Ralph L. Beals, Robert W. West, and Edward H. Spicer, cited in this chapter, represent prodigious research and, at the time of their publication, brought innovative interpretations to the study of northwestern Mexico across the disciplines of geography, history, and anthropology. Together with the *Handbook of Middle American Indians*, ed. Robert Wauchope (Austin: University of Texas Press, 1964–1976) and the *Handbook of North American Indians*, ed. William C. Sturtevant (Washington, DC: Smithsonian Institution, 1978–2008), their work has enduring value. Current methods and interpretive frameworks emphasize the historical and changing qualities of culture—which are at the core of these foundational studies—but question the descriptions of tribal practices and customs contained therein when they seem to be static and "natural."

12. Beals, *Comparative Ethnology*, 107–110, 176–177; Pérez de Ribas, *Historias*, 241; Reff, *History*, 289n12. "[Los Nevomes]: sus edificios muy de assiento; porque no son de leva, como los destos rios, que son petates: pero estos son de terrados de tierra, a manera de adobes."

13. Carl O. Sauer, *The Road to Cíbola*, Ibero-Americana 3 (Berkeley: University of California Press, 1932); Danna A. Levin Rojo, "La busqueda del nuevo Mexico: Un proceso de-migratorio en la América española del siglo XVI," in *Las vías del noroeste I: Una macrorregión indígena americana*, ed. Carlo Bonfiglioli, Arturo Gutiérrez, and María Eugenia Olavarría (México: Universidad Nacional Autónoma de México, Instituto de Investigaciones Históricas, 2006), 133–168.

14. Richard Flint, *No Settlement, No Conquest: A History of the Coronado Entrada* (Albuquerque: University of New Mexico Press, 2008); Richard Flint and Shirley Cushing Flint, eds., *Documents of the Coronado Expedition, 1539–1542: "They were not familiar with his Magesty, nor did they wish to be his subjects"* (Dallas, TX: Southern Methodist University Press, 2005).

15. *Real* ("royal") refers to authorized sites for the extraction of minerals and their refinement to separate precious metals from the ores.

16. Robert C. West, *The Mining Community in Northern New Spain: The Parral District* (New York: AMS Press, 1980), 1–4.

17. West, *Mining Community*, 10–12, Map 2, "Parral Mining Area," facing p. 5. Deeds, *Defiance and Deference*; Chantal Cramaussel, *Poblar la frontera: La provincia de Santa Bárbara en Nueva Vizcaya durante los siglos XVI y XVII* (Zamora, Michoacán [Mexico]: El Colegio de Michoacán, 2006); Salvador Alvarez, "Agricultores de paz y cazadores-recolectores de guerra: Los tobosos de la cuenca del río Conchos en la Nueva Vizcaya," in *Nómadas y sedentarios en el norte de México: Homenaje a Beatriz Braniff*, ed. Marie-Areti Hers, José Luis Mirafuentes, María de los Dolores Soto, and Miguel Vallebueno (Mexico City: Universidad Nacional Autónoma de México,

2000); and Clara Bargellini, with Michael J. Komanecky, curators, *The Arts of the Missions of Northern New Spain* (Mexico City: Antiguo Colegio de San Idlefonso, 2009) have advanced research on the social history of Spanish agricultural and ranching settlements, mining, *encomiendas*, and missions for this region. Their archival research and interpretations have opened rich ethnohistorical innovations and contributed in important ways to our knowledge of the colonial fabric of Nueva Vizcaya.

18. West, *Mining Community*, 12–14, 36–44, Map 5, "Sources of Reagents Used in the Parral Mines," 28. For estimates of deforestation due to the consumption of timber and the production of charcoal for fuel in the refining process at San Luis Potosí, see Daviken Studnicki-Gizbert and David Schecter, "The Environmental Dynamics of a Colonial Fuel-Rush: Silver Mining and Deforestation in New Spain, 1522 to 1810," *Environmental History* 15 (2010), 94–119.

19. West, *Mining Community*, 47–53, Map 6, "Source of Native Labor in the Parral District," 50. See the chapter by Chantal Cramaussel in this volume.

20. Pérez de Ribas, *Triunfos*, 39–40; Reff, *History*, 115–116; Peter Gerhard, *The North Frontier of New Spain* (Norman: University of Oklahoma Press, 1993), 274–276. Franciscan missionaries had accompanied Ibarra and, since the earliest iteration of Carapoa, had attempted to evangelize among the Indians of the Zuaque Valley, followed by Franciscans based in Culiacán. The Jesuit missions of the 1590s, in the Sinaloa watershed, served an ethnically mixed population of migratory Nevome (Pima) in Bamoa, as well as Cahitan, Ocoroni, and other tribal peoples.

21. Pérez de Ribas, *Historia*; Edward H. Spicer, *Cycles of Conquest: The Impact of Spain, Mexico, and the United States on the Indians of the Southwest* (Tucson: University of Arizona Press, 1962); Edward H. Spicer, *The Yaquis: A Cultural History* (Tucson: University of Arizona Press, 1980).

22. Daniel T. Reff, "Critical Introduction: The *Historia* and Jesuit Discourse," in Reff, *History*, 11–42. The translation, annotation, and critical introduction to Pérez de Ribas's *Historia* by Reff, Ahern, and Danford provide invaluable resources for historical and anthropological research on the greater Mexican Northwest. The linkage between the human and the divine is palpable in Pérez de Ribas's "Prologue to the Reader": "En la Historia destas Misiones están tan enlazados los medios de la divina Providencia, con los humanos y políticos, que no devo, ni puedo, desunirlos, ni desatarlos: y no dudo será de gusto el verlos juntos" [In the history of these missions the means employed by divine providence are so intertwined with human and political means that I must not, nor am I able to separate them. And I have no doubt that the reader will enjoy seeing them united] (*Historia*, 64).

23. Francisco Javier Alegre, *Historia de la Provincia de la Compañía de Jesús*, 4 vols. (Roma: Institutum Historicum, 1956-), 2: 115–120; Pérez de Ribas, *Historia*, 163–169.

24. Pérez de Ribas, *Historia*, 170–179.

25. See, for example, Pérez de Ribas's account of the "repentant *cacique*" Don Cristóbal Anamei, in *Historia*, book 3, chapter 13, 168–171.

26. *Gentiles* are non-Christians or unbaptized Indians.

27. "En el vestido [los Çuaques] se han reformado mucho, y muchos dellos compran y tienen cavallos en que caminar y llevar sus cargas. / [The Zuaques] have changed their mode of dressing noticeably, and many of them buy and keep horses for transport and carrying their loads. / It is worth noting that the use of horses would have altered the Indians' use of the environment, requiring the pasturing of the animals and supplying them with sufficient grass and water; in addition, it may well have changed or deepened social inequalities within the communities" (Pérez de Ribas, *Historia*, 170–171).

28. Reff, *History*, 286n3.

29. Pérez de Ribas, *Historia*, 237–240.

30. Daniel Reff, *Disease, Depopulation, and Culture Change in Northwestern New Spain, 1518–1764* (Salt Lake City: University of Utah Press, 1991); Reff, *History*, "Critical Introduction"; Elsa Malvido, "Cronología de epidemias," in *Ensayos sobre la historia de las epidemias en México*, ed. Enrique Florescano and Elsa Malvido (Mexico City: Instituto de Seguro Social, 1982), 171–176; Robert Jackson, *Indian Population Decline: The Missions of Northwestern New Spain, 1687–1840* (Albuquerque: University of New Mexico Press, 1994); and Suzanne Austin Alchon, *A Pest in the Land: New World Epidemics in a Global Perspective* (Albuquerque: University of New Mexico Press, 2003) argue that the devastating impact of pathogens among New World populations was due in large measure to the destructive consequences of colonialism.

31. Pérez de Ribas, *Historia*, 253–254.

32. Ibid., 267–268; Reff, *History*, 312n66. The Chínipas may have migrated to Sinaloa in 1637–1638; Jesuit Francisco Torices took the surviving Guazapares and Varohío families to the Sinaloa missions as well. Upon the death of Martínez de Hurdaide, Pedro de Perea became the governor and captain of the province of Sinaloa.

33. Pérez de Ribas, *Historia*, 254–261; Reff, *History*, 301–304; Gerhard, *North Frontier of New Spain*, 174–175; Deeds, *Defiance and Deference*, 16–34, Map 1 on p. 14, and Table 1, "Chronology of Epidemic Diseases," on p. 16.

34. Sauer, *Aboriginal Population of Northwestern Mexico*, accepted Pérez de Ribas's figure of thirty thousand (see Table I, on p. 5), and it has been repeated in a number of studies since the publication of his classic monograph. Gerhard, *North Frontier of New Spain*, 267–268, elevates that figure to fifty thousand for the Yaqui population and forty thousand for the lowland Mayos at contact. Reff, *Disease*, and Thomas Sheridan, "Prelude to Conquest: Yaqui Population, Subsistence, and Warfare during the Protohistoric Period," in *The Protohistoric Period in the North American Southwest*, AD 1450–1700, ed. D. R. Wilcox and W. B. Masse (Tempe: Arizona State University, 1981) have argued persuasively that the base-line figure of thirty thousand for each of the Mayo and Yaqui contact populations did not take into account the destructive impact of disease prior to direct encounters with Spaniards.

35. Pérez de Ribas, *Historia*, 286–294; Reff, *History*, 330–334.

36. Pérez de Ribas, *Historia*, 301–310.

37. The rebellion of 1739–1741 simmered during the previous decade. Yaqui governors' formal and repeated complaints about missionaries' arbitrary actions, their defense of their own prerogatives as governors and captains-general, and their demands to have nonindigenous *vecinos* leave their pueblos but, at the same time, to travel freely to the mining centers, bear witness to their knowledge of the environment in which they lived and to the pressures that bore down on them in these contested spaces. Archivo General de la Nación (hereafter, AGN), Indiferente Virreinal, Caja 1273, Exp. 21–23, 1727–1739; Exp. 25, 1741; Exp. 26, 1736.

38. Spicer, *Yaquis*; Evelyn Hu-Dehart, *Missionaries, Miners, and Indians: Spanish Contact with the Yaqui Indians of Northwestern New Spain, 1533–1820* (Tucson: University of Arizona Press, 1981); Alejandro Figueroa Valenzuela, *Los que hablan fuerte: El desarrollo de la sociedad Yaqui* (Hermosillo, Mexico: Instituto Nacional de Antropología e Historia, 1986), Noroeste de México #7. See also Thomas E. Sheridan, "How to Tell the Story of a 'People Without History': Narrative Versus Ethnohistorical Approaches to the Study of the Yaqui Indians Through Time," *Journal of the Southwest* 30, no. 2 (1988), 168–189.

39. Pérez de Ribas, *Historia*, 299; Reff, *History*, 340n19.

40. Pedro de Perea arrived in Sinaloa as Capitán de Infantería in 1625; upon the death of Martínez de Hurdaide (1626), Perea assumed command of the province of Sinaloa, as lieutenant governor and, in 1636, as governor and captain-general. Don Pedro de Perea, *Gouernador y capitan a guerra de la Prouincia de Sinaloa y la Nueua Andaluzia* (Mexico, 1637) from the *Catálogo Colectivo de Impresos Latinamericanos hasta 1851* (hereafter, CCILA), accessed through http://cbsrdb.ucr.edu.

41. Ibid.; West, *Sonora*, 44–47, Figure 16.

42. Ibid., Figures 16 and 18.

43. Ibid., 50–53.

44. Ibid., 52–58, citing Luis Navarro García, *Sonora and Sinaloa en el siglo XVII* (Seville, Spain: Escuela de Estudios Hispanoamericanos, 1967), Figure 19 and 38–39.

45. Cynthia Radding de Murrieta, *Catálogo del Archivo de la Parroquia de la Purisima Concepción de los Alamos, 1685–1900* (Hermosillo, Mexico: INAH, Centro Regional del Noroeste, 1976), 4–5; Archivo Parroquial de la Concepción de los Alamos, Libro de Bautismos/Matrimonios/Defunciones 17, 1685–1700.

46. Pedro Quiles de Cuéllar, *Sermón de la Purissima Concepción, de la Virgen María, Madre de Dios, y Señora Nuestra* (México, 1667), accessed through CCILA, http://cbsrdb.ucr.edu.

47. José de Tapia, *La mina rica de Dios en un sermón que predicó el P. Joseph de Tapia de la Compañía de Jesús* (México, 1692), accessed through CCILA, http://cbsrdb.ucr.edu.

48. Pedro de Perea, *Gouernador y capitan a guerra*; West, *Sonora*, 46.

49. AGI Indiferente General 130, No. 42, 1684. Méritos de Josef Fernández de la Canal, 3 fojas útiles. Fernández de la Canal's tenure in Ostimuri was brief, because in 1679 he followed Siena Osorio to Guatemala, where he became Capitán de la Sala de Armas. See also Gerhard, *North Frontier of New Spain*, 252–256.

50. Documented judicial cases in the Real Audiencia de Nueva Galicia (Guadalajara) and in the Governorship of Nueva Vizcaya in Parral attest to the presence of Afromestizo slaves and to the practices of manumission. See, for example, "Juana Miranda, esclava . . . por livertad" en Ostimuri," University of Texas at Austin (Parral 1720B, f. 2023, NLBLAC microfilm); "Juicio de intestado de Rodrigo del Campo, en Río Chico," University of Texas at Austin (Parral 1720B, Nettie Lee Benson Latin American Collection microfilm); "Nicolasa de Ibarra," Biblioteca Pública del Estado de Jalisco, Archivo Real de al Audiencia de Guadalajara, Ramo Civil 20-8-275, 32 fojas (1711–1719).

51. West, *Sonora*, 60–62; Radding, *Wandering Peoples*, 70–75.

52. The Jesuit visitador P. Luis Mancusso argued in his report to the viceroy that Indian laborers in the mines of Sonora should be paid more than the standard wage of six pesos per month and that Indians in the pueblos bordering on the Apache frontier should be exempt from repartimiento, in view of the high costs of living and the dangers of "la frontera" in this province. AGN, *Indios* Tomo 39, Exp. 143, ff. 209–210. The miners' response is in AGN, *Indios* Tomo 40, Exp. 33, ff. 56–70, in 1716, refuted the Jesuits' accusations and reiterated their dependence on indigenous labor, while declaring that mine workers were not paid a standard wage, rather some earned as much as ten or fifteen pesos per month according to their skills.

53. West, *Sonora*, 62–66, Figure 20; Appendix D, "Sellos, 1684 and 1714." West's research is based on documentation in AGN, Archivo Histórico de Hacienda, *Temporalidades*. See also AGN Indiferente Virreinal Caja 975, Exp. 16, 1738–1740: "Pueblo de Nío, Sinaloa. Órdenes del Theniente Gral Martín Cayetano Fernández de Peralta a los gobernadores indígenas para que envíen

tapisques para servir a diferentes vecinos de la provincia." José Luis Mirafuentes argues that Sonoran Indians sought labor and market opportunities in the *reales de minas*, in "Tradición y cambio sociocultural. Los indios del Noroeste de méxico ante el dominio español, siglo XVIII," in *Las vías del noroeste II: Propuesta para una perspectiva sistémica e interdisciplinaria*, ed. Carlo Bonfiglioli, Arturo Gutiérrez, Marie-Areti Hers, and María Eugenia Olavarría (Mexico: Universidad Nacional Autónoma de México, Instituto de Investigaciones Antropológicas, 2008), 149–188.

Chapter 5

1. *Acuerdos del extinguido Cabildo de Buenos Aires [. . .] Serie II, tomo VIII [. . .] Años 1739–1744* (Buenos Aires: G. Kraft, 1930), 190–191.
2. Ibid., 193.
3. Thomas Falkner, *A Description of Patagonia, and the Adjoining Parts of South America: Containing an Account of the Soil, Produce, [. . .] the Religion, Government, [. . .] and Some Particulars Relating to Falkland's Islands* (Hereford, England: C. Puch, 1774), 106–107.
4. ". . . haciendo tan fiera carnicería en todos los habitantes que se ocupan en las labranzas de aquellas campañas que [se] internaron hasta la distancia de cinco leguas de esta ciudad, matando cuantos encontraron" in "Copia de los autos que siguió el Procurador General de esta Ciudad . . . sobre que [. . .] se sacase Dinero para la defensa [. . .] 1740," *Archivo General de la Nación* (Buenos Aires), IX, 19–8-2.
5. Falkner, *A Description of Patagonia*, 107; "Copia de los autos," 1740.
6. "Estrago nunca visto ni experimentado que dichos infieles ejecutaron en el pago de la Magdalena . . . , con mucha mortandad de vecinos de dicho pago, cautivando muchas mujeres y niños y robando muchas haciendas" (*Acuerdos*, 259, 264).
7. Elizabeth A. H. John, "The Taovayas Indians in Frontier Trade and Diplomacy, 1719 to 1768," *Chronicles of Oklahoma* 31, no. 3 (1953), 268–289; Elizabeth A. H. John, *Storm Brewed in Other Men's Worlds: The Confrontation of Indians, Spanish and French in the Southwest, 1540–1795* (1975; reprint, Norman: University of Oklahoma Press, 1996), 297–303; Donald E. Chipman, *Spanish Texas, 1519–1821* (Austin: University of Texas Press, 1992), 161–163; *The San Saba Papers: A Documentary Account of the Founding and Destruction of San Saba Mission*, ed. Lesley Byrd Simpson (San Francisco: John Howell, 1959).
8. Raúl J. Mandrini, "Guerra y paz en la frontera bonaerense durante el siglo XVIII," *Ciencia Hoy* 22 (1993), 26–35.
9. In Spanish the word "frontera," or frontier, is indistinctly used to designate "limit," "boundary," or "borderland." On the old historiography on frontiers in Argentina, see Raúl J. Mandrini, "Indios y fronteras en el área pampeana (siglos XVI–XIX): Balance y perspectivas," *Anuario del IEHS* 7 (1992), 61–66.
10. I consider here the Indian peoples of the great southern plains, or pampas, particularly their eastern regions. In this territory, the ethnic situation was complex and it deeply changed over time. These changes were partially caused by (1) the contacts with the Europeans and with other Indian peoples settling in the Araucanía, to the east of the Andean Cordillera (Reche, Mapuche), and in Patagonia (Tehuelche), but especially by (2) the adaptation of the different peoples to the new historical conditions, (3) the high mobility of the Natives, and (4) the complex processes of cultural crossing. Moreover, our sources are partial and very confused, and the subject provoked heated debates. See David J. Weber, *Bárbaros: Spaniards and Their Savages in*

the Age of the Enlightenment (New Haven, CT: Yale University Press, 2005), 295n47. Surely, processes of ethnogenesis also took place in the southern territories as it happened in different parts of America. The cases of the Araucanía and the transformation of the Reche in Mapuche are well known; for the case of the Pehuenche, see Weber, *Bárbaros*, 59–61.

11. By 1600, the core of the Spanish Empire was ancient Mesoamerica (Mexico) and the Central Andes, where the main and more valuable mineral resources, silver and gold, were. From Mexico, the Spanish had expanded to Central America, and they had advanced into northern Mexico and had begun to explore New México. In South America, they had expanded along the highlands of the Andes from Venezuela to central Chile. But, except in the Rio de la Plata region where they had founded some small towns, the conquerors failed in their attempts to penetrate the South American lowlands, especially in the eastern forests and in the southern plains. The Spanish advance in the continent seemed to have stopped and reached its limits near 1600. Thus, Native societies maintained by that time the control over extensive regions. The resistance of the aboriginal peoples, the absence of resources that were valuable for the Europeans, and the environmental difficulties were all discouraging for the Spaniards.

12. Raúl J. Mandrini, *La Argentina aborigen: De los primeros pobladores a 1910* (Buenos Aires: Siglo XXI, 2008), 175–180.

13. Zacarías Moutokías, *Contrabando y control social en el siglo XVII* (Buenos Aires: Centro Editor de América Latina, 1988), 47–48.

14. Raúl Fradkin and Juan C. Garavaglia, *La Argentina colonial: El Río de la Plata entre los siglos XVI y XIX* (Buenos Aires: Siglo XXI, 2008), 64. Demographic figures are partial and estimated before 1778; they were calculated by the historians by using different types of sources. Juan C. Garavaglia, *Pastores y labradores de Buenos Aires: Una historia agraria de la campaña bonaerense 1700–1800* (Buenos Aires: Ediciones de la Flor, 1999), 42–51.

15. As an economic resource, these exotic and big herbivorous mammals were fundamental to the pampas and to both the Indians and Spaniards. Here, there was nothing comparable to the bison that lived on the North American central Plains. The guanaco (*Auchenia huanaco*), also an herbivorous mammal, was intensively hunted by the prehispanic bands, especially in the arid, mountainous regions of Patagonia where it was very important until the nineteenth century. But it is difficult for the guanaco to live in the soft soils and the humid environment of the eastern pampas, and its population is smaller.

16. Juan de Garay, "Carta al Consejo de Indias . . . [1582]," in E. Ruiz Guiñazú, *Garay, fundador de Buenos Aires: Documentos referentes a las fundaciones de Santa Fe y Buenos Aires* (Buenos Aires: Municipalidad de la Capital Federal, 1915), 88. See also Juan de Rivadeneyra, "Relación [. . .] al Consejo real de Indias [c. 1581]," and Hernando Montalvo, "Carta del tesorero de la Real Hacienda [1587]," both in *Documentos históricos y geográficos relativos a la conquista y colonización rioplatense. Tomo primero* (Buenos Aires: Comisión Nacional del IV Centenario, 1941), 75–76, 139.

17. On *Ciudad de los Césares*, see Ramiro Martínez Sierra, *El mapa de las pampas* 2 vols. (Buenos Aires, 1975), 1: 51–68. Jerónimo Luis de Cabrera entered the pampas in 1620. In attempting to find it, he departed from Córdoba, crossed the pampas, and reached the Andean *cordillera*. See Juan F. Jiménez, "Encomenderos arruinados, incas fugitivos, beliches y corsarios holandeses: Los orígenes de la expedición en búsqueda de los Césares de Jerónimo Luis de Cabrera (1620–1621)," *Anuario del IEHS* 13 (1998), 173–192.

18. Rodolfo E González Lebrero, *La pequeña aldea: Sociedad y economía en Buenos Aires 1580–1640* (Buenos Aires: Biblos, 2002), 152–163.

19. *Reche* was an ethnic term used by the people of the Araucanía at the time of the Conquest to refer to themselves. It meant "the true people" or "the true men." It was replaced in the eighteenth century by the term *Mapuche* ("the people of the land"), which their descendants use today (Guillaume Boccara, *Guerre et ethnogenèse Mapuche dans le Chili colonial: L'invention du soi* [Paris: L'Harmattan, 1998]). The battle of Curalaba conditioned the later history of the southern borders, especially the Bío Bío frontier (Margarita Gascón, "Fluctuaciones en las relaciones fronterizas en el sur del Imperio Español (Siglo XVII)," *Atekna [En la tierra]* 1, no. 1 [2003], 13–45; and "La defensa del sur del Virreinato del Perú en el siglo XVII: La estrategia imperial y la agenda de la naturaleza," *Revista TEFROS* 6, no. 1 [2008], 1–20).

20. Leonardo León Solis, *Maloqueros y conchavadores en Araucanía y las Pampas, 1700–1800* (Temuco, Mexico: Ediciones Universidad de la Frontera, 1991), 22–24.

21. See Antonio, "Carta al Rey,"; Suárez Cordero, "Carta a la Reina,", and "Carta al Rey,"; Robles, "Carta al Rey [1673]," in *Documentos históricos y geográficos*, 316, 288–89, 291, 297.

22. Margarita Gascón, "The Southern Frontier of the Spanish Empire, 1598–1740" (Ph.D. thesis, Université d'Ottawa/University of Ottawa, 1994); and "La articulación de Buenos Aires a la frontera sur del Imperio español, 1640–1740," *Anuario del IEHS* 13 (1998), 193–213. According to Gascón, during the seventeenth and early eighteenth centuries Santiago de Chile, Mendoza, Córdoba, and lastly Buenos Aires went from being "peripheral colonies" (i.e., modest settlements in the geographical borders of colonial dominion for the purpose of being launching pads for advancing the colonial world) to full-fledged "frontier societies." This process began with the rebellion of the *reches* of the Araucanía frontier and operated from west to east (i.e., from the Pacific to the Atlantic). Buenos Aires was integrated into this frontier at the beginning of the eighteenth century through the networks that had linked it with these other settlements. These frontier societies were characterized by a flow of material resources (such as the *situado*) as well as human resources (military and administrative corps) destined to retain control over a geographical frontier in which different types of contacts operated. These stimulated social mobility and had an important economic and political impact on the Indian societies that went beyond the militarized boundary. Finally, a broad commercial circulation of goods that linked all settlements was fomented. In these societies emerged an ideological system based on the exaltation of warrior values: indeed, military activity was a system of social control as well as the main path to social mobility.

23. D. A. Brading, "Bourbon Spain and Its American Empire," in *The Cambridge History of Latin America*, vol. 1, *Colonial Latin America*, ed. Leslie Bethell (Cambridge: Cambridge University Press, 1984), 389–439; see also Weber, *Bárbaros*.

24. The main conflicts for the appropriation of wild cattle in the pampas had been before this moment, among the concessionaries of *vaquerías* from Buenos Aires, Córdoba, and Santa Fe. The *cabildos* of these towns claimed rights over these wild herds that apparently did not have owners. Buenos Aires supported its claim over these herds by the fact that the animals were descended from those left behind by the town's first founders, and the *vecinos* in Buenos Aires considered themselves to be legitimate heirs. González Lebrero, *La pequeña aldea*, 171–172; Gascón, "La articulación de Buenos Aires," 206–208, and "Fluctuaciones en las relaciones," 36–37.

25. Raúl J. Mandrini, "Procesos de especialización regional en la economía indígena pampeana (siglos XVIII–XIX): El caso del suroeste bonaerense," *Boletín Americanista* 41 (Barcelona: Universitat de Barcelona, 1991), 113–136; and "Las transformaciones de la economía indígena bonaerense (ca. 1600–1820)," in *Huellas en la tierra: Indios, agricultores y hacendados en la pampa*

bonaerense, ed. Raúl Mandrini and Andrea Reguera (Tandil, Argentina: IEHS/UNCPBA, 1994), 45–74.

26. The appropriation of resources of vanquished enemies was a common practice in the Indian tradition. Such appropriations such as the execution of warriors and the capture of women constituted, beyond the motives and reach of the conflict itself, habitual manners of destroying the enemy, and they contributed to the prestige of valiant warriors. Boccara, *Guerre et ethnogenèse*, 109–175.

27. Juan Beverina, *El virreinato de las Provincias del Río de la Plata: Su organización militar. Contribución a la "Historia del ejército argentino"* (1935; Buenos Aires: Círculo Militar, 1992); Roberto Marfany, "Frontera con los indios en el Sud y fundación de pueblos," in *Historia de la Nación Argentina*, vol. 4 (Buenos Aires: Academia Nacional de la Historia/El Ateneo, 1940), 307–333; *Política seguida con el aborigen (1750–1819)* 4 vols. (Buenos Aires: Círculo Militar, 1973), 1: 107–144.

28. Raúl J. Mandrini, "Desventuras y venturas de un gallego en el Buenos Aires de fines de la Colonia: Don Blas Pedrosa," in *Vivir entre dos mundos: Las frontera del sur de la Argentina. Siglos XVIII–XIX*, ed. Raúl Mandrini (Buenos Aires: Taurus, 2006), 43–72.

29. Marfany, *Frontera con los indios en el Sud*, 309–310.

30. Garavaglia, *Pastores y labradores*, 42–70.

31. There are many cases in which Indian chiefs call for missionaries and the establishment of missions. San Sabá Mission, in Texas, was founded to protect Apache groups from attacks by Comanches. Traditionally, historians have studied why Europeans founded missions, but they seem to have forgotten another key question: why did Indians ask for or accept missions? See Matthew Babcock, "Blurred Borders: North America's Forgotten Apache Reservations," in this volume. This issue is important because it reinforces my position. The Native people did not have a passive role, and they made their own political decisions.

32. Missionaries such as José Sánchez Labrador, José Cardiel, and Thomas Falkner tried to describe these ethnic realities in order to understand them and fix them in space by introducing order in a world that seemed chaotic and ever changing. So they elaborated complex frames for classifying these Native populations. These classifications were themselves a type of appropriation—intellectually speaking, or course—of these ethnic realities. But the classificatory frames are not social or ethnic realities, and the partial and confused understanding of such realities made such a goal illusory. See Raúl J. Mandrini, "Estudio preliminar," in *Descripción de la Patagonia y partes adyacentes de la América del Sur*, ed. Thomas Falkner (Buenos Aires: Taurus, 2003), 44–53. To formulate these classificatory frames, the missionaries used their own observations as well as information given to them by Indians who arrived at the missions. But the missionaries only knew a small grouping of the southern Indians.

33. The *cabildo* represented the interests of the elite, connected mainly with commerce. The missions tried to monopolize relationships with the Indians and serve as intermediaries between the Indians and the traders of Buenos Aires.

34. The mentioned project by Cevallos to advance the frontier until the Negro River and other proposals to occupy the island of Choele Choel in the same river were not very realistic and had almost no possibility of success. The Patagonian littoral area was also explored, and some forts and ports were established, such as El Carmen o Patagones in 1779 (Martínez Sierra, *El mapa de las pampas*, 123–269). These explorations were the result of possible English attempts to establish a foothold there and in order to forge an alliance with local Indians and establish a

deeper presence in the area. See Raúl J. Mandrini, "El viaje de la fragata San Antonio en 1745–1746: Reflexiones sobre los procesos políticos operados entre los indígenas pampeano-patagónicos," *Revista Española de Antropología Americana* 30 (2000), 236–238. The fears of a British invasion, especially after Lord Anson's expedition in 1740, were reawakened when Thomas Falkner's book was published in England in 1774. Falkner thought that the occupation of Patagonian lands was relatively easy. Mandrini, "Estudio preliminar"; Daniel Villar, "Estudio preliminar: Indígenas, españoles e ingleses en el Río de la Plata y Chile durante el siglo XVIII. Acerca de *Una narración fiel de peligros y desventuras que sobrellevó*," in Isaac Morris, *Una narración fiel de los peligro y desventuras que sobrellevó* (Buenos Aires: Taurus, 2004), 9–68. The proposals for offensive war against Indians did not disappear and are found until the end of the colonial era as an option between a good war and a bad peace. See Weber, *Bárbaros*, 138–143. For the Rio de la Plata, see Francisco de Serra y Canals, *El celo del español y el indiano instruido* (1800; Buenos Aires: Librería Editorial Platero, 1979), 40–66.

35. "Tratados que deberá observar con este Superior Gobierno el cacique Callfilqui" [1790], Archivo General de la Nación (Buenos Aires, Argentina), VII, Manuscritos de la Biblioteca Nacional, 198, 1877.

36. This situation clearly appeared in the testimony of Coluhuanque, an Indian captured in 1780 near the guard of Chascomus: Coluhuanque affirms that the southern chiefs are prepared to attack the frontier but really they do it to enforce the authorities to sign the peace. "Declaración tomada a el indio Coluhuanque [. . .] en Chascomús, 29 de noviembre de 1780," Archivo General de la Nación 9 (Buenos Aires, Argentina), 1–4-3.

37. Daniel Villar and Juan F. Jiménez, "Botín, materialización ideológica y guerra en las pampas durante la segunda mitad del siglo XVIII. El caso de Llanketruz," *Revista de Indias* 60, no. 220 (2000), 687–707; and "La tempestad de la guerra: Conflictos indígenas y circuitos de intercambio. Elementos para una periodización (Araucanía y las pampas, 1780–1840)," in *Las fronteras hispanocriollas del mundo indígena latinoamericano en los siglos XVIII–XIX. Un estudio comparativo*, ed. Raúl Mandrini and Carlos Paz (Tandil, Argentina: IEHS/CEHIR/UNS, 2003), 123–143.

38. Villar and Jiménez, "La tempestad de la guerra"; Raúl J. Mandrini and Sara Ortelli, "Los 'araucanos' en las pampas (c. 1700–1850)," in *Colonización, resistencia y mestizaje en las Américas (siglos XVI–XX)*, ed. Guillaume Boccara (Quito, Peru: Abya Yala/Instituto Francés de Estudios Andinos, 2002), 246–250.

39. Villar and Jiménez, "Botín, materialización ideológica."

40. Juan F. Jiménez, "Llanketruz: El sino de un 'corsario,'" in Mandrini, *Vivir entre dos mundos*, 73–93.

41. "Tratados que deberá observar," 1790.

42. Mandrini, "Guerra y paz en la frontera bonaerense."

43. Eduardo Crivelli Montero, "Malones: ¿Saqueo o estrategia? El objetivo de las invasiones de 1780 y 1783 a la frontera de Buenos Aires," *Todo es Historia* 283 (1991), 6–32; "Declaración tomada a el indio Coluhuanque"; Antonio Galarza, personal communication.

44. Miguel Lastarría, "Declaraciones y expresas Resoluciones Soberanas [Madrid, Agosto 31 de 1804]," in *Colonias orientales del Río Paraguay o de la Plata* (Buenos Aires: Compañía Sud-Americana de Billetes de Banco, 1914), 121; Félix de Azara, *Viajes por la América meridional. Contiene la descripción geográfica, política y civil del Paraguay y del Río de la Plata* (Madrid: Espasa-Calpe, 1969), 199; Pedro Andrés García, *Diario de la expedicion de 1822 á los campos del*

Sud de Buenos-Aires, desde Moron hasta la sierra de la Ventana (Buenos Aires: Imprenta del Estado, 1836).

45. Mandrini, "Procesos de especialización," 113–136, and "Transformaciones de la economía," 45–47; Miguel A. Palermo, "Indígenas en el mercado colonial," *Ciencia Hoy* 4 (1989), 22–26; Sara Ortelli, "La frontera pampeana en las últimas décadas del período colonial: Las delegaciones de indios y el comercio con Buenos Aires," in *Territorio, frontera y región en la historia de América. Siglos XVI al XX*, ed. Marco A. Landavazo (Mexico City: Porrúa, 2003), 71–110.

46. "Ynformación hecha sobre la Reducción [Buenos Aires, 1752]," Archivo General de Indias (Sevilla, España), Audiencia de Charcas, 221 (copy in the Museo Etnográfico, Buenos Aires, Argentina, folder J, 16, 1752). See also "Carta de Juan Blas Gago al Señor gobernador Don Alonso de la Vega, Zanjón, 5 de octubre de 1757," Archivo General de la Nación (Buenos Aires, Argentina), IX, 1.5.3., f. 52; "Carta de Bartolomé Gutiérrez de Paz al Gobernador don Alonso de la Vega, Salto, 16 diciembre de 1759," Archivo General de la Nación (Buenos Aires, Argentina), IX, 1.5.2., f. 39; "Orden del gobernador [Alonso de la Vega] a José Antonio López, comandante de La Matanza, Buenos Aires, 29 de octubre de 1760," Archivo General de la Nación (Buenos Aires, Argentina), IX, 1–4-5, f. 308.

47. Mandrini, "Desventuras y venturas."

48. "Informe del marqués de Loreto al Secretario Diego de Gardoqui [29 de octubre de 1792]," Archivo General de Indias (Sevilla, España), Audiencia de Charcas, 497; Mandrini, "Desventuras y venturas," 62–63.

49. Ortelli, "La frontera pampeana."

50. "Orden del gobernador a José Antonio López, 1760"; "Comunicación del marqués de Loreto al Comandante de Monte, Jaime Viamonte; 7 de enero de 1785," Archivo General de la Nación (Buenos Aires, Argentina), IX, 1–4-6, f. 219.

51. Sebastián L. Alioto, *Indios y ganado en la frontera. La ruta del río Negro (1750–1850)* (Rosario, Mexico: Prohistoria/Universidad Nacional del Sur, 2011).

52. Gabriel Darío Taruselli, "Las expediciones a Salinas: Caravanas en la Pampa colonial rioplatense (siglos XVII y XVIII)," *Quinto Sol. Revista de Historia Regional* 9/10 (2006), 125–149.

53. Mandrini, "Transformaciones de la economía," 65–71, and "Desventuras y venturas," 45–48; Ortelli, "La frontera pampeana," 88–105. To learn about Indian movements, Francisco de Viedma recommended in 1784 that Loreto send spies as if they were merchants that traveled through Indian lands. See *Memoria dirigida al Sr. marquez de Loreto, virey y capitán general de las provincias del Rio de la Plata sobre los obstáculos que prometen establecimientos proyectados en la costa Patagónica* [1784] (Buenos Aires: Imprenta del Estado, 1836).

54. The reasons for this change were complex and are related to the rise in the demand for animals, as well as the decrease in the supply of wild cattle herds, which was affected by the increase in demand and cycles of drought. The rise in demand in Araucanía was related to peace along the Bío Bío frontier, with a possible concomitant rise in the population of Araucanía and changes in the patterns of consumption, of both food and status goods (Léon Solis, *Maloqueros y conchavadores*, 88, 96; Gladys Varela and Ana María Biset, "Los Pehuenche en el mercado colonial," *Revista de Historia* 3 [1992], 156; Daniel Villar and Juan F. Jiménez, "Saca de ganados mayores y menores para la tierra de indios: Convites, consumo y política entre los indígenas de la Araucanía y las pampas [segunda mitad del siglo XVIII]," paper presented in *Encuentro de la Red de Estudios Rural* [Buenos Aires: Instituto de Investigaciones Dr. Emilio Ravignani, 2003]).

As far as the decrease in wild cattle herds, the situation remains unclear. Some eyewitnesses from the beginning of the century suggest a slow decrease in the number of animals, though it is impossible to be exact due to the nature of the sources. But the process was not linear: the stock of wild cattle could have recovered during some periods. Furthermore, bovine herds were not as affected as horses, and there were also regional differences. Thus, at the start of the nineteenth century, there were still plenty of wild mares (*castas*) in the geographical arch stretching from the west of Buenos Aires to south of Córdoba, and that fed a brisk commerce with groups from Araucanía whose barter consisted mostly of wool *ponchos* (Juan F. Jiménez, "Castas y ponchos: Comentarios a las observaciones de Luis de la Cruz sobre el comercio de ganado entre la cordillera y Mamil Mapu (1806)," in *Entre médanos y caldenes de la pampa sea*, ed. Ana Aguerre and Alicia Tapia [Buenos Aires: Universidad de Buenos Aires, 2002], 201–230). In addition, when the sources speak of wild cattle herds, or *cimarrones* (animals able to reproduce without human intervention), these must be distinguished from domesticated animals, which in periods of drought migrated to the south of the Rio Salado where water was more abundant and which many eyewitnesses confused with *cimarrones*.

55. Indian herds included mainly horses and mares and cows and bulls. Sheep also were very important; they were famous for the quality of their wool, and their importance increased over time. This is similar to the situation of the Navajo in the American Southwest. See Edward K. Flager, "Las relaciones interétnicas entre los navajos y los españoles de Nuevo México," *Revista de Antropología Americana* 18 (1988), 129–157; Peter Iverson, *The Navajos* (New York: Chelsea House, 1990), 30–31. See also Mandrini, "Transformaciones de la economía," 56–62.

56. Mandrini, "Procesos de especialización," 123.

57. Villar and Jiménez, "Botín, materialización ideológica," 698; María Eugenia Alemano and Florencia Carlón, "Prácticas defensivas, conflictos y autoridades en la frontera bonaerense: Los pagos de Magdalena y Pergamino (1752–1780)," *Anuario del Instituto de Historia Argentina* 9 (2009), 28–29.

58. Indians soon accepted European rules, at least in interchanges with the Spaniards or in long-distance commerce. We have clear references about this dating from the nineteenth century. Raúl Mandrini, "Pedir con vuelta ¿Reciprocidad diferida o mecanismo de poder?" *Antropológicas* 1 (1992), 59–69.

59. See, for example, García, *Diario de la expedicion de 1822*, 70, 101–102, 112–113, 124, 135, and 156.

60. "La buena acogida que dais a nuestros frutos, y permiso libre con que sacamos lo que necesitamos," in *Acuerdos del extinguido Cabildo de Buenos Aires, publicados bajo la dirección del Archivo de la nación, serie II, tomo II, Años 1805 a 1807* (Buenos Aires: G. Kraft, 1926), 277–278; also 303–304, 362–363, 373.

61. Kathleen DuVal, *The Native Ground: Indians and Colonists in the Heart of the Continent* (Philadelphia: University of Pennsylvania Press, 2006), 5–6.

62. William Merrill, "God's Saviors in the Sierra Madre," *Natural History* 92, no. 3 (1983), 58–67; Donna J. Guy and Thomas E. Sheridan, "On Frontiers: The Northern and Southern Edges of the Spanish Empire in the Americas," in *Contested Ground: Comparative Frontiers on the Northern and Southern Edges of the Spanish Empire*, ed. Donna Guy and Thomas Sheridan (Tucson: University of Arizona Press, 1998), 12–13; Weber, *Bárbaros*, 128.

63. Miguel A. Palermo, "Reflexiones sobre el llamado 'complejo ecuestre' en la Argentina," *RUNA. Archivo para las Ciencias del Hombre* 16 (1986), 167–170; Daniel J. Santamaría, "La puerta

amazónica: Los circuitos mercantiles del Madeira y del Guaporé en la segunda mitad del siglo XVIII," *Memoria americana. Cuadernos de Etnohistoria* 2 (1993), 51–61; Ana A. Teruel and Daniel Santamaría, "Fronteras y mercados: La economía de la misión de Miraflores en el Chaco salteño," *Siglo XIX. Revista de Historia* 15 (1994), 48–81.

64. Daniel J. Santamaría, "La guerra Guaykuru: Expansión colonial y conflicto interétnico en la Cuenca del Alto Paraguay, siglo XVIII," *Jahrbuch für Geschichte von staat, wirtschaft und gesellschaft Lateinamerikas* 29 (1992), 121–148; Santamaría, "La puerta amazónica."

65. Pekka Hämäläinen, "The Western Comanche Trade Center: Rethinking the Plains Indian Trade System," *Western Historical Quarterly* 29 (1998), 485–513; Hämäläinen, *The Comanche Empire* (New Haven, CT: Yale University Press, 2008); DuVal, *Native Ground*.

66. DuVal, *Native Ground*, 4–5; Richard White, *The Middle Ground. Indians, Empires and Republics in the Great Lakes Region, 1650–1815* (Cambridge: Cambridge University Press, 1991), 51–93; Richard White, "Creative Misunderstandings and New Understandings," *William and Mary Quarterly* 63, 1 (2006), 9–14.

Chapter 6

1. El Conde de Revillagigedo to El Conde del Campo de Alange, Mexico, February 8, 1791, Archivo General de Simancas, Guerra Moderna, Legajo 7020, Simancas, Spain (hereafter, AGS-Simancas, GM, Legajo number). For a brief summary in English, see Max L. Moorhead, *The Apache Frontier: Jacobo Ugarte and Spanish-Indian Relations in Northern New Spain, 1769–1791* (Norman: University of Oklahoma Press, 1968), 262–263.

2. David J. Weber, "Bourbons and Bárbaros: Center and Periphery in the Reshaping of Spanish Indian Policy," in *Negotiated Empires: Centers and Peripheries in the Americas, 1500–1820*, ed. Christine Daniels and Michael V. Kennedy (New York: Routledge, 2002), 79.

3. The percentages are my own and derive from numerical data in Max L. Moorhead, *The Presidio: Bastion of the Spanish Borderlands* (Norman: University of Oklahoma Press, 1975), 260–261; Elizabeth A. H. John, ed., and John Wheat, trans., "Views from a Desk in Chihuahua: Manuel Merino's Report on Apaches and Neighboring Nations, Ca. 1804," *Southwestern Historical Quarterly* (October 1991), 166; William B. Griffen, *Apaches at War and Peace: The Janos Presidio, 1750–1858* (1988; reprint, Norman: University of Oklahoma Press, 1998), 267–268. For a higher estimate, see William B. Griffen, "The Chiricahua Apache Population Resident at the Janos Presidio, 1792 to 1858," *Journal of the Southwest* 33 (Summer 1991), 155, 81, 89; William B. Griffen, "Apache Indians and the Northern Mexican Peace Establishments," in *Southwestern Culture History: Collected Papers in Honor of Albert H. Schroeder*, ed. Charles Lange (Santa Fe, NM: Ancient City, 1985), 188–189.

4. Commander-in-Chief Jacobo Ugarte to Viceroy Manuel Antonio Flores, Arizpe, December 10, 1787, Archivo General de la Nación, Mexico, Provincias Internas, Legajo 76, para. 38, microfilm, Bancroft Library, University of California at Berkeley (hereafter, AGN, PI, Legajo number, BL-microfilm); Fray Diego Bringas to [Commander-in-Chief] Pedro de Nava, Chihuahua, March 13, 1796, and Bringas to King Charles IV, Apostolic College of Santa Cruz de Querétaro, [no day, month] 1797, paras. 79, 90, both in Daniel S. Matson and Bernard L. Fontana, trans. and eds., *Friar Bringas Reports to the King: Methods and Indoctrination on the Frontier of New Spain 1796–97* (Tucson: University of Arizona Press, 1977), 93, 115, 118.

5. James L. Haley, *Apaches: A History and Culture Portrait* (Garden City, NY: Doubleday, 1981), 31; Gary Clayton Anderson, *The Indian Southwest, 1580–1830: Ethnogenesis and Reinvention* (Norman: University of Oklahoma Press, 1999), 111; William B. Carter, *Indian Alliances and the Spanish in the Southwest, 750–1750* (Norman: University of Oklahoma Press, 2009), 188.

6. Moorhead, *Apache Frontier*, 275; Bernardo de Gálvez, "Instrucción formada en virtud de Real Orden de S.M, México," August 26, 1786, paras. 46, 52, in Donald E. Worcester, trans. and ed., *Instructions for Governing the Interior Provinces of New Spain, 1786* (Berkeley, CA: Quivira Society, 1951), 42–44. See also Capt. Antonio Cordero to Capt. Manuel Casanova, Chihuahua, January 17, 1791, and "Noticia de los Prisioneros," Chihuahua, April 28, 1791, Folder 7, Section 1, Janos Presidio Records, Benson Latin American Collection, University of Texas at Austin (hereafter, JPR-UTA).

7. Moorhead, *Apache Frontier*, 97–99; David J. Weber, *The Spanish Frontier in North America* (New Haven, CT: Yale University Press, 1992), 228.

8. Pedro de Nava, "Instrucción que han de observar los Comandantes," Chihuahua, October 14, 1791, AGN, PI 66, BL-microfilm, paras. 10, 16–18, 27. The quotations are from paras. 27, 10, and 16. For an English translation, see Pedro de Nava, "Instructions for Dealing with Apaches at Peace in Nueva Vizcaya, Chihuahua, October 14, 1791," in Rick Hendricks and W. H. Timmons, *San Elizario: Spanish Presidio to Texas County Seat* (El Paso: Texas Western Press, 1998), 102–109. On Apache "deportation," see Mark Santiago, *The Jar of Severed Hands: Spanish Deportation of Apache Prisoners of War, 1770–1810* (Norman: University of Oklahoma Press, 2011); Paul Conrad, "Captive Fates: Displaced American Indians in the Southwest Borderlands, Mexico, and Cuba, 1500–1800" (Ph.D. diss., University of Texas at Austin, 2011); David J. Weber, *Bárbaros: Spaniards and Their Savages in the Age of Enlightenment* (New Haven, CT: Yale University Press, 2005), 149–150; Christon I. Archer, "The Deportation of Barbarian Indians from the Internal Provinces of New Spain, 1789–1810," *The Americas* 29 (January 1973), 376–385; and Max L. Moorhead, "Spanish Deportation of Hostile Apaches: The Policy and the Practice," *Arizona and the West* 17 (Autumn 1975), 205–220.

9. Daniel R. Mandell, *King Philip's War: Colonial Expansion, Native Resistance, and the End of Indian Sovereignty* (Baltimore: Johns Hopkins University Press, 2010), 118; Brett Rushforth, *Bonds of Alliance: Indigenous and Atlantic Slaveries in New France* (Chapel Hill: University of North Carolina Press, 2012), 10, 13; R. David Edmunds and Joseph L. Peyser, *The Fox Wars: The Mesquakie Challenge to New France* (Norman: University of Oklahoma Press, 1993), 80; Eve Ball, *Indeh: An Apache Odyssey* (1980; reprint, Norman: University of Oklahoma Press, 1988), 131–139; Troy R. Johnson, *The Occupation of Alcatraz Island: Indian Self-Determination and the Rise of Indian Activism* (Urbana: University of Illinois Press, 1996), 3.

10. Matthew Babcock, "Rethinking the Establecimientos: Why Apaches Settled on Spanish-Run Reservations, 1786–1793," *New Mexico Historical Review* 84 (Summer 2009), 366, 91–92; Weber, *Bárbaros*, 183, 93–95; Moorhead, *Presidio*, 243–266.

11. Nava, "Instrucción," paras. 15, 23–24, 26. The quotation is from para. 26.

12. For "Spanish escorts to hunt buffalo," see, e.g., Lt. Col. Manuel Muñoz to Commander-in-Chief Teodoro de Croix, Cuartel de Dolores, June 16, 1781, Audiencia de Guadalajara, Legajo 282, Archivo General de Indias, Seville, Spain, Max L. Moorhead Collection, Western History Collections, University of Oklahoma, Norman (hereafter, AGI Guadalajara, Legajo number, MLMC); Moorhead, *Presidio*, 246–247; and Moorhead, *Apache Frontier*, 212–213, 20. For a comparative Jicarilla case in New Mexico, see Ronald Benes, "Anza and Concha in New Mexico,

1787–1793: A Study in New Colonial Techniques," *Journal of the West* 4 (January 1965), 68. For raiding, see, e.g., Jacobo Ugarte to the Marqués de Sonora, Arizpe, August 14, 1787, AGS-Simancas, GM, 7031. For mescal harvesting, see Auditor of War Pedro Galindo Navarro to Croix, February 23, 1780, Arizpe; April 23, 1780, AGI Guadalajara, 276, Seville, Spain; and Griffen, *Apaches*, 27.

13. Hendricks and Timmons, *San Elizario*, 38–39. David Weber characterizes Spanish efforts to turn Navajos and Comanches into farmers in pueblos as failures but withholds final judgment on Apache reservations. See Weber, *Spanish Frontier*, 233; Weber, *Bárbaros*, 194.

14. Ned Blackhawk, *Violence over the Land: Indians and Empires in the Early American West* (Cambridge, MA: Harvard University Press, 2006), 1.

15. "Juan Bautista De Anza (the Elder) to Manuel Bernal De Huidobro, Ures, August 13, 1735," in *The Presidio and Militia on the Northern Frontier of New Spain: A Documentary History*, vol. 2, part 1, *The Californias and Sinaloa-Sonora, 1700–1765*, ed. Charles W. Polzer and Thomas E. Sheridan (Tucson: University of Arizona Press, 1997), 305–306; John L. Kessell, *Kiva, Cross and Crown: The Pecos Indians and New Mexico, 1540–1840*, 2nd ed. (Tuscon, AZ: Southwest Parks and Monuments Association, 1995), 361; Robert H. Jackson, *From Savages to Subjects: Missions in the History of the American Southwest* (Armonk, NY: M. E. Sharpe, 2000), 98. See also Teodoro de Croix, "General Report of 1781," October 30, 1781, Arizpe, paras. 202–208 in Alfred Barnaby Thomas, ed. and trans., *Teodoro de Croix and the Northern Frontier of New Spain, 1776–1783: From the Original Document in the Archives of the Indies, Seville* (Norman: University of Oklahoma Press, 1941), 126.

16. For a similar period of "relative peace" from 1785 to 1820 in Argentina, which reached its height during the same two decades as the Spanish-Apache peace from 1790 to 1810, see Raúl Mandrini's essay in this volume.

17. José Luis Mirafuentes Galván, "Los dos mundos de José Reyes Pozo y el alzamiento de los Apaches chiricahuis (Bacoachi, Sonora, 1790)," *Estudios de Historia Novohispana* 21 (2000), 104–105.

18. Ugarte to Flores, Chihuahua, March 21, 1789, AGN, PI, 66, f. 416, BL-microfilm. On Hispanicization, see William Roseberry, *Anthropologies and Histories: Essays in Culture, History, and Political Economy* (New Brunswick, NJ: Rutgers University Press, 1989), 87, 93–94; and Edward H. Spicer, *Cycles of Conquest: The Impact of Spain, Mexico, and the United States on the Indians of the Southwest, 1533–1960* (Tucson: University of Arizona Press, 1962), 570.

19. Ugalde to Flores, Santa Rosa, April 1, 1789, AGN, PI, 159, ff. 237–261, Moorhead transcription, MLMC.

20. Tato to Juan Caneva, Bavispe, April 24, 1789, Janos Historical Archives, Special Collections, roll 9, University of Texas at El Paso Library (hereafter, JHA-UTEP).

21. Cordero to Ugarte, San Diego, September 14, 1789, AGN, PI, 193, f. 251v; Lt. José Manuel Carrasco to Ugarte, Hacienda del Carmen, October 9, 1789, AGN, PI, 193, ff. 278–279, microfilm, Mexico City, roll courtesy of Brian DeLay (hereafter, Mexico microfilm).

22. Ugarte to Flores, March 13, 1788, AGN, PI, 128, ff. 363–366, summary and partial translation, MLMC. For the quotation, see Carrasco to Ugarte, San Buenaventura, May 25, 1789, AGN, PI, 193, f. 162, Mexico microfilm.

23. Ugarte to Flores, Chihuahua, February 28 and March 7, 1789, AGN, PI, 193, ff. 105–107, 162v, Mexico microfilm.

24. Ugarte to Governor Juan Bautista de Anza, Hacienda de San Salvador de Orta, December 2, 1788, AGN, PI, 128, f. 522, Mexico microfilm; [Commissioner] Leonardo Escalante, "Padrón

del número de Apaches bajos de paz," Bacoachi, December 1, 1788, AGN, PI, 193, ff. 4–4v, Mexico microfilm.

25. William B. Griffen, "The Compás: A Chiricahua Family of the Late 18th and Early 19th Centuries," *American Indian Quarterly* 7 (1983), 26, 30. For Mescalero service as military auxiliaries at Presidio del Norte from 1790 to 1795, see Moorhead, *Presidio*, 259.

26. There is no evidence that any Apache chief who received a house at Janos ever occupied one. See Griffen, *Apaches*, 105–106. For comparative cases at Bacoachi and Sabinal, respectively, see Moorhead, *Apache Frontier*, 185; and Marc Simmons, *Coronado's Land: Essays on Daily Life in Colonial New Mexico* (Albuquerque: University of New Mexico Press, 1991), 58.

27. Cordero to Janos Commander, Pueblo del Paso, August 12, 1791, F7, S1, JPR-UTA. See also Nava, "Instrucción," para. 4. For the similar privileging of Pinal Chief Chilitipagé as "indio General" at Tucson, see Lt. Antonio Narbona to Commander-in-Chief Alexo García Conde, Arizpe, May 26, 1819, facsimile in Sidney B. Brinckerhoff and Odie B. Faulk, eds. and trans., *Lancers for the King: A Study of the Frontier Military System of Northern New Spain, with a Translation of the Royal Regulations of 1772* (Phoenix: Arizona Historical Foundation, 1965), 116.

28. Griffen, "Compás," 26–29. Three Mescalero bands moved inside Presidio del Norte in 1780 amid flooding and a smallpox epidemic. See Moorhead, *Presidio*, 248.

29. Salcedo to the Janos commander, Chihuahua, July 21, 1804, F17, S2, JPR-UTA; Griffen, "Chiricahua Apache Population," 153–154, 57; Griffen, "Compás," 33, 39; Richard J. Perry, *Western Apache Heritage: People of the Mountain Corridor* (Austin: University of Texas Press, 1991), 168; Ball, *Indeh*, 22.

30. For the first quotation, see Nava to Casanova, Chihuahua, June 8, 1792, F8, S1, JPR-UTA. For the second quotation, see Nava, "Instrucción," para. 35. For a closer look at the long-standing debate over baptizing unacculturated Indians across Spanish America, see Weber, *Bárbaros*, 93, 103.

31. Nava to Casanova, San Diego, May 14, 1792, roll 10, JHA-UTEP.

32. Domínguez to Nava, Janos, July 1, 1792, roll 10, JHA-UTEP. For the first identification of the trend of "peaceful" Apache headmen at Janos requesting baptism for their children in the 1790s, see Griffen, "Compás," 28.

33. For two Chiricahua cases at Bacoachi, see Fray Pedro de Arriquibar to Fray Francisco Antonio Barbastro, Bacoachi, May 20, 1795, in Matson and Fontana, *Friar Bringas*, 121. Only 11 percent (15 of 135 people) that the Janos chaplain Domínguez baptized between 1799 and 1802 were Apaches. See Domínguez, Janos, Baptisms, April 30, 1799, to June 30, 1802, roll 14, JHA-UTEP. Of twenty-two baptisms performed by Mexican chaplains in the Janos district from 1833 to 1834, only one was an Apache. See Fray Rafael Echeverría and Fray Alejo Bermudes, Casas Grandes baptism book, F35, S3, JPR-UTA.

34. Griffen, *Apaches*, 110.

35. Father Antonio Rafael Benites, Bacoachi, April 9, 1787, AGI Guadalajara, 287, MLMC. In May 1785 an epidemic causing deaths from pleurisy or "inflammation of the lungs" struck New Mexico. See Ann L. W. Stodder and Debra L. Martin, "Health and Disease in the Southwest Before and After Spanish Contact," in *Disease and Demography in the Americas*, ed. John W. Verano and Douglas H. Ubelaker (Washington, DC: Smithsonian Institution, 1992), 66.

36. Morris E. Opler, "The Apachean Culture Pattern and Its Origins," in *Handbook of North American Indians*, vol. 10, *Southwest*, ed. Alfonso Ortiz (Washington, DC: Smithsonian Institution, 1983), 373; Morris E. Opler, *An Apache Life-Way: The Economic, Social, and Religious Institutions of the Chiricahua Indians* (Chicago: University of Chicago Press, 1941), 242–257; Kenneth W.

Morrison, *The Solidarity of Kin: Ethnohistory, Religious Studies, and the Algonkian-French Religious Encounter* (Albany: State University of New York Press, 2002), 123–126, 43; H. Henrietta Stockel, *On the Bloody Road to Jesus: Christianity and the Chiricahua Apaches* (Albuquerque: University of New Mexico Press, 2004), 85.

37. Nava to Barbastro, Chihuahua, March 28, 1795; Barbastro to Nava, Aconchi, June 29, 1795, both in Matson and Fontana, *Friar Bringas*, 121, 28.

38. Domínguez, Janos, Baptisms, April 30, 1799, to June 30, 1802, roll 14, JHA-UTEP.

39. Galindo Navarro to Nava, Chihuahua, December 9, 1796; Nava to Galindo Navarro, Chihuahua, December 20, 1796, both in Matson and Fontana, *Friar Bringas*, 74–75.

40. Archer, "Deportation," 377. For an argument that the deportation policy began earlier in 1787, see Moorhead, "Spanish Deportation," 208–209.

41. Nava to Galindo Navarro, Chihuahua, December 20, 1796, in Matson and Fontana, *Friar Bringas*, 75.

42. Nava to the Janos commander, Chihuahua, August 12, 1794, F10, S1, JPR-UTA. For the *collera*, see Juliana Barr, *Peace Came in the Form of a Woman: Indians and Spaniards in the Texas Borderlands* (Chapel Hill: University of North Carolina Press, 2007), 169.

43. The data are based on Spanish archival documents from JPR-UTA and JHA-UTEP; from AGN, PI, 76, BL-microfilm; from AGI Guadalajara, 289, Seville, courtesy of David Weber; from the Archivo Parroquial de San Felipe El Real de Chihuahua, courtesy of Chantal Cramaussel; and from Moorhead, "Spanish Deportation of Hostile Apaches," 205–220. See also Mary Lu Moore and Delmar L. Beene, eds. and trans., "The Interior Provinces of New Spain: The Report of Hugo O'Conor, January 30, 1776," *Arizona and the West* 13 (1971), 265–282; and William E. Dunn, "Apache Relations in Texas, 1718–1750," *Southwestern Historical Quarterly* 14 (January 1911), 198–274. For similar percentages and a much higher estimate of 2,266 Apaches deported to Mexico City from 1773 to 1809 that omits the fates of captives extradited to Veracruz and Havana, see Santiago, *Jar of Severed Hands*, 201–203. For the finding that 70 percent of indigenous miners in Nueva Vizcaya in the 1680s, who included Apaches, were adult women, see Chantal Cramaussel's essay in this volume.

44. For *piezas*, see James F. Brooks, *Captives and Cousins: Slavery, Kinship, and Community in the Southwest Borderlands* (Chapel Hill: University of North Carolina Press, 2002), 374. Frontier Spaniards were likely borrowing from the term *pieza de india* for the perfectly healthy young adult male in the African slave trade. See Philip D. Curtin, *The Atlantic Slave Trade: A Census* (Madison: University of Wisconsin Press, 1969), 22. On captives' varying fates and the difference between war captives and slaves, see Catherine M. Cameron, "Introduction: Captives in Prehistory," in *Invisible Citizens: Captives and Their Consequences*, ed. Catherine M. Cameron (Salt Lake City: University of Utah Press, 2008), 2, 5, 20; Orlando Patterson, *Slavery and Social Death* (Cambridge, MA: Harvard University Press, 1982), 106–109; and Daniel K. Richter, *The Ordeal of the Longhouse: The Peoples of the Iroquois League in the Era of European Colonization* (Chapel Hill: University of North Carolina Press, 1992), 69–70. On the variety of forced and salaried indigenous labor in Spanish America, see Weber, *Bárbaros*, 245–247. For a similar conclusion on Apache miners in late seventeenth-century Nueva Vizcaya, see Cramaussel's essay in this volume.

45. For the comparative use of captive indigenous labor in *obrajes* in New Mexico, see Ned Blackhawk's essay in this volume and Blackhawk, *Violence over the Land*, 47–58.

46. Antonio Cordero y Bustamante, "Noticias relativas a la nación Apache, que en el año de 1796 extendió en el Paso del Norte, el Teniente Coronel D. Antonio Cordero, por encargo del Sr.

Comandante General Mariscal de Campo D. Pedro Nava," in *Geografía de las lenguas y carta etnográfica de México*, ed. Manuel Orozco y Berra (Mexico City: Impr. de J. M. Andrade y F. Escalante, 1864), 379. For an English translation, see Daniel S. Matson and Albert H. Schroeder, eds. and trans., "Cordero's Description of the Apache—1796," *New Mexico Historical Review* 32 (October 1957), 350.

47. On "captured kinsmen," see Moorhead, *Apache Frontier*, 274–275. For Tidaya, see Nava, "Extracto y resumen de hostilidades," Chihuahua, April 24, 1793, AGI Guadalajara, 289, Seville, Spain; Nava to Lt. Dionisio Valles, Valle de San Bartolomé, May 22, 1795, F11, S1, JPR-UTA.

48. Moorhead, *Presidio*, 260–261; Griffen, *Apaches*, 268–269, 72–73; Nava, "Estado que manifiesta de rancherias Apaches existentes de paz," Chihuahua, May 2, 1793, AGI Guadalajara, 289, Seville, Spain; Henry F. Dobyns, *Spanish Colonial Tucson: A Demographic History* (Tucson: University of Arizona Press, 1976), 105; Benes, "Anza and Concha," 71–72.

49. Asst. Inspector Diego de Borica to the Janos commander, Chihuahua, August 1, 1791, F7, S1, JPR-UTA; José Tapia, "Compañia de Janos: Distribución del primer medio . . . de tesoreria," Chihuahua, January 17, 1796, roll 10, JHA-UTEP; Capt. Joseph Manuel de Ochoa, "Cuenta seguida a los Apaches de Paz," Janos, December 31, 1799, F15, S2, JPR-UTA.

50. Odie B. Faulk, *The Last Years of Spanish Texas, 1778–1821* (The Hague: Mouton, 1964), 29–31, 124; Donald E. Chipman, *Spanish Texas, 1519–1821* (Austin: University of Texas Press, 1992), 277; Luis Navarro García, *Don José de Gálvez y la Comandancia General de las provincias internas del norte de Nueva España* (Seville, Spain: Escuela de Estudios Hispano-Americanos, 1964). For more on Antonio Narbona, including his role in an 1804 campaign against the Navajos, see Brian DeLay's essay in this volume and Dobyns, *Spanish Colonial Tucson*, 129.

51. For Tucson, see Dobyns, *Spanish Colonial Tucson*, 105. For the Sonoran frontier, see James E. Officer, *Hispanic Arizona, 1530–1856* (Tucson: University of Arizona Press, 1987), 79–80.

52. Dobyns, *Spanish Colonial Tucson*, 41–42.

53. See Joseph F. Park, "Spanish Indian Policy in Northern Mexico, 1765–1810," *Arizona and the West* 4 (1962), 343, and reprinted in *New Spain's Northern Frontier: Essays on Spain in the American West, 1540–1821*, ed. David J. Weber (Albuquerque: University of New Mexico Press, 1979), 231. Numerous borderlands scholars, drawing on Park, have inadvertently repeated this error. See, for example, Brinckerhoff and Faulk, *Lancers*, 92; Moorhead, *Apache Frontier*, 289; and Moorhead, *Presidio*, 265.

54. Cynthia Radding, *Landscapes of Power and Identity: Comparative Histories in the Sonoran Desert and the Forests of Amazonia from Colony to Republic* (Durham, NC: Duke University Press, 2005), 288; Officer, *Hispanic Arizona*, 87, 108, 12; Ray H. Mattison, "Early Spanish and Mexican Settlements in Arizona," *New Mexico Historical Review* 21 (October 1946), 288.

55. Griffen, *Apaches*, 87, 120; Griffen," Compás," 33.

56. Capt. Laureano de Murga to Capt. José Ignacio Ronquillo, Namiquipa, July 27, 1816, F22, S1; Capt. Miguel Ortiz to the Janos commander, Carrizal, August 27, 1816, F22, S1; Capt. Alberto Maynez to Bernardo Bonavia, Janos, October 3, 1816, F22, S1; Maynez to the Commander-in-Chief, Janos, October 9, 1816, F22, S1; Maynez et al. "Ración," August 3, 1818, F23, S3; José Antonio Vizcarra et al. "Ración," Janos, March 18, 1822, F25, S1; Ronquillo, "Hoja de Servicio," December 31, 1821, F24A, S2, JPR-UTA.

57. Luis Aboites Aguilar, *Norte precario: Poblamiento y colonización en México, 1760–1940* (Mexico City: Colegio de México, Centro de Estudios Históricos, Centro de Investigaciones y Estudios Superiores en Antropología Social, 1995), 49.

58. Janos censuses from January 1, 1793; December 31, 1799; December 31, 1800 (includes Casas Grandes); [no day, month], 1804; December 31, 1807; December 31, 1812; December 31, 1818; [no day, month], 1819; December 31, 1822, all in JPR-UTA; Janos censuses from December 31, 1798, and Janos census from December 31, 1801 (includes Casas Grandes), all on roll 14, JHA-UTEP.

59. Ross Frank, *From Settler to Citizen: New Mexican Economic Development and the Creation of Vecino Society, 1750–1820* (Berkeley: University of California Press, 2000), 119.

60. Kieran McCarty, ed., *Desert Documentary: The Spanish Years, 1767–1821* (Tucson: Arizona Historical Society, 1976), 134; Kieran McCarty, ed., *A Frontier Documentary: Sonora and Tucson, 1821–1848* (Tucson: University of Arizona Press, 1997), 51; Lt. José Romero to Narbona, Tucson, May 21, 1819, facsimile in Brinckerhoff and Faulk, *Lancers*, 116. For the reconciliation with the Arivaipas, see García Conde to the Count of Venadito, Durango, July 19, 1819, translated in Dobyns, *Spanish Colonial Tucson*, 104.

61. For the 1840s, see Hubert Howe Bancroft, *History of Arizona and New Mexico, 1530–1888* (San Francisco: History Company, 1889), 402. For the 1860s, see David Longstreet's testimony in Grenville Goodwin, *Western Apache Raiding and Warfare*, ed. Keith H. Basso (Tucson: University of Arizona Press, 1971), 192. See also "Resumen breve y explicatoria de los pueblos del Partido de Arizpe," *Boletín de la Sociedad de Geografía y Estadística* (BSMGE) (Mexico), tomo II, 1861, reprinted in José Agustín de Escudero, *Noticias estadísticas de Sonora y Sinaloa (1849)*, ed. Héctor Cuauhtémoc Hernández Silva (Hermosillo, Mexico: Universidad de Sonora, 1997), 368.

62. On mutual acculturation or transculturation, see Ramón A. Gutiérrez and Elliott Young, "Transnationalizing Borderlands History," *Western Historical Quarterly* 41 (Spring 2010), 36.

63. For two examples among Chiricahuas, see Griffen, *Apaches*, 71.

64. For an example at Namiquipa, see Nava to the Conde de Revillagigedo, Chihuahua, July 29, 1791, AGN, PI, 66, BL-microfilm, f. 358.

65. For an example in 1793, see Rick Hendricks, "Massacre in the Organ Mountains: The Death of Manuel Vidal de Lorca," *Password* 39 (Winter 1994), 172; and Hendricks and Timmons, *San Elizario*, 34, 37. For examples at Janos from 1795 to 1817, see Griffen, *Apaches*, 80–81, 91–92.

66. Griffen, "Compás," 32–33; Griffen, *Apaches*, 91.

67. Griffen, "Compás," 27.

68. Narbona to Gov. Cordero, Arizpe, March 8, 1819, translated in Dobyns, *Spanish Colonial Tucson*, 103.

69. Griffen, *Apaches*, 103.

70. Bringas to the king, para. 92, in Matson and Fontana, *Friar Bringas*, 119.

71. Griffen, *Apaches*, 109.

72. Arriquibar to Barbastro, Bacoachi, May 20, 1795, and Barbastro to Nava, in Matson and Fontana, *Friar Bringas*, 122, 26–27. For another translated excerpt of the Arriquibar document, see Dobyns, *Spanish Colonial Tucson*, 44–45.

73. See, e.g., Bringas to the king, para. 93, in Matson and Fontana, *Friar Bringas*, 119.

74. For environmentally induced supply shortages, see Capt. Domingo Díaz to Ugarte, March 29, 1787, AGI Guadalajara, 287, MLMC; Gálvez, "Instrucción," para. 141, in Worcester, *Instructions*, 65; and Sara Ortelli, *Trama de una guerra conveniente: Nueva Vizcaya y la sombra de los Apaches (1748–1790)* (Mexico City: El Colegio de México, 2007), 193. Moorhead, *Presidio*, 79, 212. For eating soldiers' horses, see Borica to the Janos commander, Chihuahua, July 23, 1792, F8, S1, JPR-UTA. For a parallel case of this among Apaches and Yavapais at the San Carlos reservation

in 1876, see Timothy Braatz, *Surviving Conquest : A History of the Yavapai Peoples* (Lincoln: University of Nebraska Press, 2003), 184.

75. Opler, *Apache Life-Way*, 465; Nava to the Janos commander, Chihuahua, November 10, 1796, roll 10, JHA-UTEP.

76. Lt. Col. Roque de Medina to the Janos commander, Chihuahua, January 17, 1795, F11, S2, JPR-UTA.

77. Nava, "Instrucción," para. 22.

78. Paul Hagle, "Military Life on New Spain's Northern Frontier" (M.A. thesis, University of Texas at Austin, 1962), 33; Griffen, *Apaches*, 102.

79. Although Barbastro and Arriquibar use the term "Christians," Bringas states, "Apaches continue to suffer from the bad example of the other Indians." See Bringas to the king, para. 99, in Matson and Fontana, *Friar Bringas*, 130.

80. Ibid., 122.

81. Mayor José Leon, "The Republic of Tucson," February 1, 1825, in McCarty, *Frontier Documentary*, 2.

82. Arriquibar to Barbastro in Matson and Fontana, *Friar Bringas*, 122.

83. For "Apacheanization," see Anderson, *Indian Southwest*, 106. On the spiritual significance of Apache dancing, see Opler, *Apache Life-Way*, 100–113. For an earlier Spanish take, see José Cortés, *Views from the Apache Frontier: Report on the Northern Provinces of New Spain by José Cortés, Lieutenant in the Royal Corps of Engineers, 1799*, ed. Elizabeth A. H. John, trans. John Wheat (Norman: University of Oklahoma Press, 1989), 62–64. On gambling, see Virginia Wayland, Harold Wayland, and Alan Ferg, *Playing Cards of the Apaches: A Study in Cultural Adaptation* (Tucson, AZ: Screenfold, 2006), 53; and Opler, *Apache Life-Way*, 299. On polygyny, see ibid., 416–426; Grenville Goodwin, *The Social Organization of the Western Apache* (Chicago: University of Chicago Press, 1942), 352; and Haley, *Apaches*, 145.

84. Griffen, "Compás," 32, 36; William B. Griffen, *Utmost Good Faith: Patterns of Apache-Mexican Hostilities in Northern Chihuahua Border Warfare, 1821–1848* (Albuquerque: University of New Mexico Press, 1988), 311; Griffen, *Apaches*, 81, 89.

85. Griffen, "Compás," 30.

86. Although Griffen offers both of these interpretations, he fails to note the significance of El Compá's band's continued residence at Janos. See Griffen, *Apaches*, 78.

87. For *Nantan* as chief, see Haley, *Apaches*, 155. For the first attack, see Moorhead, *Apache Frontier*, 192–196. For the second attack, see Sec. Pedro Garrido y Duran to the king, Madrid, February 8, 1792, AGI Guadalajara, 390, Seville, Spain, para. 61, courtesy of David Weber. Despite periodic hostilities between independent Apaches and "apaches mansos" at Tucson, the peaceful Apaches remained. See Dobyns, *Spanish Colonial Tucson*, 45.

88. Hendricks, "Massacre in the Organ Mountains," 174.

89. Bringas to the king, para. 94, in Matson and Fontana, *Friar Bringas*, 120; Navarro García, *Don José de Gálvez*, 493; John and Wheat, "Views from a Desk in Chihuahua," 163.

90. Navarro García, *Don José de Gálvez*, 493; Moorhead, *Presidio*, 259.

91. For evidence that inadequate rations were a significant factor in the initial Apache desertions at Bacoachi, see Int. Gov. Pedro Garrido y Duran to Escalante, February 8, 1788, AGN, PI, 234, translated in Dobyns, *Spanish Colonial Tucson*, 100.

92. Barbastro to Nava in Matson and Fontana, *Friar Bringas*, 127.

93. Griffen, *Apaches*, 79; Lance R. Blyth, "The Presidio of Janos: Ethnicity, Society, Masculinity, and Ecology in Far Northern Mexico, 1685–1858" (Ph.D. diss., Northern Arizona University, 2005), 84.

94. For the uneven breakdown of the system after 1810, see Weber, *Bárbaros*, 360n60; and Ignacio Zúñiga, *Rápida ojeada al estado de Sonora: Dirigida y dedicada al supremo gobierno de la nación* (Mexico: Juan Ojeda, 1835), 22–26. For the ending of meat rations and the 1824 policy change, see Janos ration lists, 1822–1827, JPR-UTA; Griffen, *Apaches*, 125, 31; and Griffen, *Utmost Good Faith*, 21.

95. On Comanche expansion, see Pekka Hämäläinen, *The Comanche Empire* (New Haven, CT: Yale University Press, 2008).

96. Griffen, *Apaches*, 81; August, "Balance-of-Power Diplomacy," 156; Simmons, *Coronado's Land*, 60; Benes, "Anza and Concha," 70.

97. Griffen, *Apaches*, 82.

98. Moorhead, *Apache Frontier*, 263.

99. Edwin R. Sweeney, *Mangas Coloradas: Chief of the Chiricahua Apaches* (Norman: University of Oklahoma Press, 1998), 5, 312.

100. Officer, *Hispanic Arizona*, 177, 190, 206, 264. For Gervacio Compá, see Griffen, *Apaches*, 226, 32–33, 42–43; and Sweeney, *Mangas Coloradas*, 171, 252, 79.

101. García Conde, "Manifiesto que dirige á los habitantes del departamento de Chihuahua," Chihuahua, September 23, 1842, in Jorge Chávez Chávez, "Construcción de una cultura regional en el norte de México" (Ph.D diss., Universidad Nacional Autónoma de México, 2007), 258–266; Griffen, *Apaches*, 147–151, 89–99, 233–235, 49–59.

102. García Conde, "Manifiesto," in Chávez, "Construccíon de una cultura regional," 269–270.

103. Moorhead, *Presidio*, 243.

104. Numerous scholars have treated U.S.-Apache relations in these years. See, e.g., Dan L. Thrapp, *The Conquest of Apachería* (Norman: University of Oklahoma Press, 1967), 6–14; Haley, *Apaches*, 191–230; Griffen, *Apaches*, 248–249; Sweeney, *Mangas Coloradas*, 137–158, 220–390; and Edwin R. Sweeney, *Cochise: Chiricahua Apache Chief* (Norman: University of Oklahoma Press, 1991), 99–141.

105. On the lack of scholarly understanding of Indian politics in the Southwest in the 1830s and 1840s, see Brian DeLay, *War of a Thousand Deserts: Indian Raids and the U.S.-Mexican War* (New Haven, CT: Yale University Press, 2008), xix.

106. David Meriwether, *My Life in the Mountains and on the Plains*, ed. Robert A. Griffen (Norman: University of Oklahoma Press, 1965), 217.

107. Griffen, *Apaches*, 250; Sweeney, *Mangas Coloradas*, 328, 31, 62–64, 80.

Chapter 7

I thank José Gabriel Martínez Serna, for the initial translation, and Paul Liffman and Paul Kersey, who helped me to edit this essay in English.

1. Undergraduate and postgraduate programs opened in many cities in northern Mexico, while students who specialized in this region earned their doctoral degrees at Universidad Nacional Autónoma de México (hereafter UNAM), Colegio de Michoacán, and Colegio de México. Most of their research has been published. Among dissertations, recently published, and studies in print (besides my own, which is quoted later in this essay), see, in chronological order, Clara Bargellini, *La arquitectura de la plata: Iglesias monumentales del centro-norte de México, 1640–1750* (Barcelona: Turner-UNAM, 1991); Guy Rozat, *América, imperio del demonio: Cuentos y recuentos*

(Mexico City: Universidad Iberoamericana, 1995); Carlos Manuel Valdés, *La gente del mesquite: Los nómadas del noreste en la colonia* (Mexico: CIESAS-INI, 1995); José Marcos Medina Bustos, *Vida y muerte en el antiguo Hermosillo, 1773-1828: Un estudio demográfico y social basado en los registros parroquiales* (Hermosillo, Mexico: Gobierno del Estado de Sonora, 1997), and "La representación política de antiguo régimen y la transición al liberalismo en una zona de frontera Sonora, 1650-1824" (Ph.D. diss., El Colegio de Michoacán, 2008); Patricia Osante, *Orígenes del Nuevo Santander, 1748-1772* (Mexico City: UNAM, 1997); Luis Aboites, *Demografía histórica y conflictos por el agua; dos estudios sobre 40 kilómetros de historia del río San Pedro, Chihuahua, México* (Mexico City: CIESAS, 2000); José Refugio de la Torre Curiel, *Vicarios en entredicho* (Zamora, Mexico: El Colegio de Michoacán, 2001); Valentina Garza, "Poblamiento y colonización en el noreste novohispano" (Ph.D. diss., El Colegio de México, 2002); Miguel Vallebueno, *Civitas et urbs: La conformación del espacio urbano de Durango* (Ph.D. diss., UJED/Gobierno del Estado de Durango, 2005); Sara Ortelli, *Trama de una guerra conveniente: Nueva Vizcaya y la sombra de los Apaches (1748-1790)* (Mexico City: El Colegio de México, 2007); Salvador Álvarez, *El indio y la sociedad colonial norteña, siglos XVI-XVIII* (Durango, Mexico: Universidad Juárez del Estado de Durango, El Colegio de Michoacán, 2009); Martín González de la Vara, *Breve historia de Ciudad Juárez y su región* (Chihuahua, Mexico: El Colegio de Chihuahua, 2009); Mario Alberto Magaña Mancillas, *Indios, soldados y rancheros: Poblamiento, memoria e identidades en el área central de las Californias (1769-1870)* (La Paz, Mexico: Gobierno del Estado de Baja California Sur, Instituto Sudcaliforniano de Cultura, El Colegio de Michoacán, Consejo Nacional para la Cultura y Las Artes, 2010); and Tomás Dimas Arenas, *Migración a corta distancia: La población de la parroquia de Sombrerete de 1677 a 1825* (Zacatecas, Mexico: Universidad Autónoma de Zacatecas, 2012).

2. There is a coincidence between the main uprisings and severe epidemics. New Mexico was recovered after measles epidemics in 1693. Spaniards expanded in the sierra west of Durango, Mexico, after the droughts and epidemics of 1785-1787. See Chantal Cramaussel, "Ritmos de poblamiento y demografía en la Nueva Vizcaya," in *Demografía y poblamiento del territorio: La Nueva España y México (siglos XVI-XX)*, ed. Chantal Cramaussel (Zamora, Mexico: El Colegio de Michoacán, 2009), 171-201.

3. Ignacio del Río, "Sobre la aparición y desarrollo del trabajo libre asalariado en el norte de la Nueva España (siglos XVI y XVII)," in *El trabajo y los trabajadores en la historia de México*, ed. Elsa Frost et al. (Mexico City: UNAM, 1979), 92-111.

4. Northeast New Spain (Nuevo León, Coahuila, and Nuevo Santander, all in what is now Texas) is not considered in this essay because the Indian transfers to that region were not connected with the ones in the rest of the borderlands. The Sinaloa and Sonora provinces, which first belonged to Nueva Vizcaya, had their own governor from 1733. Álamos, in the present-day state of Sonora, was part of the province of Sinaloa during colonial times.

5. See Matthew Babcock, "Rethinking the Establecimientos: Why Apaches Settled on Spanish-run Reservations, 1786-1793," *New Mexico Historical Review* 84, no. 3 (2009), 363-397.

6. David Carbajal López, *La población en Bolaños, 1740-1848: Dinámica demográfica, familia y mestizaje* (Zamora, Mexico: El Colegio de Michoacán, 2008). Raúl García discovered the same phenomenon in Linares (Nuevo León) at the end of colonial times: "Población, familia y calidad en San Felipe de Linares (1760-1810)" (thesis, Universidad Autónoma de Nuevo León, 1989). This topic has been developed by different historians. Multiethnic families existed throughout New Spain, as was seen during the conference that took place at El Colegio de Michoacán on June 18

and 19 of 2010. The articles from this conference are in David Carbajal, ed., *Familias pluriétnicas y mestizaje* (Guadalajara, Mexico: University of Guadalajara, in press).

7. For the case of Nuevo Santander, see Osante, *Orígenes*. San Antonio and Nacogdoches and the nearby missions were tiny outposts scattered in a huge territory: see Peter Gerhard, *The North Frontier of New Spain* (Norman: University of Oklahoma Press, 1993), 341, in which he mentions 3,550 Indians and 700 non-Indians living in Texas in 1800.

8. It is very difficult to know if the word *Apache* matches a particular Indian group during colonial times. Spaniards often referred to all seminomadic Indians as Apaches. See Albert H. Schroeder, *A Study of the Apache Indians* (Garland: New York, 1974), and Ortelli, *Trama de una guerra conveniente*.

9. Salvador Álvarez, "Manuel San Juan de Santa Cruz: Gobernador, latifundista y capitán de guerra en la frontera norte," *Revista de Indias* (January–April 2010), 101–126. The great importance of horses for the Indian population on the borders of the Spanish Empire has been stressed by David Weber, *Bárbaros: Spaniards and Their Savages in the Age of Enlightenment* (New Haven, CT: Yale University Press, 2005). The great numbers of stolen horses and of Spaniards captured are highlighted by Matthew Babcock, in "Rethinking the Establecimientos," and by Joaquín Rivaya-Martínez, "Captivity and Adoption Among the Comanche Indians, 1700–1875" (Ph.D. diss., University of California, Los Angeles, 2005).

10. This type of war went on during the nineteenth century when the governments of Chihuahua and Sonora fixed a price for every Apache head/scalp: see Ricardo León and Carlos González Herrera, *Civilizar o exterminar: Tarahumaras y Apaches en Chihuahua, siglo XIX* (Mexico City: CIESAS, INI, 2000).

11. We are not taking into account Guarisamey (a *real de minas* that experienced a boom at the end of the eighteenth century, in what is today Durango) because in the sacramental sources housed in the Archive of the Archbishopric of Durango there is only a single category for "Indian" to distinguish them from other ethnic groups, without specifying their places of origin. The Indian groups of the mountain, such as Xiximés and Tepehuanes, were subjected to *repartimiento* and their populations quickly dwindled: see Chantal Cramaussel, "La vertiente occidental de la Sierra: El último frente de colonización (1760–1830)," in *Historia de Durango*, 2 vols., ed. Miguel Vallebueno (Mexico City: El Gran Número Once–Universidad Juárez del Estado de Durango), 2: 200–257.

12. I base the facts presented here on my book *Poblar la frontera: La provincia de Santa Bárbara en Nueva Vizcaya durante los siglos XVI y XVII* (Zamora, Mexico: El Colegio de Michoacán, 2006).

13. This has already been discussed by Robert West in *The Mining Community in Northern New Spain: The Parral Mining District* (Berkeley: University of California Press, 1949), 49.

14. The first *alcalde mayor* assigned to the province of Sonora was named in 1640: see Luis Navarro García, *Sonora y Sinaloa en el siglo XVII* (Mexico City: Siglo XXI, 1992), 219.

15. The Topia road was prehispanic but this was not the case for the rest of the colonial roads that connected Mexico City with the main mining centers in the north. The road between Mexico and Zacatecas, for instance, did not exist before the Spanish conquest. See Chantal Cramaussel, ed., *Rutas de la Nueva España* (Zamora, Mexico: El Colegio de Michoacán, 2006).

16. *Encomienda* was a system of tribute labor extracted from Indians living on specific tracts of land; the king granted to a Spaniard (called a *encomendero*) the rights to the labor or products of an Indian village for one, two, three or more generations. *Repartimiento* was a system of forced

labor recruited from Indian villages and sent to Spanish ranches and mines for stipulated periods of time. In Opatería the issue of Indian mobility and its causes have been studied by Cynthia Radding, *Wandering Peoples: Colonialism, Ethnic Spaces, and Ecological Frontiers in Northwestern Mexico, 1700–1850* (Durham, NC: Duke University Press, 1997).

17. Several of these hideouts for fugitives were the Sierra de Barajas; the Babococo Cliffs (west of Batopilas, by the headwaters of the Mayo River: see Gerhard, *North Frontier*, 186); Tararecuo (an unknown location); and Guérachi (on the Verde River, north of Baborigame). These were mentioned in the report on the state of the province that Felipe de Neve sent to the king on December 1, 1783 (Archivo General de Indias, Guadalajara [hereafter, AGI], 268). A century and a half earlier, in a report describing the merits of the conduct of Mateo de Vesga, a hacienda owner from Santa Bárbara named Pedro Sánchez de Chávez wrote that "the rebels must be in the mountains around the Villa de las Culebras and in the Sierra de las Salinas where they always retreat in order to be beyond reach because it's a very dry land and there is no water." Spaniards could not reach them there because there was no water for their horses, and they complained of being unable to reach the Indians there (*hacer entrada*): AGI, 37, "Información de méritos de Mateo de Vesga," 1620.

18. Guillermo Porras Muñoz, *El nuevo descubrimiento de San José del Parral* (Mexico City: UNAM, 1988).

19. For a list of *encomiendas* granted in the seventeenth century, see Cramaussel, *Poblar la frontera*, 363–366. Some of these were granted for three generations, though several were petitioned "in perpetuity." There is no mention of Indians from the western flanks of the Sierra in the available documentation for either Parral or Chihuahua.

20. Silvio Zavala, *El servicio personal de los indios en la Nueva España* (Mexico City: Colegio de Mexico, 1984), 584–587.

21. Cramaussel, *Poblar la frontera*, 209–210.

22. The document was first cited by Oscar Alatriste, *Desarrollo de la industria y la comunidad minera de Hidalgo del Parral durante la segunda mitad del siglo XVIII (1765–1810)* (Mexico City: UNAM, 1983), 91n144; Archivo Histórico de Parral (hereafter, AHP), *Civil*, October 4, 1977, "Testimonio de superior despacho de cordillera librado por el señor gobernador de este reino por el que manda que los alcaldes mayores, justicias y sus tenientes se abstengan de repartir a hacienda, minas ni otro algún servicio u ocupación a los indios de los pueblos de sus respectivas jurisdicciones."

23. *Reales ordenanzas para la dirección, régimen y gobierno del importante cuerpo de la minería de Nueva España y de su tribunal general* (Madrid, 1783); there is a facsimile edition published by the UNAM in 1983. Unlike the *encomienda*, the *repartimiento* lasted all through the colonial era in agricultural zones such as San Bartolomé. A version of *repartimiento* was used for mining areas discovered in the late eighteenth century, such as San Diego del Río and Guarisamey, both located in the western parts of what is now the state of Durango. Xiximé and Tepehuan Indians from Sierra Madre Occidental had to work on these two sites as part of their tributary duties: see Cramaussel, "La vertiente occidental de la Sierra."

24. Cramaussel, *Poblar la frontera*, 205–219. At the beginning of the eighteenth century, the *repartimientos* authorized by the governor of Nueva Vizcaya corresponded only to the surrounding or nearby villages, but all the Indians were assigned to agricultural work in haciendas and none to mining duty, and their length of service varied. A new set of laws in 1746 limited the movement of Indians for *repartimiento* to ten leagues from their homeland, but other changes

included a rise in the allotted quota for each Indian population center to provide Indians for labor from one man in six to one in three; women were exempt and furthermore small settlements were allowed to keep up to twenty men to look after the crops and ensure their livelihood. By the middle of the eighteenth century, all the war *encomiendas* as well as *repartimiento* of non-Christianized Indians had all but disappeared, and an attempt was made to shift the source of labor to the mission Indians being ministered to by Franciscans and Jesuits.

25. It is estimated that about a thousand Indians were condemned to personal service in Santa Bárbara from 1631 to 1680. Most of these prisoners were sold to merchants, who took them to the main population centers of New Spain to be sold. See Cramaussel, *Poblar la frontera*, 200–203. For the Apaches at the end of the eighteenth century, see Matthew Babcock's essay in this volume.

26. AGI, Indiferente 102, Padrón de Parral, 1777, Archivo Parroquial de San Felipe El Real de Chihuahua.

27. Biblioteca Nacional de México, Lafragua Collection, no. 2/207.1, chapter 22, ff. 13–84 v. Cuihuiriachi was a *real de minas* close to the modern-day city of Cuahutémoc. It was discovered in 1686 and many settlers from Parral, as well as some coming from Sonora, settled there. The discovery of this *real de minas* is considered a precursor to the rise of Santa Eulalia and San Francisco del Cuellar de Chihuahua, where many miners moved in the early part of the eighteenth century.

28. The term "Ópata" never appears in the parish records. Ópata Indians were probably included in the "Sonoran" category. For the Ópatas, see Radding, *Wandering Peoples*, 24.

29. Sebastián González de Valdés, a Parral miner, obtained a work force from Sahuaripa during the second half of the seventeenth century (Archivo de San José del Parral, registros de matrimonios); he also claimed, however, never to have possessed an encomienda (AHP, 1655b, 882 in microfilm).

30. "Cuaderno de las cuentas de los indios yaquis y tarahumares que trabajaron en faenas desde 24 de febrero de 1776 como también de los que pasaron a las del Caiman" (Alatriste, *Desarrollo*, 89).

31. AHP, 1777, Civil, "Detención del gobernador de los indios yaquis y 18 indios de la nación citada por no llevar papel para trabajar en las haciendas" (Alatriste, *Desarrollo*, 80n134). Land was granted by the Crown (although not always titled) to all Indian pueblos, which usually got a square league. That is the reason why the Yaqui settlement in Parral is called a *barrio* (neighborhood) and not a *pueblo* (village).

32. AGI, Indiferente 102, "Padrón de Parral de 1777." The *real* of Aguacaliente was close to Cerro Gordo (the modern-day Villa Hidalgo, Durango), but this mining center's life was short-lived and its precise location is unknown.

33. AGI, Indiferente 102, "Padrón de San José del Parral de 1778."

34. Gerhard, *North Frontier*, 270–271.

35. The demographic decline during the sixteenth century was steep, and the population was reduced to one-fourth of the original, with many nations disappearing altogether; see Navarro García, *Sonora y Sinaloa*, 57–58.

36. For a study of regional history, see Benito Ramírez Mesa, *Economía y sociedad en Sinaloa, 1591–1900* (Culiacán, Mexico: Dificur/Universidad Autónoma de Sinaloa, 1992).

37. The Guasabe Indians lived on the banks of the Sinaloa River. No one has yet located the homeland of the Bacoregui Indians. Cahita is a linguistic subfamily spoken by those Indians but

it was divided in several languages, most of them extinct nowadays: see Gilberto López Castillo, *El poblamiento en tierras de indios cahitas: Transformaciones de la territorialidad en el contexto de las misiones Jesuitas, 1591–1790* (Mexico City: El Colegio de Sinaloa/Siglo XXI, 2010).

38. Tahua was a Taracahita language that was spoken in the Culiacán region (Gerhard, *North Frontier*, 257); Archivo Parroquial de Nuestra Señora del Rosario, Rosario, Sin., Book 1 of Marriages, 1688–1707. The pueblos that appear more often are San Pedro de Culiacán and Sinaloa. In the province of Culiacán there were also Abuya, Olangueruto, Guepaca (?), Navolato, Capirato, Contiaca, Santiago de Diabuto (location unknown), San Lorenzo de Távala, Santiago Beyavito (?), Badiraguato, and Yacobita. Those along the Sinaloa River included Mocorito, San Pedro Guasabe, Tamazula, Chicorato, Bamoa, and Vaca y Toro. The same pueblo names appear in the baptismal records. As for the information taken from marriage records, scholars have consulted only part of the files. The parish archive remains unclassified and many of these records have seriously deteriorated and are in very fragile conditions.

39. Copala and San Sebastián had been the property of Francisco de Ibarra during the sixteenth century, but as was the case for El Rosario, the local Indian population never recovered from the demographic collapse of the sixteenth century: see Gerhard, *North Frontier*, 252–256. For Chiametla, see Álvarez, *El indio y la sociedad colonial norteña*, 67–101.

40. Luis Carlos Quiñones, "Composición demográfica de los asentamientos tepehuanos de la región sur de la Nueva Vizcaya: Una aproximación a partir de las uniones matrimoniales," in *La Sierra Tepehuana: Asentamientos y movimientos de población*, ed. Chantal Cramaussel and Sara Ortelli (Zamora, Mexico: El Colegio de Michoacán/Universidad Juárez del Estado de Durango, 2006), 189–205.

41. Another example that does not involve *reales de minas* but that supports the importance of political boundaries within the viceroyalty's provinces in the transfer of Indian labor is the case of Sombrerete, located in the central part of the *altiplano*, between Zacatecas and Durango. During the eighteenth century, miners from Sombrerete asked in vain to receive Indian workers from the jurisdiction of Nombre de Dios (an enclave abutting the borders of Nueva Galicia and Nueva Vizcaya, but under the direct control of viceregal authorities in Mexico City) or Indians from the valley of Guadiana, which was part of Nueva Vizcaya (Dimas Arenas, Migración a corta distancia).

42. Cramaussel, "La vertiente occidental de la Sierra."

43. In the baptismal records there is a reference to a *ranchería* of Yaqui Indians in 1736 (from the marriage entries for May 30, 1736). It states that the governor, Joseph de la Cruz, a native of Torichi, in the jurisdiction of Ostimuri, asked to marry María Yoquiqui. Mentioned alongside them are several Indian mine workers. In 1752 there is a mention of a marriage license for a groom who had come from the *"pueblo de yaquis"* to be a miner's servant (Archivo Parroquial de Nuestra Señora del Rosario, "Partida de matrimonio del 8 de mayo de 1752").

44. Gerhard, *North Frontier*, 268 (Gerhard uses as his source a document from the Bibliothèque Nationale de Paris, Fonds Mexicains, 201, fol. 29v). Other authors offer different data. The number of Spaniards in the coastal provinces of Sonora and Sinaloa during the 1760s reached barely twenty-five thousand, while the Indians in the Yaqui missions numbered around twenty-one thousand, though sources indicate that in some of these missions eight out of ten Indians lived outside of them. See Sergio Ortega Noriega, "Crecimiento y crisis del sistema misional" and Martha Ortega Soto, "Colonización al inicio del siglo XVIII," both in *Tres siglos de historia sonorense (1530–1830)*, ed. Sergio Ortega and Ignacio del Río (Mexico City: UNAM, 1993), 167,

235. The Yaqui diaspora was studied by Edward Spicer in *Los yaquis: Historia de una cultura* (Mexico City: UNAM, 1994), map on p. 158. As Cynthia Radding mentioned, Yaquis and Mayos were already the most numerous Indian groups in northwestern New Spain in 1637.

45. Measles, smallpox, and typhus lowered population growth in Mexico until the second half of the nineteenth century; later, those diseases tended to be endemic and less lethal. For a recent study on smallpox during this time period, see Chantal Cramaussel, Mario Alberto Magaña, and David Carbajal, eds., *El impacto demográfico de la viruela en México de la época colonial al siglo XX*, 3 vols. (Zamora, Mexico: El Colegio de Michoacán, 2010). On the population decrease caused by epidemics in the Mandan case, see Elizabeth Fenn's essay in this volume.

46. Archivo Parroquial de Álamos, Álamos, Son., Entry of April 6, 1776, Marriage, Book no. 7; see the reference to Cocorim in Book no. 2 (1708–1736).

47. Bernd Hausberger, *Für Gott und König: Die Mission der Jesuiten in kolonialen Mexiko* (Munich: R. Oldenburg, 2000), 533.

48. At the beginning of the nineteenth century, Ignacio Zúñiga commented on this issue: "The Yaquis and Mayos are the same nation that speaks the same language that is entirely understood and intelligible by both groups . . . their pueblos . . . follow the flood valleys of the Sinaloa, Fuerte, Mayo, and Yaqui rivers for over 140 leagues." See Ignacio Zúñiga, *Rápida ojeada al Estado de Sonora* (Hermosillo, Mexico: Gobierno del Estado de Sonora, 1985), 93.

49. The precise locations of these pueblos are unknown.

50. Real Academia de la Historia (in Madrid), *Memorias de la Nueva España, Tome XIX*, "Relación de las misiones . . . por el visitador Juan Ortiz Zapata (1678)," ff. 255–356v.

51. Radding, *Wandering Peoples*, 154.

52. This had also been the case in Parral during the previous century.

53. Documents cited by Alatriste, *Desarrollo*, 80.

54. See, for example, Archivo Parroquial de Nuestra Señora del Rosario, Marriage Books 3 and 4 (from 1754–1773 and 1776–1796, respectively). In 1776 Bernardo Torres, a "free mulatto" and *barretero*, wanted to marry María Guadalupe Mendoza, whom the parish priest referred to also as a "free mulatto" even though later in the same document she was called a daughter of *caciques* (*india cacique*; her parents are called *indios caciques*); see also the uncatalogued marriage records.

55. There is a very good catalogue of documents for this parish archive by Cynthia Radding, *Catálogo del Archivo de la Parroquia de la Purísima Concepción de los Álamos, 1685–1900* (Hermosillo, Mexico: Centro Regional del Noreste/ INAH, 1976).

56. Silver was registered and given the royal imprimatur first in Parral (until 1695) and later in El Rosario. The average number of baptisms per year for the period between 1745 and 1754 was twenty-six, but the number increases almost fivefold by the 1760s. The history of Álamos has had no academic study but there are important bits of information in the bibliography of Juan Vidal Castillo, *Álamos: Por los siglos de los siglos* (Hermosillo, Mexico: Private printing, 2007). See also Roberto Acosta, "Ciudad de Álamos," *Memoria de la Academia Mexicana de Historia* 5 (1946), 38–67. The best treatment of the subject (though it focuses only on the time period of the mining boom) is a thesis by Luis Arrioja Viruell, "Minería y comercio en Álamos, 1769–1785" (Escuela Nacional de Antropología e Historia, 1999). Complementary information exists in López Castillo, *El poblamiento*, and in my article "Poblar en tierras de muchos indios: La región de Álamos en los siglos XVII y XVIII," *Región y Sociedad* 53 (2012), 11–54. Robert West, in *Sonora: Its Geographical Personality* (Austin: University of Texas Press, 1995), 55, mentioned that in 1776 nearly two-thirds of the silver produced in Sonora and northern Sinaloa came from the Álamos district.

57. As was the case in other mining centers, in Álamos there are numerous baptismal entries for Indians without references to their places of origin (and that therefore could be incorporated into haciendas) or for Indians from neighboring *rancherías*, but the number of these entries was always much lower than the number of mission Indians. See Cramaussel, "Poblar en tierras de muchos indios."

58. The document relating to this population movement has been described in Navarro García, *Sinaloa y Sonora*, 128–137.

59. These were Nuestra Señora de Guadalupe de Tabaca, Nuestra Señora del Pilar de Osobampo, and Nuestra Señora de Aranzazu de Tábelo. During the eighteenth century the first two of these haciendas had a higher number of baptized Indians than the settlement itself. The Mayo River was wide and fast flowing before dams were built in modern times, and it was therefore hardly navigable.

60. The first *encomiendas* in Sinaloa were granted during the sixteenth century (Gerhard, *North Frontier*, 275). These most likely corresponded to the numerous "nations" mentioned in the sources, though they really referred to specific pueblos and not different ethnic groups (such as Guasabe, Huite, Macoyahui, Basiroa, Conicari, and Tehueco). The same thing happened in the Sierra with names such as Chínipas, Témoris, and perhaps also the Tubare Indians. There were Mayo Indians still living in Basiroa in the eighteenth century. Regarding the relationship between *encomiendas* and Indian "nations" for central Nueva Vizcaya, see Chantal Cramaussel, "De cómo los españoles identificaban a los indios: Naciones y encomiendas en la Nueva Vizcaya central," in *Nómadas y sedentarios en el norte de México: Homenaje a la Dra. Beatriz Braniff*, ed. Marie Areti Hers, José Luis Mirafuentes, and Miguel Vallebueno (Mexico City: UNAM, 2000), 175–303.

61. The hacienda of San Antonio de Basiroa was first mentioned in the records in 1670, while Tapizuelas is listed in 1682. The *estancia* of San José de Maquipo is alluded to in 1699, as well as those of Yoricaichi, Los Mezcales, Taimuco, and Cerro Colorado. The following year, there is a reference to Guircoba, and in 1701 Tobaca and El Tábelo are mentioned; by 1707, there are references to Santa Ana del Arroyo Hondo, Osobampo, and Gerocoa, and in 1709 Plomosas is discussed. During the seventeenth century, Tapizuelas comprised three *sitios*, making it the largest (a *sitio de ganado mayor* was a unit of measurement equivalent to approximately 4,338 acres intended for cattle); Santa Lucía was two and a half *sitios* in area, and Osobampo two and three quarters *sitios* plus five *caballerias de labor*. But in the following decades, the largest and most populated hacienda was Tobaca, with twelve *sitios*, followed by San Antonio del Chino with eight and a half *sitios* (López Castillo, *El poblamiento*, 288–292).

62. Archivo de la Parroquia de la Purísima Concepción de Álamos, Marriage Book 1 (1788–1793, 186 pp.) and Marriage Book 2 (1793–1798, 196 pp.).

63. Those Indians "that have no domicile or dwelling anywhere" were considered vagrants, and those born outside the domains of the Spanish king were "foreigners" (Archivo de la Parroquia de la Purísima Concepción de Álamos, Libro de Edictos). This information regarding marriages was in response to an edict from the Bishop of Durango from August 31, 1754. The edict stipulates that "the parish priest can marry them as long as they are not vagrants or foreigners or from distant lands." The aspiring grooms had to prove their freedom and that they did not come from a settlement greater than twenty leagues' distance from the place where they wanted to marry. With these measures, the Crown tried to control the movement of people and especially of Indians in order to force them to live in their own pueblos and fulfill their tributary duties.

For the parish priests of Álamos these ordinances did not represent a major problem, because the Yaqui River was twenty leagues away and the Mayo River only five leagues.

64. Archivo de la Parroquia de la Purísima Concepción de Álamos, Marriage Book 7, "Libro primero en que se asientan las informaciones matrimoniales de indios de esta parroquia del real de Nuestra Señora de la Concepción de Álamos siendo cura interino D. Juan Nicolás Quiroz y Mora." It starts in October 1788 and is 187 pages long.

65. They came mostly from Echejoa, Navojoa, Santa Cruz, and Cuirimpo; there are also recurring references to nearby missions such as Tesia, Conicari, and Camoa. Others came from Tepahui, Batacosa, Bayoreca, and Maccoyahui, pueblos located south of the Ostimuri province, but also located in the Mayo River basin. There are also frequent references to people from along the Yaqui River: Potam, Vicam, Cocorim, Rahum, Huirivis; along the Fuerte River: San Miguel del Fuerte (also known as Caparoa), Toro, Vaca, Mochicagua (also known as Mochicahui, nowadays Los Mochis), Sibirijoa, and Tehueco; and along the Sinaloa River: Sinaloa and Bamoa.

66. Témoris was part of the mission of San Ignacio del Yaqui in 1678. See "Visita de Ortiz Zapata," in Evelyn Hu-Dehart, *Adaptación y resistencia en el Yaquimi: Los yaquis durante la colonia* (Mexico City: CIESAS, 1995), 95. For their part, Sivijoa, El Fuerte, and Sinaloa were the places of origin for most foreign Indian grooms. Bayoreca and Culiacán are next in the number of references. The links with Sonora were not as close: there are isolated references to Indians coming from Santa Ana, Horcasitas, San Marcial, and Tepachi. The references for those Indians coming from Ostimuri were for the most part from San Antonio de la Huerta and Bayoreca. There are scattered references to Indians from Batopilas and El Sitio. Generally speaking, non-Indians who married in Álamos came from a wider variety of places, both in Nueva Vizcaya as well as Nueva Galicia and central New Spain. Archivo Parroquial de Nuestra Señora de Álamos, Partidas de matrimonios, 1788–1798.

67. AGI, 347, "Carta del misionero franciscano del río Fuerte al obispo de Sonora" April 27, 1784.

68. AGI, 563, "Carta del Br. Manuel María de Avilés al obispo de Sonora," Bamoa, December 20, 1790.

69. Most of the Indian women from both the Yaqui and Mayo rivers used "Yoquiqui" after their first name; Indian men, on the other hand, did use last names. With the exception of *caciques*, who sometimes kept an Indian name, all males had surnames, a unique occurrence throughout the northern borderlands. Among the last names recorded in the parish records are Usacamea, Obomea, Tamisuamea, Buanamea, Baisua, Guaque, Batomea, Sequamu, Cauchenea, Tequiamea, Guanamea, Seguina, Osimea, Buitimea, Anuamoa, Tahuitimui, and Anuamea.

70. These are probably Huitis, north of Vaca mission, on the banks of the Fuerte River.

71. The location of this *ranchería* is unknown.

72. The Taymuco *ranchería* was located northeast of Álamos, at the foot of the Sierra. Gecopaco's location is unknown.

73. This was an old mission located along the Mayo River, north of Álamos, in the province of Ostimuri.

74. This was south of the Chico River, in the province of Ostimuri.

75. AGI, 2736, "Carta al rey de Bernardo Bonavia, comandante general de las provincias internas," Durango, June 28, 1803. Ostimuri and Álamos had different *alcaldes mayores* at that time.

76. Archivo de la Parroquia de Nuestra Señora de la Concepción de Álamos, baptismal records, 1782. Matus is a Yaqui last name.

77. All quotations are from Archivo Parroquial de Nuestra Señora de la Concepción de Álamos, Libro de Edictos.

78. Chantal Cramaussel, "El mestizaje, las familias pluriétinicas, de la villa de San Felipe El Real de Chihuahua, y la sorpresiva multiplicación de los mulatos en el septentrión novohispano del siglo XVIII," in *Familias pluriétnicas y mestizaje*, ed. David Carbajal (Guadalajara, Mexico: University of Guadalajara, in press).

79. Ibid. In agricultural areas with many haciendas, such as in Nombre de Dios, south of Nueva Vizcaya, at this time mulattoes constituted about 90 percent of the population; half a century earlier, they had only been about one-third of the population.

80. Multiethnic families were couples married by the Church that had offspring with different assigned categories of "quality" (*calidad*).

81. For this reason, there are doubts about the argument put forth by Susan Deeds that claims the missions were important centers of cultural exchange; see her *Defiance and Deference in Mexico's Colonial North: Indians Under Spanish Rule in Nueva Vizcaya* (Austin: University of Texas Press, 2003).

82. Some bibliographies regarding the general history of the area during the colonial era include the following: Phillip Hadley, *Minería y sociedad de Santa Eulalia, Chihuahua 1709–1750*) (Mexico City: Fondo de Cultura Económica, 1979), and Cheryl Martin, *Governance and Society in Colonial Mexico* (Stanford, CA: Stanford University Press, 1996). With regard to the early colonial period, see Salvador Álvarez, "Agricultural Colonization and Mining Colonization. The Area of Chihuahua During the First Half of the Eighteenth Century," in *In Quest of Mineral Wealth: Aboriginal and Colonial Mining and Metallurgy in Spanish America*, ed. Alan Craig and Robert West (Baton Rouge: Louisiana State University Press, 1994), 171–220; a shorter version can be found in Chantal Cramaussel, "Orígenes de la ciudad de Chihuahua," in *Atlas histórico de la ciudad de Chihuahua* (Chihuahua, Mexico: Cementos de Chihuahua, 2009), 18–58.

83. Among the most numerous groups of foreign Indians mentioned in the parish records are 154 Sonorans, 74 Tarahumaras, 46 Apaches, 20 Pananas, 19 Sinaloas, 13 Yaquis, and 8 Indians from New Mexico; see Salvador Treviño Castro, *El real de minas de San Francisco de Cuéllar de Chihuahua, 1709–1718: Imagen de una sociedad en crecimiento* (Chihuahua, Mexico: Private printing, 2009), 40.

84. This was a common occurrence in Nueva Vizcaya also and has been studied by Susan Deeds in *Defiance and Deference*.

85. Archivo Parroquial de San Felipe El Real de Chihuahua, Registro de bautizos de la parroquia de San Felipe (1736–1760).

86. A few of them kept their last name, but this appears to not be as common here as it was in Álamos.

87. AGI, 302, "Lista de ranchos y haciendas afectados por las hostilidades de los apaches," Durango, December 4, 1787, written by José Antonio de Olvera, secretary of the *Real Hacienda*. There were several small ranches in the mountains around the Chihuahua mines before the increase in attacks by the Apaches. Among these were the watering hole of San Juan, which was depopulated. Olvera claims that he "saw it settled by many Yaquis and Pimas that worked scrounging for scraps of leaded minerals (*metales plomosos*) from small but rich veins scattered throughout the Sierra they called Chihuahua El Viejo, but these have all been abandoned due to the predations of the barbarous Apaches." It is worth noting that while the descendants of captive Apaches and slaves in general were considered illegitimate, the Yaquis lived within families, with their wives and also perhaps with their children.

88. For the case of Parral, see Cramaussel, *Poblar la frontera*, chapter 4. For the wrong interpretation, see Ignacio del Río, "Sobre la aparición."

89. See the information from AGI, Indiferente 102, with the census from 1771 to 1779,where there are numerous references to the presence of Yaquis in Zape, Tesaes, Cajuirichi, Tabahueto, and San Agustín, a *real de minas* in the Sierra Tarahumara. Yaquis were also the main ethnic element of the population of Guasabas in the Ópata homeland and were also very numerous in Pitic toward the end of the colonial era (see Medina Bustos, *Vida y muerte*, 147). This was also the case for San Antonio de la Huerta and the de la Cieneguilla real (see Radding, *Wandering Peoples*, 144). Yaquis also migrated to Baja California: see Hu-Dehart, *Adaptación y resistencia en el Yaquimi*, 44–45. For a recent study, see Magaña Mancillas, *Indios, soldados y rancheros*.

90. Nonetheless, it requires long-term studies based on parish archives: José Marcos Medina published his work on Hermosillo in 1997; I have contributed on Parral, San Bartolomé, and Chihuahua since 2006; Mario Alberto Magaña Mancillas went through all the records regarding Baja California in 2010; Raúl García Flores is studying Linares in northeastern New Spain and Tomás Dimas Arenas Sombrerete (see the bibliographical references in note 1). Fortunately, new dissertations on this topic are now in process in Mexico. The foundation of the *Red de historia demográfica* in 2009, which had twenty-four members in 2012, gave a significant boost to the renewed interest in this academic field.

Chapter 8

1. Baron Carondelet to Aranda, c. 1793 ("unmeasured ambition"), in Louis Houck, ed., *The Spanish Regime in Missouri*, 2 vols. (Chicago: R. R. Donnelley and Sons, 1909), 2: 11–12.

2. Vicente Manuel de Zespedes to Luis de las Casas, June 20, 1790 ("distinguished"), quoted in David J. Weber, *The Spanish Frontier in North America* (New Haven, CT: Yale University Press, 1992), 272 for quote; Barthelemi Tardiveau to Count de Aranda, July 17, 1792 and Josef Vidal to Marquis de Casa-Calvo, September 27, 1800, in Houck, *Spanish Regime in Missouri*, 1: 360 and 2: 289–290; Stephen Aron, *American Confluence: The Missouri Frontier from Borderland to Border State* (Bloomington: Indiana University Press, 2006), 71–73; William E. Foley, *The Genesis of Missouri: From Wilderness Outpost to Statehood* (Columbia: University of Missouri Press, 1989), 57, 66; Abraham P. Nasatir, *Borderland in Retreat: From Spanish Louisiana to the Far Southwest* (Albuquerque: University of New Mexico Press, 1976), 35–36; Kathleen DuVal, "Choosing Enemies: The Prospects for an Anti-American Alliance in the Louisiana Territory," *Arkansas Historical Quarterly* 62 (Autumn 2003), 234; Francisco Rendon to Don Jose de Galvez, February 12, 1785, in *Documents of the Emerging Nation: U.S. Foreign Relations, 1775–1789*, ed. Mary A. Giunta (Wilmington, DE: Scholarly Resources, 1998), 197; Adam Rothman, *Slave Country: American Expansion and the Origins of the Deep South* (Cambridge, MA: Harvard University Press, 2005), 15.

3. Foley, *Genesis of Missouri*, 98–107; Peter J. Kastor, *The Nation's Crucible: The Louisiana Purchase and the Creation of America* (New Haven, CT: Yale University Press, 2004), 26–34.

4. John Elmsley to Peter Russell, November 26, 1797, in *The Correspondence of the Honourable Peter Russell*, 3 vols., ed. E. A. Cruikshank (Toronto: Ontario Historical Society, 1932–1936), 2: 28. For Upper Canada's population, see Douglas McCalla, *Planting the Province: The Economic History of Upper Canada, 1784–1870* (Toronto: University of Toronto Press, 1992), 15–17, 249.

5. The Zespedes quote is from Weber, *Spanish Frontier*, 275, 280. For Louisiana, see Barthelemi Tardiveau to Count de Aranda, July 17, 1792, in Houck, *Spanish Regime in Missouri*, 1: 360–

364; Gilbert C. Din, "The Immigration Policy of Governor Esteban Miro in Spanish Louisiana," *Southwestern Historical Quarterly* 73 (October 1969), 156; Gilbert C. Din, "Spain's Immigration Policy in Louisiana and the American Penetration, 1792–1803," *Southwestern Historical Quarterly* 76 (January 1973), 256–259; Nasatir, *Borderland in Retreat*, 37; Walter Nugent, *Habits of Empire: A History of American Expansion* (New York: Vintage, 2009), 50; Sylvia L. Hilton, "Loyalty and Patriotism on North American Frontiers: Being and Becoming Spanish in the Mississippi Valley, 1776–1803," in *Nexus of Empire: Negotiating Loyalty and Identity in the Revolutionary Borderlands, 1760s–1820s*, ed. Sylvia L. Hilton and Gen Allen Smith (Gainesville: University Press of Florida, 2010), 16. For Upper Canada, see David Wood, *Making Ontario: Agricultural Colonization and Landscape Re-Creation Before the Railway* (Montreal: McGill-Queens University Press, 2000), 22–28; McCalla, *Planting the Province*, 15–17; and Donald G. Creighton, *The Empire of the St. Lawrence, 1760–1850* (Toronto: Ryerson, 1956), 116–123.

6. The quote is from Patrick Murray to John Graves Simcoe, December 23, 1791, MG 23 H I 1, (Simcoe Transcripts) 3rd ser., 1: 367, National Archives of Canada; J. Leitch Wright, Jr., *Britain and the American Frontier, 1783–1815* (Athens: University of Georgia Press, 1975), 2.

7. Zenon Trudeau to Manuel Gayoso de Lemos, January 15, 1798, in Houck, *Spanish Regime in Missouri*, 2: 251; Nicolas de Finiels, *An Account of Upper Louisiana*, ed. Carl J. Ekberg and William E. Foley (Columbia: University of Missouri Press, 1989), 34–36; Aron, *American Confluence*, 69–77, 80–82, 87–89; Foley, *Genesis of Missouri*, 64; Nasatir, *Borderland in Retreat*, 41–42; Weber, *Spanish Frontier*, 282–284; Kathleen DuVal, *The Native Ground: Indians and Colonists in the Heart of the Continent* (Philadelphia: University of Pennsylvania Press, 2006), 178; DuVal, "Choosing Enemies," 235–236; Jay Gitlin, *The Bourgeois Frontier: French Towns, French Traders, and American Expansion* (New Haven, CT: Yale University Press, 2010), 43–44.

8. Zenon Trudeau to Manuel Gayoso de Lemos, January 15, 1798, in Houck, *Spanish Regime in Missouri*, 2: 255–256; Din, "Immigration Policy of Miro," 166, 173; Din, "Spain's Immigration Policy," 255, 276; Foley, *Genesis of Missouri*, 58–59; Weber, *Spanish Frontier*, 280–281.

9. Louis Guillaume Otto to Comte de Montmorin, March 5, 1787, in Giunta, *Documents of the Emerging Nation*, 210–211; Weber, *Spanish Frontier*, 281–282; James E. Lewis, Jr., *The American Union and the Problem of Neighborhood: The United States and the Collapse of the Spanish Empire, 1783–1829* (Chapel Hill: University of North Carolina Press, 1998), 14–22; DuVal, *Native Ground*, 174–175; Hilton, "Loyalty and Patriotism," 15.

10. For the nationalist teleology, see Francis S. Philbrick, *The Rise of the West, 1754–1830* (New York: Harper and Row, 1965), 178–179; and Jon Kukla, *A Wilderness So Immense: The Louisiana Purchase and the Destiny of America* (New York: Knopf, 2003), 133. For the contingency of allegiances, see John Mack Faragher, *Daniel Boone: The Life and Legend of an American Pioneer* (New York: Henry Holt, 1992).

11. Aron, *American Confluence*, 78; Din, "Immigration Policy of Miro," 161; Weber, *Spanish Frontier*, 279.

12. George Morgan to Don Diego de Gardoqui, August 20, 1789, in Houck, *Spanish Regime in Missouri*, 1: 288–290; Aron, *American Confluence*, 78, 82; Foley, *Genesis of Missouri*, 67–68; Weber, *Spanish Frontier*, 280.

13. George Morgan to Don Diego de Gardoqui, August 20, 1789, and Baron Carondelet to Don Luis de las Casas, April 7, 1794, in Houck, *Spanish Regime in Missouri*, 1: 288 and 2: 24–26; Din, "Immigration Policy of Miro," 164–165.

14. Esteban Rodriguez Miro to Campo de Alange, August 11, 1792 ("at first glance"); Miro and Martin Navarro to Antonio Valdes, September 24, 1787 ("we ought"), quoted in Hilton, "Loyalty and Patriotism," 10, and 13.

15. Aron, *American Confluence*, 82; Din, "Immigration Policy of Miro," 156–158, 162–164; William S. Coker, "The Bruins and the Formulation of Spanish Immigration Policy in the Old Southwest, 1787–88," in *The Spanish in the Mississippi Valley, 1762–1804*, ed. Francis McDermott (Urbana: University of Illinois Press, 1974), 61–71; Foley, *Genesis of Missouri*, 104; Weber, *Spanish Frontier*, 281; Jack D. L. Holmes, "Irish Priests in Spanish Natchez," *Journal of Mississippi History* 29 (1967), 176–179.

16. John Gordon to George Profit, June 25, 1785, quoted in Hilton, "Loyalty and Patriotism," 18 for "May God"; Weber, *Spanish Frontier*, 278–281.

17. Din, "Immigration Policy of Miro," 169; C. Richard Arena, "Land Settlement Policies and Practices in Spanish Louisiana," in McDermott, *Spanish in the Mississippi Valley*, 54–60; R. Douglas Hurt, *Nathan Boone and the American Frontier* (Columbia: University of Missouri Press, 1998), 25; Nasatir, *Borderland in Retreat*, 37; Hilton, "Loyalty and Patriotism," 11–12.

18. Houck, *Spanish Regime in Missouri*, 1: 275n1; Aron, *American Confluence*, 82–83; Din, "Immigration Policy of Miro," 169–170; Foley, *Genesis of Missouri*, 60–61.

19. Esteban Miro to Don Antonio Valdes, May 21, 1789, and George Morgan to Don Diego de Gardoqui, August 20, 1789 ("avaricious"), in Houck, *Spanish Regime in Missouri*, 1: 277–278, 288–297; Din, "Immigration Policy of Miro," 170–171; Foley, *Genesis of Missouri*, 62–63.

20. John Graves Simcoe to Evan Nepean, December 3, 1789, in *The Correspondence of Lieut. Governor John Graves Simcoe, with Allied Documents Relating to His Administration of the Government of Upper Canada*, 5 vols., ed. E. A. Cruikshank (Toronto: Ontario Historical Society, 1923–1931), 1: 7–8; Alan Taylor, *The Divided Ground: Indians, Settlers, and the Northern Borderland of the American Revolution* (New York: Knopf, 2006), 268–270.

21. John Graves Simcoe to Henry Dundas, August 12, 1791, and November 23, 1792, in Cruikshank, *Correspondence of Simcoe*, 1: 50–51, 264; Fred Landon, *Western Ontario and the American Frontier* (Toronto: Ryerson, 1941), 6.

22. Simcoe to Henry Dundas, June 30, 1791, and Simcoe, "Proclamation," February 7, 1792, in Cruikshank, *Correspondence of Simcoe*, 1: 27, 108; Lilian F. Gates, *Land Policies of Upper Canada* (Toronto: University of Toronto Press, 1968), 28; E. A. Cruikshank, "Petitions for Grants of Land, 1792–6," Ontario Historical Society, *Papers and Records*, vol. 24 (1927), 17–144. For prices in the United States, see David Maldwyn Ellis, *Landlords and Farmers in the Hudson-Mohawk Region, 1790–1850* (Ithaca, NY: Cornell University Press, 1946), 25; and Malcolm J. Rohrbough, *The Land Office Business: The Settlement and Administration of American Public Lands, 1789–1837* (New York: Oxford University Press, 1968), 10.

23. John Munro to John Graves Simcoe, March 14, 1792 ("the pleasure"), Simcoe Letterbook for 1792–1793, Manuscript #558, Huntington Library; Cruikshank, "Petitions for Grants of Land," 17; Gerald M. Craig, *Upper Canada: The Formative Years, 1784–1841* (Toronto: McClelland and Stewart, 1963), 46–47, 67, 70–71; Michael Smith, *A Geographical View of the Province of Upper Canada; and Promiscuous Remarks on the Government* (Philadelphia: Thomas and Robert Desilver, 1813), 51; Wood, *Making Ontario*, 23–27. For the origins of the settlers, see David W. Smith, Report, January 30, 1796, RG 1, A-II-1 (Surveyor General's Reports, Crown Lands), vol. 1: 33 (reel MS-3696), Archives of Ontario.

24. John Cosens Ogden, *A Tour Through Upper and Lower Canada By a Citizen of the United States* (Litchfield, CT, 1799), 34; J. K. Johnson, *Becoming Prominent: Regional Leadership in Upper Canada, 1791–1841* (Montreal: McGill-Queens University Press, 1989), 24, 30.

25. Smith, *Geographical View*, iii; Francis Gore to William Windham, October 1, 1806, in Douglas Brymner, ed., *Report on Canadian Archives, 1892* (Ottawa, 1893), 37.

26. Alan Taylor, *The Civil War of 1812: American Citizens, British Subjects, Irish Rebels, and Indian Allies* (New York: Knopf, 2010), 62–63.

27. Nugent, *Habits of Empire*, 47, 53; Gordon S. Wood, *Empire of Liberty: A History of the Early Republic, 1789–1815* (New York: Oxford University Press, 2009), 130–131; Malcolm MacLeod, "Fortress Ontario or Forlorn Hope? Simcoe and the Defence of Upper Canada," *Canadian Historical Review* 53 (1972), 168.

28. Din, "Spain's Immigration Policy," 266–267; Foley, *Genesis of Missouri*, 76–78; Weber, *Spanish Frontier*, 289–290; Wood, *Empire of Liberty*, 201.

29. Zenon Trudeau to Manuel Gayoso de Lemos, January 15, 1798, in Houck, *Spanish Regime in Missouri*, 2: 247–256; Finiels, *Account of Upper Louisiana*, 36–37; Foley, *Genesis of Missouri*, 77, 80–92; R. Hurt, *Nathan Boone and the American Frontier*, 25–26; David B. Gracy, *Moses Austin: His Life* (San Antonio, TX: Trinity University Press, 1987), 64–65; Nasatir, *Borderland in Retreat*, 38.

30. Landon, *Western Ontario*, 1–3, 17–20; McCalla, *Planting the Province*, 15.

31. Aron, *American Confluence*, 107–113; DuVal, "Choosing Enemies," 251; Foley, *Genesis of Missouri*, 78–79; Nasatir, *Borderland in Retreat*, 49–50; Weber, *Spanish Frontier*, 291.

32. Aron, *American Confluence*, 117–118.

33. Rufus King to Christopher Gore, September 6, 1803 ("Nothing"), in *The Life and Correspondence of Rufus King*, 6 vols., ed. Charles R. King (New York: G. P. Putnam's Sons, 1897), 4: 303; Aron, *American Confluence*, 116–120.

34. Benjamin Mortimer, Journal, May 13, 1798, in Leslie R. Gray, ed., "From Bethlehem to Fairfield—1798," *Ontario History* 46 (Spring and Winter 1954), 116; Metchie J. E. Budka, ed., "Journey to Niagara, 1805: From the Diary of Julian Ursyn Niemcewicz," *New York Historical Society Quarterly* 44 (January 1960), 105 ("I believe"); Smith, *Geographical View*, iii ("in order"), 211–212.

35. Erastus Granger to Henry Dearborn, September 14, 1807 ("no consequence"), Thomas Jefferson Papers, Image #408, American Memory Series (online), Library of Congress; John Douglas, *Medical Topography of Upper Canada* (Boston: Science Publications, 1985; reprint of London, 1819), 4.

36. Taylor, *Civil War of 1812*.

37. Craig, *Upper Canada*, 125–130; Johnson, *Becoming Prominent*, 113; Wood, *Making Ontario*, 26, 40.

38. David J. Weber, *The Mexican Frontier, 1821–1846* (Albuquerque: University of New Mexico Press, 1982), 10, 159, 162; Nugent, *Habits of Empire*, 134–136; Gary Clayton Anderson, *The Conquest of Texas: Ethnic Cleansing in the Promised Land, 1820–1875* (Norman: University of Oklahoma Press, 2005), 18–26.

39. Anderson, *Conquest of Texas*, 26–29.

40. Gregg Cantrell, *Stephen F. Austin: Empresario of Texas* (New Haven, CT: Yale University Press, 1999), 107–108; Andrés Reséndez, *Changing National Identities at the Frontier: Texas and New Mexico, 1800–1850* (New York: Cambridge University Press, 2005), 19–22; Anderson, *Conquest of Texas*, 18–42.

41. Antonio Martinez and Francisco Ruiz quoted in Reséndez, *Changing National Identities*, 27 ("too small" and "honest"); Nugent, *Habits of Empire*, 134–136.

42. Reséndez, *Changing National Identities*, 73–74; Anderson, *Conquest of Texas*, 44.

43. Reséndez, *Changing National Identities*, 28–29; Weber, *Mexican Frontier*, 162–163; Anderson, *Conquest of Texas*, 46–48.

44. Reséndez, *Changing National Identities*, 28–29; Cantrell, *Stephen F. Austin*, 117–118, 124; Nugent, *Habits of Empire*, 142–144; Weber, *Mexican Frontier*, 163.

45. Cantrell, *Stephen F. Austin*, 104–170; Weber, *Mexican Frontier*, 164; Anderson, *Conquest of Texas*, 45–46.

46. Cantrell, *Stephen F. Austin*, 104–170, 176–177; Nugent, *Habits of Empire*, 134, 136, 137–138; Weber, *Mexican Frontier*, 164–166.

47. Cantrell, *Stephen F. Austin*, 182–184, including Stephen F. Austin to John A. Williams and B. J. Thompson, December 14, 1826 ("foolish"), quoted on 183; Reséndez, *Changing National Identities*, 40–44 (Declaration of the Republic of Fredonia, December 21, 1826, quoted on 44); Anderson, *Conquest of Texas*, 60–64.

48. Reséndez, *Changing National Identities*, 44–45; Cantrell, *Stephen F. Austin*, 183–185 (p. 184 includes the quotation from Stephen F. Austin to John A. Williams and B. J. Thompson, December 14, 1826: "jeopardising"), and Austin to the inhabitants of the colony, January 22, 1827: "unnatural"); Anderson, *Conquest of Texas*, 64.

49. Manuel de Mier y Teran to Guadalupe Victoria, March 28, 1828 ("If it is bad"), in Jackson, *Texas by Teran*, 33; Reséndez, *Changing National Identities*, 37–40; Nugent, *Habits of Empire*, 139–140; Anderson, *Conquest of Texas*, 72.

50. Reséndez, *Changing National Identities*, 37–40; Weber, *Mexican Frontier*, xvii–xviii, 31, 162.

51. Cantrell, *Stephen F. Austin*, 220–221; Nugent, *Habits of Empire*, 145–148; Reséndez, *Changing National Identities*, 22–25; Weber, *Mexican Frontier*, 167, 170–171, 175 (includes Austin to S. M. Williams, August 28, 1833, quote: "to dam out").

52. Weber, *Mexican Frontier*, 171–172 (Mier y Teran quoted: "no physical force"), 177; Reséndez, *Changing National Identities*, 122–123; Anderson, *Conquest of Texas*, 79.

53. Nugent, *Habits of Empire*, 150–152; Reséndez, *Changing National Identities*, 165–169; Anderson, *Conquest of Texas*, 88, 95–96, 97–107.

54. Nugent, *Habits of Empire*, 152–153.

55. David J. Weber, *Bárbaros: Spaniards and Their Savages in the Age of Enlightenment* (New Haven, CT: Yale University Press, 2005); Reséndez, *Changing National Identities*, 207–210; Anderson, *Conquest of Texas*, 48–50.

Chapter 9

1. For borderlands as zones of plural sovereignty, see the introduction to Brian DeLay, ed., *North American Borderlands* (New York: Routledge, 2012).

2. My notion of blood talk is informed by work outside of history exploring the discursive character of violence—much of it prompted by the consequences of 9/11. See Joseph S. Tuman, *Communicating Terror: The Rhetorical Dimensions of Terrorism*, 2nd ed. (Thousand Oaks, CA: Sage, 2009); and especially Neil L. Whitehead, ed., *Violence* (Santa Fe: School of American Research Press, 2004). See in particular Whitehead's introduction and his essay "On the Poetics of Violence." For subtle meditation on the relationship between "wounds and words," see Jill Lepore's remarkable book *The Name of War: King Philip's War and the Origins of American Identity* (New York: Vintage, 1998).

3. The early history is covered in Frank D. Reeve, "Seventeenth-Century Navaho-Spanish Relations," *New Mexico Historical Review* 32, no. 1 (1957), 36–52; Reeve, "Navaho-Spanish Wars,"

New Mexico Historical Review 33 no. 3 (1958), 205–230; and Jack D. Forbes's pathbreaking *Apache, Navajo, and Spaniard* (Norman: University of Oklahoma Press, 1960). For the complex interconnections between Pueblos and Navajos in the precolonial and early colonial eras, see James F. Brooks, *Captives and Cousins: Slavery, Kinship, and Community in the Southwest Borderlands* (Chapel Hill: University of North Carolina Press, 2002), 81–88. The quote comes from David M. Brugge, *History of the Chaco Navajos* (Albuquerque, NM: National Park Service, 1980), 36. For the point about refugees, see Brugge, *Navajos in the Catholic Church Records of New Mexico, 1694–1875*, 2nd ed. (Tsaile, AZ: Navajo Community College Press, 1985), 43.

4. Francis Leon Swadesh, "Structure of Spanish-Indian Relations in New Mexico," in *The Survival of Spanish American Villages*, ed. Paul M. Kutsche (Colorado Springs: Colorado College Research Committee, 1979), 53–61.

5. American estimates of Navajo population around 1850 ranged from five to ten thousand; see Brian DeLay, *War of a Thousand Deserts: Indian Raids and the U.S.-Mexican War* (New Haven, CT: Yale University Press, 2008), 377n2. For New Mexico's population, see Ross Frank, *From Settler to Citizen: New Mexican Economic Development and the Creation of Vecino Society, 1750–1820* (Berkeley: University of California Press, 2000), 48; and David J. Weber, *The Mexican Frontier, 1821–1846: The American Southwest Under Mexico* (Albuquerque: University of New Mexico Press, 1982), 195.

6. For El Pinto, see Frank D. Reeve, "Navaho-Spanish Diplomacy, 1770–1790," *New Mexico Historical Review* 35, no. 3 (1960), 224, 331.

7. The exact timing of and reasons for the Navajo migration out of the Dinétah are a matter of dispute. See Reeve, "Navaho-Spanish Diplomacy, 1770–1790," 200–204; James F. Brooks, "Violence, Justice, and State Power in the New Mexican Borderlands, 1780–1880," in *Power and Place in the North American West*, ed. John M. Findlay and Richard White (Seattle: University of Washington Press, 1999), 49; and Ronald H. Towner, *The Archeology of Navajo Origins* (Salt Lake City: University of Utah Press, 1996). A further factor in the decision for Navajo families to move to the Tsoodzil region was likely the material benefits of Franciscan missionary activity there. See Frank D. Reeve, "The Navaho-Spanish Peace: 1720s–1770s," *New Mexico Historical Review* 34, no. 1 (1959), 9–28.

8. For the pattern of early land grants around Tsoodzil and Spanish concerns over Navajo rights, see Reeve, "Navaho-Spanish Peace," 29–39. The quote is from p. 32. For Delgadito and Segundo, see J. Lee Correll, ed., *Through White Men's Eyes: A Contribution to Navajo History—A Chronological Record of the Navaho People from Earliest Times to the Treaty of June 1, 1868*, 6 vols. (Window Rock, AZ: Navajo Times, 1976), 1: 105.

9. For a survey of the treaties, see David M. Brugge, "The Story of the Navajo Treaties," ms. in box 11 of the McNitt Collection, New Mexico State Records Center, Santa Fe, New Mexico (hereafter McNitt). For a wonderfully suggestive comparative study of judicial regimes on borderlands, see Lisa Ford, *Settler Sovereignty: Jurisdiction and Indigenous People in America and Australia, 1788–1836* (Cambridge, MA: Harvard University Press, 2010).

10. Correll, *Through White Men's Eyes*, 1: 93.

11. The classic account is Richard White, *The Middle Ground: Indians, Empires, and Republics in the Great Lakes Region, 1650–1815* (Cambridge: Cambridge University Press, 1991), 50–93.

12. The data for Figure 9.1 and a very brief discussion of the sources and limitations of this data are available at http://history.berkeley.edu/people/brian-delay.

13. Average rainfall in the lower Colorado Plateau region for the period 1709–1846 was 27.63 centimeters. The figure for 1773 was 17.74 centimeters, making it the driest year since 1752. (Precipitation returned to average levels in 1774, the year the violence erupted.) In nineteen of these

years precipitation fell below 20 centimeters, and in only about a quarter of these dry spells did conflict erupt within a year. See M. W. Salzer and K. F. Kipfmueller, "Southern Colorado Plateau Temperature and Precipitation Reconstructions," IGBP PAGES/World Data Center for Paleoclimatology Data Contribution Series #2005–066, 2005, NOAA/NCDC Paleoclimatology Program, Boulder, CO, ftp://ftp.ncdc.noaa.gov/pub/data/paleo/treering/reconstructions/northamerica/usa/colorado-plateau2005.txt.

14. For the emphasis on material opportunity, see Brooks, *Captives and Cousins*, 27. The quote is from Gladys Amanda Reichard, *Social Life of the Navajo Indians, with Some Attention to Minor Ceremonies* (New York: Columbia University Press, 1928), 114. There is a large literature on death in Navajo culture and religion. For a comparative introduction, see David M. Brugge, "A Comparative Study of Navajo Mortuary Practices," *American Indian Quarterly* 4, no. 4 (1978), 309–328; see also the companion articles in this special issue dedicated to Navajo mortuary practices. For a foundational text on the Enemy Way, see Bernard Haile, *Origin Legend of the Navajo Enemy Way* (New Haven, CT: Yale University Press, 1938). For Comanche and Kiowa killings in wartime, see DeLay, *War of a Thousand Deserts*, 114–138.

15. Brugge, *Navajos in the Catholic Church Records*, 48–49; Reeve, "Navaho-Spanish Diplomacy, 1770–1790," 206–213. For details of Navajo raids during these years, see Myra Ellen Jenkins and Ward Alan Minge *Navajo Activities Affecting the Acoma-Laguna Area, 1746–1910* (New York: Garland, 1974), 7–10.

16. Frank D. Reeve, "Navaho Foreign Affairs, 1795–1846," *New Mexico Historical Review* 46, nos. 2–3 (1971), 108–109; Correll, *Through White Men's Eyes*, 1: 95.

17. Though based on later ethnographic evidence that might not capture eighteenth-century or early nineteenth-century realities, a lucid description of political and social organization may be found in Gary Witherspoon, "Navajo Social Organization," in *Handbook of North American Indians, 10: Southwest*, ed. Alfonso Ortiz (Washington, DC: Smithsonian Institution, 1983); and Klara B. Kelley, "Navajo Political Economy Before Fort Sumner," in *The Versatility of Kinship*, ed. Linda S Cordell and Stephen Beckerman (New York: Academic Press, 1980). For the *naach'id*, see David M. Brugge, "Documentary Reference to a Navajo Naach'id in 1840," *Ethnohistory* 10 (1963), 186–88; and Brugge, "Early Navajo Political Structure," *Navajo Times* 1966 Tourist Guide (Window Rock, AZ, 1966), 22c–23c. On the scope of Navajo political integration in the pre-reservation era, see Lynn R. Bailey, *If You Take My Sheep . . . : The Evolution and Conflicts of Navajo Pastoralism, 1630–1868* (Pasadena, CA: Westernlore, 1980), 130–132.

18. "Become" is a 1781 quote from Governor Anza, taken from Brooks, *Captives and Cousins*, 114.

19. The quote is from Reeve, "Navajo Foreign Affairs," 110.

20. See Narbona to Chacón, Laguna, December 10, 1804, Spanish Archives of New Mexico (hereafter, SANM), 15: 359; Narbona to Chacón, Zuni, January 24, 1805, SANM, 15: 392; Correll, *Through White Men's Eyes*, 1: 100–102. A Navajo oral tradition maintained that Narbona's success had come from his discovery in a canyon of a high cave where women, children, and elderly had been hiding from the invaders. According to this version of events, an elderly Navajo woman who had been captive among the Spanish as a girl drew attention to the cave when she taunted the Spanish troops marching down the canyon floor below "as men who walked without eyes." Narbona's men responded by emptying hundreds of rounds of ammunition into the cave above. The bullets that ricocheted off the cave's roof and walls were said to have killed seventy women and children inside. See Reeve, "Navaho Foreign Affairs," 116; Frank McNitt, *Navajo Wars: Military Campaigns, Slave Raids, and Reprisals* (Albuquerque: University of New Mexico Press, 1972), 93–94.

21. For the reach of campaigns and transhumance, see Bailey, *If You Take My Sheep*, 153–159. For ears, see Reeve, "Navaho Foreign Affairs," n30; and McNitt, *Navajo Wars*, 41, 44.

22. Though unusual, the massive display of force at Cebolleta was not unique. In 1837 Navajos reportedly organized one thousand men who "almost annihilated" the Hopi pueblo of Oraibi (Correll, *Through White Men's Eyes*, 1: 158). In 1860, between one thousand and two thousand Navajo men attacked American troops at Ft. Defiance. See David M. Brugge, "Zarcillos Largos: Courageous Advocate of Peace," *Navajo Historical Publications Biographical Series* 2 (1970), 32.

23. For the quote, see Frederick Adolph Wislizenus, *Memoir of a Tour to Northern Mexico* (Fairfield, CT: Ye Galleon, 1992), 28.

24. For sheep wealth and exports, see Brooks, "Violence, Justice, and State Power," 36. For more on the sheep industry generally, see John O. Baxter, *Las Carneradas: Sheep Trade in New Mexico, 1700–1860* (Albuquerque: University of New Mexico Press, 1987). For exports in 1821–1846, see Baxter, *Las Carneradas*, chapter 5. During the decades prior to the campaigns culminating in the Long Walk and imprisonment at Ft. Sumner, only in the 1820s did Navajos begin accounting for the majority of baptized Indian captives in New Mexico. See Brugge, *Navajos in Catholic Church Records*, iii.

25. New Mexico's flocks enjoyed explosive growth in the 1810s and 1820s, but clashes with Navajos forced most of the growth east, onto the Plains. See Baxter, *Las Carneradas*, 90–94.

26. The quote from 1812 is from Pedro Bautista Pino, in Horace Bailey Carroll and Juan Villasana Haggard, eds., *Three New Mexico Chronicles: The Exposición of Don Pedro Bautista Pino, 1812; The Ojeada of Lic. Antonio Barreiro, 1832; and the Additions by Don José Agustín de Escudero, 1849* (Albuquerque: Quivira Society, 1942), 68–69. For "Señor," see John P. Wilson, *Military Campaigns in the Navajo Country, Northwestern New Mexico, 1800–1846* (Santa Fe: Museum of New Mexico Press, 1967), 16. For a contrary view, see Brooks, "Violence, Justice, and State Power," 34.

27. For the suspicions, see Ignacio Maria Sanchez Vergara to Pedro María de Allande, Jémez, August 20, 1816, box 12, McNitt (document translations by J. M. Martines). Spanish officials in Laguna, Jémez, and elsewhere fully expected Navajo hostilities as soon as word of their suspicions got out, and they sent emissaries to convince Diné of Spanish goodwill. See Mariana de la Pena to Pedro María de Allande, Pajartio, August 20, 1816, SANM, 18: 684; Sanchez Vergara to Allande, Jémez, August 20, 1816, SANM, 18: 686; Allande to Vergara, Santa Fe, August 21, 1816, SANM, 18: 688; and Vergara to Allande, Jémez, December 26, 1816, SANM, 18: 731. See also Reeve, "Navaho Foreign Affairs," 223–224; and Jenkins and Minge, *Navajo Activities*, 29. Spanish administrators found the Comanche-Navajo situation all the more delicate at that moment because they were trying to convince the Western Comanches (likely the ones who attacked the Navajo) to discourage their eastern kinsmen from allying with American traders and Mexican independence fighters. See Bernardo Bonavia y Zapata to Allande, Durango, August 13, 1816, SANM, 20: 682.

28. Vergara to Allande, Jémez, June 24, 1818, SANM, 19: 141; Allande to Vergara, Santa Fe, June 25, 1818, SANM, 19: 145; Reeve, "Navaho Foreign Affairs," 224–236; Brugge, *Navajos in the Catholic Church Records*, 56–57.

29. Vizcarra to Comandante General de Chihuahua, Santa Fe, November 12, 1831 (copy), Mexican Archives of New Mexico (hereafter, MANM),13: 476.

30. Brugge, in contrast, attributes the mounting hostilities after 1820 to the fact that the Mexicans "had decided to conquer the Navajos as well as their land." See *Navajos in the Catholic Church Records*, 161.

31. The Jémez massacre was long remembered in New Mexico as a critical moment in Mexican-Navajo relations. The U.S. trader and traveler Josiah Gregg recalled the event in his popular book, though he mistook Cochití Pueblo as the location of the massacre. See Max L. Moorhead, ed., *Commerce of the Prairies* (Norman: University of Oklahoma Press, 1954), 199. See also Reeve, "Navaho Foreign Affairs," 239. For the name, see Dolores A. Gunnerson, *The Jicarilla Apaches: A Study in Survival* (Dekalb: Northern Illinois University Press, 1974), 73. Despite the massacre, Jémez would continue to be a site of diplomacy in the future.

32. The murderers were tried and sentenced in New Mexico, but the Mexican congress overturned the sentence upon appeal in 1824. See Reeve, "Navajo Foreign Affairs," 239. For treaty terms, see ibid., 245.

33. For Joaquin, see Correll, *Through White Men's Eyes*, 1: 114; and Brooks, *Captives and Cousins*, 111, 212. For a thoughtful essay on one of Joaquin's successors, see J. Lee Correll, *Sandoval: Traitor or Patriot?* (Window Rock, AZ: Navajo Parks and Recreation, 1970).

34. For figures, see Brooks, "Violence, Justice, and State Power," 36. Bailey makes the important point that the term *rico* cannot meaningfully apply to individuals, given that Navajos conceived of wealth as something held by families. See *If You Take My Sheep*, 132–133. For the dating of the rhetoric of division, see David Brugge to Frank McNitt, Window Rock, AZ, May 19, 1966, box 11, McNitt. In 1835, headmen to be spared included Narbona, Sandoval, José Tapia, El Negrito, and, tellingly, Caballado Mucho. See Wilson, *Military Campaigns*, 20. For "dissidents," see Correll, *Through White Men's Eyes*, 1: 166–169.

35. My data only show eleven New Mexicans taken by Navajos during these years (this includes Pueblos except for Hopi, who remained outside of Spanish or Mexican control throughout the period under consideration). No doubt this is an underestimate, but my educated guess is that the actual figure was not more than twenty. Navajo negotiators often insisted that they had very few Mexican captives in their possession. For example, when drawing up peace terms with the Navajo in 1805, Governor Joaquín del Real Alencaster proposed that two Navajo captives be exchanged for the *two* Mexicans they held (Reeve, "Navaho Foreign Affairs," 111). During treaty negotiations in January 1824, Navajo spokesmen claimed that there was only one Mexican captive among their people (ibid., 244). Following a treaty with the new U.S. administrators of New Mexico in 1849, Navajos were able to produce only five captives, two of them young adults captured many years before as small children (Annie Heloise Abel, ed., *The Official Correspondence of James S. Calhoun While Indian Agent at Santa Fé and Superintendent of Indian Affairs in New Mexico* [Washington, DC: Government Printing Office, 1915], 29). Finally, Mexican authorities seemed to believe the Navajo when they said they had very few captives. While New Mexicans consistently put captive return at the top of their demands to the Navajo during peace talks, there is little indication they suspected Diné were withholding any captives following the conclusion of these talks.

36. Surviving treaty drafts from 1805 and 1819 both contain provisions for a complete return of captives. See Brugge, "Story of the Navajo Treaties."

37. This is not to say that authorities in Santa Fe had no problems with Navajo captives during this era. Spaniards in New Mexico often obtained Navajo captives from Utes, and it was not unusual for the Navajos to become aware of this arrangement and to demand that their kin be returned. See, for example, a case involving custody of a Navajo girl mentioned by José de la Prada to Joaquín Real Alencaster, Abiquiú, August 18, 1805, SANM, 15: 780; another involved three Navajo women, described by Francisco de Hocio to Alencaster, Santa Fe, August 23, 1805, SANM, 15: 795.

38. For Independence, see Weber, *Mexican Frontier*, 5. It was common practice to baptize captive Indians and to record their tribal affiliation insofar as the New Mexicans understood it. See Brugge, *Navajos in the Catholic Church Records*, 22–23.

39. Brugge, *Navajos in the Catholic Church Records*, Table 13, p. 122. The largest holder in the period had eight Navajos in his household. For the ambiguities in status among captive Navajo and their very limited opportunities to escape bondage, see ibid., 109–125.

40. For Gregg's estimate, see Moorhead, *Commerce of the Prairies*, 199. For the second observer, see James William Abert, *Abert's New Mexico Report, 1846–'47* (Albuquerque, NM: Horn and Wallace, 1962), 52. For similar praise from a northeast Mexican vantage point, see Jean Louis Berlandier, *The Indians of Texas in 1830*, ed. John C Ewers, trans. Patricia R Leclercq (Washington, DC: Smithsonian Institution, 1969), 47, 49, 139. By way of comparison, the historian Lansing Bloom noted nearly a century ago that Indian women and children sold for $100 to $300 each in mid-nineteenth-century New Mexican markets. See "New Mexico Under Mexican Administration, 1821–1846," *Old Santa Fe* 1–2, no. 14 (1913). Enslaved Navajos seem to have produced blankets that fused Mexican and Diné motifs and production techniques. See Brooks, *Captives and Cousins*, 239.

41. For New Mexico's divergent policy regarding Apaches and Comanches, see DeLay, *War of a Thousand Deserts*, 198–199. For changing conditions and sentiments in post-Independence New Mexico more broadly, see Weber, *Mexican Frontier*, and Andrés Reséndez, *Changing National Identities at the Frontier: Texas and New Mexico, 1800–1850* (Cambridge: Cambridge University Press, 2005).

42. A translation of Vizcarra's journal of his 1823 raiding campaign may be found in David M. Brugge, "Vizcarra's Navajo Campaign of 1823," *Arizona and the West* 6, no. 3 (1964), 223–244.

43. McNitt, *Navajo Wars*, 54–65. For quotes, see Reeve "Navaho Foreign Affairs," 243–245.

44. Vizcarra to Comandante General, Santa Fe, March 5, 1825 (letterbook), MANM, 3: 957; Vizcarra to Comandante General, Santa Fe, March 5, 1825 (letterbook), MANM, 3: 958. See also McNitt, *Navajo Wars*, 68–69; and Brugge, *Navajos in the Catholic Church Records*, 64.

45. Jenkins and Minge, *Navajo Activities*, 68.

46. For ransom, see Correll, *Through White Men's Eyes*, 1: 178; Ward Alan Minge, "Frontier Problems in New Mexico Preceding the Mexican War, 1840–1846" (Ph.D. diss., Uiversity of New Mexico, 1966), 77–85; McNitt, *Navajo Wars*, 81–82; Brugge, *Navajos in the Catholic Church Records*, 68–70; Jenkins and Minge, *Navajo Activities*, 71–78. For the suicides, see Correll, *Through White Men's Eyes*, 1: 166–169.

47. J. Sarracino to Armijo, Pajarito, June 1, 1843, MANM, 33: 487–489. See also Brugge, *Navajos in the Catholic Church Records*, 70; and Jenkins and Minge, *Navajo Activities*, 79–80.

48. Minge, "Frontier Problems," 52, 93; Brugge, *Navajos in the Catholic Church Records*, 71.

49. Comandante General to Inspector of the 2nd District, Santa Fe, April 21, 1844, MANM, 35: 591.

50. Jenkins and Minge, *Navajo Activities*, 81–83.

51. Comandante General to Dept. Treasurer, Santa Fe, January 22, 1844 (letterbook), MANM, 35: 578.

52. Minge, "Frontier Problems," 86–87.

53. Brugge, *Navajos in the Catholic Church Records*, 72; Jenkins and Minge, *Navajo Activities*, 86–87; Minge, "Frontier Problems," 89. The reference to scalp hunters comes from a letter by George Bent (published in the *New Orleans Picayune*, November 9, 1844), which claimed that in

1843 Armijo had contracted with a Frenchman named Portalance and an Englishman named Montgomery to raise a force and kill Navajos. Unable to find their intended quarry, the pair fell upon a party of Utes at peace with New Mexico, killing several and stealing their animals. Months later, kin of the slain came to Santa Fe to demand restitution, and their heated conference with the newly appointed governor, Mariano Martínez, ended in massacre when the governor's guards killed several of them. For the consequences of the massacre, see Ned Blackhawk, *Violence over the Land: Indians and Empires in the Early American West* (Cambridge, MA: Harvard University Press, 2006), 121–133.

54. Jenkins and Minge, *Navajo Activities*, 90–91; Brugge, *Navajos in the Catholic Church Records*, 72.

55. Correll, *Through White Men's Eyes*; Jenkins and Minge, *Navajo Activities*, 93. For the Armijo quote, see McNitt, *Navajo Wars*, 90.

56. W. W. Hill, "Navajo Warfare," *Yale University Publications in Anthropology* 5 (1936), 3–4.

57. For scholarly expressions of this argument, see, for example, Brooks, "Violence, Justice, and State Power"; and Kelley, "Navajo Political Economy Before Fort Sumner," 314–315. Lynn Bailey offers a subtle portrait of *los ladrones* as a cohort with varied interests and motives. But Bailey, too, sees most all of them as "young and usually uncontrollable by the wisdom and eloquence of the elders" (*If You Take My Sheep*, 133).

58. It is worth noting in this context that while Hill's informants reveal precious information unobtainable in colonial archives, some of their claims are directly contradicted by copious and compelling documentary evidence from the eighteenth and nineteenth centuries. These include the assertions that "real hostilities" first began with the Mexicans around 1840; that the Navajos enjoyed the upper hand militarily against New Mexicans until the latter aligned with Utes; that even the largest (revenge) expeditions topped out at two hundred warriors and were "always" made up of men from a single locality or district; and that Navajos first came into military contact with Comanches while at Ft. Sumner in the 1860s. See Hill, *Navajo Warfare*, 3–4.

59. J. Greiner to James S. Calhoun, Santa Fe, January 31, 1852, in Abel, *Official Correspondence of James S. Calhoun*, 466–469.

Chapter 10

I would like to thank the editors of this volume and Kathleen DuVal for helpful comments on an early draft. I would also like to thank the participants of the "Contested Spaces" symposium for intellectual engagement and helpful suggestions.

1. Brad D. Lookingbill, *The War Dance at Fort Marion: Plains Indian War Prisoners* (Norman: University of Oklahoma Press, 2006); Joyce M. Szabo, *Art from Fort Marion: The Silverman Collection* (Norman: University of Oklahoma Press, 2007); Phillip Earenfight, "Introduction: Images from Fort Marion," in *A Kiowa's Odyssey: A Sketchbook from Fort Marion*, ed. Phillip Earenfight (Seattle: University of Washington Press, 2007), 3–11; Herman J. Viola, "Captive Artists, Compelling Art," in *Warrior Artists: Historic Cheyenne and Kiowa Indian Ledger Art Drawn by Making Medicine and Zotom*, ed. Herman J. Viola (Washington, DC: National Geographic Society, 1998); Karen Daniels Petersen, *Plains Indian Art from Fort Marion* (Norman: University of Oklahoma Press, 1971); John C. Ewers, "Introduction," in *Howling Wolf: A Cheyenne Warrior's Graphic Interpretation of His People*, by Karen Daniels Petersen (Palo Alto, CA: America West, 1968), 5–33.

2. Scholarship on indigenous forms of writing in the Americas has been gaining critical mass in the past few decades. I discuss at length this scholarship, the implications for American literary studies, and the colonial roots of the common misperception that Native American peoples did not have writing, in *Queequeg's Coffin: Indigenous Literacies and Early American Literature* (Durham, NC: Duke University Press, 2011).

3. Phillip Earenfight, ed., *A Kiowa's Odyssey: A Sketchbook from Fort Marion* (Seattle: University of Washington Press, 2007).

4. Ibid. This history of fragmentation and dispersal is not atypical of extant indigenous texts.

5. On the material history of the manuscript, see Phillip Earenfight, "Reconstructing *A Kiowa's Odyssey*: Etahdleuh, Bear's Heat, and the Yale-Dickinson Drawings from Fort Marion–," in Earenfight, *A Kiowa's Odyssey*, 57–91.

6. See Pekka Hämäläinen, *The Comanche Empire* (New Haven, CT: Yale University Press, 2008).

7. Brad Lookingbill, "'Because I want to be a Man': A Portrait of Etahdleuh Doanmoe," in Earenfight, *A Kiowa's Odyssey*, 32.

8. Ibid., 30–56.

9. Ibid., 31.

10. For a reproduction of a book made by Zotom at Fort Marion, see Viola, *Warrior Artists*, 52E115.

11. Earenfight, *A Kiowa's Odyssey*, 158.

12. Berlo also notes this fact in her caption. See Earenfight, *A Kiowa's Odyssey*, 157–158.

13. Earenfight, *A Kiowa's Odyssey*, 158.

14. Lookingbill, "'Because I want to be a Man," 46.

15. Earenfight, *A Kiowa's Odyssey*, 160.

16. Szabo, *Art from Fort Marion*, 31. Hertha Wong has argued that even individual exploit narratives should be considered as communal texts, proposing terms like "communobiooratory" and "auto-ethnography." See Hertha Dawn Wong, *Sending My Heart Back Across the Years: Tradition and Innovation in Native American Autobiography* (New York: Oxford University Press, 1992), 6 (emphasis in original).

17. See Garrick Mallery, *Picture-Writing of the American Indians* (Washington D.C.: Smithsonian Institution, 1893), 266.

18. Robert M. Utley, ed., *Battlefield and Classroom: An Autobiography by Richard Henry Pratt* (Norman: University of Oklahoma Press, 2003), 40.

19. Ibid.

20. Doanmoe manuscript, 3.

21. Viola, *Warrior Artists*, 53.

22. Szabo, *Art from Fort Marion*, 72.

23. Viola, *Warrior Artists*, 69.

24. Ibid., 71.

25. In addition to Ignace J. Gelb, *A Study of Writing* (Chicago: University of Chicago Press, 1963), and John DeFrancis, *Visible Speech: the Diverse Oneness of Writing Systems* (Honolulu: University of Hawaii Press, 1989), some of the classic and most influential studies of writing include James Février, *Histoire de l'écriture* (Paris: Payot, 1948); Marcel Cohen, *La grande invention de l'ecriture et son evolution* (Paris: Imprimerie Nationale, 1958); Hans Jensen, *Sign, Symbol and Script: An Account of Man's Efforts to Write* (New York: G. P. Putnam's Sons, 1969); David

Diringer, *The Alphabet: A Key to the History of Mankind* (New York: Hutchinson's Scientific and Technical Publications, 1948) and *Writing* (London: Thames and Hudson, 1962).

26. Brander Rasmussen, *Queequeg's Coffin*; Birgit Brander Rasmussen, "Negotiating Peace, Negotiating Literacies: A French-Iroquois Encounter and the Making of Early American Literature," *American Literature* 79, no. 3 (2007), 445–473.

27. "Textual contact zones" link and revise Galen Brokaw and Mary Louise Pratt's work. Brokaw extends Mary Louise Pratt's influential notion of "contact zones" to consider "textual contact zones." See Galen Brokaw, "*Khipu* Numeracy and Alphabetic Literacy in the Andes: Felipe Guaman Poma de Ayala's *Nueva corónica y buen gobierno*," *Colonial Latin American Review* 11, no. 2 (2002), 276. I revise Pratt because "contact" can sometimes elide the degree of violence that "structured cross-cultural exchanges in the context of colonialism." See Brander Rasmussen, *Queequeg's Coffin*, 12.

Chapter 11

1. Brian DeLay, "Independent Indians and the U.S.-Mexican War," *American Historical Review* 112 (February 2007), 64.

2. Stephen Aron, "Frontiers, Borderlands, Wests," in *American History Now*, ed. Eric Foner and Lisa McGirr (Philadelphia: Temple University Press, 2011), 261–284.

3. Gottfried Hotz, *Indian Skin Paintings from the American Southwest: Two Representations of Border Conflicts Between Mexico and the Missouri in the Early Eighteenth Century*, trans. Johannes Malthaner (Norman: University of Oklahoma Press, 1970). For accounts of the hides' return to New Mexico, see Thomas E. Chávez, "The Villasur Expedition and the Segesser Hide Paintings," in *Spain and the Plains: Myths and Realities of Spanish Exploration and Settlement on the Great Plains*, ed. Ralph H. Vigil et al. (Niwot: University of Colorado Press, 1994), 109–110.

4. Gottfried Hotz, *The Segesser Hide Paintings: Masterpieces Depicting Spanish Colonial New Mexico* (Santa Fe: Museum of New Mexico Press, 1991), viii.

5. Karl Jacoby, *Shadows at Dawn: A Borderlands Massacre and the Violence of History* (New York: Penguin, 2008), 3. See also R. Brian Ferguson and Neil L. Whitehead, "The Violent Edge of Empire," in *War in the Tribal Zone: Expanding States and Indigenous Warfare*, ed. R. Brian Ferguson and Neil L. Whitehead (Santa Fe: School of American Research Press, 1992), 1–30.

6. Ned Blackhawk, *Violence over the Land: Indians and Empires in the Early American West* (Cambridge, MA: Harvard University Press, 2006).

7. See, for example, Pekka Hämäläinen, *The Comanche Empire* (New Haven, CT: Yale University Press, 2008), and Brian DeLay, *War of a Thousand Deserts: Indian Raids and the U.S.-Mexican War* (New Haven, CT: Yale University Press, 2008).

8. James C. Scott, *The Art of Not Being Governed: An Anarchist History of Upland Southeast Asia* (New Haven, CT: Yale University Press, 2009), 39.

9. Ibid., 26.

10. Ibid.

11. Hotz, *Indian Skin Paintings*, 19–21.

12. Ibid., 11.

13. Chávez, "The Villasur Expedition and the Segesser Hide Paintings," 90.

14. George E. Hyde, *Indians of the High Plains: From the Prehistoric Period to the Coming of Europeans* (Norman: University of Oklahoma Press, 1959); James F. Brooks, *Captives and Cousins:*

Slavery, Kinship, and Community in the Southwest Borderlands (Chapel Hill: University of North Carolina Press, 2002); John L. Kessell, *Spain in the Southwest: A Narrative History of Colonial New Mexico, Arizona, Texas, and California* (Norman: University of Oklahoma Press, 2003).

15. Gottfried Hotz, *Indianische Ledermalereien: Figurenreiche Darstellungen von Grenzkonflikten zwischen Mexiko und dem Missouri um 1720* (Berlin: Verlag Von Dietrich Reimer, 1960); Hotz, *Segesser Hide Paintings*; Editors of Time-Life Books, *The Old West: The Spanish West* (New York: Time-Life, 1976), 72–73. For an additional reprinting that uses Segesser images on its cover, see also Vigil et al., *Spain and the Plains*.

16. For varying interpretations of the combatants in Segesser I, see Ned Blackhawk, "The Displacement of Violence: Ute Diplomacy and the Making of New Mexico's Eighteenth-Century Northern Borderlands," *Ethnohistory* 54, no. 4 (Fall 2007), 738–739, and notes therein.

17. Hyde, *Indians of the High Plains*, 77. See also David J. Weber, *The Spanish Frontier in North America* (New Haven, CT: Yale University Press, 1992), 168–171; and Kessell, *Spain in the Southwest*, 208–214. For accounts of the Villasur campaign, see "A Portion of the Diary of the Reconnaissance Expedition of Colonel Don Pedro de Villasur Along the Platte River, 1720"; and "Confession of Valverde, Santa Fé, July 5, 1726," in *After Coronado: Spanish Exploration Northeast of New Mexico, 1696–1727*, ed. and trans. Alfred Barnaby Thomas (Norman: University of Oklahoma Press, 1935), 133–137, 230–234.

18. Hotz, *Indian Skin Paintings*, 73, 78.

19. Ibid., 228.

20. Kessell, *Spain in the Southwest*, 209, 214. For New Mexico's evolving and complex structures of patriarchal authority and honor-laden systems of subjectivity, see Ramón A. Gutíerrez, *When Jesus Came, the Corn Mothers Went Away: Power, Sexuality, and Marriage in New Mexico, 1500–1846* (Stanford, CA: Stanford University Press, 1991), 176–240.

21. Thomas, *After Coronado*, 33–39; Hämäläinen, *Comanche Empire*, 35. As Thomas A. Britten has also recently suggested, prior to their displacement by Plains equestrians, "the sixteenth and seventeenth centuries were a 'Golden Age' of sorts" for Apache communities in the region. See Britten, *The Lipan Apaches: People of Wind and Lightning* (Albuquerque: University of New Mexico Press, 2009), 55. For Valverde's account of his 1719 campaign, see "Diary of the Campaign of Governor Valverde, 1719," in Thomas, *After Coronado*, 110–133.

22. See, for example, W. L. Grant, ed., *Voyages of Samuel de Champlain, 1604–1618, Original Narratives of Early American History*, ed. J. Franklin Jameson (New York: Charles Scribner's Sons, 1907); John Underhill, *News from America*, ed. Dorothy M. Greninger (Syosset, NY: Underhill Society, 1981).

23. Richard White, *The Middle Ground: Indians, Empires, and Republics in the Great Lakes Region, 1650–1815* (New York: Cambridge University Press, 1991); R. David Edmunds and Joseph L. Peyser, *The Fox Wars: The Mesquakie Challenge to New France* (Norman: University of Oklahoma Press, 1993).

24. Brett Rushforth, *Bonds of Alliance: Indigenous and Atlantic Slaveries in New France* (Chapel Hill: University of North Carolina Press, 2012), 272.

25. Michael Witgen, "The Rituals of Possession: Native Identity and the Invention of Empire in Seventeenth-Century Western North America," *Ethnohistory* 54, no. 4 (Fall 2007), 647.

26. Ibid., 641.

27. Scott, *Art of Not Being Governed*, 238–239.

28. "With the exception of the border, Segesser I was the work of an Indian, as was Segesser II" (Hotz, *Indian Skin Paintings*, 78).

29. Richard White, "The Winning of the West: The Expansion of the Western Sioux in the Eighteenth and Nineteenth Centuries," *Journal of American History* 65 (September 1978), 319–343.

30. Kessell, *Spain in the Southwest*, 159.

31. Gertz, as quoted in, Scott, *Art of Not Being Governed*, 67.

32. In a recent public television series, the New Mexico station KNME produced a six-minute "Moments in Time" interview with Thomas E. Chávez in which he describes the many legacies of this conflict.

33. Oakah L. Jones, Jr., *Pueblo Warriors and Spanish Conquest* (Norman: University of Oklahoma Press, 1966).

34. James H. Merrell, *The Indians' New World: Catawbas and Their Neighbors from European Contact to the Era of Removal* (Chapel Hill: University of North Carolina Press, 1989).

35. James Tully, *Strange Multiplicity: Constitutionalism in an Age of Diversity* (New York: Cambridge University Press, 1995), 203–205, emphasis added.

36. Juliana Barr, "Geographies of Power: Mapping Indian Borders in the 'Borderlands' of the Early Southwest," *William and Mary Quarterly* 68, no. 1 (January 2011), 9–10.

37. Pekka Hämäläinen, "Rise and Fall of Plains Indian Horse Cultures," *Journal of American History* 90 (December 2003), 859–862. For further analysis of the ecological force prompting equestrian migration and raiding prior to the U.S. war with Mexico, see Hämäläinen, "The Politics of Grass: European Expansion, Ecological Change, and Indigenous Power in the Southwest Borderlands," *William and Mary Quarterly* 67, no. 2 (April 2010), 173–208.

38. Scott, *Art of Not Being Governed*, 34.

39. For identities in Segesser I, see Blackhawk, "Displacement of Violence," 738–739.

40. KNME, "Moments in Time" interview with Thomas E. Chávez.

41. Hotz, *Indian Skin Paintings*, 34–66. While following many of Hotz's suggestions, Chávez does break with Hotz on the identities of the women and children in Segesser I—that the Apache "defenders shown in Segesser I are not on the warpath. They have their women with them." See Hotz, *Indian Skin Paintings*, 35, and KNME, "Moments in Time."

42. "Rivera to Casa Fuerte, Presidio Del Paso Del Río Del Norte, September 26, 1727," in Thomas, *After Coronado*, 216. See also ibid., 39–47.

43. For Navajo-Spanish relations prior to 1720, see Frank McNitt, *Navajo Wars: Military Campaigns, Slave Raids, and Reprisals* (Albuquerque: University of New Mexico Press, 1972). See also Jack D. Forbes, *Apache, Navaho and Spaniard* (Norman: University of Oklahoma Press, 1960).

44. See Scott, *Art of Not Being Governed*, 22–26. As Scott contends, "The effect of (many) state-making projects . . . was to create a shatter zone or flight zone to which those wishing to evade or to escape bondage fled. These regions of refuge constituted a direct 'state effect'" (24). For recent studies on the American Southeast that utilize similar nomenclature and conceptual frameworks, see Robbie Ethridge, *From Chicaza to Chickasaw: The European Invasion and the Transformation of the Mississippian World, 1540–1715* (Chapel Hill: University of North Carolina Press, 2010); Robbie Ethridge and Sheri M. Shuck-Hall, eds., *Mapping the Mississippian Shatter Zone: The Colonial Indian Slave Trade and Regional Instability in the American South* (Lincoln: University of Nebraska Press, 2009); and Joseph M. Hall, Jr., *Zamumo's Gifts: Indian-European Exchange in the Colonial Southeast* (Philadelphia: University of Pennsylvania Press, 2009). See also Christina Snyder, *Slavery in Indian Country: The Changing Face of Captivity in Early America* (Cambridge, MA: Harvard University Press, 2010); and Allan Gallay, ed., *Indian Slavery in Colonial America* (Lincoln: University of Nebraska Press, 2010).

45. See, for example, Brooks, *Captives and Cousins*, and Juliana Barr, *Peace Came in the Form of a Woman: Indians and Spaniards in the Texas Borderlands* (Chapel Hill: University of North Carolina Press, 2007).

46. Scott, *Art of Not Being Governed*, x.

47. Malcolm Ebright, "Advocates for the Oppressed: Indians, Genízaros, and Their Spanish Advocates in New Mexico, 1700–1786," *New Mexico Historical Review* 71 (1996), 315. See also Russell M. Magnaghi, "The Genízaro Experience in Spanish New Mexico," in Vigil et al., *Spain and the Plains*, 114–130.

48. Fray Angelico Chavez, "Genízaros," in *Handbook of the North American Indian*, ed. Alfonso Ortiz, vol. 9, *Southwest* (Washington, DC: Smithsonian Institution, 1979), 198.

49. Blackhawk, *Violence Over the Land*, 47–58.

50. Thomas P. Campbell, ed., *Tapestry in the Baroque: Threads of Splendor* (New York: Metropolitan Museum of Art, 2007).

51. See, for example, "Diary of the Campaign of Governor Valverde, 1719," in Thomas, *After Coronado*, 110–133.

52. For the evolution of New Mexico's racial caste system, see Gutiérrez, *When Jesus Came, the Corn Mothers Went Away*, and Ilona Katzew, *Casta Painting: Images of Race in Eighteenth-Century Mexico* (New Haven, CT: Yale University Press, 2004).

53. E. Boyd, *Popular Arts of Spanish New Mexico* (Santa Fe: Museum of New Mexico Press, 1974), 118.

54. Ibid.

55. Hotz, *Segesser Hide Paintings*, 77.

56. Katzew, *Casta Painting*, 136–137, 31. See also Maria Concepcion Garcia Saiz, *Las Castas Mexicanas: Un Genero Pictorio Americano* (Milan: Olivetti, 1989).

57. Katzew, *Casta Painting*, 137, 10.

58. See Chantal Cramaussel, "The Forced Transfer of Indians in Nueva Vizcaya: A Hispanic Method of Colonization," in this volume; Katzew, *Casta Painting*, 31.

59. KNME, "Moments in Time."

Chapter 12

1. I use "traditional frontier histories" as a shorthand for a genre of white "pioneering" histories that emerged in later eighteenth-century U.S. accounts of national lands west of the Appalachians and then moved west to new regional venues over the course of the nineteenth century (often through regional historical societies)—a genre that Frederick Jackson Turner brought to the center of U.S. history in "The Significance of the Frontier in American History," *Annual Report of the American Historical Association for the Year 1893* (Washington, DC: Government Printing Office, 1894), 199–227. Richard White and Patricia Nelson Limerick have discussed the ways that this genre permeated American culture in their essays in *The Frontier in American Culture: An Exhibition at the Newberry Library, August 26, 1994–January 7, 1995*, ed. James R. Grossman (Chicago: Newberry Library/University of California Press, 1994). If Turner's frontier history drew on ideas that were already in the air in the 1890s, eighteenth-century frontier histories (Filson's history of Boone, for instance) did the same; I mean to keep the notion of "frontier history" loose enough to capture these earlier, prenational currents as well.

2. Works that look at the U.S. national fascination with American antiquity include Steven Conn, *History's Shadow: Native Americans and Historical Consciousness in the Nineteenth Century* (Chicago: University of Chicago Press, 2004); Don D. Fowler, *A Laboratory for Anthropology: Science and Romanticism in the American Southwest, 1846–1930* (Albuquerque: University of New Mexico Press, 2000); Terry A. Barnhart, *Ephraim George Squier and the Development of American Archaeology* (Lincoln: University of Nebraska Press, 2005); David R. Wilcox and Don D. Fowler, "The Beginnings of Anthropological Archaeology in the North American Southwest: From Thomas Jefferson to the Pecos Conference," *Journal of the Southwest* 44, no. 2 (Summer 2002), 121–234; James E. Snead, *Ruins and Rivals: The Making of Southwest Archaeology* (Tucson: University of Arizona Press, 2001); and R. Tripp Evans, *Romancing the Maya: Mexican Antiquity in the American Imagination, 1820–1915* (Austin: University of Texas Press, 2004).

3. For a discussion of spatial and temporal divides in American borderlands history, see Pekka Hämäläinen and Samuel Truett, "On Borderlands," *Journal of American History* 98, no. 2 (September 2011), 338–361.

4. For the specifics of John Filson's life and career, I draw on John Mack Faragher, *Daniel Boone: The Life and Legend of an American Pioneer* (New York: Henry Holt, 1992), 1–7; and Thomas Hallock, *From the Fallen Tree: Frontier Narratives, Environmental Politics, and the Roots of a National Pastoral, 1749–1826* (Chapel Hill: University of North Carolina Press, 2003), 56–65.

5. Faragher, *Daniel Boone*, 3–5; and John Filson, *The Discovery, Settlement, and Present State of Kentucke: and An Essay Towards the Topography, and Natural History of that Important Country* (Wilmington, DE: James Adams, 1784), 7. For a discussion of the "first white man" trope, see Richard White, "Are You an Environmentalist or Do You Work for a Living? Work and Nature," in *Uncommon Ground: Rethinking the Human Place in Nature*, ed. William Cronon (New York: W. W. Norton, 1996); but also see Jean M. O'Brien, *Firsting and Lasting: Writing Indians Out of Existence in New England* (Minneapolis: University of Minnesota Press, 2010).

6. Filson, *Discovery, Settlement, and Present State of Kentucke*, 57–58, 33, 97–98. For the broader interest in British antiquities leading up to (and including) this time, see Graham Perry, *The Trophies of Time: English Antiquarians of the Seventeenth Century* (Oxford: Oxford University Press, 1995); Sam Smiles, *The Image of Antiquity: Ancient Britain and the Romantic Imagination* (New Haven, CT: Yale University Press, 1994); and Philip Schwyzer, *Archaeologies of English Renaissance Literature* (New York: Oxford University Press, 2007).

7. *The Boston Weekly News-Letter*, June 12, 1740; *The Welch Indians; Or, A Collection of Papers, Respecting a People Whose Ancestors Emigrated from Wales to America, in the Year 1170, with Prince Madoc* (London: T. Chapman, 1797), 11, 17, 22–23.

8. Richard Hakluyt, *A Particular Discourse Concerninge the Greate Necessitie and Manifolde Commodyties That Are Like to Growe to this Relme of Englande by the Westerne Discoueries Lately Attempted, Written in the Yere 1584; by Richarde Hakluyt of Oxforde; Known as the Discourse of Western Planting*, ed. David B. Quinn and Alison M. Quinn (London: Hakluyt Society, 1993), 88; and *The History of Cambria, Now Called Wales: A Part of the Most Famous Yland of Brytaine, Written in the Brytish Language Aboue Two Hundreth Yeares Past; Translated into English by H. Lhoyd, Gentleman; Corrected, Augmented, and Continued out of Records and Best Approoued Authors, by Dauid Powel, Doctor in Diuinitie* (1584; London: Harding and Wright, 1811), 166–167. See Peter C. Mancall, *Hakluyt's Promise: An Elizabethan's Obsession for an English America* (New Haven, CT: Yale University Press, 2007), 151, for a discussion of Hakluyt's use of the Madoc tale as a propaganda piece, which many European readers even into the eighteenth century fully remembered it to be.

9. Filson, *Discovery, Settlement, and Present State of Kentucke*, 98. For a record of how the Welsh Indian story persisted, expanding ever-farther west, I draw on a compilation of sources in John Russell Bartlett, "Essay on the Welsh Indians," ms. in John Russell Bartlett Papers, John Carter Brown Library, but the tale was perhaps most famously perpetuated by George Catlin among the Mandan Indians. See George Catlin, *Letters and Notes on the Manners, Customs, and Condition of the North American Indians* (London: Author, 1842), 257–261. For the interwoven interest in archaeology and linguistics, see Conn, *History's Shadow*.

10. John Lawson, *A New Voyage to Carolina* (London, 1709), 62. It is worth noting that the Hatteras Indian and Welsh Indian tales both emphasize relics of the written word (i.e., books).

11. Hans Sloane to John Ray, January 29, 1786, in *Correspondence of John Ray: Consisting of Selections from the Philosophical Letters Published by Dr. Derham, and Original Letters of John Ray in the Collection of the British Museum*, ed. Edwin Lankester (London: Ray Society, 1848), 189; and Hans Sloane, *A Voyage to the Islands Madera, Barbados, Nieves, S. Christophers, and Jamaica*, 2 vols. (London: Printed by B. M. for the Author, 1707). For Sloane's life and career, see G. R. de Beer, *Sir Hans Sloane and the British Museum* (Oxford: Oxford University Press, 1953).

12. Sloane, *Voyage to the Islands*, lxx–lxxi, xiv, lviii; de Beer, *Sir Hans Sloane*, 29–30. Sloane's attention to Spanish loss extended also to the ruins of Spanish shipwrecks, in which visions of lost empires dovetailed with dreams of lost treasure. These spaces had also been consumed by nature. Sloane's illustrator sketched pieces hauled to the surface: algae-encrusted pieces of eight and a giant Spanish nail in a wood plank overgrown by feathery coral. Sloane, *Voyages to the Islands*, lxxix–lxxx; unnumbered plate.

13. Bernard Romans's *A Concise History of East and West Florida* (New York: Author, 1775) echoed Sloane's attention to crumbling forts and plazas, overgrown orchards and fields, and even lost ships. For Bartram, see Edmund and Dorothy Smith Berkeley, *The Life and Travels of John Bartram: From Lake Ontario to the River St. John* (Tallahassee: University Press of Florida, 1982); *The Correspondence of John Bartram, 1734–1777*, ed. Edmund and Dorothy Smith Berkeley (Gainesville: University Press of Florida, 1992); and William Bartram, "Some Account of the Late Mr. John Bartram of Pennsylvania," *Philadelphia and Medical Journal* 1, no. 1 (Philadelphia: J. Conrad and Co., 1804), 115–124.

14. Sir Hans Sloane to Bartram, January 16, 1742; Bartram to Sloane, November 14, 1742; and J. F. Grovonius to Bartram, July 25, 1744, in William Darlington's *Memorials of John Bartram and Humphry Marshall, with Notices of Their Botanical Contemporaries* (Philadelphia: Lindsay and Blakiston, 1849), 152, 302–304, 351. Darlington's *Memorials* also provide my insights into the business relationship between Collinson and Bartram.

15. John Bartram, *Observations on the Inhabitants, Climate, Soil, Rivers, Productions, Animals, and Other Matters Worthy of Notice; Made by Mr. John Bartram in His Travels from Pensilvania to Onondago, Oswego, and the Lake Ontario, in Canada* (London: J. Whiston and B. White, 1751), 74–75; and Cadwallader Colden to Bartram, May 9, 1746, in Darlington, *Memorials*, 331. To situate this journey, James Logan, and the larger context of British-Iroquois relations at this time, see James H. Merrell, *Into the American Woods: Negotiators on the Pennsylvania Frontier* (New York: W. W. Norton, 1999).

16. Bartram to Collinson, December 3, 1762, and Bartram to Collinson, November 11, 1763, in Darlington, *Memorials*, 243, 256. Collinson already had an interest in mastodon sites on the Ohio River: he had received two molars several years earlier. See the discussion of Collinson and like collectors in Paul Semonin, *American Monster: How the Nation's First Prehistoric Creature Became a Symbol of National Identity* (New York: New York University Press, 2000), 84–110.

17. Drawn from John Bartram's account of the journey, printed in William Stork, *An Account of East-Florida, with a Journal, Kept by John Bartram of Philadelphia, Botanist to His Majesty for the Floridas; Upon a Journey from St. Augustine up the River St. Johns* (London: W. Nicoll, 1767), 5–7, 10–12, 50–51. The "old madam" flora quote is from Bartram to Collinson, November 11, 1763, in Darlington, *Memorials*, 256.

18. For the devastation and cultural loss of colonial-native Florida and environs, see, for instance, *Mapping the Mississippian Shatter Zone: The Colonial Indian Slave Trade and Regional Instability in the American South*, ed. Robbie Ethridge and Sheri M. Shuck-Hall (Lincoln: University of Nebraska Press, 2009). For the rising British romantic obsession with Indians, see Tim Fulford, *Romantic Indians: Native Americans, British Literature, and Transatlantic Culture, 1756–1830* (Oxford: Oxford University Press, 2006). Fulford traces this interest back to the encounters and acquisitions of the French and Indian War. With Sloane and Grovonius (as for both of the Bartrams and Jefferson), the vogue for Native American antiquities bridges Enlightenment and romantic eras and sensibilities, drawing on aspects of both (thus my use of "romantic" with a small "r").

19. The first edition of *Notes on the State of Virginia* was published in May 1785; this is the version I use here. Due to a growing demand, he published a corrected copy in 1787, the copy that most edited versions of the *Notes on the State of Virginia* are based on. The full title of the version I use is Thomas Jefferson, *Notes on the State of Virginia; Written in the year 1781, somewhat corrected and enlarged in the winter of 1782, for the use of a foreigner of distinction, in answer to certain queries proposed by him* . . . (Paris: s.n., 1785). For a discussion about the production of *Notes on the State of Virginia*, see the introduction in *Notes on the State of Virginia*, ed. William Peden (Chapel Hill: University of North Carolina Press, 1955). For Buffon and the debates about the American climate and environment, see Antonello Gerbi, *The Dispute of the New World: A History of a Polemic, 1750–1900* (Pittsburgh: University of Pittsburgh Press, 1973). For Jefferson's scientific milieu, start with John C. Greene, *American Science in the Age of Jefferson* (Ames: Iowa State University Press, 1984).

20. Jefferson, *Notes on the State of Virginia*, 173–179 (the quotes are from various places among these pages). Reports on spoils retrieved from Old World sites can be found in various newspaper articles: see, for instance, *Boston Gazette*, December 1, 1747; *Boston News-Letter*, August 2, 1750; *Pennsylvania Gazette*, February 11, 1755; *New Hampshire Gazette*, October 8, 1762; *The Providence Gazette*, July 18, 1772; and *New York Journal*, September 23, 1784. For the timing of Jefferson's excavation, I draw on Doug Wilson's "The Evolution of Jefferson's *Notes on the State of Virginia*," *Virginia Magazine of History and Biography* 112, no. 2 (September 2004), 99–133. Wilson proposes, based on printing notes, that Jefferson excavated in the summer or fall of 1783.

21. Jefferson, *Notes on the State of Virginia*, 181–182.

22. Ibid., 71. For the earlier circulation of mastodon bones, see Peter Collinson and George Crogham, "An Account of Some Very Large Fossil Teeth, Found in North America, and Described by Peter Collinson, F.R.S.," *Philosophical Transactions of the Royal Society of London* 57 (1767), 464–467; and William Hunter, "Observations on the Bones, Commonly Supposed to Be Elephants Bones, Which Have Been Found Near the River Ohio in America," *Philosophical Transactions of the Royal Society of London* 58 (1768), 34–45.

23. Jefferson, *Notes on the State of Virginia*, 69–71.

24. Indeed, it is telling that Jefferson instructed Meriwether Lewis and William Clark to keep an eye out for such vestiges of human and nonhuman American antiquity during their

westward journey into Louisiana in 1804. By this point, Ohio River assemblages of mastodon bones (most famously at Big Bone Lick) and precolonial burial sites (such as the large Grave Creek mound in what is now West Virginia) had become standard road markers for such westward travelers, conditioning them for what presumably lay ahead.

25. See Mikhail Bakhtin, "Epic and Novel: Toward a Methodology for the Study of the Novel," in *The Dialogical Imagination: Four Essays by M. M. Bakhtin*, ed. Michael Holquist (Austin: University of Texas Press, 1981), 13–14. See a slightly different application of Bakhtin's notion of epic distance to borderland narratives in Samuel Truett, "Epics of Greater America: Herbert Eugene Bolton's Quest for a Transnational American History," in *Interpreting Spanish Colonialism: Empires, Nations, and Legends*, ed. Christopher Schmidt-Nowara and John M. Nieto-Phillips (Albuquerque: University of New Mexico Press, 2005), 213–247. For a broader discussion of the relationship between empire and epic, see David Quint, *Epic and Empire: Politics and Generic Form from Virgil to Milton* (Princeton, NJ: Princeton University Press, 1993).

26. For a particularly robust discussion of the interest in Native American antiquities along the Mississippi and beyond, see Michael J. O'Brien, *Paradigms of the Past: The Story of Missouri Archaeology* (Columbia: University of Missouri Press, 1996); for a nineteenth-century view of the Mississippi region and its Native antiquities, see Ephraim G. Squier and Edwin H. Davis, *Ancient Monuments of the Mississippi Valley: Comprising the Results of Extensive Original Surveys and Explorations* (Washington, DC: Smithsonian Institution, 1848). For U.S. visions of lost Native worlds in New Mexico in the 1820s and 1830s, see, for instance, Josiah Gregg, *Commerce of the Prairies: or the Journal of a Santa Fé Trader, During Eight Expeditions Across the Great Western Prairies, and a Residence of Nearly Nine Years in Northern Mexico* (New York: Henry G. Langley, 1844), 267–273, 282–286. For U.S. visions of the French-American past, see Edward Watts, *In This Remote Country: French Colonial Culture in the Anglo-American Imagination, 1780–1860* (Chapel Hill: University of North Carolina Press, 2006). For U.S. views of the Spanish-American past, start with David J. Weber, *Myth and the History of the Hispanic Southwest: Essays* (Albuquerque: University of New Mexico Press, 1988).

27. Antoine-Simon Le Page du Pratz, *The History of Louisiana, or of the Western Parts of Virginia and Carolina*, 2 vols. (London: T. Becket and P. A. de Hondt, 1863). I draw my sense of backcountry rumor versus "metropolitan" archives/texts from what I am able to access through a range of digital newspaper databases (most significant among these is *America's Historical Newspapers*, 1690–1922), using a variety of relevant keywords. For the role of rumor as a borderland dynamic during the eighteenth century, and the continental scale at which it could transmit information, see Gregory Evans Dowd, "The Panic of 1751: The Significance of Rumors on the South Carolina-Cherokee Frontier," *William and Mary Quarterly* 53, no. 3 (July 1996), 527–560. The precise "circuitry" of rumor in this context bears further study.

28. See Gordon M. Sayre, *The Indian Chief as Tragic Hero: Native Resistance and the Literatures of America, from Moctezuma to Tecumseh* (Chapel Hill: University of North Carolina Press, 2005), 203–248, together with his *Les Sauvages Américains: Representations of Native Americans in French and English Colonial Literature* (Chapel Hill: University of North Carolina Press, 1997), as a starting point for situating Le Page du Pratz's career. See also Joseph Treagle's introduction to *The History of Louisiana, or of the Western Parts of Virginia and Carolina* (Baton Rouge: Louisiana State University Press, 1983).

29. Le Page du Pratz, *History of Louisiana*.

30. "An Account of the Travels of Monchat-Ape," *Boston News-Letter*, February 7, 1754, and "The Remaining Part of the Travels of Moncacht-Ape," *Boston News-Letter*, February 14, 1754.

This article was taken from the *London Daily Advertiser*, November 10–13, 1753. For Moncacht-Apé's narrative, see Andrew McFarland Davis, "The Journey of Moncacht-Apé," *Proceedings of the American Antiquarian Society* 2 (April 1883), 321–348; and Gordon Sayre, "A Native American Scoops Lewis and Clark: The Voyage of Moncacht-Apé," *Common-Place* 5, no. 4 (July 2005). For tales of cataclysmic loss of former lands, see Sumathi Ramaswamy, *The Lost Land of Lemuria: Fabulous Geographies, Catastrophic Histories* (Berkeley: University of California Press, 2004).

31. "Remaining Part of the Travels."

32. Ibid. If the newspaper assumed the bearded men to be from Russia, Le Page du Pratz assumed them to be "the Inhabitants of some Isles in the Neighborhood of Japan." The important thing is not where the men are actually from (the truth value of this tale is impossible to assess), but rather that the encounter serves as a kind of imperial Rorschach ink-blot test. People see what they want to see.

33. On their expedition west Meriwether Lewis carried a copy of the 1774 English-language edition of Le Page du Pratz, which he borrowed from the Philadelphia intellectual Benjamin Smith Barton. Gary E. Moulton, ed., *The Journals of the Lewis and Clark Expedition*, vol. 2, *August 30, 1803–August 24, 1804* (Lincoln: University of Nebraska Press, 1986), 352n5.

34. The view of Moncacht-Apé as a precursor to Lewis and Clark traces back at least to Edward Gaylord Bourne, "The Romance of Western History," *Missouri Historical Review* 1, no. 1 (October 1906), 20. Gaylord, like others of his generation, found the tale hard to stomach. But it mattered less that the story was questionable and more that it prepared the ground for the later travel narrative of Lewis and Clark.

35. Le Page du Pratz, *History of Louisiana*, 110–113.

36. Benjamin Smith Barton, *Observations on Some Parts of Natural History* (London: Author, 1787), 14–17, 42–49. For Benjamin Smith Barton's life, I draw on Francis W. Pennell, "Benjamin Smith Barton as Naturalist," *Proceedings of the American Philosophical Society* 86, no. 1 (September 25, 1942), 108–122, but also see Benjamin Rush, James W. Wallace, and Jeannette E. Graustein, "The Eminent Benjamin Smith Barton," *Pennsylvania Magazine of History and Biography* 85, no. 4 (October 1961), 423–438.

37. Francesco Saverio Clavigero, *Storia antica del Messico*, 2 vols. (Cesena: G. Biasini, 1780–1781), for the original Italian version; Francisco Saverio Clavigero, *The History of Mexico*, 2 vols., trans. Charles Cullen (London: G. G. J. and J. Robinson, 1787). For Clavijero's quasi-nationalism—I use this term to indicate that his text anticipates elements of Mexican nationalism, without being a fully fledged proto-nationalist text—see D. A. Brading, *The First America: The Spanish Monarchy, Creole Patriots, and the Liberal State, 1492–1867* (Cambridge: Cambridge University Press, 1991), and Jorge Cañizares-Esguerra, *How to Write the History of the New World: Histories, Epistemologies, and Identities in the Eighteenth-Century Atlantic World* (Stanford, CA: Stanford University Press, 2002). For Barton's use of Clavijero, see Barton, *Observations*, 50–64.

38. Barton, *Observations*, 50–66. Barton was fickle in his attempts to place frontier antiquities, so Toltecs ended up sharing this ancient western landscape with other lost tribes. See also, for instance, Winthrop Sargent and Benjamin Smith Barton, *Papers Relative to Certain American Antiquities* (Philadelphia: Thomas Dobson, 1796), and Benjamin Smith Barton, *New Views of the Origin of the Tribes and Nations of America* (Philadelphia: Author, 1797).

39. For Kino, see Herbert Eugene Bolton, *Kino's Historical Memoir of Pimería Alta*, 2 vols. (Cleveland, OH: Arthur H. Clark, 1919), 1: 128; for Anza and Font, see Herbert Eugene Bolton, *Anza's California Expeditions*, 3 vols. (New York: Russell and Russell, 1966), 3: 214–15, but also see

2: 126–127, 3: 15, and 4: 34–41. Tales of travels and lost worlds had also lured Spaniards northward previously; take, for instance, Coronado's search for Cíbola and its fabled Seven Cities, a journey inspired by tales dating from the medieval era. Visions of Casa Grande and Casas Grandes as stopping places on the road from Aztlán take on cartographic form in Alexander von Humboldt's *Atlas géographique et physique du Royaume de la Nouvelle-Espagne* (Paris: F. Schoell, 1811), a vision of the region that informed many nineteenth-century U.S. maps. For the general European-American obsession with the Aztecs, see Benjamin Keen, *The Aztec Image in Western Thought* (New Brunswick, NJ: Rutgers University Press, 1971), but also see Eric Wertheimer, *Imagined Empires: Incas, Aztecs, and the New World of American Literature, 1771–1876* (Cambridge: Cambridge University Press, 1999).

40. Clavigero, *History of Mexico*, 113–115, for a discussion of Aztlán by way of ruins on the Gila River (i.e., Casa Grande). For Rivera and Lafora, see Pedro de Rivera, *Diario y derrotero de lo caminado, visto, y observado en la visita que hizo a los presidios de la Nueva España Septentrional el Brigadier Pedro de Rivera*, ed. Vito Alessio Robles (Mexico: Taller Autográfico, 1948), 68; and Lawrence Kinnaird, *The Frontiers of New Spain: Nicolás de Lafora's Description, 1766–1768* (Berkeley, CA: Quivira Society, 1958), 98–100. Pictographic representations of the journey from Aztlán are contained in the Codex Boturini and the Aubin Codex, both produced by Mexican authors in the generation after the Spanish conquest of Tenochtitlan; the Aztec migration story also circulated in compilations, most famously Juan de Torquemada's 1615 *Monarchia Indiana*. For a modern edition, see Juan de Torquemada, *Monarchia Indiana*, introduced by Miguel Leon Portilla, 5th ed. (Mexico: Editorial Porrua, 1975).

41. See Brading, *The First America*, 293–313, for a discussion of "creole patriots."

42. Alexander von Humboldt, *Researches Concerning the Institutions and Monuments of the Ancient Inhabitants of America* (London: Longman, Hurst, Rees, Orme, and Brown, 1814), but also see Humboldt, *Political Essay on the Kingdom of New Spain* (London: Longman, Hurst, Rees, Orme, and Brown, 1811), which fueled desires on both sides of the Atlantic for commercial expansion into Mexico. For Humboldt's cultural milieu (and a broader vision of America), see Laura Dassow Walls, *The Passage to Cosmos: Alexander von Humboldt and the Shaping of America* (Chicago: University of Chicago Press, 2009); Mary Louise Pratt, *Imperial Eyes: Travel Writing and Transculturation* (London: Routledge, 1992), 111–143; Aaron Sachs, *The Humboldt Current: Nineteenth-Century Exploration and the Roots of American Environmentalism* (New York: Viking, 2006); and Cañizares-Esguerra, *How to Write the History of the New World*, 55–63, 124–129. Humboldt's *Institutions and Monuments* was the English translation of his *Vues des Cordillères, et monumens des peuples indigènes de l'Amérique* (Paris: F. Schoell, 1810 [1813?]).

43. I should add here that the 1837 idea that Aztalan was somehow connected to sites farther south was not at all far-fetched. Archaeologists today consider it to be a northern outlier of the Mississippian material-cultural complex (having more in common with sites along the Mississippi River than with Late Woodland sites more common to this part of Wisconsin). For quotes, see "Letter to Editor, with Illustration," *Milwaukee Advertiser*, February 25, 1837; and Stephen Taylor, "Description of Ancient Remains, Animal Mounds, and Embankments: Principally in the Counties of Grant, Iowa, and Richland, in Wisconsin Territory," *American Journal of Science* 44 (1842), 22. For a treatment of the Aztalan site within a larger context of Mississippian cultures, see Robert A. Birmingham and Leslie E. Eisenberg, *Indian Mounds of Wisconsin* (Madison: University of Wisconsin Press, 2000), 142–162. Also see Robert A. Birmingham and Lynne G. Goldstein, *Aztalan: Mysteries of an Ancient Indian Town* (Madison: Wisconsin Historical Society Press, 2005).

44. "Excerpts from Letters of Dr. I. A. Lapham," in S. B. Barrett, "Ancient Aztalan," *Bulletin of the Public Museum of the City of Milwaukee* 12 (April 1933), 376–378; and Birmingham and Goldstein, *Aztalan*, 2.

45. For the classic midcentury work that saw the Mississippian system pointing toward Mexico, see Ephraim G. Squier and Edwin H. Davis, *Ancient Monuments of the Mississippi Valley: Comprising the Results of Extensive Original Surveys and Explorations* (Washington, DC: Smithsonian Institution, 1848). Now archaeologists tend to be much more skeptical of the strong claims of Mexican-Mississippian interconnection that prevailed in the nineteenth century. See, for instance, Nancy Marie White and Richard A. Weinstein, "The Mexican Connection and the Far West of the U.S. Southeast," *American Antiquity* 73, no. 2 (April 2008), 227–277.

46. Gregg, *Commerce of the Prairies*; and James H. Simpson, *Journal of a Military Reconnaissance, from Santa Fé, New Mexico, to the Navajo Country* (Philadelphia: Lippincott, Grambo, and Co., 1852). For new white Indians, see, for instance, Albert Pike, *Prose Sketches and Poems, Written in the Western Country* (Boston: Light and Horton, 1834); Rufus B. Sage, *Scenes in the Rocky Mountains, Oregon, California, New Mexico, Texas and Grand Prairies* (Philadelphia: Carey and Hart, 1846); and Lt. Amiel Weeks Whipple, *Report of Explorations for a Railway Route, Near the Thirty-Fifth Parallel of North Latitude, from the Mississippi River to the Pacific Ocean* (Washington, DC: Tucker, 1853–1854).

CONTRIBUTORS

Matthew Babcock is Assistant Professor of History at the University of North Texas at Dallas. Working with David Weber, he received his Ph.D. at Southern Methodist University. He is completing his book *Relocation and Resilience: Apache Adaptation to Hispanic Rule* as a Dornsife Fellow at the Huntington Library.

Juliana Barr is Associate Professor of History at Duke University. She is the author of the award-winning *Peace Came in the Form of a Woman: Indians and Spaniards in the Texas Borderlands* and is now at work on a book about women, religion, and slavery in the Southwest during the sixteenth and seventeenth centuries.

Ned Blackhawk is Professor of History and American Studies at Yale University. He won the Clements Prize for *Violence over the Land: Indians and Empires in the Early American West*.

Edward Countryman has written widely on early American history, American identity, and film studies. He won the Bancroft Prize for *A People in Revolution: The American Revolution and Political Society in New York, 1760–1790*, and he is University Distinguished Professor at Southern Methodist University.

Chantal Cramaussel has a doctorate from the École des Hautes Études en Sciences Sociales in Paris. She is Professor of History at the Colegio de Michoacán and is the author of books and many articles on northern Mexican history.

Brian DeLay is Associate Professor of History at the University of California, Berkeley. He is the author of the award-winning *War of a Thousand Deserts: Indian Raids and the U.S. Mexican War* and the editor of *North*

American Borderlands. He is working on a book about guns, business, and freedom in the Americas.

Elizabeth Fenn is Associate Professor at the University of Colorado, Boulder, where she holds the Walter and Lucienne Driskill Chair of Western American History. She is author of *Pox Americana: The Great Smallpox Epidemic of 1775–1782*.

Allan Greer is Professor and Canada Research Chair at McGill University. The most recent of his five books is *La Nouvelle France et le Monde*. He is spending the academic year 2013–2014 as a Fellow at the Institut d'Études Avancées in Paris.

Pekka Hämäläinen studied in Finland and, like several other contributors to this volume, was a Fellow of the William P. Clements Center for Southwest Studies at Southern Methodist University. He won the Bancroft Prize for *The Comanche Empire* and is now Rhodes Professor of American History and Fellow of St. Catherine's College, Oxford.

Raúl José Mandrini studied at the Universidad de Buenos Aires and was a professor in the department of history at the Universidad Nacional del Centro de la Provincia de Buenos Aires between 1984 and 2009. Now he is an honorary researcher at the Museo Etnográfico de la Universidad de Buenos Aires. The most recent of his many books is *La Argentina aborigende los primeros pobladores a 1910*.

Cynthia Radding is Gussenhoven Distinguished Professor of Latin American Studies and Professor of History at the University of North Carolina, Chapel Hill. Most recently she published *Landscapes of Power and Identity: Comparative Histories in the Sonoran Desert and the Forests of Amazonia from Colony to Republic*.

Birgit Brander Rasmussen is Assistant Professor of American Studies and Ethnicity, Race, and Migration at Yale University. She is the author of *Queequeg's Coffin: Indigenous Literacies and the Making of Early Literature* and a coeditor of *The Making and Unmaking of Whiteness*.

Alan Taylor won the Pulitzer, Bancroft, and Beveridge prizes for *William Cooper's Town: Power and Persuasion on the Frontier of the Early American*

Republic. He holds the Thomas Jefferson Memorial Foundation Chair at the University of Virginia, and is the author of many other books, as well as a regular contributor to the *New Republic*.

Samuel Truett is Associate Professor of History at the University of New Mexico and the author of *Fugitive Landscapes: The Forgotten History of the U.S.-Mexico Borderlands*. His coedited collection *Continental Crossroads: Remapping U.S.-Mexico Borderlands History* emerged from a previous Clements Center symposium.

INDEX

Acaxée Indians, 120, 125
Africans, 41, 124, 137, 209
agency, of small groups, 32
"age of exploration," 5
agriculture, 26, 97, 120, 124, 125, 346n12
Ahler, Stanley, 106
Alabama Indians, 65
Alamos (*real de minas*), 187, 188, 198–203, 206, 207, 382n56, 383n57
alcaldes, 39, 135, 243
alcohol, 41, 88
Algonquian speakers, 52, 80, 171
Álvarez, Salvador, 187
American Fur Company, 108, 352n75
American Revolution, 89, 208, 209, 216; debt of European empires and, 210; westward expansion following, 301, 311
Ancán Amún, 152
Andros, Edmund, 85
Anglocentrism, 31–32
Anishinaabeg Indians, 52, 56
Antonio, Bishop, 146
Antonio de Merlo, Miguel, 143
Antonio el Pinto, 233
Antuna, Chief, 175
Anza, Juan Bautista de, 319
Apache Indians, 16, 59, 67, 230, 242, 399n21; "Apaches del Nabajú," 232; as auxiliaries of Spanish army, 289, 290, 296, 297; Comanche raids on, 44, 282, 364n31; disease outbreaks among, 178; exile of Apache prisoners, 172, 372n43; farming and, 167, 168, 370n13; Gila (Gileño), 59, 165, 179, 232; Hispanicized and Christianized, 168–176; Mimbreño, 59, 165, 177, 182, 183; in mining centers, 204, 206; missionization of, 289, 292; New Mexico culture of Indian slavery and, 247; raiding and nomadic mobility of, 36, 289; received notions of, 26; resistance to United States, 70; Spanish treaties with, 92; Western Apaches, 164, 175. *See also* Chiricahuas; Mescaleros; reservations, Apache
Apachería, 166, 167, 169; buffalo hunting in, 177; failed missionization of, 282; map of, 165; Spanish military campaigns in, 171
Appalachian mountains, 35, 89, 90, 311
Arapaho Indians, 45, 48, 113, 257
Araucanian Indians, 16
archaeology, 101, 102, 322, 407n43, 408n45
Arellano, Manuel, 296
Argentina, 2, 144, 185
Arikara Indians, 44, 48, 95; drought and, 97; ecological problems and, 348n28; population of, 110, 353n97; smallpox among, 106, 113, 354n102
Arizona, 301, 319, 320, 322
Arkansas Valley, Native peoples of, 160
Armijo (Navajo headman), 255–56
Armijo, Governor, 251, 252, 396n53
asientos, 148
Assiniboine Indians, 106, 108
Atlantic Ocean, on map, 7
Atsina Indians, 113
Augustinian order, 39
Austin, Moses, 217, 221–22, 224
Australia, land appropriation in, 77
Aviles, Manuel María de, 201
Avilés, Viceroy, 153
Azara, Félix de, 153
Aztec empire, 13, *14*, 319
Aztlán, 319–322, *323*, 407n43, 407nn39–40

Babcock, Matthew, 26, 186
Baca, Bartolomé, 249
Baca, Francisco, 246
Bacon's Rebellion, 40
Bacoregui Indians, 196, 380n37

Bailey, Lynn, 246, 396n57
Bakhtin, Mikhail, 311
Ball, Eve, 170
Banner, Stuart, 73, 341n19
baptisms, 127, 128, 130, 213; of Apaches, 170, 171, 249; of Navajos, 248, 395n38; parish records of mining districts, 192, 195, 196, 197, 199, 382n56, 383n57; *reducciones* and, 134; statistics on, 135
Bárbaros (Weber), 92
Barbastro, Antonio, 180
Barr, Juliana, 288
Barton, Benjamin Smith, 316, 319, 320, 406n38
Bartram, John, 306–8, 309, 310–11, 312, 316
Bartram, William, 307, 308, 316
Basilio, Tomás, 133
Battlefield and Classroom (Pratt), 271
Bear's Heart, 258
Beaver Wars, 231
Benites, Antonio Rafael, 171
Bent, George, 395n53
Berlo, Janet Catherine, 260, 265, 266, 267
Big Bow, 264, 266, 272
bison (buffalo), 26, 44, 110, 177; Comanche-Apache relations and, 164; in economy of Great Plains, 287; float bison, 97, 345n10; horses and hunting of, 104; on northern Plains, 97, 345n8; Sioux control of hunting territories for, 106, 107; staged "buffalo" hunts, 269; warrior identity and, 259
Blackfeet Indians, 48, 106, 113
Blackhawk, Ned, 27
Black Legend, 25, 76, 77–78
blood talk, 230, 231, 237, 240, 245, 252
Boller, Henry, 352n74
Bolton, Herbert E., 23
Bonaparte, Napoleon, 217
Boone, Daniel, 217, 301–2, 304, 401n1
borderlands, 1, 24, 31, 115–16, 123; academic studies on, 184; beyond control of European empires, 60; commercial exchanges in, 154; contact zones in, 55; ecological transitions in, 140; historians of, 278; homelands as, 32; Indian autonomy and, 47, 330n5; Indian uprisings in, 143; Jesuit missions in, 127; of New Mexico, 285; overlapping communities in, 291; Pampean, 144, 146, 148; plural sovereignties in, 229; of U.S. Southwest, 300–301; vegetation and climate in, 121, 122; violence in, 186, 338n52
borders, 1, 8, 18; imperial leading to national zones, 22; redefinition of, 23; stabilization of, 145
Borrows, John, 344n55
Boston News-Letter, 313, 314
Bourbon Reforms, 147
Boyd, E., 294
Brading, David, 320
Brazil, 22, 78, 145, 159. *See also* Portuguese empire
Bridenbaugh, Carl, 31
Brokaw, Galen, 274
Brooks, James, 246, 280
Brugge, David, 248
Buenos Aires province, 26, 142, 145; economy of, 148, 155, 157; establishment of southern border of, 149; as frontier society, 147, 363n22; thin Spanish settlement of, 185
Buffon, Comte de, 308, 309, 316
burial mounds, Indian, 308–9, 316
burial records, 202
Burt, Jonathan, 108
Bustamante, Carlos de, 289, 292

cabildos (town councils), 143, 149, 150, 156, 364n33
Cacapol, 142–43, 159
caciques, 128–29, 130, 134, 151, 384n69; missions requested by, 150; raids on colonial commerce and, 156; trade and, 154; warfare rituals and, 131; Yaqui uprising and, 133
Caddo Indians, 257
Cahitan speakers, 120, 125, 137, 186, 195, 380–81n37
Cahokia, 8, 10, 311
California, 35, 37, 224, 320
Callpisqui, 151, 152
Calvinists, Dutch, 79
Canada, 2, 73; British conquest of, 341n18; as French colony, 42, 79, 335n34; land appropriation in, 77; maps of, 25; modern national borders of, 22; U.S. bid to annex, 66. *See also* Upper Canada
Cangapol, 159
Canonicus, 81–82, 83
Can-slude, 172
capitalism, 27, 60, 63

Index

captivity stories, 27, 258
Caribbean plantations, 34
Carlana (Jicarilla chief), 289, 290
Carlisle Indian School, 262
Carlos III, king of Spain, 147
Carolina colonies, 46, 62, 63, 67, 304
Carondelet, Baron de, 208
Carrilipi, 152
Carrying a Quarter of Meat, 264
Carson, Kit, 252
cartography, 4, 5, 8, 9, 16
Casa Fuerte, Marqués de, 289
Casa Grande de Moctezuma, 319
Casanova, Capt. Manuel de, 170, 172
caste paintings, 296–97
Catawba Indians, 36–37, 49
Catholicism, 39, 76, 170, 213, 221, 222, 223. See also Franciscan order; Jesuit order
Catlin, George, 107, 108, 305, 352n74
Catlin Painting the Portrait of Mah-to-toh-pa—Mandan, 1861–16 (Catlin), 305
cattle, wild, 26, 148, 155, 363n24, 366–67n54
Cayuga (Iroquois) Indians, 45
Cevallos, Pedro de, 149, 364n34
Chacoans, 10
Chacón, Fernando de, 239
Champlain, Samuel de, 16, 19, 283
Chardon, Francis, 109, 110–11, 112, 353n97
Charles II, king of England, 76
Charles IV, king of Spain, 239
Chavez, Fray Angelico, 292
Chávez, Thomas E., 277, 280, 286, 288, 297, 298, 400n41
Cherokee Indians, 49, 62, 91, 230; immigrants to Texas, 220, 222; peace treaties with Creeks, 65; white squatters in lands of, 90
Chesapeake Bay, 40, 42, 64, 85
Cheyenne Indians, 45, 48, 257, 259, 266, 270
Chiapas, 25
Chickasaw Indians, 11, 20, 62; in colonial proxy wars, 64, 65; immigrants to Texas, 220; Spanish alliance with, 210
Chiganstegé, Chief, 179
Chihuahua (*real de minas*), 187, 188, 204–6, 207, 385n87
Chile, 145, 146
Chilitipagé, Chief, 175, 176
Chinipas Indians, 120, 130–31, 359n32
Chiricahuas, 164, 167–68, 169, 179, 181–83
Chitimacha Indians, 312

Chizo Indians, 192
Choctaw Indians, 13, 20, 49, 62; in colonial proxy wars, 64, 65; immigrants to Texas, 220; Spanish alliance with, 210
Christianity, 40, 41, 70, 87, 130
Christianization, 39, 176, 181
cimarrone animals, 145–46, 367n54
city-states, Native, 8, 10
civilization, 22, 301, 324
Clark, William, 107, 314–15, 316, 320, 404n24
Clavijero, Francisco Javier, 316, 318–19, 320, 321
climate, 101–2, 121
Coahuilteco speakers, 35–36
Coddington, William, 83
Collinson, Peter, 306, 307, 403n16
"colonial America," 1, 25, 50; mutual dependency of Indians and Europeans in, 51
colonial era, 20, 23; eclipsed by Revolutionary era, 31; search for "ancient" American past, 27; settler ideology and, 66
colonialism, 4, 20, 24, 60, 140, 275, 277; dialectics of, 286; incorporation of Natives and, 40; militarized indigenous powers and, 290; Native confrontation with, 43; slavery and, 62; slow colonization of North America, 34–35
Columbian exchange, 43
Columbus, Christopher, 2, 103, 276, 318
Comanche Indians, 16, 45, 49–50, 242; Apache reservations and, 163, 164, 180–81; components of power complex, 46–47; confederacy of, 44; domination of southern Great Plains, 220; exiled prisoners of war, 257; farming and, 167, 370n13; Navajos in conflict with, 244, 393n27; political landscape rearranged by expansion of, 59; power complex of, 159–160; raiding and nomadic mobility of, 36, 58, 61, 159; smallpox among, 106; Spanish expansion limited by, 47–48, 282; uprising in Spanish borderlands, 143; U.S. expansion and, 67; Ute alliance with, 289, 293
Compá, El, 169–70, 176, 179
Compá, Gervacio, 182
Compá, Juan Diego (Nayulchi), 170, 176, 178
Compá, Juan José, 170, 182
Concho Indians, 189, 190, 191–92
Concise Natural History of East and West Florida (Romans), 306, 403n13

Conestoga Indians, 76
Conicari Indians, 120, 130
Connecticut colony, 85, 86, 87–88
conquest, 70, 74, 123, 274
contact zones, 55, 89, 338n52
Cook, Capt. James, 314
Cordero, Antonio, 169, 173, 174
Coronado, Francisco Vásquez de, 10, 407n39
Cortés, Hernán, 5, 8, 13, 102
cotton economy, 65, 67
coureurs de bois, 52
Covenant Chain, 46, 47
Cramaussel, Chantal, 26–27, 115, 247, 296
Cree Indians, 106
Creek Indians, 49, 65, 210, 220, 230, 339n59
creoles, 23, 320
criollos (Spaniards born in the Americas), 147, 156, 318
Crow Indians, 45, 48, 113
Cuba, 65, 166, 172, 212
Cutshamekin, 84

Dakota Sioux Indians, 44, 283
Décadas (Herrera y Tordesillas), 127
Declaration of Independence, 90
Delaware Indians, 90, 91, 210
DeLay, Brian, 27, 276
dependency theory, 158
Diaz, Domingo, 181
diphtheria, 102
diplomacy, 46, 55, 58, 233, 243, 252
Discourse of Western Planting (Hakluyt), 303
"discovery," 5, 15, 65
diseases (pathogens, microbes), 42–43, 64, 70, 82, 130, 139, 371n35; labor supply disrupted by, 191; in mining centers, 197; "mourning wars" and, 45; nonequestrian populations devastated by, 291; slave trade and, 67; Spanish conquest and, 102; spread of contagion, 103, 104–5, 107–8; violence and, 184, 377n2
dispossession, 23, 42, 71, 78, 80, 91, 341n19; in Catholic empires, 78; by degrees, 20; ideology and, 79–80; Royal Proclamation and, 90; treaty system and, 72, 73, 75, 76, 77
Doanmoe, Etahdleuh, 103, 258, 260, 274, 275; family of, 258–59; literacy of, 260–61
Domínguez, Atanasio, 170, 171
Dominican order, 39

Double Ditch (Yellow Bank Village), 95, 99, 350n55; aerial view of, *100*; contraction and collapse, 101, 102, 103; founding of, 101, 106; population of, 100, 106, 347n23
drought, 96, 99, 101, 102, 348n30; labor supply disrupted by, 191; in mining centers, 202; in northern New Spain, 164, 177; in pampas of South America, 366n54; violence and, 184, 391–92n13
Dunkers (Tunkers), 215
Dutch empire, 76, 77, 79, 82; documented land purchase introduced by, 85; land use agreement with Indians, 83–84. *See also* New Netherlands
DuVal, Kathleen, 158, 160

Earenfight, Philip, 258, 259, 261, 265, 274
early American history, 22, 31–33, 276
Ecueracapa, Chief, 181
Edwards, Haden and Benjamin, 222
Elliott, J. H., 23
El Rosario (*real de minas*), 187, 188, 195–98, 206, 207
El Turco, 10
empires, 4, 23, 60, 301, 324; Mexican indigenous empires, 320; Native confederacies as, 44–50, 159–160; United States as empire, 309, 310
encomienda system, 38, 57, 191, 378n16, 383n60; *repartimiento* system and, 195; war *encomiendas*, 189–190, 380n24
English/British empire, 20, 156, 159; borderlands of, 55, 89; colonial proxy wars and, 64; as dominant sea power, 147; Dutch rivalry with, 82, 85; Haudenosaunee confederacy and, 46; ideology of Anglophone superiority, 74–77, 341n18; Indian incorporation into, 40–41; land transfer in English common law, 73; Native confederacies' relations with, 230; outposts in Africa and Asia, 35; penetration into interior of North America, 103; policy in Canada after War of 1812, 219, 226; sphere of influence, 38; trading posts, 34; treaty system, 89, 92; U.S. expansion and, 66. *See also* New England
English language, 84
Enlightenment, 92, 153, 308, 404n18
"epic distance," 311

equestrianism, 279, 285, 286, 293; autonomous spaces governed by equestrians, 292; history of Indian power reorganized by, 288; violence attending rise of, 288. *See also* horses
Erie Indians, 46
establecimientos (settlements), 164, 166, 169, 171, 173, 181–83. *See also* reservations, Apache

Falkner, Thomas, 142–43, 364n32
Fallen Timbers, Battle of (1794), 66
famine, 99
Faulkner, William, 28
Fauntleroy, Thomas, 70
Fenn, Elizabeth, 25–26
Fernández de la Canal, Joseph, 138, 360n49
feudalism, European, 20, 340n8
Fields, Richard, 222
Filson, John, 301–4, 307, 310, 311, 314, 318, 321
fish, 35
Five Nations. *See* Iroquois Confederacy
floods, 177
Flores, Manuel Antonio, 172
Florida, 37, 42, 62, 64; Bartram's travels in, 307–8, 310; Franciscan missions in, 34; Spanish loss to England, 306
folklore, 27
Font, Pedro, 319
Fort Marion, Indians detained at, 257, 258, 259, 272, 274–75
Fort Sill, 265, 271
Fox Indians, 52, 57, 166, 283
Fox Wars, 283
Franciscan order, 38, 39, 124, 188, 206, 358n20; hide paintings and, 294–95; in mining centers, 204; Navajos (Diné) and, 238; *repartimiento* system and, 201; reservation system in New Spain and, 174
Francisco Güermes, Viceroy, 198
Franklin, Benjamin, 90
"free Indians" (*indios libre*), 192
French and Indian Wars, 90, 302, 307, 312, 404n18
French empire, 42–43, 46, 78, 159; borderlands of, 55; colonial proxy wars and, 64; French America as proto-West, 312; indigenous power as limit on, 36; maps and, 13; middle ground and, 53; Native land possession in, 78, 79; outposts in Africa and Asia, 35; overlap with Spanish empire, 286; penetration into interior of North America, 103; romance of loss and, 308; seigneurial property forms in, 78; sphere of influence, 38; trading posts, 34. *See also* New France
French empire, Indian allies of, 42, 52–53, 56–57, 291, 335n34; fur trade and, 16, 45; Pawnees, 280, *281*, 283; situational identities and, 284
French Revolution, 216
frontiers, 18, 35, 144, 309, 361n9; frontier societies, 147, 363n22; mythologies of, 300, 301, 322; in north of New Spain, 184; reclamation of frontier space, 311, 313; softening into borderlands, 37; Turner's frontier history, 401n1
fur trade, 16, 35, 42, 81; clashes between Natives over, 106; Dutch payment to Indians for access to, 83–84; Indian deeds procured through, 88; Iroquois bid for access to, 45; northward expansion of, 108

Gálvez, Bernardo de, 59, 164, 182
Garay, Juan de, 145, 146
García, Pedro Andrés, 153
García Conde, Francisco, 182
Gardoqui, Diego de, 213–14
Geertz, Clifford, 286
Geib, Philip, 106
General Courts, 86, 87, 89
genizaros, 172, 232, 292, 296, 297, 298
geopolitics, 16, 34, 35, 60, 61, 67
Georgia colony, 62
González, José María, 169
Good Boy, 106
Grand Settlement (1701), 49
Grave Creek mount, *317*
Grea Peace (1701), 56
Great Basin, 44, 60, 61, 62
Great Lakes region, 34, 344n55; Dakota Sioux expansion in, 44; "family of nations" allied to France in, 284; French explorers and trades in, 52; fur trade in, 45; middle ground in, 53, 55, 58; U.S. expansion into, 66
Great Plains, 26, 35, 192, 280; Comanche domination of, 65; Lakota Sioux confederacy in, 44; Native equestrian regimes, 49
Greer, Allan, 25, 26–27

Gregg, Josiah, 248, 322, 324
Grierson, General (Fort Marion commander), 271
Grovonius, Jan Frederick, 306, 307, 308, 404n18
Guamán Poma de Ayala, Felipe, 13
guanacos, 155, 362n15
Guasabe Indians, 195, 380n37
Guaykurú Indians, 159
Guazapare Indians, 120, 126, 131, 135, 359n32
guns, 43, 288
Gutiérrez, Joaquín, 168
Gutiérrez de Gandarilla, Esteban, 201
Guzmán, Nuño de, 195

Habsburg dynasty, 147
hacendados (Spanish ranchers), 78, 139, 159, 188, 191, 203
Hakluyt, Richard, 303
Hall, Charles, 114
Hämäläinen, Pekka, 25, 159–60, 282
Hasinai Confederacy, 36
Haudenosaunee confederacy, 44, 46, 56
hemorrhagic fever, 102
Henry, Alexander, 111
Henry, Patrick, 90
Herrera y Tordesillas, Antonio, 127
Hiaqui Indians, 117
Hidatsa Indians, 44, 95, 107; drought and, 97; Mandans in proximity to, 100, 347n22, 351n65; smallpox among, 106, 111–12, 354n102
Hill, Willard Williams, 252–53, 255, 396n58
Hispanicization, 39, 170, 176, 181
Histoire de la Louisiane [*History of Louisiana*] (Le Page du Pratz), 312–15
Historia de los triunfos de nuestra santa fé (Pérez de Ribas), 117, 126–27, 358n22
historiographies, 24, 31, 79, 184, 338n52; Argentine, 157; of indigenous art history, 277
history, hemispheric, 23
Hopi Indians, 324
horses, 43, 45, 128, 169, 349nn46–47, 378n9; depicted in Segesser hide paintings, 285; in economy of Great Plains, 287; loads hauled by, 104, 350n48; in Mexico, 129, 358n27; militarization of "nonstate spaces" and, 288; nonequestrian populations devastated by, 291; as object of raids, 180, 187, 253; Plains peoples' embrace of, 103–4; reintroduced to North America by Spaniards, 103; reversion to wild status (*cimarrones*), 145–46. *See also* equestrianism
horticulture, 96, 112, 115, 122, 288
Hotz, Gottfried, 277, 279–280, 282, 289, 295, 400n41
Howling Wolf, 258
How the Indians Lost Their Land (Banner), 73, 341n19
Hudson's Bay Company, 107
Huilliche Indians, 151, 158
human geography, 23, 115, 116, 122
Humboldt, Alexander von, 320–21
Hurdaide, Capt. Diego Martínez de, 126, 128, 129, 130, 134, 360n40; on military valor of Yaqui Indians, 131; moves against Yaqui uprising, 132–33
Huron Indians, 45, 46, 52, 57
Hyde, George, 280
Hyer, Nathaniel, 321

Ibarra, Francisco de, 124, 126, 138, 358n20
identities, 8, 27, 41, 284; Athapaskan, 170; colonial, 116; Indian confederacies and, 50; kinship networks and, 52; loss of ancestral identity, 195; Mandan, 114; masculine warrior, 259, 266, 267, 269, 270; *mestizo*, 320; mixed marriages and, 201; national, 13, 211, 320; preservation of, 160, 178; primacy of familial and communal ties, 33; Puritan, 36; regional and cultural, 139–40; in Segesser hide paintings, 280, 288, 291, 297; shared history and, 287; situational, 284, 286; symbolic meanings and, 140; territorial integrity and, 131; use rights and, 81
Illinois Indians, 8, 57, 283
imperialism, 4, 72
"Indian affairs," 89
"Indian Country," 20, 66, 67, 315
Indian Removal, in United States, 65
Indians (Native people), 4–5, 13, 25, 131–33, 142–43, 359n37; cartographic images of, 8, 9, 12, 22; Christian converts, 87; in colonial proxy wars, 64–65; denial of knowledge to Europeans, 18; deracinated, 231; enslavement of, 26–27, 41, 42, 43; flight from colonial encroachment, 42; herds of animals maintained by, 155, 367n55;

"immigrant Indians," 221; independent, 25, 43; Indian–Indian relations, 53, 65; *indios bárbaros*, 43, 296, 297; intermarriage with Europeans, 55, 57–58; internecine wars of, 44, 151, 158, 364n31; land cessions and treaties with United States, 71, 89; migrations and migration narratives of, 52, 315–16, 320; militarized confederacies, 62; mortality rates among, 42–43; Native warfare practices, 364n26; neglected by historians, 35, 331n7; in northern New Spain, 186; in Pampean borderlands, 148–49; peacemaking rituals, 63; place-names of, 10, 11; power of, 6, 16, 17, 36–37; raids on colonial commerce, 156; Spanish labor demands and, 70, 79, 130; transportation of defeated Indians to Caribbean islands, 166; War of 1812 and, 225
Indians of the High Plains (Hyde), 280
Indian trade, 79, 149, 154–57
indigenous people, 74, 80, 116, 277, 298; erasure of, 5; incorporated into Catholic empires, 78; religious conversion of, 38
influenza, 102
Institute of Early American History, 31
Institutions and Monuments of the Ancient Inhabitants of America (Humboldt), 321
Iroquois Confederacy, 10–11, 16, 44, 45, 49–50, 306; British North Americans' relations with, 230; Fort Stanwix conference and, 91; French empire as adversary of, 52–53, 56; hunting operations in Great Lakes region, 49; raiding of neighbors by, 61, 63
Isosé, Chief, 179

Jacoby, Karl, 277–78
Jamaica, 304, 306, 310
Jay Treaty (1794), 216
Jefferson, Thomas, 90, 217–18, 311, 314, 404n24, 404nn18–19; Humboldt and, 320; on Indian burial mounds, 308–9, 316, 318; journey narratives and, 315; mastodon fossils and, 309–10, 322; as pioneer of American archaeology, 322
Jennings, Francis, 85
Jesuit order, 8, 42, 80, 138, 188, 319, 360n52; Buenos Aires elite and, 150–51; expulsion of, 200; in Mexico, 124, 126, 128; mining districts and, 199, 204; Native uprising in Mexico and, 131, 132; perceived as shamans, 171; resettlement of Indians and, 198; Spanish, 117
Johnson, Sir William, 91
Jones, Morgan, 303
Jones, Oakah, 286
Julime Indians, 192

Katzew, Ilona, 296
Kentucky, 91, 208, 212, 221, 301, 302, 304; Indian burial mounds in, 315, 316; Welsh Indian vestiges in, 322
Kessell, John L., 280, 286
Key into the Language of America, 80, 81
Kickapoo Indians, 52, 220
King, Rufus, 218
King Philip's War, 88, 166
Kino, Eusebio Francisco, 319
kinship networks, 34, 43, 52, 57, 238
Kiowa Indians, 27, 45, 103; in Doanmoe's narrative, 265–66; exiled prisoners of war, 257, 258, 259, 270
Kiowa's Odyssey, A (Earenfight), 258, 270–71, 273–75; illustrations in, *268*; indigenous literary practices and, 262, 264; photographs added by Mason Pratt, 262, *263*; Pratt's interference with narrative, 260–62, 270, 273; traditional Kiowa life in, 264–67, 269; on warriors' transformation into prisoners, 267, 269; Zotom's narrative compared with, 270, 272–73

Lakota Sioux Indians, 44–45, 48, 50; raiding of neighbors by, 61; smallpox among, 105, 106, 108, 113; United States humiliated by, 49
land rights and purchase, 72–74; Native tributary hierarchies and, 83; personal relationship and use rights, 81–82; private property and state jurisdiction, 86–87; Protestant and Catholic empires' approaches to, 76–80; Royal Proclamation and land cessions, 89; written documents (deeds), 84–89, 343n39
landscapes, 28, 139
languages, indigenous, 80–81, 120, 309, 343n39
Lapham, Increase A., 321, 322, 323
Larson, town of, 99, 101, 105, 106, 350n55, 350n58

Lastarría, Miguel, 153
La Vérendrye, Pierre de, 104, 105, 107
Law, John, 312
Lawson, John, 304, 306
Lefebvre, Henri, 116
Lenni Lenape (Delaware) Indians, 74, 75, 76
Le Page du Pratz, Antoine-Simone, 312–16, 319, 321, 322, 406nn32–33
Lewis, G. Malcolm, 5
Lewis, Meriwether, 107, 314–15, 316, 320, 404n24, 406n33
Line of Property, 91
L'Isle, Guillaume de, 11, 13, 15, 20
literacy, 34, 257, 262, 274
Llanketruz, 152, 153
Llwyd, Humffrey, 303, 319
Locke, John, 20
Logan, James, 306
Lone Wolf, 266
Louisiana, French, 36, 312; Anglo-American polemics against, 76–77; as Caribbean-based colony, 62; Indians and, 42; restoration of, 217
Louisiana, Spanish, 44, 211–14, 221. *See also* Upper Louisiana
Louisiana Purchase, 48, 65, 217–18, 315
Loyalists, in American Revolution, 209, 214, 217; "Late Loyalists," 215, 217, 218, 219; pietists labeled as, 215–16

Madoc legend, 303–4, 316, 318
Making Medicine, 258
Mandan Indians, 25–26, 44, 105–6, 113–14, 346n17; in Catlin painting, 305; disease epidemics among, 106, 107–8, 110–12, 351n70, 353n99; drought and, 97, 99; ecological challenges faced by, 96–97, 99–102; homeland of (map), 98; horses and, 104; mobility of, 111, 354n109; origin story of, 345n10; population of, 107, 351n67; rats as challenge to, 108–9, 352nn74–75; Sitting Rabbit's map, 95–96, 345n1
Mandrini, Raúl José, 26
Mangas Coloradas (Red Sleeves), 182, 183
Mani Land Treaty, 12
maps, European, 2, 3, 4, 11; English, 18, 20, 21; European border claims and, 22; indigenous people erased from land, 5, 18; of Lewis and Clark, 107; monsters and blank spaces on, 7; Native power represented on, 6, 17; Spanish map of California, 119
maps, Native, 8, 9, 12, 36–37; memory mapping, 10; of Mississippi River, 9; of Sitting Rabbit (Little Owl), 95–96, 114, 345n1, 345n4
Mapuche Indians, 361n10, 363n19
Marquette, Jacques, 8
Martinez, Antonio, 220
Martínez, Manuel, 130
Massachusetts Bay colony, 46, 81, 82, 342n25
Massasoit, 83, 342n29
mastodon fossils, 307, 309–10, 310, 314, 322, 403n16, 405n24
Maximilian, Prince Alexander, 107, 109, 352n85
Mayhew, Thomas, 82
Mayo Indians, 117, 129–33, 138, 140, 186, 359n34; *reales de minas* and, 195, 197–98; territories and population of, 135
Mayupilquiyan, 151
McBride, James, 302
McHugh, Paul G., 74
McKenzie, Charles, 107
measles, 102, 103, 108, 112, 178, 382n45
memory, 27, 79
Méndez, Padre Pedro, 129
Mendoza, Pedro de, 145
Mennonites, 215
Merriwether, David, 70, 71
Mescaleros, 163, 179; homeland of (map), 165; raiding by, 180; revolts by, 181; wars with Spanish, 164
Meso-America, 2, 10, 362n11
mestizos and *mestizaje*, 57, 67, 186, 320
Metacom's War, 40, 231
metals, as colonial technology, 43, 288, 291
metropolitan networks, 312, 405n27
Mexican War, 67
Mexico, 1, 2, 67, 320; American settlers in Texas and, 220–24; ancient history of, 318–19; antislavery constitution of Republic, 221, 224; Aztlán-Mississippian connection and, 319–322, 323, 324, 408n45; Catholic monastic orders in, 39; *Comanchería* in, 49; as focal point of colonial ambitions, 34–35; as heart of Spanish empire, 209; land appropriation in, 78; liberals in, 226; maps of Native areas, 13; modern national borders of, 22; Spanish

conquest of, 70; as strongest New World colony, 34
Mexico, Independence of, 175, 180, 220, 222, 231; Indians allied with independence fighters, 393n27; Indian wars in New Mexico and, 244, 248; trade with United States opened by, 248
Miami Indians, 52
Miantonomo, 81–82, 83, 342n32
middle ground, 24, 53, 54, 283; diluted meaning of, 335n36; resurrected in War of 1812, 66; as short-lived relation in New England, 81, 84; survival of, 57; violent overthrow of, 90; western boundaries of, 285
Mier y Teran, Gen. Manuel de, 223–24
Miguel, map of, 16, *18*
Mih-Tutta-Hangkusch, village of, 108–10, 112, 113, 352n75, 354n102
militias, Spanish, 116, 126, 129, 132, 149, 242–43
mines, 26, 115, 123, 131, 136–39, 185. See also *reales de minas* (mining centers)
Miro, Esteban Rodriguez, 212
missionaries, 55, 114, 116, 128, 138, 359n37
missions, Spanish, 26, 38, 39, 64, 124; in Buenos Aires, 150–51; failed missionization of *Apachería*, 282, 289, 292; Jesuit, 126, 150; population transfers and, 198; San Sabá (Texas), 143, 159, 364n31
Mississippi River and Valley, 20, 37, 42, 46, 158, 322; American settler trade on, 211, 216; French-Indian borderlands along, 55; French traders in, 315; Indian slave raiding in, 64; L'Isle's map of, *15*; on Native map, 8, *9*; Royal Proclamation and, 91; Spanish colonists in, 209
Missouri River and Valley, 44–45, 95, 303, 311; French traders in, 315; horticulturalists on, 96; U.S. traders in, 48
Mitchell, John, map of, 20, *21*
Mocobíe Indians, 92
Mohawk (Iroquois) Indians, 45, 46, 210
Monarchia Indiana (Torquemada), 407n40
Moncacht-Apé, 313, 314, 315, 406n34
Monica (Mimbreño Apache woman), 183
Montero, Crivelli, 152
Montes, Lt. Ventura, 163
Morgan, George, 213–14
moros de paz ("peaceful Moors"), 166

"mourning wars," 45
mulattoes, 186, 198, 203, 382n54
multiethnic families, 203, 385n80
mumps, 102
Mundy, Barbara, 5
Muñoz, Manuel, 173
Muscogulge (Creek) Indians, 43

Nahua people/language, 5, 303, 316, 319, 320
Nahuatl speakers, 187
Narbona, Antonio, 173, 239, 240, 247, 392n20
Narragansett Indians, 80, 83, 342n32
narratives, continental and localized, 32, 33
Nasaws, 36
Natchea Indians, 65
Natchez Indians, 312, 315, 316, 321
National Cowboy and Western Heritage Museum (Oklahoma), 273
nationalism, 25
nation-states, 2, 20, 22, 24, 276
Native Americans. *See* Indians (Native people)
Native American studies, 275
Nava, Pedro de, 164, 166, 170, 172, 176, 181
Navajo (Diné) Indians, 62, 63, 164, *241*, 324; farming and, 167; Long Walk and, 252, 255, 393n24; migration out of traditional homeland, 233–34, 391n7; *naach'id* tribal council, 238, 246; resistance to United States, 393n22; Spanish treaties with, 92
Navajo–New Mexican relations, 230–31, 252–56; Apaches and, 232, 233; Jémez massacre, 245–46, 248, 394n31; judicial dispute resolution, 234–35; land disputes, 233–34; peace agreements, 251; power asymmetries in, 232–33; slave-raiding culture and, 245, 247, 248–252; violence blamed on thieves (*ladrones*), 247, 250, 254, 255, 396n57; wars, 235, 236, 237–40, 242–44, 252, 254
Nbayá Indians, 159
Never Got Shot, 264
Nevome speakers, 115, 120, 135, 137
New England, 1, 4, 34; boundaries between colonies in, 85; dreams of landed power in, 40; fenced landholdings in, 36; invention of, 5; map of, *18*; Native Americans and formation of, 23; "praying-Indian" towns, 87. *See also* English/British empire

Index

New France, 1, 42, 230, 283; Anglo-American polemics against, 76–77; Champlain's map of, 16, *20*; Haudenosaunee confederacy and, 56; Indian relations with, 49; invention of, 5; as name on maps, 4; Native Americans and formation of, 23; western reaches of, 285. *See also* French empire

New Laws (1542), 26

New Mexico, 34, 35, 37, 103, 173, 279, 320; annexed to Spanish empire, 69–70; annexed to United States, 224, 232; Comanche raids in, 58; *Comanchería* in, 164; conflict with French-allied Indians, 280, *281*, 282, 285; dependence on *Comanchería*, 47–48; as enduring colonial borderland, 230; *genízaros* in, 292, 298; Indian slave market in, 62–63; population of, 232, 391n5; precolonial antiquities of, 322; racial caste system of, 294. *See also* Navajo–New Mexican relations

New Netherlands, 5, 37, 85. *See also* Dutch empire

New Orleans, city of, 209, 211, 212, 216, 312

New Spain, 1, 59, 67, 145, 319; academic studies on history of, 184, 376n1; Apache reservations in north of, 167; equestrianism in, 279; Indian land tenure and, 78; Indians as strategic threats to, 249; internal borderlands of, 115; invention of, 5; mining in, 124; multiethnic families in, 186, 377n6; as name on maps, 4; national identity for, 13; Native Americans and formation of, 23. *See also* Spanish empire

New Sweden, 77

New York colony, 47

New Zealand, 73, 77

Nicarson, William, 87

Nicholson, Francis, 11, 36

North America, 16, 32, 42, 43, 60, 68; biography of power in, 33; borderlands of Spanish empire in, 92; European maps of, 4, 11; imperial histories of, 311; Indian reservations in, 20; market in land in, 72; nation-states of, 276; Native control in, 37; Native maps in, 8; pre-Columbian, 72; slow colonization of, 34–35; Spanish Franciscan missions in, 38

North Carolina colony, 62

Northwest Ordinance, 65

Northwest Passage, search for, 35

Notes on the State of Virginia (Jefferson), 308, 404n19

Nueva Vizcaya province (Mexico), 125, 131, 137, 173, 377n4; Apache reservations in, *165*, 180; colonization of, 185; mines in, 139, 204; missions in, 134

obrajes (colonial workshops), 292, 294, 295, 298

Ocoroni Indians, 128, 132

Ogden, John Cosens, 215

Ohio Company, 90

Ohio Country, 46, 56, 60; American defeat of Indians in, 216; Bartram's travels in, 307; Indians mounds in, 316, *317*; Indian war in, 216; mastodon fossils in, 309; U.S. westward expansion into, 66

Omaha Indians, 113

On-A-Slant ("Old Mandan Village"), 106–7

Oñate, Juan de, 16, 69–70, 71

Oneida (Iroquois) Indians, 45

Onondaga (Iroquois) Indians, 45

Onontio (French "father" of Indians), 53

Ópata Indians, 164, 167, 169, 193, 201, 239, 240

Osage Indians, 43, 113, 210, 218, 283

Ostimuri province (Mexico), 115–17, 123, 134, 139–40; Indians hiding in remote areas of, 202; Jesuit missions in, 126; map of, *118*; mining and formation of, 136–39; as transitional space, 117

Otoe Indians, 113

Oto Indians, 283

Otomí Indians, 187

Ottawa Indians, 52, 57

pacification (Spanish policy), 39, 69, 71

Pacific Northwest, 314, 315

Pacific Ocean, 8

Paiute Indians, 62, 63, 242

pampas, 26, 146, 148, 158, 361n10, 363n24

Pampas Indians, 16, 146, 150

Paraguay, 145

Paris, Treaty of, 66

Parral (*real de minas*), 187, 188, 191, 206, 207; Indian labor force in, 189, 191; missionization and, 136; as prinicipal mining center, 124–25; royal tax and, 137; traffic of captive indigenous laborers and, 296

Pascual, Julio, 130

Pawnee Indians, 48, 113, 280
Paxton Boys, 76
Payaguá Indians, 159
pays d'en haut ("the upper country"), 52, 53, 54, 283; forging of, 284; intermarriage in, 55; violence in, 56–57
"peace camps," 166
Pehuenche Indians, 151, 153, 158
Penn, John, 74
Penn, William, 74, 75, 76, 79–80, 89, 90
Pennsylvania colony, 60, 74, 76, 91
Peoria Indians, 57
Pequot massacre (1637), 18
Pequot War and massacre (1637), 283
Perea, Capt. Pedro de, 131, 134–35, 136, 138, 360n40
Pereira, Antonio, map drawn by, 2, 3, 16, 23
Pérez, Francisco, 163
Pérez, Martín, 126
Pérez de Ribas, Andrés, 117, 126–27, 128, 356n7, 358n22; indigenous spirituality and, 129; on missions and indigenous migrations, 130; *reducciones* organized by, 133
Peru, 1, 22, 25, 39, 70
Philip II, king of Spain, 69
Philip III, king of Spain, 13
Philippines, 65
Philosophical Transactions of the Royal Society, 304
Pima Indians, 193, 198, 200, 201, 205
plague, 102
plantations, 40, 79
Plymouth colony, 83, 87, 342n29
Ponca Indians, 113
Popple, Henry, 11, 20
Portuguese empire, 4, 78, 79, 145, 159. *See also* Brazil
Potawatomi Indians, 52, 57
Powel, David, 303, 319
power, 62, 81; asymmetries of, 232, 235; biography of, 33; disparity of, 88; parity of, 82; traditional sources and forms of, 34
Powhatan Indians, 40
Pratt, Mary Louise, 274
Pratt, Mason, 258, 261
Pratt, Capt. Richard Henry, 258, 264, 265–66, 275; Doanmoe's relationship with, 259; interference in Doanmoe's narrative, 260–62, 270, 273; memoir of, 271
pre-Columbian America, 10

property rights, 70, 85, 89
Protestantism, 40, 89, 225
proxy wars, colonial, 64
Pueblo Indians, 38, 58, 69–70, 101, 253; as auxiliaries of Spanish army, 280, 285, 296, 297; captives of Apache raiders, 289; detribalized exiles, 292; Spanish "pacification" of, 71
Pueblo Revolt, 54, 104, 192, 282, 286
pueblos de indios, 10
Puritans, 36, 79, 82, 84, 86
Pynchon, John, 90
Pynchon, William, 88, 90

Quakers, 74, 79, 215, 225
Quapaw Indians, 43
Quiles de Cuéllar, Pedro, 138
Quivira Indians, 10, 192

Radding, Cynthia, 26
radiocarbon dating, 105
rancherías, 115, 117, 120, 130, 134, 168, 291; Apache, 173; disappearance of, 200; *encomienda* Indians from, 190, 191; Jesuit missions and, 128; Navajo (Diné), 237, 247
ranches, 70, 123, 124, 145
Rasmussen, Birgit Brander, 27
reales de minas (mining centers), 115, 124, 140, 187–88, 206–7; founding of, 123; indigenous migrations and, 130; Jesuit missions and, 134; labor force in, 138, 187, 378n11; map of, *118*; *repartimiento* system and, 193. *See also* Álamos; Chihuahua; El Rosario; mines; Parral
reche ("true people"), 146, 361n10, 363n19, 363n22.
Reconquista (1694), 285, 286
reducciones, 41, 127, 128, 133
Refugia (Mimbreño Apache woman), 183
repartimiento system, 57, 124, 125, 192, 195; defined, 378–79n16; forcible relocations of Indians and, 190; Indian resistance to, 203; labor for mines and, 139, 194, 196, 201, 378n11; longevity of, 379n23
rescue Indians (*indios de rescate*), 192, 206
reservations, Apache, 26, 59, 67, 163–64, 166–67, 180–83; Apache interests and, 176–80; Hispanicization and Christianization of Indians, 168–76; map of, *165*;

reservations (*continued*)
  precedents in Spanish policy, 166. See also *establecimientos*
reservations, in United States, 20, 97, 182, 252–56
Revillagigedo, Conde de, 172
Rhode Island, 83, 85, 88
Richter, Daniel, 330n5
Rio de la Plata region, 144, 147, 153, 154, 362n11
Río de Loza, Rodrigo del, 124, 126
Rio Grande River and Valley, 10, 38, 44, 54, 55; cross-cultural relations in, 57; U.S. expansion into, 67
Rittenhouse, David, 316
Rivera, Pedro de, 289
Roanoke, lost colony of, 304
Romans, Bernard, 306
Royal Proclamation (1763), 73, 89–90, 344n55
Royal Society of London, 304, 306, 309
Rushforth, Brett, 283
Russian explorers, 314

Saenz de Carriosa, Francisco, 199
St. Lawrence Valley, 34, 37, 42, 45, 66, 78
St. Louis, city of, 209
Salcedo, Nemesio, 170, 176
Salinero Indians, 198
Sandoval, Cebolla, 246
San Lorenzo, Treaty of (1795), 216
Santa Fe Trail, 248
Sauk Indians, 52
Saulteaux Indians, 57
scalp hunting, 64, 66–67, 251, 395–96n53
Scattered Village, 347n22
Scott, James, 278, 279, 283, 284, 286, 299, 400n44
Segesser, Philip von, 277, 279–280
Segesser hide paintings, 277, 279; Segesser I, 280, 282, 288–295, 297–99, 400n41; Segesser II, 280, *281*, 282–89, 292–95
Seminole Indians, 65, 220
Seneca (Iroquois) Indians, 45
Serrano Indians, 150
settlers/settler societies, 24, 37, 90, 150, 287
Seven Cities of Cibola legend, 146, 407n39
Seven Years' War, 89
sexuality, 39, 53
Shaw, Nate, 102
Shawnee Indians, 65, 90, 91, 210, 220

Shermer (Village Where Turtle Went Back), 95, 345n1n4
Shoshone Indians, 62, 63, 106
Simcoe, John Graves, 214–15, 216
Simpson, James H., 324
Sinaloa Indians, 195
Sinaloa province (Mexico), 117, *118*, 123, 377n4; areas included in, 189; estimated indigenous population of, 137; mining and ranching in, 131; missions in, 126, 130, 134
Sitting Rabbit (Little Owl), 95, 114, 345n1, 345n4
slavery, African, 42, 64, 148; in Buenos Aires, 148; in Louisiana, 209; in Mexico, 137, 138, 360n50; slave rebellion in Saint Domingue, 217; in Texas, 223, 224, 248
slavery, Indian, 41, 62–64, 66–67, 172–73, 395n40; equestrian trafficking networks, 298; in French empire, 42–43; Native slave raiding, 46, 47, 49, 62–64, 192, 242, 248; New Mexico culture of, 245, 247, 248–49, 250–52
Sloane, Sir Hans, 304, 306, 308, 310–11, 403nn12–13
smallpox, 102, 105, 106, 110, 178, 350n53, 382n45; acquired immunity to, 112–13, 355n122; incubation period of, 103, 349nn42–43; in mining centers, 202; quarantines against, 111–12, 354n102; U.S. federal vaccination campaign and, 113
Smith, John, 5, 18
Smith, Michael, 215, 218
sociograms, 13
Sonora Indians, 204
Sonora province (Mexico), *118*, 136, 192, 377n4; Apache reservations in, *165*; founding of, 189; Jesuit missions in, 126; missions in, 134
South Africa, land appropriation in, 77
South America, 2, 3, 6, 16, 92, 276
South Carolina colony, 36, 62
Southeastern Slave Wars, 231
sovereignty, 24, 35, 74, 278; extension of, 74; land title and, 86; preservation of Native sovereignty, 160; territorial, 36
space, 2, 11, 35; contested, 2, 20, 116, 139; control of, 33; historiographies of, 23; of Mandans, 26, 96; maps and, 4, 5, 7, 22; militarization of "nonstate spaces," 288; Native maps of, 8; pre-Columbian, 10;

proto-nationalist, 22; viewed in European terms, 5
Spanish empire, 4, 79, 362n11; African slave trade and, 203; "black legend" about, 25, 76, 78; colonial proxy wars and, 64; enslavement of Indians and, 26–27; French revolutionary wars and, 216; incorporation of Natives as goal, 40; indigenous power as limit on, 36, 47–48, 58; labor demands on Indians, 185; Latin American wars for independence and, 225; overlap with French empire, 286; penetration into interior of North America, 103; romance of loss and, 304, 306, 308, 403n12; southern frontiers of, 153; sphere of influence, 38; treaties with Indians after Age of Conquest, 91–92. See also New Spain
Spanish language, 174
steamboats, 109, 110, 352n74
Steck, Michael, 182–83
Storia di Messico [History of Mexico] (Clavijero), 318, 320
sugar plantations, 34
Susquehannock Indians, 46
Sutton, Benjamin, 303
Swedish empire, 77, 79
Szabo, Joyce M., 270, 272

Tabeau, Pierre Antoine, 111
Tahue/Tahua speakers, 196, 381n38
Tapia, Gonzalo de, 126
Tapia, José de, 138
Tarahumara (Rarámuri) speakers, 115, 120, 159, 186; labor supplied for mines by, 191; in mining centers, 204; resistance to labor in mines, 201
Tarascan Indians, 187
Taylor, Alan, 27
Taylor, Stephen, 321
technology, 34, 43, 50, 63, 141, 291
Tegueco Indians, 117, 120, 126, 129, 132
Tegüima (southern Ópata and Eudeve) speakers, 115, 120, 125, 135, 138
Tehuelche Indians, 150
Tenochtitlan, 8, 123, 407n40; Aztlán and, 319; Spanish map of, 5, 13, 14
Teotihuacan, 8
Tepahue Indians, 120, 128, 129, 130
Tepehuán (Tepima or O'odham) speakers, 120, 124

Tepehuane Indians, 186, 189, 196, 206
terra nullius doctrine, 37
Tewa language, 245
Texas, 35, 37, 60; American settlers and republic of, 220–24, 226; Comanchería in, 164; in Confederate secession, 226; in Spanish empire, 44
textual conflict zone, 274
Thomas, Alfred Barnaby, 282
Thompson, David, 107, 351n67
Tidaya, 173
tobacco, 35, 42, 213
Toltecs, 318, 320, 406n38
topography, 34, 121
tourism industry, 27
township grants, 85
treaties/treaty system, 73, 84, 89
tribute payments, 61, 81, 83
Truett, Samuel, 27
Truteau, Jean Baptiste, 105
Tsenacommach, 5
Tully, James, 287
Tuscarora Indians, 48–49, 303
typhus, 102, 382n45

Ugalde, Juan de, 168
Ugarte, Jacobo, 163, 168, 169, 202
Underhill, John, 283
United States, 2, 159; empire building of, 65–66; Indian Removal policy, 65; land appropriation in, 77; maps of, 25; Mexican territory annexed by, 224; modern national borders of, 22; Southwest borderlands taken over by, 70; treaties with Indians, 71, 89; wars with Plains Indians, 49; westward expansion of, 27, 50, 66–67, 208–9, 301
Upper Canada, 209, 214–16, 218–19, 224–25
Upper Louisiana, 209–10, 214, 218, 225–26
Upper Peru, 145
Ute Indians, 58, 62, 63, 230, 242, 396n53; as Comanche allies, 282; Navajos in conflict with, 233, 237, 238, 396n58; New Mexico culture of Indian slavery and, 247; resistance to United States, 70–71
Uto-Aztecan languages, 120

Valverde Cosio, Antonio, 282, 289, 290, 292, 293, 294, 295
Van Develder, Paul, 97

Varohío (Guajiro) Indians, 120, 122, 130, 131, 359n32
Vértiz, Juan José de, 149, 152
Vidal de Lorca, Manuel, 179
Villalta, Cristóbal de, 128
Villasur, Pedro de, 281, 283, 285, 287; New Mexico shaken by defeat of, 282, 292–93, 295–96; Pueblo allies of, 280, 290
Virginia colony, 36, 63, 86, 309; as center of speculation in western lands, 90; dreams of landed power in, 40; Indian slave market in, 62–63; slave trade in, 67; Smith's map of, 5
Virginia Indian Treaty (1646), 344n56
Vizcarra, José Antonio, 249–50
Volante, Chief, 163, 181
Voyage to the Islands (Lawson), 304, 306

"Walking Purchase," 76
Wampanoag Indians, 83, 87, 166, 342n29, 343n39
Wanamatraunemit, 83
War of 1812, 66, 108, 219, 225
War of Austrian Succession, 76
War of Spanish Succession, 147–48
Warohio Indians, 126
Washington, George, 90
wealth, 34, 104, 116, 308
Weber, David J., 1–2, 23, 25, 325n1; on Bourbon officials' relations with Indians, 163–64; on Spanish treaties with Indians, 92
Welsh or white Indian tales, 309, 312, 314, 321, 322, 403n9; Madoc legend and, 303–4, 305; in Southwest, 324
West, Benjamin, 74–76
Westphalian system, 20

White, Richard, 53, 160
whites: color line against Indians, 41–42; "going Native," 27; landownership and, 87; white supremacy, 226
whooping cough, 107, 108, 351n70
Wichita Indians, 143
wilderness, 18, 22, 302, 307
Wilkinson, James, 212
William Penn's Treaty with the Indians (West painting), 74–76, 75
Williams, Roger, 80–82, 83, 89, 342n32
Winthrop, John, 81, 82
Wisconsin, 321, 323, 407n43
Witgen, Michael, 284
writing, European conquest and, 274

Xiximé Indians, 120, 125, 196

Yagonxli (Ojos Colorados), 177
Yamasee Indians, 65
Yamasee War, 287
Yankton Dakota Indians, 48
Yaqui Indians, 131–33, 135, 140, 186, 359n37, 381nn43–44; of Chihuahua mining center, 204–5; of El Rosario mining center, 196–98; Mayo confused with, 198–99, 382n48; migrations of, 386n89; of Parral mining center, 193–95
Yati, 151
Yazoo Indians, 313, 315
Yoreme speakers, 115, 131, 134, 140
Yucatec Indians, 12
Yuman languages, 120

Zavala, Silvio, 23
Zespedes, Vicente Manuel de, 209
Zotom, Paul, 258, 259, 265, 266, 269, 272–75
Zuni Indians, 239, 324

ACKNOWLEDGMENTS

This volume is the latest in a series of collections sponsored by the William P. Clements Center for Southwest Studies at Southern Methodist University (SMU), always in collaboration with a similar institution elsewhere. In our case the collaborator has been the McNeil Center for Early American Studies at the University of Pennsylvania. We are most grateful to the staffs at both centers for the extensive help they have given us, not just their general sponsorship but also their help in organizing preliminary conferences in Philadelphia and Dallas. At the Clements Center, we need to thank the former director Benjamin Heber Johnson, the current director Andrew Graybill, the former associate director Andrea Boardman, and the current assistant director Ruth Ann Elmore. At the McNeil Center, our gratitude is great to Daniel Richter, the Richard S. Dunn Director and a coeditor of the Early American Studies monograph series, and to the associate director Amy Baxter-Bellamy. Michael Jarvis and Kathleen DuVal commented on the conference presentations to good effect and from two very distinct perspectives. More Penn and SMU graduate students than we can name took time from their own busy schedules to help with the conference arrangements. We thank both Dan Richter and Andrés Reséndez for readings of the nearly finished manuscript. Their thoughtful comments helped both us and the individual authors to bring the project to completion. Robert Lockhart of the University of Pennsylvania Press offered many wise comments at the preliminary conferences and as we saw the project to completion. Rachel Taube at the press gave us invaluable direction in collecting, managing, and placing all our illustrations and permissions. When the project was in the early planning stage we did our best to keep it secret from David Weber. But he figured out that something was going on, pitched in, arranged the collaboration with the McNeil Center, and left his own imprint on this volume just as he left an imprint on each one of us. This book holds David's memory and his influence, and we dedicate it to him.

Juliana Barr and Edward Countryman

www.ingramcontent.com/pod-product-compliance
Lightning Source LLC
LaVergne TN
LVHW040730250326
834688LV00031B/235